THE JPS GUIDE TO JEWISH TRADITIONS

Honoring Joseph Neubauer

on the occasion of his 60th birthday

and celebrating a life filled with
boundless love for family

and extraordinary commitment
to community

Miles and Chris Lerman
David Lerman and Shelley Wallock

A JPS DESK REFERENCE

THE JPS GUIDE TO JEWISH TRADITIONS

RONALD L. EISENBERG

The Jewish Publication Society
Philadelphia
2004 • 5765

The Jewish Publication Society
2100 Arch Street
Philadelphia, PA 19103

Composition by Pageworks.

Manufactured in the United States of America

04 05 06 07 08 09 10 10 9 8 7 6 5 4 3 2 1

Library of Congress Cataloging-in-Publication Data

Eisenberg, Ronald L.
The JPS guide to Jewish traditions / Ron Eisenberg—1st ed.
p. cm.
Includes bibliographical references and index.
ISBN 0-8276-0760-1
1. Judaism—Encyclopedias. I. Title: Jewish Publication Society guide to Jewish traditions. II. Jewish Publication Society. III. Title.
BM50.E49 2004
296.4—dc22
2004006399

Acknowledgments

We gratefully acknowledge the following publishers for their kind permission to reprint material from their works:

Dietary Laws: reprinted with permission from *The Jewish Dietary Laws* by Samuel Dresner and Seymour Siegel. Copyright © 1982 by The Rabbinical Assembly.

Marriage Ceremony; and Memorial or Headstone: reprinted with permission from *Teaching Jewish Life Cycle: Traditions and Activities* by Barbara Binder Kadden and Bruce Kadden. Copyright © 1984 by A.R.E. Publishing, Inc., 1997. A.R.E. Publishing, Inc., Denver, CO. 800-346-7779, www.arepublish.com.

Maimonides' Thirteen Principles of Faith; "Vidui"; and text of various blessings reproduced from *ArtScroll Siddur* "Kol Yaakov" with permission from the copyright holders ArtScroll/Mesorah Publications, Ltd.

Aninut: reprinted from *The Jewish Way in Death and Mourning* by Maurice Lamm. Copyright © 2000. By arrangement with Jonathan David Publishers, Inc., Middle Village, NY 11379. www.jdbooks.com.

Premarital Sex: reprinted from *The Jewish Way in Love and Marriage* by Maurice Lamm. Copyright © 1991. By arrangement with Jonathan David Publishers, Inc., Middle Village, NY 11379. www.jdbooks.com.

Dietary Laws, and Prohibitions of Work on the Sabbath: reprinted with permission from *Exploring Jewish Tradition* by Abraham B. Witty and Rachel Witty. Copyright © 2001. Doubleday, Random House, Inc.

Material adapted for the section on Torah Ornaments: reprinted with permission from *The Encyclopedia of Jewish Symbols* edited by Frankel and Teutsch. Copyright © 1992. Published by Jason Aronson.

Material adapted for the section on Women and Mitzvot: reprinted with permission from *Women and Jewish Law* by Rachel Biale. Copyright © 1984 by Schocken Books, Inc. Used by permission of Schocken Books, a division of Random House, Inc.

Material adapted for the section on Superstitions: reprinted with permission from *The Book of Jewish Customs* by Harvey Lutske. Copyright © 1986. Published by Jason Aronson.

To my wife Zina,

and to our daughters

Avlana Kinneret and Cherina Carmel,

whom we pray will continue to embrace their Jewish tradition

and will transmit it with love to the next generation

Contents

Jewish Literature

Mitzvot

Preface

The JPS Guide to Jewish Traditions originated from my own search for answers to questions relating to a variety of Jewish issues, and thus it is ultimately a book that I wanted to read. As proven by my own experience, I am convinced that many Jews could gain a substantially greater spiritual satisfaction from the rituals and life-cycle events they observe by understanding the profound meanings underlying them. This is somewhat analogous to reading the prayers in Hebrew. Only with a grasp of the language can one fully appreciate the depths of the prayers; only with the knowledge of how the prayers developed and interrelate can one see the brilliance and inspiration of the sages who wrote them.

The book opens with a discussion of the major life-cycle events, encompassing the first 16 years of life, from birth through confirmation, marriage, and death. The next major section deals with the Sabbath and festivals, detailing the historical development of this superstructure of the Jewish year. This is followed by a section on synagogue and prayers, which afford Jews the opportunity for a formalized approach to a relationship with the Divine. The next major topics are the Bible and rabbinic literature, the written and philosophical cornerstones of Jewish belief; and the mitzvot, which detail the prescribed daily activities and the ethical value system that are the essence of traditional Jewish behavior. Following a discussion of symbols of Judaism and the State of Israel, there are alphabetically arranged sections on a broad spectrum of topics of Jewish interest that do not conveniently fit into any other area. The final parts of the book deal with the role of food in Jewish tradition and daily life, as well as those plants and animals that are mentioned in the Bible and Talmud. For the convenience of the reader, the appendix contains a listing of the Torah and haftarah readings for Sabbaths and festivals as well as a listing of the tractates of the Mishnah and their major topics. Bible passages quoted throughout the book are most often from The Jewish Publication Society translation (NJPS). My preferred translations are noted accordingly in the endnotes.

I want to thank Rabbi Robert Layman, former Regional Director of the United Synagogue of Conservative Judaism; Candace Levy; and Daniel Septimus for their valuable editorial contributions. I would like to acknowledge Professor Byron Sherwin at Spertus Institute in Chicago, whose superb lectures have been the source of my inspiration to pursue my writings in Judaica. I gratefully appreciate the ceaseless efforts of Carol Hupping, publishing director at JPS, who displayed unswerving dedication to making this project a reality. I also wish to thank the following people at JPS who have contributed their efforts and talents: Janet Liss, production editor; Robin Norman, production manager; and Jamie Temple, designer and typesetter. Immeasurable gratitude is due to my wife, Zina Schiff, who not only read the manuscript carefully and posed challenging questions, but also has created the ideal Jewish environment in which to write this book.

I hope that the reader will share the joy I felt while delving deeply into the fascinating richness that constitutes the traditions of the Jewish people.

Ronald L. Eisenberg
June 2004

Language

No knowledge of Hebrew, Aramaic, or Yiddish is required to use this book, since all words in these languages are transliterated into English. Transliteration is a difficult task, because the sounds of one language often cannot be reproduced precisely in another. The basic guidelines used in this book are as follows:

a	as in f<u>a</u>ther (shalom, *baruch*)
e	as in m<u>e</u>n (*lechem, beracha*)
ei	as in s<u>ay</u> (*Aleinu, Kol Nidrei*)
i	as in k<u>e</u>y (mitzvot, *rimonim*)
o	as in g<u>o</u> (Torah, shofar)
u	as in t<u>u</u>ne (Yom Kippur, *tikkun olam*)
ch	as in Ba<u>ch</u> (guttural "h" sound in *rachum, berachot*) (in Yiddish words such as *cholent*, it may also be pronounced as ch as in <u>ch</u>ip)
'	indicates the sound of the "i" in "v*i*m" at the beginning of a word to mean "and" (*v'ahavta*), or indicates a pause between two adjacent sounds (Tu b'Shevat)
h	used at the end of a transliterated term when the Hebrew word ends in the letter "*hei*"; used between the definite article "*ha*" (the) and the word it modifies (Yom ha-Din)

Some exceptions to this pattern have been required by the JPS general style. Although in the vast majority of cases the guttural sound in Hebrew has been rendered as "ch," some common words such as *hodesh, hametz,* and *huppah* appear in the book beginning with the letter "h." For a few words, such as *halakhah* and *melekh,* the guttural sound is transliterated as "kh" rather than "ch."

Life-Cycle Event

The Stages of Life

Describing the stages of life, Rabbi Yehudah ben Tema said (Avot 5:25):

At five, a child begins [the study of] Torah
At ten, Mishnah
At thirteen, [he is responsible for performance of] the mitzvot
At fifteen, he begins [the study of] Talmud
At eighteen, [he is ready for] marriage
At twenty, he begins the pursuit [of a livelihood][1]
At thirty, [a person is at the fullness of] strength
At forty, [he reaches the time of] understanding
At fifty, [he can offer] counsel[2]
At sixty, he enters his senior years[3]
At seventy, he attains a ripe old age[4]
At eighty, [his survival indicates] strength[5]
At ninety, he becomes stooped over [in anticipation of the grave]
At one hundred, it is as if he were dead, passed away, and withdrawn from the world.[6]

According to the commentators, up to age 15 represents the period of education through Torah and mitzvot. From 15 to 50 is the time of raising a family and social responsibility; from 50 to 80 is the period of wisdom and counsel; and after 80 is the time to prepare for the end, when a wise person withdraws from the scene and allows the new generation to take over.[7]

A popular expression is to wish another person, whether young or old, to live until 120—the life span of Moses (Deut. 34:7), the greatest Jew who ever lived. To reach this age is to be granted not only the great gift of length of days but also the supreme honor of being linked to the life of the most revered figure in Jewish history.[8]

First 16 Years of Life

Birth (לֵידָה)

The birth of a child is a joyous event in Judaism. In addition to reflecting the participation of the parents in the ongoing process of creation, childbirth is also the fulfillment of the first mitzvah in the Torah—to "be fruitful and multiply" (Gen. 1:28). According to the Mishnah (Yev. 6:6), this commandment is incumbent only on the male and is minimally fulfilled when he has fathered two children, one son and one daughter. However, Jewish law and historical practice urge Jews to have as many children as possible (Yev. 62b).

The ceremonies associated with the birth of a male child include circumcision (*brit milah;* see p. 7) and the redemption of the firstborn (*pidyon ha-ben;* see p. 20), but these do not take place until 8 and 31 days, respectively, after birth. Traditional Judaism has developed virtually no rituals for the process of childbirth. The pain associated with childbirth is related to the sin of Eve in the Garden of Eden (Gen. 3:16), while Rachel (Gen. 35:18) and Michal, the wife of King David (Sanh. 21a), were reported to have died during childbirth. After birth, the mother was deemed ritually impure for 40 days if the child was a boy and 80 days if the child was a girl, after which the mother was obligated to bring sin and burnt offerings (Lev. 12:2–8). The Talmud indicates that the sin offering is required because, while suffering the pangs of childbirth, the woman may have rashly vowed to spare herself such pain in the future by abstaining from further sexual relations with her husband (Nid. 31b).

According to the Talmud (Shab. 2:6), death during childbirth was related to the lapses of women in fulfilling their three classic roles: observance of family purity (see p. 560), separating the challah (dough offering; see p. 141) and kindling the Sabbath lights (see p. 136). Although the ancient Rabbis were convinced that an eight-month-old fetus could not survive, they established six months and a day after conception as the moment life began. Abortion was prohibited as a form of birth control, but was permitted to save the life of the mother, since "her life comes before that of the child." However, the mother's life no longer took precedence once the head of the newborn was delivered, because the child was considered a separate living being "and one may not set aside one person's life for that of another" (Oho. 7:6). The biblical distinction (Exod. 21:22–24) between the penalties incurred for causing the death of a mother ("life for life") and her unborn child (monetary payment) led the Rabbis to conclude that abortion is not considered a capital crime. Indeed, it was not even deemed murder to kill a newborn unless it was certain that it could survive for 30 days (the talmudic definition of viability) (Nid. 5:3).

Desecration of the Sabbath is permitted for delivery of a healthy baby (Shab. 18:3), even if the mother has already died during labor (Ar. 7a). A child delivered by cesarean section did not have either the rights or the responsibilities of the firstborn (Bek. 8:2), since it was not considered as being "the first issue of [the] womb" (Exod. 13:2).

Customs

Because of the significant danger inherent in childbirth, many folk customs surrounding birth were adapted from local non-Jewish traditions to protect the mother and child from evil spirits. These included (1) leaving the doors of the house and all its cupboards open, as well as unbuttoning buttons and untying knots, so that the mother's womb would also open; (2) having the mother wear around her abdomen a string that measured seven times the circumference of the grave of a renowned rabbi or the perimeter of the cemetery, or having her wear the sacred belt or other garments of a holy sage; (3) placing in her hand the key to the synagogue; (4) tying a variety of inscribed amulets (especially with red stones) around the mother's foot, thigh, belly, or forehead; (5) reciting special biblical passages (especially from Psalms) while the mother was in labor; (6) giving her a piece left over from the *afikoman* at the seder (see p. 287) or letting her chew on the *pitam* of the *etrog* (see p. 231); (7) having the mother drink water from the inverted finials (*rimonim*) crowning the staves of the Torah scroll; and (8) swinging a hen in circles around the mother's head to atone for her sins (a

Kurdistani practice), similar to the *kaparos* ritual performed on the eve of Yom Kippur (see p. 223).[1] In some communities, a man whose wife is in the ninth month of pregnancy is given the honor of opening the ark in the synagogue, with the hope that the merit of her husband performing this mitzvah may make her labor pains easier.[2]

A variety of charms and amulets inscribed with magic formulas were placed above the bed of the mother and on the doorposts of the room to guard against Lilith—the female evil spirit and natural enemy of newborns—who was the legendary first wife of Adam. The new mother was kept awake for the first three days after birth to prevent Lilith from harming her. In Oriental communities, it was customary to hang a *hamsikah* (an amulet shaped like outstretched hands) over the crib to protect against Broshah, a female demon who stole newborn children. Another Middle Eastern tradition for safeguarding newborns was to place sweets under the bed so that the evil spirits would be distracted from the infant while eating the treats. Among the customs believed to protect the child were (1) drawing a magic circle with chalk or charcoal on the floor of the room to guard against evil spirits, (2) hanging garlic in the baby's room, (3) tying a red thread onto the crib, (4) hanging blue beads or pieces of ivory and coral above the cradle, (5) sounding the shofar to drive the demons away by the loud noise, and (6) calling the child by a "code name" to confuse the evil spirits.

On the first Friday evening after the birth of a boy, the joyous ceremony *shalom zachar* (peace to the male child) is traditionally held, since "as soon as a male comes into the world, peace comes into the world" (Nid. 31b). Guests visit the new baby's home to join the family in prayer, a festive meal, and a discussion of words of Torah.[3] According to the Talmud, the ceremony of *shalom zachar* developed during the Roman Empire, when Jews were forbidden to circumcise their sons (Sanh. 32b). A feast was held shortly after the child's birth in an attempt to convince the Romans that no circumcision was to follow on the eighth day.

The Talmud states that when a baby is in the womb, "he is taught the entire Torah. However, as soon as he enters the air of this world, an angel comes and strikes him on his mouth, causing him to forget the entire Torah" (Nid. 20b). This is done so that children are able to study Torah on their own and know that their achievements are due solely to their own individual efforts. Nevertheless, the baby who has forgotten all the Torah he or she has learned is regarded as being like a mourner. Just as we customarily visit mourners in their home to comfort them during the period of bereavement, we visit the child as well. At the meal, it is traditional to serve chickpeas, a sign of mourning. Another custom is to have a group of children stand near the newborn's bed and recite the *Shema* together, to symbolically "train" the new arrival to accept the yoke of the commandments.[4]

The night preceding circumcision (see below) was the time for another home ceremony, *Leil Shimurim* (Night of Watching; *Vach Nacht* in Yiddish). This probably developed because friends and relatives, who were visiting the new parents, commonly joined the *mohel* on his rounds as he checked on the health of the infant. Later, this custom reflected the perceived need to guard the newborn throughout the night against malevolent spirits, especially Lilith. In the glow of candlelight (because evil spirits were said to avoid light), a festive meal featuring cooked beans and peas (to scare away demons) was eaten, and the participants held a vigil around the crib, reciting prayers and studying Torah. Before departing, all recited the *Shema* near the mother.

Because childbirth now usually takes place in modern hospitals, most of these traditional childbirth customs have tended to disappear, particularly since they were primarily based on medieval folklore and superstition.

Circumcision (בְּרִית מִילָה)

Circumcision (*brit milah*, popularly pronounced in its Yiddish form, *bris*), the ceremony of removing the foreskin of the penis on the eighth day of life, is the first life-cycle ritual commanded in the Torah (Gen. 17:11–12). The Hebrew word "*brit*" means "covenant," and thus this procedure symbolizes the entry of the infant boy into the covenant that God made with the patriarch Abraham almost 4,000 years ago. Judaism has long regarded circumcision as the primary symbol of male membership within the Jewish people. At age 99, Abraham circumcised himself, his 13-year-old son Ishmael, and every male of his household in response to God's command (Gen. 17:9–14, 23–27); in the next year, Abraham circumcised Isaac when the boy was eight days old (Gen. 21:4). The tradition maintains that Abraham's circumcision occurred on the 10th of Tishrei, which later became Yom Kippur—the day on which God forgives the transgressions of the Jewish people and welcomes them back into the covenant (PdRE 29).[1]

History

Circumcision was performed in many ancient cultures, primarily on adolescents as a puberty rite symbolizing a boy's sexual maturity and marking the passage from childhood to adulthood. However, the Jewish practice of performing circumcision in infancy reflects a sanctification of the body of a newborn male to the divine service, committing him to control his sexual urges and channel them toward providing for the perpetuation of his people. For the ancient Israelites, circumcision may have been a symbolic wish for fertility. This concept is supported by the similarity in the Bible between the language describing circumcision and that used for pruning fruit trees to increase their productivity, for example: "When you enter the land and plant any tree for food, you shall regard its fruit as its foreskin. Three years it shall be uncircumcised for you, not to be eaten .... [O]nly in the fifth year may you use its fruit—that its yield to you may be increased" (Lev. 19:23–25). Each circumcision is a symbolic re-enactment of the divine covenant, in which God promised Abraham to "make you exceedingly fertile" (Gen. 17:6) and to "make your descendants as numerous as the stars of heaven and the sands on the seashore" (Gen. 22:17).[2]

Circumcision plays a major role in several biblical stories. When Shechem raped Dinah and then wanted to marry her, Jacob's sons insisted that this would not be possible until after the prince and his people were circumcised (Gen. 34:14). However, three days after Shechem and the other males underwent this procedure and were in intense pain, Simeon and Levi (two of Dinah's brothers) killed Shechem's men in revenge. When Moses was returning to Egypt from Midian, God sought to kill him, apparently for failing to circumcise his own son (Exod. 4:24–26). Only when his wife, Zipporah, performed the circumcision was Moses spared. Circumcision was not merely a religious practice but also a sign of national identity, for only circumcised males were permitted to join in eating the Passover sacrifice (Exod. 12:43–48).

Although circumcision has been a significant act throughout Jewish history, it has not been practiced at all times. Because of the dangers they faced during their wanderings, none of the Jews born in the Sinai wilderness were circumcised until God commanded Joshua that this rite should be fulfilled before the people could enter the Land of Israel (Josh. 5:2–8). Circumcision was apparently abandoned in the Northern Kingdom during the reign of King Ahab and his Phoenician wife, Jezebel. By convincing the Israelites to resume this lapsed practice, the prophet Elijah earned the title "messenger (angel) of the covenant" (see Chair of Elijah; p. 11).

During Hellenistic times, circumcision was widely neglected; some Jews even had their foreskins restored in a painful surgical procedure so as to participate nude in Greek athletic events. The first ruler to prohibit circumcision was Antiochus Epiphanes, the Syrian-Greek tyrant at the time of the Hanukkah story (1 Macc. 1:48). Nevertheless, some mothers refused to obey this decree and had their sons circumcised, often at the cost of the lives of both mother and child (2 Macc. 6:10). Owing to the influential Jewish community, circumcision became widespread in the Roman Empire. Hadrian's forbidding this ceremony was a cause of the Bar Kokhba revolt, and circumcision became a crucial distinction between Jews and Christians.

Laws

According to the Shulchan Arukh (YD 260:1), the Jewish father is responsible for having his son circumcised. Should he fail to do so, it becomes the duty of the son to have himself circumcised when he reaches the age of bar mitzvah. Nevertheless, circumcision is not a requirement for membership in the Jewish people—any male child born of a Jewish mother is a Jew, whether circumcised or not. According to *halakhah*, circumcision ideally should be performed by a *mohel* who is specially trained in the medical procedure and is familiar with the Jewish ritual. In the traditional community, a *mohel* must be ritually observant in all respects; among more liberal Jews and in remote communities where *mohalim* are not readily available, a physician may be called on to perform the circumcision while a rabbi conducts the ritual. However, circumcision may be performed by any Jew, including a woman if no male is available.[3]

Circumcision is traditionally performed at home on the eighth day—with the day of birth counting as the first day—even if it falls on the Sabbath, Yom Kippur, or a festival, unless the boy was born by cesarean section, in which case the circumcision is postponed to the next weekday. It is customary for the circumcision to take place early in the morning, to emulate Abraham's eagerness in undertaking this divine command. The primary justification for delaying circumcision is concern for the health of the child. A delay also may be justified by the unavailability of a *mohel* on a Sabbath or holiday because of the need to travel. If the child is premature or in poor health, it is necessary to delay the circumcision until seven days after he has recovered (and in these cases it is not performed on the Sabbath or a holiday).

For a healthy newborn male who for some reason was circumcised before the eighth day or who was born without a foreskin, it is traditional to perform the ceremony of "shedding the blood of the covenant" (*hatafat dam brit*) on the eighth day, as long as it is a weekday. This procedure is performed by nicking the skin of the penis with a scalpel or needle to produce a small drop of blood.

Ritual

As a prelude to the circumcision ritual, the child is handed from the mother to the *kvaterin,* and then to the *kvater* (Polish-Yiddish corruptions of German words meaning "godmother" and "godfather," respectively), and then to the father. These intermediate steps are required because the father is not permitted to take the child directly from the mother, who is still in a state of ritual impurity from childbirth. While this is occurring, all present rise and welcome the child with the phrase "*baruch ha-ba.*" This common welcoming greeting is usually translated as "Blessed be he who comes"; however, since the numerical value of the word "*ha-ba*" in Hebrew is eight, in this context those assembled are effectively welcoming "the eight-day-old."

The father recites a formula in which he declares that he is ready to fulfill the mitzvah of circumcising his son according to the divine commandment (Gen. 17:12). He then delivers his son to the *sandek,* usually one of the infant's grandfathers, who holds the boy on a pillow placed on a table or on his lap during the procedure. In many communities, the *sandek* sits on a special "chair of Elijah"; in some traditions the chair remains unoccupied at his immediate right.

As a surrogate for the father, the *mohel* then recites the blessing for circumcision and performs the procedure. The father, or both parents

CHAIR OF ELIJAH (כִּיסֵא שֶׁל אֵלִיָּהוּ)

The chair of Elijah (*kisse Eliyahu*) is a special chair, usually richly carved and ornamented with embroideries, that was traditionally left unoccupied and symbolically meant for Elijah the prophet at the circumcision ceremony. In some communities, it is now occupied by the *sandek* (godfather). Elijah is depicted as the protector of the Jewish child, probably based on the biblical story in which he revived the son of a widow (1 Kings 17:17–24). Another reason for the symbolic presence of Elijah at every circumcision is the traditional belief that the prophet will ultimately announce the crowning of the Messiah to redeem humankind. Therefore, Elijah must appear at each circumcision to determine whether this child will be the awaited one.

in some communities, recites a blessing entering the child into the covenant "of Abraham our father." All present then respond: "As he has entered the covenant, so may he be brought to *Torah, huppah, u-ma'asim tovim* [to the study of Torah, to the marriage canopy, and to the practice of good deeds]." After reciting a blessing over wine, the *mohel* says a blessing for the welfare of the child and his family. During the course of this benediction, the Hebrew name of the child is announced (see p. 14). Finally, the *mohel* or parents drink the wine and a few drops are given to the infant. Sometimes, the ritual concludes with a recitation of the Priestly Blessing (see p. 432). The ceremony is followed by a festive meal (*seudat mitzvah*), after which blessings are recited for the *sandek*, the *mohel*, the parents, and their son in a special *Birkat ha-Mazon* (Grace after Meals).

Several interesting customs are related to circumcision. Because of the prohibition against carrying objects on the Sabbath, it was customary to keep the knife of the *mohel* under the mother's pillow before sunset on Friday evening for a circumcision to be held on Saturday morning. In the 16th century, the kabbalists extended this practice to all circumcisions, based on the belief that the demons who attack newborn infants are scared away by knives and similar objects made of iron. In some Central and Eastern European communities, it was customary to cut and sew the richly embroidered linen cloth on which a boy was circumcised into a wimple, which was presented to the congregation on the child's first visit to the synagogue. It later was used to wrap the Torah scroll when the boy was called for an aliyah on his bar mitzvah and on the Sabbath before his wedding.[4]

The lighting of candles at a *brit milah* recalls the times when repressive rulers issued decrees preventing circumcision. To obtain the necessary minyan (quorum of 10 men) without making a public announcement, candles would be lit and placed by the windows so that those passing by would know that a circumcision was about to take place and would come in to witness the ceremony.[5]

The *Shehecheyanu* blessing is not recited at a circumcision because the procedure produces considerable pain and distress for the infant. In some communities, the foreskin is placed into ashes or dust after it has been removed. This relates to the mass circumcision of the Israelites when they first entered the Land of Canaan after their 40-year journey through the wilderness. The site where this took place was named Givat ha-Aralot (Josh. 5:3), which literally means "Hill of Foreskins." According to a midrash, this implies that Joshua gathered together all the foreskins of the Israelites into a mound, which he then covered with earth.[6]

Rationale

Circumcision is the physical sign of the everlasting covenant between God and Abraham and, by extension, his descendants. Among the many rationales later given for the practice of circumcision are the following: (1) to safeguard cleanliness and health (Philo), (2) to weaken the sex drive of a man and counteract excessive lust (Maimonides), and (3) to make a sacrifice to God, somewhat akin to having the blood of an animal atone for one's sins (Nachmanides). This last reason connects circumcision with the *Akedah* (the binding of Isaac), the biblical scene that often appears on the circumcision knife. Cutting off the foreskin and ritually offering it to God enables the Jewish male symbolically to protect his entire body by "sacrificing" a small portion of it. According to the Midrash, circumcision enables human beings to become partners with God in completing the divine work of Creation (Gen. R. 11:6).[7] As the *Sefer ha-Hinnukh* observed: "The Holy One, blessed be He, wanted man to perfect himself by human action. Therefore, He did not create man in his completed state in the womb [man is born uncircumcised] to indicate that, just as man completes his physical form by his own hand, so, too, it is given to man to perfect the form of his soul by his own actions."[8] Indeed, the Rabbis noted that despite "all the precepts [religious duties] which Abraham fulfilled, he was not designated 'perfect' [Gen. 17:1] until about to circumcise himself" (Ned. 31b). By extension, in the Bible the word "uncircumcised" often refers to body organs that are "spiritually obstructed" and cannot function properly. Thus Moses attempts to justify his reluctance to be God's prophet by describing himself as having "uncircumcised lips" (impeded speech; Exod. 6:12),[9] and he urges the Israelites to "circumcise the foreskin of your heart" (Deut. 10:16)[10] so that they will no longer stubbornly refuse to accept the divine laws. Similarly, Jeremiah (6:10) railed against the Israelites for failing to heed his warnings, accusing them of having "uncircumcised ears" that do not listen.

Medical Correlation

Although the eighth day seems to be an arbitrary time to perform a circumcision, there actually is a good medical reason for this practice. In a newborn, the factor that allows blood to clot does not mature until about the eighth day. Performing a *brit milah* before this time could result in the infant bleeding to death.[11] Nevertheless, most traditional Jews would simply cite Rabbi Akiva's explanation for performing circumcisions on the eighth day. In response to this question of a Roman emperor—Since a child is born uncircumcised, why should what has been divinely created not be left exactly so?—Akiva noted that God purposely did not create a perfect world so as to enable people to play a role in ongoing creation. After fashioning the world in seven days, on the eighth day God said to human beings: "Now you take over and continue what I have begun."[12]

Simchat Bat (שִׂמְחַת בַּת)

As a response to the demand of modern feminists for equality between the sexes in religious ritual, the custom has developed in liberal and even some modern Orthodox circles to celebrate the birth of a girl on her eighth day of life (or later) at a home gathering called *simchat bat* (rejoicing of a daughter). In the absence of an established ritual, the parents can design a ceremony that is meaningful for them. Many include passages from Song of Songs and Psalms, as well as biblical selections featuring such famous women as the seven prophetesses (Sarah, Miriam, Deborah, Hannah, Abigail, Huldah, and Esther), followed by a special blessing over wine and a festive meal.[13]

Names (שֵׁמוֹת)

A person's name is thought to define and control his or her soul and destiny (Ber. 7b). Therefore, the selection of an appropriate name is a critical decision. "One should ever examine names, to give his son a name worthy for him to become a righteous man, for sometimes the name is a contributory factor for good as for evil."[1] A symbolic change of name often accompanies a change in personal status, such as relating to adoption, marriage, or conversion.[2]

Until the Emancipation, Jews had no family names. They possessed only the Hebrew name given to a boy on the occasion of his *brit milah* (circumcision) and to a girl when her father was honored with an aliyah in the synagogue shortly after her birth. A person's complete Hebrew name is his or her first name (and middle name) followed by *ben* (son of) or *bat* (daughter of) and then the first (and middle) name of the father (and in some liberal circles today, often also that of the mother). If the father is a Kohen or Levite, the child's name ends with the word *ha-Kohen* or *ha-Levi*, respectively. Even today, these Hebrew names are used during Jewish ceremonies and rituals—when called to the Torah for an aliyah, on the *ketubah* (marriage document; see p. 44), and in a special memorial prayer at the funeral and later on the gravestone in the cemetery.[3]

Biblical Period

Many biblical names have deep significance related to an event that accompanied the birth, the life of the parents, their hope for the newborn's good fortune, or simply an expression of thanks to God for the blessing of a child.[4] The sons of Rachel and Leah were named in response to the rivalry of the sisters for Jacob's love (Gen. 29:32–35, 30:6–24). Thus Leah called her first son Reuben (meaning, "see, a son") saying, "The Lord has seen my affliction; ... Now my husband will love me" (Gen. 29:32). After years of barrenness, the exultant Rachel named her firstborn "Joseph" (meaning, "may He add") saying, "May the Lord add another son" (Gen. 30:24). As Rachel was dying in childbirth, she named her second son "Ben-oni" (meaning, "son of my suffering"). Fearing that this name would doom the child to a dismal fate, Jacob changed it to "Benjamin" (meaning, "son of my right hand"; Gen. 35:18). When Pharaoh's daughter adopted the Hebrew child she found in the bulrushes along the Nile, she named him "Moses," which the Torah interprets as meaning "I drew him out of the water" (Exod. 2:10). (The name actually is of Egyptian origin from a root relating to "birth," which was commonly added to the name of a god as in Moses' contemporary Ramses, which means "born of Ra" [the sun god].[5])

Biblical names often contain some form of one of the names of God (see p. 624) in the parents' effort either to praise God or to secure divine protection for their child. Among these are *El*; abridged forms of YHVH (the Tetragrammaton, or four-letter name of God), such as *Yah* and *Yehu*; *Melekh* (King); *Baal* (Master); *Shaddai* (Almighty); *Tzur* (Rock); and *Adon* (Lord). Many biblical personalities received new names after transforming experiences with the Divine. Thus Abram and Sarai became Abraham and Sarah, respectively, after the covenant symbolized by circumcision (Gen. 17:5,15), and Jacob was renamed Israel after wrestling with a mysterious "man" (Gen. 32:29). Surprisingly, Isaac, whose near sacrifice forever altered his relationship with God, did not receive a new name after the *Akedah*. Places also may receive new names after an encounter with the Divine. For example, the site of Jacob's dream of the ladder with ascending and descending angels, originally called Luz, was renamed *Beit El* (house of God) by the Patriarch (Gen. 28:19).[6]

In the early biblical period, first names were uniquely coined at the child's birth and considered his or her exclusive possession. For example, the names of the Patriarchs and other major figures are never repeated in the Bible. This even applied to the royal family, in which none of the 21 kings of Judah was named after David, the first of the dynasty.[7] Some children were named for animals and plants, such as Rachel (ewe), Jonah (dove), Deborah (bee), and Tamar (palm tree).[8]

Talmudic Period

The Talmud complains that "most Jews in foreign parts [the Diaspora] bear heathen names [have the same names as the gentiles]" (Git. 11b). Faced with the prevalent tendency of Jews adopting foreign names, the Rabbis stressed that one of the reasons why the Israelites were delivered from Egyptian bondage was that "they did not change their names" (Lev. R. 32:5). It is unclear whether they were attacking the change from a previously given Hebrew name to a gentile name—a custom that was decried as a sign of deliberate assimilation—or the initial giving of non-Jewish names. Several late biblical figures were known both by their Hebrew and non-Jewish names, such as Hadassah–Esther; Daniel–Balshazzar; and his three friends Hananiah–Shadrach, Mishael–Mishach, and Azariah–Abed Nego. Under Hellenistic influence, it apparently became a widespread custom for an individual to have two names, one Semitic (Hebrew or Aramaic) and one Greek. Examples include such Hasmonean rulers as John (Yochanan) Hyrcanus, Judah Aristobulus, and Salome Alexandra, as well as the five sons of Mattathias (e.g., "Judah, called Maccabeus"; 1 Macc. 2:2). Some Greek names were direct translations from the Hebrew, such as Philo (the famed philosopher) from Yedidiah and Theodorus from Nathaniel. Other talmudic era names were authentic Hebrew appellations that were Hellenized in form or spelling, such as Joseph becoming Jose and Shimon changing into Simon.[9]

The Rabbis recommended that children be given names of major biblical figures—the Patriarchs and Matriarchs; several of Jacob's sons; Moses, Miriam, and Aaron; and various judges, prophets, and kings. Despite this, there is the puzzling absence in the Talmud of names that one would expect. Not a single Rabbi is known by the name of Abraham, Israel, Moses, David, or Solomon. Similarly, the names of the prophets are also rare among the talmudic sages. Instead, obscure biblical names became fashionable because of the accomplishments of those who bore them, such as Hillel and Gamaliel. New nonbiblical Hebrew names were developed, such as Akiva, Meir, and Nachman; others were chosen from Hebrew words with positive associations, such as Chaim (life), Simcha (happiness), and Ari (lion). The Talmud prohibited giving a child the name of a wicked person (Yoma 38b), but this often appears to have been disregarded. Several high priests and *tannaim* were named Ishmael; some rabbinic scholars were called

Menachem (a biblical king who "did what was displeasing to the Lord"; 2 Kings 15:18).[10]

Medieval Period

Medieval Jews continued to prefer Hebrew names, which usually could be easily adapted to the language of the surrounding society. For example, Jews living in Arab-speaking countries used Ibrahim for Abraham and Dawud for David.[11] Some Jewish children were given "abstract" names, such as Emunah (faith) and Nissim (miracles), or names related to their day of birth. Thus boys born on the seventh day might be named Shabbetai, while those born during a festival could be called by the generic name Yom Tov or the more specific Pesach or Mordecai (for Purim).[12] In general, there was a greater likelihood of girls being given non-Hebrew names.

By this time, the use of non-Jewish names had become so widespread that the rabbis ordered that every Jewish boy be given a purely religious name at his circumcision. This led to the custom, still prevalent today, in which the Jew has a "religious" name for being called up to the Torah (and in religious documents) and a non-Jewish name for civil and business purposes. At times, the non-Jewish name was a direct translation of the Hebrew one, such as the Hebrew–German/Yiddish combinations Dov Baer or Zvi Hirsch. Another approach, especially common in the United States today, is to give the child an English name with the same first letter as his or her Hebrew name. Thus Reuben can be transformed into Robert, Ronald, or Ralph, while Deborah could become Doris, Denise, or Deirdre.[13]

It became increasingly popular to add an additional term to the given name to identify the individual more precisely. The most traditional of these "surnames" was the patronym (father's name). Thus the Hebrew *ben* (son of) was transformed into the Arabic *ibn* (as in Ibn Ezra and Ibn Shaprut). Another typically Arab usage was to identify the father by his firstborn son (designated by *abu*). Some surnames derived from the bearer's birthplace or adult residence (such as Isaac Alfasi, i.e., "of Fez"). This practice became particularly widespread when periodic expulsions led Jews to select names that recalled their earlier homes (such as de Leon and D'Alvo). Other sources of widely used surnames were occupations (such as ha-Rofe, "the doctor"), character traits (such as he-Hasid, "the pious"), and physical characteristics (size, age, complexion). Eventually, these surnames became family names that were passed on through the generations.

Some children were given two genuinely Jewish names. The primary motivation for this practice was to honor two deceased relatives at the same time. However, this could lead to conflict if both the father and the mother wanted to name the child for relatives in their respective families. Eventually, it became the custom that the name of the first child belonged to the father, while that of the second child could be chosen by the mother. Another compromise was to permit one parent to give the child the sacred name and the other the ordinary name.[14]

Two types of designations were especially popular among Jews during the Middle Ages and early modern period. Some names derived from an acronym consisting of abbreviations of a title (e.g., rabbi or *ha-gaon*), the given name, and the surname. Well-known examples include such illustrious scholars as Rashi (**R**abbi **Sh**lomo **I**tzhaki), Rambam (**R**abbi **M**oses **b**en **M**aimon), Ramban (**R**abbi **M**oses **b**en **N**achman), Malbim (**M**eir **L**oeb **b**en **Y**ehiel **M**ichael), and Hagra (**Ha**-**G**aon **R**abbi **E**lijah). Other rabbis were known by their major scholarly works. As in the cases of the Tur (Jacob ben Asher), the Kli Yakar (Shlomo Efrayim), and the Imrei Bina (Meir Auerbach), these names virtually replaced their given names and surnames.

Modern Period

With the increasing tendency of Jews to engage in conventional European life after the onset of the Emancipation, the use of permanent surnames became important. Common choices included patronyms (Isaacson, Davidson) as well as names based on localities (Wien, Warshaw), on occupation (Fiedler [fiddler], Sofer [scribe], Schneider [tailor], Sandler [shoemaker]), on physical characteristics (Gross [big], Klein [little], Weiss [white], Schwartz [black]), and even on a distinguishing feature of a house (Rothschild [red shield]). When the government assigned names, Jews with the means to bribe officials could receive "beautiful" names such as Goldberg (gold mountain), Rosenthal (valley of roses), Margulis (pearls), and Rubinstein (rubies) or Bernstein (amber).[15]

Jews increasingly adopted first names prevalent in general society, while rejecting more traditional names that were considered "too

Jewish." This also applied to surnames, especially in the United States, where the family names brought from Eastern Europe generally branded their bearers as immigrants. Cumbersome Slavic endings were dropped to form short, American-sounding names. Millions of immigrants, many ignorant of the English language, flooded into the United States, and the practical necessity of registering their names resulted in the creation of a host of new surnames owing to the language barrier between foreigners and immigration officers. The classic example is the immigrant who, when asked for his name, responded *shen forgessen* (already I forgot) and promptly became "Sean Ferguson."

The rise of Zionism and the revival of the Hebrew language engendered a new interest in Hebrew names, which have evolved over time. Successive generations within the Jewish community of Palestine, and subsequently the State of Israel, tended to reject older names. Instead, they preferred to select biblical names not commonly used in the Diaspora (such as Gideon, Yael, Amnon, and Bilhah) or names commemorating geographic locations and flora of the Land of Israel (such as Sharon, Carmela, Ilanah, and Erez). Some chose names that are directly related to the joy of the modern return of the Jewish people to their ancestral land—Geula (redemption), Yigal (He will redeem), Aviva (spring), and variants of Shir (sing) and Rina (rejoice).[16] Although most American Jews, as part of the assimilatory process, choose secular names for their children—Steve instead of Shlomo, Mary instead of Miriam—biblical and other Hebrew first names have become increasingly popular. The Zionist experience led to the Hebraization of family names, as with such major political figures as David Ben-Gurion (formally Greun), Golda Meir (Myerson), and Yitzhak Ben-Zvi (Shimshelevitz). The changes in surnames during the past two centuries have been so extensive that brothers and cousins in the Diaspora and Israel now often have totally different family names.

Customs and Rituals

While there are no laws pertaining to the choosing of a Hebrew name for a child, there are important traditions that differ among various Jewish communities. Ashkenazim generally name a child for a deceased relative, both to perpetuate that person's memory and with the hope that the child will manifest the spiritual qualities of the beloved who is no longer alive. Thus names in certain families recur every few generations, causing each person to feel spiritually close to his or her recent and remote namesakes. This tradition began among the royal family and aristocracy during the Hasmonean period and gradually spread to the general public. Ashkenazim consider it bad luck to name a child after a living relative. This is probably based on the ancient notion that names give power over the souls and fates of others, so that this practice would rob the previously named individual of his full life. In contrast, among Sephardim it is customary to name children after living relatives, particularly the grandparents.[17]

In the shtetls of Eastern Europe, when someone was gravely ill, members of the community would change the person's name as a last desperate measure. They reasoned that if, for example, God had ordained that a person by the name of David was to die, the divine judgment might not extend to a person by the name of Moshe. A copy of the Hebrew Scripture would be opened at random, and the patient would be given the name of the first meritorious Jew that appeared. If he or she recovered, the individual would carry the new name from then on. Although this may seem like merely a vain superstition, it reflected the Jewish belief that God was waiting for only a loophole to extend divine mercy.[18]

Pidyon ha-Ben (פִּדְיוֹן הַבֵּן)

Pidyon ha-ben (redemption of the [firstborn] son) allows a firstborn male to be exempt from certain traditional responsibilities. As a consequence of the miracle of the 10th plague, when God smote all the firstborn males in Egypt (both man and beast) but passed over those of the Israelites dwelling in Goshen, the firstborn son was to be dedicated to God and perform religious services for the *Kohanim* in the Temple (Num. 3:13). (Firstborn Jewish males traditionally fast on the day before Passover to commemorate this miraculous sparing of their ancestors in Egypt; see p. 291.) However, it was possible to release a firstborn male from this obligation by redeeming him through the payment of five shekels to the Kohen (as the representative of God).

According to the Midrash (Num. R. 4:6), the sacrificial rituals were originally performed by all firstborn males, who were to serve as the assistants to the priests. However, after the shameful episode of the Golden Calf, this privilege was taken away from the firstborn of every tribe and awarded solely to the Levites. The Levites qualified for this special privilege because they had not participated in this sin, instead being the only ones to step forward when Moses, angered by the calf, smashed the tablets and delivered an ultimatum: "Whoever is for the Lord, come here" (Exod. 32:26).

Historical Origins

Ancient peoples believed that the gods were entitled to the first yield of field and womb, and thus the firstborn of cattle and of children were sacrificed to them. Abraham unquestioningly accepted the divine claim to Isaac (his firstborn child with Sarah) and was prepared to give up the life of his child. The *Akedah*, with the sparing of Isaac at the last moment once Abraham had passed the test, showed that Judaism had at an early age transcended this primitive and brutal concept. Having a child belong to God no longer meant its death; instead, the concept was transformed into the assumption of a leadership position in the divine service.[1]

Ceremony

Pidyon ha-ben takes place on the 31st day after the child's birth (with the day of birth counting as the first day). The reason for this delay is that Judaism considers a child viable only after 30 days. The redemption ritual is postponed if the 31st day falls on the Sabbath or a festival, when all business transactions are prohibited. The ceremony takes place in the synagogue or at home in the context of a festive meal (*seudat mitzvah*). Traditionally, the father presents his son (often on a silver tray decorated with jewelry, to indicate love for the mitzvah) to a Kohen, who is a descendant on his father's side from Aaron, the high priest. After being officially presented with the child, the Kohen asks the father whether he prefers to redeem his son or leave him. The father selects the former alternative and gives the Kohen five silver coins (originally shekels, but today typically five silver dollars or coins of the country). The Bank of Israel, in conjunction with the Israeli government, has minted special "redemption coins" that can be used for this purpose. Following this transaction, the father recites the blessing for performing the mitzvah of *pidyon ha-ben* and *Shehecheyanu*, a prayer thanking God for allowing him to live to see this day. After the redeemed child has been returned to his father, the ceremony concludes with a blessing over wine and the Priestly Blessing (see p. 432).

Pidyon ha-ben is performed only if the firstborn son "is the first to open the mother's womb" (*peter rechem*), as is biblically prescribed (Exod. 13:1). Thus it does not apply to a boy who was delivered by cesarean section or to a second boy who was subsequently delivered vaginally. Similarly, the ritual is not performed if the mother had previously miscarried or had an abortion of a fetus that existed more than 40 days in utero. The first son of a Jewish mother must be redeemed, even if he has an older half-brother born to the father from a previous marriage. Conversely, it is not necessary to redeem a son who is the firstborn of the father but not the mother. Thus if a man marries a woman who already has a son from a previous marriage, any son issuing from their marriage need not be redeemed.

The requirement of *pidyon ha-ben* does not apply if the father or the maternal grandfather is a Kohen or Levite, since in this case the child would be obligated to serve in the Temple and could not be exempted. If the father fails to redeem his son because of negligence or death, it becomes the duty of the son to redeem himself when he grows up.

Today, *pidyon ha-ben* is usually practiced by Orthodox and Conservative Jews. However, it is not observed by Reform Jews, who do not recognize priestly status in modern times.[2]

Adoption (אִמּוּץ)

Although not a precisely defined institution in Jewish law, adoption is an option available to a couple who cannot have children.[1] As the "parent of all orphans," the rabbinic court has the authority to appoint a guardian who has essentially the same responsibilities as a biological parent—to provide for the upbringing, education, and shelter of the child and to administer his or her property. If the guardian dies, the estate remains responsible for continuing to provide for the care of the child. Unlike under American law, however, the biological parents remain obligated to the child and the guardian fulfills these obligations on their behalf.

According to Jewish religious law, the status of the adoptee is entirely hereditary. Although the child may assume the name of his new family, the privileges and obligations of being a Kohen or a Levite depend solely on birth. Conversely, the child retains the priestly classification regardless of the status of his adopted family. For the same reason, marriage to a natural member of the adopted family is permissible and would not violate the prohibitions against incest, although such unions are discouraged. Once adopted, the child is treated as if he or she were a biological child. In accordance with the rule that if one raises an orphan, one is considered to have given birth to that child, there is no halakhic objection to the adopter calling the adopted child son or daughter and the child calling the adopter his or her parent. The adoptee should love, respect, and honor his or her adoptive parents and observe all the laws of mourning, including the saying of *Kaddish*. An adopted child who is not definitely known to be Jewish must undergo formal conversion to be considered a Jew. At the age of bar or bat mitzvah, the child may choose to annul the conversion, but must do so promptly.

Bar Mitzvah (בַּר מִצְוָה)

Bar mitzvah (lit., "son of the commandment") is the celebration of a boy's 13th birthday according to the Jewish calendar, when he officially attains his legal and religious majority. Upon reaching this age, the boy is obliged to fulfill all the commandments and observe the religious duties incumbent on a Jew (Yoma 82a).

The special synagogue observance of the bar mitzvah as it is known today did not exist during biblical or rabbinic times. In the Bible, the age of 13 was not even recognized as a major milestone in a boy's life. Instead, the primary age of significance was 20, when a male was fit for military service, counted in the census, and obligated to give a half shekel for the upkeep of the Temple (Exod. 30:14; Num. 1:3). Twenty was also important because those this age and older were condemned to die in the wilderness because of the sin of the spies, whereas those who were younger were permitted to enter the Promised Land (Num. 13:31–33, 14:29).[1]

Although the term "bar mitzvah" occurs in the Talmud, it was purely a legal concept. A boy of 13 was required to fast for a full day on Yom Kippur (Yoma 82a). His vows were considered valid (Ned. 5:6), and he was deemed responsible for observing the mitzvot (Avot 5:25). A boy of this age could perform acts having legal implications, such as being a member of a *beit din*, being counted as part of a minyan, and buying and selling property.

According to the Midrash, 13 was the age at which Abraham rejected idolatry and set out on his own spiritual path and Jacob committed himself to a life of Torah study (PdRE 26).[2] The Rabbis understood age 13 as a milestone of physical maturity. Each individual is born with both a *yetzer ha-ra* (inclination toward evil) and a *yetzer ha-tov* (inclination toward good). However, since the *yetzer ha-tov* did not completely develop until age 13, only at that age could the boy be expected to keep his desires and passions entirely under control (ARN 16).[3]

Today, reaching the age of 13 is not simply when a boy becomes *obligated* to observe the commandments but rather the time when he is first *allowed* to participate in and perform the various rituals associated with full membership in the community. Before this age, he does not wear tallit and tefillin, and he cannot lead the congregation in prayer or be accorded the honor of being called up to the Torah. In earlier times, however, a child under 13 was permitted to perform these rituals if he understood their significance and was considered capable of doing them. The Talmud explicitly states: "If a minor knows how to wrap himself in the tallit, he is subject to the obligation ... if he knows how to look after tefillin, his father must acquire them for him" (Suk. 42a). Similarly, if knowledgeable, he was qualified to be called up to read from the Torah (Meg. 23a). Therefore, many young boys had performed these activities on numerous occasions before their 13th birthdays, so that there was effectively no religious distinction between a minor and an adult in talmudic times.

At some time in the Middle Ages, minors were deprived of the religious rights that had been granted them during the talmudic period. This served to heighten the significance and momentous nature of reaching the age of 13.[4] From the 14th century on, the bar mitzvah celebration became a permanent and festive part of the synagogue service. On the first Sabbath after his 13th birthday, a boy is called to the Torah to read the final *maftir* portion and chant the haftarah selection from the prophets. In some communities, it was and still is customary for the young man to read the entire Torah portion of the week.

After the bar mitzvah boy concludes the second Torah blessing, it is customary in Orthodox synagogues for his father to declare: "Praised is [God] who has relieved me from punishment because of this child [when he misbehaved]" (Gen. R. 63:10). The reason for saying this blessing is that before age 13 it is the responsibility of the father to make certain that his son studies Torah and performs mitzvot. However, once the boy reaches the age of maturity, this becomes the son's personal responsibility. If the son fails to pursue Torah studies, the father is exempt from any spiritual punishment resulting from this sin of omission.[5]

On a Sabbath when a bar mitzvah is celebrated, the morning service assumes a more festive atmosphere. Members of the boy's family are called up for the reading of the Torah, and the rabbi often delivers a special sermon stressing the boy's new responsibilities and privileges. In former times, it was customary for the bar mitzvah to deliver a learned address before the invited guests. Although sons of traditional families may still give a talmudic discourse, a more general talk is now the rule. In many modern synagogues, the rabbi ends the sermon by invoking the Priestly Blessing over the boy, who also is given a gift from the congregation. After the service, a festive *Kiddush* is held. The all-too-frequent practice of making extravagant parties with excessive expenditure to celebrate the bar mitzvah detracts from the spiritual significance of the day. Instead, making a contribution to charity of even part of the money typically spent on a lavish celebration would make a powerful impression on the young man and give him some idea of the values by which he should lead his life.[6]

It has now become common for Jews who were denied religious training in their childhood to celebrate a bar mitzvah as adults, symbolizing their full membership in the community. Although these ceremonies can be moving experiences and the extensive preparatory study should be encouraged and praised, it is important to remember that the essence of the bar mitzvah is only the *age* of the individual; the transition to legal and religious responsibility is automatic at age 13 and does not depend on any special initiation rites. Some Jews have made it a tradition to chant their Torah or haftarah portions each year on the anniversary of their bar mitzvah. Those reaching the age of 83 may celebrate the 70th anniversary of the occasion by chanting their original portions at a Sabbath service and then sponsoring a *Kiddush* in honor of their symbolic recommitment to the tradition.[7]

Bat Mitzvah (בַּת מִצְוָה)

Since the Rabbis assumed that girls matured physically and emotionally earlier than boys, they were deemed to have reached the age of Jewish responsibility by 12 years and a day. However, since women in Orthodox Judaism do not have the same ritual obligations and privileges as men (such as being counted in the minyan or being called up to the Torah for an aliyah), there was no need for girls to have a formal ceremony like the bar mitzvah.[1] Nevertheless, by the 19th century some families celebrated a girl's 12th birthday, according to the Jewish calendar, with a special meal (*seudat mitzvah*) and other nonsynagogue rituals.[2] Today, the practice in most non-Orthodox synagogues is for girls to become bat mitzvah at age 13.

The first recorded bat mitzvah celebrated with a formal synagogue service took place in 1922 for Judith Kaplan, the daughter of Rabbi Mordecai Kaplan, a professor at the Jewish Theological Seminary and later the founder of the Reconstructionist movement. During the service, she read the Torah blessings and some of the Torah portion from a book, after her father had read the same section from the Torah scroll. As the bat mitzvah ceremony has evolved, girls in Conservative, Reform, and Reconstructionist congregations now participate in all of the synagogue rituals performed by boys.[3]

It has now become common for Jewish women who were denied religious training in childhood to celebrate a bat mitzvah as adults, symbolizing their full membership in the community. Although these ceremonies can be moving experiences and the extensive preparatory study should be encouraged and praised, it is important to remember that the essence of the bat mitzvah is only the *age* of the individual; the transition to legal and religious responsibility is automatic and does not depend on any special initiation rites.[4]

Confirmation

Judaism traditionally has no confirmation ceremony, since the word implies the mastery of a specific belief system and the Jewish religion has no official creed. In the 19th century, the early Reform congregations in Germany attempted to replace the bar mitzvah with a ceremony termed "confirmation," a Jewish adaptation of Christian church practice. Unlike bar mitzvah, in which a 13-year-old boy is called to the Torah for an individual aliyah to signify his accepting responsibility for performing the mitzvot, confirmation was conceived as a group ceremony celebrated by both male and female religious school students at the completion of their studies at age 16 or 17. This was based on the belief that a child of bar or bat mitzvah age (13 for boys, 12 for girls) rarely has attained sufficient religious, intellectual, and social maturity to become an adult member of the Jewish community.

In modern times, especially in the United States, confirmation has been adopted as a supplement to, rather than a substitute for, the bar or bat mitzvah ceremony—a rite of passage that is almost universally observed throughout the Jewish world. The main intention of confirmation is to extend Jewish education by several years, enhancing the commitment of young adults to Judaism. The ceremony is generally held on Shavuot, the holiday celebrating the giving of the Torah on Mount Sinai (see p. 298), since confirmation students symbolically accept the Torah during the ceremony and publicly declare their dedication to Jewish ideals. The confirmands frequently receive a special certificate, testifying to their acceptance into the Jewish community.

Marriage

Jewish Marriage

The Jewish tradition views marriage as the ultimate human condition and basic to a healthy life. As the Talmud observes, "One who does not have a wife lives without joy, without blessing, and without goodness" (Yev. 62b) as well as without Torah, protection, and peace. Marriage is believed to have been established by God at the time of Creation both to provide humans with warm companionship and to allow them to fulfill the divine plan for procreation. It is considered a holy covenant between a man and woman, with God as the intermediary. As the mystical Zohar notes, "God creates new worlds constantly. In what way? By causing marriages to take place."

Biblical Period

The Bible stresses that one of the principal purposes of marriage is to nurture the intimate bond between man and woman. God declared: "It is not good for man to be alone; I will make a fitting helper for him" (Gen. 2:18). The relationship is to be so close that "[h]ence a man leaves his father and mother and clings to his wife, so that they become one flesh" (Gen. 2:24). Although marriage was thought to be the ideal state, it was not considered to be an unbreakable sacrament. If the relationship was fraught with grave problems, especially when the wife had committed adultery, the couple was permitted to divorce (see p. 62).

The other main purpose of marriage is for bearing and raising children. In fact, the first commandment in the Torah is "Be fruitful and multiply, fill the earth and master it" (Gen. 1:28).[1] A marriage with numerous children was considered blessed; thus barrenness was cause for intense sadness (as demonstrated by Sarah, Rachel, and Hannah). Marriage is so important that the Rabbis ruled that one may even suspend the study of Torah to rejoice with and bring joy to a bride and groom.

According to the biblical tradition, compassion and modesty were two essential qualities of the ideal Jewish wife. When Eliezer, the servant of Abraham, anxiously waited at the well to select a suitable wife for Isaac, he prayed that God send a woman who was generous, hospitable to strangers, and kind to animals (Gen. 24:12–14). Indeed, the Hebrew term "*rachmanut*" (compassion) comes from "*rechem*" (womb), indicating that such kindness is a quintessential female trait, akin to the love of a mother for her child. Modesty (*tzeniut*) is also a core value. This not only refers to attire but also to a reserved dignity—"discreet habits, quiet speech, and affections privately expressed ... intended to preserve the sanctity of the inner human being from assault by the coarseness of daily life."[2]

In biblical times, marriages were usually arranged by parents, as when Abraham sent Eliezer to find a wife for Isaac (Gen. 24). Sometimes, however, the bride had a say in the matter; for example, Rebecca was asked if she would agree to travel to Canaan to marry Isaac (Gen. 24:58). Love was not overlooked when finding a marriage partner. Well-known biblical romances include Jacob and Rachel (Gen. 29:20), Samson and Delilah (Judg. 16:4), Michal and David (1 Sam. 18:20), and David and Bathsheba (2 Sam. 11:2–4). The Song of Songs is essentially an allegorical paean to the romantic love between God and Israel.

During this time, most people married someone from their own clan; in fact, this was a requirement for levirate marriages (see p. 52). However, certain marriages within the group were forbidden, such as those involving close relatives and those between male *Kohanim* and women who had been divorced (see p. 48). Unions with individuals from other nations and cultures were discouraged to guard against idolatry and to avoid diluting the customs and language of the Jewish people. Thus Isaac and Rebecca were distraught when their son Esau married Hittite women (Gen. 26:34–35); Jacob's sons reacted violently against the possibility of their sister, Dinah, marrying the uncircumcised Shechem (Gen. 34:14); and Samson's parents attempted to convince him not to marry a Philistine woman (Judg. 14:3).

Rabbinic Perspective

Unlike the Christians of the rabbinic era, who regarded celibacy as the ideal and marriage as merely a concession to humankind's weakness and libidinous nature, the Rabbis championed marriage, including its sexual aspects, as the essential human relationship. Sexual desire, when properly channeled in the marriage relationship, was a powerful positive force, rather than an emotion that was inherently shameful or evil. "Were it not for the *yetzer ha-ra* ["evil inclination"; used here for the sexual urge], no man would build a house, marry a wife, or beget children" (Gen. R. 9:7). The person at risk for transgression was rather the unmarried man who "spends all his days in sinful thoughts" (Kid. 29b). Indeed, the Rabbis condemned the man who rejected his normal human impulses and failed to produce children, charging that it was "as if he shed blood, diminished the Image of God, and made the *Shekhinah* depart from Israel" (Shab. 31a).

In addition to the biblical concept of marriage as an institution to provide companionship and an opportunity for procreation, the Rabbis viewed marriage as critical for the complete development of one's human potential. As the Talmud states, "He who has no wife is not a proper man" (Yev. 63a). Consequently, according to tradition an unmarried man was forbidden to officiate as *Kohen Gadol* on Yom Kippur (Yoma 1:1) or to serve as *shaliach tzibbur* (prayer leader) on the High Holy Days.

The Rabbis believed that a woman's desire to marry was stronger than a man's, and she would be willing to endure an unhappy marriage rather than remain alone (Yev. 113a). "A woman prefers to be impoverished and be married than be wealthy and unmarried" (Sot. 20a). Marriage is a serious undertaking, a task as difficult as parting the Red Sea and one requiring divine wisdom (Gen. R. 68:3–4). Even those who believed that marriages are predestined must take enough time to make a prudent choice: "Hasten to buy land; deliberate before taking a wife" (Yev. 63a).

For the Talmud, a respectable family was a reliable indicator of the moral quality and temperament of a prospective wife: "Do not look for beauty, look for family" (Taan. 26b).

> A man should sell all of his possessions, if necessary, to marry the daughter of a scholar. If he does not find [cannot obtain] the daughter of a scholar, let him marry the daughter of [one of] the great men of the generation [one distinguished for his righteous deeds]. If unsuccessful, then a synagogue president's daughter; or of a trustee of charitable funds; or an elementary schoolteacher. Under no circum-

stances should he marry the daughter of an ignoramus (*am ha-aretz*), because they are detestable and their wives are vermin (Pes. 49b).

After Rebecca successfully passed the test of compassion, Eliezer's first question to Isaac's future bride was "Whose daughter are you?" (Gen. 24:47). As the Rabbis observed, before marriage "one should pay close attention to the wife's brothers, because her children will probably be like them." As with Sarah, Rebecca, and Rachel, the ideal wife should possess beauty (Ber. 57b; Yoma 74b), but this should not be her only quality. As Proverbs (31:30) warns, "Grace is deceitful, beauty is vain, but a woman who fears the Lord, she shall be praised." Although the Rabbis considered wealth to be desirable, they cautioned that "He who takes a wife for the sake of money will have unworthy children" (Kid. 70a).

Early marriages were strongly preferred, as long as one made proper preparations: "First build a house, then plant a vineyard, and after that marry" (Sot. 44a). A father should find a suitable match for his daughter at a young age, lest she become unchaste and he have violated this biblical commandment: "Do not degrade your daughter and make her a harlot" (Lev. 19:29).

For the Rabbis, marriage was a sacred relationship (*kiddushin*), in which both parties were to treat each other with consideration and respect. In exchange for her faithfulness, a husband was to provide his wife with food and clothing and attend to her conjugal rights. He should seek his wife's counsel, not cause her to weep, and love and honor her more than himself.

The wife is responsible for running the home and raising the children, for "in the affairs of the household, a man should follow his wife's advice" (BM 59a). Therefore, her background and upbringing were deemed of primary importance. The Rabbis urged the need to "investigate the girl's mother and brothers" (Ket. 43a). According to the Talmud, Moses was not concerned with his wife's background (BB 109b); he married Zipporah, daughter of an idolatrous Midianite priest, and his sons did not amount to much. Conversely, Aaron married the sister of a prince in Israel, and his sons became the *Kohanim*.

The wife also sets the moral tone of the home: "The pious man married a wicked woman, and she made him wicked. The pious woman married a wicked man and she made him righteous. We can conclude that all depends on the woman" (Gen. R. 17:12). When a marriage is happy and the spouses respectful of each other's needs, God dwells with them; if this is not the case, there will be a "consuming fire" between them (Sot. 17a; PdRE 12). For the Rabbis, marriage symbolized other perfect relationships, such as those between God and Israel, Israel and the Torah, and Israel and the Sabbath.

Marriage Ceremony

A wedding is the symbolic union of a man and a woman who enter into a covenant of mutual responsibility, protection, and caring.[1] The Jewish marriage ceremony is a complex series of formalities and customs that have developed over the centuries.

Biblical Period

Although there are numerous biblical references to marriage, none provides any information about the marriage ceremony. The act of marriage is simply called "taking," as in the verse: "A man takes a wife" (Deut. 24:1). Based on the weddings of Jacob and Leah (Gen. 29:27) and of Samson (Judg. 14:12,17), there were apparently seven days of feasting in celebration of a marriage, a practice that continues among many traditional Jews to this day. Processions were held for both the bride and the groom, accompanied by music (1 Macc. 9:39). Deuteronomy (22:13–21) notes the practice of demonstrating a blood-stained sheet or garment as evidence if the husband complains that his bride was not a virgin.

Talmudic Period

In Jewish law, marriage consists of two separate acts—*kiddushin* (or *erusin*) and *nisuin*.

Kiddushin (קִדּוּשִׁין)

"*Kiddushin*" is often translated as "betrothal," but it does not correspond to the modern conception of the word. Instead, it creates a special legal and personal relationship between a man and a woman that can be dissolved only by divorce or the death of either party. For all practical purposes, the *arusah* (affianced bride) is regarded as a married woman (*eshet ish*) and thus is prohibited to any other man (any such relationship would be considered adultery). However, *kiddushin* alone does not bring into being the mutual rights and duties between husband and wife. In particular, cohabitation between them is strictly prohibited. At this stage, the prospective bridegroom is not liable for the maintenance of his future bride, and she has no *ketubah* (see p. 44).

According to the Mishnah (Kid. 2a), there are three ways to effect *kiddushin*: *kesef* (money), *shetar* (deed), and *bi'ah* (cohabitation). All at some point require the presence of two competent witnesses. For *kiddushin* by *kesef*, the bridegroom transfers to his bride money or its equivalent that has a value of at least one *perutah* (the lowest coin). Today, this is usually an unadorned ring, which he places on the forefinger of her right hand while addressing her with the words "*Harei at mekudeshet li be tabba'at zo ke-dat Moshe ve-Yisrael*" (Behold, you are consecrated to me with this ring, according to the law of Moses and Israel).

The other two ways to accomplish *kiddushin* have long been obsolete. In *shetar*, the bridegroom handed his bride a written document listing the names of the parties and other relevant details; it also contained the words "Behold, you are consecrated to me with this "deed" [not "ring"], according to the law of Moses and Israel." Just as divorce is accomplished by the husband handing his wife a writ (*get*; see p. 67), so the Rabbis reasoned a woman could become a man's wife by a formal document ratifying the marriage.

The third way to effect *kiddushin* was *bi'ah*, a word derived from two common biblical euphemisms for sexual intercourse (*ba aleha*, "he came upon her," and *ba eleha*, "he came unto her").[2] After addressing her by saying, "Behold, you are consecrated to me with this "cohabitation" [not "ring"], according to the law of Moses and Israel," the groom took the bride into a private place; after they had intercourse, she was reserved to him. Although technically valid, the Rabbis regarded this mode of *kiddushin* as equivalent to prostitution (Git. 81b), and any man using it was subject to flogging (Kid. 12b).

The concept of *kiddushin* forbidding a person to all others applied only to women. Legally, the groom was not prohibited from having relations outside of marriage with another woman, as long as she was not married. This reflected the permission of polygamy in the early *halakhah*, which allowed a man to have several wives while a woman could have only one husband. The justification for this difference was apparently to protect children from any questions concerning paternity.[3]

In medieval times, the parents of the bride and the parents of the groom agreed to a set of conditions (*tenaim*), which included "the date and place of the wedding, the dowry, the gift for the groom, the parents' financial commitment to the couple, delineation and separation of the bride's estate, and inheritance rights."[4] Although initially agreed to orally, these terms eventually were committed to writing in a formal document and signed at the *kiddushin* ceremony.[5]

Nisuin (נִישׂוּאִין)

Nisuin, the second part of the marriage ceremony, took place sometime after *kiddushin* (usually one year later in the case of a virgin, to give her time to prepare her trousseau). The bride was brought to the groom under the *huppah* (wedding canopy). The wedding ceremony was a time for celebration and dancing. Indeed, the Talmud reports that one Rabbi amazed his colleagues by dancing with the bride on his shoulders (Kid. 17a). Distinctive headdresses, sometimes of gold, were worn by both bride and groom until the destruction of the Temple.

Medieval Period

During the Middle Ages, the two parts of the marriage ceremony were combined and thus celebrated on a single day. This change solved several practical problems. First, it was possible that during the year between *kiddushin* and *nisuin*, one or both of the betrothed could be deported or die. Furthermore, during this time, the bride and groom were legally fully married but were not permitted to live together as husband and wife. Thus there was the danger of elopement, a change of heart by either party, or another man snatching away the bride.[6] In addition, intimacies inevitably occurred when a poor groom, who was commonly housed by his wealthier in-laws, was placed in the same house as his prospective bride.[7] Furthermore, if the groom-to-be were to be taken captive or die in battle without witnesses, the betrothed woman would become an *agunah* (see p. 70) and be prohibited from marrying any other man.[8]

According to Rashi, two separate ceremonies meant the need for two

HUPPAH (חֻפָּה)

The word "*huppah*" refers either to the wedding canopy, which is usually made of beautiful fabric and supported by four firm poles, or to the marriage ceremony itself. During the biblical period, the *huppah* was the groom's room or tent in which the marriage was consummated.[1] Consequently, one possible explanation of the word "*huppah*" is that it was a combination of two Hebrew words: "*(c)hai po*," meaning "live here."[2] According to the Talmud, "it was the custom when a boy was born to plant a cedar tree and when a girl was born to plant a pine tree, and when they married, the tree was cut down and a canopy [*huppah*] made of the branches" (Git. 57a). Thus the *huppah* represented the fulfillment of the parents' hopes for their children. Even today, children receiving their Hebrew names are blessed with the hope that they will grow to "Torah, the wedding canopy (*huppah*), and good deeds (*ma'asim tovim*)."[3]

In medieval France and in North Africa, it was common for the groom to place his tallit over the bride's head to symbolize that he would shelter and protect her. The origin of this custom is found in Ruth's (3:9) words to Boaz, "Spread your robe over your handmaid, for you are a redeeming kinsman"; and, in fact, during the biblical era, such an act constituted a formal betrothal.[4] Later, German Jews based this practice on a verse from Ezekiel (16:8): "[Y]our time for love had arrived. So I spread my robe over you."[5]

The *huppah* symbolizes the groom's home and the bride's new domain.[6] The *ketubah* often reflects this metaphor, as the parchment on which it is written may be decorated with a doorway that frames the text of the marriage contract.[7]

separate banquets, which imposed financial difficulties on all but the wealthiest and would shame those who could not afford them. This concept may explain the old custom of holding the *kiddushin* on Friday afternoon, so that the Sabbath dinner doubled as the betrothal celebration, while the wedding was held on Saturday night after sundown.[9] Therefore, from the beginning of the 12th century it became customary to perform both ceremonies together, a practice that is now universally followed.

The wedding ceremony may be performed anywhere, but it most commonly takes place in the hall where the subsequent festivities are to be held. Ultra-Orthodox Jews, Hasidim, and Ashkenazim in Israel usually hold wedding ceremonies outdoors after nightfall. This relates to the divine assurance to Abraham that God would "make your descendants as numerous as the stars of heaven" (Gen. 22:17). Weddings may not be performed during twilight hours, since the date might actually change if night falls while the ceremony is in progress.

In the West, the most popular day for weddings is Sunday because of the convenience of the guests. Orthodox couples often select Tuesday because the phrase "And God saw that it was good" is repeated in the biblical account of the Creation on that day (Gen. 1:10–12). Conversely, Monday was generally avoided because this phrase does not appear. However, any day of the week is valid except the Sabbath, when legal transactions are forbidden and work and travel are not permitted. In addition, the two celebrations (Sabbath and wedding) should be observed individually and not combined, based on the talmudic principle that "we should not mix joy with joy" (MK 1:7). For the same reason, two members of the same family cannot be married on the same day. Weddings also are not celebrated on major festivals, the three weeks (mourning period) between the 17th of Tammuz and the 9th of Av (see p. 304), and the *sefirah* period between Passover and Shavuot (with the exception of Lag ba-Omer; see p. 294). Rosh Hodesh traditionally was considered a propitious time for weddings, since the waxing moon was a symbol of growth and fertility.

The bride and groom have a wide choice of attire. In the West, the bride typically wears white and has a headdress and veil (see p. 38). Some Orthodox bridegrooms wear a white *kitel* (see p. 619), since the wedding day is comparable in its gravity to Yom Kippur when that garment is worn. In many Middle Eastern communities (especially Yemenite), a particularly beautiful or skillfully embroidered costume may be saved to be worn by other brides.

Because marriage presents a new beginning for the bride and groom, it has become traditional to enter this new phase of life with fasting and prayers for the forgiveness of past sins, much like on Yom

Kippur. The custom of fasting on one's wedding day, except if the wedding occurs on Rosh Hodesh, Purim, or another day of joy on which fasting is not allowed, can be traced to the Jerusalem Talmud, which noted that the sins of a king, a prince, and a groom are forgiven on the days they enter their new lives. In some communities, both bride and groom fast; in others, only the groom does so. According to one explanation, if the groom were not required to fast he might go out with friends on the night before the wedding (i.e., a bachelor party) and become so drunk that he could not recover in time to properly carry out the legal formalities involved in the wedding ceremony. In contrast, the bride is not required to fast, since it was thought to be less likely that her friends would encourage her to drink to excess.[10] Traditionally, brides and some grooms immerse themselves in the *mikveh* (ritual bath; see p. 555) before the wedding as an act of spiritual purification.

Before being led to the *huppah*, the bridegroom traditionally engages in a handkerchief ceremony, symbolizing the ancient act of *kinyan* (acquisition), in which a man "acquired" a woman. In ancient Israel, trade agreements that are now frequently sealed by a handshake were instead confirmed by passing a piece of cloth from seller to buyer. Before the wedding ceremony, one of the witnesses represents the bride and holds up a handkerchief. The bridegroom takes hold of the handkerchief and raises it, thus formally completing the transaction and indicating his agreement to fulfill the obligations of the *ketubah* (marriage document; see p. 44).[11] The witnesses then sign the marriage document; in many communities, including the State of Israel, the groom also signs.

The ancient concept of *kinyan* in relation to marriage is difficult for modern Jews to comprehend. Even nonfeminists bristle when women appear to be regarded as mere property. However, the Rabbis viewed marriage in terms of the acquisition of *Temple* rather than *secular* property. *Kiddushin* denotes the fact that the wife is exclusively reserved to her husband. This is not as a consequence of any "ownership" of her person, as in civil law, but instead reflects a change in her *status*, as when a property was dedicated to the Temple. Property became sanctified exclusively for Temple use and could not be used for secular purpose. Consequently, the traditional Jewish concept of *kinyan* does not envision a change in ownership, since no person owns another, but rather the bride receiving her a new status as *eshet ish* (a married woman).[12]

The groom is then escorted to the place where the bride is waiting, often a special bride's room, and lets down the veil over her face. The groom is led to the *huppah* by his parents, and the bride is then brought to the wedding canopy by hers. A common variation is for the two fathers to escort the groom and the two mothers to walk with the bride. According to one explanation, the groom arrives at the *huppah* first based on a tradition associated with the giving of the Ten Commandments at Mount Sinai. Just as God (the bridegroom) came

BRIDAL VEIL

Bedeken (*di kallah*), or "covering (the bride)" is an old Jewish tradition in which the groom lets down the veil over the face of his bride in her dressing room before the marriage ceremony. Today, the bride is generally ushered out of her room, attended by the female members of the bridal party, and seated in a special bride's seat, usually at the end of the reception hall where the guests are gathered. The groom enters, and he and the bride see each other for the first time in up to a week.[1] After the groom gently draws the veil over his bride's face, the rabbi pronounces the blessing invoked on Rebecca by her mother and brother when she left her home in Haran for Canaan to marry her cousin Isaac: "O sister! May you be the mother of thousands of myriads" (Gen. 24:60).[2]

The major reason for the *bedeken* ceremony is that it permits the groom to clearly identify his bride before she is veiled so that he is not fooled as was Jacob when he received Leah instead of his beloved Rachel (Gen. 29:23–38). Another reason for this tradition is that Rebecca immediately veiled herself after seeing her future husband, Isaac (Gen. 24:65), and so Jewish brides throughout the ages have worn this symbol of female modesty during the marriage ceremony. Among Middle Eastern Jews, the bride's veil is made of opaque material. Effectively led blindfolded to the *huppah*, this indicates her complete trust in the man who will soon become her husband.[3]

forward to receive Israel (the bride), it became customary for the groom to take his place under the wedding canopy first, so that he can welcome his bride as she walks down the aisle.[13]

The roles of best man and maid or matron of honor have an ancient precedent in Judaism. Gabriel and Michael, two angels who attended the wedding of Adam and Eve, are the classic friends of the bride and groom, who respectively may be in charge of holding the ring and the *ketubah* during the ceremony.[14]

Since ancient times, when it was customary to play a flute before the bride and groom, it has been traditional to perform music at a wedding. Processional music should be joyful but stately; it is customary to use a single melody, though this may be changed to heighten the drama just before the entrance of the bride. Couples often select classical music, though many rabbis specifically request that it not be the two most conventional selections—from Wagner's *Lohengrin* and Mendelssohn's *Midsummer Night's Dream*—pieces written by, respectively, a notorious anti-Semite and a Jew who converted to Christianity.[15]

A popular custom in the wedding procession was for candles to be held by two people escorting the bride and groom. Light was always associated with celebration, as in the verse, "The Jews enjoyed light and gladness" (Esther 8:16), which is recited as part of the *Havdalah* ceremony that concludes the Sabbath. In keeping with the comparison of the wedding to the covenant between God and the Jewish people at Mount Sinai, candles represent the thunder and lightning that accompanied the Revelation. Moreover, the numerical value of the Hebrew word "*ner*" (candle), when multiplied by the two people escorting the bride and groom (500), is exactly the same as that of the biblical phrase *p'ru u-r'vu* (be fruitful and multiply; Gen. 1:28).[16]

Among Ashkenazim, it is customary for the bride to be led in seven circuits around the groom, based on the phrase, "a woman shall go around [encompasses] a man" (Jer. 31:21). In medieval times, this practice was thought to produce a magic circle of protection for the groom to keep away malevolent spirits. Some believe that this tradition was related to the custom of defining and securing ownership of real property by walking around it.[17] The number seven comes from the times in the Torah where it is written: "And when a man takes a wife."[18] In some communities, the bride makes only three circuits around the groom, primarily based on the verses in Hosea (2:21–22) in which God (the groom) speaks to Israel (the bride) using the word "betroth" three times. Other explanations for this number include the three ways in which a man may legally betroth a woman and his three basic biblical obligations to her (food, clothing, and conjugal relations).[19] The bride then stands at the right hand of the groom, the opposite of the common practice in non-Jewish weddings, based on the verse: "The princess stands at your right hand, decked in gold of Ophir" (Ps. 45:10), for in Jewish tradition the bride is a queen and the groom a king.[20] It is customary to face east under the *huppah*, so as to turn one's heart to Jerusalem.

In some communities, the rabbi delivers a sermon before the ceremony begins. The rabbi or cantor recites the blessing over a goblet of wine, from which both the groom and bride drink. The groom then places the ring on the forefinger of the bride's right hand (see p. 43) and recites the marriage formula (for *kiddushin*; see p. 33), after which the *ketubah* is read out loud. In many communities, the marriage document is read in the original Aramaic and followed by a summary in the vernacular.

The rabbi then recites the *Sheva Brachot* (seven marriage benedictions). The first is said over a second cup of wine, from which the bride and groom drink. The shared cup of wine is symbolic of holiness, joy, and union. The other blessings praise God for Creation (particularly of human beings), invite Jerusalem (Zion) to rejoice as her children marry, and speak of the joy and happiness of the groom and bride.[21]

The ceremony concludes with the rabbi proclaiming the couple "husband and wife" and offering a closing blessing (such as the Priestly Blessing; see p. 432). The groom crushes a glass, wrapped in a cloth, under his right foot (see p. 45), and those assembled shout *mazel tov*. The bride and groom are then escorted to a room where they remain alone for about 10 minutes (*yichud*, "union, joining"), breaking their fast and spending a few quiet moments together. Rather than a mere custom, *yichud* is a halakhic requirement that must be testified to by two qualified witnesses specifically given this role. This private act, which in ancient times included sexual consummation, seals the marriage. The couple emerges as man and wife, and the bride and groom then rejoin their families and friends for the wedding feast.[22]

It is an obligation to rejoice with the bride and groom on their wedding day. According to the Midrash (PdRE 12), the angels themselves danced and played musical instruments at the wedding of Adam and Eve. In the Talmud, the House of Shammai asked, "What words must we use when dancing before the bride?" to which the School of Hillel answered, "Beautiful and graceful bride." Shammai then asked, "What shall we do if she is lame or blind ... for does not the Torah direct: 'keep away from any lie?'" Hillel replied: "If a person has purchased some bad merchandise in the marketplace, should one praise it [to make it look good to him] or disparage it [so it looks bad to him]? Surely, one should praise it in his eyes" (Ket. 17a).[23]

One also must rejoice with the groom, for "anyone who partakes of the wedding meal of the bridegroom and does not make him rejoice violates the spirit of the five voices" (Ber. 6b). This is a reference to Jeremiah (33:11), who prophesied that when the desolate streets of Jerusalem and the cities of Judah would be restored to their former glory, one would again hear the five voices (or sounds)—joy, gladness, the groom, the bride, and people thanking God.[24]

Other Customs

Often initially based on non-Jewish practices, various folk customs have been incorporated into the Jewish marriage ceremony to protect the couple from evil spirits or to ask God to bless the marriage with children.

Among Ashkenazic Jews, customs seen as a defense against evil spirits include the breaking of the glass at the end of the ceremony (see p. 45), women carrying lighted candles while leading the bride to the *huppah*, and the seven circuits the bride makes around the groom under the wedding canopy. In most Middle Eastern communities, the *hinnah* is celebrated the night before the wedding. In this strictly feminine ceremony, relatives and friends of the bride gather at her home and paint her hands with red henna to ward off the evil eye.

In many communities, the bride and groom do not see each other preceding the wedding for a time varying from one day to one week. On the Sabbath before the wedding, the bridegroom is honored by being called to the Torah (in Yiddish this is called "*aufruf*," meaning "call up"). On these days, the bridegroom has precedence over all others, including a bar mitzvah, in being called for an aliyah. In the synagogues of medieval Europe, this was an opportunity to publicly announce the forthcoming wedding and to make certain that no congregant was aware of anything that would invalidate the marriage. This practice has its origins in the time of the First Temple, when the public sat between two special gates—one for mourners and one for grooms. The mourners were welcomed with words of con-solation, while the grooms were greeted with the blessing: "May He whose Presence dwells in this house make you happy with sons and daughters."[25]

The custom of the bride presenting the groom with a tallit is an inference drawn from the biblical juxtaposition of the commandment to wear fringes (tzitzit) and the phrase "a man takes a wife" (Deut. 22:12). In talmudic times, a married man covered his head with a tallit during prayer to indicate his marital state. In later years, it became customary for a single man not to wear a tallit at all (unless leading the service), a practice still followed in many Orthodox congregations.[26]

In many communities, it is customary to throw rice, wheat, nuts, and candies at the groom during the wedding and when he is called to the Torah on the preceding Sabbath. Rice and nuts are considered symbols of fertility in many cultures, and throwing these items is an expression of the hope that the couple will "be fruitful and multiply." This tradition may have evolved from a talmudic comment that toasted grains and nuts were to be thrown before the bride and groom, presumably as a symbol of good fortune (Ber. 50b).[27] Indeed, in Hebrew the words "*egoz*" (nut) and "*tov*" (good) have the identical numerical equivalent (17). However, the word "*chet*" (sin), when spelled without the final *aleph*, also has the same numerical value, implying that a marriage has the potential to be either extremely good or horribly bad.[28]

As early as the Middle Ages, it was traditional to shout congratulations at the bride and groom at the conclusion of the wedding ceremony. Among Ashkenazim, the words used are "*mazel tov*" (lit., "good star"). This hearkens back to biblical and talmudic times, when "*mazel*" could refer to a star, a constellation of the zodiac, or a planet. Because it was widely believed that a person's fate depended on the position of the stars, the phrase "*mazel tov*" took on the secondary meaning of "good luck." Sephardim use the words "*siman tov*" (good omen). In American synagogues, the two expressions are often joined together in the song *Siman Tov u-Mazel Tov*, which is also sung after a bar or bat mitzvah concludes chanting the haftarah.

In traditional communities, the wedding celebrations continue for an entire week. The *Sheva Brachot* are recited as part of the *Birkat ha-Mazon* after each meal where there is a minyan and a new guest present, as a way of extending the joyous festivities associated with the wedding.

Wedding Ring (טַבַּעַת)

The custom of the groom giving a ring to the bride reflects the ancient understanding of marriage as essentially a business transaction, in which the groom "acquired" his bride and sealed the deal by the payment of a silver or gold coin that had a value of at least one *perutah*, the smallest unit of currency in talmudic times. Although Yemenite Jews still use a coin at the wedding ceremony, most Jewish traditions have substituted a ring. The ring must belong to the groom and be a simple solid band, preferably gold, without jewels or ornaments. If a groom presents his naive bride with a ring bedecked with inexpensive stones that he misrepresents as fine jewelry, the marriage can be invalidated if she accepts his proposal on false pretenses.[29]

The groom places the wedding ring on the forefinger of the bride's right hand and then recites the marriage formula: "Behold, you are consecrated to me with this ring, according to the law of Moses and Israel." In Hebrew, this phrase has 32 letters, the numerical equivalent of the word "*lev*" (heart); thus the groom is symbolically giving his heart to his bride as he recites these words. The ring is placed on the forefinger, the most prominent digit, which is used for pointing, so that witnesses to the ceremony can clearly see that the groom has performed this act.[30] After the ceremony, the ring is transferred to the traditional fourth finger of the left hand, a practice that may be based on the ancient belief that a vein runs directly from this finger to the heart.[31]

In many modern non-Orthodox congregations in the United States, a double-ring ceremony is performed in which the bride also presents a ring, placing it on the groom's finger, saying "*Ani l'dodi v'dodi li*" (I am my beloved's, and my beloved is mine; Song 6:3). Because according to *halakhah* it is the groom who acquires the bride, this innovation has only sentimental value. Most Orthodox couples save the groom's ring for later. However, when the bride wants to give the groom a ring under the *huppah*, she generally does so after the reading of the *ketubah* and does not recite the ancient marriage formula. If the bride wishes to make an oral declaration as she gives the ring, another option is for her to recite selected verses from the Bible to the groom and have him respond to her in kind.[32]

Ketubah (כְּתֻבָּה)

The *ketubah* (lit., "written document") is the Jewish marriage contract. Written in Aramaic, it sets forth in detail the financial obligations that a husband undertakes toward his wife as her inheritance should he die or as her alimony should he divorce her. If either of these events occurred, the woman would have money and resources of her own and not be made destitute without any financial support. Today, a standardized *ketubah* is read before the bridegroom and two witnesses and signed by them. The witnesses may not be relatives of the bride or groom. This is consistent with the general rule in Jewish jurisprudence that a witness must not be related to the parties involved, an extension to civil law from the biblical prohibition against a father being put to death on the testimony of his son (Deut. 24:16).[33]

Just as the bridegroom is forbidden to cohabit with his bride after marriage unless he has written and delivered the *ketubah* to her, so the husband is forbidden to live with his wife for even one hour if she no longer has it in her possession. Therefore, if the *ketubah* is lost or destroyed, the husband is obliged to write a new one with the same terms as in the original. Thus, when the Jews were expelled from France in 1306 and robbed of all their possessions, Rashba ordered that his followers refrain from conjugal relations until every man gave his wife a replacement *ketubah*.[34]

The Rabbis viewed the *ketubah* as an important deterrent to rash and irrational divorces by ensuring the financial integrity of the economically vulnerable woman. After the edict of Rabbenu Gershom requiring that the wife must consent to a divorce, the function of the *ketubah* became more psychological than legal. At a time when most marriages were arranged based on family background, class, and learning and involved prospective spouses and families who scarcely were acquainted with each other, the *ketubah* was a testimony to the honorable intentions and worthiness of the husband.[35] Today, the *ketubah* represents the covenant of the couple's marriage and their new household.[36]

From 10th-century Egypt to the present day, the Aramaic text of the *ketubah* has often been decorated with an illuminated border. These works of art have been prized for generations as family heirlooms. Popular subjects in European countries included biblical or mythological motifs, portraits of the bride and groom in contemporary costume, family coats of arms, symbols representing conjugal bliss (occasionally even nude figures), priestly symbols for the family of a Kohen or Levite, crowns, and even biblical figures representing the name of the bride or groom.[37]

Ketubot from Sephardic communities were usually written on paper and typically decorated with geometric patterns, which reflected the prohibition in the Muslim host culture against pictorial representation. It is customary in these communities to read a special *ketubah* on Shavuot, marking the "wedding" of God and Israel when the Torah was given at Mount Sinai.[38]

Breaking the Glass

At the conclusion of the wedding ceremony, the groom traditionally crushes a glass under his right foot. The most popular explanation is that this is a sign of mourning for the destruction of the Temple in Jerusalem. This also serves as a reminder that unbridled joy can be suddenly erased by overwhelming grief. (A less common wedding custom that also symbolizes mourning for the Temple is the placing of a small amount of ash on the forehead of the groom.)

Of the many other rationales offered for this well-known custom, all have some relation to the underlying purpose of creating noise. According to the Talmud, a great scholar shocked the guests at his son's wedding when he deliberately smashed expensive glassware to reduce the excessive gaiety of those rabbis in attendance (Ber. 31a). This action also may have been related to the ancient belief that it is wise to temper joy to prevent disaster. The broken glass is also interpreted as symbolic of the mystical concept of the shattered vessels, a tangible reminder of the need for the new couple to engage in the mitzvah of *tikun olam*, the repairing of our imperfect world.[39]

Originally, the glass was broken to create a loud noise to frighten away evil spirits and demons. This belief is consistent with popular traditions in many cultures, including such current practices as the ringing of church bells and the smashing of a bottle against the hull of a ship before it is launched.[40] During the Middle Ages, it was customary for the groom to taste the wine after the seven wedding benedictions had been recited. After allowing his wife to also taste from the glass, he would turn to the north wall and throw the glass against it. The choice of direction reflected the superstitious belief that evil spirits came from the north, just as the prophets saw the evil enemy descending upon Israel from that direction. In Germany, synagogue facades were inlaid with a special stone for the express purpose of smashing a glass at the end of weddings. The practice of throwing a glass against the wall has long been abandoned. Today, instead of using the glass from which the wine was drunk, in most weddings a separate glass is prepared for the ceremony and is crushed under foot.

Shadchan (שַׁדְּכָן)

The Talmud indicates that marriages are preordained. "Forty days before the birth of a child, a voice in heaven announces: 'The daughter of so-and-so will marry the son of so-and-so'" (Sot. 2a). According to a classic legend, a Roman matron asked Rabbi Yosi, "What has your God been doing since finishing the creation of the world?" He replied, "God has been busy making matches" (Gen. R. 68:4; PdRE 2:4). The mystical Zohar maintained that each soul is created both male and female, divided before birth, and ultimately reunited when a man and woman marry.[41]

According to the Midrash, once a match is made God does not disappear. After Eve's creation, Adam was called *esh* (fire). Eve was also called *esh*, but when they married each received one of the letters of God's name (*yud* and *he*). With the addition of a *yud*, Adam became *ish* (man); an added *he* changed Eve's name to *ishah* (woman). Thus whenever God's presence is absent from a marriage, there is only a destructive, all-consuming fire.[42]

Nevertheless, for much of Jewish history, the responsibility for selecting the destined mate (*bashert* in Yiddish) has been given to the matchmaker (*shadchan*). In return for a fee, this individual would arrange and assist the union between a man and a woman, taking into consideration not only the scholarship and piety of the groom and the compatibility of the couple but also the financial status, suitability, and *yichus* (lineage) of their families. During talmudic times, most marriages were arranged directly by the heads of the two families involved. A few were even decided on by the couple themselves, though the Rabbis strongly discouraged this practice (Kid. 12b–13a).

Because matchmaking was considered "God's work," the profession was once regarded as a worthy endeavor. It also was a well-paid profession, with the amount paid varying from 1 percent to 3 percent of the dowry. In some locations the *shadchan* was paid after the wedding; in others, he received his compensation as soon as the match was arranged.[43] Some of the most illustrious rabbis earned a living from arranging marriages. Although Jews during the 15th and 16th centuries were often severely limited in their ability to travel, the *shadchan* was given relative freedom and thus could bring together members of different communities who otherwise would not have met.[44] To increase their chances of obtaining an educated and religious son-in-law, parents with eligible daughters often asked rabbis and scholars, especially heads of yeshivot, to act as matchmakers.

By the end of the 16th century, the attitude toward matchmakers had shifted. No longer deemed a paragon of integrity, the *shadchan* became an object of derision, viewed as a miserly opportunist who misrepresented potential suitors.[45] Indeed, the *shadchan* became notorious for being able to glibly play down or divert attention away from any flaws, physical or otherwise, the potential spouse may have.

Today, numerous individuals and many Jewish organizations offer matchmaking services, and some keep computerized databases. In traditional circles, it is still considered completely acceptable for young people to meet their mates with the help of a third party. In ultra-Orthodox communities, arranged marriages continue to be in vogue.[46]

Harmonious Married Life

The Rabbis believed that happiness in married life could be attained through proper behavior and attitude. "A man who loves his wife as himself, who honors her more than himself," will achieve the biblical blessing (Job 5:24), "You will know that your tent is at peace" (Yev. 62b). A husband "should always be heedful of wronging his wife; since her tears are frequent and she is quickly hurt" (BM 59a). The Rabbis urged the husband to "[a]lways observe the honor due to his wife, because blessings rest on a man's home only on account of his wife" (BM 59a), a conclusion they inferred from the biblical verse noting that Pharaoh treated Abram well for Sarai's sake (Gen. 12:16). The husband should also demonstrate his affection by providing his wife with appropriate clothes, cosmetics, and jewelry, particularly on the festivals (Ket. 64b).[1]

As a reflection of the patriarchal society in which they lived, the Rabbis believed that a strong marriage depended on the wife adopting a subservient attitude toward her husband. As Maimonides noted: "The sages commanded the woman to honor her husband to excess, and she should fear him; all her actions should conform to his wishes, and she should regard him as a minister or a king."[2] This is consistent with women being halakhically exempt from performing the time-bound positive mitzvot. As Jacob Anatoli wrote in the 13th century: "If a woman were to occupy herself performing a mitzvah at a fixed time, her husband would be without a helpmate at that moment and this would lead to quarrels between them."[3]

Obligations and Rights of the Husband

According to Jewish law, a man who marries becomes obligated to his wife for 10 things in addition to the statutory *ketubah*.[1] Of these, three are biblical in origin—food, clothing, and conjugal rights (Exod. 21:10). The other seven obligations are rabbinic: "to treat her if she falls ill; to ransom her if she is captured; to bury her if she dies; to provide for her maintenance out of his estate after his death; to let her dwell in his house after his death for the duration of her widowhood; to let the daughters sired by him receive their maintenance out of his estate until they become espoused; to let her male children sired by him inherit her *ketubah*, in addition to their share with their half brothers in his estate."[2]

In addition to the use of his wife's property, the husband's rights are those entitling him to "her earnings, to anything she finds, and to inheritance of her estate."[3] These legal obligations and rights are inherent in the marriage relationship, regardless of whether there is a written *ketubah* or any separate agreement between the parties.

Prohibited Marriages

Some forbidden relationships render a marriage null and void from its inception. In other cases, they do not invalidate the marriage but provide justification for having it terminated by divorce.

Prohibited and Void

Marriages that are forbidden as incestuous according to Torah law or for other reasons are considered as having never existed. Thus there is no need for the couple to be divorced; any children are *mamzerim* (see p. 51).

According to the Rabbis, before the Revelation at Sinai, the only relationships that were prohibited were those between a man and his mother, his father's wife, a married woman, and a sister on his mother's side. Therefore, Abraham was permitted to marry his half-sister Sarah (the daughter of his father, according to Gen. 20:12); Jacob could wed two sisters, Rachel and Leah; and Amram was allowed to marry his aunt Yocheved (the parents of Aaron, Moses, and Miriam).

The Torah lists a series of marriages between parties related to one another by prohibited degrees of kinship, all of which are punishable by *karet* (divine punishment of premature death) (Lev. 18:6–17). A man is specifically prohibited from marrying the following relatives:

Mother
Stepmother
Sister (whether born of a legal marriage or out of wedlock)
Half sister
Granddaughter (daughter is not specifically mentioned, but is obviously included)
Aunt (sister of his mother or father or the wife of his father's brother)
Daughter-in-law (either after divorce or his son's death)
Sister-in-law
Wife's sister (while the wife is still alive)

A few of these forbidden relationships deserve further study. In the Near East, it was a regular practice for an heir apparent to take possession of his father's wife to assert his right to the throne and to become identified with the ruler's personality in the eyes of the people.[1] This explains Reuben's conduct in bedding Bilhah, the concubine of his father, Jacob (Gen. 35:22), which resulted in Reuben earning the unending wrath of his father and his being forced to forfeit his privilege as the firstborn. The prohibition against having a sexual relationship with the wife of one's brother did not apply when he died childless, in which case there was the obligation of either levirate marriage or *halitzah* (see p. 52). The act of marriage brought into force more forbidden relations—the wife's mother, grandmother, daughter, or granddaughter—all of which were prohibited even after the divorce or death of the wife.

Marriage to a wife's sister was forbidden as long as the wife was alive (even if they had been divorced), lest the two sisters become "rivals" (Lev. 18:18). Ironically, after a wife's death, marriage to the surviving sister was not only permitted but even deemed praiseworthy by the Rabbis, who maintained that no other woman would show the same deep affection for the orphaned children of the deceased sister.

The Rabbis expanded the primary forbidden relationships in the ascending and descending line (Yev. 21a). Known as "secondary prohibited marriages," these unions included the following: just as a man was forbidden to have relations with his mother, so was he forbidden to marry his grandmother or great-grandmother. Similarly, since his stepmother was forbidden, so was his grandfather's wife; as his daughter-in-law was prohibited, so was his grandson's wife. Marriages of the secondary prohibited degree are prohibited but valid (see below); they must be dissolved by a divorce and any children are legitimate.

Other marriages that are prohibited and void under Jewish law are those between a man and a woman who is already married (especially since such adultery results in bigamy) and those between a Jew and a non-Jew.

Prohibited but Valid

Although valid, some marriages are prohibited because they are a violation either of a biblical law that was not punishable by *karet* or death or of a later rabbinic enactment. According to *halakhah*, either party is entitled to demand a divorce, which may be compelled if the other refuses. Because the marriage was valid, the woman requires a *get* (see p. 67) before she can remarry.

The Talmud states that a married woman who commits adultery by having consensual sexual relations becomes prohibited to her lover and must be divorced by her husband (Sot. 27b). He is forbidden to remarry her, even if she has not married anyone else in the interim. A wife who has been raped may remain married to her husband, unless he is a Kohen.

According to biblical law, a divorced woman who has remarried and had her second marriage also terminated (by divorce or death) may not remarry her first husband (Deut. 24:4). If this were not the case, people might feel free to divorce one another at will to sample other mates, before subsequently getting together again. Abravanel (citing Ralbag) suggested that this prohibition was intended to prevent the possibility of a man conspiring with his wife to leave him, marry another man, and make life so miserable for her second husband that he would agree to make a cash settlement and divorce her, thus enabling her to return to her first husband with a financial windfall.[2]

The Torah contains special regulations expressly prohibiting a *Kohen* (as chief religious functionary of the Jewish people) from marrying a divorced woman, a *zonah*, or a *chalalah* (Lev. 21:7). Although usually translated as "harlot," the term "*zonah*" in this context applied specifically to a woman who had intercourse with any man who was not permitted to her as a husband because of a negative commandment. According to Rashi, such forbidden relationships included not only those punishable by death or *karet* but also the living with a *mamzer* or a non-Israelite woman.[3] The term "*chalalah*," generally translated as "desecrated" or "profaned," referred to a woman who was forbidden to marry a *Kohen* but had previously married one anyway (such as a divorcée who had married a *Kohen* or a widow who had married the *Kohen Gadol*) or to any daughters born of such unions (Rashi).[4]

A Jew is forbidden from marrying a *mamzer* (Deut. 23:3). Contrary to popular misconception, a *mamzer* (often mistranslated as "bastard") is not someone born out of wedlock. Rather it is the child of a sexual relationship between a man and woman whose marriage could never be valid under Jewish law (Kid. 3:12). Examples include the offspring of a union between a brother and sister or other incestuous relationship, a child born to a married woman by some man other than her lawful husband (adultery), and a child born of a woman who had remarried without having obtained a valid divorce (*get*) from her first husband. According to the Bible, a *mamzer* and all of his or her descendants may never marry a Jew. However, a marriage between two *mamzerim* is permitted.

Addressing the issue of why the child was penalized for the immoral action of his or her parents, Maimonides viewed it as a deterrent against such behavior, for "in order to create a horror of illicit marriages, a *mamzer* was not allowed to marry an Israelite woman; the adulterer and the adulteress were thus taught that by their act they bring upon their seed irreparable injury."[5] Realizing that this law was overly harsh and unfair to both the *mamzer* and his or her descendants, the Rabbis eventually allowed a *mamzer* to marry a convert as a way of becoming more quickly integrated into the Jewish community. They believed that the offspring of a *mamzer* who had married a convert would, within a generation or so, begin to be referred to as a descendant of the convert (not the *mamzer*) and become fully accepted.

Except in regard to marriage, the personal status of a *mamzer* is not adversely affected in any way. He can be called up to the Torah, has equal rights of inheritance as other heirs, and can hold public office. The Mishnah even states that "a *mamzer* who is a scholar (*talmid hakham*) takes precedence over a *Kohen Gadol* who is an ignoramus (*am ha-aretz*)" (Hor. 3:8).

According to the decree of Rabbenu Gershom,[6] a married man is prohibited from marrying a second woman (bigamy). If contracted, the second marriage is valid but the parties are compelled to divorce.

After a woman is divorced or widowed, she cannot be remarried for 90 days so that there will be no doubt about the paternity of her offspring. The Rabbis also prohibited a man from marrying a pregnant woman or nursing mother until her offspring reached the age of 24 months, deeming this to be best for the "good of her child." If such a marriage occurs, however, a divorce cannot be compelled if either party refuses.

Levirate Marriage (יִבּוּם)/*Halitzah* (חֲלִיצָה)

Levirate marriage is the obligation of a surviving brother to marry the widow of his brother if he died without having sired children (Deut. 25:5–6). The corollary is that the widow must marry a brother-in-law rather than anyone outside the family. The oldest of the surviving brothers had the first obligation to perform this commandment, which also allowed him to inherit all his dead brother's property.

The explicit purpose of this commandment was to have the surviving brother produce an heir to perpetuate the name of his dead brother, so that it would not "be blotted out of Israel." The literal meaning of the biblical text implies that the firstborn child of a levirate marriage would be named after the dead brother, to carry on his memory. However, this is true only in the spiritual sense, for there was no requirement to name the newborn son after the dead brother.

The duty of levirate marriage was obligatory only on one who was alive at the time of the death of his childless brother; it did not apply to one born after his brother's death. Furthermore, both brothers must have the same father. If either of these conditions was not fulfilled, the childless widow was immediately free to marry anyone she chose.[1]

The institution of levirate marriage also served to protect the wife. In numerous verses, the Torah lumps widows with orphans and strangers as the disenfranchised members of society to whom special kindness must be shown. The situation of a widow without children was especially dire, for she had no one to care for her and provide material support. The levirate law guaranteed her a new family, enhanced status, and financial resources.[2]

The most famous story about levirate marriage in the Bible is that of Tamar, who was an ancestor of King David (Gen. 38). After the death of his older two sons (who had both married her), Judah refused to allow his third son to perform this obligation with the childless Tamar. Eventually, Judah himself unknowingly fulfilled the commandment when he had relations with Tamar, and she subsequently gave birth to a child.

As an alternative, the surviving brother could perform *halitzah* (lit., "taking off the shoe") instead of levirate marriage (Deut. 25:9). If the brother-in-law refused to marry the childless widow, she would (in the presence of the elders) take off his shoe—a symbol of mourning, since his failure to perform levirate marriage meant that his brother was now irrevocably dead—and spit on the ground in front of him (indicating contempt), declaring that "thus shall be done to the man who will not build up his brother's house" (Deut. 25:9). From then on, the widow was free to marry anyone she chose.

Whereas in the Torah it is clear that levirate marriage is approved and *halitzah* a shameful way out, the Talmud prefers *halitzah* (Bek. 13a). The Rabbis believed that the brother should marry his sister-in-law only out of a sincere desire to perform the commandment and not for monetary or sensual motives. However, they realized that such lofty thoughts are difficult except for the "most elevated people."[3]

The two greatest medieval scholars took opposite points of view on this issue, with Maimonides favoring levirate marriage[4] and Rashi preferring *halitzah*. This led to a split in the *halakhah* between the two traditions, with Sephardim following Maimonides and his preference for levirate marriage and Ashkenazim upholding Rashi's view that *halitzah* supersedes it. This dichotomy was not permitted in the State of Israel, where the rabbinate ruled in favor of *halitzah* and effectively outlawed levirate marriage. If the surviving brother refuses *halitzah* and insists instead on a levirate marriage, a court may compel him to perform *halitzah* and even threaten him with imprisonment if he fails to comply. The situation is similar in the United States, where Sephardic rabbis do not permit levirate marriage and require *halitzah* in all cases.[5]

The institutions of levirate marriage and *halitzah* may result in the widow finding herself "in limbo." If the brother-in-law is under the age of 13 and thus not competent by reason of youth to perform either procedure, the widow is forced to wait until he reaches adulthood. If the brother-in-law is mentally incompetent to participate in *halitzah*—under Jewish law either because he is insane or is a deaf-mute—the widow becomes an *agunah* (see p. 70), a "chained woman" who is forbidden to marry anyone else. Similarly, if the brother-in-law is known to exist but his location is unknown, or if he refuses to perform either procedure out of maliciousness or contempt for Jewish law (as with an apostate), the woman's situation is like that of an *agunah* whose husband has disappeared or has refused to issue her a *get*, respectively. If any of these problems apply, the Talmud requires that any other brother who was present and available must immediately grant the widow her freedom through *halitzah*. Nevertheless, in traditional circles, a man whose brother has converted or is said to be insane or a wanderer may be deemed so risky that it is difficult for him to arrange a good marriage.[6]

Intermarriage

Intermarriage is the union of a non-Jew and a Jew—one born of a Jewish mother or who has converted in accordance with Jewish law. According to *halakhah*, a person who has converted from Judaism to another religion is still considered Jewish with respect to the law on mixed marriages, based on the talmudic dictum: "An Israelite, even if he has sinned, is still an Israelite" (Sanh. 44a).

Since biblical days, intermarriage has been opposed because it weakens the essential core of Judaism. From the time Abraham sent his servant to choose a wife for Isaac from among his own people, through Ezra's expulsion of the non-Jewish wives of the Jews who returned from Babylonian exile to establish the Second Commonwealth, to the recent practice of severing all ties with and even observing a period of mourning for intermarried children as if they were dead, marrying out of the faith has been one of the most strenuously discouraged and forcefully condemned acts that a Jew could perform. Marriage with a non-Jew was forbidden as a negative commandment by the Torah (Deut. 7:3) because of the fear that this would lead to idolatry, with the heathen spouse causing the Israelite to "lust after their gods" (Exod. 34:16). The declining fortunes of King Solomon were directly attributed to his marriage to foreign wives "who sacrificed to their gods," thus leading him to "do what was displeasing to the Lord" (1 Kings 11:1–6). The prophet Malachi (2:11–12) severely castigated his generation: "Judah has broken faith; abhorrent things have been done in Israel and in Jerusalem. For Judah has profaned what is holy to the Lord—what He desires—and espoused daughters of alien gods."[1] Attempting to prevent what was deemed one of the most severe breaches in the Jewish tradition, the Shulchan Arukh prohibited consuming many kinds of food prepared by non-Jews—bread (YD 112), cooked dishes (YD 113), milk (YD 115), wine (YD 123–128)—and even eating with non-Jews at a festive meal (YD 152). Nevertheless, the Rabbis stressed that Jews should work with their non-Jewish neighbors for the mutual betterment of all in the community; they tried only to limit "excessive familiarity" that could lead to intermarriage.[2] Today, intermarriage is viewed as a major threat to the stability of the family structure and the continuity of the Jewish people.

The Rabbis declared that mixed marriages are not legally valid, because the non-Jewish party to the contract is incapable of contracting a marriage with a Jew within Jewish law. Therefore, the Jewish partner of a mixed marriage does not halakhically require a divorce before subsequently marrying a Jew. Conversely, if one (or both) of the parties to a halakhically valid marriage subsequently converts out of Judaism and the union is then dissolved by a civil decree, neither party can marry a Jew until the previous valid marriage is terminated by a *get* (see p. 67).

According to Jewish law, the status of children from a mixed relationship is determined exclusively by the faith of the mother. If the mother is Jewish and the father non-Jewish, the children are considered Jewish in every respect; if the father is Jewish but the mother is not, the children are not considered Jews. In 1983, the Reform movement broke with this tradition and formally adopted the principle of patrilineal descent. They view this as a way to compensate for demographic decline by broadening the definition of a Jew and extending a welcome and a sense of legitimacy to people who otherwise would most likely be lost to the Jewish community. However, by defining Jews differently from traditional Jewish law, this practice has effectively established a new category of people who are deemed Jewish by the standards of some Jews but not by the standards of the majority.

Throughout much of Jewish history, intermarriage usually meant that the Jewish spouse was lost to the community, for there was little chance that a non-Jew would accept the religion and enter the community of a people reviled and persecuted by the outside world. Today, however, some Jews who marry non-Jews maintain ties to Judaism and to the Jewish community. Although most Conservative and many Reform rabbis request conversion from the non-Jewish spouse, a growing number of Reform rabbis are prepared to officiate at mixed marriages. While affirming their opposition to intermarriage, the official arm of the Conservative movement has allowed the Jewish partner of a mixed marriage (but not the non-Jewish spouse) to become a member of a congregation. Most congregations also welcome the participation of non-Jewish spouses, though usually with certain restrictions as to their ritual and leadership involvement. On the other hand, Reform practice is to accept both spouses as members of the congregation, requiring that children of the marriage be brought to the temple school to receive training in Judaism and not simultaneously be enrolled in a non-Jewish religious school.

Sex

Premarital Sex

Although the talmudic Rabbis considered premarital sexual activity sinful, they recognized the strength of the human desire for sexual gratification and the difficulty many people have in controlling it. Consequently they advised, "18 is the proper age for marriage" (Avot 5:25).

According to Biale,[1] the biblical prohibitions that form the basis of the sexual codes in the *halakhah* prohibit only incestuous and adulterous relations. When polygamy was permissible, as during biblical times, a married man was not forbidden from having sexual relations with an unmarried woman as long as he could theoretically marry her. If he did not attempt to marry her, the man would be condemned and even flogged in some communities, but he was not guilty of a sexual transgression. Similarly, an unmarried and not betrothed woman who had sexual relations with a man did not violate any explicit sexual prohibition.

Nevertheless, the *halakhah* condemns nonmarital sexuality as "promiscuity" (*zenut*). The Talmud uses the term in multiple ways to refer to a spectrum of relationships such as professional prostitution; sexual relations of an unmarried woman not in the pursuit of marriage but merely for pleasure; any type of illicit sexual relationship, including adultery; and a specific type of woman whom a Kohen is forbidden to marry (*zonah*) but who is permitted to all other men.

As Maurice Lamm[2] observed:

> For Judaism, the value in human sexuality comes only when the relationship involves two people who have committed themselves to one another and have made that commitment in a binding covenant recognized by God and society. The act of sexual union, the deepest

personal statement that any human being can make, must be reserved for the moment of total oneness.

Male Homosexuality

Considering it an unnatural and depraved activity, the Bible is unequivocally explicit on the subject of male homosexuality: "Do not lie with a male as one lies with a woman; it is an abhorrence" (Lev. 18:22). This verse comes at the conclusion of the list of prohibited sexual relationships, but is the only one (other than bestiality) that uses the harsh term "abhorrence" (*to-eivah*). According to some commentators, this stresses the special disgust in which God holds those who engage in these unnatural practices, for all the other prohibited relationships involve normal sexual activity, though with prohibited mates.[1]

The Bible refers to only two actual incidents involving homosexuality. The most famous deals with the threatened homosexual rape of the angels who have come to Lot to urge him to escape with his family from the wicked city of Sodom (the source of the common use of the term "sodomy" for male homosexuality) before it and all its inhabitants are destroyed (Gen. 19). In the other, a threatened homosexual rape by a group of Benjamites eventually resulted in a devastating civil war that decimated that tribe (Judg. 19–20).

The rarity of homosexuality among Jews is suggested by the history of a legal decree designed to prevent it. Rabbi Judah forbade two bachelors from sleeping together under the same blanket, for fear that this would lead to homosexual temptation (Kid. 4:14). However, the other sages permitted it, deeming homosexuality so rare among Jews that such preventive legislation was unnecessary (Kid. 82a). This view was adopted by Maimonides, who observed that "Jews are not suspect to practice homosexuality."[2] However, by the 16th century, Yosef Karo[3] cautioned against being alone with another man because of the "lewdness rampant in our times" (S.A. EH 24). A century later, Rabbi Joel Sirkes[4] reverted to the original ruling, suspending the restriction on the ground that "in our lands [Poland] such lewdness is unheard of."[5]

The Rabbis offered three basic reasons for the strict ban on homosexuality. They considered it an unnatural perversion, defying the very structure of the anatomy of the sexes (which they deemed as obviously designed for heterosexual relationships) and thus debasing the dignity of human beings created in the image of God. Homosexuality frustrates the procreative purpose of sex, just as does masturbation and other forms of "spilling the seed in vain." Finally, a homosexual might abandon his wife and severely disrupt the integrity of the family, a core principal in Jewish life. For all these reasons, traditional Jewish law rejects the concept that homosexuality is to be regarded as morally neutral. It is unwilling to countenance the increasingly prevalent "politically correct" view that homosexual acts are acceptable as long as they are between two consenting adults and merely constitute an alternative lifestyle.

Since the 1980s, the rise of the gay pride movement has forced the Jewish community to confront the issue of homosexuality. Synagogues have been established by and for homosexuals. Requests have been made to accept homosexuality as an alternative lifestyle and for rabbinic sanctification of homosexual commitment ceremonies, based on the argument that procreation is the primary but not the only purpose of Jewish marriage.[6] It is interesting that the question of gay marriage was addressed in talmudic times, when the Rabbis stated that even those gentiles who engage in homosexual practices "do not draw up a *ketubah* for males"—that is, they do not write a marriage deed for gay couples (Hul. 92b).[7]

Among the Orthodox, Norman Lamm[8] argued that, although homosexuality between consenting adults should not be treated as a criminal offense, it was outrageous to believe it was morally neutral.[9] Moses Tendler[10] decried as profane the establishment of a gay synagogue or any institution designed to place the mantle of acceptability or respectability on homosexuality. He noted that homosexuals should be given every possible opportunity to take their place within the Jewish community, in conformity with the rabbinic adage that a Jew remains a Jew—no matter how serious his sin.[11] More recently, Barry Freundel, after comparing the Orthodox gay movement to "a group of Orthodox Sabbath violators or Orthodox ham eaters," argued that "we cannot close our eyes and pretend that a problem of this magnitude will go away. It is our task to present a legitimate Jewish response, balancing our opposition to homosexual activity with our concern for the human beings involved."[12] He urged the traditional Jewish community to motivate homosexuals to change their orientation, stressing that gays should be kept within the Torah community by the creation of a situation that "offers a positive alternative to the gay synagogue and to the even worse choices of complete abandonment and assimilation."[13]

The marginalization of gays exists to a much lesser degree in the other denominations within Judaism. As far back as 1977, Reform rabbis passed a resolution "encourag[ing] legislation which decriminalizes homosexual acts between consenting adults and prohibits discrimination between them as persons"; 14 years later, the Conservative movement followed suit with similar resolutions. Reform rabbis endorsed same-sex civil marriages in 1996, and the movement recently voted to allow rabbis to conduct same-sex marriages and to permit the ordination of admittedly gay men (and women).[14] While the Conservative movement does not ordain openly gay men or women as rabbis and officially prohibits same-sex commitment ceremonies, this latter policy is being increasingly flouted.

Female Homosexuality

The Torah does not mention female homosexuality, either because lesbianism was not widely practiced or because it was considered merely a minor offense. In the Talmud, however, Rabbi Huna said that if a woman performs a sex act with another woman, both are no longer considered to be virgins and thus cannot marry a *Kohen Gadol* (Shab. 65a on Lev. 21:13). Continuing that discussion, Rashi observed that the underlying concern was not whether lesbians may marry a *Kohen Gadol*, an office that had ceased long before the third century when Rabbi Huna lived, but with the basic immorality of the practice. Indeed, the term used is "for the priesthood" and not "for the High Priesthood," leading the Tosa-fists to understand Rabbi Huna as meaning that women who indulge in these practices are treated as harlots, who are forbidden to all *Kohanim* (Lev. 21:7). However, elsewhere in the Talmud it is noted that Rabbi Huna's ruling is not followed (Yev. 76a). The women would not be treated as harlots but rather as indulging in obscene practices.

Maimonides maintained that this lenient approach reflected the belief that lesbianism does not involve genital intercourse.[1] He argued that, although prohibited, a married woman guilty of female homosexuality did not become automatically forbidden to her husband.

Nevertheless, he stated that a husband should object to his wife indulging in such activities by preventing her from associating with women known to engage in lesbian practices. In addition, he urged a court dealing with a case of lesbianism to apply the punishment of flogging prescribed for rebelliousness, since the women had performed a forbidden act.[2]

Divorce (גֵּרוּשִׁין)

Jewish Concepts of Divorce

The dissolution of a marriage in Jewish law is a formal legal procedure with a host of specific details that must be observed.

Biblical Period

In early biblical times, an Israelite male could simply divorce his wife at will and send her from his home. The Jewish law of divorce is based on the verse: "A man takes a wife and possesses her. She fails to please him because he finds something obnoxious [or a matter of indecency] about her, and he writes her a bill of divorcement, hands it to her, and sends her away from his house" (Deut. 24:1). The term used for divorce in the text is "*keritut*" (cutting off), implying that a divorce must unconditionally sever all legal bonds between the husband and the woman with whom he had previously lived as "one flesh" (Gen. 2:24). According to the verse in Deuteronomy, every Jewish divorce requires the husband to write a formal legal document, generally known by its later talmudic term "*get*" (see p. 67), and hand it to his wife. Divorce was no longer to be at the arbitrary whim of the husband; instead, there had to be a reason given, though the vague grounds listed were later to give rise to extensive controversy.

Although not formally noted in the biblical text, the Israelite woman was probably entitled to some financial settlement (later formalized in the *ketubah*; see p. 44), which decreased the likelihood of her husband arbitrarily divorcing her without cause. This would explain the willingness of a husband to falsely accuse his wife of not being a virgin, risking fine and flogging and subjecting his household to shame (Deut. 22:13–21)—because by establishing a valid reason, he could divorce her without incurring any monetary penalty.

The unfortunate divorcée typically returned to her father's home (Lev. 22:13) and was forced to leave her children with her former husband. She was permitted to remarry, but not to a *Kohen* (Lev. 21:7), suggesting that the mere fact of having undergone a divorce left her with some dishonor or shame. The Bible cites only two situations in which a husband was forbidden to divorce his wife—if he had falsely accused his wife of not being a virgin before marriage, and if he had engaged in sexual intercourse with a virgin who was not betrothed to another man (Deut. 22:28–29).

The biblical ideal of marriage was a permanent union; divorce was only countenanced under exceptional circumstances, primarily when the marriage produced no children.

Later Developments

An entire volume of the Talmud (*Gittin*, or "divorces") elaborates the specific details instituted by the Rabbis concerning the divorce procedure. This requirement of complex legal formalities served to protect women to some degree against rash and irrational divorces. Despite permitting divorce, the Talmud included pronouncements and anecdotes exalting a first marriage as faithfulness to "the wife of your youth" and condemning divorce and remarriage in such statements as "A divorced man marries a divorced woman—four minds [opinions] in bed" (Pes. 112a), and "If a man divorces his first wife, even the altar sheds tears" (Git. 90b). The precise meaning of the term "*ervat davar*" (something obnoxious or a matter of indecency) in the biblical verse was the subject of a dispute between Beit Hillel, Beit Shammai, and Rabbi Akiva (Git. 90a–b). Beit Shammai argued that it meant adultery, so that the only proper ground for divorce was sexual impropriety. Beit Hillel disagreed, maintaining that "something obnoxious" might refer to any act that made the husband unhappy, even something as minor as his wife's cooking.[1] Although Beit Hillel prevailed in the law of divorce, the concept of Beit Shammai still has an effect. Whereas in the case of "something obnoxious" the husband has the *right* to divorce his wife, in the case of sexual transgression he has an *obligation* to do so, even if he would prefer to forgive her (Sot. 27b).[2] Rabbi Akiva took a different approach, interpreting the biblical verse as including two separate statements regarding the grounds for divorce. For him, the exact nature of *ervat davar* is immaterial, for the first part of the clause, "she fails to please him," stands as an independent justification. Thus a man was permitted to divorce his wife "if he finds another woman more beautiful than she is" (Git. 90a).

In addition to being unable to initiate a divorce action, until about 1000 C.E. a woman could be compelled to accept a divorce against her will. Despite an explicit talmudic statement—"A woman may be divorced with her consent or without it [while a man can give divorce only with his full consent]" (Yev. 112b)—an edict traditionally attributed to Rabbenu Gershom was issued declaring that a man may not divorce his wife except with her consent. This was closely linked to Gershom's prohibition of polygamy. Before this ruling, a man could either end his marriage unilaterally or drastically change its dynamics by taking a second wife. From this time on, marital strife could be resolved only through negotiations with his wife. However, in practice a woman could not refuse divorce indefinitely by withholding her consent, since by making her life unbearable a vindictive husband could effectively force her to accept it. Nevertheless, Rabbenu Gershom's ruling did improve the wife's bargaining power in negotiating the terms of the divorce.[3]

Unlike many other legal systems, in Jewish law the mutual consent of the parties is sufficient for dissolution of the marriage and delivery of the *get*. There is no requirement for a court to become involved in the process.

Divorce Other Than by Consent

If only one spouse wishes to divorce, the court must decide whether there are specific grounds to compel the husband to give (or the wife to receive) a *get*.

Right of the Wife to Demand a Divorce

According to the Talmud (Ket. 77a), a wife is entitled to demand a divorce in two general situations. The first is when her husband is physically repulsive to his wife, because of either a loathsome medical condition (e.g., "afflicted with boils and leprosy") or a malodorous occupation (e.g., gathering dog's dung, smelting copper, or tanning hides). It is immaterial whether the offensive condition arose before or after the marriage, for mere knowledge from a distance is not like being forced to live under adverse circumstances every day. Until the end of the gaonic period, the claim that "my husband is distasteful to me" was recognized as satisfactory grounds for a woman to compel her husband to divorce her. However, in the 12th century this was rejected by Rabbenu Tam, whose chief concern was to preserve the institution of marriage and minimize the number of divorces. So overwhelming was his personality and so cogent his legal reasoning that his ruling influenced all subsequent halakhic authorities so that even now a woman who finds her husband distasteful has no legal recourse and must remained married to a husband she abhors.[1]

A wife may compel her husband to divorce her if he refuses to fulfill to the best of his abilities his marital obligations to provide her with food, clothing, shelter, and conjugal relations (S.A. EH 76:11). Similarly, she may be granted a divorce if her husband physically or mentally abuses her so that she cannot be expected to continue living with him. Finally, the wife has legitimate grounds for divorce if her husband is unfaithful to her or if he "transgresses the Law of Moses"—for instance, if he causes her to violate the dietary laws knowing that she observes them, or if he has intercourse with her against her will during her menstrual period.[2]

The Talmud records a critical disagreement between two prominent sages (Ket. 77a). Samuel argued that a man should first be compelled to fulfill his duty to maintain his wife before he is required to divorce her. He consistently attempted to use the powers of the court to preserve the marriage as long as possible rather than dissolve it, hoping that there might be reconciliation and resolution of the conflict. Rav disagreed, stating that the husband's refusal to support his wife is merely one sign of his hostile attitude toward her. Convinced that by the time the situation had deteriorated to such a point the marriage should be ended immediately, Rav added that forcing her to remain with him would be like living "with a serpent in a basket."

In Israel today, the rabbinate generally takes the position advocated by Samuel. Couples seeking a divorce are usually urged by the court to attempt to live together for an additional period to ascertain whether they can achieve reconciliation (*shalom bayit*; lit., "peace in the house"), before requiring the husband to give his wife a *get*.[3]

Right of the Husband to Demand a Divorce

A husband may demand a divorce on the basis of defects or disabilities that prevent the husband from cohabiting with his wife (Nid. 12b) and failure of his wife to bear children within 10 years of their marriage (Yev. 6:6). This latter justification applies only if the husband has no children, even from another woman, and can persuade the court of his sincere desire to have children to fulfill the biblical commandment to be "fruitful and multiply" (Gen. 1:28).[4]

Unworthy conduct on the part of the wife also can be grounds for the husband to compel a divorce. This includes knowingly misleading him into "transgressing the Law of Moses"—for which the Mishnah gives the examples of feeding him untithed food and having intercourse with him during her menstrual period—and her personal transgressions, such as "not setting apart her dough offering (challah); making vows and not fulfilling them; going out with uncovered head [immodesty]; spinning in the street; and conversing with every man" (Ket. 72a). Another sage added various affronts to his honor, for example, "a wife who curses her husband's parents in his presence ... and one who is regarded as a screamer [a woman whose voice can be heard by her neighbors when she speaks inside her house]." A wife proven to have voluntarily committed adultery becomes prohibited to her husband, and she can be required to accept a *get* against her will (i.e., she is no longer protected by Rabbenu Gershom's edict) and forfeits the monetary protection of her *ketubah* (Ned. 90b).

Consequences of Divorce

Men and women who divorce are generally free to remarry anyone they please unless it is halakhically forbidden. The divorced woman is not permitted to marry a Kohen, nor is she allowed to marry a man with whom she is suspected of having committed adultery. Furthermore, she may not marry any person who served as a witness at the delivery of her *get* and may not marry within a period of 90 days following the divorce (lest there be doubt as to the paternity of her first child from her second marriage).[1] The husband is required to pay his ex-wife her dowry and the money stipulated in the *ketubah*, unless she has forfeited it as in the case of her adultery, but he no longer has any legal obligation to maintain her.

To prevent promiscuity, after divorce the parties are forbidden to reside together in their former common home. If owned or rented by one of them, that party is allowed to remain. If the home is the property of both, the wife is required to leave, based on the somewhat questionable concept that "moving about is harder for a man than for a woman" (Ket. 28a), although the court has the right to allow the wife to remain if necessary for an equitable settlement of financial disputes between the parties. Continuing to occupy the dwelling jointly (or later returning to it) can have unexpected and serious consequences. According to the presumption in traditional Jewish law that a man should not live with a woman for the sake of promiscuity and since both parties could have validly remarried according to *halakhah*, it will inferred that they had intended to enter into a *new* marital relationship! If either or both wish to marry third parties, they must formally divorce again.

Under Jewish law, as in secular society, divorce does not relieve a husband from his obligations for the support of the children of his marriage.[2] Traditionally, all children under age six are put in the custody of their mother, for they are primarily in need of the physical care and attention that mothers typically give children at that age. Boys who are older than six years must be with their father so that he can carry out his obligation to teach his male children Torah; conversely, girls older than six years must be with their mother so that she can instruct them in the ways of modesty.[3] However, in terms of modern civil divorce, most children remain with their mothers.

Get (גֵּט)

"*Get*" is the talmudic term for a formal divorce document that is written and signed by the husband and then delivered to his wife. Just as a Jewish marriage is entered into by a contract between husband and wife (*ketubah*), it can be terminated only by a legal document nullifying the original contract. A *get* may not be issued until a civil divorce is first obtained, just as a Jewish marriage ceremony may not be conducted without first fulfilling all civil requirements. Like all legal documents of the mishnaic and talmudic periods, a *get* is written in Aramaic, the everyday language of the time. The document follows a standard format and must be handwritten by a scribe, as originally was the *ketubah*.[1] A *get* is written in 12 lines, because this is the sum of the numerical value of its two Hebrew letters (ג = three, ט = nine). The writing and hand delivery of the *get* to the wife by the husband (or his agent) must be properly witnessed. The rules pertaining to the writing, signing, and delivery of a *get* are very precise to avoid mistakes, and thus they must be stringently observed. After the formal ceremony of handing over the *get*, the wife is officially divorced from her husband and both are issued a certificate of divorce (*p'tur*) stating that their marriage has been terminated and that each is free to marry again. The wife can marry any man except one to whom she is prohibited by law—such as a Kohen or a man with whom she had an adulterous relationship. The husband can remarry immediately after a divorce, but the wife cannot do so for a minimum of 90 days; if she is pregnant, the wait will eliminate questions about the paternity of the child.[2]

After the ceremony, the wife returns the *get* to the court, where the corners of the document are cut with scissors or a knife to indicate that it has been delivered and may never be used by anyone else. The document is then filed away in its torn state by the court to avoid any later suspicion that it was not absolutely legal. This custom began during Hadrian's rule over the Land of Israel in the first century C.E., when the Jewish community was denied all legal authority but Jewish courts continued to function secretly. Cutting the *get* enabled the Jews to deny that it was a legal document if later discovered by the Roman authorities. After the *get* has been returned, the Jewish court presents the wife with a document verifying the divorce.[3]

According to *halakhah*, a divorced woman cannot be remarried if she does not have a *get*. A woman who does so is regarded as an adulteress, and any child of her second union is considered a *mamzer*, who is permitted to marry only another with this same status or one who has converted to Judaism. This is the sole instance in which the Torah punishes an innocent party (the *mamzer*) for the sin of another (his or her parents).

All too frequently, religious men have taken advantage of their estranged wives' need for a *get* and have refused to grant it. Although this can be the act of a vindictive husband, refusal to issue a *get* more commonly is a form of blackmail to secure a more favorable financial settlement or even an actual cash payment if the wife comes from a wealthy family.[4] A woman who has been refused a *get* is known as an *agunah*, or "chained woman" (see p. 70).

Compelled Delivery/Receipt

To be valid, a *get* must be given by the husband of his own free will. Therefore, it is invalid if the husband is of unsound mind or under duress "contrary to law." A wife can appeal to the rabbinic court to compel her husband to grant her a divorce on the basis of his offensive physical condition, violation of marital obligations, or "unworthy conduct" (see p. 64). However, this is an inherently problematic procedure because it violates the requirement that a *get* be given with the husband's "full consent." The Rabbis used a variety of tortuous arguments to escape this conundrum. In essence, they maintained that although the husband initially did not wish to divorce his wife, once ordered to do so by a court he is under legal obligation to follow the order. Although it strains credulity, the Rabbis reasoned that because the husband would not wish to violate the law by disregarding their orders, he is considered to have genuinely consented to divorcing his wife.[5] Another rationale was offered by Maimonides, who argued that the husband's refusal to obey a court order to give a *get* must be due to an "evil disposition." Therefore, the court may apply duress to weaken or drive away his evil inclination, so that when the husband finally gives his consent, he does so of his own free will.[6]

According to Israeli law, the rabbinic courts have the authority to appeal to the civil courts and the police and request the incarceration of a recalcitrant husband. Even within the Orthodox world in the Diaspora, civil authorities are not infrequently requested to force a stubborn husband to grant a divorce. Rather than appealing to a court to compel the husband directly, the approach is to use threats of other legal actions against him, particularly an investigation of tax evasion.[7]

Conditional

In exceptional cases, a *get* may be written and delivered conditionally, designed to take effect only if a specific event occurs. This is usually applicable only in times of severe persecution (such as pogroms or the Holocaust) or war, when husband and wife may become separated and there is a danger of her becoming an *agunah* (see next page) if the husband does not return and no one can unequivocally attest to the fact that he has died. Consequently, a soldier preparing for war may issue a conditional *get* that would be effective if he failed to return by a certain date, thus permitting his wife to remarry.[8]

A conditional *get* may also be written if the husband of a childless couple becomes seriously ill. Such a document would free the wife from the law of levirate marriage (see p. 52). The husband may give his wife a *get* on condition that it be effective only if he dies from his present illness; if so, she would be considered divorced on the day she received the *get* (Git. 72a).[9]

Agunah (עֲגוּנָה)

An *agunah* (chained woman) is a woman whose marriage has in fact ended or been suspended but who legally remains a married woman (bound to a husband who no longer lives with her) and thus is unable to remarry. The *halakhah* prescribes that a marriage can be dissolved only by divorce or by the death of either spouse. According to Jewish law, divorce is effected not by decree of the court, but by the parties themselves—the delivery by the husband of a *get* (see p. 69) to his wife. If the marriage is untenable but the husband either willfully refuses to deliver a *get* (despite the threats and punitive measures of a Jewish court) or is legally incompetent to grant it (usually because of insanity), divorce is not possible and the wife becomes an *agunah*. Similarly, if the husband deserts his wife and disappears or if he dies but there is no valid testimony to that fact, the woman remains legally married and cannot marry another.[1]

On the other hand, a husband is not seriously affected by his wife's refusal to accept a *get* or her disappearance without a trace. In this situation, although the first marriage remains valid, the court may release the husband from Rabbenu Gershom's prohibition against bigamy by granting him exceptional permission to contract an additional marriage (*heter nisuin*). If the wife is mentally incompetent, the husband has recourse to a *heter me'ah rabbanim* (permission of 100 rabbis). In this procedure, a document is drawn up by a *beit din* and circulated to the other rabbis for their signatures. Traditionally, these rabbis were from at least three different countries; today, in North America it is generally accepted that the rabbis can be from three of the U.S. states or Canadian provinces.[2]

The *halakhah* has long been torn between the need to find a way to permit the *agunah* to remarry and the grave concern of ruling incorrectly and permitting a still-married woman to marry another man. The consequences of allowing an adulterous marriage by mistake are catastrophic—should the first husband eventually turn up, the woman must be divorced by her second husband and is also barred from remarrying the first—so that she is forbidden to *both* men. Moreover, any children she had with the second husband would be branded as *mamzerim* (see p. 51).[3]

Many rabbis have urged their colleagues to be as lenient as possible in finding a way for an *agunah* to remarry. The general halakhic principle is that the testimony of two competent witnesses is required to establish any fact. However, the need to quickly resolve the problem of an *agunah* led the Rabbis to accept testimony that would not be permitted in other cases. Not only is the testimony of a single witness sufficient but the rabbinic court will accept the evidence of a woman and a relative—classes usually deemed incompetent as witnesses—as well hearsay evidence (overheard conversation among non-Jews).

The woman herself can be a legitimate witness to her husband's death, even though she obviously is not a disinterested party to the case. The rationale for this ruling is that were she to give false testimony, she would be setting herself up for disaster if the husband she had reported as dead ever returned. However, the woman is deemed a reliable witness only "under normal circumstances," which the Mishnah defines as "when there is peace between him and her and peace in the world" (Yev. 114b). If there has been known marital friction between husband and wife, there would be reason to suspect the woman of deception in an attempt to simply be rid of her husband.[4]

Despite this general leniency, *circumstantial* evidence is not permitted in the case of a husband suspected of being deceased. Sufficient testimony must include *direct* evidence of his death. A man seen drowning in a large body of water whose shores are beyond the horizon cannot be presumed to have perished unless his body is found. Although highly unlikely, there is always the possibility that he survived by swimming to land at a point beyond the view of the witness.[5] However logical may be the presumption of death, it may not be accepted by the court as irrefutable proof. Although obtaining direct evidence of death was always difficult in times of war and pogrom, the problem became especially acute in the aftermath of the Holocaust, in which there were a staggering number of deaths for which no one survived to provide direct testimony.[6]

According to the Talmud, every soldier in King David's army gave a conditional *get* to his wife before going out to battle, so that if he were killed or captured she would be free to remarry (Ket. 9b).[7] The commentators have differed in their interpretations of such a "pre-battle" divorce. Rashi deemed it a valid conditional *get*, written out but not delivered to the wife (see p. 69). If the husband failed to return from the war and was presumed dead, the document could be given to the widow to "effectuate" the divorce. However, this approach poses several halakhic difficulties. First, a *get* is designed to end a marriage that is currently failing, not as insurance against one that is still viable. Moreover, once a *get* is written it must be delivered as soon as possible, since a man is forbidden to remain with his wife after deciding to divorce her. According to Rabbenu Tam,[8] the *get* in question was a real one but there was a mutual agreement that the husband and wife would remarry if he returned from the war. Among the problems with this view are (1) if the husband is a Kohen, he could not remarry his wife, since she would be technically a divorcée; and (2) if either party reneged on the promise to remarry, the initially unwanted divorce would be unconditionally binding, so that the spouse who desired to remain married would have no legal recourse.[9]

The Conservative movement in America has attempted to combat the problem of the *agunah* whose husband has disappeared or refused to grant a divorce by inserting a clause into the *ketubah* (see p. 44) in which the husband and wife agree to allow the *beit din* to decide the issue. The woman would be explicitly permitted to bring a civil lawsuit against her husband if he refused to give her a *get* or agree to its terms. This approach has been severely criticized by the Orthodox, and its validity and enforceability remain questionable.[10]

There currently are three halakhic options to the *agunah* problem.[11] One is to impose communal sanctions—both social and financial—on the recalcitrant party, including the synagogue recital on the Sabbath of a "curse against those who make others suffer" (the opposite of the *Mi She Berach* blessing for those who work for the needs of the community; see p. 462). Another is to solve the problem through the civil legal system, either by taking into account the husband's refusal to issue a *get* in the judicial determination of the equitable distribution of the marriage property[12] or by awarding damages to women whose husbands have refused to give them a *get* based on such torts as "infringement on the right to personal autonomy" and "intentional infliction of emotional distress."[13] Probably the most effective approach is the prenuptial agreement. This preventive measure may make the marriage conditional on certain defined circumstances, such as the husband remaining present and continuing to support his wife; providing for substantial damages for failure to issue a *get*; or binding the parties to appear before a specific *beit din* and abide by the court's decision.[14] Like the addition to the *ketubah*, prenuptial agreements may suffer from some technical halakhic problems and are of no help to women who marry without them.[15] Moreover, they are also rejected by many couples who, for emotional reasons, strongly believe that the wedding day is not the time to consider the possibility of divorce. The Reform movement does not require couples to obtain a *get* and considers a civil divorce agreement as sufficient.[16]

Despite the biblical requirement that a husband deliver a *get* to effectuate a divorce, there are five instances in the Talmud in which the Rabbis have canceled the marriage, even retroactively. The considerations that caused them to do so were to prevent *agunot*, to strengthen rabbinic authority, and to punish a husband "who acted improperly" (Git. 33,73; Ket. 3; BB 48; Yev. 110). Commentators have argued that a rabbinical court is empowered to sever a relationship of personal status based on the marriage formula—"behold you are consecrated unto me with this ring in accordance with the laws of Moses and Israel"—which makes the rabbis, as guardians of the law, "silent partners" to every marriage. Therefore, in extreme cases, a divorce can be granted by a religious court, though it should be one that is authoritative and, as much as possible, universally accepted. Consequently, Riskin[17] urged the establishment of a special Jerusalem court empowered by a decree of the chief rabbinate to abrogate marriage unilaterally in the case of a recalcitrant husband who has flouted the ruling of a regular rabbinical court and not granted his wife her freedom.

Unless some workable solution is accepted, the *agunah* is faced with three terrible choices. She can resign herself to her desperate fate, embark on an arduous and often unsuccessful search to find a halakhic authority willing and able to find some technicality to release her from an untenable marriage, or be forced to abandon the observant Jewish community to attain personal fulfillment in a new marriage.[18]

Death

Death and Dying (מָוֶת)

In Jewish thought, both life and death are part of the divine plan for the world. Life is deemed the highest good, and human beings are obliged to cherish it and preserve it. Every person is mandated to marry and procreate to share in perpetuating the human species (Yev. 63b). One must preserve oneself in a state of health. The Talmud not only includes many rules of hygiene but also cautions against making one's home in a community where there is no competent doctor: "A scholar should not reside in a city where the following 10 things are not found: A court of justice that imposes flagellation and decrees penalties, a charity fund collected by two and distributed by three, a synagogue, public baths, a convenience, a circumciser, a surgeon, a notary, a slaughterer, and a schoolmaster" (Sanh. 17b). As a renowned physician, Maimonides included a chapter on rules of health in his code *Mishneh Torah*. The Rabbis ruled that the preservation of life supersedes the fulfillment of all commandments, except the prohibitions against murder, adultery, and idolatry (Yoma 82a).

One should be concerned as much with the preservation of the lives of others, based on the mitzvah to love one's neighbor as oneself (Lev. 19:18), which Rabbi Akiva regarded as the most fundamental precept of the Torah. The Rabbis taught that whoever saves the life of a single person is as one who saves the whole world, and whoever destroys a single person is as one who destroys the whole world (JT Sanh. 22a)—for every person bears the divine image, and every person was created unique and irreplaceable. Each one, therefore, has a right to say: "The world was created for my sake" (Sanh. 4:5).

In view of the high value attached to life, the most baffling phenomenon is death, which puts an end to a human being and his or her achievements. The account of Adam's sin (Gen. 2) is the biblical attempt to deal with the problem. Rabbinic literature contains a variety of views on the subject. Some of the sages echoed the biblical concept that death was a punishment meted out to Adam and his descendants because of his sin in the Garden of Eden (Gen. R. 16:6), but others maintained that death was an appropriate termination for a finite creature and had been preordained at the time of Creation. A response to the fear of death was the concept that individuals survive as incorporeal spirits. Related to this was the belief in retributive judgment, with the righteous rewarded with eternal bliss in Paradise while the wicked are punished in Hell. The final mitigation of the terror of death in rabbinic literature was the belief in the resurrection of the dead and the world to come (see p. 114).

The Dying Process

Jewish tradition emphasizes respect for the dying and the dead as well as deference and adherence to the last wishes of one who is dying. Thus the final requests of Jacob (Gen. 49:29) and Joseph (Gen. 50:25) to have their remains taken out of Egypt so that they could be buried in the land of their fathers were respectfully followed, and Solomon heeded the deathbed advice of his father David (1 Kings 2:1–9) to take revenge on his enemies. The verbal instructions of a dying person (*goses*) are legally binding, even a deathbed change of last will and testament. Family members should be present when death is imminent, because it is a matter of great respect and even a religious act to watch over a person as he or she passes from this world to the next. According to the Talmud, a sick person nearing the end should be encouraged to confess his or her sins before God (called "*vidui*" in Hebrew; Shab. 32a). As noted in Proverbs (28:13), "He who confesses and gives them [his sins] up will find mercy." This is the traditional text of such a confession:

> I acknowledge before You, my God and God of my ancestors, that my recovery and my death are in Your hand. May it be Your will to heal me completely, but if I should die, may my death be an atonement for all sins that I have committed. May You grant my share in the Garden of Eden, and privilege me for the world to come that is concealed for the righteous.[1]

According to the Shulchan Arukh, this rite may be performed on a Sabbath or festival. Lest one frighten the patient and hasten death (which is prohibited), it is permissible to remind the person that recitation of the confession does not mean that death is at hand but merely is one possibly last opportunity to acknowledge the divine judgment. The patient who is too ill to speak can say the confession with his or her "mind and heart." If even this would be too much of an emotional strain, a person should not be forced to confess, in view of the assurance that "all Israel is guaranteed a portion in the world to come" (Sanh. 9:1).[2] With the last breath, the Jew is to pronounce the affirmation of faith, the *Shema*, timing it so that the final word he utters in life is *Echad* (One).[3]

According to Jewish law, death is presumed to occur when breathing has stopped and there is no evidence of heartbeat, peripheral pulse, or corneal reflex (see p. 113). Those present at the time recite the blessing *Baruch Ata Adonai, Dayyan ha-Emet* (Praised are You, Lord, the True Judge). To make absolutely certain that cardiac and respiratory functions have ceased, the body must be left untouched for about eight minutes while a feather is laid across the lips and nose and those present watch carefully for the slightest sign of movement. When death is finally established, the eyes and mouth of the deceased are gently closed by the eldest son (or nearest relative), an action performed by Joseph at the death of his father, Jacob (Gen. 46:4). A mystical explanation is that this prevents the eyes from seeing anything after beholding the Divine Countenance at the moment of death. In some communities, it is a tradition for the son to place some soil from the Land of Israel on the eyes of his dead father. The arms and hands of the departed are extended alongside the body. The face of the deceased is covered with a sheet, for it is considered disrespectful to allow others to see the ravages of death on it. A cloth is tied around the head to close the lower jaw and prevent the mouth from opening. The body is placed on the floor, feet toward the door (a position that, according to custom, was never assumed by a living person), and covered with a black sheet, while a lighted candle is set close to the head. On the Sabbath or a festival, the body must not be moved, although the chin may be lightly bound. Some Orthodox Jews have retained the custom of pouring water on the floor as a sign to friends and neighbors that a death has occurred. Originally, all the water in the house was poured out to prevent the spread of death, based on the belief that the Angel of Death cleansed his dripping knife in water. Another custom observed in some circles is for relatives and friends to ask forgiveness of the deceased for any harm or discomfort they might have caused during his or her lifetime.[4]

From the moment of death until burial, the deceased may not be left alone. A reliable *shomer* (watcher), preferably a member of the family or a personal friend, must remain with the body at all times, reciting psalms throughout the night. While engaged in this mitzvah, the watcher is exempt from the performance of other positive commandments (Ber. 18a). Smoking, eating, drinking, and unnecessary or derogatory conversation are forbidden in the room that contains the body.[5]

Angel of Death (מַלְאַךְ הַמָּוֶת)

Unlike the polytheistic belief in an independent deity who is responsible for causing death on earth, in Judaism God alone is the master of life and death. Nevertheless, there is the allegorical figure of an Angel of Death (*Malach ha-Mavet*), a messenger charged with carrying out divine decrees. In the Bible, the Angel of Death is described as "the Destroyer" (Exod. 12:23)—an "angel of the Lord standing between heaven and earth, with a drawn sword in his hand" (1 Chron. 21:15–16), whose function is to terminate the life of mortal human beings. The Talmud describes the Angel of Death as "full of eyes," standing at the head of the dying person and wielding a sword from which hangs a drop of gall. "As the sick person beholds it, he trembles and opens his mouth [in fright]; he [the Angel of Death] then drops it into his mouth. It is from this that he dies" (Av. Zar. 20b).[1]

Because in Jewish tradition the Angel of Death is merely a messenger carrying out God's decrees, its powers are severely limited and can be overcome in several ways. The study of Torah or some exceptional act of piety or goodness can be used to thwart the Angel of Death; there is no need to resort to the magical weapons and potent potions generally used against death in other cultures. Many heroes, especially in the Bible, are described as having defeated the Angel of Death with their fervent prayer, constant study, and outstanding acts of charity. The three Patriarchs, Moses, Aaron, and Miriam were said to have died by a kiss from God, rather than from the sword of the Angel of Death.

According to legend, other exceptionally meritorious persons were spared the agony of death and entered Paradise during their lifetimes.[2]

There are numerous tales depicting how mortals deceived the Angel of Death by trickery, such as by changing the doomed person's name on his or her deathbed. In one classic scenario, the Angel of Death appears on a bride and groom's wedding night with one of the couple preventing the death of the other.

Many Jewish customs associated with death and burial developed from the belief that the soul of the deceased needs to be protected from the Angel of Death or his agents. The image of the Angel of Death continues to play a role in the Passover haggadah, both in the story of the 10th plague (see p. 250) and in the folk song *Had Gadya* (see p. 290). In the world to come, after the resurrection of the dead, God will slaughter the Angel of Death and bring to fulfillment the words of the prophet, "He will destroy death forever. My Lord God will wipe the tears away" (Isa. 25:8).[3]

Preparation for Burial

Hevra Kadisha (חֶבְרָא קַדִּישָׁא)

The *hevra kadisha* (lit., "holy society") is the group that is charged with the responsibility of preparing the body for burial in accordance with Jewish customs. Membership in a *hevra kadisha* is considered a great communal honor, bestowed only on those who are truly pious and can display the proper respect for the deceased.

The Aramaic term "*hevra kadisha*" originally applied to any mutual aid society that provided a broad spectrum of charitable activities for its members. Among Ashkenazic Jews, the term became restricted to a society formed for the sole purpose of preparing the body for burial. The first recorded *hevra kadisha* that provided for the burial of all members of the community was in 16th-century Prague. It established specific government-approved regulations concerning fees to be paid, allocation of graves, and rules for erecting tombstones. However, its most important duty remained the preparation of the body for burial, which the Rabbis regarded as "the true kindness," since there could be no expectation of a reward.

During the Middle Ages, it became customary for the *hevra kadisha* to devote one day each year to fasting and prayer, to atone for any inadvertent disrespect shown to the dead. This typically took place on the Seventh of Adar, the traditional anniversary of the death of Moses, and was followed by a *seudah* (festive meal).[1]

Today, most Jewish communities with a significant Jewish population have a *hevra kadisha*. For reasons of modesty, the *hevra* is divided according to gender, with men attending male deceased and women attending females. However, many modern Jews use a Jewish funeral home or even a non-Jewish funeral home that practices Jewish burial customs.

Tahara (טָהֳרָה)

Tahara (cleansing or purification) is the ceremony of washing the dead before burial, which is performed by members of the *hevra kadisha* (see above). The basis for this ritual cleansing of the body is the verse, "As he came out of his mother's womb, so must he depart at last, naked as he came" (Eccles. 5:14). This means that just as a baby is washed immediately after birth and enters this word clean and pure, so must the body be washed before burial. The body is laid on a special board with the feet toward the door to indicate the escape of all impurity. While the body is undressed and thoroughly cleansed with lukewarm water, the attendants recite a series of biblical verses. In ultra-Orthodox circles, the head and the front part of the body are rubbed with a beaten egg, a symbol of the perpetual wheel of life.

The essential part of the ritual purification of the *tahara* ceremony is the pouring of warm water over the entire body, while it is held in an upright position. The body is then thoroughly dried and dressed in shrouds (see below). It is crucial that these and the following sacred tasks of preparing the body for burial should be performed by members of the *hevra kadisha* and never by non-Jews, for these are traditional Jewish acts and not done merely for hygienic purposes.[2]

In addition to washing the body, the hair is combed and the fingernails and toenails are cut. After performing *tahara*, the members of the *hevra kadisha* clean their hands with salt water. Most Jewish cemeteries have a special annex for *tahara*, though in recent years the ceremony usually takes place at a hospital mortuary or at the funeral home.

Shroud (תַּכְרִיכִים)

In the early talmudic period, it became customary for all Jews to be buried in the same type of garment—a simple shroud (*tachrichim*) made of inexpensive muslin, cotton, or linen—to indicate that rich and poor are equal before God. Since the 16th century, the accepted color for a shroud has been white, to symbolize purity. Shrouds are made without seams, knots, or buttons and have no pockets, signifying that it is a person's soul, not his or her wealth, that will be judged in the world to come.[3] This view was diametrically opposite to that of Egyptian and other early civilizations, which were as concerned with death as with life and whose tombs were filled with jewelry, food, and implements for the deceased to use in a new life after death. In contrast, *Pirkei Avot* (6:9) well illustrates the Jewish belief that "when a person departs from this world, neither silver, nor gold, nor precious stones, nor pearls escort him, but only Torah study and good deeds."[4]

At one time, the dead were dressed in costly garments of gold or silver. However, according to the Talmud, "formerly the [expense of] taking the dead out [to his burial] fell harder on his near-of-kin than his death, so his relatives abandoned him and fled [to escape the expense], until at last Rabban Gamaliel, disregarding his own dignity, [insisted that he be buried] in a plain linen shroud [instead of costly garments]" (MK 27a–b).

Traditionally, a man's shroud consists of seven parts—a headpiece, pants, shirt, belt, *kitel* (robe; see p. 619), tallit, and sheet. The Hebrew terms for some of these garments derive from the clothing of the *Kohen Gadol* in the ancient Temple.[5] A man is often buried in the *kitel* that he wore in his lifetime during High Holy Day services and at the Passover seder. When the body is dressed by members of the *hevra kadisha* (see above) various ties are looped without knots into the form of the Hebrew letter *shin*, standing for *Shaddai*, one of the names of God. The *kitel* is stripped of its snaps or buttons, and the tallit of its ornaments (*atarah*). One of the tzitzit (fringes) is cut (deliberately rendering it ritually unfit) and placed in a corner of the tallit, indicating that this Jew is no longer required to perform the mitzvot and symbolizing the severing of the bond of life.[6]

Coffin (אֲרוֹן)

Coffins were not used by the ancient Israelites. The deceased was simply buried on a bed of intertwined reeds, literally fulfilling the requirement of the biblical verse, "for dust you are, and to dust you shall return" (Gen. 3:19). Coffins were used only to honor specific individuals (such as a *Kohen*), to hide the horrific sight of a badly burned or maimed person, or to avoid a public health hazard (such as an individual who died of a contagious disease).[7] The only reference to a coffin in the Bible is the one in which the embalmed body of Joseph was kept (Gen. 50:26), reflecting an Egyptian custom and serving the purpose of preserving the body until it could be brought back to the Land of Israel for burial many years later. The custom of burying the dead in wooden coffins is recorded in the Talmud (Sanh. 98a–b). However, during talmudic times, it was more common to bear the body to the cemetery on a *mittah* (bier), and coffins were used only to transport corpses to distant places (MK 25a; Ket. 111a).

In Israel today, the common practice is to wrap the body in linen and bury it directly in the ground, a custom popularized by the 16th-century kabbalists. In Western countries, however, local law generally demands that coffins be used. Among nontraditional Jews in the United States, elaborate wooden or metal coffins are often employed. Where the earth is unstable and shifting, coffins may have to be enclosed in concrete vaults.

The Talmud reports that at one time "they used to bring out the deceased for burial, the rich on a tall state bed, ornamented and covered with rich coverlets, the poor on a plain bier (or box); and the poor felt ashamed. Therefore, they instituted [a law] that all should be brought out on a plain bier, out of deference for the poor" (MK 27a–b). Consequently, traditional Jews use a plain wooden coffin—with no nails, metal, or any decoration—usually made of pine or other inexpensive soft wood that decomposes more rapidly than a hardwood like oak.[8] The use of wooden coffins can be traced back to a midrash (Gen. R. 19:8), in which Rabbi Levi interpreted the biblical phrase that Adam and Even hid themselves among the trees in the Garden of Eden when they heard the divine judgment for committing the first sin (Gen. 3:8) as meaning that their descendants would be placed within coffins of wood when they died and were prepared to receive their reward.[9] Wood is also preferred over metal, which is a symbol of war and inconsistent with the hope of a loved one "resting in peace." The coffin should be simple and inexpensive as a reminder that all are equal in death.[10]

When municipal law requires the use of coffins, Orthodox Jews use coffins with loose bottom boards or with holes drilled into them to bring the corpse into direct contact with the earth and allow more rapid decomposition of the body. This is based on Judah ha-Nasi, whose will requested that "holes be drilled in my coffin" (JT Kil. 9:4, 32b).

Earth from the Land of Israel is sometimes placed in the coffin. This custom arises from medieval Jewish folklore, which maintained that when the Messiah comes at the end of days, the dead will be resurrected on the Mount of Olives in Jerusalem. Since those who are buried outside of Israel will roll underground to that site, the earth from the Holy Land will enable the body to know when it has arrived at the proper place. Another explanation for including a bag of Jerusalem earth in the coffin is that it teaches us that even in death we are still connected to the Land of Israel; some believe that earth from the Holy Land possesses atoning power.

Another tradition is to put into the coffin *Sheimot* (sacred books containing the Divine Name) that can no longer be used. The Jerusalem Talmud describes the custom of placing small sticks in the hands of the deceased (Kil. 9:3). It was ascribed to Rabbi Jeremiah, who requested that a staff be put into his hand when lowered into the grave so that he would be ready to march to Jerusalem at the announcement of the coming of the Messiah.[11]

The Hebrew word for coffin (*aron*) has the same base as that used for the ark in the synagogue (*Aron Kodesh*) that holds the Torah scroll. The body is honored as the holy vessel that contained the soul and thus is treated with the utmost reverence and respect.

Funeral Service (הַלְוָיָה)/Burial (קְבוּרָה)

The purpose of the funeral service is to pay tribute to the departed and to console the mourners. For centuries, funerals took place either at the residence of the deceased or at the cemetery. Today, most families choose to have the service in a funeral chapel and then go directly to the graveside for burial.[1] Although it is permissible to hold a funeral in the synagogue, this is generally reserved for rabbis and prominent leaders of the community.

Biblical Period

In ancient Israel and elsewhere in the Middle East (especially Egypt), receiving a decent burial was of great importance. As nomadic wanderings slowly gave way to more settled existence during the time of the Patriarchs, the acquisition of a grave site in the vicinity of a settlement was a significant indication of its permanence. Therefore, the Bible allots an entire chapter (Gen. 23) to Abraham's purchase of the Cave of Machpelah as a family tomb, and Jacob on his deathbed instructs his sons to bury him there (Gen. 49:29–33). Being buried in the land of his fathers was so important to Joseph that he made his brothers swear to "carry up my bones from here" (Gen. 50:25). No one wished to be buried in a strange place, and regardless of how long a person was away, his real home remained the site where his ancestors rested in the family grave. Thus Barzillai refused to join King David in Jerusalem because he was 80 years old and wanted to "die in my own town, near the graves of my father and of my mother" (2 Sam. 19:38). God Himself buries Moses in the last chapter of the Torah (Deut. 34:6), and biblical biographies ordinarily end with the statement that a man died and give an account of his burial (e.g., Josh. 24:30; 1 Kings 2:10 [David],11:43 [Solomon]).[2]

It was considered a sign of disrespect to leave unburied the deceased, whose soul has returned to God but whose body is left to linger in the land of the living.[3] Providing a decent burial for a stranger ranked with giving bread to the hungry and garments to the naked. However, no distinctively Israelite burial practices developed during almost the whole of the biblical period. Euphemistic biblical expressions for "to die"—including "to rest (or sleep) with one's fathers" (1 Kings 11:21) and "to be gathered to one's kin" (Gen. 25:8)—indicate the practice of family burial. During the Israelite period, the typical tomb was a natural cave or a chamber cut into soft rock, located near the city. Instead of being buried in the ground, bodies were laid on the floor or on rock shelves specially constructed on three sides of the chamber. As the tomb filled with the deceased from generations of the same family, it was necessary to pile up the skeletons or to extend the tomb into a side chamber to make room for new burials. In the rabbinic period, bones were collected after a year and placed in an ossuary, a small stone container.

Customs

Jewish tradition insists on prompt burial as a matter of respect for the dead (*kavod ha-met*). The Bible recounts that Sarah (Gen. 23) and Rachel (Gen. 35:19) were buried promptly. This token of respect was even extended to the body of a man who had been hanged; rather than permit the corpse to remain on the tree all night, "you … must bury him the same day" (Deut. 21:23). A corpse found unattended (*met mitzvah*) had to be buried promptly, even by the *Kohen Gadol* who was otherwise forbidden to become ritually unclean through contact with the dead. Therefore, Jewish law generally requires that burial take place within 24 hours after death. However, proper "honor of the dead"—to allow for preparation of a coffin, for shrouds to be made, and to await the arrival of close relatives—may justify some delay, but never for more than three days. Certain delays are unavoidable, because funerals may not take place on the Sabbath, on Yom Kippur, or in many communities, on the first day of festivals.[4] Where there is a need to bury two people at the same time, the interment of a scholar takes precedence over an *am ha-aretz* (average citizen), and the burial of a woman is always performed before that of a man.

In the past, fragrant flowers and spices were used at funerals to mask the smell of the decaying body. However, Jewish tradition discourages this practice, as well as the placing of flowers on the grave, as non-Jewish customs. Instead of sending flowers, it is proper to send a donation in honor of the deceased to a synagogue or to a charity selected by the mourning family.[5] Jewish tradition opposes the practice of viewing the body before burial, considering it incompatible with the principle of showing proper respect for the dead.[6]

Funeral Service

The funeral service normally begins with one or more psalms, often numbers 23 ("The Lord is my shepherd") and 121 ("I will lift up my eyes to the mountains"). For a woman, "A woman of valor" (selections from Prov. 31; see p. 129) is traditionally recited. A central part of the funeral service is the eulogy to pay tribute to the deceased without overstating his or her character traits or achievements. The Talmud states, "Just as the dead are punished [if they were sinners], so the funeral orators are punished [for delivering false eulogies]" (Ber. 62a), implying that just as it is wrong to praise excessively in a eulogy so it is incorrect not to eulogize a deserving person properly. Although normally offered by the officiating clergy, family members or close friends may choose to speak. In traditional circles, the eulogy is omitted when the funeral takes place on festivals or other days when *Tachanun* (see p. 435) is not recited. The service in the funeral home is usually concluded with the chanting of *El Malei Rachamim* (see p. 87), the traditional memorial prayer, which beseeches God to "grant perfect rest under the wings of Your Presence."[7]

The body is then transported to the cemetery (see p. 88), where relatives and close friends are honored by being the pallbearers who carry the coffin to the grave site. Escorting the dead (*levayat ha-met*), especially a deceased scholar, to his or her last resting place is considered an extremely important symbol of respect. The Rabbis included this among those acts "the fruit of which a man enjoys in this world while the stock remains for him in the world to come" (Pe'ah 1:1). Escorting the dead warranted even interrupting the study of Torah and was called "the true kindness" (*hesed shel emet*), an act of genuine selflessness since one can expect no reciprocation. The minimum duty is to rise as the funeral cortege passes and symbolically accompany it by walking in the direction of the hearse some six or eight feet to indicate respect for the deceased and sympathy for the mourners.[8]

In former days, barefoot pallbearers carried the bier on their shoulders. Many stops were made, so that they could be relieved by others who wished to participate in this religious act. The funeral procession was accompanied by hired mourners (professional wailers, who were usually women), who chanted dirges and lamentations and added their voices to the cries of the women of the household.[9]

Today, the procession traditionally pauses at least three times en route to the grave site to recite Psalm 91, indicating their unwillingness to part from the deceased.[10] In talmudic times, seven stops were made to allow the procession to sit on the ground and offer comfort and consolation to the mourners or to weep and lament for the departed. This number reflected either the seven times that the word "*hevel*" (vanity) occurs in Ecclesiastes 1:2 (BB 100b)—three times in the singular and twice in the plural, equaling four—or the seven stages of life (Eccles. R. 1:1). Each stop reminds those in the processional that death is inevitable and thus one should avoid a life of vanity, eschew evil, and walk in the path of goodness.[11]

As the coffin is lowered into the grave, those present say, "May he (or she) come to his (or her) place in peace." Those gathered then help fill the grave with dirt so that they can physically take part in the mitzvah of burying the dead. The practice is usually only symbolic, each person adding just a small amount of dirt. In some communities, however, those attending the burial add enough dirt to cover the coffin or even to completely fill the grave.[12] If a shovel is used, it is customary for each person to place the shovel in the pile of dirt, rather than hand it to the next person. This is a silent symbolic gesture expressing the prayer that the tragedy of death be not "contagious" and that the remainder of the family and friends may live long and peaceful lives.[13]

The mourners say the traditional *Mourner's Kaddish* or the "burial *Kaddish*," which includes in its first paragraph a reference to God "reviving the dead and raising them to eternal life." Those present at the ceremony then form two rows, between which the mourners walk, and offer words of consolation: "May God comfort you among all the mourners of Zion and Jerusalem."[14] The purpose of this recessional is to change the theme of the day—from honoring the dead to comforting the survivors.

In some congregations, each of those assembled at the graveside pulls up a blade of grass at the border of the cemetery, acknowledging the frailty of life and expressing the hope of resurrection based on these verses: "Let men sprout up in towns like country grass" (Ps. 72:16); "He is mindful that we are dust. Man, his days are like the grass; he blooms like a flower of the field; a wind passes by, and it is no more" (Ps. 103:14–16); and "And they of the city shall flourish like the grass of the earth" (Ps. 72:16).

Because of the sacredness of his role in the service of the Temple in Jerusalem, for which he was required to be ritually pure, a *Kohen* was subject to a number of restrictions. These included a prohibition against physical contact with the dead or even being under the same roof with a corpse (Lev. 21:1). Since these regulations are still in effect, a Kohen may not approach nearer than four cubits (about six feet) to a grave. However, the Torah lifts these restrictions when the deceased is one of the close relations for whom the Kohen has to observe shivah—father, mother, son, daughter, brother, sister, or wife.[15]

El Malei Rachamim (אֵל מָלֵא רַחֲמִים)

El Malei Rachamim (God full of compassion) is a prayer for the departed that is recited with a haunting chant at the funeral service, on visiting the graves of relatives (especially during the month of Elul), and after having been called up to the reading of the Torah on the anniversary of the death of a close relative (yahrzeit; see p. 100). In some Ashkenazic synagogues, *El Malei Rachamim* is also a part of the *Yizkor* memorial service (see p. 101) on Yom Kippur and on the last days of the three pilgrimage festivals. The prayer originated in the Jewish communities of Western and Eastern Europe, where it was recited for the martyrs of the Crusades and of the Chmielnicki massacres.

If one or both parents of either the bride or the groom is dead, it is customary to visit the grave before the wedding and to recite *El Malei Rachamim*. At one time this memorial prayer was recited during the wedding service under the *huppah*. Although a dramatic and effective way to remember the deceased, this practice marred the joy of the wedding. Consequently, the fashion has changed and the memorial prayer is now usually recited (if at all) before the wedding ceremony in the presence of the immediate family, usually in the rabbi's study.[16]

El Malei Rachamim is a plea that the soul of the departed be granted *menuchah nechonah* (proper rest), since the mere fact that a soul is in *Gan Eden* (Paradise) does not guarantee it complete contentment. According to tradition, the level of the soul in *Gan Eden* depends on its prior achievements on earth. Through our prayers and good deeds, we hope to earn God's compassion for the departed souls of those who were dear to us.[17] The statement is made that the worshiper resolves to "contribute to charity in remembrance of his (or her) soul." *El Malei Rachamim* includes the phrase "*on* the wings of the Divine Presence," rather than the more common "*under* the wings of the Divine Presence." The latter phrase implies heavenly protection from danger by using the analogy of a bird spreading its protective wings over its young. The analogy is reversed when speaking of spiritual elevation—God's presence is compared to a soaring eagle that puts its young on top of its wings and carries them aloft.[18]

Cemetery: House of Eternity (בֵּית עָלְמִין)/ House of Graves (בֵּית קְבָרוֹת)

During the biblical era, Jews generally buried their dead in family plots on their own property, either in caves (Land of Israel) or in the earth (Babylonia). Thus Abraham bought the Cave of Machpelah to become his family sepulchre (Gen. 23:20) and Manasseh was buried "in the garden of his palace " (2 Kings 21:18), while Rachel was interred on the road near Bethlehem (Gen. 35:19). The primary impetus to the development of communal cemeteries was the traditional laws of ritual purity, which forbid *Kohanim* from touching a corpse or coming within four cubits (about six feet) of a grave. A *Kohen* may enter a cemetery only for the burial of a close relative—parent, child, wife, brother, or unmarried sister (Lev. 21:2–4). Therefore, *Kohanim* are customarily buried in a special row close to the cemetery wall, so that their relatives can visit the graves without entering the confines of the cemetery itself.

In talmudic times, great care was lavished on the cemetery, leading the Rabbis to observe that "the Jewish graveyards are fairer than royal palaces" (Sanh. 96b). Although not "hallowed ground" in any religious sense, a cemetery may not be used for any other purpose. Multiple provisions were enacted to prevent *kalut rosh*, a spirit of levity and undignified behavior that would show disrespect to the dead. Suitable head covering must be worn; eating, drinking, and smoking are forbidden; care should be taken not to tread on a grave or lean on a headstone; a path through it cannot be used as a shortcut; and animals are not permitted to graze there. It is inappropriate to wear tallit or tefillin or read a Torah scroll in a cemetery, lest one "shame" the dead who are no longer able to perform these mitzvot (Ber. 18a).

In the confined quarters of the ghetto, little room could be allotted for a cemetery. This often led to the need to bury bodies on top of each other, giving rise to the general rule that each layer of graves must be separated by a space of six handbreadths (also the minimum space that must be left between adjoining graves). Lack of space in cemeteries required that the dead be interred in rows in the order of their burial, though a special area was generally reserved for rabbis and other prominent and pious members of the community. Men and women often were buried in separate rows. To segregate them from the righteous members of the community, apostates (especially baptized Jews), persons of evil repute, and suicides (see p. 103) were buried in a separate corner of the cemetery.

A widespread custom that has persisted to this day is visiting cemeteries on public fast days to offer prayers at the graves of the departed. Although the apparent rationale for this practice is "that they may intercede on behalf of the living," the Talmud stresses that one is forbidden to pray to the dead and that all pleas must be addressed to God alone. Visiting the cemetery is especially observed on Tisha b'Av, during the month of Elul before the High Holy Days, and on the days before Yom Kippur. In conjunction with each visit, one is supposed to make a contribution to charity.

The custom of decorating graves with flowers was strongly opposed by Orthodox rabbis, who considered this merely an imitation of gentile practice. However, planting flowers and shrubs in the cemetery does not bother non-Orthodox Jews, who view it merely as a manifestation of reverence for the dead.

Today, many communities have established large cemeteries with separate sections for members of different religions. This is acceptable under Jewish law as long as the portion of the cemetery allocated to the Jewish community is given as a permanent possession, is fenced off, and is separated by at least four cubits (six feet) from the general sections. In the United States, burial plots are typically sold in advance, rather than assigned in rotation at the time of death.

Memorial or Headstone (מַצֵּבָה)

Since ancient times, graves have been marked with a stone or monument. The first tombstone mentioned in the Bible is the *matzevah* (monument) that Jacob erected over the grave of his beloved wife Rachel (Gen. 35:20). In biblical times, the primary purposes of the monument were to protect the body from wild beasts and to identify the position of the grave so that a *Kohen* could avoid approaching too close and becoming ritually unclean. Today, the monument also serves to identify the grave so that relatives can find it when they visit the cemetery and to honor the memory of the departed.[19]

Initially, a pile of stones, a pillar, or merely a distinctive sign served to indicate the site of a grave. Only during the Hasmonean period, under Greek and Roman influence, did the custom develop of erecting ornate monumental tombstones for the nobility, such as *Yad Avshalom* (Monument of Absalom) in the Kidron Valley in Jerusalem. Decrying this practice, Rabbi Shimon ben Gamaliel declared: "one does not erect *nefashot* [monuments] to the righteous, for their words are their memorial" (Gen. R. 82:10). The burial places of outstanding religious leaders often became pilgrimage sites for their disciples, and tent-like canopies (*ohalim*) were usually erected over the grave. This practice was designed to treat great sages like royalty, as in the elaborate *ohel* for Maimonides in the cemetery in Tiberias.[20]

Sephardic tombstones typically lie horizontal on the grave and often portray events connected with the biblical character whose name was borne by the deceased. In contrast, Ashkenazim have traditionally used symbols illustrating the religious status (hands raised in the Priestly Blessing for a *Kohen*; a ewer and basin or musical instrument for a Levite) or occupation of the deceased (pair of shears for a tailor; a violin or harp for a musician). A recent tendency, especially among the Orthodox, is to use simple tombstones to emphasize that all are deemed equal in death.[21]

In the United States, the tombstone usually includes the name and dates of birth and death of the deceased (according to the Jewish calendar) in both English and Hebrew, as well as the relationship to other family members—father, mother, husband, wife, grandfather, grandmother, sister, brother. The inscription is generally headed by the letters פ״נ (standing for *po nikbar*) for a man and פ״ט (short for *po temunah*) for a woman, both of which mean "here lies buried." Sephardim use the letters מ״ק, which stand for *mekom kevurat* (the place of burial of). At the bottom of the tombstone are the letters תנצבה, which make up the abbreviation of the phrase *t'hee nishmato (nishmatah) tzerurah bitz'ror ha-chayim*, meaning "may his (or her) soul be bound up in the bond of eternal life."[22]

In the Diaspora, it is customary to erect and consecrate the grave marker during the 12th month after death. While many families wait until almost the full year has passed, it may be done sooner. The reason for waiting is that family members think of the deceased daily as they say *Kaddish* for the first 11 months after death. A more practical reason to delay the erection of a monument is to allow the earth around the grave a chance to settle, so that the heavy tombstone does not sink into the ground.[23] In Israel, the stone is usually placed on or soon after the 30th day (*sheloshim*) after burial.

In Western Europe and especially in the United States at the beginning of the 20th century, it became the custom to formally "consecrate" the monument with a service, though there is no religious obligation to do so. Since in the United States the tombstone is covered with a cloth, which is removed by the family during the service, the ritual has been termed "the unveiling." The ceremony also consists of several psalms, a brief eulogy noting the most important characteristics of the deceased, and the recitation of *El Malei Rachamim* (see above) and the *Mourner's Kaddish* (said aloud only if there is a minyan).[24]

A custom when leaving the grave site is to place a small stone on the marker. This may hearken back to the ancient tradition of marking the grave with a pile of stones. Conversely,

> it may be the end result of the custom of writing notes to the deceased and pushing them into crevices in the headstone (just as notes are pushed into cracks in the Western Wall in Jerusalem). When no crevice could be found, the note was weighted down with a stone. In time, the paper disintegrated or blew away leaving only the stone.[25]

Later visitors probably assumed that leaving a stone was the prevailing custom.

Mourning (אֵבֶל)

"Mourning" refers to the expression of grief and sorrow over the death of a close relative, friend, or national leader. The Rabbis distinguished four stages in the mourning period: *aninut*, the period between death and burial; shivah, the seven days following burial; *sheloshim*, the time until the 30th day after burial; and the first year (JT MK 3:7, 83c).

Excessive mourning was discouraged based on this verse: "Do not weep for the dead and do not lament for him" (Jer. 22:10). Consequently, intensive mourning ceased after *sheloshim*. To one who continued to mourn thereafter, God declared: "You are not more compassionate toward him [the departed] than I" (MK 27b). According to the Rabbis, a person who indulged in excessive grief over his dead would only have to weep for another. Indeed, the Talmud reported that a neighbor of Rabbi Huna lost all seven of her sons because she "wept excessively" for each one (ibid.).

Keriah (קְרִיעָה)

Keriah is the tearing of a garment as a sign of grief, a traditional Jewish mourning custom based on the actions of several figures in the Bible. These include Reuben on finding his brother Joseph missing from the pit (Gen. 37:29), Jacob upon seeing Joseph's bloodstained cloak and assuming that his favorite son was dead (Gen. 37:34), the brothers when the goblet was found in Benjamin's sack (Gen. 44:13), David on hearing of the death of King Saul (2 Sam. 1:11), Mordecai when he heard news of the decree of genocide arranged by Haman (Esther 4:1), and Job on learning of the death of his children (Job 1:20). Although the rending of garments initially may have been simply a manifestation of natural feelings of grief and anger, it also developed as a symbolic substitute for the pagan practice of mutilating one's flesh upon learning of a relative's death, an action that is expressly forbidden in two biblical passages (Lev. 19:28; Deut. 14:1–2).

At the death of one of the seven relatives for whom mourning is decreed—father, mother, children (at least 30 days old), brother, sister, husband, wife—a rent of at least four inches long is made in the lapel of an outer garment before the funeral. Divorced mates may cut their clothing, but they are not obligated to do so. A bride or groom should not perform *keriah* during the first seven days after the wedding, for this is deemed a time of joy even in the face of grief.[1] In talmudic times, it also was customary to express grief by *keriah* at the death of the *nasi* (president of the Sanhedrin) or of a great scholar (MK 22b) or upon seeing Jerusalem and the Temple Mount in ruins.

The torn garment is usually a vest, suit jacket, or tie for a man and a dress, blouse, or scarf for a woman.[2] A member of the *hevra kadisha* or officiating clergyman usually makes the incision with a knife, and the mourner tears it to the required length. This is at least one hand's breadth long, for "then David took hold on his clothes and rent them" (2 Sam. 1:11). The mourner stands during this procedure, based on this verse in Job (1:20): "Then Job arose and tore his robe." This posture also symbolizes both strength in the face of crisis and respect for the deceased.[3] The mourner says "Blessed are You ... the Righteous Judge" (*Dayyan ha-Emet*), bearing testimony that he does not blame God for his misfortune and accepts the divine judgment as a necessary part of life.

According to the Talmud, *keriah* should be done at the moment of death (MK 25a). Today, the general practice is to defer *keriah* until just before the funeral service or burial. Among non-Orthodox Jews, it is common to cut and tear a black ribbon, which is pinned to a garment of the mourner as a substitute for destroying the garment itself. For parents, the *keriah* is made on the left side, closest to the heart; for other relatives, it is made on the right. Although the tear must be exposed during the entire mourning period, it may be roughly stitched together after the seven-day shivah period and completely sewn up after the 30-day *sheloshim*. When mourning for parents, however, the *halakhah* is that the *keriah* may be stitched only after 30 days and may never be sewn up. For reasons of dignity and modesty, women may stitch the *keriah* together as soon after the funeral as they wish.[4]

Aninut (אֲנִינוּת)

Aninut is the status of a bereaved person (*onen*) during the period between the death and burial of a close relative. Although still required to observe the negative commandments of the Torah, the *onen* is not responsible for performing many of the positive religious duties, such as the recital of the *Shema* and the wearing of tallit and tefillin (MK 23b). According to the Talmud, this indicates respect for the memory of the deceased, since the *onen* is too distraught to discharge these religious obligations (Sem. 10). Moreover, this permits the *onen* not to be distracted while dealing with the mitzvah of attending to the burial needs of the deceased, in keeping with the talmudic dictum that "he who is engaged in a religious act is exempt from performing other religious duties" (Suk. 25a). The *onen* may not eat in the presence of the body; is forbidden to consume meat or drink wine; may not recite the Grace after Meals (MK 23b); may not partake of a festive meal or attend a party; must eschew the luxuries of self-adornment, bathing for pleasure, having a haircut, or engaging in conjugal relations; may not conduct business; and cannot even study Torah (which is considered a source of enjoyment). If death occurred on the Sabbath or if the Sabbath is part of the *aninut* period, the *onen* is obligated to discharge all of his or her religious obligations and is even permitted to eat meat and drink wine on that day (MK 23b). However, the *onen* is not to study Torah or be given an aliyah. *Aninut* is terminated with the burial, which commences the official mourning period.[5]

Lamm describes the *onen* as one who is "in deep distress, a person yanked out of normal life and abruptly catapulted into the midst of inexpressible grief. He is disoriented, his attitudes are disarrayed, his emotions out of gear. The shock of death paralyzes his consciousness and blocks out all regular patterns of orderly thinking."[6] Consequently, one is discouraged from trying to comfort the *onen* before the burial. As *Pirkei Avot* (4:23) teaches, "Do not console him while his dead lies before him." Therefore, the common Western (primarily American) customs of visitation and viewing the body to pay one's last respects to the deceased are against traditional Jewish practice.[7]

Meal of Consolation

Upon returning from the funeral to the home where shivah will be observed, it is traditional to ritually wash one's hands with water from a pitcher placed outside the door. This custom is based on the biblical concept that contact with a corpse is a major cause of ritual impurity (Num. 19:11).[8] It also stresses that Judaism is concerned with the value and dignity of life, rather than excessive attention to or worship of the dead. The washing is performed with a cup of water poured alternatively on both hands; as with the shovel at the filling of the grave, the cup is not passed directly from hand to hand.[9]

It is the obligation of the community to provide a meal of condolence (*seudat havra'ah*) for the mourners on their return from the cemetery. Indeed, the Jerusalem Talmud criticized neighbors who caused the bereaved to prepare their own meal, cursing them for being so callous to the plight of the mourners.[10]

It is customary to serve foods that are round to symbolize the cyclical and continuous nature of life. Among the most common are hardboiled eggs (a symbol of the close connection between life and death), lentils, garbanzo beans, and even bagels. According to some, the egg is the only food that hardens the longer it is cooked, stressing that human beings must learn to steel themselves when death occurs.[11] Similarly, the egg is completely sealed inside its shell, reminding the mourners to remain silent and refrain from casual talk.[12] Lentils are especially significant because, unlike most beans, they have no eye—symbolic of the deceased no longer being seen. Also, just as lentils have no mouth, so are mourners forbidden to open their mouths to greet people (Gen. R. 63:14). The critical importance of the *seudat havra'ah* to the mourners is that it is served by friends and other family members who care deeply for them. In modern times, guests now share in this meal, but it was once limited to those in mourning.[13]

Shivah (שִׁבְעָה)

Shivah (lit., "seven") is the most intense period of mourning. In computing the seven days, Jewish tradition follows the principle of deeming a fraction of a day as a complete day. Thus the day of burial is considered the first day, even if the interment was concluded only a few minutes before nightfall. Similarly, the seventh day is considered a full day after the morning service.

Shivah is suspended for the duration of the Sabbath, though that day is counted as one of the seven days of mourning, because the Sabbath is a day of joy and delight in which not even death may intrude. On the Sabbath, the mourner attends synagogue and may not show any outward signs of mourning, though private observances such as the prohibition against bathing remain in force.

If the burial took place before a major holiday (Rosh Hashanah, Yom Kippur, Passover, Shavuot, or Sukkot) and the mourner observed shivah for even a short period before the festival, the remainder of the shivah period is canceled by the holiday. However, if the burial occurred during *hol ha-mo'ed* (intermediate days of the festival), the entire shivah is observed after termination of the festival. Conservative Judaism has curtailed this observance to three days, with the last day of the holiday counting as the first day of shivah.

The initial seven-day period of mourning was instituted by the Rabbis (MK 20a), based on an interpretation of this verse in Amos (8:10): "I will turn your festivals into mourning and all your songs into dirges." Just as the major festivals of Passover and Sukkot were celebrated for seven days, so they decreed that the first portion of the mourning ritual last seven (*shivah*) days. This later Jewish custom had actually been observed by Joseph, who mourned his father, Jacob, for seven days (Gen. 50:10). A mystical reason offered by the Zohar is that for seven days the soul goes to and fro between the house and the grave, as it mourns for the body.

Shivah must be observed for father, mother, wife, husband, son, daughter, brother, and sister (including half-brother and half-sister). It is not observed for an infant who was younger than 30 days old when he or she died, because the child is regarded as having been born prematurely or as not having been viable at birth. The responsibility to mourn for their relatives is incumbent on boys from the age of 13 and a day and on girls from the age of 12 and a day.[14]

Customs

The bereaved family gathers to "sit shivah" in the home of the deceased; if necessary, shivah may be observed in the home of a close relative. In the past, the practice was to sit on overturned couches or beds (Sem. 6:1); it is now traditional for mourners to sit on low stools or benches. This may be a symbol of the mourner's awareness that life has suddenly changed or of the desire to stay close to the earth where his or her departed loved one is now buried.[15] In the Bible, the typical posture for the mourner was either sitting (Ezek. 26:16; Jon. 3:6; Job 2:13) or lying (2 Sam. 13:19; Lam. 2:21) on the ground. This practice is still observed by some Sephardic Jews, who sit on the floor during the shivah period.[16] Elderly people, the physically weak, and pregnant women may sit on normal seats. Nevertheless, if possible, they should make an effort to sit on a low stool whenever people come for short visits to comfort the bereaved.[17]

It is considered an obligation for relatives and friends to visit mourners during the shivah period, comforting them and providing them with food and other needs. Mourners do not extend greetings to the comforters or rise to meet them, a tradition derived from God's urging Ezekiel to "sigh in silence" (24:17). Based on the actions of the three friends of Job—the classic mourner—who sat with him for seven days without uttering a word (Job 2:13), the Rabbis noted that discreet individuals express their condolences in sympathetic silence. Therefore, visitors are advised not to speak until the mourner begins the conversation and to refrain from frivolous talk and customary greetings. When leaving, it has become customary for the visitor to approach the mourner and say, "May God comfort you among the other mourners of Zion and Jerusalem." This reinforces the concept that *all* Jews are mourners since the destruction of the Temple.

The Rabbis considered the first three days of mourning as the most intense: "Three days for weeping and seven for lamenting" (MK 27b). Therefore, tradition dictates that mourners be left alone with their thoughts and members of their immediate family for the first two days of mourning (after the funeral, which counts as the first day of shivah), deferring condolence calls until the third day unless this will prevent a person from visiting the mourner at all during the shivah period.

The activity of mourners is strictly limited while they are sitting shivah. Mourners do not bathe (except to wash for basic cleanliness), anoint the body, or engage in sexual intercourse. As a sign of their withdrawal from society, they do not use cosmetics, shave, cut the hair, or wear new clothes. Slippers of cloth, felt, or rubber are worn instead of comfortable leather footwear because the mourners remain indoors. Mourners do not leave the house, perform manual labor, or conduct business transactions. A mourner who must leave to conduct urgent business to prevent irreversible financial loss—such as distributing perishable goods that would be unusable if not sold that week—may place a bit of sand or earth in his shoes as a constant reminder of his status as a mourner and the need to return to sitting shivah as soon as possible. Mourners must refrain from such enjoyable activities as attending parties, including wedding and bar or bat mitzvah receptions, listening to music, and watching television. They are even forbidden from studying Torah, except for sorrowful portions of the Bible and Talmud such as Job, Lamentations, parts of Jeremiah, and the laws of mourning.[18]

In the house of mourning, it is customary to cover mirrors or turn them to the wall. The most popular reason for this practice is that mirrors are a symbol of vanity, and the mourner should not be concerned with personal appearance. Because prayer services are held in the house of mourning, the reflection might distract the attention of the worshipers. Indeed, it is forbidden to pray in front of a mirror, and synagogues are not decorated with them.[19]

A memorial candle is kept burning in a house of mourning throughout the seven-day shivah period, even on the Sabbath, during which no demonstrable mourning is observed. In Jewish tradition, the candle is symbolic of the body, while the flame represents the soul that is always reaching upward (Prov. 20:27). Lighting a candle and keeping it burning throughout the shivah period is thus an attempt to aid the soul of the departed in its journey heavenward.[20]

By the end of the Middle Ages, praying in the house of mourning was a well-established custom. Today, a minyan gathers for morning and evening prayers so that the mourners may recite the *Kaddish*. For the reading of the Torah during these home services, a scroll may be borrowed from the community synagogue as long as there are proper facilities for its care. If it is not possible to assemble a minyan in the home, the mourner may attend the synagogue for services and the recitation of the *Kaddish*.

Out of sensitivity to the those sitting shivah, *Hallel* (see p. 162) is not recited in the house of mourning on Rosh Hodesh, because it contains such verses as: "The dead cannot praise the Lord, nor any that go down into silence" (Ps. 115:17) and "This is the day that the Lord has made—let us exult and rejoice on it" (Ps. 118:24). In some communities, however, it is recited when the mourners leave the room. If Rosh Hodesh coincides with the Sabbath, *Hallel* is recited even if the service is being held in the house of those sitting shivah, since no public display of mourning is permitted on this day.

Tachanun (see p. 435) is omitted because its theme—"I have sinned before You"—is inappropriate for mourners, since it would make them feel guilty rather than comforted. The mourner is not called up for an aliyah during the week of shivah, even if the only Kohen or Levite in the congregation, because the Torah blessings express a feeling of good fortune that is not in keeping with the person's true emotions at the time. However, a mourner who is accidentally called up to the Torah should not refuse the aliyah, since this would be considered public mourning, which is forbidden. On Friday evening, mourners omit the six psalms of the *Kabbalat Shabbat* service (see p. 145), remaining in an anteroom until the last verse of *Lekhah Dodi* (see p. 146), at which time they enter the synagogue from the rear door and join the congregation. The congregation then offers a greeting of consolation: "*Ha-Makom yenachem*." The mourners do not take their usual seat (if they have one), an indication that there has been a major change in their life.

At one time, it was customary to bring gifts to the house of mourning during the shivah period. However, this tradition was later prohibited because it was viewed as emulating non-Jewish practices. The most appropriate gift is a contribution to the favorite charity of the deceased or to the synagogue where he or she worshiped.

Shivah concludes after the morning service on the seventh day. The mourner leaves the house and takes a walk around the block to symbolize his or her resumption of some of the normal functions of daily life.[21]

Sheloshim (שְׁלוֹשִׁים)

Sheloshim (lit., "30") refers to the 30 days of mourning after the death of close relatives (parents, child, brother, sister, husband, wife), counted from the time of the burial. This period may reflect the 30 days of mourning observed by the Israelites in the wilderness after the deaths of Aaron (Num. 20:29) and Moses (Deut. 34:8). One month was also the period prescribed by the Bible for a captive gentile maiden to mourn for her parents before she could be wed by her Jewish captor (Deut. 21:13). During this period of modified mourning, the bereaved begins to return to normal life and may resume work. Mourners may sit on regular chairs; mirrors are uncovered; and the prohibitions against wearing leather shoes, studying Torah, and engaging in sexual intercourse are lifted. Services are no longer held in the home, and mourners go to the regular synagogue minyan to say *Kaddish*.[22]

Some prohibitions of the initial seven-day shivah period are continued during *sheloshim*. According to *halakhah*, the bereaved is not allowed to wear new clothes, or even festive clothes, on Sabbaths and festivals; shave or have a haircut, though most authorities now permit it; attend weddings, dances, and parties or participate in any other form of merriment; or embark on a business journey. In addition, during *sheloshim* one may not listen to instrumental music or play a musical instrument (unless one earns a livelihood by playing an instrument or is playing it in order to learn); furthermore, the mourner may not listen to radio, watch television, or attend a movie, theatrical performance, or concert. A mourner may not get married during *sheloshim*, although an exception is made in the case of a bride or groom whose wedding preparations had already been made before the death occurred. If at all possible, however, the wedding should be postponed at least until after the shivah period. If a man is in mourning for his wife, he must wait until three pilgrimage festivals (Passover, Shavuot, Sukkot) have passed before remarrying, unless there are small children who need care.[23]

At the same time, however, *sheloshim* limits mourning by not permitting the mourner to visit the grave, thus preventing excessive expressions of grief.[24] Although during talmudic times mourners may have worn black throughout the *sheloshim* period, Jews today do not dress in black clothing or wear black armbands as signs of mourning because these are considered non-Jewish customs. During the *sheloshim* period, mourners traditionally do not change their regular synagogue seat (if they have one) for weekday services.

If the mourning rites of shivah are observed for at least one hour before the commencement of Passover or Shavuot, the shivah is waived and the observance of *sheloshim* is reduced to 15 days after the festival. In the case of Sukkot, the mourner has to observe the *sheloshim* for only eight days after the festival. If the mourner observes at least one hour of shivah before the commencement of Rosh Hashanah, the shivah is waived and Yom Kippur annuls the *sheloshim*. If one hour of mourning is observed before Yom Kippur, shivah is waived and the subsequent Sukkot festival annuls the *sheloshim*. The minor festivals of Hanukkah and Purim do not shorten the *sheloshim*.

For all but parents—who are mourned for 11 months—*sheloshim* constitutes the entire period of mourning.

Yahrzeit

The first biblical reference to a yearly memorial to the departed was the custom of the daughters of Israel, who "[went] every year, for four days in a year, and chant[ed] dirges for the daughter of Jephthah the Gileadite" (Judg. 11:40). During talmudic times, many people fasted on the anniversary of a parent's death (Ned. 12a). However, the current practice of yahrzeit (lit., "year time") as the annual memorial observed by Jews for the deceased members of their immediate families dates back to the Middle Ages. The Jewish communities of the Rhineland, rebuilding after the catastrophic devastation of the Crusades, mourned the thousands of martyrs who had died for *kiddush ha-Shem* (sanctification of the Name) and memorialized them each year on the anniversaries of their deaths.[25]

The commemoration of the yahrzeit on the Hebrew date of the anniversary of death is observed for parents. Many extend it to the other five close relatives for whom mourning is required—brother and sister, son and daughter, and spouse. Yahrzeit is also observed for outstanding scholars and other individuals. The only yahrzeits that occur in the standard calendar are the Seventh of Adar, the traditional date of the death of Moses; Lag ba-Omer, the 33rd day of the counting of the Omer (see p. 294) and the traditional date of the death of Shimon bar

Yochai, which is observed by popular pilgrimages to his grave at Meron; and the Third of Tishrei (Fast of Gedaliah). Hasidic communities observe the yahrzeits of the leaders of their specific dynasties, though they are festive occasions celebrating the day that these *tzadikim* ascended to the spiritual realm. In modern times, annual commemorations have been instituted in Israel for such prominent figures as Theodor Herzl, Vladimir Jabotinsky, Rav Kook, Chaim Nachman Bialik, and Yitzhak Rabin.

A person observing yahrzeit recites the *Mourner's Kaddish* at each of the three daily services and even leads them when able to do so. If the Torah is read on that day, the mourners are given *aliyot*; otherwise, they are called to the Torah on the preceding Sabbath. A 24-hour memorial candle is lit at home in accordance with this biblical verse: "The soul [spirit] of man is the candle of God" (Prov. 20:27).

Among Sephardim, the memorial ritual was unknown until the 16th century, when Isaac Luria of Safed gave it a kabbalistic explanation.[26] Although called *nachalah meldado* or *Annos*, the Yiddish term "yahrzeit" has become so widespread that it is often found in Sephardic religious works.

Non-Jewish cultures usually commemorate the birthday of the deceased. However this date is only an indication of the person's potential, rather than a celebration of what he or she has actually accomplished during life.[27]

Yizkor (יִזְכּוֹר)

Yizkor (May [God] remember) is the commonly used term for *Hazkarat Neshamot* (remembrance of the souls), the memorial service for the departed. In the Ashkenazic ritual, *Yizkor* is recited after the reading of the Torah during the morning service on the last days of each of the three pilgrimage festivals (Passover, Shavuot, and Sukkot) and on Yom Kippur. Sephardim also recite the memorial service (*Hashkabah*) during the evening service immediately preceding the Day of Atonement. Rather than a congregational recitation of the memorial prayers after the holiday Torah service, in the Sephardic ritual each person called to the Torah says a memorial prayer for his own relatives.

The custom of performing a memorial service for the dead developed among the Jews in Germany at the time of the Crusades, when thousands were massacred by mobs. Initially, a communal service was held once a year, on Yom Kippur, when lists were read detailing the men and women who had been martyred for *kiddush ha-Shem* (sanctification of God's Name). Today, the memorial service consists of three prayers that are recited while standing and with the Torah scrolls taken out from the ark. The first prayer, *Yizkor Elohim* (May God remember [the soul of]) expresses the mourner's hope that the departed souls will enjoy eternal life in the presence of God. Although the *aggadah* suggests that good deeds and generous donations to charity by living descendants can atone for the departed, this was opposed by some of the *Ge'onim*, who argued that only the deeds performed by people during their lifetimes count before God.[28]

In the Ashkenazic ritual, the second prayer in the memorial service is *El Malei Rachamim* (see p. 87). In modern times, a special prayer is frequently added for the victims of the Holocaust and for those Jewish soldiers who have died in war, particularly in defense of the State of Israel. The traditional memorial service concludes with the recital of *Av ha-Rachamim* (see p. 461).

It is customary for individuals whose parents are both living not to participate in the *Yizkor* service and to actually leave the sanctuary until it has concluded. To rise and stand silent when others are praying is awkward, and it is embarrassing to be the focus of envy for still having one's parents alive.[29] Some have derided this as a mere superstitious practice, arguing that it is contrary to the original intent of the prayers, which was for the community to pay homage to the martyrs of Judaism. Moreover, it ignores the need to commemorate the victims of the Holocaust, the terrible 20th-century tragedy in which many of the millions slaughtered have no living relatives to remember them.[30]

In the Conservative ritual, introductory readings and verses from the psalms are read in Hebrew and English. In the Reform rite, the memorial service is held only on the last day of Passover and on Yom Kippur as part of the late afternoon service before *Ne'ilah*. It consists of a shortened version of the traditional text plus various classic and modern readings expressing the transience of existence and the merits of those who have lived an exemplary life. Both the Conservative and Reform rituals end the memorial prayer with a congregational recitation of the *Mourner's Kaddish* (see p. 394).

Suicide

Because the duty of preserving life (*pikuach nefesh*), including one's own, is a paramount injunction in Judaism, suicide is prohibited. This is ultimately based on the belief that God created and thus owns the entire universe, which includes the bodies of all human beings. Therefore, the individual does not have the right to destroy or damage divine property. A stark description of the reasons for Jewish revulsion at suicide was provided by Yechiel Tuchinsky:[1]

> The sin of one who murders himself is greater than that of one who murders someone else for several reasons. First, through this murder he has left no possibility for any remorse and repentance. Second, death is the greatest form of repentance (Yoma 86), but he, on the contrary, has committed through his death the greatest sin, namely murder. Third, through his act he has made clear his repudiation of his Creator's ownership of his life, his body, and his soul... He is like one who actively (and intentionally) burns a scroll of the Torah, for our sages ... compared the creation of the soul to a scroll of the Torah that (now) has been burned and he must therefore face judgment in the future for this as well.

Suicide must be sharply differentiated from martyrdom, which, under certain extremely rare circumstances, is the greatest mitzvah of Judaism. The Talmud teaches that we must kill ourselves (or let ourselves be killed) rather than be forced to commit idolatry, adultery, or murder (Sanh. 74a). In each case, these are choices of death for the sake of God, not for oneself. Saul took his own life because he knew that the Philistines would put him to death anyway (1 Sam. 31:4–5), but only after parading him as a captive to shame the Israelite people. The suicide of Samson (Judg. 16:30), in which he brought down the pagan temple and killed many of the enemy, is extolled as an act of *kiddush ha-Shem* (sanctification of God's Name). The most famous act of suicide in Jewish history is the mass self-destruction of more than 900 Jews on the hilltop fortress of Masada in 73 C.E., who killed themselves rather than be enslaved and subjected to a foreign power (Rome). Another instance of mass suicide considered to be martyrdom occurred in York, England, in 1190 and was motivated by a desire to avoid forced conversion.

A poignant ruling from the Holocaust demonstrates the extent to which suicide is to be avoided if at all possible, except in dire circumstances of martyrdom. A man knew that he was to be tortured by the Nazis to force him to reveal the whereabouts of other Jews. Ephraim Oshry permitted him to commit suicide lest he betray those other Jews, but the rabbi did not permit this ruling to be published for fear that it would undermine the commitment to life of the other Jews of the Kovno ghetto.[2] Despite the poem about the 93 young women in Warsaw that appears in the martyrology section for Yom Kippur in modern *machzorim*, several authors have taken pride in the fact that so few Eastern European Jews committed suicide in the midst of the horrors of Nazi terror.[3]

Although suicide was not explicitly forbidden in the Talmud, later authorities considered suicide an even more heinous sin than murder. The murderer has the possibility of repenting for his terrible deed, while for the suicide the act is final. Death is traditionally considered a punishment that atones for the evil one has committed in life; the suicide has used this atoning action to commit his or her terrible crime. Suicide was thought to be a denial of the doctrines of reward and punishment and the sovereignty of God, and thus the suicide was said to forfeit his or her share in the world to come.[4]

The formal laws regarding suicide first appear in the late post-talmudic tractate *Semachot*. These mandate that no rites be performed in honor of the dead (e.g., *keriah*, eulogy), provided that the surviving mourners are not aggrieved by such denials (Sem. 2:1). However, a distinction is made between suicide while of sound mind (*la-da'at*), to which these severe restrictions apply, and suicide while of unsound mind (*she-lo la-da'at*), to which they do not apply. In most cases, a suicide is considered as being of sound mind only when there is clear evidence of deliberate intent. As the Talmud explains:

> Who is a suicide of sound mind? It is not so regarded if a man climbed a tree or a roof and fell to his death, but only where he states, "I am climbing the roof or the tree and I am going to throw myself to my death," and one sees him acting accordingly ... a man found strangled or hanging from a tree or cast upon a sword is regarded as a suicide while of unsound mind (Sem. 2:2–3).

According to *halakhah*, a person who takes his or her own life is *presumed* to do so without the necessary premeditation, whether from pathological depression, substance abuse (liquor, narcotics, barbiturates), or duress. The broad category of "duress" includes not only compulsion, such as the necessity to kill oneself rather than surrender to the enemy or violate God's laws, but also extreme suffering, anxiety, or fear of punishment, identification with a person who has just died, or real or imagined sinfulness.[5]

It was, and in some places still is, the custom to bury suicides in a special section of the cemetery, near its outer limits and at least six feet from other Jewish dead. In recent years, however, there is a growing tendency to remove this stigma from one who takes his or her own life; if there is even the slightest indication, the verdict is usually suicide while of unsound mind.

Euthanasia and Assisted Suicide

Euthanasia

"Euthanasia" (mercy killing) is a term denoting "the action of inducing gentle and easy death." The precise Hebrew equivalent of the Greek word is "*mitah yafah*" (beautiful death). It occurs several times in the Talmud, though always in connection with the duty to minimize the agony of those convicted of capital crimes before their execution (Sanh. 45a). The term is never applied to deliberately hastening the end of individuals dying from natural causes. The sanctity of human life is a supreme value in Judaism, based on the biblical concept of humans being created "in the image of God" (Gen. 1:27) and the talmudic dictum that "one who destroys a single soul is regarded as having destroyed an entire world" (Sanh. 37a). Each second of human life is unique and of equally infinite value. However, this value may come into direct conflict with the fundamental principle of preventing pain and suffering and preserving human dignity.

The Talmud appears to take different views on the issue of euthanasia. The statement "we do not worry about mere hours of life" implies that if one is dying of a terminal disease it is permitted to cease aggressive medical treatment, even if it is effective in prolonging vital organs, and concentrate instead on relieving pain and allowing the person to die. A contrary source depicts the scenario of a building collapsing on a person on the Sabbath. Potential rescuers are required to violate the Sabbath to save even a small amount of life, implying that it is justified to employ every possible medical technique to do the same. The Tosafists attempted to reconcile these views by observing that the proper objective of medical care is to act "for his or her benefit [*l'tovato*]" (Av. Zar. 27b), indicating that sometimes one may have to abandon attempts to save a life if they are doomed to failure, merely prolong suffering, and thus are not in the patient's general best interests.

Two Hebrew terms are used to describe people nearing the end of life. "*Terefah*" refers to an individual who, as a result of congenital anomaly or trauma, suffers the loss or perforation of one or more specified organs and, as a result, is presumed to be incapable of surviving for a period of 12 months. A "*goses*" is one who is moribund and expected to die within 72 hours, described as a flickering candle that cannot be moved for fear of extinguishing life (Sem. 1:1–4). According to the Shulchan Arukh, "a patient on his deathbed is considered as a living person in every respect ... and it is forbidden to cause him to die quickly ... or to move him from his place (lest this hasten his death); ... and whoever closes his eyes with the onset of death is regarded as shedding blood" (YD 339:1 and gloss). Maimonides agreed, legally codifying as murder the killing of any innocent person, "whether he is healthy or about to die from natural causes."[1]

Nevertheless, although a person is forbidden to do a positive act to *hasten* death, one is also prohibited from performing an act that would *delay* the death of a *goses* by artificial means when he or she has no hope of living. In his *Sefer Hasidim*, Judah the Pious (12th century) recognized permission to "remove the impediment"—any object or action that prevents the *goses* from dying. For example, one is permitted to remove a woodchopper from the vicinity of a dying person, if the noise is preventing his or her soul from departing. The prohibition against needlessly prolonging the dying process is dramatically illustrated by the ruling that those attending at the moment of death are forbidden to cry, lest the noise restore the soul to the deceased. However, it is forbidden to move the *goses* to another place if the person says he or she cannot die until placed somewhere else or to remove the *goses*'s pillow, even if one believes that the feathers of a certain bird are delaying his or her death. These examples are generally interpreted as implying that it is permissible to withhold or withdraw "heroic" methods to prolong a lingering life if there is no reasonable hope of recovery, especially if the person is in severe pain.

Some have made a distinction between established medical therapy (which must be given) and nonscientific practices (*segullot*), which are mistakenly believed to have some metaphysical effect that keeps the *goses* alive.[2] Another possibility is that the removal of an impediment to dying applies only to the very end of the *gesisah* period, when a person's soul is trying to escape the body and, according to the Talmud, the *goses* is experiencing severe pain.[3] Indeed, the very concept of the *goses* is somewhat problematic in view of modern medical interventions (e.g., respirator), which can keep even a moribund patient alive for far longer than 72 hours. Therefore, the number of true *gosesim* is now relatively small.[4] Although neither the patient nor others may induce death, they may pray to God to permit an extremely ill person in great pain to be released from suffering.

A classic talmudic text concerning the martyrdom of Chananiah ben Teradion encapsulates the rabbinic view of euthanasia (Av. Zar. 18a). When the renowned sage was to be burned at the stake, the Romans secured tufts of wet cotton around his heart to prolong his suffering. As the fire raged, the rabbi's disciples urged him to "open your mouth so you can end it quicker." However, he refused, saying that only God who gave him life could take it away. This is the primary argument against *active* euthanasia, any attempt to accelerate death by taking a step that would terminate life faster than it would naturally cease. However, the rabbi did permit removal of the wet cotton around his heart, which was applied only to sadistically prolong his suffering. This is interpreted as meaning that in some circumstances *passive* euthanasia is permitted, the removal of artificial life support keeping alive a person who will soon perish (i.e., not shortening life, but rather removing any impediment to the natural process of dying, especially if one is in severe pain).

In modern practical terms, most Jewish authorities would permit the withholding or disconnecting of artificial respirators and other machines that maintain the vital bodily functions of a *goses* but do not offer any reasonable chance of cure; they reason that these therapies merely prolong the dying process and do not serve the interests of the patient. Also falling in this category are cardiopulmonary resuscitation, surgery, dialysis, chemotherapy, and radiation therapy if they are merely palliative, especially if they increase pain and suffering or if the patient does not consent. However, the majority would not permit the removal of artificial nutrition and hydration from one who is terminally ill and cannot or will not ingest food and liquids through the mouth, making a distinction between "unusual" medications and the nutrition and hydration that are required by everyone. A minority would disagree, claiming that intravenous or enteral nutrition and hydration are not providing food and water in the "usual" sense, which we must do, and thus are similar to medications that are effectively prolonging the dying process. One is also required to administer beneficial procedures for complications that any other patient would willingly accept, such as antibiotics for pneumonia and blood for severe hemorrhage.

A controversial issue is the amount of medication that can be administered to relieve pain. Some argue that a physician may give whatever is necessary to alleviate pain, even if it may hasten a person's death, as long as the intention is to relieve pain. Others take the opposite approach, maintaining that as long as a physician knows that the dose is strong enough to kill the patient, he would be liable for injuring the patient indirectly even if the primary intent was to relieve pain. A few even take the bizarre stance of minimizing pain medication of a dying person for fear of inducing drug addiction! However, all would agree that if the primary intent is to cause the patient's death, it is forbidden to give that amount of medication, even at the request of the patient.

Assisted Suicide

Since suicide is forbidden in Jewish law, so is assisting one to end his or her own life.[5] This applies even if one merely hands an overdose of pills to an individual or sets up a machine so that a person can administer a lethal substance intravenously (i.e., so that once provided with a mechanism to commit suicide, the person acts completely on his or her own).

One who assists a suicide violates the proscription, "You shall not insult the deaf or place a stumbling block before the blind" (Lev. 19:14). The Rabbis interpreted this verse as extending to those who are morally blind, and thus it is forbidden to mislead those whose medical conditions are causing them such suffering that they think that a prohibited act is permissible. By actively making it possible for such individuals to do what is forbidden, the assistant is also guilty of the more serious crime of "strengthening or aiding those who commit a sin." One who assists a suicide could be considered as having injured that person indirectly. While not liable in a human court of law, the assistant would be guilty of a prohibited act in the divine tribunal. Referring to an incident in which a person who placed deadly poison before the animal of a neighbor was subject to divine retribution, the Talmud stresses that God would certainly be angry at an individual who jeopardized the life of a human being in that way. An assistant who knowingly administers a lethal dose of medication or poison with the intent to bring about the person's death has committed murder, even if the ultimate motive was benign.

Cremation

Disposal of the dead body by burning is not a Jewish custom. From earliest recorded time, interment in the earth has been considered obligatory, based on God's statement to Adam (the first human): "for dust you are, and to dust you shall return" (Gen. 3:19). Therefore, cremation is prohibited because it interferes with the natural decay of the body. The Talmud (Sanh. 46b), Maimonides (*Sefer ha-Mitzvot*), and the Shulchan Arukh (YD 362) all deemed burial to be a positive commandment, derived from the biblical verse "you must not let his corpse remain on the stake [hanging] overnight, but must bury him the same day" (Deut. 21:23). Because "burning" was one of the four biblical types of capital punishment meted out for a number of offenses (Lev. 20:14, 21:9), cremation was considered a humiliation inflicted on criminals (Josh. 7:15,25; Isa. 30:33). The Rabbis regarded the burning of a corpse to be an idolatrous practice, an affront to humankind as the highest form of creation, and a denial of the belief in bodily resurrection.[1]

When cremation is performed, the ashes of the deceased are typically scattered at sea or saved in a special urn. According to Orthodox practice, cremated ashes may not be buried in a Jewish cemetery. Furthermore, those who choose not to be buried in the ancient Jewish manner, as a final defiance of tradition, are not to be mourned.[2] Although more liberal denominations also discourage cremation in favor of the traditional practice of burial, many of these rabbis will officiate at a memorial service for a person who has been cremated and permit the ashes to be buried in the cemetery.[3]

As Dorff[4] observed, in the generations after the gas chambers and ovens, it is difficult to understand why Jews would willingly do to their beloved what the Nazis maliciously did to so many during the Holocaust, thus communicating disdain for the dead instead of love and respect. Some Jews have elected cremation, claiming that it is less expensive than burial; however, it is not necessarily less than the cost of the plain wooden box mandated by Jewish law. In those cases of hardship where burial is truly unaffordable, some Jewish funeral directors perform this service for little or no cost.

Modern Issues Concerning the Dead

Autopsy

Whether autopsies are permitted is an extremely controversial issue among traditional Jews. It brings into direct opposition two fundamental principles—*kavod ha-met* (reverence for the human body after death) and *pikuach nefesh* (the preservation of life). Many rabbis have argued that the biblical requirement for burial as soon as possible (Deut. 21:22–23), combined with the prohibition against desecrating the corpse (*nivvul ha-met*), forbids mutilation of the body for postmortem examination. However, others have countered that reverence for the corpse must yield to the superior value of life and its preservation. Indeed, the duty of saving and maintaining life, which includes even cases of a doubtful nature, overrides all but three commandments of the Torah (against idolatry, adultery, and murder).

It was not until the 18th century, when human bodies began to be commonly used systematically for medical research, that the permissibility of autopsies for medical research and saving lives became a practical halakhic question. The first clearly recorded ruling permitting an autopsy in the interest of the living was issued in a responsum by Ezekiel Landau of Prague. However, it was strictly limited to a situation in which, at the time of death, there was in the same hospital another patient suffering from the same symptoms, so that the autopsy could be of immediate value in saving a life. The problem became an important issue in Israel with the establishment of the Medical School of the Hebrew University in Jerusalem. Rav Kook, the usually liberal Ashkenazic chief rabbi of Palestine, entirely forbade the autopsy of Jewish bodies for medical purposes. However, a 1949 agreement between Hadassah Hospital and Chief Rabbi Isaac Herzog, which was incorporated into Israeli law four years later, permitted autopsies in the following situations: (1) when the civil law demanded it in cases of crime or accidental death, (2) to establish the cause of death when it was doubtful, (3) to save lives (i.e., when an autopsy may yield medical information that would directly benefit another person), and (4) in cases of hereditary disease, when an autopsy may directly benefit the survivors.[1] Before an autopsy could be performed, it was necessary to obtain the signatures of three doctors. The medical dissection must be performed with the utmost respect for the deceased. Any organs dissected were to be handed over to the *hevra kadisha* for burial after the necessary examinations had been performed.

As autopsies became more routine and after allegations of widespread abuse of the legal safeguards, certain Orthodox circles in Israel agitated to have the law amended by reverting to the strictly limited permission given by Rabbi Landau. Consequently, in 1980 (despite strenuous opposition by Israeli medical researchers), the law was changed to make it more difficult to justify the need for performing an autopsy. Autopsies are now permissible only if there is a specific legal or medical reason to warrant one in a given case.[2]

Although from the halakhic point of view the objections that apply to autopsies also apply to dissection for the purpose of anatomic study, enough people bequeath their bodies for this purpose that it has not sparked substantial religious opposition. The only restrictions are that the remains be buried in a timely fashion according to Jewish law and custom and that the decision be in accord with the wishes not only of the deceased but also of his or her family. Today, medical schools in the United States have a sufficient supply of bodies of unknown, abandoned individuals from county morgues. Therefore, Jews should not volunteer to have their bodies dissected, for there is no medical need to override the respect for a corpse required by the concept of *kavod ha-met*.[3]

There is general agreement among halakhic experts that autopsies are permitted in the case of violent or accidental death or when a crime is suspected.

Organ Donation

As with autopsies, the issue of organ donation revolves around the often-conflicting principles of *kavod ha-met* and *pikuach nefesh*.[4] In this instance, however, these two basic tenets work in tandem, for it is assumed that deceased persons would be honored if their organs were used to preserve the life of another. Giving a person the opportunity to live by donating an organ is also the ultimate act of *hesed*, lovingkindness to one's fellow human being.

Despite this predominant opinion that delaying burial to permit organ transplantation does not diminish respect for the dead but, on the contrary, enhances it, some rabbis have limited this practice to varying degrees. The most restrictive opinion permits donations only when there is a specific patient who stands to lose his or her life or an entire physical faculty. According to this view, if a person can see out of one eye, a cornea may not be removed from a cadaver to restore vision in the other eye. A corneal transplant would be permitted only if both eyes were failing and the prospective recipient would be in danger of losing all vision, thus incurring serious potential danger to life and limb. Moreover, since the patient for whom the organ is intended must be known and present, donation to an organ bank would not be permitted.

Nevertheless, since there now is a shortage of donated organs and it is certain that all will be used for transplantation, most Orthodox rabbis have relaxed the restrictions on organ donations. However, there are still major problems associated with giving permission for transplantation. One is precisely defining the moment of death. According to classical Jewish sources, there were two criteria to determine when death occurred. The majority rule was the breath test, in which a feather was placed beneath the nostrils of the patient; movement of the feather indicated life, whereas lack of movement signified death (Yoma 85a; PdRE 52). This test was based on two biblical verses: "God breathed life into Adam" (Gen. 2:7), and the Flood killed "all in whose nostrils was the merest breath of life" (Gen. 7:22). A minority view in the Talmud maintained that the cessation of heartbeat was also required to determine death (Yoma 85a). Later codifiers insisted on both respiratory and cardiac manifestations of death.

Moses Isserles,[5] acknowledging the difficulty of accurately distinguishing death from a fainting spell, argued that even after the cessation of breath and heartbeat one should wait a period of time before assuming that the patient is dead. In a 1988 ruling approving heart transplantation, the chief rabbinate of Israel effectively accepted the modern definition of death as a completely flat electroencephalogram (both cortical and brainstem function), which indicates the cessation of spontaneous brain activity.

Some Orthodox Jews resist organ donation because of the concept that death does not come at a clear, definable moment but rather occurs in stages over time. According to rabbinic lore, the complete severing of the relation between body and soul does not take place until three days after death (Gen. R. 100:7; Lev. R. 18:1; MK 3:5). During that time, the soul hovers over the grave in the hope that it may be restored to the body, departing only when decomposition begins. This was an explanation for the belief that the grief of mourners naturally becomes most intense on the third day after the death of a loved one. Moreover, this concept led the Rabbis to permit relatives to watch graves for three days in case the interred body was still alive, "for once it happened that they watched one who thereupon continued to live for 25 years and another who still had five children before dying" (Sem. 8:1). Some even believed that the soul continues to have some relationship with the body for 12 months, until the body has disintegrated (Shab. 152b–153a). Medieval folklore often spoke of the "spirit community," in which life continued after physical death. Thus the combination of all these factors makes it understandable why some families are hesitant to donate the organs of their relatives.

The Talmud (Av. Zar. 29b) and Maimonides[6] clearly indicate that it is forbidden to use a cadaver for some other purpose or extraneous benefit. Modern rabbis have employed ingenious reasoning to argue that organ donation and transplantation do not violate this rule against deriving benefit from the body (*hana'ah min ha-met*). Some of the arguments are as follows:

1. The prohibition against deriving benefit from a cadaver is of rabbinic origin and thus may be overridden for medical purposes.

2. Even if the prohibition is of biblical origin, what was forbidden was only conventional uses of the cadaver, not such "nonconventional" ones as medical treatment.
3. The prohibition was designed to ensure a timely burial that would prevent dishonoring the cadaver so that, once the bulk of the remains have been properly buried, individual organs can be used for transplantation without violating the original prohibition.
4. Once an organ has been transplanted, it is no longer considered as dead tissue, since it literally has been revitalized in the body of the recipient.

Another objection to organ transplantation is the belief among some that one must be buried complete to be resurrected whole. According to this view, donating an organ would leave the deceased without that part when the dead are brought back to life. Medieval philosophers ridiculed this concept. For example, Saadiah Gaon pointed out that if one believes that God created the world from nothing, one should surely believe that God can revive the dead even if a few parts are missing. Except for the most extreme branches of ultra-Orthodoxy, virtually all rabbis agree that saving life in the here and now clearly and unequivocally takes precedence over whatever one believes about future resurrection.

Afterlife and the World to Come (עוֹלָם הַבָּא)

Judaism has always maintained a belief in an afterlife, though there has been a broad spectrum of views in different historical eras concerning such core issues as the immortality of the soul, the resurrection of the dead, and the nature of the world to come (*olam ha-ba*) after the messianic redemption.[1]

Biblical Period

According to the older books of the Hebrew Scripture, the sojourn of a human being on earth is followed by a descent to She'ol, a kind of Hades, a netherworld where the dead live an ethereal, shadowy existence. A vast region located deep beneath the earth, She'ol was enclosed with gates and a place of eternal silence. When Jacob heard that his favorite son, Joseph, had been torn to pieces by a wild beast, he

PARADISE (*GAN EDEN*) (גַּן עֵדֶן)

The term "Paradise" is a Greek word that the Septuagint used to translate the Hebrew word "*pardes*," which refers to *Gan Eden* (the Garden of Eden). The early prophets figuratively depicted the end of days as a return to the original peace and joy of the Garden of Eden before the sin of Adam and Eve (Isa. 11:6–9, 51:3; Ezek. 36:35), rather than the "heavenly" abode of God. As with Gehenna (see p. 117), the Rabbis disagreed as to when the entry of the righteous into *Gan Eden* would occur—immediately after death or only at the time of resurrection.

In this eschatological Paradise, the righteous would sit at golden tables (Taan. 25a) or under elaborate canopies and participate in lavish banquets (BB 75a). For the medieval philosophers, *Gan Eden* and Gehenna were both figures of speech. Maimonides[1] maintained that the former referred to communion with God, while the latter meant to be deprived of eternal life. For Joseph Albo,[2] Gehenna was the state of the soul that, having sought only material gratifications in this life, had no means of obtaining satisfaction in the nonmaterial world beyond the grave.

moaned that he would "go down mourning to my son in She'ol" (Gen. 37:35). The prophets pictured it as a dreary, gloomy place, a land of the shades. In the *Hallel* (see p. 162), the Psalmist (115:17) observed: "The dead cannot praise the Lord, nor any who go down into the silence [of the grave]." Job (14:12) viewed death as the ultimate finality with no hope of an afterlife: "So man lies down never to rise; he will awake only when the heavens are no more." An explicit biblical formulation of the doctrine of the resurrection of the dead occurs in the Book of Daniel (12:2): "Many of those that sleep in the dust of the earth will awake, some to eternal life, others to reproaches, to everlasting abhorrence." However, the most dramatic portrayal of this bodily resurrection is found in the Valley of the Dry Bones prophecy in Ezekiel (37), which envisions the future redemption of Israel.

During the Second Temple period, the idea of heavenly immortality, either for all Israel or for the righteous alone, vied with the resurrection of the dead as the dominant theme. One part of the Book of the Maccabees promised everlasting life with God to those Jewish martyrs who preferred death to the violation of the divine Torah but was silent on the subject of resurrection. Conversely, in another section a tortured Israelite on the point of death says to the wicked king: "Better to be killed by men and cherish God's promise to raise us again. There will be no resurrection to life for you!" The philosopher Philo[2] stressed the immortality of the individual soul, which is imprisoned in the body here on earth. The souls of the righteous return to their home in God, whereas those of the wicked suffer eternal death.

Talmudic Period and Midrash

According to the Rabbis, when a person dies, the soul leaves the body. However, for the first 12 months the soul retains a temporary relationship to the body, coming and going until the body has disintegrated. Thus the prophet Samuel could be raised from the dead by the witch of En-Dor within the first year of his demise (1 Sam. 28). This 12-month period is a time of purgatory for all souls or, according to another view, only for those of the wicked. The righteous then go to Paradise (*Gan Eden*; see p. 115), while the wicked are consigned to Hell (*Geihinnom*; see p. 117). Some sages believed that the soul remains quiescent, with those of the righteous "hidden under the Throne of Glory"; others viewed the souls of the dead as having full consciousness. The Midrash declares: "The only difference between the living and the dead is the power of speech" (PR 12:46). There also was controversy as to how much the dead know of the world they have left behind (Ber. 18b).

The Rabbis realized that the biblical principle that people are either rewarded or punished during their life for good or evil deeds seemed to be contradicted by ordinary experience. The problem of why the innocent suffer and the wicked prosper in this life, especially as presented in the Book of Job, appeared to be an enigmatic mystery that could be understood only by the wisdom of God. A rabbinic solution to this conundrum was the concept of the resurrection of the dead. Rabbi Jacob remarked that "there is no reward for precepts [virtuously fulfilling the mitzvot] in this world" (Kid. 39b), while several talmudic statements indicate that "the righteous will receive their reward in the world to come" (Taan. 11a). The Talmud unequivocally states: "He who

GEHENNA

"Gehenna" is the Greek form of the Aramaic "*Geihinnom*" and the Hebrew "*Ge* (*Bene*) *Hinnom*" (the Valley of [the sons of] Hinnom), the ravine in the south of ancient Jerusalem (Josh. 15:8, 18:16). Defiled by being the site of the cult of Moloch, which involved the burning of children, Gehenna was cursed by Jeremiah, who predicted that the Babylonian destruction of Jerusalem would fill this valley with the corpses of the city's inhabitants, who would burn there and rot like "dung upon the face of the earth" (Jer. 8:2). Isaiah (66:24) alluded to these words when he spoke of the punishments of the wicked at the end of days: "They shall go out and gaze on the corpses of the men who rebelled against Me: Their worm shall not die, nor their fire be quenched; they shall be a horror to all flesh." Later writings added further gruesome details of the torments suffered by the wicked in this fiery pit, where their bodies burn eternally while at the same time rotting away with worms and maggots.

The traditional rabbinic view of Gehenna was a purgatory, where even the worst of sinners would spend only a year. There was some support for a doctrine of eternal damnation, but this was disputed by the talmudic claim that "there will be no *Geihinnom* in future times." Saadiah Gaon argued that both reward and punishment were everlasting, with perpetual torment reserved for nonbelievers, polytheists, and the "impertinent perpetrators of grave sins." As a strong believer in the immortality of the soul, Maimonides viewed the punishment of the sinner not as torment but as complete annihilation of the soul. Modern Jewish thought has essentially abandoned the notion of eternal punishment and has virtually eliminated the entire concept of Gehenna as a place of torture for one's sins.[1]

maintains that resurrection [of the dead] is not a biblical doctrine [i.e., intimated in the Torah]" (Sanh. 90a) has no portion in the world to come. Indeed, the concepts of an afterlife and eventual divine justice became pillars of the Pharisees and their rabbinic descendants and one of the chief points of difference between them and the Sadducees, who asserted that the soul died together with the body. To paraphrase the Talmud, if those who never lived before can live, then why cannot God make those who have already lived live again (Sanh. 91a)?

Some Rabbis maintained that the resurrection of the dead would be only for the righteous, while others believed that the wicked also would be temporarily resurrected, only to be judged and destroyed, with the ashes of their souls being scattered under the feet of the righteous. The Rabbis offered various views as to the nature of human existence in the world to come. The third-century Babylonian *amora* Rav viewed the future life as a world of purely spiritual bliss, where "there is neither eating, nor drinking, nor any begetting of children, no bargaining or jealousy or hatred or strife. All that the righteous do is to sit with their crowns on their heads and enjoy the light of the [Divine] Presence" (Ber. 17a). However, most of his contemporaries and followers believed in the restoration of the souls into the bodies of the resurrected, who would rise from their graves fully clothed (Ket. 111b).

Rabbinic and later liturgical texts viewed the afterlife as a "Torah academy on high," a *yeshivah shel ma'alah* as in the preamble to the *Kol Nidrei* on Yom Kippur. This concept of an eternal house of study reflected the highest values of the Jewish people. The medieval comment "in *prayer* we speak to God; in *study* God speaks to us" indicated the belief that the Torah represents both the link of the Jew to God and the pathway to eternity.

The Talmud raises many questions about the precise way in which the body would be resurrected. For example, the decision that an amputee would be resurrected *with* a lost limb (Sanh. 91b) led to the tradition of burying amputated limbs of the deceased in the same grave so that they would be available at the time of resurrection. Another discussion dealt with the eventual living arrangements of a widow or widower who remarried—would that person spend eternity with the first or second spouse?[3] The concept of resurrection of the body was also a source of the strong opposition in Jewish law to the practice of cremation.

Medieval Period

Medieval Jewish philosophers faced the problem of logically integrating the conflicting notions of the immortality of the incorporeal soul with a physical resurrection. The concept of a disembodied afterlife was especially strong among these individuals, who were heavily influenced by Greek tradition. As the part of a human being that is most like God, the soul was considered the seat of the intellect, spirituality, creativity, and the divine spark. Thus the soul can survive bodily death, being transported to a spiritual realm beyond the dimensions of time and space, where it enjoys eternal repose. The soul and body were seen as natural enemies, with the soul being a veritable prisoner of the body. Life was a struggle, a test of how well the individual could develop the soul despite the pernicious influence of the body.

If taken to the extreme, however, this belief could lead to asceticism and severe deprivation of the body to best prepare the soul for eternity. Maimonides noted that if the body triumphs over the soul, there is eternal oblivion. Only if the soul triumphs over the body can it achieve eternal repose in heaven. Nevertheless, doctrinal considerations made the belief in resurrection, not the immortality of the disembodied soul, one of Maimonides' 13 fundamental principles of Jewish faith (see p. 509). In his later *Guide of the Perplexed*, however, Maimonides indicated that the immortality of the soul is paramount by describing two stages of the afterlife.[4] In the first, with the advent of the Messiah, there would be physical resurrection on earth. The body, reunited with the soul, would eat, drink, marry, and procreate. After a long life span characteristic of the messianic age, the body would die again. Only the soul that had achieved "intellectual cohesion with God" would be immortal and enjoy an eternity of spiritual bliss. Nachmanides did not support this two-tiered approach, arguing instead that individuals would be resurrected into "specially refined bodies" and live forever in *this* world (i.e., the revived dead will not die again).

Kabbalistic Concepts

The kabbalists conceived of the soul as having its origin in divine emanation and being incarnated on earth with a specific task to fulfill. The soul of the wicked—one who has failed in his or her assigned task—is punished and purified in Hell or reincarnated (*gilgul*; lit., "rolling") to complete its unfinished work. In certain cases, however, the wicked soul is denied even Hell or reincarnation and is exiled without the possibility of finding rest. This mystical view, which became normative in

Judaism between the 16th and 18th centuries and has had even longer influence in the Hasidic community, may have developed as a response to the problem of theodicy. Since some individuals are born disadvantaged, either physically or mentally, it would seem unjust to expect the same achievement of everyone. In effect, this concept maintains that each soul deserves more than one opportunity at life, and thus it is placed in a variety of bodies to realize its potential. The body to which the soul is assigned in any given life reflects the moral quality of its former life. When fully developed, the soul breaks out of the wheel of transmigration and finds final repose with God.

According to the mystics, after death the soul does not necessarily go into a new human body. The worse the sins committed, the lower the life form to which the soul is assigned. If it is transformed into an animal, the fate of that creature affects the next transmigration. For example, if the animal is eaten by a person who uses the energy to study Torah or for another sacred purpose, this helps the soul within to be liberated from its lower bodily life form. Indeed, the mystics made detailed lists of which sins led to one coming back as which animal. They also showed which heroes of the Bible and of later Jewish history, including the great rabbis, were transmigrations of earlier figures. For example, the soul of Cain entered the body of Jethro and the soul of Abel, the body of Moses. When Moses and Jethro met they rectified the sins caused by the two brothers. Furthermore, the mystics claimed that they could read the lines of a person's face to determine the state of that individual's soul in this life and in all past lives.

Modern Jewish Thought

Orthodox Judaism has maintained a consistent belief in both the future resurrection of the dead as part of the messianic redemption and in some form of immortality of the soul after death. In the *Amidah*, Jews praise God who "faithfully revives the dead." Similar sentiments are expressed in the *Birkot ha-Shachar* (morning blessings; see p. 401), *Yigdal* (see p. 470), and *Ani Ma'amin*. In the *Modeh Ani* (see p. 473), which is recited upon awaking, one thanks God for the "mini-resurrection" that occurs as the soul is returned to the body after sleep. However, Reform and Conservative prayer books (but only in its English translation) have eliminated any literal belief in the future resurrection of the dead, modifying the previous liturgical passages to relate only to the belief in a spiritual life after death. An unequivocal belief in the survival of the soul after death is implicit in the various prayers said in memory of the dead and in the custom of mourners reciting the *Kaddish* (see p. 394).

Who Merits an Afterlife?

The Talmud states that "all Israel have a portion in the world to come" (Sanh. 90a), while Maimonides[4] asserted that this also applied to "the pious of the nations." The afterlife has traditionally been viewed as a time of ultimate judgment and reckoning, with each person held accountable for his or her own actions. Thus, instead of serving as a way to moral and social escapism (i.e., since this world is not the essential one, why be concerned with moral and social responsibility), the opposite is true. Accountability in the *future* world is based on one's actions in *this* world, which can be seen as a preparation for the world to come. The concept of an afterlife is also a valuable response to the vexing theodicy problem, providing a notion that regardless of what occurs in this *temporary* world, justice will emerge triumphant in the *everlasting* future. The Talmud describes a scenario in which a person goes before the heavenly tribunal for a final day of judgment and is asked five questions (Shab. 31a). Rather than the questions one might expect—Did you keep the Sabbath? Did you maintain a kosher home? Did you give to charity?—they are (1) Were you honest in your business dealings? (2) Did you set aside time to study Torah? (3) Did you have children? (4) Did you hope for redemption? and (5) Did you search for wisdom? The sages have related these questions to the innate human desire to perpetuate the self beyond the grave in terms of honestly begotten wealth, wisdom and experience, children as "biological" redemption, and perpetuation of one's hopes and dreams.

Summary

Though firmly convinced of the reality of a world to come, Maimonides wisely stated that we mortals can have no real knowledge about its nature. Even if we did have some information concerning the afterlife, we would be incapable of comprehending it, since the world to come would have a different dimension of existence beyond time or space and thus it would be beyond our ability to describe it or even conceive of it. Nevertheless, the Jewish tradition assures us that, even in this life, one can experience a sample of the world to come. As the Talmud states, "three things give us a foretaste of the world to come—the Sabbath, a sunny day, and sexual intercourse" (Ber. 57b).

Sabbath and Festivals

Sabbath (שַׁבָּת)

Overview

The Sabbath (*Shabbat*, related to the Hebrew verb "*shavat*," meaning "cease, rest") is the seventh day of the week, a day of rest and refraining from work.

Historical Antecedents

Scholars have related the word "Sabbath" to the Babylonian "*sapattu*," the full moon at mid-month, which apparently was a day of favor, or to the "unlucky day" occurring at seven-day intervals when the king's activity was severely restricted.[1] However, there is no convincing explanation of how it became separated from the lunar cycle to become the weekly "Sabbath of the Lord" observed as a joyous day by the Israelites. The striking difference in the Jewish understanding was the positive sanctity of the day, in which resting from work was regarded as obedience to a divine command.

In the Torah

After creating the world in six days, God ceased work on the seventh day (*shavat mi-kol melachto*), blessing the day and declaring it holy (Gen. 2:1–3). In addition to being a celebration of Creation, an imitation of God's own day of rest, the Sabbath is called an everlasting sign of the divine covenant with the Jewish people (Exod. 31:13,17). The Fourth Commandment mandates the observance of the Sabbath as a remembrance of the redemption from slavery in Egypt (Deut. 5:15). This commandment declares that the Sabbath must be "remembered" (Exod. 20:8) and "observed" (Deut. 5:12). "Six days you shall work, but on the seventh day you shall cease from labor" (Exod. 34:21) prohibited the Israelites from working on the Sabbath. The second half of this verse, "you shall cease from labor even at plowing time and harvest time," implied that even during those periods of the year when there was urgent pressure in the fields, when the Israelites felt that their livelihood demanded continuous work without a break on the Sabbath, they must nevertheless rest and not desecrate the holy day. This concept was reinforced by having an admonition to keep the Sabbath immediately precede the divine instructions concerning the building of the Tabernacle and Moses' transmission of them to the people. Thus resting on the seventh day took priority even over the duty of constructing the Sanctuary, the place where God was to dwell among the people.

The requirement to refrain from work was emphasized in connection with the manna, which nourished the Israelites during their years of wandering in the wilderness. On each of the first five days of the week, God supplied the required amount of manna and the Israelites gathered it. On the sixth day, however, twice as much manna appeared because none was provided on the seventh day when gathering would have constituted work. The severe consequence of violating the prohibition against work on the Sabbath was graphically illustrated by the tale of a man who was sentenced to death by stoning for gathering sticks on the Sabbath (Num. 15:32–36).

Prophetic Perspective

In the prophetic books, there are scattered references to the Sabbath. It was a day when people visited prophets (2 Kings 4:22–23) and, in later times, the Temple (Isa. 1:13). Commerce ceased on the Sabbath (Amos 8:5–6), and the Israelites were enjoined not to carry things out of their houses or into the gates of Jerusalem (Jer. 17:21–22). In accordance with biblical prescriptions, additional offerings were sacrificed in the Temple on the Sabbath (Ezek. 45:17), and the showbread was changed (1 Chron. 9:32).

Sabbath observance gained prominence during the period of the Babylonian exile, possibly because this practice was a way to distinguish the Israelites and their relationship to God from the gentile nations, thus decreasing the likelihood of assimilation. While the Five Books of Moses considered idolatry as the worst sin of the Jewish people (Exod. 23:24; Deut. 4:25), the exilic and post-exilic prophets considered profanation of the Sabbath the most damaging religious violation. Both Jeremiah and Ezekiel linked the fate of Jerusalem to proper Sabbath observance. Indeed, Ezekiel (20:11–12) equated the Sabbath with all the other commandments. Second Isaiah (58:13–14) considered honoring the Sabbath the essential step to both personal and national redemption.

Rabbinic Period

The Rabbis of the talmudic period furthered the centrality of the Sabbath by articulating intricate laws that embellished the biblical idea of a day of rest. (A whole talmudic tractate is devoted to the Sabbath.) They also ascribed great theological significance to the Sabbath. Like the Bible, the Talmud describes the Sabbath as a precious gift from God to the Israelites (Shab. 10b). The Sabbath was so important that observing it properly was equivalent to fulfilling all the commandments (Exod. R. 25:12). A person who "profanes the Sabbath publicly" was to be treated as an idolater (Hul. 5a). Conversely, one who prays on the eve of the Sabbath is considered a partner in the creation of the world, is blessed by the angels, and is purged of all sin (Shab. 119b). According to Rabbi Judah, "He who delights in the Sabbath is granted his heart's desire" (Shab. 118b).

Observance of the Sabbath was critical to the redemption of the Jewish people. "If Israel truly were to observe two Sabbaths according to the laws thereof [requirements of *halakhah*], they would be redeemed immediately [the Messiah will come]" (Shab. 118b). The Rabbis considered the Sabbath metaphysically different from other days. In a famous exchange, the Roman emperor asked Rabbi Joshua ben Chananiah why Sabbath dishes have such a good smell. Rabbi Joshua replied that there is a special spice called Sabbath, but the Roman emperor couldn't have any because it is effective only for those who hallow the seventh day (Shab. 119a). Jews are also said to have an extra soul on the Sabbath (Betz. 16a). The Rabbis decreed that, because it was a festive day, three meals should be eaten on the Sabbath (Shab. 118b), and they instituted the *Kiddush* over wine to sanctify the beginning of the Sabbath (Pes. 106a; see p. 138) and the *Havdalah* ceremony to separate the Sabbath from the regular days of the week (Ber. 33a; see p. 147).

Later Jewish Thought

The medieval Jewish philosophers focused on the symbolic nature of the day. For Maimonides, proper observance of the Sabbath was equal to all of the other commandments in the Torah.[2] He viewed the Sabbath as testimony to the fact that God created the world and as a day for providing human beings with well-needed bodily rest and renewal to enable them to better serve God.[3] The *Akedat Yitzhak* considered the Sabbath as teaching three fundamental Jewish beliefs—in the creation of the world from nothingness (*creatio ex nihilo*); the Revelation of the Torah at Mount Sinai, because Jews study the Torah on their day of rest; and the world to come, of which the Sabbath is a foretaste.

According to Samson Raphael Hirsch,[4] the prohibition of creative activity on the Sabbath is a critical acknowledgment of God as the Creator. Human beings are permitted to rule over the natural world for six days by divine decree, but on the seventh day they are forbidden to make anything for their own purpose. In effect, on the Sabbath humans relinquish their temporary control over the world and return it to the ultimate Creator of all.

In the 20th century, Abraham Joshua Heschel described the Sabbath as "a sanctuary in time."[5] For Ahad Ha-Am, the father of cultural Zionism, the Sabbath was the key to the centuries of Jewish national survival in the Diaspora. "More than Israel has kept the Sabbath, the Sabbath has kept Israel."[6] A similar sentiment was expressed by the national poet of Israel, Chaim Nachman Bialik, who wrote: "Without Shabbat, there is no people of Israel, no Land of Israel, no culture of Israel. Shabbat is the culture."[7]

Kabbalistic Perspective

As a reflection of Creation, the seven days of the week symbolize the seven lower *sefirot*. The kabbalists interpreted numerous biblical verses and rabbinic teachings about the Sabbath as referring to the divine union of the masculine and feminine aspects of God. By linking the verse "And God blessed the seventh day and declared it holy (*va-y'kadesh*)" (Gen. 2:3) with *kiddushin* (betrothal; see p. 32), they conceived of the Sabbath as representing a wedding of the *Shekhinah* (feminine aspect of the Divine) and the Godhead, whose union brings heavenly bliss to the Jewish people. On the Sabbath, each Jew receives an additional soul, and the *Sitra Atra* (Other Side) is incapable of doing evil. Just as the masculine and feminine aspects of God achieve union on the Sabbath, so conjugal relations between husband and wife are doubly blessed on this day.[8]

The kabbalists introduced several customs that have become universally accepted over the centuries. They developed the service of *Kabbalat Shabbat* (Welcoming of the Sabbath) to greet the Sabbath Queen (see p. 145) on Friday evening. In Safed, it was customary to go out to the fields and face west to receive the Divine Presence. This was symbolically represented as the relationship between the bride (*Shekhinah*) and groom (Israel) in *Lekhah Dodi* (Come, my beloved) (see p. 146). The kabbalists introduced the recitation of *Eshet Chayil* (Woman of valor; see below) and a variety of *zemirot* to be sung at the three

ESHET CHAYIL (WOMAN OF VALOR; אֵשֶׁת חַיִל)

Eshet Chayil (Woman of Valor) is a poem taken from Proverbs (31:10–31) that enumerates the qualities of the virtuous woman. It is traditionally recited or chanted by the husband, alone or together with the children, before the *Kiddush* on Friday evening. In *Eshet Chayil,* the woman of valor is praised for being dignified, respected, practical, hardworking, charitable, speaking with wisdom and kindness, and facing life with optimism and confidence. The ideal wife, she is trusted and praised by her husband and beloved by her children. The poem concludes with the lines: "Grace is deceptive, beauty is illusory; it is for her fear of the Lord that a woman is to be praised. Extol her for the fruit of her hand, and let her works praise her in the gates."[1]

Initially, the singing of *Eshet Chayil* was a kabbalistic ritual, and the intended object of the song was the *Shekhinah,* the Divine Presence and a feminine mystical symbol. Today *Eshet Chayil* honors the wife and mother of the family who has worked hard all week and especially on Friday to prepare everything for the Sabbath day. Verses of *Eshet Chayil* are often recited at the funerals of pious women and appear as inscriptions on their tombstones.[2]

Sabbath meals (see p. 143). They also gave great importance to the fourth meal after sundown, a farewell feast in honor of the departing Sabbath termed *melaveh malkah* (escorting the queen).

Restrictions

Work

The Bible does not specifically list those labors that are prohibited on the Sabbath, although it alludes to field labor (Exod. 34:21; Num. 15:32–36), treading in a winepress and loading animals (Neh. 13:15–18), doing business and carrying (Isa. 58:13; Jer. 17:22; Amos 8:5), traveling (Exod. 16:29–30), and kindling fire (Exod. 35:2–3) as forbidden work. In the Mishnah, the Rabbis enumerated 39 major categories (with hundreds of subcategories) of labor that were forbidden (*avot melakhah*) based on the types of work that were related to the construction of the Tabernacle in the wilderness, which ceased on the Sabbath (Shab. 7:2). Activities that cannot be performed on the Sabbath are basic tasks connected with preparing the showbread (sowing, plowing, reaping, binding, threshing, winnowing, selecting, grinding, sifting, kneading, baking), work related to making the coverings in the Tabernacle and the vestments used by the *Kohanim* (shearing [sheep], bleaching, carding [changing tangled or compressed material into separate fibers], dyeing, spinning, stretching [material], making two loops [meshes], threading needles, weaving, separating, tying [a knot], untying [a knot], sewing, tearing), activities concerned with writing and the preparation of parchment from animal skin (trapping or hunting, slaughtering, flaying [skinning], treating skins [curing hides], scraping pelts, marking out [to make ready for cutting], cutting [to shape], writing, erasing), construction (building, demolishing), kindling a flame (lighting, extinguishing), carrying (from private to public domain, and vice versa), and putting the finishing touches to a piece of work already begun before the Sabbath.[1]

The Rabbis decreed that one not only should avoid forbidden acts but also must not do anything that (1) resembles a prohibited act or could be confused with it, (2) is a habit linked with a prohibited act, or (3) usually leads to performing a prohibited act. The rabbinic enactment of measures to prevent these possibilities was termed "putting a fence around the Torah" (Avot 1:1). For example, ripping up a piece of paper was forbidden since it resembles "cutting to shape" or could be confused with it. Similarly, agreeing to buy something was prohibited, because most agreements are confirmed in "writing"; climbing a tree is forbidden, because it may lead to breaking twigs or tearing leaves, which could be construed as "reaping" (i.e., separating part of a growing plant from its source).[2]

Other activities that by extension are prohibited on the Sabbath include the following:[3]

- Adding fresh water to a vase of cut flowers (sowing—any activity that causes or furthers plant growth).
- Making a bouquet of flowers (making a sheaf).
- Removing good fruit from spoiled fruit (winnowing, selecting, sifting).
- Brushing dried mud from boots or clothes (grinding).
- Adding cold milk directly to hot tea or coffee (baking—cooking in any form, including adding ingredients to a boiling pot).
- Cutting hair or nails (shearing sheep—removing outer covering of a human or animal).
- Applying makeup (dyeing).
- Braiding hair (weaving).
- Drawing blood for a blood test (slaughtering).
- Rubbing soap to make lather, applying face cream, polishing shoes, using scouring powder for utensils or other surfaces (scraping—smoothing the surface of any material by grinding, rubbing, or polishing).
- Sharpening a pencil (cutting to shape—altering the size or shape of an item to make it better for human use).
- Painting, drawing, typing (writing—making durable marks on a durable material).
- Tearing through lettering on a package (erasing).
- Opening an umbrella or unfolding a screen (building).
- Smoking a cigarette, using the telephone (kindling a fire).
- Switching off an electric light (extinguishing a fire).
- Setting or winding a clock or watch (finishing off).
- Wearing eyeglasses not permanently required (carrying from private to public domain and vice versa).

For an activity to be considered as work forbidden on the Sabbath, the violation must be intentional. Therefore moving a chair from one place to another is permissible, even though it may produce an impression on the ground. Similarly, walking on the grass is allowed, even though this may result in some of it being crushed underfoot and thus technically constitute the prohibited activity mentioned above or the forbidden cutting of blades of grass. One has not violated the Sabbath as long as the original purpose was solely to move the chair or to walk on the grass. In contrast, one is not permitted to engage in a task that always results in forbidden work. Thus washing oneself on a lawn is prohibited because it inevitably will result in watering the grass, which is forbidden on the Sabbath.[4]

Any items that may not be used on the Sabbath may not even be handled on that day, lest one unintentionally perform one of the forbidden types of work. These objects are termed *muktzeh*, meaning to "set aside" or "store away." Among the many things considered *muktzeh* are money and checks; scissors, hammers, and saws; pencils and pens; battery-operated toys and flashlights; radios and CDs; telephones and computers; and religious objects such as shofar, tefillin, and *lulav*. Even the Sabbath candlesticks are *muktzeh* and thus should not be touched on the Sabbath after the candles have been lit.[5]

Even if not strictly classified as forbidden work, certain "mundane matters" should be avoided on the Sabbath. These include weekday chores (such as packing suitcases and rearranging furniture, which are not in keeping with enjoyment of the restful spirit of the Sabbath), opening mail, and discussing business issues or matters of everyday concern. One is forbidden to even think about or make plans for the week ahead, such as preparing equipment, mapping out a route, readying a briefcase for the next day, or setting the table for a party on Saturday night. Based on Isaiah's exhortation that one "honor it [the Sabbath] by not doing your usual ways" (Isa. 58:13),[6] the Rabbis recommended that a person should even walk differently on the Sabbath, avoiding the long strides and rushing about that characterize the pace of most people on weekdays.[7]

In addition to the general forbidding of all manner of work on the Sabbath, there is a special prohibition against making a fire (Exod. 35:3). The Rabbis considered this to include everything that pertains to the kindling of light, even if no actual work is involved. In modern times, there is a controversy regarding whether the switching on of electric lights and appliances is equivalent to making a fire. There are two reasons to think that switching on an electric light may not be considered kindling. First, switching on a light does not create electric power; the power exists already. Second, there is no combustion in the filament of an electric light. Nevertheless, Orthodox Jews do not use electric appliances on the Sabbath, believing that the prohibition against kindling a fire was not based on the physical effort involved in rubbing two stones together to produce a spark but rather on the thought and planning that resulted in its generation. For the Hazon Ish,[8] the activation of an electric current and its transmission to sources of power, heat, and light that is produced by turning on a switch is forbidden because it falls under the category of "building"—intentionally causing something to happen. An exception is the refrigerator, which may be opened and closed because any electric current that this produces is incidental and without conscious intent. However, many observant Jews unscrew the refrigerator bulb for the Sabbath. Lights that have been kindled before the Sabbath, such as the Sabbath candles, are allowed, as are an oven for keeping previously cooked food warm and a burner to keep water warm for coffee or tea. Similarly, it is permitted to leave an electric appliance running during the Sabbath and to use a timer to automatically turn an appliance on or off, as long as the timer is set before the Sabbath begins.

One mechanism to ease the difficulty of complying with the prohibition against work on the Sabbath was the concept of the *Shabbos goy*—a non-Jew hired by an observant family to perform certain activities forbidden to Jews on the Sabbath, such as starting a fire and turning lights on and off.[9] However, the proliferation of electronic timers has virtually eliminated the need for the *Shabbos goy*.

Carrying

On the Sabbath, it is forbidden to carry any object (even a house key or handkerchief) outside a private domain, though carrying is permitted inside a private residence or a synagogue. An ingenious way to get around this restriction is to change an object that is usually carried into something that can be worn, such as converting a house key into a tie clip. The prohibition against carrying is especially difficult for mothers of infants or young children. Forbidden to carry a child outside the house, they are effectively confined to their homes on the Sabbath.[10]

To overcome these restrictions, under certain circumstances the Rabbis permitted the establishment of an *eruv*. Literally meaning "blending" or "intermingling," an *eruv* converts a large public area into a "private domain" where carrying is permitted on the Sabbath. For example, it is forbidden to carry an object from one house to another. However, if all the tenants living around a large courtyard contribute food and place it at a central point before the Sabbath, the entire area is symbolically transformed from a series of individual private homes into one common group dwelling that belongs to the entire community. Today, a common way of making an *eruv* is to extend a wire or nylon cord around the perimeter of a community, by connecting it to telephone or utility poles. In this way, the entire area becomes a single domain, in which it is permitted to carry and push baby carriages. In Israel, *eruvim* have been constructed in all cities. In the United States, they have been established in cities that have a substantial Orthodox Jewish population.[11]

Travel

The Rabbis interpreted the verse prohibiting the gathering of manna on the seventh day (Exod. 16:29) as forbidding one from journeying on the Sabbath. Unlike the Karaites, who took the verse "let no person go out of his place on the seventh day" literally and did not allow anyone to leave home on the Sabbath, the Rabbis did not restrict movement within one's town. However, they prohibited Jews from walking more than 2,000 cubits (approximately ½ mile) beyond the town boundaries on the Sabbath, "because traveling interrupts the rest of both man and beast."[12] As Menachem ha-Babli[13] observed, because Jews have an "extra soul" on the Sabbath, they must devote their free time to the study of Torah and not waste the day in going from place to place.[14]

Orthodox rabbis forbid driving an automobile on the Sabbath, based on the fact that it involves turning on the ignition, which in turn ignites sparks—an act that violates the Torah law against making a fire on the Sabbath (Exod. 35:3). Conservative rabbis generally permit Jews to drive on the Sabbath, but only to synagogue. This ruling was made in response to the migration of Jews to the suburbs, where most no longer live within walking distance of a synagogue. Continuing to forbid driving on the Sabbath would have forced many congregants to remain at home or to pursue nonreligious activities. Fearing an erosion of Jewish identity if synagogue attendance dropped precipitously, these rabbis permitted driving as the lesser of two evils. Orthodox rabbis denounced this decision, arguing that Conservative rabbis should instead encourage their congregants to live within walking distance of their synagogues.[15]

In Israel, public transport does not operate on the Sabbath in Jerusalem and Tel Aviv, but it does run in Haifa. Except for specifically non-Jewish sections of the country, the Sabbath is the official day of rest on which all businesses and stores must close.

Pikuach Nefesh

All of the Sabbath restrictions may be violated to preserve life (*pikuach nefesh*). Those who are seriously ill must be given any necessary medical treatment. As Maimonides[16] noted: "The commandments of the Sabbath, like all other commandments, may be set aside if human life is in danger," based on the verse "You shall keep My laws and My rules, by the pursuit of which a man shall *live* [and not die]" (Lev. 18:5). Even if unclear whether a life will be saved, a person is permitted to violate the Sabbath, "for the mere possibility of danger to human life overrides the Sabbath." As an example, Maimonides observed that it was permissible, and even mandatory, to exceed the 2,000-cubit limit to rescue one or more Israelites whose lives were in danger from heathens, a flooding river, a collapsed building, or physical or mental illness.[17] As the Talmud concluded, "Violate one Sabbath [in order that someone may live] to observe many Sabbaths" (Yoma 85b). The deliberate desecration of the Sabbath to save a life is more than outweighed by the potential for future sanctification of the Sabbath and God's Name. Thus, according to the Rabbis, if a building collapsed on top of someone on the Sabbath and it is unclear whether the person is alive or dead, it is required to dig the person out, even though digging is a violation of the Sabbath (Yoma 8:6). However, in situations that are not life threatening, medical treatment that violates the Sabbath should be minimized or administered by a non-Jew.

The concept of *pikuach nefesh* is so highly regarded that if a seriously ill person needs food on the Sabbath, the *halakhah* requires that one should slaughter animals and prepare them according to the dietary laws, rather than feed the individual ritually forbidden food. It is even permitted to give patients forbidden food if physicians consider it necessary for their recovery. For three days after giving birth, a woman is considered in a weakened and vulnerable condition. If one of these days falls on the Sabbath, it is an obligation to do everything possible to alleviate her pain and ease her discomfort, including lighting a fire to keep her warm. In Israel, the concept of *pikuach nefesh* also applies to the Israel Defense Forces, border patrol, and home guard, which are permitted to violate the Sabbath by traveling and carrying weapons when necessary for security purposes to protect life.[18]

Observances

The Rabbis ruled that the Sabbath should be made the specific object of honor (*kavod*) and delight (*oneg*), based on this verse in Isaiah (58:13): "If you call the Sabbath a 'delight,' the Lord's holy day 'honored.'"[1] Traditionally, "honor" implied the duties of bathing immediately before the Sabbath, wearing special Sabbath clothes, and receiving the Sabbath with joy. "Delight" meant lighting candles on Friday night, enjoying special delicacies, eating a minimum of three Sabbath meals, cohabiting with one's spouse, and engaging in general repose and added sleep.[2] According to the Bible, the agricultural bounty of ancient Israel was reflected in its harvest of grain, wine, and oil. Each week, Jews symbolically experience these divine blessings as they eat challah, drink wine, and kindle the Sabbath lights (originally oil lamps).[3]

Kindling the Sabbath Lights

The kindling of lights has long been viewed as adding to the joy of the Sabbath. While the sages may have disagreed about which precise oils and wicks were appropriate for use as Sabbath lights, they unanimously rejected the practice of the Karaites, who sat in the dark on Sabbath eve because they literally followed the biblical injunction against kindling fire on the seventh day (Exod. 35:5).[4]

Traditionally, the woman of the house lights at least two candles on Friday evening, corresponding to the two ways in which the Fourth Commandment is phrased—"remember" (Exod. 20:8) and "observe" (Deut. 5:12) the Sabbath day—two phrases that the Talmud relates were miraculously "pronounced in a single utterance" by God (Shev. 20b). Two candles also symbolize the unity underlying all apparent duality: man and woman, body and soul, speech and silence, Creation and Revelation. In many families, an additional candle is lit for each child in the family; it is customary never to decrease that number.[5]

So as not to desecrate the Sabbath by miscalculating the precise time that night falls and the seventh day begins, it is customary to light the candles 18 minutes before sunset on Friday evening. Unlike most commandments, for which the recitation of a blessing precedes the activity and any benefit that can be derived from it, the lighting of the Sabbath candles is performed before the blessing is said. Were the woman to recite the blessing first, she effectively would have welcomed the Sabbath before actually having kindled the candles, which would violate the prohibition against making a fire on this day. Before reciting the blessing, some women pass their hands three times over the candles to symbolically draw in the essence of light and the spirit of holiness, thus enhancing the powerful emotion of ushering in the Sabbath. It is customary for women to cover their eyes while reciting the blessing after lighting the Sabbath candles. One explanation is that this enables the woman to exclude all extraneous thoughts and concentrate her full attention on the words she is saying. An alternative is that this practice is consistent with the prohibition against enjoying the subject of a blessing until after it has been recited. Covering her eyes permits the woman to delay (until after finishing the blessing) the spiritually elevating experience of gazing on the glowing light of the Sabbath candles.[6]

The moment at which the Sabbath candles are lit is considered a favorable time for God to hear a woman's personal prayer. Therefore, it is customary for her to thank God for the blessings of the past week and ask for continued good fortune for her family. After praying that her children be imbued with Torah and observe the mitzvot, she may beseech God to heal the sick and remember the souls of her departed relatives.[7] Finally, she greets all at the table with *Shabbat shalom* ([may you have a] Sabbath of peace), or the Yiddish *gut Shabbos* (good Sabbath).[8]

Based on a literal translation of the Yiddish *"bentsch licht,"* the candle-lighting ceremony is often misunderstood as "blessing the candles." The Sabbath candles are not inherently holy, and the blessing stresses that God "has sanctified *us*" by the commandment to kindle the Sabbath lights. Like all mitzvot, this ritual act is designed to enable us to experience holiness, rather than to make any material object holy.[9]

Kindling the Sabbath lights is not a biblical commandment, but rather one of the seven ritual mitzvot legislated by the Rabbis (Shab. 25b). Although the duty to light candles for the Sabbath falls equally on men and women, in a family setting it traditionally has been considered the responsibility of the women "because they usually are at home taking care of the household at that time."[10] Indeed, the lighting of Sabbath candles is generally regarded as one of the three "women's commandments," along with observing the laws of family purity through immersion in a ritual bath (*mikveh*; see p. 555) and separating out a portion of dough (challah) when baking bread. According to Rabbi Moses Isserles, a woman who fails to light the pair of Sabbath candles must henceforth light three Sabbath candles for the rest of her life, to remind her to always be scrupulously careful in fulfilling this important mitzvah.[11]

Kiddush (קִדּוּשׁ)

Kiddush (sanctification) is the prayer recited over a cup of wine to consecrate the Sabbath (or festival) in accordance with the biblical commandment to "Remember the Sabbath day and keep it holy" (Exod. 20:8). When first instituted by Ezra and the men of the Great Assembly, the *Kiddush* was not an independent ritual but a part of the *Amidah*, where it still remains in the middle blessing for Friday evening. Later, when the impoverished Jewish community became wealthier and wine was readily available, the Rabbis decreed that the *Kiddush* also should be recited over a cup of wine. This symbol of joy and celebration was considered most appropriate for the Sabbath and festivals. The use of wine in this ceremony may have related to the sacrificial ritual in the Temple, for the Talmud notes that the *Kiddush* may be recited only over "wine that is fit to be brought as a drink offering on the altar" (BB 97a).[12]

The Rabbis debated whether the *Kiddush* over wine should be recited in the synagogue or the home. The decision was that *Kiddush* should be said at the table just before sitting down to eat the Sabbath dinner (Pes. 101a).[13] Rashbam[14] maintained that this was based on this verse, "And you shall call the Sabbath a 'delight'" (Isa. 58:13), explaining that "Where there is delight [i.e., a festive meal], there shall you recite the *Kiddush*."[15] However, because the synagogues of Babylonia had annexes that served as community hostels and provided food and lodging for travelers, it became customary to also recite the *Kiddush* in the synagogue at the end of the Friday evening service. According to Kol Bo,[16] this tradition (which persists among Ashkenazim) was established for the sake of those who cannot read Hebrew; if they hear the *Kiddush* enough in the synagogue, they eventually will learn how to recite it correctly at home.[17]

In addition to the principal evening *Kiddush*, the Rabbis mandated that a minor *Kiddush* be recited before the noon meal on the Sabbath (or festival). Although termed the "Great *Kiddush*" (Pes. 106a), it is essentially the customary blessing over wine. Some include an appropriate scriptural verse before the blessing. For the Sabbath, one says: "Therefore the Lord blessed the Sabbath day and hallowed it" (Exod. 20:11). For festivals, the additional verse is: "So Moses declared to the Israelites the set times of the Lord" (Lev. 23:44). Some further enhance the stature of the Great *Kiddush* by adding the prayer *Ve-shamru* (And they shall keep [the Sabbath]) (Exod. 31:16–17), a passage in which the Sabbath is labeled "an everlasting sign" between God and the children of Israel. Strong drink other than wine may be used for this *Kiddush*, for which the word "great" may originally have referred to the amount of drink rather than the length of the prayer.[18]

In modern times, the Saturday morning *Kiddush* has assumed new importance. Sponsored by the entire congregation or by specific members to celebrate a special event in their lives, it also serves as a communal social hour.

Text

The Friday evening *Kiddush* begins with an introductory paragraph (*va-yechulu ha-shamayim*) describing the seventh day of Creation (Gen. 2:1–3). This is preceded by the words "*yom ha-shishi*" (the sixth day), the last two words of the preceding biblical verse (Gen. 1:31), so that the first four letters spell out YHVH (the Tetragrammaton). The blessing over wine (*borei peri ha-gafen*) is then recited, followed by the blessing for the sanctification of the day. Concluding with "Praised are You, O Lord, who hallows the Sabbath," the core of this longer blessing refers to both the Creation of the world and the Exodus from Egypt. This double memorial is in accordance with the variant texts of the commandment in Exodus (20:11) and Deuteronomy (5:15).

On festivals falling on weekdays, the introductory scriptural passage is omitted; all that is recited are the blessings over wine and for the sanctification of the day, which ends "Who hallows Israel and the festive seasons." On all full festivals, except the last days of Passover, one recites the *Shehecheyanu* blessing, thanking God for having "kept us in life, sustained us, and enabled us to reach this season" (see p. 479). When a festival immediately follows the Sabbath, a special benediction marking the termination of the Sabbath (*Havdalah*; see p. 147) is added.

Customs

Although women are generally exempt from observing the positive mitzvot that depend on a set time, this does not apply to the *Kiddush* (or kindling the Sabbath and festival lights; see above). The Talmud states that the biblical commands to "remember" (*zakhor*; Exod. 20:8) and "observe" (*shamor*; Deut. 5:12) the Sabbath day include women, for "Whoever has to 'observe' has to 'remember'; and since women have to 'observe' [by performing no work], they also have to 'remember' " (Ber. 20b). Because women have an equal obligation to say the *Kiddush*, according to *halakhah* they may do so even on behalf of men who are present.[19]

Opinions differ as to whether the *Kiddush* should be said while standing or seated at the dinner table. The Sephardic tradition prefers standing during the *Kiddush*, viewing it as a form of testimony to the loving relationship between God and Israel (and in a Jewish court, testimony is always given while standing). Ashkenazim more commonly sit, based on the concept that if the person saying the *Kiddush* is fulfilling the ritual obligation of the others in the room, all must sit down together to form a group. Hasidim tend to follow the kabbalistic tradition, which advocates standing because of the comparison of the Sabbath to a bride and the fact that the wedding blessings are said while standing.[20] Moshe Feinstein offered a compromise—reciting the *Kiddush* while standing, but drinking the wine while sitting down.

The blessing for bread usually precedes that for wine, because the Torah mentions wheat before the vine when describing the seven species of agricultural produce that symbolize the fertility of the Land of Israel (Deut. 8:8). On the Sabbath and festivals, however, this sequence is reversed. While the *Kiddush* over wine is being recited, the two challot on the Sabbath table remain covered, which is considered equivalent to having removed the bread from the table.

According to the Talmud, it is preferable to recite the evening

Kiddush over wine (Pes. 107a). However, if wine is not available, or if one may not drink it for health reasons, it is permissible to say the *Kiddush* over grape juice or over the two loaves of challah. In the latter situation, the only difference is that the blessing for bread is substituted for that of wine. When the *Kiddush* is said over the challot, they do not have to be covered, and it is customary to place one's hands on the bread during the recitation of the blessing.[21]

Challah

For each Sabbath meal, two whole loaves of bread (challah) are placed on the table and covered with a cloth. These are reminiscent either of the double portion of manna that fell on Friday and sustained the Israelites over the Sabbath or of the two rows (12 loaves) of the show-bread (*lechem panim*) eaten on the Sabbath by the *Kohanim* (Exod. 25:30). The Hebrew word "*challah*" is mentioned in the Bible (Num. 15:20) as the small portion of dough ($^1/_{24}$ for an individual; $^1/_{48}$ for a baker) that was to be set aside when baking bread and then offered to the *Kohanim* in the Temple. Because *Kohanim* can no longer observe the laws of priestly purity and thus are disqualified from eating anything related to a holy sacrifice, in observant households (and kosher bakeries) where bread is baked, an olive-size challah portion is now thrown into the fire and burned. According to the Mishnah, Jews are responsible for separating the challah portion when baking bread from at least three pounds of flour of any of the five grains—wheat, barley, spelt, oats, and rye (Hal. 1:1).[22]

According to one explanation, placing two loaves of bread on the Sabbath table may relate to the ancient practice of serving a loaf of bread with every cooked dish. On weekdays, the family ate only one cooked food at a meal, so that only one loaf was placed on the table. However, as befits the joyful quality of the Sabbath, each meal included two cooked dishes, both of which required its own loaf of bread.[23]

The Sabbath challot are usually covered with a decorative cloth, a symbol of the layer of dew that protected the manna in the wilderness. Covering the challah also prevents it from being "slighted" by having its blessing preceded by the *Kiddush* over wine—for if bread is served at a meal, at all other times the blessing over it takes precedence (see p. 474). Another explanation of this practice relates to the traditional likening of the Sabbath to a bride. Just as the bridal veil is removed after reciting the blessings under the wedding canopy, so the "veil" of the challot is lifted after their blessings have concluded and before the bread is cut. All the people at the table do not have to make their own blessing over the challah, since they have fulfilled their obligation by listening to the blessing and responding "amen." Because the dinner table is considered to be symbolic of the altar in the Temple (Ber. 55a), where salt was brought with all offerings, the custom developed of sprinkling salt on the challah to commemorate the sacrificial system.[24]

In some communities, 12 challot are placed on the table to symbolize the showbread, 12 large loaves of wheat flour (corresponding to the number of the tribes of Israel) that were placed in two rows on the table in the sanctuary each Sabbath and left there until the next Sabbath, when they were removed (miraculously still fresh) and eaten by the *Kohanim*. An alternative is to bake two long challot in the shape of the Hebrew letter "*vav*" (numerical value of six which, when doubled, equals the 12 showbreads).[25]

Sabbath Meals

It is customary to invite guests and sing special table hymns (*zemirot*; see below) at the three main Sabbath meals—Friday evening, Sabbath lunch, and a third meal (*seudah shelishit*, or *shal'shudes*) before the close of the day. This tradition stems from the threefold repetition of the word "*ha-yom*" (today) in the verse, "Then Moses said: 'Eat it [the manna] today, for today is a sabbath of the Lord; you will not find it today on the plain'" (Exod. 16:25).[26]

The Sabbath table is traditionally covered with a white tablecloth, reflecting either the white manna that covered the earth or the "pure table" (symbolized by white) on which the showbread was laid out in the Temple. The third meal at home is usually quite simple. However, when held in the synagogue, it is often sponsored by a member of the congregation in honor of a special event such as a marriage or yahrzeit. Hasidim assemble around the rebbe's table for the third meal, sharing a morsel of food and listening to words of Torah wisdom.[27]

Since it is forbidden to cook food on the Sabbath, though it can be kept warm until served, a popular Sabbath lunch dish among European Jews is *cholent* (see p. 681), a slow-cooking stew that can be kept warm overnight. Sephardim also have a traditional slow-simmered stew known either as *chamin* (or *chamim*; from "*cham*," the Hebrew word for "hot") or *adafina* (or *dafina*; from the Arabic word for "covered"). The tradition of eating fish on the Sabbath is based on a midrash that reasons that because fish were created on the fifth day and humans on the sixth, followed by the seventh day of rest, this relationship should be continued by having fish eaten by Jews on the Sabbath. In Eastern Europe, a classic dish was gefilte (stuffed) fish (see p. 684), which received its name because originally several types of boned fish (usually carp, pike, and whitefish) were ground up, seasoned, and then stuffed back into the skin of the fish before cooking. Another fish that was used for Sabbath dinner was chopped herring, which was popular because of its appetizing taste and ability to be stretched to feed family and guests.[28]

Some communities traditionally eat onion and garlic on the Sabbath. According to one interpretation, the manna that the Israelites ate in the wilderness contained all the flavors in the world except for onion and garlic, which were excluded because they were believed to be harmful to pregnant women. Consequently, the custom arose of eating onion and garlic on the Sabbath to make the pleasures of the palate complete.[29]

Zemirot (זְמִירוֹת)

"*Zemirot*" is the term for the table hymns sung during or immediately after Sabbath meals. These medieval songs represent a unique blend of the holy and the secular, the serious and the playful, and allow family and friends to enhance the Sabbath experience.

The most famous of the *zemirot* is *Shalom Aleichem* (Peace be upon you), which traditionally is sung as the family gathers around the table on Friday night to welcome the "angels of peace." This hymn, sung only among Ashkenazim and believed to have been written in the 17th century, was inspired by talmudic legend (Shab. 119b). Rabbi Yosi ben Yehuda taught: "Two ministering angels—one good, one evil—accompany every Jew from the synagogue to his home on the Sabbath eve. If they find the candles burning, the table set, and the bed covered with a spread, the good angel exclaims, 'May it be God's will that it also be so on the next Sabbath,' and the evil angel is compelled to respond 'amen.' But if everything is disorderly and gloomy, the evil angel exclaims, 'May it be God's will that it also be so on the next Sabbath,' and the good angel is forced to say 'amen.'"[30] After extending our wishes for peace to the ministering angels "of the Most Exalted, the Supreme King of kings, the Holy One, blessed be He," in the final three verses we successively pray "May your coming be in peace," "Bless me with peace," and "May your departure be in peace."

Most *zemirot* were composed by the kabbalists, who considered it proper to chant table hymns in honor of the spiritual guests visiting the Jewish home on Sabbath eve. Among those authors whose *zemirot* are still sung in Jewish homes was Isaac Luria, the master kabbalist, who composed table hymns for each of the three Sabbath meals. The most popular of these, *Yom Zeh l'Yisrael* (This day is for Israel), describes a mixture of spiritual and physical pleasure, a divine commandment coupled with bodily enjoyment that concludes with a vision of the messianic age when life will become one great Sabbath. The second verse refers to the additional soul that is given to each Jew on Friday evening and then taken away when the Sabbath ends (Taan. 27b).[31]

Another major liturgic poet belonging to the Safed circle of mystics was Damascus-born Israel Najara, who wrote 650 hymns, the best known of which is *Yah Ribon Olam* (God, Master of the universe). This table hymn is written in Aramaic and has the author's first name as an acrostic formed by the opening letters of the verses. The song praises the glorious and powerful "King who reigns over kings" whose "powerful and wonderful deeds it is beautiful to declare." It continues by extolling God as the Creator of all life and a worker of wonders. Finally, it concludes with a request that God redeem the Jewish people from exile and allow them to rebuild the Temple in Jerusalem, "the city of beauty." It is interesting that the song does not mention the Sabbath at all.

Yom Zeh Mechubad (This day is honored) urges Jews to observe the Sabbath for God will provide those who do with everything they need to enjoy the day—the ceremonial wine for *Kiddush*; two loaves of challah; meat and fish, rich foods, sweet drinks, and "all appetizing things"; and even proper clothes to wear. It is based on the talmudic statement promising that all Sabbath expenses would be restored: "The Holy One, Blessed be He, said unto Israel: 'My children, borrow on My account and celebrate the holiness of the day and trust in Me, and I will repay'" (Betz. 15b). The refrain to the six stanzas is a reminder that "This day is honored more than all other days, because on it the Eternal rested."[32]

Tzur Mishelo (lit., "Rock from whose store [we have eaten]"), is an anonymous hymn that introduces the *Birkat ha-Mazon* (see p. 476) on the Sabbath. The refrain recalls the invitation to the Grace after Meals, while the four stanzas summarize the contents of that prayer—praising God for providing food, giving thanks for the "good land" bequeathed to Israel, and asking God to have mercy on the Jewish people and restore the Temple and the kingdom of David.

By the 16th century, the singing of *zemirot* at Sabbath meals had become a widespread custom. In addition, special *zemirot* were sung in honor of the departing Sabbath Queen as the day grew to a close. These table hymns, whose melodies were usually borrowed from folk songs, Jewish and non-Jewish alike, have remained popular to this day. Many Jewish families sit around the dinner table for hours joyfully singing them.[33]

Liturgy

On Friday evening, the regular prayers are preceded by *Kabbalat Shabbat* (Welcoming the Sabbath), which is a series of psalms, and the hymn *Lekhah Dodi* (see p. 146), introduced by the kabbalists in 16th-century Safed. A special prayer, *Ve-shomru* ([the Children of Israel] shall keep [the Sabbath]), which is also recited on Saturday morning, stresses the obligation of the Jewish people to observe the Sabbath as an eternal covenant between them and God, the Creator of heaven and earth (Exod. 31:16–17). To increase attendance at services, many Reform and Conservative synagogues in the United States have instituted a late Friday evening service that starts after the close of the business day. This service features a sermon by the rabbi and is typically followed by refreshments at an *Oneg Shabbat*, a term coined by famed poet Chaim Nachman Bialik to describe a popular study session that he initiated on Sabbath afternoon.

The Saturday morning service includes readings from the Torah (see p. 438) and haftarah (see p. 456), and there is an additional (*Musaf*) service. During the afternoon (*Mincha*) service, there also is a Torah reading from the next Sabbath's portion. In many congregations, it is a custom to study *Pirkei Avot* (Ethics of the Fathers) following the afternoon service from Passover to Rosh Hashanah. This is a collection of the moral and practical teachings of about 60 sages whose lives spanned nearly five centuries. In all Sabbath services, petitions are eliminated from the *Amidah* and replaced with special blessings in honor of the day. When the Sabbath concludes and three stars can be seen in the night sky, *Havdalah* (see p. 147) is recited. In addition to a blessing over wine, special blessings are made over spices (to restore the soul saddened by the departure of the day) and over light (which could be neither lit nor blessed on the Sabbath).

Lekhah Dodi (לְכָה דוֹדִי)

Lekhah Dodi (Come, my beloved) is the climax of the *Kabbalat Shabbat*, the set of prayers in which the congregation welcomes the Sabbath before the official Friday evening service. It was composed by Solomon ha-Levi Alkabetz, the best-known liturgic poet of the Safed circle of kabbalists in the early 16th century. The author's Hebrew name—Shlomo ha-Levi—is formed by the initial letters of the first eight stanzas.

The opening line and refrain of *Lekhah Dodi*—"Come, my beloved, to greet the bride; let us welcome the Sabbath presence"—was inspired by the talmudic account of how the sages honored and welcomed the Sabbath, which was compared to a princess or bride (Shab. 119a). Isaac Luria and his disciples used to form a procession every Friday afternoon and go to the outskirts of Safed to receive the Sabbath Bride (Sabbath Queen) with song and praise. This mystical ceremony spread to other communities, where the Sabbath Bride was welcomed not in the fields but in the synagogue immediately before the Friday evening service. Eventually, the *Kabbalat Shabbat* was standardized to consist of six psalms that correspond to the regular days of the week (Ps. 95–99, 29) and contain 65 verses (the numerical equivalent of *Adonai*) and *Lekhah Dodi*, followed by *Mizmor Shir*, the psalm (92) for the Sabbath day.[1] Some congregations open the Friday evening service with the singing of *Yedid Nefesh* (Beloved of the soul), composed by Eleazar Azikri, a 16th-century kabbalist of Safed. With the first letters of its four stanzas spelling out YHVH (the Tetragrammaton), the poem extols the love between God the Creator and human beings, who humbly yearn for divine mercy and favor.[2]

In the Torah, there are two different versions of the Fourth Commandment: "remember" and "observe" the Sabbath day to keep it holy (Exod. 20:8; Deut. 5:12). According to tradition, "remember" refers to fulfilling the positive mitzvot associated with the Sabbath, whereas "observe" refers to not violating the negative commandments related to the day. The first stanza opens with the talmudic statement that God simultaneously spoke the words "remember" and "observe" to link them forever in the collective mind of the Jewish people (Shev. 20b).

The second stanza notes that although the Sabbath was the final divine act of Creation, it was ordained by God even before the universe was created. In the next verses of *Lekhah Dodi*, the poet urges Jerusalem to wake up, cease her weeping, and return to her former glory. Eventually the Messiah will come if, as the Talmud states, "Israel observes two Sabbaths according to the laws thereof [*halakhah*]" (Shab. 118b).[3]

According to the Midrash, because God united the Jewish people with the Sabbath, that day of the week is eagerly anticipated and ecstatically welcomed like a beloved bride (Ber. R. 11:9).[4] When reciting the final stanza of *Lekhah Dodi*—"Enter in peace ... come, O bride"—it is customary to turn toward the rear of the synagogue (traditionally facing westward in the direction of the setting sun that signals the arrival of the Sabbath), bowing slightly to symbolically welcome the Sabbath Bride. At this point, the glory of the Sabbath enters and with it the additional soul that enhances the Jew's experience of this sacred day.[5] Turning around at the end of *Lekhah Dodi* also allows congregants to comfort the mourners, who traditionally wait behind the rear door to the synagogue until the beginning of *Mizmor Shir*, which follows immediately. In this way, it is readily apparent which of their fellow worshipers are in mourning and in need of consolation.[6]

In some synagogues, *Lekhah Dodi* is not recited when a festival falls on the Sabbath, lest the congregation feel shamed when worshipers say, "Let us welcome the presence of the Sabbath" but not the arriving *yom tov*.[7]

Havdalah (הַבְדָּלָה)

Havdalah is a ritual ceremony that is rich in symbols and religious significance and marks the conclusion of the Sabbath (or a festival). The

Hebrew term (lit., "separation") is the same word used several times in Genesis to signify God's original creative act of distinguishing light from darkness (1:4), the primordial waters from the heavens (1:6–7), and day from night (1:14).[1] An ancient ceremony that goes back more than 2,000 years, *Havdalah* emphasizes the distinction between the sacred and the ordinary, the departing Sabbath (or festival) and the following regular weekday.

The conclusion of the Sabbath is a time of apprehension and sorrow, when Jews must relinquish their extra Sabbath souls and return to their ordinary states. The Zohar relates that Joseph, Moses, and David all died before sundown on the Sabbath day. As three stars appear in the sky (about 42 minutes after sunset), ending the 25-hour respite from the pressures of daily life, Jews must once again shoulder the stress and burdens of the workday world.

Havdalah consists of three blessings—over wine, sweet-smelling spices, and light—followed by the major benediction that deals with the separation or distinction that God has made "between the holy and the profane, between light and darkness, between Israel and the other nations, and between the seventh day and the six working days." In the Middle Ages during the period of the Crusades, the pupils of Rashi added an introductory set of seven scriptural verses (from Isaiah, Psalms, and Esther) to be recited when *Havdalah* is said in the home. Beginning with "Behold, the God who gives me triumph" (Isa. 12:2),[2] these verses stress that in the past Jews have successfully trusted in God and relied on divine assistance in times of trouble, expressing confidence that in the future God will continue to be a fortress of strength when needed. Although not an obligatory part of the ceremony, the recitation of these verses is regarded as a "good omen" and has become standard practice.[3]

According to a midrash, Adam became frightened as the skies darkened at the end of the first Sabbath, as he contemplated the unknown dangers that he and Eve would face as they emerged from the sheltered confines of the Garden of Eden. To allay his fear, God taught the first couple how to strike two flints together to make fire, and Adam gratefully declared, "Praised be He, the Creator of Light!"[4] This was the origin of the custom of kindling fire in the form of a candle at the end of the Sabbath.[5] This legend may have been a response to the ancient Greek myth of Prometheus, who after stealing fire from heaven and giving it to humans, was chained to a rock and tortured by order of Zeus. In contrast to the Greek gods, who were jealous of the accomplishments of mortals, the God of Israel personally gave the gift of fire to human beings and has provided them the opportunity for continual progress.[6]

Wine is the preferred beverage for the *Havdalah* ceremony. However, one may also use any drink "common to the land" (except water), which many authorities consider to include beer, milk, coffee, tea, and fruit juice.[7] The cup of wine is filled to overflowing to symbolize the wish for abundant blessings. This is based on an aggadic interpretation of the biblical verse that God "will bless your bread and your water" (Exod. 23:25). A household where "wine flows like water" is regarded as within the framework of this divine blessing (Er. 65a), and this may be emphasized by pouring some wine on the ground. At the end of the *Havdalah* ceremony, some Jews dampen their fingertips with the last drops of wine in the cup and touch them to their eyelids and pockets to bring good luck during the upcoming workweek.[8]

The fragrant spices refresh and revive the spirit and dispel the sadness accompanying the end of the Sabbath day. A mystical reason is that the spices either provide spiritual compensation for the additional soul that each observant Jew figuratively possesses on the Sabbath day,[9] which Rashi defined as a unique feeling of rest and contentment, or that they symbolize the spiritual farewell "feast" for that extra soul.[10] In ancient times, before forks came into use, it was customary to cleanse the hands after a meal by passing them over spices on hot coals. On the Sabbath, this custom could not be performed. However, after the third Sabbath meal was eaten at dusk, the spices could be brought in and thus they became associated with the *Havdalah* service.[11]

A braided multi-wick candle is customarily used for *Havdalah*, based on the talmudic recommendation that the ideal way to perform the mitzvah is to employ a "torch" that sheds a greater light (Pes. 103b). If this is not available, it is permissible to use two ordinary single-wick candles held so that their flames merge together.[12] A compound light is required in keeping with the blessing *borei me'orei ha-esh* (Who creates the flaming lights). Unlike Sabbath, festival, and memorial candles, the *Havdalah* candle is extinguished at the end of the ceremony.[13]

A popular explanation for holding the candle and reciting a blessing over it is that light was God's first creation on the first day of the week. While saying the blessing for the light, it is customary to spread one or both hands toward the flame and examine the shadows playing on the palm of the hand and the nails of the fingers.

The order of the blessings in the *Havdalah* ceremony may reflect a hierarchy in the human senses. The sense of taste (wine) is the lowest and least refined. Smell (spices) is more sensitive than taste (an odor also can be detected at a distance) but less advanced than the sense of sight (candle). Even higher than the senses is the intellect, which can distinguish between two things (Sabbath and regular weekdays).[14]

According to tradition, the prophet Elijah, the messenger of the good tidings of the coming of the Messiah, will not arrive on Friday when everyone is busy preparing for the Sabbath or on Saturday, when Jews are at rest. Consequently, he is expected immediately after the Sabbath ends. Therefore, at this time many Jews sing *Eliyahu Hanavi* (Elijah the prophet), which expresses the hope that Elijah will arrive during the coming week and usher in the era of redemption for Israel and all humanity.[15] Another hymn that is frequently sung at the conclusion of the *Havdalah* ceremony is *Hamavdil* (Who distinguishes), which asks the God who differentiates between the holy and the profane to pardon our sins and to multiply our offspring (and our wealth), making them as numerous "as the sand and as the stars in the night." These are the same biblical symbols for limitlessness as in God's promise to Abraham concerning his descendants (Gen. 22:17). Finally, it is customary to wish one another a good week, typically in either Hebrew (*shavuah tov*) or Yiddish (*gut voch*).

If a person cannot recite *Havdalah* on Saturday evening or forgets to do so at that time, it is permissible to perform the ceremony any time through Tuesday of the coming week (from Wednesday on, Jews are presumably making preparations for the next Sabbath).[16]

Throughout the ages, many people have preferred to eat their main meal after *Havdalah*, when they could have freshly cooked food. Since the Rabbis could not prevent this practice, they insisted that this meal be considered a farewell feast in honor of the departing Sabbath Queen and termed it *melaveh malkah* (escorting the queen). The Saturday evening meal is also associated with King David, the ancestor of the Messiah. The Talmud relates that in answer to his plea, "Tell me, O Lord, what my term is" (Ps. 39:5)[17], David was informed that his

SPICE BOX (קוּפְסַת בְּשָׂמִים)

The blessing over aromatic spices is one of the rituals of *Havdalah,* the ceremony that marks the conclusion of the Sabbath. During the Middle Ages, perhaps in memory of the incense used in the Temple service, it was customary to greet and bid farewell to the Sabbath with fragrant spices, initially myrtle and later precious spices that were often stored in special glass containers. Smelling the spices at *Havdalah* also compensates the Jew for the loss of the "extra soul" that departs with the close of the Sabbath day. According to an ancient legend, the fires of *Geihinnom* (netherworld) that are rekindled at the end of the Sabbath produce such an appalling odor that the *Havdalah* spices are needed to guard against it.[1]

Today, the spice box is a favorite creation of ceremonial artists, and over the centuries it has been constructed in a multitude of ways. Because spices came from the faraway Orient and were extremely expensive, Europeans guarded them as treasures, often in spice towers. Therefore, Ashkenazic spice boxes were sometimes made in the shape of a tower topped with a pennant and having a clock face to indicate the time when the Sabbath ended that week. Other spice boxes took the form of fruit, animals, and (later) even trains. During the Inquisition, Conversos disguised spice boxes as ornamental pieces or children's toys to hide their Jewish symbolism from the authorities.

death would occur on a Sabbath. Therefore, after each Sabbath, King David would celebrate because he knew he would live for at least one more week.[18]

At the end of a festival that does not fall on a Saturday night, only the blessing over wine and the major *Havdalah* blessing are said. The introductory verses and the blessings for spices and light are omitted. If the end of the Sabbath coincides with the onset of a festival, *Havdalah* is still recited. However, the blessing for spices is omitted, since the festival (*yom tov*) is regarded as sufficient "fragrance" to compensate for the loss of the Sabbath (Pes. 102b).[19]

Special Sabbaths

Throughout the year, some Sabbaths commemorate specific events and are distinguished by variations in the liturgy and special customs. Two of these Sabbaths recur—Shabbat Mevarchim (see p. 167), which immediately precedes each new month and announces its date, and Shabbat Rosh Hodesh, when the Sabbath coincides with the new moon. The other special Sabbaths are discussed in chronological order, according to the Jewish calendar.

Shabbat Shuvah

Shabbat Shuvah (Sabbath of Return) occurs during the Ten Days of Repentance between Rosh Hashanah and Yom Kippur (see p. 204). The name derives from the initial word of the week's haftarah: "Return (*shuvah*) O Israel, to the Lord your God" (Hos. 14:2).

Shabbat Shirah

Shabbat Shirah (Sabbath of Song) is applied to the day when the Torah reading includes *Shirat ha-Yam* (The Song at the Sea; Exod. 15:1–18)—the prayer of thanksgiving chanted by the Israelites after safely crossing the Sea of Reeds during the Exodus from Egypt (see p. 409). The haftarah on Shabbat Shirah contains another triumphal hymn, the "Song of Deborah" (Judg. 5).

The Torah portion for Shabbat Shirah includes the story of the manna that sustained the Israelites during their wanderings in the wilderness. According to legend, some ungrateful individuals rebelled against the authority of Moses by violating his command not to gather manna on the Sabbath. They took half of the double portion from Friday and spread it on the ground early on Saturday morning, planning to gather it and thus prove Moses a false prophet. However, the birds immediately swooped down from the skies and cleared the fields, so that not a trace of manna was left. To demonstrate our eternal appreciation for their prompt action, it is customary on Shabbat Shirah to scatter seeds outside the home to feed the birds.[1]

Shabbat Shekalim

Shabbat Shekalim (Sabbath of Shekels) is the Sabbath that falls on or immediately precedes the First of Adar, the month of Purim (Second Adar in a leap year). Besides the weekly Torah portion, the additional reading from a second scroll (Exod. 30:11–16) recounts the commandment to donate a half shekel toward the upkeep of the Temple. On the First of Adar in ancient days, messengers were sent out to all Jewish communities to collect these funds (Shek. 1:1).

Shabbat Zakhor

Shabbat Zakhor (The Sabbath of Remembrance) immediately precedes the festival of Purim. Its name derives from the additional Torah reading from a second scroll (Deut. 25:17–19), which commands the Israelites to remember Amalek, the tribe that perpetrated a cowardly and unprovoked attack on weary stragglers at the rear of the Israelite column as they wandered in the wilderness soon after the Exodus from Egypt. The recitation of the divine commandment to "blot out the memory of Amalek from under heaven. Do not forget" (Deut. 25:19) is most appropriate at this time since, according to *Megillat Esther*, the arch-villain Haman was a direct descendant of Agag, the king of the Amalekites.

Shabbat Parah

Shabbat Parah (the Sabbath of the [Red] Heifer) immediately precedes Shabbat ha-Hodesh (see below). The additional Torah reading from a second scroll (Num. 19:1–22) relates the ritual purification with the ashes of the Red Heifer, which was required in Temple times for all those who had been defiled by contact with a dead body. Originally, this was a call for all those planning to participate in the Passover pilgrimage to Jerusalem to ritually cleanse themselves; today Shabbat Parah reminds Jews to begin the extensive cleansing of *hametz* from their homes, which must be accomplished before the celebration of Passover.

Shabbat ha-Hodesh

Shabbat ha-Hodesh (Sabbath of the Month) is that Sabbath that falls on or precedes the First of Nisan, the month of Passover. The additional Torah reading from a second scroll (Exod. 12:2) notes that the month of Nisan "shall mark for you the beginning of the months; it shall be the first of the months of the year for you"; describes the sacrifice of the paschal lamb on the first Passover in Egypt; and details many of the rules and preparations required for the yearly celebration of that festival.

Shabbat ha-Gadol

Shabbat ha-Gadol (the Great Sabbath) occurs at the beginning of the week when Passover will be observed. Its name reflects the immense historical and religious significance of the upcoming festival. Although there is no additional Torah portion, the special haftarah (Mal. 3:4–24) ends with the announcement that God will send Elijah the Prophet as the herald of the messianic age. "I will send the prophet Elijah to you before the great (*ha-gadol*) and awesome day of the Lord. He shall reconcile parents with children and children with their parents, so that when I come I do not strike the whole land with utter destruction." This reference to the promise of ultimate redemption is most appropriate to the upcoming festival of Passover, which celebrates the historical deliverance of the Jewish people from slavery in Egypt.

Shabbat Hazon

The Sabbath of Vision (Shabbat Hazon) immediately precedes Tisha b'Av (see p. 304). The name derives from the initial word of the week's haftarah, in which Isaiah (1:1–27) prophesies the terrible afflictions that God will inflict upon the Israelites as punishment for their sins. Shabbat Hazon occurs during the period of mourning (Nine Days) for the destruction of the Temple, which is commemorated on Tisha b'Av.

Shabbat Nachamu

Sabbath of Comfort (Shabbat Nachamu) immediately follows Tisha b'Av. It derives its name from the initial word of the week's haftarah (Isa. 40:1) and is the first of the seven "*haftarot* of consolation" leading up to the observance of Rosh Hashanah. These selections prophesy the redemption of Israel, the ingathering of the exiles and the restoration of the Jewish people to their land, and the coming of the messianic days of peace and justice.

Festivals (חַגִּים) and Fasts

Overview

The generic Hebrew term for the festivals is *"hagim"* (sing., *hag*), which comes from a verb meaning "to celebrate." The word is related to the Arabic *"haj"*—the pilgrimage to Mecca. The Torah describes the festivals as *"mo'adim"* (appointed times or seasons), which some simply refer to as *"yom tov"* (good day). The festivals allow the Jew to recognize the role of God in nature and history, to identify with the Land of Israel and the holy city of Jerusalem, and to vicariously experience both the triumphs and the tragedies of their people over the millennia.[1]

The festivals can be divided into those commanded by the Torah (major) and those that were added later (minor). The Torah-mandated festivals are the three pilgrimage festivals (Passover, Shavuot, and Sukkot), Rosh Hashanah, and Yom Kippur. Those festivals that were added later are Purim, Hanukkah, Lag ba-Omer, Tu b'Av, Tu b'Shevat, and the modern commemorations of Yom ha-Atzmaut (Israel Independence Day) and Yom Yerushalayim (Jerusalem Day). Ironically, Tisha b'Av, the national day of mourning, is also regarded as a festival (termed *"mo'ed"* in Lam. 1:15), since according to tradition it will become the greatest festival with the coming of the Messiah.

Pilgrimage Festivals

"Three times a year ... all your males shall appear before the Lord your God" (Deut. 16:16) is the commandment requiring every Israelite to come up to Jerusalem on Passover, Shavuot, and Sukkot. These three pilgrimage festivals marked, respectively, the spring (barley), summer (wheat), and autumn (fruit) harvests of the agricultural cycle. They are known as the *Shalosh Regalim* (lit., "three feet") because most people went up to Jerusalem on foot. According to Josephus, on one occasion more than 2½ million pilgrims came to Jerusalem for Passover. All males were expected to fulfill the commandment of appearing before the Lord and bringing a burnt offering on these festivals. Exceptions were made for minors and those who were deaf, mute, insane, blind, crippled, uncircumcised, aged, sick, in a delicate state of health, or in a state of ritual impurity. The pilgrimage to Jerusalem was qualified by the verse, "none shall appear before Me empty-handed" (Exod. 23:15). The Rabbis interpreted this as requiring the bringing of offerings, not only a burnt offering and a special peace offering for the specific holiday (*Hagigah*) but also a second peace offering that could be shared by its owner, family, and guests at a festive meal.

The commandment to appear before the Lord on the three pilgrimage festivals was obligatory only for men. However, the Talmud declared that the requirement to "rejoice" on the festivals (Deut. 16:14) was also binding on women (Hag. 6b). Maimonides recounted the rabbinic statement that Jews must rejoice on their festivals in every way possible, including "by eating meat, drinking wine, putting on new garments, distributing fruits and sweetmeats to children and women, and making merry with musical instruments and dancing in the sanctuary (though not elsewhere)."[2] He added, "The most binding of these (modes of rejoicing) is the drinking of wine," since "wine ... cheers the hearts of men" (Ps. 104:15).[3] Nevertheless, the holiness of the festival always prevented Jewish celebrations from descending into the wild orgies characteristic of pagan festivals at the time.

The Torah obligated the Israelites to include the poor, the needy, and the strangers, as well as orphans and widows, in this rejoicing (Deut. 16:11). It was also important to invite the Levites to join in the festivities, for they did not receive any portion of the meat from the offerings brought to the Temple. Indeed, Maimonides warned that "he who while eating and drinking in the company of his children and his wife bars the entries of his home, and fails to offer food and drink to the poor and the wretched, rejoices not in a manner suitable on the occasion of fulfilling a commandment, but merely to gratify his own belly."[4]

During biblical times, the *Kohanim* were commanded to sound silver trumpets in the Sanctuary in conjunction with the communal offerings for the festivals (and the Sabbath) (Num. 10:10). This was in addition to the musical accompaniment of the Levites at appropriate parts of the sacrificial service.[5] According to *Sefer ha-Hinnukh*, trumpets were sounded to stir and arouse the emotions; just as they sounded the alarm as a call to arms before battle, so the trumpets blared to awaken the people to a critical moment in their spiritual lives. By becoming aware of the importance of the impending occasion by the sounds of the trumpet, the Israelites would pray for divine assistance with greater intensity.

Common Features of Festivals

Three basic factors characterize the festivals: rejoicing, changes in the liturgy, and special ceremonies.

Rejoicing

Rejoicing in the festival primarily takes the form of ceremonial meals, with the obvious exception of Yom Kippur. On the more important biblical festivals, there is both the positive commandment to rest (to abstain from work) and the negative commandment prohibiting *m'lechet avodah*, which is generally rendered as "laborious or servile work," in contrast to the more restrictive prohibition "you shall do no work" that applies to the Sabbath and Yom Kippur. According to Rashi, *m'lechet avodah* means "essential work that will cause a significant loss if it is not performed." Nachmanides considers it "burdensome" work, such as ordinary farm or factory labor; in contrast, a person may engage in "pleasurable work," such as the preparation of food.[6] Whatever the interpretation of the term, all agree that the preparation of food—including such labors as slaughtering, cooking, and baking—is permitted on festivals (other than Yom Kippur) that fall on a weekday, based on the verse, "only what every person is to eat, that alone may be prepared for you" (Exod. 12:16).

While preparation of holiday meals is permitted on festivals, it is forbidden to prepare food for another day. Strictly speaking, if a festival occurs on Friday, one would not be permitted to prepare food for the Sabbath. To overcome this problem, the Rabbis instituted the *eruv tavshilin*. On the day before the festival, one prepares a special dish consisting of two items of food (such as bread and a piece of fish) for the Sabbath. In this way, a "blending" (*eruv*) of the Sabbath and festival foods occurs, making it permissible to prepare food on Friday for the Sabbath.[7] According to another talmudic view, the prohibition against preparing food for the Sabbath without an *eruv tavshilin* was intended to stress the importance of the ban against working on a festival to prepare for the subsequent weekdays.[8]

Changes in the Liturgy

Changes in the liturgy generally correspond to the importance of the festival. In Temple times, there was an additional (*Musaf*) sacrifice particular for the day. For example, the offerings of Sukkot were unique in three ways. There were offerings to invoke protection for the gentile nations; the offerings were slightly different for each day of the festival; and finally, there was a special water libation, in which water was poured into pipes at the top of the southwest corner of the altar every morning of the festival. The Water-Drawing Ceremony (see p. 236) was performed either every night (except the Sabbath) or only on the first night (the sources vary), accompanied by intense, night-long festivity, led by the most distinguished sages of the land.

Other special festival offerings were the meal offering of the new

MACHZOR (מַחְזוֹר)

The *machzor* is the prayer book used on the major festivals of the Jewish year. The best-known *machzor* is the one for the High Holy Days (Rosh Hashanah and Yom Kippur). There is also a *machzor* for the three pilgrimage festivals (Passover, Shavuot, and Sukkot) as well as separate prayer books for each. The Hebrew word means "return" or "cycle," appropriate because each of these festivals occurs once a year.

Like the siddur, the *machzor* contains the basic prayer service with special changes and additions for each festival. The *machzor* for the High Holy Days is especially enriched with *piyyutim*, a sampling of the thousands of prayer-poems composed by *hazzanim* who were deeply inspired by the liturgy of these days. Although rabbinic leaders were largely opposed to the inclusion of *piyyutim* in the service, many philosophical and mystical poems were inserted because they were both popular and beautiful.

barley on the second day of Passover, when the counting of the Omer begins, and the bringing of two loaves of bread from the new crop of wheat on Shavuot.

Today, a listing of the appropriate additional offerings constitutes the *maftir* portion of the Torah reading for each festival (see p. 459). This is read in a second scroll from the relevant verses in Numbers 28–29. During the *Musaf* service, a recitation of the required offerings for that specific festival (or the Sabbath) effectively serves as a replacement for the additional offerings that were brought to the Temple on that day. It is also customary to read one of the *megillot* on certain festivals: the Song of Songs on the Sabbath during Passover (see p. 269), the Book of Ruth on Shavuot (see p. 299), Ecclesiastes on the Sabbath of Sukkot (see p. 234), the Book of Esther on Purim (see p. 257), and Lamentations on Tisha b'Av (see p. 306).

A special *Amidah* is recited on Passover, Shavuot, and Sukkot, and there are different versions of the *Amidah* for both Rosh Hashanah and Yom Kippur. The standard *Amidah* is recited on Rosh Hodesh, *hol ha-mo'ed* (intermediate days of the festival; see below), Hanukkah, and Purim, with the addition of *Ya'aleh v'Yavo* (see p. 431) on Rosh Hodesh and *hol ha-mo'ed*, and *Al ha-Nissim* on Hanukkah and Purim. *Ya'aleh v'Yavo* and *Al ha-Nissim* (whose two versions recount the miracles of Hanukkah and Purim) are also inserted into the *Birkat ha-Mazon* on the appropriate days. The complete *Hallel* (see p. 162) is recited on Shavuot, Sukkot (including *hol ha-mo'ed*), Shemini Atzeret, Hanukkah, and the first day(s) of Passover. Only the "half" *Hallel* is recited during the rest of Passover and on Rosh Hodesh, and the *Hallel* is omitted entirely on Rosh Hashanah, Yom Kippur, and Purim.

Special Ceremonies

Most festivals are associated with special ceremonies. These may be biblical injunctions (eating matzah on Passover), talmudic commandments (lighting candles on Hanukkah), or customs (planting saplings on Tu b'Shevat). On the pilgrimage festivals and High Holy Days (as well as the Sabbath), it is customary for the woman of the house to light candles accompanied by a special blessing and (except on Sabbath) to recite the *Shehecheyanu* prayer (see p. 479); men customarily make *Kiddush* (sanctification) over wine, except on Yom Kippur.

Intermediate Days (*Hol ha-Mo'ed*)

The Torah mandates that Passover and Sukkot be celebrated for seven days, with an additional day (Shemini Atzeret) celebrated after the final day of Sukkot. Leviticus 23 uses the term "*mikrah kodesh*" (lit., "holy gathering") to refer to the first days of Passover and Sukkot, the seventh day of Passover, and Shemini Atzeret and prohibits work on these days only. The permissibility of work on the intermediate days, known as *hol ha-mo'ed*, therefore, became a matter of debate. According to Maimonides,[9] work is permissible on *hol ha-mo'ed*. Those Rabbis who disagreed were nevertheless lenient when financial loss could be caused by delays, though they discouraged heavy labor and work deliberately deferred to the mid-festival days. The days of *hol ha-mo'ed* are still festive days, marked by liturgical changes (see above) and set aside for rejoicing. It is customary to greet people by saying *mo'adim l'simcha* (joyous times).

Second Festival Days in the Diaspora

In ancient Israel, the Sanhedrin in Jerusalem announced the new moon each month. After two reliable witnesses had actually sighted the crescent moon, special messengers were sent to disseminate the information, but they often were unable to reach distant communities in time to inform the people of the correct day. Therefore, in the Diaspora, an extra day was added to Passover, Shavuot, Sukkot, and Rosh Hashanah to prevent any chance of people mistakenly failing to celebrate it on the mandated date. In about 360 C.E., Hillel II established a fixed Jewish calendar (still used today) based on precise mathematical and astronomical formulations, so that everyone knew the specific day of the festival in advance. Nevertheless, the sages decided to continue the custom of celebrating second days of festivals in the Diaspora, to "preserve the customs of their forefathers" (Beit. 4b). Yom Kippur was the exception, since a double fast day was considered too difficult (though some observed it). Rosh Hashanah, on the other hand, gradually came to be observed as a two-day festival even in the Land of Israel.[10]

On Passover and Sukkot, the first day of *hol ha-mo'ed* was observed as a full festival day in the Diaspora, and an additional day was added at the end. Thus on Passover a seder is also held on the second night and an eighth day is added. The day after Shemini Atzeret at the completion of Sukkot became known as Simchat Torah (Rejoicing of the Law). Despite the fact that the date of Shavuot could never have been in doubt, even in ancient times—because it always falls on the 50th day from the beginning of the counting of the Omer on the second day of Passover—Shavuot was also celebrated for a second day in the Diaspora.

Although the second day of the festival is rooted in rabbinic ordinance and is not prescribed in the Torah, it has nevertheless been preserved with equal sanctity throughout the centuries, long after the original doubt was resolved. In contrast, the *halakhah* does not regard the second day of Rosh Hashanah as a "second festival day" but rather as an "extended day," which is equivalent to the first day in every respect.

In Babylonia, the talmudic sages contemplated eliminating the second day of festivals as soon as a permanent calendar was fixed. In our day, the Reform movement has dropped the second day of festivals and there has been some debate in the Conservative movement about following suit, primarily based on the realization that the overwhelming majority of its members do not observe both days. However, one Conservative rabbi has written that the second day is critical in affirming the special sacredness that being in the Land of Israel adds to a Jew's very existence, based on the verse "For man is the tree of the field" (Deut. 20:19). Just as a tree depends on two factors in its growth—the earth in which it is rooted and the air in which it lives, so the spiritual growth of human beings requires the earth on which they are born and the environment that is breathed into their inner beings. Those living in Israel get both kinds of nourishment from the land and its surrounding environment. In the Diaspora, however, one cannot live and exist as a Jew except by creating synagogues and houses of study to produce a Torah-centered holy environment. Consequently, in the Diaspora it is necessary to compensate for the lack of sanctified land by adding an extra day to the sacred environment of the festivals.

According to the Shulchan Arukh and its commentaries, people traveling between the Land of Israel and the Diaspora follow the practice of the place to which they have arrived if they intend to live there (OH 496:3).

Hallel (הַלֵּל)

The recital of *Hallel* (Ps. 113–118) immediately after the morning *Amidah* is a hallmark of the festival liturgy. According to the Talmud, the prophets ordained that the six psalms of *Hallel* (lit., "praise"), which express thanksgiving and joy for divine redemption, be recited on each festival and to commemorate times of national redemption from peril (Pes. 117a). Long before King David redacted them into the Book of Psalms, tradition says *Hallel* was known to the nation. Various sages observed that *Hallel* was joyously exclaimed by Moses and Israel at the Sea of Reeds after being saved from the chariots of the Egyptians; by Joshua after conquering the kings of Canaan; by Deborah and Barak after defeating Sisera; by Hezekiah after successfully repelling the attack of Sennacherib; by Hananiah, Mishael, and Azariah after being saved from Nebuchadnezzar; and by Mordecai and Esther after defeating the wicked Haman who attempted to destroy the Jewish people.[11]

According to the Talmud, these psalms of joy and praise stress five fundamental themes of Jewish faith (Pes. 118a): the Exodus from Egypt ("When Israel went out of Egypt"; Ps. 114:1), the dividing of the sea ("The sea saw it and fled"; Ps. 114:3), the giving of the Torah at Sinai ("The mountains skipped like rams, the hills like young sheep"; Ps. 114:4), the future resurrection of the dead ("I shall walk before the Lord [in the land of the living]"; Ps. 116:9), and the birth pangs of the Messiah ("Not unto us, O Lord, not unto us"; Ps. 115:1., which is interpreted as a prayer to be spared the great distress preceding the arrival of the Messianic Age).[12]

In the Temple, *Hallel* was chanted by levitical choirs on the first day of Passover, while the sacrificial lambs were slaughtered, and at the seder; on the eight days of Sukkot, when the *lulav* was waved during the recitation of portions of Psalm 118; and on the eight days of Hanukkah, in remembrance of the rededication of the Temple after the Hasmonean victory. When the Temple was destroyed, *Hallel* was transferred to the synagogue. Later, it was added to the Shavuot service as a substitute for the levitical singing of the "Songs of Ascent" (the pilgrim psalms; Ps. 120–134), which used to be chanted when the first fruits were brought to the Temple. Around the beginning of the third century C.E., Babylonian Jews initiated the practice of reciting *Hallel* on the last six days of Passover and on Rosh Hodesh. To distinguish these new occasions from those on which *Hallel* had been traditionally recited, they omitted the first 11 verses from Psalm 115 and all of Psalm 116. This resulted in the current distinction between the "full" and "half" *Hallel*.[13]

The Midrash offers an ethical, humanitarian explanation for limiting *Hallel* on the last six days of Passover. God is pictured as rebuking the ministering angels who wished to sing praises to celebrate the deliverance of the Israelites: "My creatures are drowning in the sea, and you would sing to Me!" (Yalkut Sh. 247). Thus the abridged *Hallel* reflects the mitigation of Israel's joy because of the death of the Egyptians who had pursued them.

Hallel is not recited on Rosh Hashanah and Yom Kippur, because they are somber days of judgment and thus inappropriate times for singing psalms of joy (Ar. 10b). *Hallel* also is omitted on Purim because, despite the miracle of the day, the deliverance of the Jewish people was only partial and they remained in exile as subjects of Ahasuerus. However, *Hallel* is read on Hanukkah, not only because the military victory was more complete but also because this festival commemorates the miracle of the lights, which marked the rededication of the Temple.

The jubilance and celebration expressed in *Hallel* make it most appropriate for days of national rejoicing. Therefore the chief rabbinate in Israel has ruled that *Hallel* should be recited on Yom ha-Atzmaut (Israel Independence Day) and Yom Yerushalayim (Jerusalem Day). This practice has not been adopted by the small group of non-Zionist, ultra-Orthodox Jews who refuse to recognize the validity of the secular State of Israel (or its chief rabbinate).[14]

Although Sephardim also recite *Hallel* at evening festival services, this apparently was not the original intent, because its first paragraph (Ps. 113) speaks of praising the name of God "from the rising of the sun until its setting" (Meg. 20b). An exception is the first night(s) of Passover, since the climax of the Passover miracle took place at night and Psalm 114 makes special reference to the Exodus from Egypt. Although the usual practice in the synagogue is to stand for *Hallel* (based on the verse: "Praise the name of God, you servants of the Lord who *stand* in the house of the Lord"; Ps. 135:1–2), it is not the custom during the seder because of the duty to recline as a symbol of freedom.[15] Moreover, the blessing before *Hallel* is not recited at the seder—an indication of the immediacy of the experience of the Exodus from

Egypt. Rather than merely celebrating an event of the distant past, the participants in the seder should feel that they themselves were redeemed from slavery, so that the thanksgiving psalms become a natural outpouring of gratitude to God for which no preliminary blessing is recited.[16]

The festival *Hallel* must be distinguished from the *Hallel ha-Gadol* (Great *Hallel*), a talmudic term that refers only to Psalm 136, which is recited during *Pesukei de-Zimra* at the morning service on Sabbaths and festivals (Pes. 118a). This psalm praises God for mercifully sustaining all creatures and for saving the Israelites from Egyptian bondage and mighty kings who sought to destroy the people. Each of its 26 short lines is followed by the refrain, "*ki l'olam hasdo*" (for His kindness endures forever). According to the Mishnah, it was sung on joyous communal occasions, such as a long-awaited rain after a period of severe drought (Taan. 3:9). The Great *Hallel* was also recited on Passover eve when the sacrificial lamb was eaten, and therefore it is now said at the seder (Pes. 118a).[17]

Jewish Calendar (לוּחַ)

The Jewish calendar is based on 12 lunar months, whose names are of Babylonian origin and came into use among Jews only after the destruction of the First Temple.

The time span between one new moon and the next is 29 days, 12 hours, 44 minutes, and 3⅓ seconds. In the Jewish calendar, a month must be composed of complete days, thus they vary between 29 and 30 days. Five months (Nisan, Sivan, Av, Tishrei, and Shevat) have 30 days, five (Iyar, Tammuz, Elul, Tevet, and Adar) have 29 days, and two (Heshvan and Kislev) have either 29 or 30 days. However, the lunar year is approximately 11 days shorter than the solar year (365 days, 48 minutes, and 46 seconds). Without any adjustments, the festivals would "wander" and shift from their appointed seasons of the year. For example, Passover could fall in the autumn, winter, or summer, whereas according to the Torah it must be observed in the spring (Deut. 16:1). Therefore, an additional month is added seven times in every 19 years.[1] This added month, which is called Adar Sheni (Second Adar), immediately precedes the month of Nisan (the first month in the Jewish year). During Second Temple times, the Sanhedrin was respon-

Month	*Time of Year*	*Days*	*Date of Festivals and Fasts*
Nisan (נִיסָן)	March–April	30	15th: Passover (first day) 27th: Yom ha-Shoah
Iyar (אִיָּר)	April–May	29	5th: Yom ha-Atzmaut 18th: Lag ba-Omer 28th: Yom Yerushalayim
Sivan (סִיוָן)	May–June	30	6th: Shavuot (first day)
Tammuz (תַּמּוּז)	June–July	29	17th: Fast day
Av (אָב)	July–August	30	9th: Tisha b'Av 15th: Tu b'Av
Elul (אֱלוּל)	August–September	29	*Selichot*[1]
Tishrei (תִּשְׁרֵי)	September–October	30	1st: Rosh Hashanah (first day) 3rd: Tzom Gedalyah 10th: Yom Kippur 15th: Sukkot (first day) 22nd: Shemini Atzeret 23rd: Simchat Torah
Heshvan (חֶשְׁוָן)	October–November	29/30	None[2]
Kislev (כִּסְלֵו)	November–December	29/30	25th: Hanukkah (first day)
Tevet (טֵבֵת)	December–January	29	10th: Fast day
Shevat (שְׁבָת)	January–February	30	15th: Tu b'Shevat
Adar (אֲדָר)	February–March	29[3]	13th: Fast of Esther 14th: Purim

[1]Several possible dates (see p. 178).

[2]This month is often called "Mar Heshvan," based on either of two meanings of the Hebrew word "*mar*"—"bitter" and "mister." One tradition is that because Heshvan contains no holiday or special observance, it has a taste of bitterness to it. A more endearing explanation is that the Rabbis felt sorry for the month because of its lack of any special day and, therefore, gave it some honor by calling it "Mister Heshvan" (Greenberg, 303).

[3]In a leap year, Adar has 30 days and Adar Sheni (the extra month) has 29 days. The fast of Esther and Purim are observed in Adar Sheni.

sible for keeping track of discrepancies in length between the solar and lunar years and intercalating the extra month when needed according to agricultural conditions. As the Sanhedrin was about to be disbanded (mid-fourth century C.E.), there was a need to establish a permanent calendar based on astronomical calculations to adjust the solar and lunar years. This fixed calendar, published by Hillel II, has been used by Jews ever since.

In its description of Creation, the Torah repeatedly states: "There was evening and there was morning, a ... day" (e.g., Gen. 1:5). Therefore, Jews count every day starting with the preceding evening, so that the Sabbath begins on Friday night.

The numbering of years in the Jewish calendar is based on the time since the "Creation of the world" on Rosh Hashanah (Tishrei). To calculate this, the Rabbis combined the life spans of the early generations listed in the Bible—starting with Adam—with the time that had elapsed since then. To determine the current Jewish year, add 3,760 to the year in the civil calendar from January to Rosh Hashanah and 3,761 from Rosh Hashanah until the end of December. Thus the first part of the year 2005 in the civil calendar is the year 5765 in the Jewish calendar; after Rosh Hashanah, it would be the year 5766. In Hebrew, the year is usually written with just the last three numerals, using letters to represent the numbers. Thus 5765 would be written תשס״ה (ת = 400, שׁ = 300, ס = 60, ה = 5). Although they realize that this way of numbering the years does not accurately reflect the true age of the earth, Jews use it out of respect for their remote ancestors. This is somewhat similar to the subsequent customs of Christians and Muslims, who date their calendars back to the birth of Jesus and to Muhammad's flight from Mecca to Medina, respectively.

Rosh Hodesh (רֹאשׁ חֹדֶשׁ)

Rosh Hodesh (lit., "head of the month") is the first day of the month, which correlates with the sighting of the crescent of the new moon. In a lunar calendar, each month has a little more than 29 days (see p. 164). Originally, it was the Sanhedrin's task to determine whether a particular month had 29 or 30 days, based on the visual observation of witnesses. The members of the Sanhedrin gathered on the 30th of each month and awaited testimony. If witnesses appeared, Rosh Hodesh was celebrated, and that day was counted as the first day of the next month. If no witnesses appeared, the next day was celebrated as Rosh Hodesh. To spread word that the new month had begun, fires were lit on the Mount of Olives and then successively throughout Israel. Jews living far from Jerusalem always celebrated Rosh Hodesh on the 30th day of the month. When informed that it had been postponed to the next day, they also celebrated that day.

In ancient times, Rosh Hodesh was considered an important holiday, observed with great seriousness. Work was suspended, special sacrifices were offered in the Temple, the shofar was blown, and it was customary to visit the prophet. When predicting the disasters that will befall the Jewish people, Hosea (2:13) conveys God's stern warning, "I will cause all her joy to cease, her feast days, her new moons, and her Sabbaths." Conversely, Isaiah (66:23) declared that, at the time of the redemption, "and New Moon after New Moon, and Sabbath after Sabbath, all flesh shall come to worship Me, said the Lord." This verse is the conclusion of the special haftarah that is recited when Rosh Hodesh falls on the Sabbath.

After the destruction of the Temple, the power to declare the day of the New Moon passed to the head of the court at Yavneh. During the fourth century C.E., however, the Christian authorities in the Land of Israel prohibited the dissemination of information regarding the day of the New Moon. Consequently, in about 360, Hillel II published a fixed calendar based on astronomical calculations (see p. 165), thus freeing Jewish communities from having to rely on the declaration by the high court in the Land of Israel.[1]

Work is permitted on Rosh Hodesh. Since earliest times, however, it was customary for women to abstain from work as a reward for not having surrendered their jewelry for the fashioning of the Golden Calf (JT Taan. 1:6, 64c). In certain communities, no work was done; in others only heavy work was forbidden. In recent years, women have formed Rosh Hodesh groups to study and worship together.[2]

Although the importance of Rosh Hodesh as a religious festival has declined and it retains only a shadow of its former prominence, the Rosh Hodesh service contains three liturgic elements that raise it to the level of the intermediate days of the major festivals.[3] *Ya'aleh v'Yavo* (see p. 431) is included in the morning *Amidah* (and the *Birkat ha-Mazon*), the half *Hallel* is recited (see p. 162), and there is a *Musaf* service that recounts the sacrifices that were offered in the Temple on that day. As a joyous, though minor, festival, *Tachanun* (see p. 435) is not recited, fasting is forbidden, any funeral service is abbreviated, and it is traditional to partake in a festive meal.[4]

Birkat ha-Hodesh (בִּרְכַּת הַחֹדֶשׁ)

Birkat ha-Hodesh is the public announcement mentioning the name of the new month and the day(s) on which Rosh Hodesh will be celebrated. It is recited on the Sabbath before the new moon, following the reading of the haftarah. Traditionally, the *shaliach tzibbur* (prayer leader) holds the Torah during *Birkat ha-Hodesh*.

Initially, *Birkat ha-Hodesh* was only a simple announcement on the Sabbath before the upcoming new moon. During the eighth century, a group of Jewish sectarians known as the Karaites denied the validity of all rabbinic enactments and insisted on strict and literal adherence to the biblical legislation. They decried the rabbinic procedure of determining the day of the New Moon by calculation and demanded a return to the old system of direct visual observation. Thus the act of announcing the new moon on the preceding Sabbath took on increased importance as a way of asserting rabbinic authority, and the ceremony was embellished with two special prayers for the coming month.[5] The first, recited before the announcement of the new month, recalls the divine miracles performed for our ancestors and prays that God will "gather in our dispersed from the four corners of the earth." The second, recited after the announcement, is a prayer that the new month will bring life, peace, gladness, joy, salvation, and consolation for the house of Israel.

In the 18th century, Ashkenazim added the prayer *Yehi Ratzon* (May it be your will) as an introduction to *Birkat ha-Hodesh*. Taken from the Talmud, it is essentially a private petition that was recited daily after the completion of the *Amidah* by Rav, the illustrious third-century Babylonian sage (Ber. 16b). To make it more appropriate for the announcement of the new month, the prayer was rewritten in the first person plural and preceded by the phrase "renew for us this month for good and for blessing."[6] The congregation rises for *Birkat ha-Hodesh*, a custom that hearkens back to the Sanhedrin's sanctification of the day of the New Moon, which was performed while standing. On the Sabbath preceding Rosh Hashanah (the First of Tishrei), *Birkat ha-Hodesh* is not recited in order to "confound the heavenly adversary."

Kiddush Levanah (קִדּוּשׁ לְבָנָה)

Kiddush Levanah (Sanctification of the Moon) is the prayer of thanksgiving recited at the monthly reappearance of the crescent moon. In the Talmud, Rabbi Yochanan taught that one who blesses the new moon in its proper time is like one who greets the *Shekhinah* (Divine Presence), for a person can appreciate the existence of God only through the divine works (Sanh. 42a). In addition to the miracles and revelations to Israel, the actions of God in nature are manifest by the "orderly functioning of the enormously complex heavenly bodies" that is most evident to human beings in the cycles of the moon.[7]

Kiddush Levanah also symbolizes the regenerative capacity of the Jewish people, as suggested in the verse, "It [David's throne] shall be established forever as the moon" (Ps. 89:38). Just as the moon remains in the sky even though temporarily absent from our view, so David's throne will eventually reappear with the coming of the Messiah. After the destruction of the Temple, it was vital for the Jewish people to nurture the confident hope for a future Messianic Age with the ingathering of the exiles, the rebuilding of the Temple, and the re-establishment of Jewish sovereignty under a descendant of King David.[8] As Rabbi Shimon ben Gamaliel observed, "Just as the new month sanctifies and renews itself in this world, so shall Israel sanctify and renew itself in the distant future" (PdRE 51).

A code message relating the rebirth of the moon, the Davidic dynasty, and the perpetual existence of the Jewish people developed during the talmudic era. When the Romans abrogated the authority of the rabbinical court in Jerusalem to consecrate the day of the New Moon, this ceremony had to be carried out clandestinely. Judah ha-Nasi sent an emissary to the place in Judea where the *beit din* met, instructing them to sanctify Rosh Hodesh on the 30th day. The return message indicating that the mission had been accomplished contained the watchword *David, Melech Yisrael, chai v'kayam* (David, King of Israel, lives and endures; RH 25a). This phrase has become the lyrics of a popular song and is repeated three times during the *Kiddush Levanah* service as a symbol of Israel's renewal and national redemption. Another phrase (also the words of a well-known song) that has entered the *Kiddush Levanah* service and reflects the symbolism of the new moon is *siman tov u-mazel tov, yehei lanu u-l'chol Yisrael* (May it be a good sign and good fortune for us and for all of Israel).[9] These words are also sung to celebrate such joyous activities as weddings and bar and bat mitzvah ceremonies.

As a ceremony stressing God as the Creator and Israel's rebirth, *Kiddush Levanah* should be recited joyously, preferably at the conclusion of the Sabbath when people are still in a good mood and dressed in their finest clothes. Also, according to tradition, it was on a Saturday night that the Temple was destroyed and the *Shekhinah* went into exile—and thus with the renewal of the moon Jews pray that Israel and even the Divine Presence will also be revived as in days of old.[10] Ideally, it should be said with a minyan under the open sky, when the moon is clearly visible and not hidden by clouds. It is customary to delay recitation of *Kiddush Levanah* until after Tisha b'Av (Ninth of Av) and Yom Kippur (10th of Tishrei), because the gloom of Av and the trepidation associated with the Days of Judgment are not conducive to the requisite joy. The blessing of the moon is not recited on Sabbath and holiday eves—either because of the prohibition against carrying prayer books outside the house or synagogue building when there is no *eruv* (see p. 134) or because we do not set two different causes for joy in competition with one another.[11]

High Holy Days

Repentance (Teshuvah; תְּשׁוּבָה)

Repentance (*teshuvah*) is a prerequisite for divine forgiveness.[1] It requires a combination of genuine remorse for the wrong committed plus evidence of changed behavior. The Bible uses numerous phrases to indicate the need for human beings to play an active role in the process of repentance—"direct your hearts to the Lord" (Josh. 24:23), "circumcise your heart" (Jer. 4:4),[2] "wash your heart" (Jer. 4:14), "get yourselves a new heart" (Ezek. 18:31). However, all these expressions of penitential activity can be summarized by the Hebrew root *"shuv"* (return), which encompasses both a turning away from evil and a turning toward the good and ultimately developed into the rabbinic concept of *teshuvah* as repentance.

Rabbinic Period

The Talmud states that repentance was one of the seven things created before the world itself (with the Torah, the Garden of Eden, Gehenna, the Throne of Glory, the Temple, and the name of the Messiah) (Pes. 54a) and "reaches up to the Throne of Glory" (Yoma 86a). God urges Israel not to be ashamed to repent, just as a son is not embarrassed to return to his loving father (Deut. R. 2:24). On public fast days, the elder of the congregation would declare, "Brethren, Scripture does not say of the men of Nineveh: 'And God saw their sackcloth and their fasting' but: 'And God saw their works, that they turned from their evil way' [Jon. 3:10]" (Taan. 2:1).

The Rabbis were aware of the basic theological difficulty in the whole concept of repentance—for once a wrong has been done, how can it be put right? The general rabbinic answer is that it is a matter of divine favor. As the Jerusalem Talmud explains, "They asked of wisdom: 'What is the punishment of the sinner?' Wisdom replied: 'Evil pursues sinners' [Prov. 13:21]. They asked of prophecy: 'What is the punishment of the sinner?' Prophecy replied: 'The soul that sins it shall die' [Ezek. 18:4]. Then they asked of the Holy One, blessed be He: 'What is the punishment of the sinner?' He replied: 'Let him repent and he will find atonement'" (Mak. 2:7, 31d).

In a discussion concerning whether the repentant sinner or the wholly righteous man who has not sinned is greater, Rabbi Shimon ben Lakish opted for the former. In one version he is quoted as saying that when sinners repent, their sins are accounted as if they had been committed unintentionally; in another, the sins are even accounted as virtues. The Talmud reconciles these two versions by explaining that the first refers to repentance out of fear, while the second alludes to repentance out of love (Yoma 86b). Even those who have been wicked all their days are pardoned if they repent for their sins at the end of their lives (Kid. 40b). The talmudic dictum "Repent one day before your death" (Shab. 153a) means it is necessary to spend every day in repentance, for we do not know which will be our last.

Yom Kippur brings pardon for sin if there is repentance (Yoma 8:8). This applies only to transgressions between human beings and God (*bein adam la-Makom*). For transgressions between one human being and another (*bein adam la-chavero*), Yom Kippur does not secure atonement unless one has sought forgiveness from the other person and redressed the wrongs done to him or her (Yoma 85b). If necessary, one must attempt three times to seek forgiveness from another. According to the Talmud (Yoma 87a), this is based on the triple repetition of the word "please" in the message that the brothers, fearful of Joseph's exacting revenge after Jacob's death, contended was given to them by their father just before he died (Gen. 50:17).[3] If forgiveness is not granted—itself a grave sin—the burden of seeking exoneration is removed from the transgressor. According to Judah ha-Nasi, the Day of Atonement brings pardon for transgressions against God even without repentance, except in cases of very serious sin (Yoma 85b). However, the forgiving quality of Yom Kippur is ineffective if one thinks: "I will sin and the Day of Atonement will procure atonement." Similarly, the person who says "I will sin and repent, and sin again and repent" will not be afforded any opportunity to repent (Yoma 87a). In the second century C.E., Rabbi Ishmael stated:

> If a man transgressed a positive precept and repented, he is forgiven right away. If he has transgressed a negative commandment and repented, then repentance suspends punishment and Yom Kippur procures atonement. If he has committed a sin punishable by *karet* (premature death by heavenly decree) or death at the hand of the court and repented, then repentance and the Day of Atonement suspend the punishment, and suffering cleanses him from the sin. But if he has been guilty of profaning the Divine Name, then penitence has no power to suspend punishment, nor Yom Kippur to procure atonement, nor suffering to finish it, but all of them together suspend the punishment and only death finishes it (Yoma 86a).

Repentance requires true remorse for having committed the sin. Rabbi Judah defined a true penitent as one who encountered the object that caused his original sin on two subsequent occasions and yet was able to keep away from it. As he specified, "With the same woman, at the same time, in the same place" (Yoma 86b). It is essential that the penitent sinner confess his or her sins, though the sages debated how this should be accomplished. Rabbi Judah ben Bava required that the details of each sin be stated explicitly, considering a mere general confession to be insufficient. In contrast, according to Rabbi Akiva a general confession of sins was enough. The Rabbis frowned on public displays of confession, unless the sins were committed in a public forum or, in the view of some, were offenses against other people (Yoma 86b). Convinced that confession without true repentance was a worthless endeavor, the Rabbis compared such behavior to the ancient parable of a man who immerses himself in the purifying waters of the *mikveh* (ritual bath; see p. 555) while still grasping in his hand a defiling reptile (Taan. 16a).

The sinner must be encouraged to repent for his or her past actions. One is forbidden to rebuke a penitent by saying, "Remember your former deeds" (BM 4:10). According to the Talmud, a person who stole a beam and incorporated it into his house was not required to demolish the house; to encourage him to repent, he instead was permitted to pay cash for the value of his theft (Git. 5:5). Moreover, if robbers or usurers repented and wanted to return their illicit gains, the Rabbis urged that their victims not accept restitution, lest this discourage other potential penitents from returning to the right path (BK 94b).

Medieval Period

Underlying the philosophical approach to repentance is the doctrine of "free will," for if there is no moral choice, there can be no sin for which one has to repent. Given the existence of free choice and the inherent fallibility of human beings, at times they will choose wrongly and thus sin is *inevitable* ("to err is human ..."). Therefore, repentance is necessary to repair the mistakes that mortals inevitably will make. Because true repentance requires that a person not repeat a sin when subsequently faced with the same situation, this implies that *sin can be overcome*, as expressed in the phrase "sin crouches at the door ... yet you can be its master" (Gen. 4:7). Finally, lest repentance be a vain action, it must be true that God is willing to forgive us for our sins ("... to forgive, divine").

The great Sephardic philosophers Saadiah Gaon (10th century), Bahya ibn Pekuda (11th century), and Maimonides (12th century) pursued an "anthropomorphic" approach to repentance, focusing on the human being. For them, repentance was a way of attaining moral self-fulfillment, the realization of individual human potential. Based on the Aristotelian belief that the health of the soul parallels the health of the body, Maimonides (an accomplished physician) argued that just as a physical illness could produce a sickness of the body, so the moral vices (i.e., sin) led to a sickness of the soul. Similarly, just as medications could be used to treat a physical illness, a spiritual sickness could be cured with the "medicine" of *teshuvah*. This entailed a three-step process encompassing remorse (intellectual), confession (speech), and physical deeds (behavior modification). He emphasized the importance of *vidui*—publicly confessing those sins committed against one's fellow human beings—though he stressed that a verbal confession without inner conviction is worthless.[4] For Maimonides, the basic goal of repentance was to dispel spiritual illness, while a cultivation of the moral virtues was designed to improve the health of the soul.

Saadiah's basic premises were (1) whatever we do affects our spiritual health and well-being, (2) a benevolent God wants what is good for us, and (3) rational people would want to do what is good for themselves. Given these assumptions, the only possible reasons why rational people would do something harmful is that they simply do not know what is good and bad. This knowledge can be discovered only by studying the Torah and observing its commandments. Therefore, divine punishments for transgressions are not punitive but rather pedagogical, designed to instruct us in the right path so that through repentance we can continually move to a higher and more rational moral and spiritual level. Saadiah believed that there were four aspects of *teshuvah*, based on Hosea 14:2–5—renunciation of sin (awareness, confession, rejection), remorse, quest for forgiveness from the one wronged, and resolve not to relapse into sin again (*Emunot ve-Deot* 5:5). Nevertheless, he maintained that some sins were so terrible that punishment in this world is inevitable despite repentance.

For Bahya, the conditions necessary for repentance included (1) recognition of the evil nature of one's sin, (2) realization that punishment for one's sin is inevitable and that repentance is the only means of averting punishment, (3) reflection on the favors previously bestowed by God, and (4) renunciation of the evil act (*Hovot ha-Levavot* 7:4).

The philosophers developed different gradations of repentance. For Saadiah, the highest level of repentance is that which takes place immediately after one has sinned, while the details of the sin are still fresh in the mind. A lower level of repentance occurs when one is threatened by disaster, and the lowest is the repentance that takes place only just before death. According to Bahya, the highest level is the repentance of one who, while still capable of sinning, has conquered his evil inclination entirely. The next level of repentance is one who manages to refrain from sin, but is nevertheless constantly drawn toward sin by his evil inclination. The lowest form of repentance is one who no longer has the power or opportunity to sin. For Maimonides, "perfect" repentance means having the opportunity to repeat the offense but refraining from doing so because one is truly penitent and not out of fear or physical weakness.[5]

Hasidei Ashkenaz

The German pietist movement known as Hasidei Ashkenaz developed in England, France, and Germany during the Crusades—a terrible time for the Jews, who were killed as "infidels" when the Christians marched to the Holy Land. Not understanding why they were suffering, the Hasidei Ashkenaz had an almost neurotic need to invent some sins that they must have perpetrated and then develop ways to repent for them. The Talmud had *explicitly* provided four "separate acts of atonement" (Yoma 2; 60a); the Hasidei Ashkenaz were convinced that their suffering meant that God also has an *implicit* will that they must discover, and this led to the development of severe approaches to repentance.

The followers of this movement reasoned that because the worst sin was conversion to Christianity the best repentance and highest virtue was to sacrifice themselves and their families for God rather than convert. The deplorable conditions under which they lived prompted the Hasidei Ashkenaz to develop the basic assumption that life in this world is transient and short, whereas life in the next world is eternal. Therefore, their goal was to cultivate life in the world to come, since life on earth is merely "preparation" for the future life.

Because the Temple rites and Sanhedrin were no longer available to atone for those sins that required lashes or even the death penalty, the Hasidei Ashkenaz developed "replacement" or "symbolic" *teshuvah* by which they inflicted on themselves the punishment the Sanhedrin would have imposed. For example, adherents who committed an offense for which death by the sword was required might cover themselves with some substance attractive to bees and walk slowly through a hive; the stings they received were a symbolic way of being stabbed to death. Expanding on the talmudic dictum of building a *fence* around the Torah, the Hasidei Ashkenaz added a *gate*—prohibiting even that which was permitted on the grounds that it could lead to forbidden activities. For example, if a man sinned by having an illicit relationship with a woman, proper *teshuvah* would entail not even looking at a woman, hearing a female voice, or going where women gather. Proper repentance must be individualized, because various people are drawn to different things—such as theft, gluttony, sex, and greed—and must construct their own protective fences and gates. In essence, each person became at the same time sinner, judge, victim, and executor of punishment.

The Hasidei Ashkenaz developed a horrendous array of punishments, including severe self-flagellation, as repentance for real or imagined transgressions. They introduced two days of Yom Kippur, and interpreted the phrase "and you shall afflict yourselves" (Lev. 16:31)[6] as requiring self-flagellation during the entire month of Elul through the Day of Atonement.

Kabbalistic Concepts

Unlike the anthropocentric approach of the medieval Jewish philosophers and the Hasidei Ashkenaz, the kabbalists were *theocentric*, focusing on the inner life of God and how human deeds influence the Divine. In essence, they considered that *teshuvah* was to be performed for the sake of God and not for humankind. The goal was to repair the torn fabric and inner balance of the Divine, rather than merely to allow human beings to reach their fullest potential. As the Zohar noted, "Repentance repairs everything, repairs the world above, repairs the world below, repairs the man himself, repairs the whole world." Employing sexual imagery to depict the inner life of the Divine, the Zohar observed that the male and female forces within God are ideally in balance. The major goal of repentance and the Jewish festivals is to cure the imbalance between the male and female forces within God that is caused by human sins, so that there could be a "holy sexual union."

A powerful concept of the kabbalists was the importance of human beings, who were crucial in maintaining both our natural world and the upper world of the *sefirot*. This idea reached its climax in the kabbalistic system of Isaac Luria in 16th-century Safed, in which repentance was deemed an essential step in the process of *tikun*—the repairing of the heavenly world. Through repentance, the Jew was able to assist God in the elevation of the holy sparks entrapped in the *klipot* (husks). This would ultimately usher in the Messianic Age, completing and perfecting the work of Creation.

Using the analogy of a series of tubes, the kabbalists maintained that our sins introduce material that can clog the pipes connecting the upper and lower worlds, forcing evil substances to flow back down to us. Repentance unclogs the pipes among the *sefirot*, so that divine love, grace, and mercy can flow down to our world. The kabbalists wanted to "restore" that which once was by correcting flaws in the cosmos and the male–female imbalance within God, unlike the philosophers, who wanted to make the world "better" and reach a level that had never existed before.

Hasidism and the Musar Movement

Hasidism emphasizes a highly personal and anthropocentric relation to the Deity, either on the part of the individual Hasid or at least in the person of the tzadik. The movement tones down the severity of the doctrine of repentance, expressing confidence in the loving response of God and divine forgiveness that help lessen the sense of overburdening sin.

By contrast, the Musar movement stressed the overpowering role of sin, teaching that repentance is the persistent task of the Jew, day after day, year after year. This turning inward to scrutinize one's deeds and motives gave the follower of the Musar movement an awareness of sin of which the average Jew or the Hasid would be totally oblivious. This process of self-scrutiny and repentance reached its pinnacle in the month of Elul preceding the High Holy Days, which was entirely devoted to soul searching and even self-inflicted physical suffering in the hope of achieving genuine repentance.

Modern Period

Rav Kook, the first Ashkenazic chief rabbi of Palestine, devoted an entire work (*Orot ha-Teshuvah,* Lights of repentance) to the concept of repentance. In addition to the traditional return of each individual to God, Kook envisioned a national *teshuvah* in the return of the Jewish people to the ancestral Land of Israel. Kook adapted kabbalistic thinking to demonstrate the cosmic significance of individual repentance. Whereas sinning causes isolation from God and disrupts the harmony in the universe, the repentance of even a single person is a valuable step in returning to the ideal unity of all existence.

The quintessential *baal teshuvah* (one who repents) was Franz Rosenzweig. Ready to convert to Christianity, after attending an Orthodox service on Yom Kippur Rosenzweig was inspired to intensively study the tradition as well as to write books that would draw other assimilated Jews to an appreciation and love for what he termed the "inner fire of the Jewish star of redemption." Stressing that fulfilling the commandments is a gradual process of personal growth, Rosenzweig's response when asked about those mitzvot he did not keep was "not yet."

Selichot (סְלִיחוֹת)

Selichot are penitential prayers for the divine forgiveness of sins. They originally were part of the liturgy for fast days, most of which commemorate tragic events. The *Selichot* were a way of recognizing God and divine punishment, an acknowledgment that all tragedies were the result of Israel's sins and that additional misfortune could be avoided with repentance. Later, the recitation of *Selichot* was applied to the preparatory period preceding the High Holy Days and eventually extended to the Ten Days of Repentance, including Yom Kippur but not Rosh Hashanah. The term "*Selichot*" is also used for the special midnight service that takes place before Rosh Hashanah.

The *Selichot* prayers stress not only the sins of the worshiper but also the suffering of Israel. They make repeated references to the afflictions, persecutions, and humiliations that have been the lot of Israel in exile. Overshadowing all is the theme of Israel's undying faith in God's mercy, the absolute conviction of the Jewish people that the ordeal of exile will ultimately come to an end and that redemption will replace the anguish of the dispersion.[1]

Some of the penitential prayers are among the oldest in the liturgy. The combination of confession and supplication for forgiveness is found as early as the fifth century B.C.E. Nehemiah (9:3) describes a great national day of fasting: "Standing in their places, they read from the scroll of the Teaching of the Lord their God one-fourth of the day, and for another fourth they confessed and prostrated themselves before the Lord their God." The Talmud specifies that for one-quarter of any fast day a person must "offer up supplications" (Meg. 30b), though the precise nature of these prayers was not decreed and thus they varied greatly from one community to another. Some penitential prayers for rain are mentioned in the Mishnah (Taan. 2), including one that is still recited today in which biblical characters from Abraham to Ezra are listed as examples of God's mercy (see p. 240). The prayer opens, "He who answered our father Abraham on Mount Moriah, may He answer us; He who answered his son Isaac when he was bound on the altar, may He answer us; He who answered Jacob at Beit El, may He answer us" and concludes, "He who answered all the righteous, the devout, the wholesome, and the upright, may He answer us."[2]

During the gaonic period, special predawn *Selichot* services were instituted for each of the intermediate days between Rosh Hashanah and Yom Kippur. Eventually, these were extended to the days immediately preceding Rosh Hashanah. Although initially brief, these services gradually lengthened as persecutions increased and numerous penitential prayers were composed. According to the Talmud, when night comes to an end ("last of the three watches") is a time of "favor and compassion" (*eit ratzon*) as the spirit of God hovers over the earth (Av. Zar. 3b). Therefore, the pious would rise before dawn and assemble in the synagogue for daily *Selichot* services at this time of the year.[3] However, this regimen was too rigorous for ordinary Jews, who were satisfied with one *Selichot* service that typically took place on the Saturday night preceding Rosh Hashanah. For the convenience of the multitude, this service was held at midnight instead of the predawn hours, possibly based on the verse: "I arise at midnight to praise You for Your just rules" (Ps. 119:62).[4]

Today, Sephardic communities begin reciting *Selichot* at the beginning of the month of Elul, and these prayers of forgiveness are continued for 40 days through Yom Kippur, which the Midrash calculated was the period that Moses stayed on Mount Sinai (PdRE 46 on Exod. 34:28). Ashkenazim begin saying the penitential prayers on the Saturday night before Rosh Hashanah. As the start of the new week and the end of a sacred day of rest and study, the conclusion of the Sabbath was considered an especially opportune time for these prayers of forgiveness.[5] However, if there are fewer than four days between this time and Rosh Hashanah, the prayers are begun the previous Saturday night. In this way, the number of days on which *Selichot* are recited varies from four to nine.

Although *Selichot* were initially inserted into the *Amidah* after the appropriate sixth blessing (a prayer for the forgiveness of sins), virtually every community has now adopted the custom developed in the Land of Israel of reciting them after the *Amidah*.[6]

Thirteen Attributes of Mercy

The core of the *Selichot* prayers is the Thirteen Attributes of Mercy, the very words that God taught Moses for the people to use whenever they needed to beg for divine compassion. Because the Talmud states that God was wearing a tallit at that time (RH 17b), it is customary for the prayer leader to wear a tallit for the recital of the *Selichot* prayers, even though they otherwise are never worn at this early hour because it is too dark to see the tzitzit (which are meant to be visual reminders, as in the verse, "And you shall see them"; Num. 15:39).[7] The Thirteen Attributes of Mercy are found after the incident of the Golden Calf, when God threatened to destroy the people of Israel rather than forgive them (Exod. 32:10). According to the Talmud, Moses felt that Israel's sin was so serious that there was no possibility of intercession on their behalf (RH 17b). At this point, God appeared to Moses and taught him the Thirteen Attributes, saying: "Whenever Israel sins, let them recite this [the Thirteen Attributes] in its proper order and I will forgive them." Thus this appeal to God's mercy reassures us that repentance is always possible and that God always awaits our return.[8]

The Thirteen Attributes of Mercy are based on two verses in Exodus: "The Lord! The Lord! God, Compassionate and Gracious, Slow to anger and Abundant in Kindness and Truth, Preserver of kindness for thousands of generations, Forgiver of iniquity, willful sin, and error, and Who Cleanses (—but does not cleanse completely, recalling the iniquity of parents upon children and grandchildren, to the third and fourth generations)" (34:6–7). The Hebrew phrase *"v'nakeh lo y'nakeh"* (and Who cleanses but does not cleanse) is a common biblical grammatical form that uses repetition to stress the action. The Rabbis ingeniously cut off the verse after *v'nakeh,* thus changing the meaning to indicate that God does forgive all sins! This remarkable midrashic transformation has become the standard format whenever this Torah verse is used in a synagogue service. Although it may go beyond the plain meaning of the biblical text, the change is consistent with the general concept of the passage—the merciful and forgiving nature of God.[9]

The Thirteen Attributes of Mercy, according to the generally accepted opinions of Rabbenu Tam and Abudraham,[10] are as follows:

- The Lord! (*Adonai*)—God is merciful *before* a person sins, even though aware that future evil lies dormant within him.
- The Lord! (*Adonai*)—God is merciful *after* the sinner has gone astray.
- God (*El*)—a name that denotes power as ruler over nature and humankind, indicating that God's mercy sometimes surpasses even the degree indicated by this name.
- Compassionate (*rachum*)—God is filled with loving sympathy for human frailty, does not put people into situations of extreme temptation, and eases the punishment of the guilty.
- Gracious (*v'chanun*)—God shows mercy even to those who do not deserve it, consoling the afflicted and raising up the oppressed.

- Slow to anger (*erech apayim*)—God gives the sinner ample time to reflect, improve, and repent.
- Abundant in Kindness (*v'rav chesed*)—God is kind toward those who lack personal merits, providing more gifts and blessings than they deserve; if one's personal behavior is evenly balanced between virtue and sin, God tips the scales of justice toward the good.
- Truth (*v'emet*)—God never reneges on His word to reward those who serve Him.
- Preserver of kindness for thousands of generations (*notzeir chesed la-alafim*)—God remembers the deeds of the righteous for the benefit of their less virtuous generations of offspring (thus we constantly invoke the merit of the Patriarchs).
- Forgiver of iniquity (*nosei avon*)—God forgives intentional sin resulting from an evil disposition, as long as the sinner repents.
- [Forgiver of] willful sin (*pesha*)—God allows even those who commit a sin with the malicious intent of rebelling against and angering Him the opportunity to repent.
- [Forgiver of] error (v'*chata'ah*)—God forgives a sin committed out of carelessness, thoughtlessness, or apathy.
- Who cleanses (*v'nakeh*)—God is merciful, gracious, and forgiving, wiping away the sins of those who truly repent; however, if one does not repent, God does not cleanse (*lo y'nakeh*).[11]

The kabbalists introduced the custom of also reciting the Thirteen Attributes of Mercy before taking the Torah from the ark during the three pilgrimage festivals of Passover, Shavuot, and Sukkot. This was followed by a silent prayer beginning, "Master of the universe, fulfill my heartfelt requests for good," demonstrating an understanding that all too often one's personal goals are not for his or her benefit. Like all personal supplications, the Thirteen Attributes of Mercy are not recited on the Sabbath or on festivals that fall on the Sabbath.[12]

Elul (אֱלוּל)

The entire month of Elul is a preparation for the High Holy Days, with its themes of renewal and return. Jewish tradition points to the very name of the month as symbolically appropriate, since the Hebrew letters of Elul are an acronym for words in the verse from the Song of Songs (6:3), *"Ani l'dodi v'dodi li"* (I am my beloved's and my beloved is mine). Believing that the "beloved" refers to God, the Rabbis took this verse to describe the particularly loving and close relationship between God and Israel. Separated from each other during the three weeks before Tisha b'Av (see p. 304), Israel and God rediscover each other beginning with Tu b'Av (see p. 307), and their love slowly intensifies. The climax of their relationship occurs on Yom Kippur, when Israel is forgiven for the shameful incident of the Golden Calf that had initially precipitated the process of mourning, repentance, and renewal.[1] According to tradition, the First of Elul is also the day when Moses ascended Mount Sinai in preparation for receiving the second tablets 40 days later on Yom Kippur. The prophetic readings on the Sabbaths of Elul are the last four of the seven "*haftarot* of consolation."

The shofar is blown daily, except on the Sabbath, during the month of Elul. Because the second tablets represented the reconciliation between God and Israel after the sin of the Golden Calf, sounding the shofar is a reminder that the month of Elul is a propitious time for us as well. The shofar is blown at the conclusion of the morning service, with the exception of the day before Rosh Hashanah.[2] Two explanations for this are to distinguish a mere custom from the Torah commandment to blow the shofar on Rosh Hashanah itself,[3] and to act as a ploy to confuse Satan, the prosecutor who is preparing the case against us before the divine court.

Special penitential psalms (*Selichot*) requiring a minyan are recited during Elul. Ashkenazim also recite the penitential Psalm 27 twice daily, in the morning and in the evening. Its opening verse—"The Lord is my light and my help; whom should I fear?"[4]—awakens the spirit and inspires repentance and reverence.[5] The psalm also expresses our confidence and trust in God, so that we enter the upcoming High Holy Day season not with fear but with faith in a favorable divine judgment.[6]

On the day before Rosh Hashanah, Jews ask forgiveness from each other. Traditional Jews observe the practice of *hatarat nedarim*, in which one person asks three others to serve as a *beit din* (court) to grant forgiveness for any unfulfilled vows from the past year. In turn, each of the four asks the other three to serve as the *beit din*.[7] In many respects this is a more halakhically defensible practice than *Kol Nidrei*, which in the Ashkenazic version requests forgiveness for *future* vows (see p. 210).

During Elul, Jews begin to wish each other *shanah tovah* (a good [new] year). Many people visit the graves of their parents, close relatives, and others who played prominent roles in their lives. This custom probably originated in the hope that the departed would intercede on our behalf before the heavenly court in an attempt to secure a favorable judgment. Some synagogues even hold public memorial services at the cemetery.[8]

Rosh Hashanah (רֹאשׁ הַשָּׁנָה)

Rosh Hashanah (lit., "head of the year"), which falls on the first and second days of the autumn month of Tishrei (September–October), is now celebrated as the beginning of the Jewish new year. The term occurs only once in the Bible (Ezek. 40:1), where it simply means the start of the year and does not refer to this specific festival. Indeed, the Torah counted the months from Nisan, the month of Passover, so that what we now call Rosh Hashanah is referred to as the festival of the *seventh* month (Num. 29:1),[1] a sacred occasion commemorated with the blast of the horns. Although originally a one-day holiday (RH 4:4), in the Diaspora a second day was added to Rosh Hashanah because of the difficulty in determining when the new moon actually appeared. After the calendar was set, Jews in Israel continued to observe only one day until the Middle Ages, when the practice of observing two days became universal. Because the Rabbis viewed Rosh Hashanah as a *yoma arichta* (one long day), there was a question whether on the second day one should say *Shehecheyanu*, the blessing expressing gratitude for special occasions. To avoid this problem, the custom arose of eating a new fruit or wearing a new garment on the second night, acts that would themselves require a *Shehecheyanu* blessing.[2]

The Mishnah designates four different days as "Rosh Hashanah," each relating to specific activities:

- The First of Nisan for reckoning the reigns of Jewish kings (the date for determining how many years a king has ruled) and for establishing the order of the festivals.
- The First of Elul for tithing animals.

- The First of Tishrei for agriculture (sabbatical years, jubilee years), passing judgment on humankind, and marking the anniversary of the Creation of the world.
- The First (but according to Hillel, the 15th) of Shevat for trees (RH 1:1).

Rosh Hashanah may have begun as a harvest festival to celebrate the beginning of the agricultural cycle. (Eventually, this function became associated primarily with Sukkot, which falls two weeks later.) Not until late biblical and rabbinic times did Rosh Hashanah begin to take on the character that it has today—as the Day of Judgment (Yom ha-Din), when the deeds of each person over the past year are weighed, and his or her fate is decided for the coming year (RH 1:2).[3] The verse "From the beginning of the year to the end of the year" (Deut. 11:12) was interpreted to mean that God determines at the beginning of the year what will transpire by its end (RH 8a). Another opinion held that on Rosh Hashanah God decides what each person will earn ("the entire sustenance of man") that year (Betz. 16a). As the *U-netaneh Tokef* (see p. 199) describes, on this day God decides "who shall live and who shall die." Rabbi Keruspedai said in the name of Rabbi Yochanan:

> Three books are opened [in heaven] on Rosh Hashanah: one for the completely wicked [whose bad deeds definitely outweigh their good], one for the completely righteous, and one for the intermediate [average persons]. The completely righteous are immediately inscribed in the Book of Life; the completely wicked are immediately inscribed in the Book of Death; the doom of the intermediate is suspended from Rosh Hashanah to Yom Kippur; if they deserve well, they are inscribed in the Book of Life; if they do not deserve well, they are inscribed in the Book of Death (RH 16b).

Although this basic concept of Rosh Hashanah as the Day of Judgment may at first appear to be totally missing from the Torah, Menachem Leibtag[4] elegantly demonstrated how the ancient agricultural holiday was transformed into it. Unlike Egypt, which enjoys a constant supply of water from the Nile River, the Land of Israel depends on rain for its water supply. Rain in this region falls only during the autumn and winter months, and it primarily determines the fate of the produce for the coming year. If the rainfall is insufficient, there will not be enough water to drink and the crops will not grow. A shortage of rain can lead not only to drought but also to famine and disease throughout the hot and dry months of the spring and summer. Furthermore, a food shortage is likely to lead to an outbreak of war between nations fighting over the limited available resources. Consequently, it may appear to human beings as though nature itself—via the early rainy season—determined "who will live and who will die," who by thirst and who by famine, who by war and who by disease (as in the *U-netaneh Tokef*).

This was clearly an unacceptable conclusion for the Torah, in which a primary theme is that the creation of nature was a willful act of God, who continues to oversee it. Although it may seem to humans that nature works independently, the Torah is adamant that they must recognize that it is God, not nature, who determines their fate. Therefore, in anticipation of the fall and winter rainy season and its effect on the fate of the entire year, the Torah commanded the Israelites to gather together in the seventh month to declare God's kingship over creation.

Of the four holidays in the seventh month (Tishrei), why was Rosh Hashanah selected to be the Day of Judgment? According to Leibtag, the explanation lies in the biblical names for the holiday—Yom Teruah ("day of blowing the horn"; Num. 29:1) and Zichron Teruah ("remembrance of blowing the horn"; Lev. 23:24). In biblical times, the shofar (ram's horn) was used primarily for war. In addition to being a means for military commanders to communicate important signals to their troops, the shofar was used to warn civilians of enemy attack and to mobilize the army. Two basic types of notes were sounded on the shofar—a long steady note (*tekiah*) to signal an "all-clear" situation and an oscillating series of short notes (*teruah*) that warned of imminent danger, like a siren sound today. (Both the *shevarim* and *teruah* used in the modern shofar service are examples of the ancient *teruah*, differing only in their frequency of three or nine notes per beat, respectively.) Therefore, in biblical times, a person hearing the shofar sounding a *teruah* would instinctively prepare for war or impending danger. As Amos (3:6) noted, "When a ram's horn is sounded in a town, do the people not tremble?"

When the Torah instructed the Israelites to make a Yom Teruah on the first day of the seventh month, it clearly did not expect them to go to war. Instead, they were commanded to create an atmosphere on this day that simulated the tension and terror of battle, a sense of imminent crisis and pending calamity. They fearfully realized that the amount of rain that would fall, and thus the fate of the upcoming year, hung in the balance. However, they were also commanded, *Zichron Teruah,* to remember that it is God and not nature who controls their destiny. Unless God remembered them and manipulated the natural forces for their benefit, the coming weeks and months could spell disaster.

Returning to the scenario of the Day of Judgment, Leibtag observes that we must not merely stand in awe that on this day our lives are judged. We must also sound the *teruah* so that God will remember us for life, just as we must remember God by acknowledging our absolute dependency on the divine force that controls all others. Therefore, on this day we proclaim the kingdom of God over all humankind, in recognition of the divine mastery over nature and our destiny.

The Rabbis taught that the world was created on the first day of Tishrei (RH 27a). This is supported by the fact that the letters in the Hebrew word *"b'reishit"* (when God began to create [the heaven and earth]) can be rearranged to spell *alef b'Tishrei* (the First of Tishrei). The theme of praying that God will inscribe us in the Book of Life is featured prominently throughout the Rosh Hashanah liturgy. The other major motifs of Rosh Hashanah—*Malkhuyot* (God's kingship), *Zichronot* (God's remembering us for good), and *Shofarot* (the blasts of the ram's horn) are expressed in the *Musaf Amidah* (see p. 197).

The Torah readings for Rosh Hashanah include the birth of Isaac on the first day (Gen. 21) and the *Akedah*, the binding of Isaac, on the second day (Gen. 22). The *haftarot* describe, respectively, the birth of Samuel (1 Sam. 1:1–2:10) and Jeremiah's vision of the deliverance of the people of Israel from exile (Jer. 31:2–20). By focusing on the themes of birth after long periods of barrenness (Sarah, Hannah), the deliverance of Israel from exile, and the rescue of Isaac from imminent sacrifice, these readings add a positive note to these fateful days. The stress on the birth of children corresponds with Rosh Hashanah being the birthday of the world. The willingness of Abraham to sacrifice his beloved son is a manifestation of his complete trust in the divine will, and we pray that God will consider the merit of our ancestor in deciding to inscribe us in the Book of Life for the coming year.[5]

Hallel (see p. 162) is not recited on Rosh Hashanah. According to a midrash, the angels asked God why on Rosh Hashanah the Jewish people do not sing these songs of praise, which are part of the usual festival service. In response, God replied: "Is it possible that the King should be sitting on the throne of Judgment with the books of life and death open before Him, and Israel should sing hymns of praise?" (RH 32b). An alternative explanation offered by the Hatam Sofer is based on the tradition that on Rosh Hashanah (and Yom Kippur) the souls of deceased parents come down to pray with their children, an idea implied by the phrase, "The books of the living and the dead are open before Him." Since the souls of "the dead cannot praise God" (Ps. 115:17), the living do not sing *Hallel* so as not to embarrass them.

Birkat ha-Hodesh, the public announcement mentioning the name of the upcoming new month and the day(s) on which Rosh Hodesh will be celebrated, is not recited on the Sabbath preceding Rosh Hashanah (First of Tishrei). The traditional explanation is that the blessing is omitted to confuse Satan, the Accuser, so that he will not be able to denounce us before the heavenly court. An allusion to this is found in a verse from Psalms, "Blow the shofar on the new moon, when it is concealed" (81:4),[6] implying that the new moon of Rosh Hashanah should be hidden and thus not mentioned. Similarly, there is no mention of Rosh Hodesh in the prayers for Rosh Hashanah, even though the day is also Rosh Hodesh Tishrei.

Rosh Hashanah never falls on a Wednesday, Friday, or Sunday. If it fell on a Wednesday, Yom Kippur would be on a Friday, and thus Jews would be unable to prepare for the Sabbath. If it fell on a Friday, Yom Kippur would be on a Sunday, and thus Jews who observe the Sabbath would be unable to get ready for Yom Kippur. Finally, if Rosh Hashanah were on a Sunday, Hoshana Rabbah (the last day of Sukkot; 21st of Tishrei) would be on a Saturday. This would preclude performance of the major ritual of the day—beating the willows during the synagogue services (see p. 237)—which would be forbidden on the Sabbath.[7]

Bris Kehunas Olam offers a related explanation of why Yom Kippur cannot fall on Sunday, Tuesday, or Friday. As a day of purity, Yom Kippur can occur only on a day in which all that was created was similarly pure and not on one associated with ritual impurity (*tumah*). Because *tumah* can be contracted by earthenware vessels and water (earth and water were created on Sunday), wooden vessels (trees were created on Tuesday), and those made of the skins or bones of land animals (created on Friday), Yom Kippur cannot fall on these days. Conversely, *tumah* does not apply to the firmament (created on Monday), the heavenly lights (created on Wednesday), or to the Sabbath, the day of rest. On Thursday, God created the birds and the fish; vessels made of their skin, bone, or feathers cannot contract *tumah*.[8]

Customs

On the first night of Rosh Hashanah it is customary to greet friends with *leshanah tovah tikatevu* (may you be inscribed [in the Book of Life] for a good year). The Sephardic version of the greeting adds the phrase "may you be worthy of abundant years." To symbolize the hope for a sweet year, pieces of challah are dipped in honey at the beginning of every meal. Similarly, a slice of apple is dipped in honey and eaten before reciting the prayer: "May it be Your will, O Lord our God and God of our fathers, to renew unto us a good and sweet year" (*she-techadesh aleinu shanah tovah u-metukah*). In Hebrew, the word for "honey" (*devash*) has the same numerical value (406) as "Father of Mercy" (*Av ha-Rachamim*), a divine attribute for which we pray on this day.[9]

The challot baked for Rosh Hashanah are round. This symbolizes both a royal crown, which is consistent with the day's ubiquitous motif of the kingship of God, and the cyclical and eternal nature of life, expressing the hope that the coming year will be complete and unbroken by tragedy. In some communities, the challot are decorated in the form of a ladder. This symbolizes our spiritual striving, like the ladder in Jacob's dream that connected heaven and earth (Gen. 28:10–22), and the recurring theme that on this day the destiny of each person is decreed—whether to ascend the ladder of life and find success in the year to come or to descend and suffer an unfortunate fate. Another popular style for the challot on both Rosh Hashanah and Yom Kippur is a bird shape. Originating in 18th-century Ukraine, the symbolism of the *faigele* (little bird) is "May our sins be carried away by the bird, and may she fly with our prayers for salvation straight up to God." To these persecuted Jews and later to those throughout Eastern Europe, who were the victims of frequent pogroms, the bird also reflected the comforting prophetic promise in which hovering birds become a metaphorical image of a protecting and rescuing God (Isa. 31:5).[10]

Pomegranates are a popular fruit for Rosh Hashanah because they contain numerous seeds, which symbolize the hopes for fertility and the privilege of performing abundant good deeds. The pomegranate is also said to contain 613 seeds, the precise number of commandments in the Torah. Carrots are frequently served because the Yiddish word for them, "*meirin*" (more), indicates our desire for a year filled with blessings. They also are a symbol of prosperity, because when sliced they resemble golden coins. Other foods frequently eaten on Rosh Hashanah are pumpkins, fenugreek, leeks, beets, and dates, because they grow in profusion and are symbols of prosperity (Hor. 12a).[11]

It is also customary to avoid certain foods on Rosh Hashanah—especially nuts (*egoz*), which in Hebrew has a numerical value (17) equivalent to that of "sin" (*het*), if spelled without the final silent *alef*. Moreover, nuts are said to increase phlegm and the flow of saliva, which interfere with the recital of the prayers.[12] Other foods generally not eaten on Rosh Hashanah include sour and bitter foods (pickles, lemons, vinegar, horseradish); black-colored food (black olives, eggplant, chocolate); and fish (*dag*), which in Hebrew is close to *da'ag* (worry). Nevertheless, many Sephardic Jews eat fish heads on this holiday to symbolize their wish to "head" their community in righteousness,[13] hoping that they will be "the head and not the tail."[14] Another custom in some communities is to eat the head of a sheep, as a reminder of the binding of Isaac.[15]

One custom is to refrain from sleeping on the afternoon of Rosh Hashanah, using the time instead to study Torah or recite psalms in synagogue. This is based on a statement in the Jerusalem Talmud: "If one sleeps at the beginning of the year [Rosh Hashanah], his good fortune likewise sleeps."[16]

Shofar (שׁוֹפָר)

On Rosh Hashanah, the Torah explicitly commands the sounding of the shofar, the most recognizable symbol of the day. "In the seventh month, on the first day of the month, you shall observe complete rest, a sacred occasion commemorated with loud blasts" (Lev. 23:24). In fact, the term "Rosh Hashanah" does not appear in the Torah at all. Instead, the holiday is referred to as Yom Teruah (day of blowing). However, the use of the shofar was not limited to this day. The shofar was blown to mark the giving of the Torah at Mount Sinai (Exod.

19:16) and the razing of walls of Jericho during the Israelite conquest of the Promised Land (Josh. 6:20). It was also used to announce the jubilee year (Lev. 25:9).

After the biblical period, the shofar no longer was used in Jewish priestly, military, and civil ceremonies. However, the shofar was blown on fast days, to announce a death, and at funerals; a special black shofar was sometimes used to announce an excommunication from the Jewish community (see p. 105).[17]

According to the Talmud, six blasts of the shofar were blown on Friday afternoon (Shab. 35b). At the first sounding, the laborers in the fields ceased their work. At the second, shops were closed and city laborers stopped working. The third signaled that it was time to kindle the Sabbath lights. The final three blasts of the shofar formally ushered in the Sabbath. In modern Israel, the shofar has been used to mark solemn occasions, inaugurate new presidents, and celebrate the liberation of the Western Wall in Jerusalem in 1967.[18]

Since biblical times, the shofar has been associated with messianic redemption. According to the Midrash, the left horn of the ram that Abraham sacrificed instead of Isaac was sounded on Mount Sinai, while the right will be blown "in a time to come at the assembling of the dispersed" (PdRE 31). Isaiah (27:13) prophesied: "And in that day a great ram's horn shall be sounded; and they who were lost in the land of Assyria and they who were dispersed in the land of Egypt, shall come and worship the Lord on the holy mountain in Jerusalem." In addition to the traditional belief that the shofar will announce the resurrection of the dead, according to a medieval legend Elijah will blow the shofar three days before the arrival of the Messiah.[19]

Description

According to the Talmud, the ritual commandment to hear the sound of the shofar on Rosh Hashanah can be fulfilled using a shofar made from an antelope, gazelle, goat, mountain goat, or ram (RH 27a). All of these are kosher animals that have horns with removable cartilage. This second feature is important because a shofar must be hollow, since it is derived from the word "*shefoferet*" meaning "tube." The Talmud explicitly forbids using a cow's horn because it is known as a "*keren,*" not a "shofar," adding that it is forbidden because our advocate on

Rosh Hashanah should not be a reminder of the Golden Calf, our great sin and accuser. We do not want our past transgressions to bias God against forgiving our current sins ("the accuser may not act as defender"; RH 26a). The Rabbis strongly recommended the use of a ram's horn as a shofar because of its association with the story of the *Akedah* (see p. 194) (RH 16a). A ram's horn is also desirable because it is curved, which is symbolic of our bowing in submission to God's will (RH 26b). The shofar may not be painted but may be covered with gold, as long as its tone is unchanged and the mouthpiece stays natural. It is permitted to pour water, wine, or vinegar into the ram's horn on Rosh Hashanah to make a clear sound, because this is not considered to be "repairing," which is forbidden on a festival.[20]

Sounds

The Torah refers to two different sounds of the shofar—*tekiah* and *teruah* (Num. 10:5–8). The Mishnah describes the *tekiah* as a long blast and the *teruah* as "three *yevavot*," a wavering crying blast (RH 4:9). It prescribes three sets of shofar sounds because the word "*teruah*" is mentioned three times in the Torah (Lev. 23:24, 25:9; Num. 29:1). During the talmudic period, doubt arose as to the exact nature of the *teruah*. The talmudic sages disagreed as to whether the *teruah* should be a wailing, moaning, undulating sound (*shevarim*) of three broken notes or a series of quick sobs (*teruah*) in at least nine staccato notes. Since a crying person may make both of these sounds, it was unclear what God wanted. The final decision was to use all three possible combinations—the first set of sounds should include both *shevarim* and *teruah*, whereas the other two sets should contain only one or the other.

One of the biblical verses relating to the commandment of blowing the shofar uses the phrases *u-tekatem teruah* (you should blow a *teruah*) and *teruah yitk'u* (and the *teruah* will be blown) (Num. 10:6). From the two placements of the word "blow" (varying forms of the Hebrew word "*tekiah*") in relation to the word "*teruah*," the Rabbis deduced that there should be a long *tekiah* sound both before and after the *teruah*. They even noted that before and after each "crying sound" a person needs to have a calm sound to regain his or her confidence. Thus evolved the pattern of blowing the shofar that persists today:

Tekiah, shevarim teruah, tekiah
Tekiah, shevarim, tekiah
Tekiah, teruah, tekiah

A long concluding note, *tekiah gedolah* (great blast), ends the two sets of shofar blasts in the service (see below).

On the High Holy Days

To herald the season of repentance, the shofar is blown from the second day of Elul (except on the Sabbath) (see p. 184). On Rosh Hashanah, the Torah prescribes the commandment of "hearing" the sound of the shofar, but does not say when or how this ritual act is to be performed. The Rabbis originally decreed that the shofar be blown during the main service of Rosh Hashanah, which in their day was the morning service. Later, this practice was changed, so that the sounding of the shofar and the reading of the biblical verses connected to it were postponed until much later in the day during the *Musaf* (additional) service. An explanation for this delay is that on one occasion the Romans, assuming that the early morning shofar blast was a signal for an uprising against them, attacked the Jews and killed them. Although the historical accuracy of the claim is in doubt, it is indisputable that the shofar, like the trumpet of the Romans, was an instrument used to signal battle as in the story of Joshua and the walls of Jericho. Consequently, the decision was made to sound the shofar later in the day to prevent any misunderstanding, for at that time it could be construed only as part of a religious ritual.[21]

Moving the shofar service from the morning service to the *Musaf* presented the problem that the main mitzvah of the day was not performed until a relatively late hour. To solve this difficulty, the Rabbis added an additional blowing of the shofar at the conclusion of the Torah service (without any recitation of biblical verses).[22]

The Rabbis decided that there should be 100 shofar blasts, equal to the number of sobs of Sisera's mother or the number of letters in her lament for her son as recounted in the Song of Deborah (Judg. 5:28). This was designed to show that, just as Jews were sensitive to the tears of the mother of an archenemy, so we hope God will be sensitive to our tears and judge us mercifully on the High Holy Days. Today, 30 sounds are blown after the Torah reading and 30 during the reader's repetition of the *Musaf Amidah* (see below)—10 at the conclusion of each of its three major sections (*Malkhuyot, Zichronot, Shofarot*). Another 30 sounds of the shofar are blown either during the silent *Musaf Amidah* (Sephardic tradition) or during the full *Kaddish* at the end of the *Musaf* service (Ashkenazic ritual). Sephardim sound the final 10 blasts during the *titkabeil* portion of the full *Kaddish* at the end of the *Musaf* service; Ashkenazim do so after the *Mourner's Kaddish*. Both the morning and *Musaf* sets of shofar blasts end with a *tekiah gedolah* (great blast).[23]

The shofar may be sounded only in the daytime. According to *halakhah*, women and children are exempt from the commandment to listen to the sound of the shofar. However, its placement in the Rosh Hashanah ritual is such that nearly all do hear it. Whether the shofar should be blown if Rosh Hashanah fell on the Sabbath was a vexing question. When this occurred, the shofar was blown in the Temple but not in the countryside. After the Temple was destroyed, there was a difference of opinion among the major Rabbis. Fearing that an inexperienced blower might go for help to a more experienced person, thus violating the law of carrying on the Sabbath, they eventually concluded that the shofar should not be blown on the Sabbath (the current practice). This decision was based on the two descriptions of Rosh Hashanah in the Bible: Yom Teruah (Day of Blowing; Num. 29:1) and Yom Zichron Teruah (Day of Remembering of the Blowing; Lev. 23:24). The former was deemed to mean any day but the Sabbath, when the shofar would *actually* be blown, whereas the latter was considered as referring to the Sabbath, when all we do is *remember* the sound of the shofar and not blow it.

At the conclusion of the *Ne'ilah* service on Yom Kippur, a *tekiah gedolah* is also blown on the shofar (see p. 221).

Reasons for Sounding

Multiple reasons have been put forth to explain why the shofar is blown on Rosh Hashanah. The most common is its connection to the *Akedah*, the binding of Isaac (Gen. 22), which is read in the synagogue on the second day of this festival. In the biblical tale, when the angel prevented Abraham from killing Isaac, God commanded Abraham to sacrifice a ram instead of his son. According to this view, the ram's horn is blown to remind God of the merits earned by our ancestors Abraham and Isaac—who were willing to unquestionably obey the divine command—with the hope that this will tip the scales of judgment in our favor. This was a popular concept among the Rabbis, who desperately tried to suppress the dominant belief in the Second Temple period that Isaac was actually killed by Abraham (who did not heed the angel's final warning to spare his son). This meant that somehow Isaac had to have been restored to life, a concept that was totally unacceptable because it was perilously close to the Christian idea of the resurrection. Interestingly, the idea of Isaac having been killed and later revived is especially seen in Yemenite midrashim, presumably because these Jews had no contact with Christians and thus no need to suppress the story.

The original reason for blowing the shofar may have been related to the pagan custom of making loud noises at the beginning of each new year to chase away demons—frightening away the evil spirits so that the forces of good would triumph and the upcoming year would be a happy one. According to the Talmud, the sound of the shofar can "confuse the avenger" and prevent Satan from testifying against Israel on these holy days (RH 16b). In line with this tradition, later-day mystics added several verses from Psalms to be read before the blowing of the shofar. One of these, *Min ha-meitzar* ("Out of the depths"; Ps. 130:1) forms an acrostic that reads *kera satan* (destroy Satan).[24]

Blowing the shofar announces the coronation of God as King, an important theme of Rosh Hashanah. It also emphasizes two other major motifs of the holiday—remembering God as the Creator of the world (after the blowing of the shofar, a prayer is recited that begins "Today the world was born") and the Revelation at Mount Sinai, where the ram's horn was sounded.

In the 10th century, Saadiah Gaon offered 10 reasons for sounding the shofar. In addition to ones already mentioned, he suggested the following:[25]

- To announce the beginning of the period of repentance and to warn people against transgressing.
- To remind us of the warnings of the prophets, who raised their voices like the shofar to touch our consciences.

- To remind us of the alarms of battle that accompanied the destruction of the Temple.
- To cause us to be in awe and do the will of God, for as Amos (3:6) asked, "When a ram's horn is sounded in a town, do the people not tremble?"
- To remind us of the great Day of Judgment, when the horn will be sounded as a summons to the heavenly court (Zeph. 1:16).
- To remind us that the shofar will herald the ingathering of Israel's scattered remnants to return to the Holy Land in the Messianic Age (Isa. 27:13).
- To remind us of the revival of the dead.

Maimonides stated that the act of blowing the shofar is the equivalent of an alarm clock, rousing us from our spiritual slumber with a call to examine our deeds, return in repentance, and remember God our Creator.[26] Others have suggested that it is a wake-up call to God and His mercy toward us. Later interpretations in the Hasidic tradition include considering the shofar as a "prayer without words," the highest form of prayer, and the concept that within each of us is a little shofar that needs to be blown (especially the broken-noted *shevarim*) to penetrate deeply into our hearts and lead to serious repentance.

Avinu Malkeinu (אָבִינוּ מַלְכֵּנוּ)

Avinu Malkeinu (Our Father, our King) is a penitential prayer that originated on fast days as a plea for rain. The Talmud ascribes the origin of this prayer to Rabbi Akiva (Taan. 25b). During a severe drought, he exclaimed before the ark, "Our Father, our King, have mercy upon us for Your own sake!" whereupon the rain fell. *Avinu Malkeinu* is included in an expanded version after the repetition of the *Amidah* in the morning and afternoon services during the Ten Days of Repentance from Rosh Hashanah through Yom Kippur. In the Ashkenazic ritual, *Avinu Malkeinu* is not recited on the Sabbath, both because penitential prayers are not said on that day and because its original association with fast days made it unsuitable for the Sabbath, which is dedicated to pleasant and joyful experiences. According to the Sephardic tradition, however, the seriousness of the Ten Days of Repentance, when a person's fate lies in the balance, justifies the recitation of *Avinu Malkeinu* on the Sabbath. Similarly, if Yom Kippur falls on a Sabbath,

Avinu Malkeinu is recited in Ashkenazic synagogues during the *Ne'ilah* service at the close of the day, when a final judgment is imminent and so a last plea is permitted.[27]

On the two days of Rosh Hashanah and the next seven days, *Avinu Malkeinu* contains five petitions asking God to "inscribe us" in the book of a good life, of redemption and salvation, of sustenance and prosperity, of merit, and of forgiveness and pardon. During the *Ne'ilah* service on Yom Kippur, this phrase is replaced by "seal us," and on fast days the words "remember us" are used.

The divine blessings and forgiveness for which *Avinu Malkeinu* pleads are not requested based on our personal accomplishments but instead on behalf of the merits of the martyrs of Israel ("act for the sake of those who went through fire and water for the sanctification of Your Name"), as well as a direct appeal to God's own continual compassion ("act for the sake of Your abundant mercies ... for we have no good works of our own").[28]

Traditionally, the congregation rises before the open ark and recites *Avinu Malkeinu* in a whisper, except for nine of the middle verses (15–23), which are chanted responsively. In some synagogues, however, all the verses are recited by the reader and then repeated in unison by the worshipers. A popular practice is to sing the final verse to a traditional melody.

The phrase "*Avinu Malkeinu*" is a combination of two apparently contradictory conceptions of God—the tender and forgiving parent and the strict and severe sovereign. The Rabbis, however, had no difficulty with this apparent dichotomy, seeing God concurrently in both relationships toward humankind. They maintained that one can acknowledge divine kingship yet at the same time appeal to God for love, understanding, and forgiveness.[29]

Musaf Amidah (מוּסָף לְרֹאשׁ הַשָּׁנָה)

On the Sabbath and the major festivals, the central benediction of the *Amidah* for the *Musaf* service describes the special temple offering of the day and contains a prayer for the restoration of the Temple and its ritual. The only exception is the *Musaf Amidah* on Rosh Hashanah, which contains three long intermediate benedictions that deal with the kingship of God over the entire universe (*Malkhuyot*), God's remembrance of Israel (*Zichronot*), and the sounding of the shofar (*Shofarot*).

These three basic themes correspond to the three names by which Rosh Hashanah is traditionally known—Yom ha-Din (Day of Judgment), Yom ha-Zikaron (Day of Remembrance), and Yom Teruah (Day of Sounding the Shofar). Each of these themes is also related to the divine role in messianic days, when God will be sovereign over the whole world and will remember Israel and redeem the people from their exile, and when the great shofar will be sounded to announce the coming of the Messiah.[30]

In ancient times, the basic elements of these three sections existed as

HINENI (הִנְנִי)

Hineni (Here I stand, [devoid of deeds]) is a special prayer recited by the *hazzan* before the *Musaf Amidah* on Rosh Hashanah. This Hebrew word, also translated as "here I am," was the simple answer given by Abraham in the story of the *Akedah* when summoned by God to sacrifice his son (Gen. 22:1), when asked by Isaac where was the lamb for the offering (Gen. 22:7), and when commanded by the angel not to slay his son (Gen. 22:11). Of unknown authorship, the prayer originated in Europe during the Middle Ages. In simple words but chanted with a stirring melody, the *hazzan* expresses feelings of fear and inadequacy because of his (or her) sins and imperfections. The *hazzan* prays that, despite his (or her) own shortcomings in conduct, voice, memory, and devotion, he (or she) will be worthy to serve as the representative of the congregation to bring its supplications before God.

In some communities, the *hazzan* begins chanting *Hineni* from the back of the synagogue and gradually comes forward to the front of the congregation. In addition to admitting his (or her) humility and hesitance to assume the awesome role of leading the people in the *Musaf* service, this gesture indicates that he (or she) has no special importance as an individual but is merely serving as the representative of all the worshipers. Some *hazzanim* have dramatized the effect by having a person in the congregation ask, "Where is the *hazzan*?"—to which the *hazzan* then would reply from the back, "*Hineni*" (here I am!).[1]

an independent prayer connected to the sounding of the shofar, the main ritual of Rosh Hashanah and the only one biblically required for this day. During the Second Temple period, the sounding of the shofar was introduced by a series of biblical verses that described the reasons for this practice. The Mishnah required that one recite "not less than 10 kingship, 10 remembrance, and 10 shofar verses," none of which "signify punishment" (RH 4:6). Even after the *Malkhuyot*, *Zichronot*, and *Shofarot* sections became part of the *Musaf Amidah*, the person blowing the shofar could select which verses to recite; eventually, the Rabbis selected specific ones and prescribed them as part of the service.[31] For the first two sections, there are three selections from the Torah, three from the Writings, and three from the Prophets, with a concluding Torah verse. In the *Shofarot* section, an extra verse from Psalms replaces the final Torah selection.

U-netaneh Tokef (וּנְתַנֶּה תֹּקֶף)

U-netaneh Tokef (We shall ascribe holiness [to this day]) is a beloved *piyyut* (hymn) recited before the *Kedushah* of the *Musaf Amidah* on Rosh Hashanah and Yom Kippur. It epitomizes the significance of the High Holy Days by describing the Day of Judgment on which all creatures pass before God, one by one, like a flock before the shepherd who decrees their fate.

According to tradition, *U-netaneh Tokef* was composed by Rabbi Amnon in the 11th century. It is said that, on many occasions, the bishop of Mainz had pressured Rabbi Amnon, his friend and adviser, to abandon his faith and convert to Christianity. Once, in a weak moment, Rabbi Amnon asked for three days to think it over but spent the time fasting and praying for forgiveness for even suggesting that he would consider such a breach of faith. When the rabbi did not return at the appointed time, the bishop summoned him to his court and demanded an answer. Rabbi Amnon replied that his tongue should be cut out for the sin of saying he would even consider conversion. Replying that the fault was the rabbi's legs for not coming as promised, the enraged bishop ordered that Rabbi Amnon's feet be chopped off. As each joint was amputated, the bishop offered to stop the dismemberment if the rabbi would convert. When Rabbi Amnon steadfastly refused, his hands were also cut off, and he returned home a mutilated cripple. A few days later, the dying rabbi was carried to the synagogue for Rosh

Hashanah services. Rabbi Amnon asked permission to recite a personal prayer before the congregation, and as he uttered the final words of the *U-netaneh Tokef*, he died. Three days later, Rabbi Amnon appeared in a dream to Kalonymous ben Meshullam (a German mystic and author of *piyyutim*) and taught him the prayer, which soon became a standard part of the liturgy. The story of the martyrdom of Rabbi Amnon, which reflected the historical experiences of German Jewry, has added to the powerful appeal of the *U-netaneh Tokef*.[32]

U-netaneh Tokef emphasizes the precarious nature of humanity and details the many possible fates that may befall us. It stresses that God alone determines the destiny of both entire populations ("how many will pass away and how many will be born") and individuals ("who will live and who will die"). For those who are condemned to die, the precise method is decided by divine decree ("who by fire and who by water"); similarly, for those who are to live, God determines "who will be serene and who will be disturbed ... who will be impoverished and who will be enriched, who will be humbled and who will be exalted." *U-netaneh Tokef* unequivocally asserts that the divine judgment is based on an assessment of each individual's actions, whether he or she warrants being inscribed in the Book of Life or the Book of Death. Even the cause of a death, whether it appears natural, accidental, or violent, is decided by God on Rosh Hashanah.[33]

This litany of deterministic fates is, however, followed by the stirringly optimistic phrase—"but repentance (*teshuvah*), prayer (*tefillah*), and charity (*tzedakah*) avert the severity of the decree" (RH 16b). This mirrors the talmudic teachings: "Everything is in the hands of God, except the fear of God" (all the qualities of individual human beings are fixed by nature, but their moral characters depend on their own choices) (Ber. 33b), and "Everything is foreseen, yet freedom of choice is given" (Avot 3:15).[34] In almost all Orthodox *machzorim*, above these three Hebrew words (in smaller type) are, respectively, the words "*tzom*" (fast), "*kol*" (voice), and "*mamon*" (money)—indicating that sincere repentance includes fasting, prayers recited in a loud voice, and contributions to charity.[35]

The optimism of the author, however, is not based on any idealistic view of the lofty nature of human beings. Rather, people are described as mere flesh and blood, who "came from dust and who shall return to dust" and whose days are "as a fleeting shadow, as a passing cloud ...

and as a dream that vanishes." Nevertheless, human beings are in the hand of a merciful God, who recognizes the faults of His creatures, is slow to anger, and waits patiently for them to return from their evil ways. Contrasting the ephemeral nature of mere mortals, the *piyyut* ends with exultant praise of the Divine: "But You are king, the living and eternal God."[36]

Malkhuyot

The *Malkhuyot* section deals with God's universal sovereignty and stresses the optimistic view that God will ultimately establish divine kingship over the entire world. It opens with *Aleinu* (see p. 466), which eloquently expresses the hope that all humanity will eventually realize the oneness and kingship of God. During the rest of the year, the prayer leader and congregants slightly bend their knees and hips and bow their heads when saying, "We bend the knee, bow in worship, and give thanks." However, when recited aloud during the *Musaf Amidah* on Rosh Hashanah (and Yom Kippur), the *Aleinu* is traditionally accompanied by complete prostration, in which one falls to the hands and knees and touches the head to the floor to physically demonstrate complete homage to God.[37] In most congregations, only the *hazzan* and the rabbi prostrate themselves.

The three Torah verses depict God as the loving king of the Jewish people, whose coronation was commemorated when the Jewish people accepted the Torah at Mount Sinai (Exod. 15:18; Num. 23:21; Deut. 33:5). The three selections from the Psalms (22:29, 93:1, 24:7–10) recall God as the ruler over all nations, the sovereign of Creation and the natural world, and the "Lord of hosts, He is the king of glory." The three prophetic verses stress the unity of the One God, who will redeem the Jewish people and ultimately be acknowledged by all the nations as "King over all the earth" (Isa. 44:6; Obad. 1:21; Zech. 14:9). The final scriptural verse is the *Shema* (Deut. 6:4), the quintessential statement of Jewish faith and an assertion of the kingship of God.[38]

Zichronot

The *Zichronot* section deals with God's role in remembering the deeds of nations and individuals, determining their destinies in justice and mercy by punishing the wicked and rewarding the good. It affirms that God will eventually remember the covenant and redeem Israel from exile and suffering.[39] The poetic prologue to this section by the *amora* Rav, the third-century head of the Babylonian academy at Sura, is based on the rabbinic concept that the First of Tishrei (Rosh Hashanah) was the day when Creation was completed and God judged Adam—and, by extension, all humankind.[40]

The three Torah verses refer to God's remembering "Noah and every living thing" when about to destroy the wicked and corrupt world by the Flood (Gen. 8:1), the covenant with the Patriarchs when hearing the groaning of the Children of Israel in their abject slavery in Egypt (Exod. 2:24), and the patriarchal covenant at some future time when the Jewish people will suffer the disasters enumerated for failure to observe the divine commandments (Lev. 26:42). The verses from Psalms (111:4–5, 106:45) also stress that God will forgive and provide for the people because of remembering the eternal covenantal relationship between them. The first prophetic verse is an appeal to the people to repent, with confident assurance that God will remember the love of the new Jewish nation when they accepted the divine covenant in the wilderness (Jer. 2:2). The other two verses allude to or directly refer to Ephraim, one of the 10 lost tribes that became a symbol of the Jewish people at the time of the Babylonian exile (Ezek. 16:60; Jer. 31:20). Despite their transgressions, God's "heart yearns for him" and "will receive him back in love." The final verse in the *Zichronot* section again refers to a future time of catastrophe, when God will recall the covenant with the ancestors of the people whom God once redeemed from slavery in Egypt (Lev. 26:45).[41]

Shofarot

The *Shofarot* section recounts some of the symbolic meanings of the shofar (see above). The three Torah verses describe the awesome experience of the Revelation at Mount Sinai, which culminated with the mighty sound of the shofar (Exod. 19:16,19; 20:15). The four selections from Psalms (47:6, 98:6, 81:4–5, 150) depict the joyous sounding of the shofar in praise of God. The prophetic verses speak of the future sounding of the great shofar, which will signal the ingathering of the Jewish people and usher in the Messianic Age (Isa. 18:3, 27:13; Zech. 9:14–15).

Except on the Sabbath, 10 blasts of the shofar are sounded at the end of each of these three sections, followed by a short prayer that describes Rosh Hashanah as *ha-yom harat olam* (today is the birthday of the world) and an entreaty that God "accept with mercy and favor" our recital of the prescribed verses.

Tashlikh (תַּשְׁלִיךְ)

Tashlikh (you will cast) is the ceremony on the afternoon of the first day of Rosh Hashanah in which Jews recite special penitential prayers and psalms and throw crumbs or small pieces of bread into a body of water (river, lake, or ocean) to symbolically cast away their sins. It is postponed to the second day of Rosh Hashanah if the first day falls on the Sabbath, because of the proscription against carrying on that day. The name derives from the verse in Micah (7:19), "You will cast (*v'tashlikh*) all their sins into the depths of the sea."

Tashlikh was not a ritual devised by the Rabbis but rather a popular practice among Ashkenazic communities that began during the medieval period and was reluctantly accepted by rabbinic authorities after they had fought against it as a superstitious custom of pagan origin designed to propitiate the spirits of the rivers on critical days of the year.[42] The Rabbis feared that Jews would consider this ceremony sufficient to absolve them of their sins, rather than appreciating the need to change their conduct and return to God's path. Although the custom is not mentioned by talmudic or gaonic authorities, it may have originated in antiquity based on the Roman practice of throwing objects representing human wealth (including stalks of grain) into the flood waters as an offering to the gods, who might otherwise resent humans taking food from the earth that belonged to them.[43]

Various explanations have been suggested for the *Tashlikh* ritual. According to *Sefer Maharil*, the earliest extant work that mentions *Tashlikh*, the ceremony is meant to recall a legend associated with the binding of Isaac. As Abraham was on his way to the mountain where he was to sacrifice Isaac, Satan made several unsuccessful attempts to dissuade the Patriarch from his mission. Finally, Satan turned himself into an impassable river, but Abraham and Isaac promptly threw themselves into it. God saw this as a sign of Abraham's dedication and caused the water to retreat. Thus the water of *Tashlikh* alludes to the river that Abraham and Isaac confronted in their service of God.

Another possibility is that the water of *Tashlikh* is a reminder of Creation (when the world was covered with water) and its purpose (Torah and the commandments). It may also symbolize the kingship of God, because in ancient Israel, the coronation of kings took place near a fountain or a body of water.

According to tradition, the body of water into which Jews symbolically cast their sins should preferably have fish within it. Fish were the first witnesses of the work of Creation, which began on Rosh Hashanah. Because fish never close their eyes, the ceremony may reflect that the ever-vigilant eyes of God see all our sins. According to Ecclesiastes (9:12), "And a man cannot even know his time. As fishes are enmeshed in a fatal net, and as birds are trapped in a snare, so men are caught at the time of calamity, when it comes upon them without warning." Fish also cannot speak and thus are unable to gossip about one's sins to others. In any event, the folk custom of *Tashlikh* effectively encompasses the essential ideas of Rosh Hashanah—praying for divine compassion and protection, self-purification, and casting off our sins.[44]

Special versions of *Tashlikh* have developed in some Jewish communities. Kurdish Jews symbolically cleansed themselves of sin by jumping into the water and swimming like fish. In Galicia, Hasidim lit small straw rafts in the water, ecstatically watching as their sins were burned up or washed away. In Jerusalem, where even small streams of water are few, *Tashlikh* is performed at a well.[45]

Ten Days of Repentance (עֲשֶׂרֶת יְמֵי תְשׁוּבָה)

The Ten Days of Repentance (*Aseret Y'mei Teshuvah*) is the inclusive period from Rosh Hashanah through Yom Kippur. According to tradition, Rosh Hashanah is the day on which God decides the fate of every individual for the upcoming year. However, since the final judgment is not "sealed" until Yom Kippur, the Ten Days of Repentance (lit., "turning" or "return") provide a time for intensive soul searching and reconciliation with God. The Rabbis recognized the difficulty of making a spiritual return when a person is burdened with unresolved guilt and resentment. Therefore, it is customary to ask forgiveness from other people whom one may have inadvertently (or even deliberately) insulted or injured during the past year, since the atonement of sins on Yom Kippur applies only to those between human beings and God.

Directly confronting the other person is necessary to achieve forgiveness or reconciliation with a fellow human being. In addition to the often painful task of directly confronting others to seek forgiveness, each person in turn must be willing to graciously grant forgiveness when requested by others.[1]

The Ten Days of Repentance offer a last chance, through one's actions, to influence God to reconsider an unfavorable decision (RH 16b)—for, as is written in *U-netaneh Tokef* (see p. 199), "repentance, prayer, and charity avert the severity of the decree." Therefore, the holiday greeting until Yom Kippur, "*le-shanah tovah tikatevu* (may you be *inscribed* [in the Book of Life] for a good year)," is changed on Yom Kippur to "*g'mar chatimah tovah* (may you be *sealed* [in the Book of Life] for good," or "may the completion of your inscription be a good one)."

Jews traditionally visit the cemetery during the Ten Days of Repentance, effectively asking the departed to intercede on their behalf in an attempt to influence God to respond favorably to their pleas for a good and healthy year.[2] Changes in the liturgy during this period include the following:

- The insertion of pleas to be inscribed in the Book of Life in the *Amidah* before the closing formulas of the first, second, and last two benedictions.
- A change from "Holy God" to "Holy King" in the eighth benediction.
- The daily recitation of *Avinu Malkeinu* (except on the Sabbath) in the morning and afternoon prayers in public worship with a minyan (see p. 196).
- The daily recitation of the special penitential prayers (*Selichot*) before the morning service.

The intermediate Sabbath between Rosh Hashanah and Yom Kippur is called Shabbat Shuvah (Sabbath of Return; see p. 152), based on the concept of *teshuvah* (repentance) that dominates this period and on the opening words of the haftarah: "Return, O Israel, unto the Lord your God" (Hos. 14:2). A long sermon on the theme of repentance is traditional on this day. Indeed, rabbis in Europe used to deliver sermons only twice a year—on Shabbat Shuvah and on Shabbat ha-Gadol before Passover.

Yom Kippur (יוֹם כִּפּוּר)

Yom Kippur (Day of Atonement), the fast day on the 10th of Tishrei, is devoted to individual and communal repentance (*teshuvah*; lit., "returning"). It is the climax of the 40-day period of self-examination that begins with a month of spiritual preparation during Elul (see p. 182) and intensifies on Rosh Hashanah and the remainder of the Ten Days of Repentance.

The Torah (Lev. 16:31) describes Yom Kippur as a *Shabbat shabbaton* (Sabbath of solemn rest), on which all manner of work is forbidden. Jews are commanded to practice self-denial (literally, "afflict your souls, Lev. 16:29), "for on this day atonement shall be made for you to cleanse you of all your sins; you shall be clean before the Lord" (Lev. 16:30). According to the sages, the duty of afflicting the soul requires the prohibition of (1) eating and drinking, (2) bathing for pleasure, (3) anointing of the body with oil, (4) wearing leather shoes, and (5) engaging in sexual relations (Yoma 8:1). Yom Kippur is characterized by a 25-hour fast—unlike most fast days, other than Tisha b'Av, which last only from dawn to dusk. However, a sick person whose health would be jeopardized by fasting is obligated to eat, according the principle of *pikuach nefesh* (saving of life; see p. 135). Even a healthy person seized by a fit of "ravenous hunger" that causes faintness must be fed on Yom Kippur with whatever food is available until he recovers. According to tradition, children under the age of nine and women in childbirth (from the time labor begins until three days after birth) are forbidden to fast even if they want to.[1]

As a general rule, the decision whether to fast on Yom Kippur depends on the subjective opinion of the patient who claims the need to eat, even if contradicted by 100 doctors. Conversely, a patient must eat if a doctor declares that it is essential for health, even if he or she thinks it is not necessary.[2]

The other prohibitions on Yom Kippur are less stringent. Although it is forbidden to wash for pleasure, one is permitted to do so for hygienic purposes such as washing the hands after going to the bathroom or cleaning the feet if they become splattered with mud. Similarly, a person may wear leather shoes for health reasons or if required to traverse muddy terrain. According to an ancient rabbinic ruling, a bride is allowed to wash within the first month after her marriage (Yoma 73b).[3]

The author of *Agra DePirka* maintains that the purpose of shoes is to separate a person's flesh from the ground, since the earth was cursed because of the sins of Adam and Eve in the Garden of Eden. Conversely, shoes are removed when walking on holy ground, as when Moses beheld the Burning Bush and was commanded by God to "remove your sandals from your feet, for the place on which you stand is holy ground" (Exod. 3:5). On Yom Kippur, the entire earth is sanctified by the holiness of the day, so one really should not wear shoes at all.[4] Indeed, the *Kohanim* were barefoot when officiating in the Sanctuary, and even today they remove their shoes before pronouncing the Priestly Blessing (see p. 432).

According to various commentators, the five "afflictions" may correspond to the five services of the Day of Atonement; the five immersions of the *Kohen Gadol* relating to the divine service for that day; the five books of the Torah, which Jews must accept without any intervening "curtain of physical pleasures"; the five senses with which human beings can perform mitzvot or transgressions; or the five times the word "*nefesh*" (soul) is mentioned during the Torah reading for Yom Kippur.[5]

In Temple times, Yom Kippur was a day of elaborate rituals to effect the atonement of the people. On this one day of the year, the *Kohen Gadol* would enter the Holy of Holies and pronounce the four-letter Name of God (YHVH; see p. 626) before the masses, who had assembled in the Temple courtyard. The sins of Israel were symbolically transferred to the scapegoat in the rite of *Azazel* (see p. 224). After the destruction of the Temple, the focus of the day shifted to the synagogue, where Jews spend almost the entire day in prayer seeking atonement. By abstaining from basic worldly needs, human beings demonstrate that they can conquer all physical cravings and overcome the bodily appetites that are the principal sources of sin.

However, fasting is not sufficient in itself to secure atonement. To gain divine forgiveness, there must be sincere repentance combining contrite confession and a solemn resolve to abandon the ways of evil (see p. 173). Yet even this secures atonement only for transgressions between human beings and God (*bein adam la-Makom*). As the Talmud notes, for transgressions between one person and another (*bein adam la-chavero*), Yom Kippur does not secure atonement unless one has sought forgiveness from the other person and redressed any wrongs (Yoma

85b). This is the source of the custom in many communities, immediately preceding the recitation of *Kol Nidrei*, of worshipers walking around the synagogue and asking forgiveness from one another for offenses committed during the past year. The sages taught that the fate of every person, which has been left pending from Rosh Hashanah, is finally determined on Yom Kippur. Thus a Jew feels that his or her entire existence hangs in the balance. Relatives and friends greet each other with the phrase "*g'mar chatimah tovah*" (may the completion of inscription be a good one).

Synagogue Services

The synagogue ritual of Yom Kippur is structured around its five services, one more than is usual for a Sabbath or festival:

- *Kol Nidrei*, the evening service (see p. 210).
- *Shacharit*, the morning service.
- *Musaf*, the additional service that includes the martyrology—remembering those who have given their lives for *kiddush ha-Shem* (sanctification of God's name) and whose memory we invoke to ensure God's blessing—and the *Avodah*, a description of the temple ritual for the day (see p. 218).
- *Mincha*, the afternoon service.
- *Ne'ilah*, the concluding service (see p. 220).

The *Yizkor* memorial prayer for the dead, which originally was said only on Yom Kippur but later was included in all the major festivals (see p. 101), is usually recited after the morning Torah and haftarah readings, though some congregations have moved it to later in the afternoon. Although traditionally a tallit is not worn for the evening service, on Yom Kippur it is put on before *Kol Nidrei*—before sundown, while it is still light enough to see the tzitzit (fringes)—and worn for all the services of the day. (If the tallit is not put on until after sunset, no blessing is said.) During the recital of the *Shema*, the words "*baruch shem k'vod malkhuto l'olam va-ed*" (praised is the name of His glorious kingdom for all eternity) are said aloud, not quietly as is the usual practice (see p. 414), in remembrance of the response of the people as they prostrated themselves when the *Kohen Gadol* uttered the holy name of

God (YHVH; the Tetragrammaton), which was spoken only on Yom Kippur after each of his three confessions (see p. 220).

A hallmark of the Yom Kippur liturgy is the confessionals (see p. 213), which are recited once in the afternoon prayer on the eve of the Day of Atonement and 10 times during the day itself.

During the morning service of Yom Kippur, six people are called to the reading of the Torah, which deals with the ancient Temple ritual of the Day of Atonement (Lev. 16). This is the only time there are six *aliyot*, which is one more than other festivals but one less than on the Sabbath; when Yom Kippur falls on the Sabbath, seven *aliyot* are called. The haftarah (Isa. 57:14–58:16) denounces those who fast out of rote ritual and fail to make a sincere commitment to alter their behavior, stressing that what God really desires is acts of justice and mercy to the poor and destitute. For the afternoon of Yom Kippur, the traditional Torah reading (with three *aliyot*) is Leviticus 18, which deals with forbidden sexual relations. This reflects the talmudic description that, in Temple times, Yom Kippur afternoon was one of the most joyful times of the year (Taan. 4:8). When the Temple ritual ended in the early afternoon, the solemn mood of the Day of Atonement evaporated and the people began to celebrate the assumed divine forgiveness. Young women would dress in white and go out into the fields to dance, and the young men would come and choose their brides. Thus the Torah reading was chosen to remind the people of their moral responsibility, so that they would not be too carried away during this period of dancing and courtship.

As an alternative reading for Yom Kippur afternoon, some congregations have selected the Holiness Code (Lev. 19:1–18), which demands proper behavior, social justice, and loving your neighbor. The haftarah for the afternoon of Yom Kippur is the entire Book of Jonah (and Micah 7:18–20). This describes how all the inhabitants of the pagan city of Nineveh successfully repented from their evil ways—indicating the universality of God's compassion and fueling the hope that our repentance will also result in God's forgiving mercy.[6]

The final *Ne'ilah* service concludes with the dramatic recitation of the *Shema* once, *baruch shem k'vod* ... (praised is His glorious name ...) three times, and *Adonai Hu ha-Elohim* (the Lord is God) seven times, followed by a final long blast of the shofar (*tekiah gedolah*). Blowing the shofar, the central symbol of the High Holy Day period, marks the definitive end to both the day and the entire period of repentance. It evokes the feeling of a successful passage from sin to repentance, from death to life. The shofar is also sounded as a reminder of the great shofar blast of the jubilee year, which was blown every 50 years on Yom Kippur to announce the freedom of slaves and the reversion of all land to its original owners (Lev. 25:8–10). This shofar blast was designed to "proclaim liberty throughout the land and to all the inhabitants thereof" (Lev. 25:10)—words selected by the American patriots to be inscribed on the Liberty Bell, which announced the signing of the Declaration of Independence and the birth of their new free land.

Kol Nidrei (כָּל נִדְרֵי)

Kol Nidrei (All vows) is the opening prayer of Yom Kippur. Chanted by the *hazzan* in a dramatic and beloved melody, *Kol Nidrei* annuls all vows made to God. Before reciting *Kol Nidrei*, the *hazzan* declares in solemn legalistic terminology: "By the authority of the heavenly court and by the authority of this earthly court, with divine consent and the consent of this congregation, we hereby declare it permissible to pray with those who have transgressed." This statement is based on a talmudic teaching: "No fast is true, unless some of the sinners in Israel participate in it" (Ker. 6b). The Rabbis compared this to the mixture of perfumes that made up the incense used in the Temple. Among the 11 aromatic spices was galbanum, which was included despite its unpleasant odor, because without it the combination cannot be considered incense.[7] Thus this preliminary to *Kol Nidrei* dispels arrogance, for each of us may be the transgressor in the congregation, and on this day the barriers between the righteous and the sinners are broken down. Some believe that the transgressors being mentioned once referred to the Marranos, the secret Jews of Spain, who officially had adopted Christianity but on Yom Kippur came furtively to join their brethren in the plea for divine forgiveness.[8]

As a legal formula written in Aramaic, *Kol Nidrei* is associated with several legal customs. Because only a *beit din* (court composed of three persons) could abrogate a vow, two people holding Torah scrolls stand on either side of the *hazzan*. This scene is also reminiscent of Aaron and Hur standing on either side of Moses and supporting his hands during the battle with the Amalekites (Exod. 17:12). In many congregations, however, all the Torah scrolls are removed from the ark and held as *Kol Nidrei* is recited. *Kol Nidrei* is repeated three times, because in Jewish law a court releasing someone from a vow was required to declare "you are released" three times. In many synagogues, the voice of the *hazzan* grows louder each time *Kol Nidrei* is chanted to emphasize the solemn implication of the plea to cancel all vows. The congregants often recite the prayer in an undertone, to absolve the *hazzan* from his personal vows, since he cannot nullify them himself. Another explanation is that *Kol Nidrei* is recited softly at first to symbolize the hesitant manner in which fearful penitents enter the palace of the divine king to plead for their life. As they gain confidence and approach the God of mercy, the prayer is chanted a little louder. As they finally become comfortable nearing the Almighty in His court, they lift their voices and make the third petition loudly.[9] As a legal procedure, *Kol Nidrei* must be chanted before sundown while it is still daylight, since a Jewish court could not make decisions at night.

After the third recitation of *Kol Nidrei*, the worshipers remind God of the biblical verse promising forgiveness—"The whole Israelite community and the stranger residing among them shall be forgiven, for it happened to the entire people through error" (Num. 15:26).[10] The *hazzan* repeats the words of Moses after the sin of the Golden Calf: "Pardon, I pray, the iniquity of this people according to Your great kindness, as You have forgiven this people ever since Egypt" (Num. 14:19). The congregation then responds in God's words: "I have pardoned [them], as you have asked" (Num. 14:20).

The origin of *Kol Nidrei* is unknown, but one suggestion is that it may have originated during the gaonic period (9th and 10th centuries) as a magical formula to remove evil spirits threatening to interfere with the sacredness of Yom Kippur. This may account for its being strongly condemned by many of the sages as a pagan-like custom totally inconsistent with traditional Jewish practice. Nevertheless, the popular appeal of *Kol Nidrei* was so great that it remained in the liturgy as one of the most beloved of all prayers.[11]

The custom of reciting *Kol Nidrei* gradually spread both to the Land of Israel and to Europe, where it also encountered rabbinic opposition and was regarded as an invalid practice that made light of vows. This primarily related to the initially accepted version that invoked divine pardon, forgiveness, and atonement for those sins "from the previous

Yom Kippur until *this* Yom Kippur" (i.e., the *past* year). The Tosafists of 12th-century France and Germany (especially Rabbenu Tam) reworded this phrase to read "from this Yom Kippur until the *next* Yom Kippur" (i.e., the *coming* year). Ashkenazim have adopted this formulation of Rabbenu Tam, whereas Sephardim generally accept the earlier gaonic version. The early Reform movement recommended eliminating *Kol Nidrei* from the Yom Kippur service, and later Reformers suggested alternative versions. However, the latest editions of the Reform prayer book retain the traditional text.

Kol Nidrei assumed special significance during the time of the Spanish Inquisition, when Jews at pain of death were forced to give up their faith and assume the rituals of the Roman Catholic Church. For the many Jews who continued to practice their religion in secret, *Kol Nidrei* provided a welcome opportunity for solemnly renouncing the vows that they had made only under duress.[12] The melody used today for *Kol Nidrei*, which originated in southern Germany during the 16th century, exquisitely voices sorrow and suffering before rising triumphantly in hope and faith.[13]

Anti-Semites often pointed to *Kol Nidrei* as proof that Jews could not be trusted and that their oaths were meaningless. To combat this, the Rabbis took great pains to stress that the *Kol Nidrei* formulation relates to vows and promises made *only* to God and was never meant to apply to oaths taken before secular courts of law.

A sense of the mood of reverence and awe that pervades the congregation during the stirring chanting of *Kol Nidrei* can best be illustrated by the effect it had on the young Franz Rosenzweig. Having decided to convert to Christianity, but before having taken the decisive step of baptism, Rosenzweig attended services on Yom Kippur. Joining the worshipers in a small Orthodox synagogue in Berlin, he was spiritually stirred by the power of the *Kol Nidrei* ritual. Rosenzweig found himself in direct communion with God and rediscovered his Jewish roots, determined to strengthen rather than reject his own membership in the house of Israel. Not only did this religious experience change his mind about baptism, but it also inspired Rosenzweig to devote his life to the study and teaching of his tradition. Eventually, Rosenzweig became a distinguished philosopher and one of the foremost spokesmen for Judaism in his generation.[14]

The melody of *Kol Nidrei* has been the subject of numerous musical compositions. The most famous is an arrangement of the Ashkenazic version for cello or violin and orchestra, composed by the non-Jewish Max Bruch as a commission from the Jewish community of Liverpool.

Confessions (*Vidui*; וִדּוּי)

According to Jewish tradition, the confession of sin is the first step on the road to atonement. Divine forgiveness, which reconciles the worshiper with God, must be preceded by a cleansing of the soul. Making confession of sins also awakens the heart to intense prayer, enabling the person to stand before God and plead for divine mercy. Therefore, the Rabbis prescribed the inclusion of the confession of sins in each of the five services for Yom Kippur (Yoma 87b).[15]

The confession of sins as a means of atonement predated the rabbinic period and originated in ancient times. The classic biblical example is King David's humble admission of guilt, when he confessed to the prophet Nathan that "I have sinned against the Lord" (2 Sam. 12:13). In his reply, Nathan indicated the effectiveness of confession in securing divine forgiveness: "The Lord also has remitted your sin; you shall not die." Nevertheless, confession alone is not sufficient to atone for sins. It must be followed by *teshuvah*, a "return" from one's sinful ways (see p. 171).[16]

The oldest formula of the confession was probably, "I have done wrong, I have transgressed, and I have sinned"—the simple words uttered by the *Kohen Gadol* in his confession on Yom Kippur (Yoma 3:8). After confessing his own sins, the *Kohen Gadol* then recited confessions for the entire priesthood and finally for all Israel. Once the Temple was destroyed and the sacrificial rites ceased, increased emphasis was placed on the synagogue service and individual prayers. Each person became required to make his or her own confession on Yom Kippur. Originally, only one confession was required at the beginning of Yom Kippur, so that worshipers would not be continually reminded of their transgressions on this sacred day. The Rabbis then added a confession in the afternoon before the final meal before the fast because "perchance some wrong has happened in the course of the meal"—the person might have become too full from food and drink to make proper confession, or unfortunately die suddenly (such as from choking on a chicken bone during the meal) before doing so (Yoma 87b). Later, the

Rabbis decreed that confessions be recited at all five services on the Day of Atonement.[17]

Some Rabbis maintained that it was necessary to specify exactly those sins that one had committed. Rabbi Akiva disagreed, arguing persuasively that a general confession was sufficient. In talmudic times, any expression of confession sufficed. During the gaonic period, however, the Rabbis formulated texts that served as the basis of the two set forms of confession that are recited today—*Al Het* (Great confession) and *Ashamnu* (Short confession). Both of these confessions are expressed in the plural, as is customary in the Jewish liturgy, in keeping with the concept of the collective responsibility that Jews have for one another (Shev. 39a). Each Jew confesses not only those sins that he or she has committed personally but also every transgression that may have been committed by any member of the congregation. Moral corruption is not merely the concern of the sinner alone but rather is a danger to the entire fabric of society. The sages compared this to one who drills a hole in a boat and then responds to the complaints of his fellow passengers that it is none of their business, since the hole is only under his seat! Therefore, the congregation rises to recite the confessions in unison.

At the mention of each transgression, all worshipers symbolically express their remorse by beating their breasts, since the heart was long regarded as the source of sin. Others have noted that "since body language is often more expressive than words, we add physical action to stress the severity of what we have done and the sincerity of our repentance."[18]

Al Het (עַל חֵטְא)

Al Het (For the sin [which we have committed before You]) are the first Hebrew words of the formula for the major confession of sins recited on Yom Kippur. It is said during the afternoon *Amidah* on the evening of Yom Kippur and in every silent *Amidah* and repetition of the *Amidah* on the Day of Atonement itself, with the exception of the closing *Ne'ilah* service.

For the sin which we have sinned before You ...
under duress and willingly

by hardening the heart
without knowing (without thinking)
with the expression of our lips
by immoral behavior
in public and in private
knowingly and deceitfully
with abusive speech
by oppressing a neighbor
with improper thoughts
with lewd association (licentiousness)
by insincere confession
by disrespecting parents and teachers
intentionally and unintentionally
by the use of power
by desecrating the Name
with unclean lips
with foolish speech
by surrendering to the evil inclination
knowingly or unknowingly (against those who know and do not know)

by fraud and falsity
by bribery
by mocking
by slander (evil tongue)
in business matters
in matters of food and drink
by usury and extortion
by arrogance
by idle gossip
by wanton looks
by haughty eyes
by shameless conduct

by throwing off the yoke of responsibility (rejecting Your commandments)
by perverting justice
by plotting against friends
with a jealous eye (envy)
by acting frivolously

by being stubborn
by running to do evil
by talebearing
by swearing falsely
by causeless hatred
by failing to extend a hand (withholding loans)
with a confused heart (confusion of values)

Al Het is a litany of 44 transgressions, which are not arranged in a logical order but rather as a double alphabetical acrostic in which two sins are allotted to every letter. In the Sephardic tradition, there is only one letter for each sin, though some follow it by a reverse-order alphabetical arrangement. Whether by design or not, the number of sins in *Al Het* is precisely the same as the lines in *Avinu Malkeinu* (see p. 196), a prayer that also plays a major role in the Yom Kippur liturgy.[19]

The recitation of *Al Het* is divided into three parts (of 20, 12, and 12 verses, respectively), each of which is followed by the formula: "And for all these, O God of forgiveness, forgive us, pardon us, grant us atonement." These words are chanted by the congregation during the reader's repetition of the *Amidah*.

After the 44 transgressions, another nine lines are added, enumerating sins according to their prescribed punishments. (These are omitted from some modern *machzorim* because the penalties are not operative in our time.)

For the sins for which we are obligated to bring ...
a burnt offering
a sin offering
a variable offering
a guilt offering
corporal punishment (lashes)

For the sins for which we are liable to ...
40 lashes
the death penalty at the hands of a heavenly court
spiritual excision and childlessness
the four death penalties of the human court (stoning, burning, beheading, or strangling)

Ashamnu (אָשַׁמְנוּ)

Ashamnu (we have trespassed) is the initial Hebrew word and name of the shorter confession of sins recited on Yom Kippur. It also is included in other penitential services, such as *Selichot* (see p. 178) and the daily morning and afternoon prayers in most Sephardic and some Ashkenazic congregations.

Ashamnu consists of 24 generic transgressions of a moral nature organized in alphabetic order in Hebrew, with the last letter used three times.

We have ...

become guilty
betrayed
robbed
slandered
acted perversely
caused wickedness
sinned willfully
been violent
falsely accused
sanctioned evil
practiced deception (been unfaithful)
scorned
rebelled
provoked
turned away
been perverse
acted wantonly
oppressed
been obstinate (stiff-necked)
acted wickedly
dealt corruptly
been abominable
gone astray
led others astray

On Yom Kippur, *Ashamnu* is repeated at all services, always preceded by the admission: "We are neither so arrogant nor so stubborn as

KI ANU AMECHA (כִּי אָנוּ עַמֶּךָ)

Ki anu amecha (For we are Your people) is a favorite *piyyut* that is recited at all services on Yom Kippur. In a series of poetical parallels, the close relationship between Israel and God is analogized to those between children and parents, servants and masters, sheep and shepherd, vineyards and their keepers, and lover and beloved. The *piyyut* is based on a midrash that interprets the verse "I am my beloved's and my beloved is mine" (Song 6:3) as a love poem of the intimate relationship between Israel and God. However, the prayer book soon departs from this idyllic vision by contrasting the stark difference between humanity and the Divine. It notes that we are "arrogant, stubborn, laden with sin, and ethereal as a passing shadow," whereas God is "gracious and merciful, patient, abounding in compassion, and eternal."

Ki anu amecha is followed by a brief admission of sin and a plea for God not to ignore our prayers, which leads immediately to the first of the confessions, *Ashamnu* (see p. 217).

to declare that we are righteous and have not sinned; for, indeed, we have sinned."

Avodah (עֲבוֹדָה)

Avodah (lit., "service"), the name for the Temple ritual, is now applied to an essential element of the *Musaf* service on Yom Kippur. It vividly describes the sacrificial ritual in the Temple on the Day of Atonement, based on Leviticus 16 and detailed in *Mishnah Yoma* (1–7) and the talmudic tractate of the same name. The *Avodah* service has preserved the quintessential rite of ancient Judaism, the most solemn moment of the Jewish year involving the holiest person (*Kohen Gadol*), the holiest time (Yom Kippur), and the holiest place (Temple in Jerusalem). Although not one of the pilgrimage festivals on which Jews were biblically required to appear at the Temple in Jerusalem (Deut. 16:16), on Yom Kippur huge throngs of worshipers came to see the awesome ritual and to hear the words of the *Kohen Gadol*.[20]

KI HINEI KA-CHOMER (כִּי הִנֵּה כַּחֹמֶר)

Ki hinei ka-chomer (Behold, like clay) is a poem in the *Selichot* prayers for the evening of Yom Kippur. This *piyyut* by an unknown author is based on a verse in Jeremiah (18:6): "Just like clay in the hands of the potter, so are you in My hands, O House of Israel," implying that God has the power to mold, create, or destroy the Jewish people. In succeeding stanzas, the poet continues this theme, comparing God to various craftsmen (masons, smiths, glassblowers, weavers, and smelters) and human beings to the raw materials that they use (stone, iron, glass, cloth, and silver, respectively). The poet implores God to use us for creative, not destructive purposes. Each couplet ends with the plea: "Recall Your covenant and do not regard our [evil] inclination," a direct reference to the Thirteen Attributes of Mercy (see p. 180).

After the destruction of the Second Temple and the cessation of the sacrificial rites, how could the people achieve atonement? The Rabbis ruled that in this emergency situation, one could perform the Temple duties by reading about them, since the utterance of a person's lips is equivalent to the actual performance of the ritual. In addition, the Rabbis were convinced that a yearly recitation of the Yom Kippur ritual in the Temple would give Jews a sense of historical continuity and an intense longing for the restoration of their ancient homeland.[21] The *Avodah* service was initially just a narration of the Temple ritual on Yom Kippur as related in *Mishnah Yoma*, but during the Middle Ages, numerous *piyyutim* were added.

Yom Kippur was the only time during the year when the *Kohen Gadol* entered the Holy of Holies in the Temple. Preparation for this event began a week before the Day of Atonement, when the *Kohen Gadol* went to a designated area of the Temple court to study the sacrificial ritual for Yom Kippur. On the day before Yom Kippur, the *Kohen Gadol* emerged and was taken to another chamber in the Temple compound, where he met with other priests and continued his study. On the Day of Atonement, the *Kohen Gadol*, dressed in gold-embroidered garments, conducted the daily cultic rituals. When performing the rituals exclusively associated with the sacrifices of atonement, the *Kohen Gadol* wore white linen vestments. During the course of the day, he immersed himself and changed his clothes five times and washed his hands and feet 10 times.

The *Kohen Gadol* first offered a bull as his personal sin offering. He confessed his sins and those of his family, then the sins of the tribe of Aaron (the *Kohanim*), and finally those of all Israel (Lev. 16:17). Every time the *Kohen Gadol* uttered the holy name of God (the Tetragrammaton), which was spoken only on Yom Kippur, the people prostrated themselves and responded: "Praised is His name, whose glorious kingdom is forever and ever." It remains a custom in some communities for worshipers to completely bow down on the floor of the synagogue when this part of the *Avodah* service is read. A cloth or piece of paper must be placed between one's head and the floor (not between one's knees and the floor, as many erroneously do), because it is forbidden to bow down on a stone floor, except in the Temple.[22]

After drawing lots to determine which of the two male goats was sent off to the wilderness for Azazel (see page 224) and which would be sacrificed as a sin offering for the Lord, and after a special incense offering was made in the Holy of Holies, the *Kohen Gadol* recited a prayer that Israel be blessed with peace, prosperity, and fertility and that no earthquake harm the inhabitants of the Sharon plain ("their houses may not become their graves").

Some modern prayer books used in liberal congregations have minimized the references to sacrifice and either abridge the *Avodah* or make it optional.

Ne'ilah (נְעִילָה)

Ne'ilah (Closing [of the gates]) is the final service of Yom Kippur. Some have suggested that the name refers to the historical fact that this extra service was recited at the end of the Day of Atonement, when the Temple gates were closing. However, the special *piyyutim* written for this service favor the idea that *Ne'ilah* reflects the more spiritual concept of the closing of the gates of Heaven, which have been kept open to receive our final prayers and supplications. This poetic image has imbued the *Ne'ilah* service with a sense of urgency. In contrast to the leisurely pace of the other Yom Kippur services, the mood suddenly changes.[23] Although Judaism teaches that the gates of prayer are always open to the truly repentant, as individuals and as a congregation we feel that this is our final chance to pour out our hearts before the divine throne of mercy. Even those who have left the synagogue because of weakness induced by the fast usually return to participate in the *Ne'ilah* service.[24] Paradoxically, as the initial hunger from fasting wears off, many worshipers feel a revitalization of their spiritual strength.[25]

Beginning with the repetition of the *Amidah,* the ark remains open throughout the *Ne'ilah* service. All who are physically capable remain standing, an act that requires additional effort and adds to the feeling of urgency and spiritual transformation. The separate members of the congregation appear as one penitent, joined in their firm conviction that the divine judge will pardon their sins at this final hour of the day.[26] In the *Amidah,* the phrase used since Rosh Hashanah, "*inscribe* us in the Book of Life," now becomes "*seal* us in the Book of Life," as the final seal is placed on the divine decree. *Ashamnu* and *Avinu Malkeinu* are again repeated, but the pressure of time forces the omission of the long *Al Het*.

As the climax of the Day of Atonement rapidly approaches, the prayer leader and congregation join in the recitation of three biblical sentences whereby they rededicate themselves to the essential theological doctrines of Judaism.[27] The first is a single recitation of the *Shema,* the quintessential affirmation of faith. This is followed by a threefold repetition of "Praised is His name, Whose glorious kingdom for ever and ever," the line that is usually recited as a silent response to the *Shema*. This recalls the threefold declaration: "The Lord is king [present], the Lord was king [past], and the Lord will be king [future]."[28] Finally, the verse *Adonai hu ha-Elohim* (the Lord is God) is repeated seven times. This unequivocal denial of all idolatry and affirmation of the One and Only God was the response of the Israelites to Elijah's triumphant victory over the priests of Baal on Mount Carmel (1 Kings 18:39). This declaration is followed by a long blast of the shofar (*tekiah gedolah*), an echo of the ancient practice of sounding the shofar to proclaim the beginning of the 50th (jubilee) year of freedom throughout the land (Lev. 25:9). Just as all lands returned to their original owners and slaves were freed from their masters with the onset of the jubilee year, so we celebrate our personal liberation from the overwhelming burden of our transgressions. The piercing blast of the ram's horn also symbolizes the certainty that we have been granted divine forgiveness and been inscribed for a good year.[29] This confidence in the future is expressed as all join in saying *le-shanah ha-ba'ah be-Yerushalayim* (next year in Jerusalem), the city that has symbolized hope and freedom for Jews throughout the ages.[30]

Customs

Numerous customs are associated with Yom Kippur. On the preceding day, many traditional Jews go to the *mikveh* (ritual bath; see p. 555) to symbolize their spiritual rebirth. A controversial ritual is *kaparos*, in which sins are symbolically carried off by a fowl twirled over the head (see below). The last meal before the fast (*seudah ha-mafseket*, the meal of separation or the concluding meal) has special significance and is considered not merely as a preparation for Yom Kippur but as an inseparable part of the Day of Atonement. The Talmud declared that "everyone who eats and drinks on the ninth [of Tishrei] is considered by Scripture as if he had fasted on the ninth and the tenth" (Ber. 8b). Some of the pious even kept candy in their mouths the entire day of the ninth, possibly to emphasize their humanity in striking contrast to the angelic qualities they would experience fasting on the 10th of the month. Since the final meal must be eaten before sunset, it is not considered a holiday meal and no *Kiddush* is recited. Nevertheless, this *seudah ha-mafseket* is considered a festive meal and the Grace after Meals begins with the recitation of *Shir ha-Ma'alot*, which is usually said only on the Sabbath, holidays, and festive occasions. Following the meal, memorial candles are kindled for departed members of the family, and the candles for Yom Kippur are lit.

The prohibitions on Yom Kippur all have symbolic meaning. Eating and drinking, sexual relations, bathing, anointing, and leather shoes are prohibited because we have given up all physical pleasures for this day, when we are to be as pure as angels. The custom of wearing white garments on Yom Kippur emphasizes our otherworldly, angelic qualities on this day. It also is reminiscent of Isaiah's (1:18) prophecy of divine forgiveness: "Be your sins like crimson, they can turn white as snow." Many wear a *kitel* (white robe; see p. 619), also donned at a wedding, which may instill a sense of purity. As the shroud in which one will ultimately be buried, the *kitel* may be worn as a foretaste of death—in view of the imminent divine decision as to who will live and who will die—or possibly even as a ruse to fool the Angel of Death into thinking that the person has already departed this life.

Kaparos (כַּפָּרוֹת)

Kaparos (lit., "atonements," but in the sense of "ransom") is the custom in which the sins of a person are symbolically transferred to a fowl. On the day before Yom Kippur, a cock (for a male) or a hen (for a female) traditionally is swung around the head three times while the following is pronounced: "This is my substitute, my vicarious offering, my atonement; this cock [hen] shall meet death, but I shall find a long and pleasant life of peace." These birds, never offered in the Temple, were selected so that no suspicion would arise that one was attempting the strictly forbidden practice of re-creating a Temple sacrifice. If for some reason a cock or hen cannot be obtained, other animals such as fish or geese, or even flowers in a planter, may be used with the substitution of the appropriate words.[31] Because the Hebrew word "*gever*" means both "man" and "cock," the *Ge'onim* explained that the latter could substitute for the former, with the fowl taking on any misfortune that might otherwise befall the person in punishment for his or her sins. After the ceremony, it is customary to donate the bird to the poor. Today, many people have substituted money for the cock or hen in performing the ceremony, changing the formula recited to "this coin shall go to charity but I shall find a long and pleasant life of peace." Therefore, this custom also serves as a last-minute form of *tzedakah*, attempting to "avert the severity of the decree."

The popular belief that evil spirits feared a closed circle (magic ring) may have been the original reason for this practice. Moreover, demons shunned the light, and the rooster frightened them away when he crowed in the morning to announce the first light of day (a power against evil spirits that eventually was transferred to the hen).[32]

Many major rabbinic authorities, both medieval and modern, have strenuously opposed the *kaparos* ceremony. They have attacked it as a pagan superstitious ritual, decrying the belief that one may substitute the death of an animal for one's own life. Yosef Karo even called *kaparos* "a stupid custom." Nevertheless, despite the objections of the great rabbis, the ceremony appealed strongly to the masses and has survived in traditional households.[33]

Azazel (עֲזָאזֵל)

Azazel is the name either of a goat-demon or the place to which one of the goats was sent in the Temple service on Yom Kippur. It appears in the verses, "And he [Aaron] shall place lots upon the two goats, one marked for the Lord and the other marked for Azazel. Aaron shall bring forward the goat designated by lot for the Lord, which he is to offer as a sin offering; while the goat designated by lot for Azazel shall be left standing alive before the Lord, to make expiation with it and to send it off to the wilderness for Azazel" (Lev. 16:8–10).

In talmudic times, a popular rabbinic interpretation was that Azazel referred to the place to which the goat was sent, the *eretz g'zera* (inaccessible region) of Leviticus (16:22). Later, Azazel became associated with another undesirable locale—Hell; and the modern Hebrew equivalent of "go to hell" is *"lech l'Azazel"* (lit., "walk [or go] to Azazel"). Modern scholars generally agree that Azazel was perceived as a goat-demon living in the wilderness, whose task was to accept the yearly accumulation of sins generated by the Israelites. Just as the first goat was set aside as a burnt offering for the Lord, so in parallel fashion the second was sent to Azazel as a literal sin offering, a messenger that returned the sins of Israel to their demonic source.

It is clear, however, that the Israelite tradition did not contemplate this ritual as a sacrifice to a demon. Not only was the goat for Azazel not slaughtered, at least according to the Torah, but the next chapter in Leviticus (17:7) specifically prohibits the offering of sacrifices "to the goat-demons after whom they [the Israelites] stray." Indeed, before the Azazel ritual was performed, the sins of the people had *already* been forgiven. Slaughtering the other goat designated for the Lord and sprinkling its blood on the atonement seat was sufficient to "purge the Shrine of the uncleanness and transgression of the Israelites" (Lev. 16:16). Once the *Kohen Gadol* had performed these acts, the Torah relates that he "made expiation for himself and his household, and for the whole congregation of Israel" (Lev. 16:17). Thus it appears that the goat for Azazel was merely a symbolic rite that formally completed the process of atonement after the cleansing of sins that had *already* occurred in response to verbal confession and ritual sacrifice.[34]

The biblical text mandates that the goat sent to Azazel be set free. During Second Temple times, however, a procession of the honored citizens of Jerusalem accompanied the goat into the wilderness. According to the Talmud, one man "divided a scarlet thread and tied one end to the rock and the other end between its horns and pushed [the goat] from behind" (Yoma 67a), and "before it reached halfway down the mountain it was already broken into pieces!" (Hul. 11b). The Tosefta adds that if the goat survived the fall, someone had to go down and kill it, possibly to prevent the evil omen if the goat managed to find its way back to the Israelite camp and symbolically return the sins back to the community. As one midrash observes, "If they saw the goat that had been sent away returning, they knew that the Holy One was angry with His world" (Song R. 3:6).[35] A messenger then declared that the red thread on the head of the goat had miraculously turned white, indicating that God had accepted the atonement of the Israelites and mercifully forgiven the people of their sins.[36]

Azazel "may be a symbol of the evil impulse, the tendency to be led astray by the animal part of our nature, by lust or appetite."[37] In biblical times, a physical act was necessary to conquer the inclination of the Israelites to sin; mere words were not sufficient. Interpreting the two goats homiletically, Hirsch observed: "We can follow our sensual instincts into the wilderness, leading to self-destruction, or we can sacrifice our instincts to the service of God."[38]

A Day Like Purim

According to the Zohar, the Hebrew name for the Day of Atonement (*Yom ha-Kippurim*) could be read as "*Yom ki-Purim*" (A day like Purim). Initially, it seems incongruous that a day of awesome self-inspection and prayer could have any relation to one that is characterized by joyful abandon. One interpretation is that it stresses the dichotomy between external appearance and inward reality—on Yom Kippur one searches behind the former to discover (and improve) the latter, whereas a major aspect of Purim is the stress on costume and Esther's hiding her Jewish origins from everyone in the Persian court. Both Purim and Yom Kippur can be thought of as a time of facing up to inevitable death. In the time of Mordecai and Esther, Haman convinced Ahasuerus to issue a decree calling for the murder of every Jew in his vast kingdom. On Yom Kippur, we recognize that all human beings have sinned and logically should not escape God's judgment. Nevertheless, just as Israel survived Haman's threat, so the Jewish people as a whole has endured for centuries of Yom Kippur observances based on God's merciful acceptance of their repentance.[39]

Fall Festivals

Sukkot (סֻכּוֹת)

Sukkot (lit., booths), also known as Tabernacles, is one of the three agricultural pilgrimage festivals (along with Passover and Shavuot) mandated in the Torah (Lev. 23:39–43). Beginning on the 15th of Tishrei, the full moon five days after Yom Kippur, this joyous harvest festival is named for the temporary shelters in which the Israelites dwelled as they wandered through the wilderness. Sukkot lasts for seven days, of which the first (and second in the Diaspora) is a *yom tov*, a festival on which work is prohibited; the other days are *hol ha-mo'ed*, intermediate days on which work is permitted. Immediately after Sukkot, on the 22nd of Tishrei, is the holiday of Shemini Atzeret (Eighth Day of Assembly; see p. 239). Simchat Torah (see p. 240) is celebrated on the same day as Shemini Atzeret in Israel and on the day after (23rd of Tishrei) in the Diaspora.

In biblical times, Sukkot was the most important holiday of the Jewish calendar. As the last of the three Israelite festivals connected with the agricultural year, it was celebrated as Hag ha-Asif (Feast of the Ingathering from the threshing floor and winepress). Like the other two major agricultural festivals, Sukkot was taken over from the Canaanites, who celebrated a joyous feast at the end of the grape harvest (Judg. 9:27). Also known as Zeman Simchateinu (Season of Our Joy), or simply *he-Hag* (the Holiday) as the main feast of the year, Sukkot was the occasion for the consecration of Solomon's Temple (1 Kings 8). On the second day of Sukkot during the sabbatical year, the king was commanded to assemble the entire people to listen to specific readings from the Book of Deuteronomy. Even in ancient times, the festival became associated with messianic redemption, because of Zechariah's (14:16) prophecy that at the end of days all the peoples of the world would acknowledge the divine kingship, make a pilgrimage to Jerusalem to worship God, and observe the feast of Sukkot.

According to the Rabbis, a special ceremony of water libation was celebrated at the end of the first day of Sukkot (but not on the Sabbath) at the Temple in Jerusalem (Suk. 51a–b). Known as *Simchat Beit ha-Sho'evah* (Rejoicing of the house of water drawing; see p. 236), this ceremony was apparently based on the verse from Isaiah (12:3), "Joyfully shall you draw water from the fountains of triumph,"[1] which is the text for the popular Israeli song and dance *Mayim* (water). The Rabbis observed that whoever had not seen the ceremony of the water drawing had never witnessed real joy (Suk. 51b).

The series of festivals extending from the beginning of Elul, the month before Rosh Hashanah, until Simchat Torah has been interpreted as an allegory symbolizing the marriage of God and the Jewish people. According to this view, "Elul is the period of courtship; Rosh Hashanah, the betrothal; Yom Kippur, the fast before the wedding; the seven days of Sukkot, the seven blessings of the marriage ceremony; Shemini Atzeret, the breaking of the glass; and Simchat Torah, the consummation." In America, the biblical harvest festival of Sukkot was the basis for the Pilgrims' celebration of Thanksgiving.[2]

Three commandments concerning Sukkot are found in the Torah: dwelling in the sukkah, gathering together the four species, and rejoicing during the holiday. Other rituals and customs include the reciting of *hoshanot* while making circuits in the synagogue, reading the Book of Ecclesiastes, inviting *ushpizin* (symbolic guests; see p. 235) to the sukkah, and the special rituals associated with Hoshana Rabbah, the seventh day of the festival (see p. 237).

The identical Torah readings for the first two days of Sukkot deal with the ordinances of this and the other pilgrimage festivals (Lev. 22:26–23:44) and detail the appropriate sacrifices (Num. 29:12–16). The haftarah for the first day (Zech. 14:1–21) includes the visionary passage that is the climax of the *Aleinu* prayer (see p. 466): "On that day the Lord shall be one and his name one." The haftarah for the second day (1 Kings 8:2–21) describes the dedication ceremony of Solomon's Temple as a house for God's name, which occurred on Sukkot.

Sukkah (סֻכָּה)

Sukkah (pl., sukkot) is the name for the hastily constructed, unsubstantial structure that Jews erect as part of the observance of the fall festival of Sukkot, in accordance with the biblical commandment, "You shall live in booths [sukkot] seven days" (Lev. 23:42). Therefore, the Talmud records a dispute as to whether the sukkot mentioned in the Torah were actual or metaphysical booths, the latter referring to the protective "clouds of glory" that accompanied and sheltered the Israelites during their 40-year journey (Suk. 11b).[3] Some believe that they originated from the temporary shelters in which workers would live in the fields and vineyards during the harvest season. Even when no longer in common use, these booths remained a powerful religious symbol of God's special care for the Jewish people.[4]

The sukkah must be a temporary structure, only strong enough to withstand normal gusts of wind. It must have a minimum of three walls (31 inches or higher), at least two of which must be complete (Suk. 6b). The sukkah may be constructed of any material, though it is usually of wood or canvas suspended on a metal frame. It must be built under the open sky, not under a tree or inside a house. The roof of the sukkah is covered with *sekhakh*—plants that cannot be used for food, are in their natural state (i.e., not wooden boards), and are detached from the ground (Suk. 1:4). Therefore, a grape arbor or any growing vine cannot be used. Typically consisting of cut branches or bamboo sticks, the *sekhakh* must be arranged so that there is more shade (covered space) than sunshine inside the sukkah during the day (Suk. 9b–10a). However, it should not be so dense that the stars cannot be seen through it at night.

It is customary to decorate the sukkah with colorful fruit, which must remain in place and not be eaten during the festival (Suk. 10a), and with signs quoting verses from the Bible or depicting beautiful scenes from Israel. The Talmud recommends decorating the sukkah with "handmade carpets and tapestries, nuts, almonds, peaches, pomegranates and branches of grape, vines, [vials of] oil, fine meal, and wreaths of ears of corn" (Betz. 30b). Some even adorn the sukkah with onions in keeping with the verse, "Mankind shelters in the shadow of Your wings" (Ps. 36:8), since the Hebrew word for "under the shadow" (*b'tzeil*) is close to that for onion (*batzal*).[5] According to tradition, the construction of the sukkah should begin immediately after the close of Yom Kippur, so as to "link mitzvah with mitzvah."

The Talmud indicates that during this festival Jews should regard the sukkah as their principal dwelling place, with the house merely a temporary residence (Suk. 2:9). A blessing is made (*leishev ba-sukkah*) every time one enters the sukkah, which refers to the commandment to dwell in the sukkah. (No blessing is made on the building of the sukkah [S.A. OH 641:1].) It is forbidden to eat any major meal or to sleep outside the sukkah, though "casual eating [a small quantity, such as a piece of fruit] and drinking [such as water]" are permitted elsewhere (Suk. 26a). However, modern rabbinical authorities, cognizant of the cold and rainy climates to which Jews have wandered during their long exile, have permitted sleeping and eating inside the house when the weather is bad.[6] Not only is a person not obliged to sleep or eat in the sukkah when rain penetrates the roof, but one is forbidden to do so, for it is improper to insist on carrying out a religious duty from which there is exemption. Synagogues often build a sukkah for the benefit of those congregants who do not have their own.

Newlyweds and the wedding party are exempt from the requirement to eat in the sukkah, probably based on the principle of not mixing two kinds of joy (the wedding and the sukkah). Moreover, the Rabbis may have felt that the sukkah was not the most comfortable spot for the couple to spend their wedding night. In traditional circles, this exemption continues for the entire seven days of celebration after the wedding. Those involved in performing another mitzvah are also freed from the obligation of dwelling in the sukkah, based on the general concept that one does not have to perform one mitzvah when engaged in another (Suk. 26a). As examples, the Shulchan Arukh lists the study of Torah, visiting a teacher, and redeeming captives. Travelers are also exempt, for just as they do not come home every night during the rest of the year, they are not obligated to return to their sukkah-home during Sukkot. According to the Rabbis, a person guarding a vineyard is not required to build a sukkah because "the breach invites the thief" (Suk. 26a)—if potential robbers knew that the owner was stationed in one area, they could simply steal from other parts of the property![7]

The sukkah has become a general symbol of divine protection, as in the evening prayer that asks God to "spread over us the 'sukkah' of Your peace" (*sukkat sh'lomecha*). The Midrash states that God protected the Israelites in sukkot during their journey in the wilderness because of the shelter that their father Abraham had provided to the three strangers beneath a tree on his land (Gen. R. 48:10 on Gen. 18:2–5).

Maimonides declared that a person should remember his bad times in his days of prosperity, so as to be induced to lead a modest and humble life. Therefore, on Sukkot we leave our comfortable homes and dwell in simple booths exposed to the elements to remind us that this once was our condition in the desert. Similarly, the festival stresses that material wealth is transitory; the only possessions that one can amass for all eternity are the future spiritual rewards for living righteously and performing mitzvot during our relatively short physical lives on earth.[8]

Four Species (אַרְבָּעָה מִינִים)

The four species (*arba'ah minim*) are plants mandated by the Torah as part of the celebration of Sukkot—"You shall take for yourselves on the first day the fruit of goodly trees, branches of palm trees, and boughs of thick trees, and willows of the brook, and you shall rejoice before the Lord your God seven days" (Lev. 23:40). According to tradition, the four species specified in this commandment refer to the *etrog* (citron; see p. 699), the *lulav* (palm tree; see p. 701), *hadas* (myrtle; see p. 700) and *aravah* (willow; see p. 704). Although it is likely that the four species were used initially in the construction of the sukkot in which Jews dwelled during the festival (Lev. 23:42), they later became employed in a separate ritual. Three myrtle and two willow branches are bound to the *lulav* with strips of palm (the myrtle on the right and the willow on the left) and held in the right hand, while the *etrog* is taken separately in the left hand (Suk. 37b).

According to Abudraham, the *lulav* is waved several times during the service as a gesture of triumph. Just as armies raise their flags over territory they have conquered from their enemies, so Jews wave their standards to indicate that they have emerged victorious over the numerous enemies who have sought to destroy them.[9]

Midrash offers several moral and homiletic interpretations of the symbolic meaning of the four species. The *etrog* is shaped like the heart, which the ancients believed was the seat of a person's intelligence; it symbolizes the hope for divine forgiveness for the murmurings and impure desires of our hearts. The *lulav* is like a person's spine, reminding us of the rabbinic ideal that the normal posture at prayer is to stand erect before God. The *myrtle* is shaped like an eye, implying that one should never go straying after temptations that one sees on the day of his heart's rejoicing and symbolizing the hope for divine forgiveness for greed and envy. Finally, the *willow* is like the lips, which a person should hold in restraint (lest they lead to idle talk and falsehoods) while focusing solely on being in awe of God.

The *etrog*, which has a taste and an aroma, symbolizes one who possesses both scholarship and good deeds; the *lulav*, a branch of the date palm, whose fruit has a taste but no aroma, symbolizes a scholar who is deficient in good deeds; the *myrtle*, which has no taste but has an aroma, symbolizes a person who is deficient in Torah but possesses good deeds; and the *willow*, which lacks both taste and aroma, symbolizes a person who has neither scholarship nor good deeds (Lev. R. 30:12). The four species are held together while making the blessing because all sorts of people must be united in the community of Israel, and the failings of one are compensated for by the virtues of the others.

The four species remind us of the four great kingdoms that conquered the Jews and afflicted them greatly—Babylonia, Persia, Greece, and Rome. Just as the Jews endured these powerful oppressors, so shall they survive others (with the help of God).[10]

Finally, each of the four species represents one of the ancestors of the Jewish people. The *etrog*, a beautiful fruit, is compared to Abraham, who had a beautiful and fruitful old age. The *lulav*, whose Hebrew name stems from a root meaning "to bind," is compared to Isaac, who was bound and ready to be offered as a sacrifice. The *myrtle*, which is thick with leaves, is compared to Jacob, who was blessed with many children. The *willow*, which dries up quickly, is compared to Joseph, who died before all his brothers. When holding the four species together, Jews pray that God show them mercy because of the merits of their ancestors—Abraham, Isaac, Jacob, and Joseph.[11]

The four species are often collectively called by the name of the largest member, and thus the blessing is *netilat lulav* ("taking" or "raising" the *lulav*). Before the blessing, the *etrog* is held with its *pitam* (stem-like protrusion) pointed downward. After the blessing, the *etrog* is inverted so that the *pitam* faces up. In the sukkah, one stands facing east with the *etrog* in the left hand and the *lulav*, myrtle, and willow in the right. The four species are shaken three times forward, to the right (south), over the shoulder (west), to the left (north), upward, and downward. In the synagogue, the four species are shaken in the same sequence during *Hallel*, but never waved during mention of the Name of God (Suk. 3:9), the unshakable center of the universe. This ritual dates back to Temple times, when the four species were shaken in every direction to acknowledge that the dominion and presence of God extends to the four corners of the universe, Heaven, and earth (Suk. 37b).

Waving of the four species during *Hallel* is as follows:

- Psalm 118:1: *Hodu* (east) *l'Adonai* (straight) *ki* (south) *tov* (west) *ki* (north) *l'olam* (upward) *chasdo* (downward) (Praise the Lord for He is good, His steadfast love is eternal).[12]
- Psalm 118:25: *Ana* (east) *Adonai* (straight) *hoshi'a* (south) *na* (west); *ana* (north) *Adonai* (straight) *hoshi'a* (upward) *na* (downward) (O Lord, deliver us).[13]
- Psalm 118:25: *Ana* (east) *Adonai* (straight) *hatzlicha* (south) *na* (west); *ana* (north) *Adonai* (straight) *hatzlicha* (upward) *na* (downward) (O Lord, let us prosper).
- Psalm 118:29—*Hodu* (east) *l'Adonai* (straight) *ki* (south) *tov* (west) *ki* (north) *l'olam* (upward) *chasdo* (downward) (Praise the Lord for He is good; His steadfast love is eternal).

Each person should have his or her own four species for the first day of Sukkot, based on the literal translation of the biblical verse, "You shall take to yourselves" (Lev. 23:40). According to *halakhah*, if one person uses another's *lulav* and *etrog*, it must be given as a present, not a loan (though with the understanding that it will be returned after the ceremony). Because children cannot legally transfer ownership of property, they should be given the four species last. On all other days of the festival, when the obligation to have one's own four species is only rabbinic, it is permitted to freely borrow and lend the *lulav* and *etrog*.[14]

Hoshanot (הוֹשַׁעְנוֹת)

After the *Musaf* service in the Ashkenazic ritual and following *Hallel* in the Sephardic rite, all congregants who have the four species follow the prayer leader in counterclockwise processions (*hoshanot*) circling the synagogue. (This is omitted on the Sabbath, when the four species are not carried.) One circuit is made each day, except for the seventh day (Hoshana Rabbah; see p. 237), on which seven circuits are made.[15] This ceremony was originally performed in the Temple, where the altar was circled as Psalm 118:25 was chanted. It was continued after the destruction of Jerusalem "in remembrance of the Temple" (Suk. 3:12).

The word *"hoshanot"* is derived from the word *"hoshana"* (or *hoshi'a na*, "Save, I pray"), the refrain sung after the six prayers for deliverance that are usually written as acrostics or in reverse alphabetical order. These prayers are derived from biblical and midrashic sources and are recited in a particular sequence, depending on the day of the week. The *hoshanot* depict the destructive forces of nature and beseech divine protection of both animal and plant life, based on the merit of the Patriarchs, Matriarchs, 12 tribes of Israel, Moses and Aaron, prophets, and kings who demonstrated their courage and faithfulness to God and whose deeds shaped Israel's national character and serve as our spiritual models.[16] They contain an array of appeals, ranging from requests for sufficient water and good crops to prayers for the return of the Jewish people from exile and ultimate redemption.

Ecclesiastes (Kohelet; קֹהֶלֶת)

The Book of Ecclesiastes (Kohelet) is read just before the Torah service on the intermediate Sabbath of Sukkot or on Shemini Atzeret. Although its composition is traditionally ascribed to King Solomon in his old age, when he was frustrated and despondent, linguistic analysis and content suggests a much later date. The sages considered this melancholy and often depressing book to be appropriate as the winter approaches, providing a note of seriousness to balance the gaiety of the festival of Sukkot. In addition, the biblical verse, "Distribute portions to seven or even to eight" (Eccles. 11:2), was deemed by the Rabbis to apply to the seven days of Sukkot and the eighth day of Shemini Atzeret (Er. 40b).

The name "Ecclesiastes," which is derived from the Septuagint (Greek translation of the Bible), means "assembler" or "convoker" and is a reasonably accurate rendering of the Hebrew word *"kohelet."* The author observes that although human beings cannot predict the phenomena of nature or their personal experiences, they are determined in advance by God: "A season is set for everything, a time for every experience under heaven: A time for being born and a time for dying, a time for planting and a time for uprooting the planted ... a time for loving and a time for hating, a time for war and a time for peace" (Eccles. 3:1–8). Looking back at the end of his life on his many accomplishments and his amassing of numerous possessions, Kohelet grimly concludes that "everything was emptiness and chasing after wind, of no profit under the sun" (Eccles. 1:11). Nevertheless, the book ends with the affirmation that there is an ultimate purpose to life: "Fear God and obey His commandments, for this is the whole of man" (Eccles. 12:13).

Ushpizin (אֻשְׁפִּיזִין)

Ushpizin (Aramaic for "guests") refers to the seven biblical personalities whom, according to the Lurianic kabbalistic tradition, we invite to visit the sukkah during the seven days of Sukkot with the words "Enter, exalted holy guests." Each of these "guests" is symbolic of one of the *sefirot* (divine emanations)—Abraham (lovingkindness, *hesed*), Isaac (strength, *gevurah*), Jacob (beauty, *tiferet*), Moses (victory, *netzach*), Aaron (splendor, *hod*), Joseph (foundation, *yesod*), and David (sovereignty, *malkhut*). All seven are guests in every sukkah throughout the seven days of the festival, but on each day one of them leads the others as the guest of honor. After reciting a special blessing, it is customary to tell stories, sing, or study traditional texts about the individual featured that night. A popular practice is to decorate the wall of the sukkah with an ornamental chart bearing an inscription that includes the names of these seven *ushpizin*.[17]

Another connection between the *ushpizin* and Sukkot is that all seven were wanderers or exiles. At God's command, Abraham left his father's house to go to the Land of Canaan (Gen. 12:1), and Isaac went to Gerar in the land of Abimelech, king of the Philistines, to escape a famine (Gen. 26:1). Jacob fled to Padan-Aram to find a wife and to escape the wrath of Esau (Gen. 28:5) and, in his last years, lived in Egypt. Joseph was sold into slavery in Egypt (Gen. 37:36). After killing the Egyptian taskmaster, Moses fled Egypt for Midian (Exod. 2:15); later, together with Aaron, he led the people during their 40 years of wandering in the wilderness. David was pursued by Saul and fled to the land of the Philistines (1 Sam. 19:10).[18] The theme of wandering and homelessness symbolized by the temporary nature of the sukkah is reflected in the lives of the *ushpizin*.[19]

The precise order of *ushpizin* is important, because of the correlation with the days of the week on which tradition tells us several of them died. The fourth day of Sukkot, on which we honor Moses (the fourth guest), falls on the same day of the week as the Seventh of Adar (the date of his death). Similarly, the fifth day of Sukkot is on the same day of the week as the First of Av (death of Aaron, fifth honored guest), and the seventh day of the festival occurs on the same day of the week as the Sixth of Sivan (Shavuot, the traditional date of the death of David, the seventh of the *ushpizin*).[20]

Water-Drawing Ceremony

A special ceremony of water libation was celebrated on the first evening of Sukkot (but not on the Sabbath) at the Temple in Jerusalem (Suk. 4:9–10, 5:1–5). Known as *Simchat Beit ha-Sho'evah* (Rejoicing of the house of water drawing), the major symbolic act was the bringing of water in a golden flask from the Pool of Siloam to the Temple, where it was poured on the altar as a supplication for an abundant rainy season.

As the Talmud relates (Suk. 51a–b):

> At the end of the first day of the festival, they descended to the Court of the Women where ... there were three golden candlesticks [each 50 cubits high] with four golden bowls on top of each and four ladders leading up to them. Four youths drawn from priestly stock held jars of oil ... which they poured into the bowls. From the worn-out undergarments of the priests they made wicks, and with them they kindled the lamps; and there was not a courtyard in Jerusalem that was not illuminated by the light. Men of piety and good deeds used to dance with lighted torches in their hands and sing songs and praises. And Levites without numbers with harps, lyres, cymbals, and trumpets and other musical instruments were there upon the 15 steps leading down from the Court of the Israelites to the Court of the Women, corresponding to the 15 Songs of Ascents in the Psalms [*Shir ha-Ma'alot*; see p. 478] ... and sang their songs.
>
> As dawn, arose, two *Kohanim* would blow trumpets and descend

the steps, sounding blasts when they came to the 10th step and once again when they reached the Court of the Women. Arriving at the eastern gate of the Temple, they would turn to the west, facing the Temple itself, and proclaim: "Our fathers [in the days of the First Temple] who were in this place [stood] with their backs toward the Temple of the Lord, and their faces toward the east, and they worshiped the sun toward the east [Ezek. 8:16]. But as for us, our eyes are turned to the Lord [we belong to God]".

At these joyful festivities, it is said that Rabbi Shimon ben Gamaliel "used to take eight lighted torches [and juggle them in the air], catching one and throwing another [so that none touched the ground]. When he prostrated himself, he used to dig his two thumbs in the ground, bend down [while still leaning on them], kiss the ground, and raise himself up again [by these two fingers while doing a headstand], a feat which no other man could accomplish" (Suk. 53a). Other reported acts of incredible dexterity were the juggling of eight knives, glasses of wine (without spilling any), and eggs (without breaking any). The Rabbis observed that whoever had not seen the ceremony of the water drawing had never witnessed real joy (Suk. 5:1).

Hoshana Rabbah (הוֹשַׁעְנָא רַבָּה)

Hoshana Rabbah (lit., "the great hoshana") is the seventh day of Sukkot. On this day, seven circuits (*hakafot*) are made around the synagogue (in Temple times, the altar) with the four species, rather than the single circuit performed on the other days of Sukkot. The Jerusalem Talmud termed Hoshana Rabbah "the day of the willow" and noted that willow branches were placed so that their leaves overlapped the top of the altar (RH 4:8, 59c).

The major ritual of Hoshana Rabbah was the striking of willow branches against the ground near the altar, which symbolized a casting away of sins and was the reason for it being considered the final Day of Judgment.[1] This ceremony took place even if Hoshana Rabbah occurred on the Sabbath, though since the fourth century C.E. the Rabbis have arranged the calendar so that this never occurs. Today, this ritual of beating a tied bundle of five willow branches against the ground (or a chair) is performed immediately after the recitation of the *hoshanot*. In most synagogues, congregants use a separate bunch of willows for this ceremony; in others, the willows are taken from the *lulav*.[2]

Liturgy

Some traditions consider Hoshana Rabbah as the end of the High Holy Day period, the last time that unfavorable judgments can be averted before the final seal is placed on the Books of Life and Death. In accordance with this concept, the *shaliach tzibbur* (prayer leader) in some synagogues wears a *kitel* (white robe) as on the High Holy Days. Ashkenazim add psalms recited only on Sabbaths and festivals to the preliminary part of the service, and some Yom Kippur melodies are often included.[3]

Customs

The Zohar states, "The seventh day of the festival [i.e., Hoshana Rabbah] is the close of the judgment of the world, and writs of judgment issue from the Sovereign" (Tsav 31b). Consequently, it is a tradition for Jews to wish each other *pikta tava*, an Aramaic phrase that literally means "a good note" (*a guten kvitel* in Yiddish) and refers to a favorable judicial decree from the divine court. One kabbalistic custom is to stay up the entire night of Hoshana Rabbah (*Tikun leil Hoshana Rabbah*; lit., "the prepared [texts] of the night of Hoshana Rabbah"), similar to the practice on Shavuot (see p. 299), but this is not as widely observed. The time is spent reading various biblical books and may be related to the practice of King David, the primary honored guest for the day (see above), who is said to have stayed awake every night except for a brief nap. However, the original purpose of this ritual was to ensure that each person finished the entire Book of Deuteronomy before the yearly Torah reading was completed and begun anew on Simchat Torah. Some visit the sukkah for a final time on Hoshana Rabbah afternoon to recite the prayer, "May we merit dwelling in the sukkah made of Leviathan [in the Messianic Age]" (see p. 724).[4]

In some Ashkenazic communities, it is a custom to eat cabbage cooked in water on Hoshana Rabbah. This is based on a phrase that occurs in several of the *piyyutim* recited on that day—"*kol mevaseir v'omeir*" (a voice announcing glad tidings says)—since in German the word "*kohl*" means "cabbage" and "*mit vasser*" means "with water."[5]

Shemini Atzeret (שְׁמִינִי עֲצֶרֶת)

Shemini Atzeret (Eighth day of assembly) is often considered as the eighth day of Sukkot, but it is actually an independent festival (Lev. 23:26). It marks the conclusion of the festivities and observances of Sukkot—though none of the Sukkot ceremonies applies to it—and as such was selected as the day for the recitation of *Yizkor* (see p. 101), the memorial service that is recited on the final day of all three pilgrimage festivals. Because "*atzeret*" comes from a root meaning "to hold back," the Rabbis deemed that God instituted this holiday so that all those who made the pilgrimage to Jerusalem for Sukkot would remain with Him in the city for one additional day (or as Rashi wrote, like a "small banquet made by the king for His beloved"). If there is no intermediate Sabbath of Sukkot on which the Book of Ecclesiastes (see p. 234) would normally be read, then it is read before the Torah reading on Shemini Atzeret.

Should Shemini Atzeret be a separate festival independent of Sukkot? After much discussion, the Talmud (Yoma 2b–3a) enumerates six signs indicating that they are separate festivals:

- The different rotation of the *Kohanim* for the Temple service.
- The recital of the *Shehecheyanu* prayer (see p. 479).
- No requirement to dwell in the sukkah or take the four species.
- Calling the day Shemini Atzeret rather than Sukkot.
- A different set of sacrifices.
- A special psalm for the day recited by the Levites.[1]

Prayer for Rain (תְּפִילַת גֶשֶׁם)

For an agrarian society like ancient Israel, nothing is more important than rain. Sufficient rainfall was perceived as demonstrating God's favor, whereas insufficient rainfall was perceived as divine punishment for the sins of the people, as in the second portion of the *Shema* (Deut. 11:13–17). Because God's grace was understood to be the source of rain, it was common for the pious—whom God would consider favorably—to pray on behalf of all Israel. On Yom Kippur, in Temple times, the *Kohen Gadol* recited a prayer for rain (Yoma 53b). A famous talmudic story is told about a righteous man named Honi who, during a drought, drew a circle in the ground and refused to move until God sent rain. Community-wide fasts were also instituted in times of drought in the hope that additional worship, devotion, and repentance would convince God to send rain. The talmudic tractate *Ta'anit* (fasts) devotes much attention to prayers for rain.

However, prayers for rain were not limited to times of trouble. Instead, they were inserted into the liturgy. From Shemini Atzeret until the first day of Passover, when the Prayer for Dew is said (see p. 270), worshipers reciting the *Amidah* add the words "*mashiv ha-ruach u-morid ha-gashem*" (Who causes the wind to blow and the rain to fall) at the beginning of the second benediction (S.A. OH 114). This addition is introduced by the extended Prayer for Rain (*Tefillat Geshem*), which is recited on Shemini Atzeret during the reader's repetition of the *Musaf Amidah* (in the Ashkenazic tradition) or before the *Musaf* service (in the Sephardic tradition). The prayer for rain is composed of a series of *piyyutim*, which vary among different traditions and stress the life-and-death importance of rain for the land and the people. In the Ashkenazic ritual, these religious hymns appeal to God to remember Abraham, Isaac, Jacob, Moses, Aaron, and the 12 tribes and "in their merit favor us with abundant water (rain)." The prayer for rain ends with three final pleas—to each of which the congregation fervently answers "Amen"—"for a blessing and not for a curse, for life and not for death, and for plenty and not for famine."

The sages decreed that the Prayer for Rain should be recited during Sukkot, the pilgrimage festival that falls closest to the rainy season in Israel. However, because of the obligation to dwell in the sukkah, rainfall would make it uncomfortable or impossible to fulfill this mitzvah. This desire for good weather while in the sukkah led the Rabbis to designate that the Prayer for Rain be postponed until Shemini Atzeret.

Simchat Torah (שִׂמְחַת תּוֹרָה)

Simchat Torah (Rejoicing of/with the Torah) is the final day of the series of festivals associated with Sukkot. Rather than a separate festival, Simchat Torah was during talmudic times simply referred to as the second day of Shemini Atzeret (Meg. 31a). Even today, it is called Shemini Atzeret in both the prayers and the *Kiddush* recited on this day. In Israel, Simchat Torah is celebrated on the same day as Shemini Atzeret (22nd of Tishrei); in the Diaspora, it falls on the next day (23rd of Tishrei) and concludes the Sukkot season.

The hallmark of the Simchat Torah services is the completion of the annual cycle of readings from the Torah scroll. This became the universal custom during the gaonic period, when the practice of the influential Babylonian community of reading the entire Torah in one year finally supplanted the triennial cycle followed in the Land of Israel (see p. 439). Originally, only the last two chapters of the Torah (Deut. 33–34) were selected as the portion for this day. However, it later became customary to also read the first chapter of Genesis on Simchat Torah so as to silence Satan and prevent him from arguing that the Jews were celebrating only because they had finally finished the Torah and did not want to start reading it again. Moreover, the last letter of the Book of Deuteronomy and the first letter of Genesis spell "*lev*" (heart), teaching that just as the heart is to the body, so is Torah to the universe (*divrei emet*).[1]

After the *Amidah* on the evening of the festival, the prayer leader recites and the congregation repeats *ata hareitah* (you have been shown [to know that the Lord is God, there is none beside Him]), a series of biblical verses praising the wonders and glory of God. All the Torah scrolls are removed from the ark; in some synagogues, a lighted candle is left in the empty ark, based on the verse: "The commandment is a lamp, the teaching {Torah] is a light" (Prov. 6:23).[2] The Torahs are carried around the synagogue in seven processions (*hakafot*), possibly related to the seven times Joshua circled Jericho before the walls of the city collapsed. Behind the Torahs follow the children, who traditionally carry flags like the tribal standards held by the Israelites as they traveled in the wilderness.[3] Prescribed alphabetical verses are recited initially, but as these finish there is an opportunity for singing popular Hebrew songs as well as dancing with the Torahs and with each other. Some consider it praiseworthy to drink alcohol at this time so as to enhance the ability to dance, the extent of the procession, and the exhilaration of the participants. When the seven circuits have been completed, all but one of the Torah scrolls are returned to the ark. Traditionally, the last section of Deuteronomy is chanted out of the remaining scroll (though not the final verses, which are read the next morning)—the only time during the year when the Torah is read at night.[4]

An innovation in some liberal synagogues is to read three Torah portions on the evening of Simchat Torah. All the men are called up for the first aliyah; all the women for the second (the end of Deuteronomy); and all the children, covered by a tallit over their heads, for the third (the first few verses of Genesis). Another practice is to have the Torah scroll completely unrolled and held by congregants in a huge circle around the room. As the beginning and end of the Torah are placed next to each other, the congregation is literally encircled by words of Torah.[5]

On the following morning, the *hakafot* are repeated. After the seven circuits, three Torah scrolls are left out of the ark. From the first scroll, the reader repeatedly chants a series of verses (Deut. 33:1–26) until all adult Jews (only the males in Orthodox synagogues) have had a chance to recite the blessings over the Torah. All the children are then called up together for an *aliyah*, and a tallit is spread like a canopy above their heads while they recite the blessings with an adult accompanying them. Those who are honored with the last two *aliyot* are popularly designated as the *hatan Torah* (bridegroom of the Law) and *hatan b'reishit* (bridegroom of the beginning). The first of these is called up for the final portion of the Torah (Deut. 33:27–34:12); this honor is usually given to the rabbi of the congregation or a scholar. The other, who is called up for the reading of the opening portion of Genesis (1:1–2:3) from the second scroll, is typically the president or a distinguished lay member of the congregation.

In medieval Europe, the *hatan Torah* and *hatan b'reishit* made generous contributions to charity and threw sweets to the children in the synagogue. Today, in many congregations it is customary for these individuals to pledge contributions to the synagogue and sponsor refreshments in honor of the event. This is based on the verse "He [Solomon] went to Jerusalem … and sacrificed burnt offerings and presented offerings of well-being; and he made a banquet for all his courtiers" (1 Kings 3:15), which the Rabbis interpreted as meaning that a feast should be given in honor of the completion of the Torah cycle.

Finally, the sacrificial rite for the day (Num. 29:35–39) is read from the third Torah scroll. It is a custom for those lifting up the scrolls after the readings on Simchat Torah to crisscross them, symbolizing the adage "Turn the Torah [study it from all sides], and turn it over again, for everything may be found in it" (Avot 5:26). The haftarah portion for Simchat Torah is the opening of Joshua (1:1–18), which begins "After the death of Moses" and continues the history of the Jewish people as they prepare to enter the Promised Land after the "completion" of the Torah.[6]

Simchat Torah can be likened to a wedding, both in symbolism and mood. The tallit held over the heads of the children is the *huppah* (bridal canopy); the last two people receiving Torah honors bear the special title of "bridegroom." Finally, worshipers dance and sing with the Torah scrolls in seven processionals that re-create the festive atmosphere of a wedding celebration.[7]

For many years, Simchat Torah was the occasion for large gatherings in Russia, primarily in and around the Choral Synagogue in Moscow, where groups of Jewish youth sang Hebrew and Yiddish songs, danced the hora, and discussed the latest events in Israel.[7] In the West, mass demonstrations were held on Simchat Torah, demanding that the Soviet authorities permit Jews to freely study their history and religion and be granted the right to emigrate to Israel.

Winter Festivals

Hanukkah (חֲנֻכָּה)

Hanukkah (Dedication) is the eight-day festival that begins on the 25th of Kislev (December) and commemorates the victory of Judah Maccabee and his followers over the army of the Syrian ruler, Antiochus Epiphanes. In the fourth century B.C.E., Greek forces under Alexander the Great conquered much of the known world, including the Near East and Israel. When Alexander died in 320, leaving no sons to succeed him, a bitter 20-year power struggle between his two leading generals resulted in Ptolemy ruling Egypt and Seleucus controlling Syria. The Land of Israel, the crossroads of the ancient world, came under Seleucid domination.

The historical basis of Hanukkah is found in the two Books of the Maccabees. These are part of the Apocrypha, a group of 14 books of the Septuagint (Greek translation of the Bible) that Judaism did not include in the Bible but were accepted by the Catholic Church. In 168 B.C.E., king Antiochus Epiphanes attempted to Hellenize all of the peoples under his rule. He outlawed the practice of such Jewish rituals as Sabbath observance and circumcision and converted the Temple into a pagan shrine by instituting the worship of Greek gods and the sacrifice of pigs on the altar. Many Jews enthusiastically accepted the Greek customs, while others resisted Hellenism and died as martyrs.[1]

When a Jew in the village of Modi'in prepared to perform the idolatrous act of pig sacrifice, Mattathias, a respected elderly *Kohen*, became so furious that he slew him. With his five sons, Mattathias retreated to the mountains and fought a guerilla war against the Syrian-Greeks and their Jewish allies. After Mattathias's death, the leadership of the band passed to his third son, Judah, who waged a brave and brilliant campaign that eventually led to the defeat of the Seleucids.[2]

Judah was given the name "Maccabee," which may have derived

from the Hebrew word *"makav"* (hammer) and thus have been a testament to his imposing strength. Another explanation is that Maccabee is an acrostic for the first letters of the Hebrew words *Mi kamocha ba'elim Adonai* ("Who is like You, O Lord, among the mighty"; Exod. 15:11), which is recited daily before the morning and evening *Amidah* and as part of the Song at the Sea (see p. 409).

Judah and his comrades finally liberated Jerusalem and began to purify the Temple. The defiled altar was demolished and a new one built, and new holy vessels were prepared. On the 25th of Kislev, the third anniversary of the harsh decrees that sparked the uprising, the Temple was joyfully rededicated and its sacrificial service renewed. According to the Mishnah, this task took eight days, and thus the festival is observed for that long. Another explanation is that the eight days of dedication ceremonies were modeled after the consecration of the Temple of Solomon during Sukkot (2 Macc. 12), a holiday that the Maccabees could not observe while they were still fighting as fugitives in the mountains of Judea (2 Macc. 10:6–8). The Torah portion for Hanukkah (Num. 7:1–8:4) describes the identical sacrifices brought by the princes of the 12 tribes at the dedication of the sanctuary as well as the kindling of the menorah. The haftarah reading (Zech. 2:14–4:7) for the Sabbath of Hanukkah contains the verse "Not by [military] might, nor by [physical] power, but by My spirit, said the Lord of Hosts"—a prophecy of the spiritual victory of God in every generation. On this joyous festival, a full *Hallel* is recited on each of the eight days, *Tachanun* (prayers of supplication) is not said, and fasting is prohibited; in traditional communities, it is forbidden to eulogize the dead.

Ironically, the ritual that is now most closely associated with Hanukkah—the kindling of lights—is not mentioned in any of the historical works describing the rededication of the Temple. Only later in the Talmud is there the first mention of the legend that, when the Maccabees entered the Temple, they discovered that the Syrian-Greeks had defiled all the jugs of oil for lighting the menorah (Shab. 21b). After much searching, they found a single small cruse of oil still bearing the unbroken seal of the *Kohen Gadol*. However, this cruse contained only enough oil to keep the menorah burning for a single day. Miraculously, the menorah flame continued to burn for eight days until new pure oil could be prepared. To commemorate this event, the Rabbis decreed that the holiday would be observed annually by kindling lights for eight days, and Hanukkah became known as the Festival of Lights.

The Talmud focuses completely on the miracle of the oil, omitting all references to the incredible military victory of Judah the Maccabee and the Hasmoneans, the family name of the Maccabees and their descendants. This may reflect the fact that it was composed after the disastrous revolts against Rome in 70 C.E., when the Second Temple was destroyed, and in 135, when the Bar Kokhba rebellion failed. By censoring the inspiring story of how a small number of Jews successfully overcame a powerful enemy, the Rabbis hoped to discourage any thoughts of another doomed attempt at overthrowing Roman rule. In addition, the Hasmonean dynasty had quickly become corrupt and Hellenized, opposing and even persecuting the Rabbis. Furthermore, the Rabbis condemned the re-establishment of the monarchy by the Hasmoneans after their victory over the Syrian-Greeks. According to Jewish tradition, only members of the House of David (descended from the tribe of Judah) could legitimately lay claim to the throne of Israel, and the Hasmoneans did not possess that lineage.[3]

Nevertheless, the tale of the Maccabees never totally disappeared from Hanukkah. On each day of the festival, *Al ha-Nissim* (For the miracles) is recited in the *Amidah* and during the Grace after Meals. This summary of the story of Hanukkah emphasizes the military victory, mentions lighting the Temple menorah only incidentally, and makes no reference to the miracle of the oil.[4] In Israel, Hanukkah has become a symbol of national liberation and the triumphant Jewish spirit. This view is reflected in a torchlight marathon from Modi'in, where the rebellion broke out and the Hasmoneans are buried, to Jerusalem.[5]

Work is permitted on Hanukkah, and there is no special synagogue service. However, influenced by the winter Christmas season in contemporary America, Hanukkah has assumed the status of a major holiday, in which gift giving has become a central focus.

Customs

The major ritual associated with Hanukkah is the kindling of the festival lights (see below) that, like the holiday itself, is rabbinically ordained. Following candle lighting, many sing the hymn *Maoz Tzur* (Mighty rock [of my salvation]; see below) and a variety of other

Hanukkah songs. To commemorate the miracle of the oil, it is customary to eat foods fried in oil, such as potato latkes (pancakes) in Ashkenazic communities and *sufganiyot* (doughnuts) among Sephardim and in Israel.

The tradition of eating cheese and other dairy foods is based on late midrashim that associate Hanukkah with the story of Judith. According to legend, Jews in a besieged city had given up hope for a successful defense. Judith left the city and entered the enemy camp, captivating the general Holofernes. The feast she prepared for him included cheese to make him thirsty; Holofernes drank wine until he fell asleep, whereupon the brave heroine decapitated him. Seeing the Jews bearing the severed head of their general, the enemy fled, and the city was saved. Although the Book of Judith (found in the Apocrypha) is set in the Babylonian period (sixth century B.C.E.) and thus seems to have no apparent connection with Hanukkah, medieval versions of the story relate it to the Hasmonean revolt. Indeed, some modern scholars have dated the book to the Maccabean period. Another woman connected with the Hanukkah story is Hannah, who with her seven sons was executed after courageously refusing to eat pig meat in defiance of Antiochus's decree. Because of Hanukkah's association with Judith and Hannah, in some communities women perform no household duties while the candles burn, or even throughout the entire festival.[6]

An old Hanukkah custom among Russian Jews was the flaming-tea ceremony. Everyone at the table pours brandy over a lump of sugar in a spoon, sets it ablaze (to symbolize the burning light of the candles), and drops it into a glass of tea. In Western Europe, goose once was a staple of the festive Hanukkah dinner, a custom borrowed from gentile neighbors celebrating Christmas at about the same time.[7]

In many communities, it has become traditional to give gifts of money, especially coins (Hanukkah *gelt*), to the children. Some have suggested that this practice relates to the minting of coins for currency by the Maccabees after restoring political autonomy to the Jewish people. In Eastern Europe, the family customarily gathered together on the fifth night of Hanukkah to give children money as a reward for their diligence in Torah study. In Western countries, Jews were influenced by the Christian tradition of exchanging gifts at Christmas. To emulate their Christian neighbors, many Jewish parents, especially in America, began giving gifts to their children on each night of Hanukkah.

In the late Middle Ages, the custom developed of yeshivah students celebrating Hanukkah by ceasing their studies and engaging in games of chance, especially cards. Despite intense rabbinic opposition to this "wasting of time," the practice has persisted to the present day. Getting into the spirit of the occasion, Rabbi Levi Yitzhak of Berditchev defended this apparent frivolity by explaining that Jews played cards on the nights of Hanukkah to accustom themselves to staying up late, so that they would have the stamina to study Torah longer during the rest of the year.[8] Today, by far the most popular game of chance played on Hanukkah is dreidel (see p. 251).

Kindling the Hanukkah Lights

The major ritual associated with Hanukkah is the lighting of the eight-branched menorah (also called a *hanukkiah*), a rabbinically ordained commandment. However, the kindling of lights in relation to Hanukkah is not even mentioned in the Books of the Maccabees or the writings of Josephus, the first-century C.E. Jewish historian. The first reference is made in a *baraita* (statement) that notes, "the precept of light on Hanukkah requires that one light be kindled in each house; the zealous require one light for each person; the extremely zealous add a light for each person each night" (Shab. 21b). It then discusses the controversy concerning the number of candles that should be lit. Beit Shammai declared that eight candles should be lit on the first night, and thereafter they should be reduced by one on each successive day. The *halakhah*, as usual, follows Beit Hillel, which argued for lighting one candle on the first night, two on the second night, and so forth. This view was based on the principle that in matters of holiness, one should increase rather than diminish.

The *halakhah* prescribes that the Hanukkah lamps be lit between "sunset and until there is no wayfarer left in the street" (Shab. 21b). The lamp should be placed outside the door of the house. A person who lives in an upper story should place the lamp at the window nearest to the street. "But in times of danger [religious persecution], it is sufficient to place [the lamp] on the table [inside the house]." Because "its purpose is to publicize the miracle," providing for the Hanukkah lights was deemed to take precedence over the purchase of wine for *Kiddush* on the Sabbath (Shab. 23b). As Maimonides observed, "Even if one has no food to eat except what he begs from charity, he should beg or sell some of his clothing to purchase the oil and lamps to light [the Hanukkah lamp]."[9] It is still customary to place the menorah by a window to publicize the miracle so that passersby can see the lights. In some cities, Hanukkah candles are lit in large menorahs erected in public places to commemorate the miracle.

The Talmud notes that the mitzvah of kindling the Hanukkah lights is best fulfilled with olive oil, to remind one of the menorah in the Temple (Shab. 23a). Nevertheless, any oil can be employed, and today most people use candles. Lighting only one menorah is sufficient to fulfill the mitzvah, but it has become customary among Ashkenazim for each person in a household to light his or her own menorah. Women are equally obliged to light the Hanukkah lamps, since they also were included in the miracle (Shab. 23a). Unlike the light cast by Sabbath and festival candles, which was originally used for illuminating the house so that one would be able to see, the light of the Hanukkah menorah is intended exclusively to publicize the miracle and is not permitted to be used for any other purpose (Shab. 21b).

The Hanukkah menorah has spaces for the eight candles (or oil and wicks), which are placed in a straight line and on the same level so that the viewer can easily determine how many candles are burning and thus what night of Hanukkah it is. A person who does not have enough candles for a given night should light only one candle, which fulfills the primary mitzvah of proclaiming the miracle and is not confusing to others. Typically, there is also space for a ninth candle, called the *shammash* (servant), which is placed higher or to one side to differentiate it from the other candles. The *shammash* is not counted as one of the eight primary lights; its only role is to kindle the other candles. The light of the *shammash* can also provide illumination for reading, thus preventing any accidental use of the light of the eight primary candles that may not be used for practical purposes.

Two blessings are recited before lighting the Hanukkah candles. The first relates specifically to the commandment to kindle the lights (*lehadlik ner shel Hanukkah*), and the second refers to the miracle itself ("Who performed miracles for our ancestors, in those days, in this season"). On the first night, as on all festivals, one also recites the *Shehecheyanu* blessing (see p. 479), which expresses thanks for being alive and well and in a position to observe the festival. The current practice is to insert the candles in the menorah from right to left (newest addition on the left), but to light them from left to right (newest addition kindled first). After the lighting is completed, it is traditional to recite a short prayer starting with the words "*ha-nerot hallalu*" (these lights).

The Hanukkah candles should burn for a minimum of a half hour. However, the general halakhic opinion is that merely kindling the lights fulfills the commandment. Therefore, if the candles do not burn for at least 30 minutes, or if they are accidentally extinguished, the mitzvah has been fully performed. Even those who say that the candles should be relit agree that the blessing should not be repeated. On Friday night, the Hanukkah candles are lit before the candles that usher in the Sabbath. Since the Sabbath candles are traditionally lit 18 minutes or more before sundown, it is customary to use bigger Hanukkah candles so that the lights will still burn for at least 30 minutes after sundown.

Maoz Tzur (מָעוֹז צוּר)

Maoz Tzur (Mighty Rock [of my salvation]) is the most popular of the Hanukkah songs traditionally sung after the kindling of the festival lights. The hymn was composed in Germany by a 13th-century poet about whom nothing is known except that his name was probably Mordecai, based on the acrostic signature spelled out by the initial Hebrew letters of the first five stanzas.[10] The most common melody was borrowed from a popular 15th-century German folk song or Protestant church hymn.

The opening stanza of *Maoz Tzur* is a prayer for the re-establishment of the Temple, the rededication of the altar, and the restoration of the sacrificial rites ("there we will bring a thanksgiving offering"). Concluding with the phrase "*hanukkat ha-mizbeach*" (dedication of the altar), this stanza is the only one known by most Jews. The next three stanzas praise God for delivering the Jewish people from various tribulations that have befallen them—Egyptian bondage, the destruction of the First Temple and the Babylonian exile, and Haman's plot in Persia.[11] The fifth stanza summarizes the miracle of Hanukkah, which commemorates the miraculous victory of the Maccabees over the Syrian-Greek army.

A final stanza, which most scholars consider a later composition by a different author, seeks divine vengeance against the enemies of the Jews. Often censored by Christian authorities, it implores God to "repel the Red One," a reference to Esau/Edom, whose descendants (Romans) were responsible for the exile of the Jewish people from the Land of Israel.[12] It also may refer to Frederick the Red, organizer of the Third Crusade, and be an indirect condemnation of the devastation caused by his and other Christian armies that destroyed hundreds of Jewish communities on their way to liberate the Holy Land from the infidels.[13]

The revenge motif explicit in *Maoz Tzur* troubled some segments of the Jewish community. In the 19th century, two well-known American rabbis, Marcus Jastrow and Gustav Gottheil, composed a considerably

DREIDEL (סְבִיבוֹן)

The dreidel, a four-sided top that is inscribed with Hebrew letters, is a popular symbol of Hanukkah. Although the Rabbis generally prohibited gambling as a waste of time that instead should be devoted to Torah study, they were more lenient during this festival of joy. "Dreidel" is a Yiddish word derived from the German "*drehen*" (to turn). In medieval Germany, gambling dice had four letters inscribed on their sides—N, G, H, and S, respectively—representing the words "*nichts*" (nothing), "*ganz*" (all), "*halb*" (half), and "*shtell arein*" (put in). After throwing the dice, the player would do the action indicated by the letter that appeared face upward. Jews transformed the dice into a spinning top and translated the letters into their Hebrew equivalents—נ (N), ג (G), ה (H), and שׁ (S)—which add up to the same numerical value (358) as *Mashiach* (Messiah). These letters also form an acronym for the phrase *nes gadol hayah sham* (a great miracle happened there). In modern Israel, the dreidel is known as *sevivon* (Hebrew for a "spinning top") and the letter שׁ is replaced by a פ (P)—the first letter of the word "*po*" (here), making the phrase "a great miracle happened *here*."[1]

toned-down English version, which they titled "Rock of Ages," deeming it more palatable to contemporary sensibilities.[14]

Tu b'Shevat (ט״ו בִּשְׁבָט)

Tu b'Shevat, which occurs on the 15th day (full moon) of the month of Shevat (January–February), is known as the "New Year of the Trees," the day on which God decides how bountiful the fruit of each tree will be in the coming year. The word "Tu" derives from the Hebrew alphabetical form for the number "15"—ט (9) plus ו (6). Although adding י (10) and ה (5) to get י״ה (15) would make more mathematical sense, this spelling is not used since it is one of the holy names of God.[1]

In ancient times, produce needed to be tithed annually. As the New Year of the Trees, Tu b'Shevat was the beginning of a new tithing cycle (RH 1:1). In the Land of Israel the rainy season precedes Tu b'Shevat, so fruits that began to form after this date were taxed in the following cycle. The determination of the age of a tree was also important because one was forbidden to eat or derive any benefit from the fruit that a tree bears during its first three years (Lev. 19:23). During the fourth year, all fruit had to be brought to Jerusalem and eaten there (Lev. 19:24); only in the fifth year were all restrictions removed (Lev. 19:25). Tu b'Shevat also corresponded to the time of the flowering of the almond tree, the first to bloom in Israel.

Long a minor festival, Tu b'Shevat became substantially more important among Sephardic Jews under the influence of the 16th-century kabbalists of Safed, who instituted the practice of eating different kinds of fruit, especially those native to the Land of Israel, accompanied by appropriate readings. The kabbalists viewed trees as symbols of humans, based on the verse: "For a human is like the tree of the field" (Deut. 20:19). Parallel to the obligation of *tikun olam* (spiritually repairing the world), the kabbalists believed that human beings could elevate their spiritual selves by the ritual consumption of various fruits on Tu b'Shevat. If done with the proper intention (*kavanah*), sparks of holy light hidden in the fruit could be liberated from their shells and ascend to their divine source, thus contributing to the renewal of life for the coming year. For the kabbalists, trees were symbolic of the Tree of Life, which carries divine goodness and blessings into the world. Attempting to stimulate the flow of positive divine energy into the world, the kabbalists of Safed created a Tu b'Shevat seder (modeled after the Passover seder) in which participants eat various kinds of fruit and nuts and drink four cups of wine.[2]

The kabbalists conceived of four worlds or levels of creation (from lowest to highest)—*asiyah* ("action," our world of physical reality), *yetzirah* ("formation," the level similar to Plato's "forms," the ideal version of our world), *beri'ah* ("creation," the site of the forces leading to the creation of these forms), and *atzilut* ("emanation," where the divine energy initially began these processes). As purely spiritual, the world of *atzilut* cannot be symbolized in any material way. However, the other three worlds are each represented by 10 *beri'ah* specific fruits, corresponding to the number of sefirot, or emanations of the Divine. The overall symbolism in this system is that the parts that can be eaten represent holiness, the inedible parts (pits) represent the impure, and the shells protect the delicate holiness inside.[3]

Beri'ah, palpable but so soft that it needs no protection, is symbolized by fruits that have neither pits on the inside nor shells on the outside and thus are totally edible (even though they have seeds)—grapes, figs, apples, *etrogim* (citrons), lemons, pears, raspberries, blueberries, carobs, and quinces. *Yetzirah* requires protection, but only at its heart, and thus is represented by fruits that have inedible pits inside but whose outsides can be eaten—olives, dates, cherries, hackberries, jujubes, persimmons, apricots, peaches, loquats, and plums. The realm of the real world, *asiyah*, needs full protection and is represented by fruits and nuts that have tough outer shells that must be discarded and an inside that can be eaten—pomegranates, walnuts, almonds, pine nuts, chestnuts, hazelnuts, coconuts, Brazil nuts, pistachios, and pecans (also bananas, avocados, and melons).

At the Tu b'Shevat seder, one eats a combination of the fruits and nuts mentioned above as well as some others. Each food is accompanied by an appropriate verse from the Bible or a quotation from the Talmud. Reciting blessings over the fruits and nuts helps release the holy sparks of life flow trapped within them. However, the act of chewing the foods produces an even more powerful effect, for humans have 32 teeth, the precise number of times the word "*Elohim*" (God) appears in the story of Creation. Participating in the Tu b'Shevat seder allows the holy sparks to be freed and return to their Creator so that the vital life force can continue to flow.[4]

The kabbalistic seder for Tu b'Shevat also includes the drinking of four cups of wine. Each cup is filled before each set of fruits or nuts is served but drunk only after each set of food has been eaten.[5] Beginning with a cup of white wine, participants at the Tu b'Shevat seder add increasing amounts of red wine so that the next three cups are pink, deep rose, and almost completely red, respectively. This sequence symbolizes the gradual transition of the land from the cold whiteness of winter through the pale buds of spring into the full blooming flowers of summer and the striking colors of the leaves before they fall from the trees in autumn. The four cups may also represent the four letters of the Tetragrammaton, the most holy name of God.[6]

In the 20th century, with the growth of Zionism, the redemption of the land, and the founding of the State of Israel, the festival of Tu b'Shevat has acquired increased significance. It also has assumed the character of Arbor Day, with thousands of school children engaging in tree-planting ceremonies. In the Diaspora, Jews plant trees in their own communities (if the ground has thawed sufficiently) and donate money to the Jewish National Fund to support the planting of trees in Israel.[7]

Purim (פּוּרִים)

Purim (14th of Adar) celebrates the deliverance of the Jews from the Persian villain Haman's plot to kill them. The name of the holiday is the plural of the Babylonian or Persian word "*pur*" (lot), referring to the lots cast by Haman to determine when the slaughter of the Persian Jewish community was to take place (Esther 3:7). The lots fell on the 13th day of the month of Adar (late February or early March), which has become a minor fast day (see below). However, the Jews' successful struggle against their enemies led the Rabbis to exclaim that "with the start of the month of Adar our joy greatly increases" (Taan. 29a).

The main feature of Purim is the synagogue reading of the *Megillah* (scroll), the Book of Esther. After banishing Vashti, King Ahasuerus selected Esther as his new queen. When Mordecai, Esther's cousin and foster father, refused to bow down to Haman, the grand vizier convinced Ahasuerus to issue a decree calling for the massacre of Jewish communities throughout the kingdom. Under Mordecai's urging, Esther invited Haman to a private gala banquet, where she revealed that she was Jewish and pleaded for Ahasuerus to save her people. The king agreed, Haman was hanged, the Jews were given permission to attack their enemies, and Mordecai and Esther established Purim as an annual holiday.[1]

Although Purim is a joyous event, the Book of Esther is a bittersweet reminder of the experience of the Jewish people in exile. Haman's description of the Jews as "a certain people scattered about and dispersed among the other peoples" (Esther 3:8) is unfortunately all too accurate. The tale of a group of Jews living in the Diaspora at the mercy and whim of the ruler has often been repeated. All too frequently, Jews have faced a variety of Hamans, but in most instances (unlike in the *Megillah*) the conclusion of the story has not been happy. The triumph of the weak over the powerful recounted in the Book of Esther has been enormously uplifting to Jews throughout their long exile. At times, specific communities have celebrated other Purims (little Purims) to commemorate their deliverance from perilous situations.[2]

Echoing the midrashic literature, Maimonides observed that "even if all the festivals should be annulled in the Messianic Era, Purim will never be annulled,"[3] since it is such a perfect example of the Jewish community being protected by divine providence.[4] Isaac Luria, the great kabbalist, stressed the importance of Purim by remarking that the Hebrew term for the Day of Atonement means "a day like Purim" (*Yom ke-Purim*).

Historical Antecedents

According to tradition, the Book of Esther recounts events that actually occurred in the Persian capital of Shushan (Susa). Evidence cited for the book's historicity are the extensive descriptions of Persian customs and court practices. Although it is also true that there was a king Ahasuerus—the Hebrew form of the Persian name (Xerxes in Greek) of a monarch who reigned from 486 to 465 B.C.E.—the story presents several historical difficulties. For example, there is no mention of Purim in Jewish literature before the first century B.C.E. Moreover, a Persian king could choose a queen only from among seven noble Persian families, making his marriage to Esther impossible. Some scholars suggest that the Jews transformed Purim from an ancient pagan festival. Support for this view is the remarkable resemblance of the names "Mordecai" and "Esther" to the major Babylonian gods Marduk and Ishtar.[5]

The Book of Esther has a dearth of explicitly religious content. In fact, the name of God is not mentioned once in the *Megillah*. This seriously troubled the Rabbis, some of whom refused to admit the Book of Esther into the Jewish canon. The Jews neither plead to God to save them in times of peril nor have a celebration of thanksgiving to God for their deliverance. In addition, the warlike tone of the concluding chapters against their gentile oppressors led the Rabbis to fear that the Book of Esther might arouse the hatred and suspicion of non-Jews. Nevertheless, it was finally admitted as part of the biblical canon, and the story of Purim was used as a model of God's hidden hand in history. By the second century C.E., Purim was clearly an established festival. Indeed, an entire tractate of the Mishnah (*Megillah*) is devoted to the details of its observance, especially to the rules governing the reading of the scroll of Esther.

Customs

The major customs of Purim are based on the verse, "They were to observe them as days of feasting and merrymaking, and as an occasion for sending gifts to one another and presents to the poor" (Esther 9:22). "Feasting and merrymaking" refers to the special festive meal (*seudah*) eaten late on Purim afternoon, toward evening (Esther 9:19). While the traditional *Kiddush* is not said on Purim, some people recite one consisting of a senseless series of biblical verses linked solely by the use of the same Hebrew word in adjacent lines. This is an example of "Purim Torah," a variety of puns, jokes, and spoofs of the Talmud and other classic texts that are characteristic of the festival. In some yeshivot, a student was selected as the "Purim rabbi" to give lectures that frivolously manipulated sacred texts and parodied his teachers, who for one day were not the objects of respect but the targets of playful or stinging satires. One rationale for this practice is that a single day of making good-natured fun of the Torah, which is so highly revered the rest of the year, prevents Jews from becoming sanctimonious about their holy text.[6]

An Ashkenazic tradition is the *Purim-spiel* (Yiddish for "Purim play"), a performance given at the traditional festive family meal held on Purim afternoon. Over time, this developed from a witty monologue to a lavish production. Today, the *Purim-spiel* often takes place in

READING OF THE *MEGILLAH* (קְרִיאַת הַמְּגִילָּה)

Megillat Esther is read from a handwritten scroll, which is frequently decorated, often with scenes from the narrative. However, if no scroll is available, it can be read from a printed text (but without reciting the blessings). Originally read only during the day, it eventually became traditional to also read the *Megillah* at night (Meg. 4a). Rather than being rolled like a Torah, the scroll of the *Megillah* is usually folded like a letter as it is read, since the Purim story includes several written decrees and news of the festival itself was spread through dispatches (Esther 9:26,29).

A special *trope* is used for reading the *Megillah*, though it can be merely recited if no one knows the proper cantillation. The four verses of "redemption" (Esther 2:5; 8:15,16; and 10:3) are enthusiastically recited aloud by the congregation and then repeated by the reader. It is customary for the reader's voice to become louder for the several verses that relate to Mordecai and mark the decisive moments in the story (Esther 1:22; 2:4,17; 4:14; 5:4; and 6:1). Verse 2:6 is chanted using the *trope* of Lamentations, since it describes the destruction of Jerusalem. According to the Talmud, the short lines listing the 10 sons of Haman (Esther 9:7–9) should be recited in one breath, because they were hanged together (Meg. 16b).

The popular custom is for the congregation to make lots of noise each of the 54 times that the name "Haman" is read in the *Megillah* to fulfill the biblical commandment to "blot out the name of Amalek" (Deut. 25:19), the ancestor of Haman. While any kind of noisemaking device is acceptable, including booing and stamping one's feet on the floor, it is traditional to use a *grager* (rattle) for this purpose. Some even write the name Haman on the soles of their shoes, so as to literally blot out the name as they stomp their feet.

the synagogue in conjunction with the reading of the *Megillah* on Purim evening. Adults join children in the religious school in the writing and producing of satires directly or indirectly related to the events that occurred in Persia more than 2,000 years ago.

Purim is a time of carnivals and masquerades, in which people are permitted to flout the commandment forbidding men to dress as women and women to dress as men (Deut. 22:5). Under the influence of the Roman carnival, Italian Jews at the end of the 15th century were the first to add masquerading to the celebration of Purim, and this custom spread throughout the Jewish world.

In modern Israel, a prominent feature of Purim observance in Tel Aviv is the huge parade of costumed revelers called *Adloyada*. This term derives from the statement of Rav, the renowned Babylonian talmudic scholar, mandating that a person get so drunk ("mellowed with wine") on Purim that "he cannot tell the difference (*ad lo yada*) between 'Cursed is Haman' and 'Blessed is Mordecai.'" (Meg. 7b). It is interesting that the Hebrew letters of these two phrases—"*arur Haman*" and "*baruch Mordecai*"—have the identical numerical value (502). In Eastern Europe, this command to become inebriated was observed so well that a proverb described a foolish person as one "who gets drunk all year and stays sober on Purim."[7]

Mishloach manot (often abbreviated as *shalach manot*) is the tradition of sending gifts (lit., "portions") to friends and acquaintances. Because the word "*manot*" is in the plural, it became traditional to send at least two kinds of food to at least two people. Similarly, there is the practice of sending *mattanot le-evyonim* (gifts to the poor) to at least two needy people, so that they also can share in the joy of the Purim festival. In most communities, this is accomplished through contributions to charities that care for impoverished Jews.[8]

Just before reading the *Megillah* on the eve of Purim, it is customary to donate three half-dollars to charity. This symbolizes the three times in which the Torah commanded the Israelites to contribute a half shekel for the upkeep of the Tabernacle (Exod. 30:13,15). Donated during the month of Adar, in which Purim falls, the half shekels affordable even by the poor were used to purchase the animals that were offered twice daily by the *Kohanim* on behalf of the Jewish people.[9] The qualification that "the rich shall not pay more and the poor shall not pay less"[10] indicated that the Tabernacle belonged to the entire community, without regard to wealth or social status, since all are equal in the eyes of God. The half-shekel tax also taught the moral lesson that one Jew alone is only half a Jew; he or she must join with another Jew to become a complete individual.[11]

A variety of special foods are associated with Purim. The most popular are the Ashkenazic triangular pastries filled with poppy seeds or fruit known as hamantashen (Haman's pockets; see p. 262) and the Sephardic fried, ear-shaped cookies called *oznei Haman* (Haman's ears). Some communities eat chickpeas, reminiscent of the vegetarian diets of Esther (and later Daniel) to avoid any infringement of the dietary laws of kashrut while in the king's palace. A bizarre pun has led some to eat turkey on Purim, since the opening line of the *Megillah* states that Ahasuerus ruled from *Hodu* (the Hebrew word for both "turkey" and "India") to Kush (Ethiopia).[12] Kabbalists and Hasidic groups often prepare sweet-and-sour dishes that reflect the inherent dichotomy of Purim—a festival that quickly shifts from a day of deep sorrow and fasting on the 13th of Adar to one of unbridled elation and celebration on the 14th of the month.[13]

Although work is not prohibited, many take the day off to fully cel-

HAMANTASHEN

Hamantashen (lit., "Haman's pockets") are triangular pastries that are traditionally eaten by Ashkenazic Jews on Purim and may represent the bribes filling the pockets of this corrupt villain of the Purim story. Although they may be stuffed with puréed dried fruits, hamantashen are traditionally filled with *mohn* (Yiddish for "poppy seeds"), a word that sounds like the Hebrew pronunciation of the second syllable of the name Haman. Hamantashen are sometimes called "Haman's hat," and European medieval drawings often anachronistically depict Haman as wearing the popular three-cornered hat of the time. Other Purim pastries, popular among Sephardim, are fried, ear-shaped cookies known in Hebrew as *oznei Haman* (Haman's ears). This name is said to have derived from the former practice of cutting off the ears of criminals before hanging them—appropriate since Haman was hanged "on the gallows that he had prepared for Mordecai" (Esther 7:10) at the conclusion of the Book of Esther.[1]

ebrate the rituals of exchanging gifts and the festive Purim *seudah*. The only change in the liturgy is the addition of *Al ha-Nissim* (For the Miracles) to the *Amidah* and the Grace after Meals. Since Purim is a joyous occasion, mourners do not observe shivah (see p. 95) in the traditional formal manner.

Jewish communities throughout the world have developed unusual Purim customs. Many made large effigies of Haman and either beat, burned, or hung them. In Afghanistan, the synagogue carpets were taken up and the congregants trampled on the floor beneath them, in case Haman were hiding there. In Germany, torches containing gunpowder would be ignited on Purim eve, exploding with a deafening roar during the *Megillah* reading. French children used to take smooth stones, write or engrave Haman's name on them, and strike them together during the *Megillah* reading whenever the villain's name was mentioned. In Bukhara, where the ground was usually covered with snow at Purim time, a large snow-Haman was built next to the synagogue. This Haman had a funny-shaped torso, long thick legs like an elephant, a large head, eyes of charcoal, a carrot for the nose, and a piece of beet for the mouth. A "gold chain" of dried watermelon peels was hung over the stomach as a symbol of office, and a broken pot was placed on the head. After the Purim feast, the whole community gathered as a large fire was made around the snow-Haman, and all sang joyfully as it melted.[14]

Shushan Purim

The Jews of Shushan, the Persian capital, continued to battle against their enemies for an extra day and did not rest until the 15th of Adar, when they celebrated their deliverance (Esther 9:18). Because Shushan was a walled city, the Rabbis ruled that Jews living in cities that had a fortified outer wall around them at the time of Joshua would observe Purim on the 15th of Adar (Meg. 1:1). Therefore, in modern Israel, Purim is celebrated on the 15th of Adar in Jerusalem (a walled city in ancient times), whereas in Tel Aviv and elsewhere the festival is observed on the 14th of the month. In leap years, when there is an extra month of Adar, Purim is celebrated in Second Adar so that the festival always falls one month before Passover.

Fast of Esther (תַּעֲנִית אֶסְתֵּר)

Purim is preceded by the Fast of Esther (Ta'anit Esther), now observed only in traditional circles, which recalls the three-day fast by the Jews of Persia (Esther 3:12, 4:16) to lend support to Queen Esther. Because the fate of her people was at stake, Esther was preparing to enter King Ahasuerus' presence without prior permission, an act punishable by death. Ironically, the fast mentioned in the *Megillah* actually occurred during Passover of the previous year, rather than just before the climactic events in the Purim story. Indeed, on the 13th of Adar of that year, the Jews were fighting against their enemies. When the day of fasting falls on a Sabbath, it is moved back to Thursday, since fasting is not permitted either on the Sabbath (except on Yom Kippur), a day of joy, or on Friday, when one is preparing for the Sabbath.

Archetypal Characters in the Book of Esther

Esther (אֶסְתֵּר)

The heroine of the Purim story was one of the four most beautiful women in the world (Meg. 15a) and a symbol of female modesty. Although her Hebrew name was Hadassah (myrtle), non-Jews called her Esther, a name that is derived from Ishtar, the Persian equivalent of Venus, the goddess of beauty (Meg. 13a). Her courage and ingenuity enabled the Jews of Persia to be saved from Haman's plot to massacre them. Some have suggested that the name Esther derived from the Hebrew word "*seter*" (hidden), a foreshadowing of her ability to disguise her Jewish identity until she had won the heart of King Ahasuerus and thus was in a position to save her people from destruction.[15]

Haman (הָמָן)

The villain of the Purim story, Haman is the prototype of the enemy of the Jews throughout the ages. He is traditionally considered a descendant of Amalek (Meg. 13a), the ancient adversary of Israel whose roots reach back to Esau.

Amalek was the predatory tribe that perpetrated a cowardly and unprovoked attack on the faint and weary stragglers at the rear of the column of Israelites, who were exhausted from the march out of Egypt (Exod. 17:8–16). Consequently, the Jews were commanded to utterly exterminate the seed of Amalek, male and female, young and old (Deut. 25:19). Hundreds of years later, this was precisely the order that the prophet Samuel gave to Saul, the first king of Israel. Saul defeated the Amalekites in battle, but he did not execute their monarch, Agag (1 Sam. 15:9). For this act of disobedience, God withdrew the kingship from Saul and replaced him with David. In the *Megillah*, Haman is designated as "the Agagite"; Esther and Mordecai were descendants of Saul.

Jews are also commanded to "Remember what Amalek did to you" (Deut. 25:17). Today, this is fulfilled by the annual reading of the Torah portion dealing with Amalek on Shabbat Zakhor (Sabbath of Remembrance), which precedes the festival of Purim.

Mordecai (מָרְדֳּכַי)

The hero of the Purim story, Mordecai was a descendant of a family of upper-class Israelite society who, in 597 B.C.E., were taken into Babylonian exile along with King Jehoiachin of Judah by Nebuchadnezzar. Although the name "Mordecai" bears a close resemblance to the name of the Babylonian god Marduk, the Talmud interprets his name as coming from the two words "*mor*" (myrrh) and "*decai*" (pure), which reflect his noble character (Meg. 10b). The foster father of his cousin Esther (Esther 2:5), Mordecai was one of Ahasuerus's consultants who "sat in the king's gate" (Esther 2:21). In this position, Mordecai was able to inquire daily about her welfare (Esther 2:10–11). When he discovered a plot to assassinate the king, Mordecai informed Esther, who passed the information to the king in Mordecai's name. Although not immediately rewarded for saving the king's life, Mordecai later was dressed in royal attire and promenaded around the city on a royal steed by Haman, his archenemy (Esther 6). When Haman's plot to destroy the Jews became evident, Mordecai urged the hesitant Esther to intercede with Ahasuerus on behalf of her people, maintaining that "Who knows, perhaps you have attained to royal position for just such a crisis" (Esther 4:14). He argued that if she failed to act decisively, "Do not imagine that you [alone], of all the Jews, will escape with your life by being in the king's palace. On the contrary, if you keep silent ... relief and deliverance will come to the Jews from another quarter, while you and your father's house will perish" (Esther 4:13–14).

In the *Megillah,* Mordecai and Haman represent polar opposites of good and evil. Yet the Rabbis decreed that one was obligated to reach a state of *ad lo yada,* the inability to distinguish between "Blessed is Mordecai" and "Cursed is Haman." Rather than a drunken daze, *ad lo yada* can imply a mystical moment of insight, when there truly is *no* difference between Mordecai and Haman—just as good and evil are encompassed within God who, as Isaiah (45:7) observed, "form[s] light and create[s] darkness, make[s] peace and create[s] evil." Support for this view comes from a midrash that declares that when all other festivals will be abolished in messianic times, Purim alone will remain.[16]

Spring Festivals

Passover (פֶּסַח)

The spring festival of Passover (Pesach) commemorates the redemption of the Jewish people from bondage and the Exodus from Egypt. One of the three pilgrimage festivals (with Shavuot and Sukkot), Passover also celebrates the spring barley harvest in Israel. The name derives from the 10th plague, when God "passed over" (*pasach*) the homes of the Israelites and slew only the firstborn of Egypt (Exod. 12:27). Other names for the festival are Hag ha-Matzot (Festival of the unleavened bread), Hag ha-Aviv (Festival of spring), and Zeman Heruteinu (Aeason of our freedom). Passover begins on the 15th of Nisan and lasts seven days in Israel and eight in the Diaspora. The first and seventh days (the first two and last two in the Diaspora) are considered festival days on which work other than cooking is prohibited; on the "intermediate days" (*hol ha-mo'ed*), work is permitted.

In the synagogue, a full *Hallel* is recited on the first day of Passover (two days in the Diaspora), but only a half *Hallel* on the remaining days of the festival (see p. 162). The reason is that on the seventh day the Egyptians were drowned in the Sea of Reeds; when the angels wanted to offer praises for the miraculous escape of the Israelites, God chastised them for singing while some divine creatures were perishing (Meg. 10b). Since a half *Hallel* is recited on the seventh day (and eighth in the Diaspora), the same must apply to the intermediate days of Passover, lest they "receive more honor" than the last festival day(s).[1] The Torah is read on all eight days.[2] There are five *aliyot* on the first two and last two days of Passover and four *aliyot* during *hol ha-mo'ed*, except on the Sabbath when there are the usual seven *aliyot*. On the first day, a special prayer for dew (*tal*; see p. 292) is recited in the *Musaf Amidah,* replacing the prayer for rain (*mashiv ha-ruach u-morid ha-gashem*), which is not resumed until Shemini Atzeret in the fall (see

p. 239). The Song of Songs (see below) is read on the Sabbath of Passover, and *Yizkor* (memorial service) is recited on the last day. The counting of the Omer (see p. 292), which connects Passover to Shavuot seven weeks later, begins on the second day.

The eating or mere possession of *hametz* (leavened products) is explicitly prohibited on Passover, and many symbolically sell it to a non-Jew through the intermediary of their rabbi (see below). At the end of the festival, some Jews refrain from eating bread or other leavened products until there has been enough time for the rabbi to buy back the *hametz*. Many wait until the next day, to avoid eating any products containing *hametz* that may have been prepared on the holiday.[3] In contrast, the Jews of North African descent hold a great celebration called *Maimuna* on the evening and day after Passover (see below).

As the paradigmatic story of freedom and redemption and God's special choosing of the Children of Israel, Passover has become the central holiday of the Jewish people. References to the Exodus are found throughout the liturgy and the mitzvot. Every morning in the *Shacharit* service, Jews recount the story of the Exodus, including Moses' Song at the Sea (see p. 409). The first of the Ten Commandments links monotheism with the divine act of saving the Israelites: "I the Lord am your God who brought you out of the land of Egypt, the house of bondage" (Exod. 20:2). The Friday night *Kiddush* describes the Sabbath as "a memorial to the Exodus from Egypt," and this day of freedom from everyday worldly pursuits is in dramatic contrast with the enslavement of the Israelites. The rationales for the numerous Jewish laws requiring ethical sensitivity and compassion are based on the fact that "you were strangers in the land of Egypt, and I took you out"; just as God heard the pleas of a desperate, enslaved people, so we are enjoined to heed the call of the downtrodden and disenfranchised among us. Finally, we are reminded of the Exodus in the tzitzit, mezuzah, certain laws of kashrut, and the laws pertaining to the harvest.[4]

Historical Antecedents

Some scholars believe that the festival of Passover originally consisted of two distinct celebrations. First was the *pesach,* or "protective sacrifice" (probably the accurate meaning of the Hebrew word) on the 14th of Nisan (Lev. 23:5; Num. 28:16), which may have developed from a no-

FAST OF THE FIRSTBORN (תַּעֲנִית בְּכוֹרִים)

The Fast of the Firstborn (*Ta'anit Bechorim*) is observed on the 14th of Nisan, the day before Passover, to commemorate and express gratitude to God for sparing the firstborn Israelites during the 10th plague in Egypt (Exod. 13:1). Traditionally, if a child was too young to fast (under the age of 13), his father fasted instead of him; if the father was also a firstborn, the child's mother would fast instead of the child. According to some authorities, firstborn females should fast as well, though women generally never acquire the status of firstborn in Jewish law. Some people who are not firstborn choose to fast to whet their appetites for their first taste of matzah at the seder.

As one of the minor fast days, *Ta'anit Bechorim* begins at sunrise, rather than the previous night. Many of those who observe it take advantage of the halakhic principle that Torah study can supersede and break off the fast. Whenever the study of a body of Jewish text is completed, such as a tractate of the Talmud, it is customary to have a *siyum* (completion)—a celebration of the special occasion with food and drink. Therefore, the tradition has evolved to finish the study of a tractate of Talmud on the morning before Passover, when a festive meal (*seudat mitzvah;* "meal in honor of a mitzvah") is arranged in the synagogue. For those firstborns who participate, the meal associated with the *siyum* concludes the fast.[1]

madic pagan custom of sacrificing animals to ensure protection of their flocks before leaving from their winter desert pasture to more cultivated areas. Second was the seven-day Feast of Unleavened Bread (Lev. 23:6; Num. 28:17), perhaps developed from a Canaanite spring festival. According to this view, these were combined at the beginning of the Babylonian exile.[5]

Hametz (חָמֵץ)

The eating of *hametz* (leavened products) is explicitly prohibited on Passover (Exod. 12:19–20, 13:3). This is a memorial to the Exodus, when the Israelites "took their dough before it was leavened" (Exod. 12:34) and left Egypt in great haste. The criterion for rendering grain *hametz* is that it ferments on decomposition. The Rabbis deemed that this characteristic applied to the five species of grain indigenous to the Land of Israel: wheat, barley, oats, rye, and spelt (see p. 477). Those grains (rice, millet) that decompose by "rotting" were not regarded as forbidden *hametz* (Pes. 35a). Nevertheless, Ashkenazic authorities forbid the use of rice and millet on Passover and included a group of foods known as *kitniyot* in the prohibition as well. *Kitniyot,* generally translated as "legumes," are foods such as beans, peas, corn, lentils, buckwheat, and, according to some authorities, peanuts. One reason for this ruling is to prevent possible confusion if flour made from these substances were stored near *hametz* flour. Otherwise, one might inadvertently bake matzah using rice or legume flour, which was not permissible because matzah theoretically may be made with only one of the five grains that are capable of becoming leavened (but, in practice, only with wheat).

Ashkenazim feared that kernels of wheat and barley might be mixed inadvertently with rice and *kitniyot,* potentially turning them into prohibited *hametz* if exposed to water. After the Ritva, a great 14th-century Sephardic Torah scholar, recorded that once wheat kernels were found mixed together with the rice in containers sold as pure rice, Sephardim in northern Spain refused to eat rice on Passover while continuing to consume beans, peas, and other *kitniyot*. Today, however, most Sephardim do eat rice on Passover.[6]

The question of what constitutes *kitniyot*—and the proper treatment of liquids and oils produced from them—has been the subject of much debate in the rabbinic literature. Most Ashkenazim forbid the use of all derivative products. Therefore, soft drinks for Passover are sweetened with sugar, rather than with the corn syrup that is used during the rest of the year. In Israel, where the majority of the religious population is of Sephardic origin and thus many of the manufactured goods for Passover contain *kitniyot* or their oils, Ashkenazim must exert great care in purchasing Passover foods to ensure that they contain no prohibited *kitniyot* or their derivatives.[7]

One excellent food that is permitted on Passover, even for Ashkenazim, is quinoa. A member of the goosefoot family, named for its three-lobed leaves, quinoa is distinguished by its curly halo when cooked and was never included in the prohibition against *kitniyot*. Quinoa is prepared like rice and is a naturally complete protein.

According to Jewish law, if forbidden food is accidentally mixed with permissible food, the concoction is permissible if the forbidden food accounts for 1/60 or less of the total amount (*batel b'shishim*; lit., "nullified in the 60"). This rule, however, does not apply to *hametz* on Passover. Even the tiniest amount of *hametz* makes forbidden everything with which it has been mixed.

In addition to the obvious breads, pastries, and pasta, *hametz* can be found in candy and gum, oils, vinegar, spices, processed meats, cereals, ice cream, whiskey, and many other products. Even paper towel wrappers may contain cornstarch, a form of *hametz*.[8] Because pots in which *hametz* has been cooked absorb and retain some of it—"imparting a flavor" into any other food cooked in them—those that have been used during the year are forbidden for use during Passover unless they have been rigorously cleansed in accordance with halakhic requirements (S.A. OH 451). For the same reason, separate dishes must be used for Passover; however, this is not required for nonpermeable glass, which merely needs to be soaked and well washed to be permissible for Passover use.

The mere possession of *hametz* during Passover is also forbidden. The first step toward ridding the home of *hametz* is a thorough general housecleaning. To symbolize the final removal of *hametz* from the home, a formal search for leaven (*bedikat hametz*) is conducted on the night before Passover. Before the search, it is customary to deposit small pieces of bread (10 pieces, according to kabbalistic lore) in rooms throughout the house where *hametz* may have been used during the year. The search is traditionally carried out by candlelight, with a feather and a wooden spoon to collect the *hametz*. The use of a candle (lamp) is required to enable an extremely rigorous and thorough search (some now use a flashlight for safety's sake) (Pes. 1:1).[9] After the search, one recites an Aramaic statement: "All *hametz* in my possession that I have not seen or removed, or of which I am unaware, is hereby nullified and ownerless as the dust of the earth." In the morning, after the last meal of *hametz*, any leftovers are added to the crumbs gathered the previous night, and all are burned or thrown out. Finally, the declaration of annulment of *hametz* said on the previous night is repeated to conclude the ritual of banishing *hametz* from our dwellings.[10]

Sale of *Hametz*

The disposal of *hametz* could produce serious financial hardship when large quantities of foodstuffs are involved, or when *hametz* is used for business purposes. To alleviate this problem, the Rabbis devised the legal formula of "selling" the *hametz* (*mechirat hametz*) to a non-Jew before Passover and then "buying" it back after the festival has concluded. This applies only to foods; utensils used for *hametz* need only be washed and stored separately.

Initially, the selling of *hametz* involved the physical transfer from Jew to non-Jew "in the market place" (Pes. 13a), though soon there developed the mutual understanding that the Jew would buy it back after Passover. To preclude the need for having to physically transfer the property, today the seller merely writes down the type of *hametz* without specifying the precise amount or exact location. The parties agree on a price and a down payment made by the non-Jew, who theoretically could choose to pay the purchase price and keep the *hametz*. Because a formal legal document is required, the sale usually is done through a rabbi, who is empowered to act as the agent in the transaction. After Passover, the agent buys back the *hametz* and restores it to the original owners.[11]

Symbolism

The Rabbis regarded *hametz* as the symbol of the evil inclination. The "yeast in the dough" (the evil impulse that causes a ferment in the heart) prevents human beings from carrying out the will of God (Ber. 17a). *Hametz* also represents human haughtiness and conceit. Just as leaven puffs up dough, so human arrogance cause us to believe that we, not God, control our destiny. Keeping away from *hametz* during Passover reminds Jews that they once languished in Egyptian bondage before being redeemed by God "with a mighty hand and with an outstretched arm."[12]

The Song of Songs (שִׁיר הַשִּׁירִים)

The Song of Songs (*Shir ha-Shirim*), one of the five *megillot*, is usually read on the intermediate Sabbath of Passover. When the first day of

PRAYER FOR DEW (תְּפִלַּת טַל)

On the first day of Passover, Jews throughout the world recite the special Prayer for Dew (*tal*), asking God to end the winter rains in Israel and to send dew to a land that depends on this source of moisture during the long, dry summers. According to legend, this is an auspicious time to pray for dew—for when Isaac bestowed the patriarchal blessing on his son Jacob (Gen 27:28–29), he declared that the future festival of Passover would be the time not only of redemption but also when the heavenly chambers of dew and blessing are open (PdRE 32). Just as the gentle dew of spring leads to the rebirth of the natural world, so it is the season when the Jewish nation was finally released from stifling bondage and allowed to flower.[1]

In the Ashkenazic ritual, the Prayer for Dew is recited during the reader's repetition of the *Musaf Amidah*. The six-stanza invocation ends "For You are the Lord our God, who makes the wind blow and the dew descend," followed by this plea: "For a blessing and not for a curse; for life and not for death; for plenty and not for famine." In Israel, all rites have adopted the Sephardic custom of inserting the phrase "Who causes the dew to descend" (*morid ha-tal*) in every *Amidah* at the beginning of the second benediction from the first day of Passover until Shemini Atzeret, when the Prayer for Rain is said (see p. 239).

Passover falls on the Sabbath, it is read in Israel on the first day and in the Diaspora on the eighth. The themes of spring and sexuality in The Song of Songs are most appropriate for Passover, the springtime festival of birth and renewal.

The Song of Songs is a series of lyric poems, in which two lovers express to each other the yearnings and delights of their mutual love. It is filled with striking, erotic imagery, such as: "Your navel is like a round goblet—let mixed wine not be lacking!—your belly like a heap of wheat hedged about with lilies. Your breasts are like two fawns, twins of a gazelle" (Song 7:3–4).[13] Unique in the Bible, The Song of Songs focuses entirely on the love between man and woman—no morals are drawn, no prophesies are pronounced, God is not mentioned, and theological concerns are never discussed. Consequently, there was intense discussion among the Rabbis regarding whether The Song of Songs should be included in the biblical canon. The argument was resolved by Rabbi Akiva, who insisted: "All the Writings are holy, but The Song of Songs is the Holy of Holies."

The Song of Songs has been interpreted both literally and as an allegory. Tradition has ascribed The Song of Songs to King Solomon, though some modern scholars reject this idea because of the complexity of its language. Rabbi Jonathan viewed it as one of the three works that Solomon composed during different stages of his life. "When a man is young, he sings songs [The Song of Songs]. When he becomes an adult, he utters practical proverbs [Proverbs]. When he becomes old, he speaks of the vanity of things [Ecclesiastes]" (Song R. 1:1, no. 10). The Song of Songs has long been considered symbolic of the love between God and the Jewish people. Beginning with the Exodus from Egypt on Passover, the romance flourished and was "consummated" seven weeks later when God gave Israel the Torah at Mount Sinai.[14]

Seder (סֵדֶר)

The seder (lit., "order") is the special home ceremony held on the first night of Passover (also the second in the Diaspora) that fulfills the biblical commandment that parents tell their children about the miraculous deliverance of their ancestors from Egypt.

Five specific mitzvot must be observed during the seder. The two biblically ordained commandments are eating matzah (Exod. 12:18) and reading the haggadah, the recounting of the story of the Exodus from Egypt (Exod. 13:8). The three practices instituted by the Rabbis are the drinking of four cups of wine (Pes. 99b); eating *maror*, the bitter herbs (Pes. 116ba); and reciting *Hallel* (Pes. 117b).[15]

The major symbols of the seder are arranged on a ceremonial plate, as follows:[16]

- *Zeroa*—roasted bone, usually a shankbone, which is a reminder of the paschal lamb (Exod. 12:2–3,5–6; Pes. 114b). It also symbolizes the *zeroa netuyah* (outstretched arm), with which God brought the Israelites out of Egypt. Some vegetarians substitute a roasted beet.

- *Beitzah*—roasted egg, which represents the special festival offering (*Hagigah*) of each Jew going up to the Temple in Jerusalem. It is also a symbol of mourning for the destruction of the Temple (the first day of Passover is always on the same day of the week as Tisha b'Av) as well as of life, birth, fertility, and regeneration.
- *Karpas*—fresh green vegetable, typically parsley, which represents the seasonal rebirth that takes place in the spring (the time of Passover) as well as the renewal of the hope for redemption. This practice may date back to ancient Rome, when banquets would begin with hors d'oeuvres.
- *Maror*—bitter herbs (discussed below).
- *Haroset*—paste of chopped fruits, nuts, wine, and spices (discussed below).
- *Hazeret*—additional *maror* for the *korech* sandwich (discussed below), usually lettuce.

Traditionally, there are 15 specific sections of the seder. According to tradition, all details of the evening have a definite purpose, even those that may seem to be superfluous. The seder follows a standard order:[17]

- *Kaddesh*—sanctification; recitation of the festival *Kiddush* (first cup of wine).
- *Urechatz*—washing the hands (without blessing); reflecting the ancient practice of ritual purification before partaking of anything dipped in liquid (Pes. 115a).
- *Karpas*—greens; eating a vegetable, typically parsley, dipped in saltwater (Pes. 114b).
- *Yachatz*—division; breaking of the middle matzah, half of which is hidden for the *afikoman* (see below) (S.A. OH 473:6).
- *Maggid*—recitation; relating the narrative of the Exodus from Egypt, which includes the second cup of wine. The seder plate is lifted for an instant, and the matzot are uncovered as the story of the redemption begins.

  Ha Lachma Anya—"This is the bread of affliction [that our ancestors ate in Egypt]"; Aramaic paragraph that invites all who are hungry to join with us and ends with a hope for the return to Israel and Jerusalem ("This year we are slaves, next year we will be free").

Mah Nishtanah—the Four Questions (see below).

Avadim Hayinu—"We were slaves [to Pharaoh in Egypt]"; the paragraph that begins telling the story of the Exodus, stressing that had God not redeemed our ancestors, we and our descendants would still be enslaved to Pharaoh. It also declares that regardless of how learned we still must relate the story of the Exodus, for whoever expands on the telling is considered praiseworthy; this is emphasized by the following paragraph, which tells of the five talmudic scholars who stayed up all night discussing the Exodus.

Four Children—discussed below.

Mi-Tehilah Ovdei—"In the beginning [our ancestors] worshiped idols."

Baruch Shomeir—"Praised is the One who keeps [His pledge to Israel]."

Arami Oveid Avi—"My father was a wandering Aramean" (Deut. 26:5–8); this core of the story was also recited by Jews bringing their first fruits to the Temple in Jerusalem.

Dayenu—"It would have been sufficient" (dicussed below).

Rabban Gamaliel Hayah Omeir—"Rabban Gamaliel would say"; the requirement to explain the three central symbols of the seder: the Passover sacrifice, matzah, and *maror.* Taken from the Mishnah (Pes. 10:5), the text was reworded into a question-and-answer form during the post-talmudic period.

B'chol Dor va-Dor—"In every generation [each person should feel personally redeemed]"; stressing that the redemption from slavery in Egypt was not only for our ancestors but for all Jews at all times, the passage was taken from the Mishnah (Pes. 10:5) and supplemented by a statement of Rava (Pes. 116b).

L'fichach—"Therefore, [since God redeemed us, we must glorify the Holy One and sing praise before Him]"; the prelude to the recitation of two sections of the *Hallel.*

- *Rachtzah*—ritual washing of the hands (with the blessing *al netilat yadayim*) made before reciting the blessing over the bread (matzah) (S.A. OH 475:1).
- *Motzi*—blessing over matzah as a food.
- *Matzah*—blessing over matzah as a special commandment of the seder.
- *Maror*—bitter herbs (discussed below).
- *Korech*—sandwich made of matzah and *maror*; a reminder of Hillel's practice (Pes. 115a) in Temple times, based on the verse, "They shall eat it [the Passover sacrifice] with unleavened bread and bitter herbs" (Num. 9:11).
- *Shulchan Orech*—prepared table; the festival meal. This is generally preceded by eating an egg dipped in saltwater as a sign of mourning for the Temple and the sacrificial system, as a symbol of joy and fertility, or as a metaphor for the response of the Jewish people to persecution (the more they are heated [oppressed], the harder they get!). Although there are no required foods, many do not eat any roasted meat, lest it appear that they are actually partaking of the Passover sacrifice. A Moroccan tradition was to barbecue foods, because grilling over a wood fire was the quickest way for the Israelites to cook their food.[18]
- *Tzafun*—hidden; ransoming and eating the *afikoman* (see below).
- *Barech*—blessing; recitation of the Grace after Meals; third cup of wine.
- *Hallel*—ceremony of the cup of Elijah (see below), reciting the remainder of *Hallel*, and drinking the fourth cup of wine.
- *Nirtzah*—acceptance; concluding prayer expressing the hope that God has accepted our observance of Passover and will speedily send the Messiah. After this, all say "*le-shanah ha-ba'ah be-Yerushalayim*" (next year in Jerusalem) and sing various Passover songs (see below).

The seder is more than a mere narration of the historical account of the Exodus. Instead, "in every generation one is obligated to look upon oneself as if he or she personally had gone forth out of Egypt" (Pes. 10:5). Consequently, a Sephardic tradition is for everyone to march around the seder table carrying a pack and staff to re-enact the Exodus. Rituals designed to enable participants in the seder to experience directly the joy of freedom include reclining in one's chair (as did free Roman citizens), eating matzah (consumed by the slaves when they first tasted freedom), and drinking four cups of wine. Conversely, inviting the poor to join in the celebration, eating bitter herbs, and the tradition among some of adding a fourth matzah for those Jews who are still oppressed are actions that remind us of the bitterness of the slavery and repression suffered by our ancestors. Ethical concern for fellow human beings is emphasized by the custom of spilling out a drop of wine at the mention of each of the Ten Plagues, diminishing our own joy while recalling the distress of the Egyptians. The cup of Elijah symbolizes our hope for messianic redemption.[19]

Haggadah (הַגָּדָה)

The haggadah (telling) is the book that contains the prayers and blessings, legends, commentaries, psalms, and songs that are traditionally recited at the Passover seder. The word derives from the phrase "*ve-higad'ta* [*le-vincha*]" (and you shall *tell* your child [on that day: "it is because of that which the Lord did for me when I came forth out of Egypt"]) (Exod. 13:8). In addition to specifying the foods and rituals required for the seder, the Mishnah (Pes. 10:4) set out four questions that children should ask their parents about this ceremony (see below). In turn, parents are advised to answer their children according to their level of understanding. Over the years, these answers became an anthology of biblical, talmudic, and midrashic sources, which were added to the prescribed order of blessings and rituals and codified into a precise order during the Middle Ages. In addition, the haggadah includes various psalms, table hymns, and popular folk songs calculated to appeal to children.

The oldest published version of the haggadah is in the prayer book of Saadiah Gaon from the 10th century. Because it is used at home rather than in the synagogue, Jews were able to embellish the haggadah with decorative and even representational art without it being subjected to rabbinic scrutiny. The 13th century saw the appearance of richly adorned *haggadot*, many of which are now regarded as masterpieces of medieval illuminated manuscripts. The haggadah has been a favorite focus of the Jewish creative spirit, and it is estimated that about 3,000 editions have appeared since the 15th century.[20]

Four Cups of Wine (אַרְבַּע כּוֹסוֹת)

Each participant at the Passover seder is required to drink four cups of wine. Indeed, the Mishnah indicates that this duty must be observed by even the poorest person (Pes. 10:1). The four cups of wine are consumed at the following times: (1) at the *Kiddush* at the start of the seder; (2) at the conclusion of the main part of the haggadah, which ends with the blessing for redemption (*ge'ulah*); (3) at the end of the Grace after Meals; and (4) at the conclusion of *Hallel* (after the hymn *Nishmat kol chai*). Only the second and fourth cups were added for the seder, since it is traditional to drink wine following *Kiddush* and *Birkat ha-Mazon* at every meal on Sabbaths and festivals.

Red wine is preferred (Pes. 108b), though white wine was often used because of the blood libel accusations against Jews in Europe (see p. 288). According to the Shulchan Arukh, each cup must contain at least a one-quarter log—equivalent to 3.3 fluid ounces or 0.137 liter (OH 472:9). It is customary to drink each of the four cups of wine while leaning to the left and reclining on a pillow (Pes. 108a), since in Roman times reclining was a sign of a free person. There are at least two practical reasons for leaning to the left side. Since the esophagus is on the left, leaning to the right could increase the danger of food going down the windpipe. Moreover, leaning to the left allows one to hold a cup steady with the right hand, which is stronger in most individuals.[21] Since one should be wide awake at the seder, rather than sleepy or slightly inebriated, it is permissible to use "Kosher for Passover" grape juice instead of wine.[22]

The general consensus among the Rabbis (Exod. R. 6:4) was that the four cups of wine reflected the four different expressions of divine deliverance used in the Torah in relation to the redemption of Israel: "I will *bring you out* [from under the burdens of the Egyptians]," "I will *deliver you* [from their bondage]," "I will *redeem you* [with an outstretched arm and with great judgments]," and "I will *take you* [to Me for a people]" (Exod. 6:6–7). Although the next verse contains a fifth expression—"And I will *bring you* [into the land that I vowed to Abraham, to Isaac, and to Jacob]"—this was not considered as warranting an extra cup (see "Cup of Elijah," below).

Other symbolic explanations for the four cups are that they correspond to the four times Pharaoh's cup is mentioned in the story of the butler, who finally brought Joseph's success at dream interpretation to the attention of Pharaoh (Gen. 40:11,13); to the four ancient kingdoms

(Babylonia, Persia, Greece, and Rome) that oppressed Israel and for which God requites Israel with four cups of consolation (JT Pes. 10:1, 37b–c); or to the four worlds (this world, the days of the Messiah, the revival of the dead, and the world to come), which are ensured to those who carry out all the requirements of the seder in the proper way (Vilna Gaon). Another explanation is that the cups relate to the four national characteristics that the Jews retained in slavery that allowed them to survive captivity in Egypt and made them worthy of liberation: they kept their Hebrew names, they refused to speak any other language but Hebrew, they maintained their moral and ethical standards, and they did not engage in vicious gossip about each other (Lev. R. 32).[23]

The number "four" plays a prominent role in the seder. In addition to the four cups of wine, there are four questions, four children, four types of food specified for the seder meal (matzah, Passover sacrifice, *maror*, *haroset*), and in some communities a fourth matzah to symbolize those Jews who are still oppressed.[24]

Four Questions (*Mah Nishtanah*; מַה נִּשְׁתַּנָּה)

The four questions asked at the Passover seder are popularly known by the first words of the introductory line—*Mah nishtanah* (What is different [about this night from all other nights?]). These questions come at the beginning of the recital of the haggadah and now are usually asked by the youngest participant. However, as late as Maimonides,[25] *Mah nishtanah* was probably said by the person leading the seder rather than asked by a child. The Four Questions date back to the time of the Mishnah (Pes. 10:4) and relate to the way festival meals were eaten at that time. If there is no child at the seder table, the woman of the house traditionally asks the questions; if there are only men at the seder, they must ask each other, even if all are talmudic scholars (Pes. 116a).

According to the Ashkenazic ritual, the questions come in the following order:[26]

1. On all other nights we eat either *hametz* or matzah. Why, on this night, do we eat only matzah?
2. On all other nights we eat all kinds of vegetables. Why, on this night, must we eat bitter herbs?
3. On all other nights we do not usually dip vegetables even once. Why, on this night, do we dip twice?

4. On all other nights we eat sitting upright or reclining. Why, on this night, do we eat reclining?

In the Sephardic ritual, the order of the four questions is dipping, matzah, bitter herbs, and reclining. Originally, the meal *preceded* the recitation of *Mah nishtanah*, thus explaining why there are questions about the matzah and *maror* even though in a modern seder the child has not yet tasted them.[27]

The answers to the first two questions (matzah, *maror*) appear in the haggadah and are discussed below. However, no specific answers to the third and fourth questions (dipping, reclining) are given in the text.

Several reasons are offered for the two dippings—the *karpas* in saltwater and the bitter herbs in *haroset*. The simplest is that although dipping once as a sort of appetizer before each meal was a routine practice, this deliberate departure from customary eating habits was designed to arouse the curiosity of children and prompt them to ask questions. According to some commentators, dipping twice refers to two historical events that are associated with the experiences of the Israelites in Egypt. After selling Joseph into slavery, his brothers dipped his coat of many colors into blood as evidence that a wild beast had devoured Jacob's favorite son (Gen. 37:31). That deed ultimately led to the Jews going down to Egypt, because as viceroy of Egypt Joseph dispensed the food that Jacob and his family required during the seven years of famine. The second dipping was the divine command that the Israelites dip a bunch of hyssop into the blood of the Passover offering and then smear it on their doorposts to signify that those inside the house should remain protected while the firstborn Egyptians were being killed in the 10th plague (Exod. 12:22–23).[28]

In ancient times, it was customary for the upper classes to eat their great banquets while reclining on couches, their left arm on the cushions while their right hand held food or wine. Therefore, during the celebration of freedom at the seder, Jews revive this custom to dramatize their status as free human beings.

Four Children (אַרְבָּעָה בָּנִים)

Children either ask or are told about the Exodus from Egypt in four biblical verses (Deut. 6:20; Exod. 12:26, 13:8,14). Based on the talmudic statement, "According to the son's intelligence his father instructs him" (Pes. 116a), the Rabbis created a system of teaching the story of the Exodus that was individualized, depending on the maturity, attitude, and age of the questioner.[29]

The haggadah speaks of four children: wise, wicked, simple, and one who does not know how to ask. It stresses that by paying close attention to the manner way in which a person asks a question, one can gain an insight into the individual's character and prepare a suitable reply.[30] (Of course, this mandate to teach one's children according to their ability applies equally to girls.)

The wise child (*hakham*) asks insightful questions, seeking to gain a deeper understanding of the proper way to observe the commandments relating to Passover. This child should be answered with precise and explicit information that satisfies his quest for knowledge.[31] Although the biblical text reads, "What are the statutes, laws, and ordinances that the Lord our God has commanded you (*etchem*)" (Deut. 6:20), the Jerusalem Talmud changed the last word to "*otanu*" (us) in order to sharpen the difference between the wise child (who unequivocally includes himself in the community) and the wicked child (who clearly excludes himself from it).[32]

According to the Torah, the only response to the wicked child (*rasha*), who effectively isolates himself from the Jewish people, is to "set his teeth on edge." Instead of directly answering his question, it is necessary to respond in his own terms—that we celebrate Passover because of what God did for *us* when we went out of Egypt. Had the wicked child lived at that time and similarly disassociated himself from the fate of the Jewish people, he would not have been redeemed and instead would have been condemned to languish among the mass of slave laborers.[33]

Although the Hebrew word "*tam*," used to describe the third child, is usually translated as the slightly derogatory "simple," it more probably is meant as a praiseworthy characteristic, as in the verse commanding the Jew to be *tam* (wholehearted) with the Lord your God (Deut. 18:13). The mystics considered this the highest level of religious consciousness, representing unquestioning faith and unsophisticated surrender to the divine will. In this way, the four children can be divided into two contrasting pairs. Two children differ in their intellectual abilities—the wise versus the one who does not know how to ask;

the other two are distinguished by their spiritual differences—the wicked versus the one who is *tam*, or "religiously naive."[34]

The fourth child not only does not know what to ask but does not even realize that there are questions about the seder that he should ask. The haggadah begins its discussion of this child with the words *"at p'-tach lo"* (you should begin for him), using the feminine gender for "you." This suggests that this child should be approached with the gentle understanding and warmth generally associated with the mother. It is necessary to patiently encourage the child to formulate questions and then provide answers at a level that the child can comprehend. The word *"at"* (את) begins with the first letter of the Hebrew alphabet and ends with the last, indicating that we must teach this child the entire expanse of Jewish life and tradition.[35]

Shlomo Riskin cites a profound interpretation ascribed to Joseph Isaac Schneerson, a former Lubavitcher rebbe:

> The Four Children represent the four generations of the American experience. The Wise Child represents the European roots, the generation of the grandparents who came to America with beard and earlocks, dressed in *shtreimel* and *kapote*, steeped in piety, with a love for learning and profound knowledge of the Jewish tradition. Their progeny (the Wicked Child), brought up within the American "melting pot," rejected his parent's customs and ways of thought ... Turning his back on the glories of the Jewish tradition, this child often became successful in business but was cynical in his outlook. The third generation, the Simple Child, is confused. He watched his grandfather making *Kiddush* on Friday night and his father standing by silently, perhaps resentfully, impatient to prepare for business on Saturday morning ... The fourth generation, the Child Who Does Not Know How to Ask, offspring of the Simple Child, is the greatest tragedy of all. He was born after his great-grandparents had died. He knows only his totally assimilated grandfather (Wicked Child) and his religiously confused father ... This is our mute American generation, the generation who thought it was someone's birthday when she saw her great-grandmother lighting the festival candles.[36]

Riskin adds that there is also a fifth generation, so far removed from Judaism that it is unaware that it is Passover. At least the wicked child is attending the seder, though he cannot fathom how it relates to his life, as is the one who does not know how to ask, despite the fact that he finds it beyond his understanding. Tragically, an increasing number of American Jews are not even present at the seder. When opening the door for Elijah the Prophet, we should also keep it open for those masses of assimilated Jews who have not yet entered. In this way, Elijah can fulfill the promise "to reconcile parents with children and children with their parents" (Mal. 3:24). These fifth-generation children must be made aware of their lost heritage before we can dare expect the redemption of the Messianic Age.[37]

Dayenu (דַּיֵּנוּ)

Dayenu (It would have been sufficient) is a song of thanksgiving in the Passover haggadah. Beginning with the words, "How many acts of kindness God has performed for us," it enumerates 15 (in some rites 16) stages of the redemption of the Jews from bondage in Egypt. These include the splitting of the sea, the providing of manna to feed them in the wilderness, the Revelation of the laws of Sabbath and the entire Torah, and finally being led into the Land of Israel and building the Temple.

The sages stressed that the word "*dayenu*" does not mean that the Jews would have been satisfied had they not received all of these blessings, especially the final ones of Sabbath, Torah, Land of Israel, and Temple. Instead, the concept is that any individual one of these gifts would have been of such great magnitude as to warrant unlimited gratitude. How much more appreciative must Jews be that God gave them *all* of these precious gifts (Malbim).[38]

In colloquial Hebrew and Yiddish, the word "*dayenu*" is often used ironically to mean "that's enough" or "I've had enough."

Ten Plagues (עֶשֶׂר מַכּוֹת)

The overriding purpose of the Ten Plagues (Exod. 7:14–11:10, 12:29–33) was that "The Egyptians shall know that I am the Lord" (Exod. 7:5; repeated in various forms in 7:17; 8:16,18; 9:14,16,29)—an answer to Pharaoh's derisive challenge, "Who is the Lord, that I should heed Him and let Israel go?" (Exod. 5:2). As agents of God, Moses and Aaron announced, signaled, and removed the plagues in the divine name. The various catastrophic events, the fact that they affected the Egyptians but spared the Israelites (starting from Exod. 8:18), and the special harshness of the last four plagues gradually crushed Pharaoh's resistance and convinced the Egyptians of the impotence of their gods and the supreme power of the God of Israel.

The Ten Plagues were as follows:

Blood (דָּם)
Frogs (צְפַרְדֵּעַ)
Vermin (lice; כִּנִּים)
Wild beasts (עָרוֹב)
Pestilence (disease of the flocks; דֶּבֶר)
Boils (שְׁחִין)
Hail (בָּרָד)
Locusts (אַרְבֶּה)
Darkness (חֹשֶׁךְ)
Slaying of the firstborn (מַכַּת בְּכוֹרוֹת)

Rabbi Judah developed three meaningless Hebrew acronyms (*det-zach, adash, b'achav*) to refer to the plagues. Although possibly only a mnemonic device, some commentators explain that this was invented to indicate that the plagues occurred at different levels, representing various aspects of divine mastery over nature and the world. As Riskin observed, "Blood, frogs, and lice affected the ground—the blood, the Nile River; the frogs, the swampland surrounding it; and the lice, the solid earth. Wild beasts, pestilence, and boils affected those who lived upon the land. Hail, locusts, and darkness involved the atmosphere. The slaying of the firstborn taught that our God is also the Lord over life and death. It was important for Pharaoh, who believed that he was a god, to understand that he was a creature, not Creator."[39]

The plagues can also be categorized into three sets of three, capped by a 10th, based on an invariably recurring order of introductory clauses. The first, fourth, and seventh plagues began with God commanding Moses to stand before Pharaoh in the morning (at the Nile) to warn him. Plagues two, five, and eight began with a command to enter Pharaoh's residence to warn him there, but the third, sixth, and ninth plagues began without warning. The plagues also can be grouped in terms of how they were brought about: Aaron summoned the first three using his staff, Moses the next three without the use of his staff, and Moses the final three using his staff.[40]

Over the centuries, the plagues have been interpreted as attacks on the principal divinities that had been worshiped since time immemorial in the Nile Valley. The plagues succeeded in humiliating the deities worshiped by the Egyptians—the Nile River, a frog-headed goddess of fruitfulness, sacred cattle, the sacred beetle, and the sun god (Ra)—clearly demonstrating that the God of the Israelites had the power to subvert the actions of these so-called gods to devastate their land. Some have suggested that the plagues represent miraculous intensification of local or seasonal phenomena that occurred by divine power in a single year. When the Nile rises each summer, the river is reddened by organisms within it. As the waters recede, swarms of frogs and insects follow in their wake. Soil contaminated by rotting frogs can become a breeding ground for disease, especially the highly infectious anthrax that affects cattle. During winter or spring, winds may blow vast swarms of locusts across Egypt that devour huge quantities of vegetation. Even the three days of palpable darkness may be explained by the severe sandstorms resulting from the hot, dry winds (*hamsin*) that blow in the early spring.[41]

When each of the plagues is recited, Jews traditionally dip their little finger into the wine and spill a drop of it (or pour some wine out of the cup) to symbolize their grief at the loss of any human life, even that of their bitter enemies. According to Midrash, as the waters of the Sea of Reeds engulfed the Egyptians, the ministering angels began to recite songs of praise. However, God promptly silenced them: "The work of My hands is perishing and you sing praises to Me?" Thus even at the time of our great celebration we cannot fill our cups to the brim, since our redemption required the destruction of others.[42] Another explanation is that the finger recalls the cry of the magicians of Egypt, "This is the finger of God!" (Exod. 8:15), when they were unable to duplicate the infestation of vermin and were forced to admit that the plagues were a supernatural phenomenon beyond human control.[43]

Matzah (מַצָּה)

Matzah is unleavened bread that is made from flour and water and is the quintessential symbol of Passover. Unlike the prohibition against eating *hametz* or even having it in one's possession, which is in force throughout Passover, there is a positive duty to eat matzah only on the first night (first two nights in the Diaspora), based on the verse "they shall eat it with unleavened bread [matzah] and bitter herbs [i.e., the Passover sacrifice]" (Num. 9:11). Eating matzah is optional thereafter (Pes. 120a). In addition to being the only bread permitted during Passover, in ancient Israel matzah was the only bread that could be offered up with sacrifices on the altar (Lev. 2:4–5).

Only grains that can ferment can be used to make matzah. This applies to the five species indigenous to the Land of Israel—wheat, barley, spelt, rye, and oats (see above)—but in practice only wheat is used. The Talmud states that under normal climatic conditions, flour mixed with water begins to ferment in the time it takes to walk 2,000 cubits (a Roman mile), which is estimated to be from 18 to 24 minutes (the shortest time is adopted today) (Pes. 46a). A water temperature above normal causes the fermentation process to speed up, but this can be slowed down by continually manipulating the mixture and perforating the dough to permit the air bubbles to escape. Exquisite care is taken to ensure that the entire process from kneading to final baking does not exceed 18 minutes. For Passover use, especially at the seder, some Jews prefer special *shmurah* (guarded) matzah. This is prepared under close supervision from the time the wheat is harvested until it reaches the oven, unlike ordinary Passover matzah, which is supervised only beginning with the milling of the wheat. Unlike the flat, uniform square sheets of regular matzah, handmade *shmurah* matzah is uneven and round, resembling the matzah baked in ancient times (and is generally more expensive because of the labor involved).[44]

The advent of the first matzah-baking machine in the 1850s—which kneaded the dough and pushed it between two metal rollers from which it emerged thin, perforated, and round—provoked an intense halakhic controversy. Because the machine reused the corners of dough that were cut off to make the matzot round, it was feared that these bits might become leavened before finally being incorporated into a sheet of matzah ready for baking. This dilemma was solved by a later machine, which produced square matzot with no leftover dough. Another rabbinic complaint was that these machines endangered the livelihood of those who earned money before Passover by working in a matzah bakery, which would require fewer manual workers. However, this was rejected by the vast majority of authorities, who lauded the efficiency of the new matzah-making process and wondered why the same concern had not been expressed for scribes who had been displaced by the printing press.[45]

The three pieces of matzah placed on the seder table may represent the three divisions of the Jewish people (Kohen, Levite, and Israel); the three patriarchs (Abraham, Isaac, and Jacob); the "three measures of fine meal" from which Sarah baked cakes (at Abraham's request) for the three angelic visitors (Gen. 18:6), who according to tradition came on the night of Passover; or a combination of the two festival or Sabbath loaves displayed in the ancient Temple plus a replacement for the former Passover sacrifice. At some modern seders, a fourth matzah is added to represent those Jews who still live under oppressive regimes and lack the freedom to openly practice their religion. Near the beginning of the seder, the leader breaks the middle matzah. This may indicate that even our freedom is not yet complete or be a reflection of the fact that the starving Israelites slaves would never eat an entire piece of bread, always saving part of it for a later meal in case the cruel Egyptian taskmasters provided no food at all. Half of this matzah becomes the *afikoman*, which is eaten to finish the meal (see below).[46]

Two blessings are made over the matzah at the seder—one over its use as "bread," and the other related to the positive commandment to eat unleavened bread on the festival. So that a person first tastes matzah at the seder iself, strict halakhah mandates that one should not eat any matzah or indeed any hametz from the morning of the 14th of Nisan. The sages compared one who eats matzah after that time to a man who seduces his betrothed while she is still in her father's house, an offense punishable by lashes, because it shows that the offender is unwilling to control his animal instincts and restrain his desire until after the wedding.[47] Most Jews refrain from eating matzah during the entire month before Passover, so as not to spoil the anticipation of that first taste.

Matzah has a paradoxical symbolism in the Passover story. The flat shape of matzah reminds us that the former Jewish slaves escaped Egypt so quickly that their bread did not have time to rise (Exod. 12:39). Conversely, matzah is described as *lechem oni* (bread of affliction) (Deut. 16:3), the minimal food provided for the Jewish slaves as they toiled under Pharaoh.[48] The Aramaic passage *"ha lachma anya"* (this is the bread of affliction), which is recited near the beginning of the seder, invites all who are needy to join with us in the meal. Thus we commence our joyous celebration of Passover with the sobering realization that hunger still persists in our unredeemed world.[49]

The Zohar labels matzah "the bread of faith," symbolizing the trust of the Jewish people in God. Without waiting for their dough to rise, the Israelites fled Egypt, putting complete faith in divine assistance without having any idea where they were going, how long it would take to get there, or how they would find the food and other material support they needed to survive.[50]

Some have questioned whether matzah made from flour mixed with grape juice, oil, or eggs instead of water may be used on Passover. Although in the absence of mixing with water there is, strictly speaking, no fermenting, the Talmud (Pes. 36a) considered such matzah to be forbidden at the seder because it constitutes "rich matzah" (*matzah ashirah*) rather than the required bread of affliction. According to *halakhah*, only the ill and elderly are permitted to eat these fancy types of matzah at the seder (S.A. OH 462).

Maror (מָרוֹר)

The Torah stipulates that the festival of Passover is to be observed by eating the Passover offering, matzah, and *maror* (bitter herbs) (Exod. 12:8; Num. 9:11). *Maror* is eaten at the seder to remember the bitterness the Israelites experienced during their period of slavery in Egypt, for as the Torah notes: "They embittered their lives with hard labor, with mortar and bricks, and with all manner of labor in the field" (Exod. 1:14).

Although the Bible does not specify the plant by name, the Jerusalem Talmud describes *maror* as a "bitter vegetable with a silvery appearance that has sap" (Pes. 2:5, 29c). The Mishnah enumerates five possibilities, including lettuce (*hazeret*); chicory; and *maror*, which might be a bitter weed native to the Middle East that the Arabs call "*murar*" (Pes. 39a). Many Jews today use horseradish for *maror*. The Rabbis preferred romaine lettuce as a bitter herb, since its stem has a milky sap and because the taste, like the experience of the Jews in Egypt, is initially sweet but then becomes bitter. Also, its Hebrew name "*chasah*" is similar to the word "*chas*" (pity), symbolizing how God heard the groaning of the Israelites and redeemed them.[51] In addition, this variety of lettuce starts as a very soft plant, but in time its core hardens, symbolizing the insidious entrapment of the Israelites by the Egyptians. Initially the Egyptians took a soft approach, hiring the Israelites as highly paid workers; but then they hardened their grasp on the Israelites as they gradually converted them into slaves. Subsequent commentaries related this concept to the *yetzer ha-ra* (inclination toward evil), which rarely conducts a frontal attack on one's spirituality. Rather we are lured into an apparently innocent activity, and the *yetzer ha-ra* imperceptibly drives us into increasingly greater indulgence, until we lose our moral compass and become a virtual slave to our passions.[52]

The *maror* also symbolizes the suffering that has beset the Jews throughout their history. Rabbi Shimon bar Yochai taught that "the Holy One, blessed be He, gave Israel three precious gifts [Torah, Land of Israel, world to come], and all of them were given only through sufferings" (Ber. 5a). The Rabbis maintained that a person truly appreciates blessings only after living through times of despair and bitterness. According to Simcha Bunam, the bitter herbs (symbol of slavery) are only eaten *after* the matzah (symbol of freedom) because the Israelites did not realize that they were laboring in servitude until Moses had promised them the hope of freedom.[53]

According to Hillel (Pes. 115a), during Temple times matzah, *maror*, and the Passover offering were eaten together in a sandwich (*korech*) in fulfillment of the verse, "they shall eat it with matzah and *maror*" (Exod. 12:8; Num. 9:11). Other authorities claimed that these three items were eaten one at a time. In deference to Hillel, one of the most prominent of the sages, Jews today eat a matzah-*maror* sandwich *after* having first fulfilled the individual mitzvot of matzah and *maror* by eating each separately. Philo termed this combination of *maror* and matzah a "moral migration from wickedness to virtue."[54] When sinners are moved to repent, they are despondent and bitterly (*maror*) dwell on their past transgressions. Eventually, the healing food (matzah) conquers their previous arrogance and allows them to become content.[55]

Haroset (חֲרוֹסֶת)

Haroset is a paste made of fruit, nuts, spices, wine, and sometimes matzah meal that is symbolic of the mixture of clay and straw from which the enslaved Israelites made bricks. The origin of the word is unknown, though it may come from "*heres*" (clay) because of the similar color and texture. The ingredients of *haroset* vary widely among different communities. Ashkenazic Jews typically use ground apples, chopped nuts, cinnamon, and red wine. The first two ingredients allude to two verses in The Song of Songs (see above), which is traditionally recited on Passover: "Under the apple tree I roused you" (Song 8:5) and "I went down to the nut grove" (Song 6:11).[56] Cinnamon recalls the spices that Adam and Eve were allowed to take with them when banished from Eden, so that *haroset* figuratively contains a "hint of Paradise lost."[57] The red wine is a reminder of the blood of the Passover offering and of the Israelite infants who were mercilessly slaughtered in Egypt.[58] Sephardim tend to use ingredients that grew in the Land of Israel during biblical times—grapes, dates, figs, olives, apricots, pomegranates, and almonds.[59] North Africans also include pine nuts, hard-boiled eggs, and spices such as ginger and cinnamon. Yemenites add chili pepper, whereas Israelis transform the relatively bland western *haroset* into a sweet dessert by adding dates, bananas, candied orange peel, and orange juice.[60]

For the second dipping at the seder, the *maror* (bitter herb) is dipped into the *haroset*. In addition to its sweetness mitigating the bitterness of the *maror*, the *haroset* is a manifestation of the continual optimism of the Jews, the idea that even the worst catastrophe contains within it a spark of redemption. Consequently, one sage confidently proclaimed that the Messiah was born on that dire day that the Temple was destroyed. The apples in *haroset* remind us of the trees under which, according to legend, Jewish mothers gave birth and hid their male infants lest the Egyptians drown them in obedience to Pharaoh's decree (Exod. 1:22).[61]

Afikoman (אֲפִיקוֹמָן)

Early in the Passover seder, the leader breaks the middle of the three matzot into two pieces and hides the larger half. This portion of matzah is known as the *afikoman*, and the seder cannot conclude until all guests have eaten a piece of it.

"*Afikoman*" is a Greek word, whose precise meaning is unclear. It is generally interpreted either as "a food eaten for pleasure" or as "dessert following the meal." The *afikoman* is first mentioned in the Mishnah, which states "one should not have any *afikoman* after the

Passover sacrifice" (Pes. 10:8). Since the destruction of the Temple, the broken half of the middle matzah has come to symbolically replace the Passover sacrifice, so that now nothing may be eaten or drunk after the *afikoman* except for water and the required last two cups of wine. As with the Passover sacrifice, the *afikoman* must be consumed before midnight.[62]

Another talmudic opinion is that *afikoman* relates to the practice of going (reveling) from house to house after the seder (Pes. 119b), which the Rabbis prohibited because it was inconsistent with the solemnity of the occasion.[63] Riskin extended this idea to reflect criticism of those who race from house to house throughout the year, keeping so busy with the needs and affairs of others that they do not have enough time to devote to themselves or their own families. Extrapolated to the national level, this can result in constant exploration of different cultures, rather than taking the time to investigate one's own in depth. As the birthday of the Jews as a people, Passover makes a powerful plea for Jews to stay home and study their own heritage.[64]

It has become customary for the seder leader to hide the *afikoman* after breaking the middle matzah and for the children to find it and then ransom it after the meal for presents or money. According to the Talmud, this practice encourages the children to keep awake during the seder (Pes. 109a).

In view of its essential role in the seder, the *afikoman* has been endowed with special powers. In various cultures it has been carried as a good luck charm to protect against the evil eye, to promise a long life, and to ensure that a pregnant woman will have a safe delivery. Some believe that eating a piece of the *afikoman* guarantees that a single woman will find a husband during the coming year. From a kabbalistic perspective, the *afikoman* can be regarded as symbol of messianic *tikun olam*, since it was formed by breaking and eventually reappears "to make the meal whole."[65] According to Mishnah Berurah, some wrap the *afikoman* in a cloth and place it on the shoulder to literally re-enact the biblical verse, "So the people took their dough before it was leavened ... wrapped in their cloaks upon their shoulders" (Exod. 12:34).[66]

Cup of Elijah (כּוֹסוֹ שֶׁל אֵלִיָּהוּ)

The cup of Elijah is a large ornate goblet that is filled with wine at the Passover seder, placed on the table, but not drunk. It is the result of a controversy among the Rabbis concerning whether the seder ritual required four or five cups. Each of the four cups of wine relate to expressions used in the Torah to describe God's imminent redemption of Israel (Exod. 6:6–7) (see p. 276). According to some opinions, there was also a requirement to drink a fifth cup at the seder in commemoration of the divine pledge in the next verse, "and I will bring you [into the land]" (Exod. 6:8). Others maintained that no fifth cup should be drunk, since this divine promise of the return of the Jewish people to the Land of Israel was still to be fulfilled. The ultimate rabbinic decision was not to drink a fifth cup; however, because the *halakhah* was in doubt, Jews pour it and leave it on the table in anticipation of Elijah's return and the final fulfillment of the divine promise in the Messianic Age. Moreover, there is a traditional belief that Elijah will provide definitive answers to all undecided halakhic questions. Thus the cup of Elijah gives expression to our fervent hope that the prophet will come soon, perhaps even on this Passover night, and our confidence that the Messiah will bring the ingathering of the exiles, the re-establishment of Jewish sovereignty over Israel, and fulfillment of the divine promise to return the people to their land.[67] Now that the State of Israel exists, some have advocated drinking five, not four, cups of wine at the seder, arguing that God's pledge has indeed been fulfilled.[68]

Once the cup of Elijah has been poured, it is customary to open the front door and recite a prayer asking God, "Pour out Your wrath upon the nations that do not recognize You and upon the kingdoms that do not invoke Your Name." This custom dates back to the Middle Ages, when the Passover season was an especially difficult period for Jews because of the proximity to Easter. Beginning in Crusader times, Christians often placed a dead body (frequently a baby) in Jewish courtyards during the seder night and then accused the Jews of using the blood of the murdered child to bake matzot and prepare wine. These blood libels became the excuse for vicious pogroms in which many Jews were killed. In an effort to protect themselves from the wrath of the mob, Jews would periodically open their doors to see if such a nefarious plot was being hatched. As they looked out, they would plead for God to "pour out Your wrath" on those who sought to destroy their people.[69] In our day we maintain the custom of our ancestors, with the hope that we will never share their fear.

Although not actually part of the haggadah, in many homes it is a custom to recite special prayers at the seder in memory of those who perished during the Holocaust, especially the martyrs of the Warsaw Ghetto Uprising that began on the first night of Passover.

Passover Songs

After the completion of the formal recitation of the haggadah, the Passover seder concludes with four songs: *Ki Lo Na'eh, Adir Hu, Echad Mi Yode'a*, and *Had Gadya*. They were incorporated into the haggadah for the amusement of the children, so that they would not fall asleep before the end of the seder.

Ki Lo Na'eh (For to Him praise is proper) is an alphabetical acrostic with a tongue-twisting refrain. *Adir Hu* (Mighty is He), also an alphabetical acrostic, contains a refrain that pleads for the rebuilding of the Temple, the symbol of Israel's restoration, and the inauguration of the Messianic Age, "speedily, in our days."

Echad Mi Yode'a (Who knows one?), which dates back to the 16th century, is the classic counting song, in which each of the 13 stanzas consists of a question "Who knows ..." followed by the corresponding answer. The reply to each succeeding question repeats the previous answers. By the final verse, the aim is to rapidly race through all the answers from 13 back to one in a single breath:

> Who knows thirteen? I know thirteen. Thirteen are the attributes of God),[70] twelve are the tribes of Israel,[71] eleven are the stars [in Joseph's dream], ten are the commandments, nine are the months of pregnancy, eight are the days to circumcision; seven are the days of the week, six are the orders of the Mishnah,[72] five are the books of the Torah,[73] four are the Matriarchs,[74] three are the Patriarchs,[75] two are the tablets of the covenant, One is our God in Heaven and on earth.

Had Gadya (One Kid) are the first words and title of a popular Aramaic song that traditionally concludes the Passover seder. Composed of 10 stanzas, the song relates what happens to a little goat that was bought by a father for two coins (*zuzim*). The goat was eaten by a cat, which was bitten by a dog, which was beaten by a stick, which was burned by fire, which was quenched by water, which was drunk by an ox, which was butchered by the slaughterer (*shochet*), who was killed by the Angel of Death, who in punishment was destroyed by God. Each stanza repeats the previous verses and closes with the refrain "*had gadya, had gadya.*"

The commentators unanimously agree that the deceptively simple folk story of *Had Gadya* has a deep hidden meaning. The classic interpretation of the song is an allegory of Jewish history, in which God originally "acquired" the people (the kid) with two coins (the tablets of the covenant). The Jews then became the subjects of various nations that conquered each other in turn—Assyria (the cat), Persia (the stick), Greece (the fire), Rome (the water), the Saracens (the ox), the Crusaders (the slaughterer), and the Turks (the Angel of Death), who at the time of the song's completion (the late 16th century) still ruled the Land of Israel. *Had Gadya* concludes with the confident assurance that the Messiah (representing the Holy One) will finally redeem the Jews from this last oppressive ruler. Thus the seder ends with this miniature morality play in which the nations that have persecuted the Jews are destroyed; all exultantly look forward to the Messianic Age and, with the demise of the Angel of Death, to everlasting life.[76]

Maimuna

Maimuna is a day-long celebration of Moroccan Jews throughout the world that begins immediately after the conclusion of the Passover holiday at sundown. The term probably derives from the Hebrew-Aramaic word "*mammon*," meaning "riches" or "prosperity," reflecting a belief that both personal and national wealth are determined on that day. Traditionally the anniversary of the death of Joseph, the father of Maimonides, *Maimuna* is characterized by an extraordinary show of hospitality in which Jews open their doors to friends and neighbors. In every home, the table is set with a white tablecloth and adorned with flowers, branches of fig trees, stalks of wheat, and a fishbowl that usually contains a live fish as a symbol of fertility. Dairy foods are eaten, especially pancake-like wafers of fried dough (*muflita*) spread with butter and honey. In Israel, Jews of Moroccan descent celebrate the day after Passover with communal picnics, and a large central gathering is held in Jerusalem.[77]

Omer Period (עֹמֶר)

From the second day of Passover until the festival of Shavuot, Jews are commanded to count seven weeks. This process of counting is known as *sefirat ha-Omer* (counting of the Omer). The omer was the measure of newly harvested grain (traditionally barley), which the Israelites were commanded to bring to the Temple as a harvest offering on the second day of Passover. The Kohen took the omer and waved it in every direction, praying that God protect the harvest from "injurious winds and harmful dews" (Men. 62a).

For the ancient Israelites, the Omer period (*Sefirah*) was the critical time when the success of the harvest was determined. The proper ripening of the grain (wheat, barley) and the growth of the other major crops native to the Land of Israel (olives [oil], grapes, pomegranates, figs, dates [honey]) depended on the proper balance of the north and south winds during this vulnerable time. The pilgrimage festival of Shavuot at the conclusion of the Omer period was in thanksgiving for God's blessing and protection of the land and its produce.[1]

The *Sefirah* is observed each evening by reciting a special blessing and counting each day of the Omer. (If forgotten at night, the count can be performed during the day, but without the blessing.) According to the Talmud, one must count the number of days and the number of weeks (Men. 65b–66a). For example, on the first day the recitation is "Today is the first day of the Omer"; a week later one says, "Today is the eighth day, making one week and one day of the Omer." To keep an accurate count of the days, special Omer calendars were developed. These contained movable numbers and were often decorated with folk art motifs.

The kabbalists considered the seven weeks of the *Sefirah* period as signifying the ascent of the Israelites through 49 gates of impurity, as they passed from the depths of their slavery in Egypt to their pure state at the time of giving of the Torah at Mount Sinai, when they were judged worthy of becoming a "kingdom of priests and a holy nation." (Exod. 19:6) The sages also associated the period of seven weeks with seven attributes personified by great ancestors of the Jewish people: lovingkindness (Abraham), strength of character and wholehearted devotion to the service of God (Isaac), glory and uprightness (Jacob), morality (Joseph), eternity and the conviction that only the Torah has lasting value (Moses), splendor and the pursuit of peace (Aaron), and God-given sovereignty (David).[2]

The Omer period is observed as a time of semi-mourning. Traditional Jews do not get haircuts, celebrate weddings, or play musical instruments during this time. Initially, these restrictions may have been related to the intense anxiety felt by the Israelites during the vulnerable weeks leading up to the harvest.[3] Ultimately, however, the mourning was connected to the plague that struck Rabbi Akiva's students during this time (see below). The Conservative movement has reduced the time of no celebrations to the few days from the end of Passover through Yom ha-Shoah.

A popular custom during the Omer period is the study of the mishnaic tractate *Pirkei Avot* (Ethics of the Fathers). Beginning after Passover, one of its six chapters is studied each Sabbath following the afternoon service. In this way, the final chapter dealing with the Torah is read just before Shavuot, the festival commemorating the Revelation at Mount Sinai. (Sephardim still continue the custom of reading *Pirkei Avot* only during this period, but most Ashkenazic congregations repeat the entire treatise three times until the Sabbath before Rosh Hashanah.) A less-observed custom is to study the talmudic tractate *Shevuot* during the Omer period. Not only are the Hebrew letters identical to the upcoming festival—though the word means "vows" instead of "weeks"—but the tractate has 49 pages so that one can be studied on each day of the counting of the Omer.[4]

Lag ba-Omer (לַ״ג בָּעֹמֶר)

The major exception to the semi-mourning during the *Sefirah* period is Lag ba-Omer, the 33rd day (ל = 30, ג = 3) of the counting of the Omer (18th day of Iyar). According to talmudic and midrashic sources, during the period between Passover and Shavuot 24,000 disciples of Rabbi Akiva died of a terrible plague (Yev. 62b). This may refer to the overwhelming defeat suffered by the forces of Bar Kokhba, whom Akiva strongly supported in the unsuccessful rebellion against the Romans. Tradition maintains that the plague ceased on Lag ba-Omer, possibly an allusion to the brief recapture of Jerusalem that is said to have occurred on this date.

The kabbalists considered Lag ba-Omer as commemorating either the rabbinic ordination (by Akiva) of Shimon bar Yochai, the reputed author of the mystical Zohar, or the anniversary of his death. Believing that many of the broken Fragments of Creation were finally reunited upon bar Yochai's death, kabbalists and Hasidim in Israel hold a festive celebration (*hillula*) on Lag ba-Omer at the sage's grave in the village of Meron, near Safed. Thousands gather there to study mystical texts and to sing and dance around large bonfires. (The Romans had banned the bonfires used by Jews to signal the new lunar months, but Bar Kokhba reinstituted this practice during his rebellion.) Because cutting one's hair is prohibited during the semi-mourning Omer period, on Lag ba-Omer it became customary for three-year-old boys to have their first haircut.

The scores of weddings performed on this day add to the festive character of this semiholiday. It is customary to eat foods made from carob (see page 679) on Lag ba-Omer, because the fruit of a carob tree sustained bar Yochai and his son during the 12 years they hid from the Romans in a cave. According to the Chatam Sofer, Lag ba-Omer was also celebrated because it was the day when manna began to fall in the wilderness.[5]

Another tradition associated with Lag ba-Omer is children playing with bows and arrows. According to legend, the rainbow, which symbolizes peace and has a Hebrew name (*keshet*) that also means the bow of an archer, did not appear during the lifetime of Rabbi Shimon bar Yochai, because he was such a saintly man. Others associate the bow with the Bar Kokhba revolt, maintaining that Rabbi Akiva's students actually died fighting the Romans (and not from the plague).

Other days that are exempted from the restrictions of the Omer period include Yom ha-Atzmaut (Israel Independence Day; see p. 296) and Rosh Hodesh (see p. 166).

Yom ha-Shoah (Holocaust Remembrance Day; יוֹם הַשּׁוֹאָה)

In 1951, the government of the State of Israel established the 27th of Nisan as the date to commemorate the Holocaust and its victims. After much debate, this date was chosen because it occurs between the anniversary of the Warsaw Ghetto Uprising (which began on the first day of Passover, the 15th of Nisan, in 1943) and Yom ha-Zikaron (Remembrance Day) and also falls during the traditional mourning period of the counting of the Omer. However, some ultra-Orthodox authorities in Israel opposed the institution of this observance, since it was the action of a secular state and because they did not favor setting aside a special day for the Holocaust.

Some congregations and individuals light six yahrzeit candles in memory of the six million Jews who were murdered. Many observances include recitation of the *Mourner's Kaddish* and *El Malei Rachamim* (see p. 87), parts of the traditional service for mourning the dead. In Israel, the day is observed by the closing of theaters and places of entertainment, schools, and most businesses. Wreath-laying ceremonies are held at Yad Vashem, the Jerusalem memorial to the victims of the Holocaust. The Israeli rabbinate has decreed the fast day of the 10th of Tevet (see p. 309) as the Day of *Kaddish*, on which Jews pray and study in honor of the yahrzeit (memorial anniversary) of relatives who were victims of the Holocaust but whose date of death is unknown. In the United States, Holocaust Remembrance Day is usually observed on April 19 (or the nearest appropriate Sunday), the day on which the Warsaw Ghetto uprising broke out according to the civil calendar.[6]

Yom ha-Zikaron (יוֹם הַזִּכָּרוֹן)

Yom ha-Zikaron (Remembrance Day) is a memorial day for those who died fighting for the State of Israel. It is observed on the Fourth of Iyar, the day before Israel Independence Day.

Following the *Kaddish* after *Aleinu* in the morning service, a memorial candle is lit, the ark is opened, and Psalm 9 ("For the leader, on the death of the son") is read. This is followed by *Yizkor* (see p. 101) for the war dead, *Mourner's Kaddish* by relatives of those killed, and the recitation of *El Malei Rachamim*. These additions to the regular liturgy are concluded with Psalm 144 ("Praised is the Lord, my rock, who trains my hands for battle, my fingers for warfare"). At 11:00 A.M., sirens are sounded throughout Israel, signaling two minutes of silence and the virtual cessation of all activity throughout the country.[7] In addition, a memorial ceremony is held at the Mount Herzl military cemetery, flags are flown at half-mast, and places of entertainment are closed.

Yom ha-Atzmaut (יוֹם הָעַצְמָאוּת)

Yom ha-Atzmaut (Independence Day) is celebrated on the Fifth of Iyar, the Hebrew date of the Declaration of Independence by Israel on

May 14, 1948. It is a day of rejoicing with fireworks, dancing in the streets, and a variety of official ceremonies and public entertainment. Until 1967, the major event was an annual military parade, but this was canceled in response to many complaints that it was stressing human heroism and power rather than the miraculous and spiritual element of the return to Zion. At the conclusion of the day, the Israel Prize is granted to individuals who have made special contributions to Israeli culture, intellectual life, and science. Other events include the International Bible Contest for Jewish Youth and the Hebrew Song Festival. In years when the Fifth of Iyar falls on a Saturday or Friday, Yom ha-Atzmaut festivities are held on the previous Thursday to avoid public desecration of the Sabbath. Yom ha-Atzmaut is immediately preceded by Yom ha-Zikaron, the day for remembering those who gave their lives in the defense of the State of Israel (see above).

Some congregations in Israel celebrate Yom ha-Atzmaut with an evening service that opens with psalms of thanksgiving (usually Ps. 97, 98, and 107) and ends with the blowing of the shofar and a prayer that soon we will hear the shofar announcing the arrival of Messiah. A festive meal is held with singing, lighting of candles, and even (in some traditions) *Kiddush*; during the Grace after Meals, *Shir ha-Ma'alot* is sung to the tune of *Hatikvah*, the national anthem of Israel.[8] The next morning, psalms added on the Sabbath and festivals are recited. *Hallel* is said, though there is controversy among the Orthodox as to whether to include the accompanying blessing. This reflects the tension between the desire to praise God for Israel's independence and the hesitance of either deducing a divine command to do so or making a major festival on a day not authorized by ancient tradition.[9] Some congregations take out the Torah and read three *aliyot* (Deut. 7:12–8:18), followed by the same haftarah portion that is read on the last day of Passover in the Diaspora (Isa. 10:32–12:6).

In the Diaspora, Yom ha-Atzmaut is celebrated with a variety of parades, cultural events, fairs, and public ceremonies designed to foster solidarity with fellow Jews in the State of Israel.

Yom Yerushalayim (יוֹם יְרוּשָׁלַיִם)

Yom Yerushalayim (Jerusalem Day) is celebrated on the 28th of Iyar to commemorate the unification of the city of Jerusalem on June 7, 1967, when the Israeli army swept to victory over Arab forces during the Six-Day War. For the first time since the Second Temple fell to the Romans in 70 C.E., the Temple Mount and the Western Wall were under Jewish control. A thanksgiving service is held at the Western Wall, and torches are lit in memory of those Israeli soldiers who lost their lives in the battle for Jerusalem. As a minor festival falling during the semi-mourning Omer period, some Orthodox circles permit weddings to take place (as on Lag ba-Omer and Rosh Hodesh).[10]

Shavuot (שָׁבוּעוֹת)

The festival of Shavuot occurs in late spring, 50 days after the beginning of Passover. Literally meaning "weeks," which reflects the seven weeks of the counting of the Omer that separate it from Passover, Shavuot is sometimes translated into English as "Pentecost" (the 50th day). It is observed on the Sixth of Sivan (plus the Seventh in the Diaspora). Coming at the end of the barley harvest and the beginning of the wheat crop, one biblical name for Shavuot is Hag ha-Katzir (Harvest Festival). The festival is also known as Yom ha-Bikkurim (Day of the First Fruits), when joyful pilgrims would march to Jerusalem to offer up baskets of their first ripe fruits and bread baked from the newly harvested wheat (Bik. 3:2–4). A remarkable transformation of the festival took place in rabbinic times, when Shavuot became observed as the anniversary of the giving of the Torah on Mount Sinai (Pes. 68b) and was referred to in the liturgy as *Zeman Mattan Torateinu* (The Time of the Giving of Our Torah).

In Temple times, two loaves of bread were "waved before the Lord" on Shavuot (Lev. 23:17–20), the only meal offering baked with leaven (*hametz*). Menachem Leibtag suggested that whereas unleavened bread (matzah) symbolizes the initial stage of a process, the fully risen *hametz* symbolizes its completion. Bringing the leavened loaves on Shavuot may indicate that the giving of the Torah at Mount Sinai on that date should be understood as the culmination of the process of redemption from slavery that began on Passover, when only matzah could be consumed. Just as the two loaves marked the staple of our physical existence, so the historical process that began with the Exodus from Egypt and culminated with the giving of the Torah reflected the essence of our spiritual existence.

To emphasize the rabbinic view of Shavuot as the anniversary of the Revelation at Sinai, the Torah reading for the day appropriately includes a recitation of the Ten Commandments (Exod. 19:1–20:26). This section was read daily in the Temple; after its destruction, however, the Rabbis discouraged its recitation in the synagogue lest some sectarians argue that only these commandments, rather than the entire Torah, were given to Moses on Mount Sinai (Ber. 12a).[1] The haftarah reading for the first day is Ezekiel's (1:1-28, 3:12) stunning mystical vision of the divine chariot (*merkavah*).

Under the influence of the kabbalists, it became customary to observe an all-night vigil (*Tikun leil Shavuot*; lit., "The prepared [texts] of the night of Shavuot") devoted to the study of passages from the Bible, Talmud, and Zohar. The popular explanation is that staying up all night on the eve of Shavuot atones for the behavior of the Israelites at Sinai, who according to tradition slept late that morning and had to be awakened by Moses (because "*tikun*" can also be translated as "rectifying").[2] An opposite view is that this practice is based on the legend that thunder and lighting kept the Israelites awake and trembling all night while Moses was on Mount Sinai receiving the Torah.[3] In some communities, the Shavuot eve study session concludes with the only sunrise service of the Jewish year, a symbol either of the light of the Torah or of the Jews as a "light unto the nations" (Isa. 49:6).[4] A less-observed custom in the Diaspora is staying up late on the second night of Shavuot to recite the entire Book of Psalms, whose author (King David), according to tradition, was born and died on Shavuot.[5] Some Sephardic communities read a special *ketubah* (marriage contract) before the ark, symbolic of the "wedding" of God and Israel that was celebrated at Mount Sinai.[6]

In the synagogue, it is traditional to read the Book of Ruth on Shavuot, because the story takes place at harvest time (Ruth 2:23). As a proselyte, Ruth accepted the Torah just as did the Israelites at Mount Sinai. This is evidenced in her name, which has a numerical value of 606—the difference between the commandments observed by Jews (613) and those incumbent on all nations of the world (the seven Noahide laws).[7] Ruth also was the great-grandmother of King David (Ruth 4:17), who is closely associated with the festival (see above). In Ashkenazic synagogues, *Akdamut* (see below), a long medieval Aramaic *piyyut*, is usually chanted after the first *aliyah* has been called but before the Torah reading begins. The Sephardic tradition is to recite a *piyyut* by ibn Gabirol called *Azharot*, which lists the 613 commandments in the Torah.[8]

It is customary to adorn the synagogue with plants and flowers. In addition to Shavuot being a harvest festival, this practice may relate to the image of the Torah as a Tree of Life (Prov. 3:18); to the legend that Mount Sinai was once a "green mountain" with trees and shrubs, as implied by the phrase "neither shall the flocks and the herds graze" (Exod. 34:3); or to the rabbinic notion of Shavuot as the Day of Judgment for the fruit of the trees (RH 1:2) when God determines the amount of fruit that each tree will produce. Greenery is also symbolic of the reeds in which the infant Moses was hidden when he was rescued on the Sixth of Sivan, the day of Shavuot. Some communities decorate the Torah scrolls themselves with roses because of a midrashic interpretation of The Song of Songs that compares Israel to the single fragrant rose among the thorns, the only nation willing to accept the Torah.[9]

Dairy foods are traditionally eaten during Shavuot. According to legend, upon learning the laws of kashrut at Sinai, the Israelites understood that their pots were not kosher and thus resolved to eat only uncooked dairy foods until they could get new ones. Some people eat dairy foods containing honey because the Torah is likened to milk and honey in the verse, "Honey and milk are under your tongue" (Song 4:11). In addition, in the Torah the law of the first fruits (offered at the Temple on Shavuot) is placed next to the biblical prohibition against boiling a kid in its mother's milk (Exod. 23:19). Another explanation is that the Israelites exposed for the first time to the wondrous world of Torah were like newborns; just as babies drink only milk, so Jews commemorate the moment at Sinai by drinking and eating only dairy foods.[10] In *gematria*, the numerical value of the Hebrew word "*halav*" (milk) equals 40, corresponding to the number of days Moses spent on Mount Sinai receiving the Torah.[11]

A popular Shavuot dish among Ashkenazim is blintzes, thin crepes filled with sweetened cheese and usually topped with fresh fruit or jams. According to a midrash, cheese is eaten on Shavuot because one of the names for Mount Sinai was *Har Gavnunim*, which is derived from the Hebrew word "*gevinah*" (cheese).[12] In some communities, it is customary to eat triangular dumplings (kreplach) stuffed with cheese—

AKDAMUT (אַקְדָמוּת)

Akdamut (lit., "prelude") is a medieval *piyyut,* written in Aramaic, that in Ashkenazic synagogues is chanted responsively by the prayer leader and the congregation just before the Torah reading on Shavuot. The poem was composed in the 11th century by Meir ben Isaac Nehorai of Worms (Germany), who according to tradition was forced to participate in one of the numerous public disputations with priests debating the truth of Judaism versus Christianity. Consequently, it emphasizes the continuing commitment of the Jewish people to the Torah, despite often-intolerable pressure from those espousing other faiths.

The poem begins with 44 lines whose first letters are a double alphabetical acrostic. This is followed by 46 lines whose initial letters spell out "Meir, son of Rabbi Isaac, may he grow in Torah and in good deeds, Amen. And be strong and of good courage!" Every line ends in the syllable תָא (the last and first letters of the Hebrew alphabet).[1] In *Akdamut,* the poet describes the angelic praise of God in the heavens and the earthly partnership between God and the Jewish people, who remain faithful even in the face of their tribulations. The poem echoes the ancient legend that, just as traditional Jews on weekday mornings wear tefillin (see p. 382) containing a parchment with the verse "Hear, O Israel, the Lord [is] our God, the Lord is one"[2] (Deut 6:4), so God also wears tefillin that reads "Great is Israel, a unique people." There is also a passage looking forward to the coming of the Messiah, when the mythical monsters Leviathan and Behemoth (see p. 724), slain by God's ultimate justice, will be fed to the righteous at the messianic banquet.[3]

because the Torah, which consists of three parts (Five Books of Moses, Prophets, and Writings), was given by God in the third month through Moses, who was the third child of his parents, to a people that is divided into three groups (Kohen, Levite, and Israelite). In some communities, the challot baked for Shavuot are long and have four corners, symbolizing the four methods of interpreting the Torah.[13]

It has long been traditional to inaugurate the education of a Jewish child on Shavuot, the festival commemorating the giving of the Torah. In the Middle Ages, a child was introduced to the Hebrew *alef-bet* on this day, usually at the age of five, and then given cakes, honey, and candies so that "the Torah might be sweet on his lips."

A modern custom is the ceremony of confirmation (see p. 26), observed by many non-Orthodox synagogues on Shavuot, in which teenagers who have completed their formal religious school studies confirm their loyalty to the teachings of Torah.

Fast Days and Summer Observances

17th of Tammuz

The 17th of Tammuz commemorates the breaching of the walls of Jerusalem by the Romans (70 C.E.), which occurred three weeks before the destruction of the Second Temple on Tisha b'Av. The Jerusalem Talmud maintains that the break in the walls of Jerusalem by the Babylonians that led to the fall of the First Temple (586 B.C.E.) also occurred on this date (JT Taan. 4:8, 68c), although the Babylonian Talmud accepts the citation of Jeremiah (52:6–7) that this event took place on the ninth of the month (Taan. 28b). According to the Mishnah, other catastrophes that occurred on the 17th of Tammuz—the only Jewish observance that begins and ends during the declining moon—include the breaking of the first tablets by Moses in response to the incident of the Golden Calf; the cessation of the daily sacrifices in the First Temple; and the burning of a Torah scroll and the erection of an idol in the Temple by the heathen Apostomos, about whom nothing is known (Taan. 4:6).

The minor fast of the 17th of Tammuz lasts just from sunrise to sunset. Only eating and drinking are prohibited; the other deprivations of the major fast days of Yom Kippur and Tisha b'Av are not observed, and work is permitted.[1]

Zechariah (8:19) prophesied that ultimately the 17th of Tammuz, along with other fast days associated with the destruction of the First Temple in Jerusalem (Tisha b'Av, Tzom Gedalyah, 10th of Tevet), "shall become occasions for joy and gladness, happy festivals for the House of Judah."

The Three Weeks

The Three Weeks is a period of mourning that extends from the 17th of Tammuz through the Ninth of Av. Also known in Hebrew as *bein ha-meitzarim* (between the straits; i.e., between the two fasts), it commemorates the period leading up to the destruction of the First and Second Temples in Jerusalem.

The traditional mourning rites during the Three Weeks include abstention from weddings and other joyous celebrations, instrumental music, and entertainment and the prohibition against the purchase or wearing of new clothing or the eating of new fruit, for which the *Shehecheyanu* blessing (an expression of joy) must be recited.[1]

Beginning with the First of Av, the mourning customs become intensified. During this period, known as the Nine Days, eating meat and drinking wine are forbidden, except for Sabbath meals. Also prohibited are cutting hair, shaving, bathing, swimming, washing clothes, or wearing freshly laundered garments. Traditional Jews generally avoid any activities that could bring joy—such as going to a concert or the theater and redecorating a room. On the Sabbaths of the Three Weeks, special *haftarot* are read from Jeremiah (1:1–2:3, 2:4–3:4) and Isaiah (1:1–27), in which the prophets warn the people that their unfaithfulness to God will lead to the impending punishment of Israel at the hands of its enemy.[2]

The Sabbath immediately preceding Tisha b'Av is called Shabbat Hazon (Sabbath of the Vision). It takes its name from the opening words of the Haftarah of Admonition, which is filled with such harsh language hurled against the people by the prophet Isaiah that in Yiddish it became known as *Schwarz Shabbos* (Black Sabbath).[3]

Tisha b'Av (תִּשְׁעָה בְּאָב)

Tisha b'Av, the ninth day of the month of Av (July–August), is the saddest day in the Jewish calendar. It is a fast day that marks the anniversary of the destruction of the First Temple by the Babylonians in 586 B.C.E. and the Second Temple by the Romans in 70 C.E. Tisha b'Av eventually became a symbol for all the catastrophes that have befallen the Jewish people throughout its history. According to the Mishnah, Tisha b'Av was the date of several other disasters for the Jewish people (Taan. 4:6):

- The 10 spies brought back to Moses their negative report about Canaan, condemning the Israelites to spend 40 years wandering in the wilderness until they were permitted to enter the Promised Land.
- The Bar Kokhba revolt was finally crushed when Betar, the last stronghold, was captured by the Romans in 135 C.E.
- One year later, the Roman emperor Hadrian rebuilt Jerusalem as a city he renamed Aelia Capitolina (from which Jews were barred) and erected a pagan shrine on the site of the destroyed Temple.

According to tradition, Tisha b'Av was also the date of the expulsions of the Jews from England (1290) and Spain (1492).

The importance of Tisha b'Av as a fast day was emphasized in the Talmud, which observes: "He who eats or drinks on the Ninth of Av must be considered as guilty as one who has eaten on Yom Kippur" (Taan. 30b). The final meal before the fast often consists of hard-boiled eggs and lentils, which are customarily prepared for mourners, and some people used to even put ashes in their food

In addition to fasting, Tisha b'Av (known as the Black Fast), like Yom Kippur (which is termed the White Fast), is observed by refraining from wearing leather shoes, anointing with perfume, bathing, and sexual intercourse. If the ninth day falls on the Sabbath, the entire Tisha b'Av observance is moved to the next day, because no mourning is permitted on the Sabbath. From sunset to sunset, the general rule in the Talmud is that a person is obliged to observe all the mourning rites that apply in the case of the death of a next of kin (Taan. 30a). It is the only day when even the study of Torah is forbidden, since this would be a source of joy. All one is permitted to study is the Book of Job and the sections of Jeremiah and the Talmud that relate to destruction, especially of Jerusalem.

In synagogue, the congregation sits on the floor, footstools, or low benches (as would private mourners in their homes), reading by the light of candles or dim lights as a symbol of the darkness that has befallen Israel on that day. The curtain covering the ark (*parochet*) is removed; in some Sephardic synagogues in which the ark normally has no curtain, a black curtain is hung and the Torah scrolls themselves are draped in black mantles. Certain congregations even place the Torah scroll on the floor and strew ashes over it, while those in attendance recite the words "the crown has fallen from our head" (Lam. 5:16).

The megillah of Lamentations (Eikhah) is recited in a haunting melody, with the next-to-last verse repeated by everyone so that the book ends on the hopeful note of "Take us back, O Lord, to Yourself, and let us come back; renew our days as of old" (Lam. 5:21). (This same verse is the final line sung as the ark is closed after the scroll has been returned to it following the Torah reading.) The chanting of Lamentations is followed by the recitation of a series of special *piyyutim* called *kinot*, medieval dirges that recount the destruction of the Temple and the sins of the Jewish people. The prayer leader recites the service in a monotonal and melancholy tune. Tallit and tefillin are not worn, since the community is considered to be as mourners, who do not wear them between the time of death of a loved one and the funeral; some sprinkle ashes on their heads as a symbol of mourning. Congregants do not exchange greetings upon entering or leaving the synagogue.[1]

Work is not forbidden, though traditionally it is minimized as much as possible in accordance with the observation of Rabbi Akiva that "anyone who does work on the Ninth of Av will never see in his work any sign of blessing" (Taan. 30b).

There is a tradition that the Messiah will be born on Tisha b'Av, reversing the centuries of travail and suffering that have been the lot of the Jewish people. Like the mystical phoenix rising from the ashes, ultimate redemption will result from the depths of destruction and despair. An expression of this surprisingly hopeful mood as the day progresses is the custom of sweeping the house on the afternoon of Tisha b'Av in case the Messiah should come. For a similar reason, women in some communities don fine clothes and put on perfume. At the afternoon service, tallit and tefillin are worn (both are usually worn during the morning service, with the exception that the tallit is worn on Kol Nidre night), a sign that the mourning practices of Tisha b'Av will end at sundown. The ark curtain and Torah mantles are restored, the Torah is read again, and the full *Kaddish* is recited (including the line requesting that God accept our pleas [*titkabeil*]). There is an additional paragraph stressing comfort and looking hopefully to the future redemption.[2] After sundown and the breaking of the fast, some go outside for the joyful service of *Kiddush Levanah* (Sanctification of the Moon; see p. 168).[3]

The Sabbath immediately following Tisha b'Av is called Shabbat Nachamu (Sabbath of Comfort). It takes its name from the opening Hebrew word of the haftarah, "Be comforted, [be comforted, My people, says your God]" (Isa. 40:1). This is the first of the seven "*haftarot* of consolation" (leading up to the observance of Rosh Hashanah), which prophesy the redemption of Israel, its restoration to the land, and the coming of the messianic days of peace and justice.[4]

Tu b'Av (ט״ו בְּאָב)

Tu b'Av, the 15th day (full moon) of the month of Av (July–August), is a minor holiday that in Second Temple times celebrated the beginning of the grape harvest in ancient Israel. The term "*Tu*" derives from the Hebrew alphabetical form for the number "15": ט (9) plus ו (6). Although adding י (10) plus ה (5) to get יה (15) would be mathematically more logical, this spelling is not used because it is one of the holy names of God.[1]

According to the Mishnah, on this day (as well as on Yom Kippur) "the daughters of Jerusalem used to dress in white garments [which they borrowed so as not to put to shame anyone who had none] and go out and dance in the vineyards [and young men would follow after them]" (Taan. 4:8; 26b). This may imply that the afternoons of Yom Kippur and the 15th of Av, which follows the mourning fast of the Ninth of Av, are periods of forgiveness. According to one tradition, during the 40th year of their wandering in the wilderness, on Tu b'Av the Israelites were finally forgiven for the sins of the spies. Those from the Exodus generation who had survived received a divine pardon sparing them from death, and thus they were permitted to enter the Promised Land (Taan. 30b).[2]

The Talmud reports other events that occurred on this date as reasons for this minor holiday (Taan. 30b–31a; BB 121a,b). No longer was an Israelite woman prohibited from marrying a man from a different tribe if she had inherited land from her father in the absence of any male heirs. Originally established in the case of the daughters of Zelophehad (Num. 36:8) to prevent land shifting from the inheritance of one tribe to another, this rule was no longer required once the land had been divided after the conquest of Canaan. Also on this date, the Benjamites were readmitted into the community and were no longer prohibited from marrying members of the other tribes (because of the incident of the concubine of Gibeah in Judges 21:18). These two events, combined with the talmudic description of young maidens dancing in the vineyards, led to Tu b'Av eventually becoming a day when women could actively search for an eligible husband.[3]

On Tu b'Av, the Romans finally permitted the burial of the remains of the Jewish soldiers who had fallen three years earlier in the defense of Betar, the last stronghold of Bar Kokhba. This event was considered so momentous for the Jews of that time that it led to the composition of a fourth blessing in the Grace after Meals (*ha-tov v'ha-meitiv*; "Who is good and does good"), which thanks God both for not permitting these corpses to decay and spread disease and for making the Romans finally allow the Jews to bury them.[4]

Tu b'Av was the last day that kindling for the Temple altar could be chopped, because thereafter the sun would no longer be hot enough to dry the wood (Taan. 31a). It therefore represented the turning point of the sun's heat from scorching to bearable—a first hint of the revivifying autumn, just as Tu b'Shevat (exactly six months earlier) was the harbinger of the upcoming spring.[5]

The prohibition against planting crops during the sabbatical year began on Tu b'Av, a month and a half before the actual beginning of the sabbatical year on the following Rosh Hashanah.

In Israel today, the radio airwaves on Tu b'Av are filled with songs of love. After the absence of weddings throughout the Three Weeks, the matrimonial season gets into high gear on Tu b'Av. As a minor festival, Tu b'Av is considered a day of joy, so that the bride and groom are not required to fast on their wedding day.

Tzom Gedalyah (צוֹם גְּדַלְיָה)

Tzom Gedalyah (Fast of Gedalyah), which occurs on the day after Rosh Hashanah (Third of Tishrei), commemorates the assassination of the last governor of Judea, who in 586 B.C.E. was named to the post by the conquering Babylonians. The murder of Gedalyah was apparently instigated with the hope of overthrowing Babylonian rule, but instead his death was the final blow to any immediate hope of restoring Jewish sovereignty and independence and led to the further dispersal of the Jewish people.[1]

Zechariah (8:19) prophesied that ultimately Tzom Gedalyah, along with other fast days associated with the destruction of the First Temple in Jerusalem (17th of Tammuz, Tisha b'Av, and 10th of Tevet), "shall become occasions for joy and gladness, happy festivals for the House of Judah."

10th of Tevet

The 10th of Tevet, which comes shortly after Hanukkah, is a minor fast day marking the beginning of the siege of Jerusalem by Nebuchadnezzar that eventually resulted in the Babylonians destroying the First Temple. Along with Tzom Gedalyah, the 17th of Tammuz, and Tisha b'Av, the 10th of Tevet is one of the four fast days mentioned by the prophet Zechariah (8:19) that commemorate the destruction of the Temples in Jerusalem and the demise of an independent Jewish state in ancient times but that ultimately will be celebrated as "happy festivals for the House of Judah."[1]

Synagogue and Prayer

Synagogue

Overview

The synagogue is considered by many Jews to be the most important institution in Judaism. The three Hebrew designations for the synagogue indicate its major functions—*beit knesset* (house of assembly), *beit tefillah* (house of prayer), and *beit midrash* (house of study). The Yiddish term for a synagogue is "*shul*" (school), reflecting the fact that Jewish worship and learning most often take place in the same building. Early Reform Jews chose the term "temple" for their synagogues, indicating that in the post-Enlightenment age they no longer yearned for a return to the Land of Israel and the rebuilding of the Temple in Jerusalem, instead considering the country of their citizenship to be their everlasting homeland.[1]

Historically, the synagogue represents the site of the first communal worship divorced from sacrifice. Unlike the Temple, which could only be in Jerusalem and was run by a specifically sanctified clergy born to the task (*Kohanim* assisted by Levites), the synagogue could be housed anywhere (not necessarily in a spot with some sacred connotation); did not have to adhere to a rigid architectural pattern; and had prayer leaders and teachers whose roles were not determined by birth, ancestry, or socioeconomic level.[2] By the end of the Second Temple period (first century C.E.), the synagogue as a house of prayer and study was a firmly established institution, though its origin is recorded neither in the Bible nor in postbiblical records.[3]

Early History

The initial sites of worship in ancient Israel were shrines established by Abraham, who erected altars to God at a site between Beit El and Ai

(Gen. 12:7–8) and at Hebron (Gen. 13:18), and by Jacob, who set up an altar at Beth El, the site of his dream of angels ascending and descending on ladders extending from the earth to Heaven (Gen. 28:18–19). Following the conquest of the Land of Israel under Joshua, there apparently were numerous regional shrines in addition to the central one, which housed the ark containing the tablets of the Ten Commandments, the most sacred object of Israel. The principal feature in each of these shrines was a sacrificial system under the control of a cadre of priests (*Kohanim*). The major limitation was that no Israelite shrine could be erected outside the Land of Israel, for even though God was viewed as the universal deity of the entire world, sacrifices to the God of Israel were permitted only on the land that had been divinely chosen for His people. The dramatic religious reformation of King Josiah (609 B.C.E.) solidified the exclusive position of the Temple in Jerusalem. Henceforth, no altar could be built beyond the boundaries of the Land of Israel; the only permissible site for an altar or sacrifice to God within Israel was the shrine in Jerusalem (2 Kings 22–23; Deut. 12:5–6).

This caused several major problems for the Israelites. As a practical matter, the slaughtering of animals and the eating of meat, which had always been connected with sacrificial worship, became extremely difficult for those who lived far from Jerusalem. The solution was to permit "profane" slaughter, solely for eating and not as part of worship (Deut. 12:15–16). A more serious problem was the requirement that communal worship with sacrifices could now take place only in Jerusalem, where all males were required to appear before the Lord on the three pilgrimage festivals of Passover, Shavuot, and Sukkot (Deut. 16:16). Those who were unable to come to Jerusalem were effectively precluded from participating in organized Jewish worship.[4]

Virtually all scholars agree that the synagogue as an institution originated during the Babylonian exile following the destruction of the Kingdom of Judah in 586 B.C.E. With the Temple destroyed, the Israelites were suddenly cut off from traditional methods of seeking divine assistance, gaining forgiveness from sin, thanking God for merciful salvation, and celebrating the holy days.[5] Not only were the exiles deprived of their Temple but they were also forbidden to build an altar and offer sacrifices outside the Land of Israel. Had this prohibition not been in effect, the exiles would probably have returned to the previous situation of erecting multiple sacrificial shrines throughout the

Diaspora. Indeed, this actually occurred at about that time, when a small group of Jewish mercenary soldiers settled on Elephantine, a small island in the Nile, and constructed a temple on Egyptian soil. The ritual system that they established, which included priests and sacrifices, survived for several hundred years. However, this was not a viable solution for the exiles in Babylonia, who accepted the Book of Deuteronomy as authoritative and could not conceive of violating one of its core precepts. In contrast to pagans who believed that their gods were exclusively associated with a given land, the exiles were convinced that the Divine Presence, later termed the *Shekhinah*, was with them in Babylonia. Although sacrifice to God was forbidden outside of the Land of Israel, the Torah did not prohibit the worship of God *without sacrifice* on foreign soil. Unlike pagan gods, the God of Israel did not depend on sacrifices for sustenance. Instead, the inability to offer sacrifices was to punish the people for their failure to scrupulously observe the commandments, and the restoration of the sacrificial service was to be the future reward for their repentance.[6]

At this stage, there was no precedent for people assembling for communal prayer services. During the years of exile, it appears likely that groups of Israelites periodically gathered together for mutual support and consolation and to maintain their connection with fellow Jews and the God of Israel. In the Land of Israel, it had been customary to visit the prophet on Sabbaths and days of the New Moon (2 Kings 4:23). Consequently, in Babylonia gatherings would take place on these days with a local leader, such as the prophet Ezekiel (who was also a *Kohen*). The prophet would probably read to the people from the forewarnings of the approaching disaster, as well as offer some words of comfort or hope. Torah portions dealing with the Exodus from Egypt would also be appropriate, to assure the people that the God who redeemed their ancestors would also redeem them if they proved worthy. There probably was recitation of the psalms that the Levites used to sing in the Temple on the day of the week corresponding to that of the gathering. Special prayers might be composed for the occasion, including confessions of sins to obtain divine mercy and redemption.

The Jews of Babylonia attended these informal meetings with increasing frequency, because they filled the religious void created by the destruction of the Temple. In time, these informal meetings became routine religious functions of the community. "Public prayer progressively became regarded as an official religious ritual, and the gatherings at the prayer houses were seen as religious requirements ... In later years, when the Jews returned to Jerusalem and rebuilt the Temple, many of them continued to attend the prayer meetings."[7] Eventually, the prayers became organized into a synagogue liturgy.

The earliest reasonably definitive reference to this precursor of the synagogue comes from the Book of Ezekiel (11:16). After the first dispersion of King Jehoiachin and the aristocracy in 597 B.C.E., the Jews who had remained in Judah taunted the exiles, saying that they were removed from the Temple, which still stood. Ezekiel responded to them, "Thus said the Lord God: I have indeed removed them far among the nations and have scattered them among the countries, and I have become to them a 'little sanctuary' (*mikdash me-at*) in the countries where they have gone" (Ezek. 11:16). The Talmud applied the term "little sanctuary" to the synagogue (Meg. 29a). Although at the time such gatherings must have seemed only a pale alternative to the splendor of the Temple and its impressive sacrificial rites, they eventually proved to be more enduring and one of Judaism's major contributions to civilization. As Shalom Spiegel wrote, "The Jews were the only people of antiquity who succeeded in divorcing prayer from sacrifice, and so were the first to evolve the modes and manners of public worship as the world knows them now."[8]

Some traditions date the development of the *beit midrash* (the house of study and, by extension, a site for prayer without sacrifice) back to early biblical times. The Midrash interprets the plural word in the verse "Jacob was a mild man who stayed in tents" (Gen. 25:27) to imply that the Patriarch spent his time in the *beit midrash* of Shem and the *beit midrash* of Eber. Philo and Josephus attributed the origin of the synagogue to Moses.[9] During the First Temple period, the prayer of Hannah at Shiloh was unaccompanied by sacrifice (1 Sam. 1:10), and Solomon's prayer at the dedication of the Temple makes no mention of any sacrificial rite (1 Kings 8:12–21).

A precursor of the synagogue may have been the *ma'amadot*, a system by which the general public was represented at the Temple during the offering of the daily sacrifices (Num. 28:1), even though they could not perform any of the priestly or levitical duties. The country was divided into 24 districts, each of which sent a delegation of eminent and pious Israelites to represent it at the daily public offerings for one week every six months. These men were known as the *anshei ma'amad* (men of standing), because their task was to "stand by" and observe the Temple ritual. They also joined together to recite prayers and read from Genesis. Those *anshei ma'amad* unable to travel to Jerusalem for the week refrained from work and assembled each day to recite prayers, which mostly corresponded to the psalms being said at the Temple. If a *Kohen* were present, he would recite the Priestly Blessing (see p. 432) at the end of these daily prayer meetings, which were timed to finish at the same time as those in Jerusalem. Eventually, these local gatherings attracted large crowds, who joined the *anshei ma'amad* in prayer. After the destruction of the Temple, some devout men would remain in the synagogue after daily services to read the same verses from Genesis that had formerly been recited by the *anshei ma'amad*. Some modern editions of the siddur (prayer book) still include a section (*ma'amadot*) that contains these scriptural passages from what may have been the origin of the synagogue service.[10]

Post-Exilic Period

There are no explicit references to the synagogue in the writings of the post-exilic prophets. Nonetheless, those who returned to the Land of Israel from Babylonia presumably brought back with them the fundamental elements of the institution. It is generally agreed that these early synagogues served primarily as centers of study, where the Torah and prophetic passages were read and explanations provided. Prayers may have been recited before and after these readings, similar to the blessings said today in relation to the chanting of the Torah and haftarah portions. The establishment of the synagogue implies the evolution of standard forms of service, and the Talmud ascribes the formulation of the earliest prayers (*Amidah*, *Kiddush*, and *Havdalah*) to Ezra and his successors, the men of the Great Assembly (Ber. 33a).

Though large masses of diaspora Jews made the pilgrimage to Jerusalem on festivals, there was a need to develop local places for study and worship outside the Land of Israel. Indeed, the earliest remains of a synagogue unearthed by archaeologists is in Egypt, in the form of a marble slab with an inscription indicating that it was dedicated by the Jews. As the Talmud describes, the synagogue in Alexandria was so large ("it sometimes held twice the number of people that went forth from Egypt" [1,200,000]) that it was often impossible to hear the voice of the *hazzan*; thus it was necessary for an attendant to wave a scarf so that worshipers in the back of the congregation would know when to respond "amen" to each of the blessings before and after the Torah reading (Suk. 51b).

Early synagogues, especially in the Diaspora, were centers of Jewish social, educational, and religious life. There, collections were made to amass funds both for local needs and to send to Jerusalem. Greek was the language of synagogues in parts of the Diaspora (not in Babylonia); even the Torah was read in Greek (using the Septuagint, the official Greek translation). In the Land of Israel, Aramaic (the vernacular) was used along with Hebrew. Since Hebrew was no longer the spoken language of the people, a free Aramaic translation accompanied the Torah reading. Yet, the synagogue was never regarded as a rival to the Temple. Although both served as a site for the worship of God, the Temple was "service" through a sacrificial rite, whereas the synagogue emphasized "the service of the heart." Moreover, the synagogues focused on educational activities under the auspices of the sages and later the Rabbis. After the destruction of the Second Temple, prayers for its rebuilding were incorporated into the synagogue service. The Rabbis observed that even during the Messianic Age, when the dispersed Jews would return to the Land of Israel and the Temple would be rebuilt, the synagogues of the Diaspora would still exist to serve the vital purpose of expounding the Torah to the masses (Meg. 29b).[11]

After the Destruction of the Temple (70 C.E.)

After the Temple was destroyed and the sacrificial service ceased, the synagogue remained as the only focal point of Jewish religious life. Many Temple customs and rituals were transferred to the synagogue—blowing the shofar at Rosh Hashanah services (see p. 190), the processions with *lulav* and *etrog* on Sukkot (see p. 231), and the eternal light (*ner tamid*) hung in front of the ark (see p. 336). Conversely, others were forbidden precisely because they had exclusively belonged to the Temple. Prayer was regarded as the substitute for sacrifice, and the word "*avodah*," which had referred to the sacrificial system, was now applied to prayer (*avodah* of the heart). Numerous talmudic statements were designed to encourage attendance at synagogue—"A man's prayer is only heard in the synagogue" (Ber. 6a), "Anybody who has a synagogue in his city and does not attend there is called a bad neighbor ... and brings exile on himself and his children" (Ber. 8a), "God becomes angry when He comes to synagogue and does not find 10 persons there" (Ber. 6b), and "Whoever has a fixed place for his prayer has the God of Abraham as his helper" (Ber. 6b). One sage attributed the longevity of Babylonian Jews to the fact that they attended synagogue; another recommended that one should pray simultaneously with the synagogue service if unable to be there physically.

Medieval Period

The medieval synagogue served multiple functions, reflecting almost all the activities in daily Jewish existence. "As a house of prayer, the synagogue was in almost constant use. It was open all day and much of the night for private and public worship. In times of adversity, Jews went to the synagogue to seek God's help; in times of rescue, they went there to rejoice in their deliverance and to chant psalms of praise and thanksgiving to God."[12] Services were relatively informal, especially in the Ashkenazic synagogues of Central and Eastern Europe. During the Torah reading, Jews felt sufficiently at home in their "little sanctuary" to walk about and greet their neighbors. They had no qualms about chanting prayers out loud, even if their favorite melodies were not the same as those of the prayer leader, and they were oblivious to the clamor around them.

The most important attachment to the synagogue was the study hall, which contained a library of sacred texts. Study groups for those at all levels of scholarship were typically taught by volunteers, whose only payment was the hope for reward in the world to come. The synagogue also housed the community school and, in some cities, an academy for advanced students (*yeshivah*) that prepared them for rabbinic ordination.

The synagogue was the center of community life, housing the community offices, courtroom, *mikveh* (ritual bath), matzah bakery, hospice for needy travelers, and hall where weddings and other festivities were held. Regulations approved by the leaders of the community were submitted for popular approval at special synagogue meetings. Mourners were officially and publicly comforted in the synagogue, a custom that persists to the present day. On the Sabbath preceding his wedding, the bridegroom was honored with an aliyah, to the joy of the members of the congregation. The rarely invoked ban of excommunication (*herem*; see p. 607) was solemnly pronounced in the synagogue, accompanied by lighted black candles, a blast of the shofar, and a host of awesome maledictions. However, the most striking practice was the permission given to any person with a private complaint, who felt helpless before the powerful establishment, to rise during congregational services and call for a halt in the prayers until he was satisfied that he would receive prompt justice. That this never became a communal nuisance attests to the integrity of the Jewish courts and the general feeling that they would provide fair treatment for all.

The synagogue was one of few medieval institutions that was relatively democratic, at least for men. Each male 13 or older was counted equally in constituting the minyan (quorum of 10) needed for a congregational service (see p. 372). Every capable person was eligible to lead the congregation in prayer. On the anniversary of a parent's death, the humblest worshiper could claim his right to be the prayer leader. Every Jew also was eligible to be called to the Torah, though the first two *aliyot* were reserved for a Kohen and Levite, respectively. On certain special occasions—such as the Sabbaths after a boy reached age 13, preceding his marriage, and before the anniversary of a parent's death—even the poorest and least educated man would be called to the Torah.

Modern Period

Unlike the small informal synagogues of the Middle Ages, many of the synagogues built by the Reform movement in the 19th century were elaborate, dignified buildings that were lavishly and formally furnished. Known as "temples," most included an organ and choir loft and a *bimah* (see p. 335), at the front of the sanctuary. Pews were arranged in straight rows, with no special section for women. Prayer leaders and rabbis were salaried employees of the congregation. Heavily influenced in both structural style and internal organization by prevailing trends in the various Christian churches, Reform synagogues succeeded in becoming paragons of decorum and dignity, though at the cost of relinquishing the warmth and spontaneity that had characterized synagogues for centuries.

Simpler, less formal synagogues still exist, but eventually even Orthodox congregations built impressive buildings and hired professional officials. Although these synagogues were constructed in accordance with Jewish law, adjustments were sometimes made to accommodate modern sensibilities. In some synagogues, women's galleries were built in a way that provided women with a full view of the service. A popular trend in the last half of the 20th century in America was the expanding synagogue, in which a hall is constructed next to the main sanctuary and is separated from it by a partition that can be removed for the High Holy Days. This provides for increased seating capacity, thus precluding the need for extra personnel to lead an overflow service.

Synagogue Architecture

Synagogue architecture has been extremely varied, usually reflecting the popular styles of the dominant culture in which Jews lived. Some structures were extremely elaborate and no less impressive than Christian cathedrals or grand mosques. In medieval Europe, Christian law mandated that synagogues have modest exteriors that would not rival the splendor of churches.[1] After the Cossack slaughter of the mid-17th century, Polish Jews built synagogues with thick walls, heavy buttresses, and crenulations for sharpshooters along the roof. In this way, the synagogue aided the Jew in achieving both "salvation of soul and safety of life and limb."[2]

Traditionally, the synagogue was built on the most elevated site in the city so that it was the tallest building in town, in keeping with the verse, "To raise the House of our God" (Ezra 9:9).[3] Indeed, as Rav observed, "any city whose roofs are higher than the synagogue will be ultimately destroyed" (Shab. 11a). However, Jews frequently have been unable to comply with this law in both Christian and Muslim countries, which reserved this prerogative for their churches and mosques, respectively.[4] Indeed, in many places synagogues were deliberately built low, so as to be as inconspicuous as possible to non-Jews. To increase the height of the interior space, the floor of the synagogue often was dug below street level, fulfilling the verse, "Out of the depths I call You, O Lord" (Ps. 130:1).[5]

Jews generally erected their synagogues within the areas they inhabited, though as early as talmudic times some were built outside the city (Kid. 73b). To eliminate the need for latecomers to return home alone on often dangerous paths, special prayers were inserted to lengthen the service so that all could finish at the same time. Synagogues often were constructed near bodies of water, possibly to preclude the need for a *mikveh* (ritual bath; see p. 555).

The orientation of the synagogue presented a major problem. Based on Solomon's prayer at the dedication of the Temple (1 Kings 8:30) and the description of Daniel praying facing Jerusalem (Dan. 6:11), the Rabbis declared that synagogues be oriented toward Jerusalem, with those in the Holy City itself facing in the direction of the Temple. The Talmud clearly demands this orientation for the recitation of the *Amidah*, so that "in this way, all Israel will be turning their hearts toward one place" (Ber. 30a). The earliest synagogues had their entrances facing toward Jerusalem. However, worshipers entering through the main doors (usually three) in this facade were required to turn around to face the Holy City in prayer. In addition, the *halakhah* mandates that the Holy Ark be placed on the side facing Jerusalem, and it would be unfitting to enter the sanctuary from the same side on which the ark stands. This apparent contradiction is probably explains the later institution of a fixed ark inside the synagogue. In the early synagogues, the ark containing the Torah scrolls was a movable object, which was carried or wheeled in for services. When the once-portable ark was finally fixed in the wall, the previous custom of synagogue entrances being oriented toward Jerusalem was abandoned—the Rabbis decided that it was better to enter the synagogue approaching the ark so that one could bow before it as a sign of respect.

When possible, one is required to go through a vestibule to the main sanctuary rather than enter directly from the street, to symbolically shed the concerns of the outside world in moving from secular to holy space. The vestibule of a traditional synagogue contains a pitcher and washbasin to enable worshipers to pour water over their hands. By physically cleansing themselves, they are reminded of their duty to be pure in conduct: "Who may ascend the mountain of the Lord? Who may stand in His holy place? He who has clean hands and a pure heart" (Ps. 24:3–4).[6]

Despite the absence of any uniformity in the external appearance of a synagogue, the interior has been subjected to rabbinic regulation. A synagogue must have windows, a halakhic requirement that derives from the description of Daniel having "had windows made [in his upper chamber where he prayed] facing Jerusalem" (Dan. 6:10). According to Rashi, windows are required because they allow the worshiper to see the sky, which inspires reverence and devotion during prayer. Some have recommended that there be 12 windows in a synagogue, corresponding to the 12 tribes of Israel. Each has a special angel who carries its prayers through a particular "window in heaven" (reflecting the distinct spirit and soul of the tribe) directly to the throne of God.[7]

Torah scrolls were housed in an enclosure or closet, known as the *Aron Kodesh* (Holy Ark; see p. 332). In ancient synagogues, it was customary to store the scrolls in an adjoining room or, for reasons of safety, in another building. The prayer leader's desk was placed immediately in front of the ark, sometimes below the floor level. The Torah was read from the *bimah* (see p. 335), an elevated platform surrounded by a railing for safety, which was situated at the center of the synagogue so that everyone in the congregation could hear the Torah reading and the sermon. The modern custom of creating additional space by placing the *bimah* at the front of the synagogue was highly controversial.

Traditionally, seats were provided for the elders to sit adjacent to the ark, facing the congregation. This gave rise to the general desire to sit near the eastern wall, because it was the most prestigious place in the synagogue.[8] Although this custom is no longer followed, in synagogues with the *bimah* in the front, major officials often sit flanking the ark. Women have traditionally sat in a separate section—either at the sides, in the rear, or in a balcony—often separated from men by a divider called a *mechitzah* (see p. 337). Reform and Conservative synagogues have abolished this separation.

The decoration of synagogue interiors has varied from simple to lavishly adorned. According to the Zohar, "a synagogue should be a place of great beauty ... wonderfully decorated, for it is an earthly copy of the heavenly original." The earliest ornamentations were mosaic floor designs, as found in Jerusalem synagogues of the Second Temple period, at Masada, and throughout the Land of Israel. Some were basic geometric patterns, while others had pictorial representations of Temple artifacts, biblical scenes, animal and floral designs, and even pictures of the zodiac (see p. 618). Outside the Land of Israel, wall and ceiling decorations have been found dating back to the talmudic era. The walls of most early synagogues had handwritten or engraved inscriptions of biblical verses or words to inspire prayer.[9] Later synagogues added stained glass windows, the Tree of Life (see p. 697), rampant lions, and the Star of David (see p. 575), as well as many biblical and rabbinic verses.[10]

From ancient times, it has been customary in many synagogues to honor donors by inscribing their names on walls, plaques, or Torah ornaments. Memorial tablets are often installed for the deceased, with adjacent tiny electric lights that are turned on for the anniversaries of their deaths and when *Yizkor* is recited. These practices are suggested in the verse, "I will give them, in My house and within My walls, a monument and a name [*yad vashem*] ... an everlasting name which shall not perish" (Isa. 56:5).[11]

Although not as holy as the Temple, as its symbolic replacement the synagogue has gained some degree of holiness. All ritual objects in the synagogue acquire sanctity by virtue of the sacred purposes that they serve. This is determined by their proximity, in space and use, to the Torah scroll, the most sacred object in the synagogue.[12] Therefore, when no longer usable, bookcases that held sacred texts, the ark in which the Torah stood, and the curtain *(parochet)* that hung in front of the ark must be stored away rather than destroyed. In many synagogues, a special storeroom (*genizah*) is set aside for the disposition of torn prayer books, Bibles, and other holy texts that have deteriorated and can no longer be used, so as to show respect for the name of God contained within them. The contents of the *genizah* are removed periodically and reverently buried in the cemetery.[13]

Torah Scrolls and Ornaments

The Scrolls

Torah scrolls (*sifrei Torah*) are works of simple beauty, written with pious care by a specially trained scribe known as a "*sofer*." This is a shortened form of the title "*sofer stam*," the last word of which is an acronym for "*sefer Torah, tefillin,* and *mezuzot*"—the three items containing texts that the *sofer stam* writes. Literally meaning "one who counts," the word "*sofer*" probably reflects the fact that some of the early scribes used to count all the letters, words, and verses of the Torah to make certain that none were inadvertently added or omitted (Kid. 30a).

Working full time, it takes a skilled *sofer* about nine months to complete the 5,888 verses and 79,976 words in the Torah.[1] As one engaged in sacred work, a *sofer* customarily begins his day by immersing himself in a *mikveh* (ritual bath), an act of spiritual purification indicating his readiness to accept the obligation of his holy task. If unable to do so, the *sofer* leaves a space for the name of God, postponing writing it for a day when he can immerse himself in the *mikveh*.[2] Before beginning to write and mindful of the sanctity of the task he is about to undertake, the *sofer* must declare out loud, "I am writing the Torah for the sake of the holiness of a Torah scroll, and all of the names of God in it for the sake of the holiness of the Name." When about to write one of the names of God, the *sofer* must pause and dip the quill into ink anew before inscribing the last letter of the preceding word, and then say aloud, "I am writing for the sake of the holiness of the Name."[3]

Although some authorities disagree, the accepted rule is that a woman may not write a Torah scroll; if she does, the scroll is invalid for public use. This is based on a talmudic dictum that "whosoever cannot serve as the representative of the public in religious matters is not permitted to write a scroll of the Torah" (Sof. 1:13), and women in post-talmudic times were not permitted to read the Torah before a congregation (see p. 452).[4]

When writing a new Torah, the scribe is forbidden to rely on his memory and must have before him a correct scroll or printed Pentateuch to serve as his guide (Meg. 18b), for any incorrect word or obliterated letter makes a scroll unfit for use (*pasul*). Despite all precautions, however, mistakes are inevitable due to the difficulty of the scribe's task. The most common errors are dittographic (writing the same letter or word twice), haplographic (omitting one or two identical letters or words that should follow each other), and homoioteleutonic (mistaking a word for the next time it appears in the passage and thus failing to include everything in between).[5] Most simple errors may be corrected by scratching out the incorrect writing with a sharp blade and pumice stone. The most serious error—the omission or misspelling of the name of God—cannot be corrected, since the divine name cannot be erased (Sof. 5:6), and the entire sheet of parchment must be discarded. When a mistake is found in a Torah, a cloth ribbon is tied around the mantle as a sign that it cannot be used until the appropriate correction is made. According to the Talmud, a Torah scroll that has fewer than 85 correct letters must be discarded (Shab. 116a). This is the number of letters in the two verses in the Book of Numbers (10:35–36) that are separated by inverted *nuns* in the scroll and sometimes regarded as a separate book (see p. 442). However, later authorities ruled that too extensive corrections rendered the scroll unsightly and therefore invalid. A scroll that cannot be repaired must be placed in an earthenware container and buried in the cemetery (Meg. 26b).

The words of the Torah are written on parchment, which must be prepared according to strict rules:

> The parchment used for a Torah scroll is made from specified sections of the hide of a kosher animal, though not necessarily one that has been slaughtered according to Jewish ritual. The hide consists of three layers, but only the flesh side of the inner layer and the outer side of the hairy layer may be used for Torah parchment (Shab. 79b). The method of cleaning and softening the hide has changed throughout the centuries. During talmudic times, salt and barley flour were sprinkled on the skins, which were then soaked in the juice of gallnuts (Meg. 19a). In the modern era, the skins are softened by soaking them in clear water for two days, after which the hair is removed by soaking the hides in limewater for nine days. Finally, the skins are rinsed and dried and the creases ironed out with presses, a process similar to the curing of leather. In keeping with the sanctity of processing material for a Torah scroll, the person handling the skins must make a verbal declaration of intent, acknowledging that all actions are being performed for the holiness of the *sefer Torah*.[6]

Individual leaves of parchment are sewn together with thread (*giddim*) made from the foot tendons of a kosher animal. To reinforce the *giddim*, thin strips of parchment are pasted on the top and bottom of the page.

The words of the Torah are inscribed with a quill pen made from the feathers of a kosher bird, usually goose or turkey. The *sofer* must painstakingly carve a point in the end of each feather, many of which are required for the writing of a Torah scroll. A metal instrument is forbidden, because iron and steel were associated with war and violence, rendering them unfit to touch a *sefer Torah*, which is an instrument of peace. The ink must be jet black and durable, but not indelible. During talmudic times, a viscous ink was made by heating a vessel with an olive oil flame, then scraping off the soot produced on both sides of the vessel and mixing it with oil, honey, and gallnuts (Shab. 23a). Today, the ink preparation is made by boiling a mixture of powdered gallnuts, gum arabic, and copper sulfate crystals. Some scribes also add vinegar and alcohol to make it glossy. Only a small amount of ink is prepared at a time, so that it is always fresh. At one time, gold lettering apparently was used for the writing of a Torah scroll, but this practice was later abandoned, presumably because of its allusion to the Golden Calf.

An ingenious tradition has developed for the scribe to test the color and viscosity of the ink and that the quill can make letters of the proper thickness. After writing on a piece of paper the name "Amalek," the scribe draws several lines through it. In addition to making certain that all is in readiness for his sacred task, the *sofer* symbolically fulfills the biblical commandment to "blot out the memory" of this treacherous tribe (Deut. 25:19), which cowardly attacked the rear of the Israelite column as they were escaping from Egypt.[7]

The Torah is written in a square script, and the precise shape, form, and method for writing each letter is prescribed. There are two basic styles of script—the Ashkenazic, which resembles the script described in the Talmud, and the Sephardic, which is identical to the printed letters of the Hebrew alphabet currently used in sacred texts. Care must be taken to ensure that each letter is surrounded by white space and does not run into the one adjacent to it. Although Hebrew is read from right to left, each individual letter in the *sefer Torah* is written from left to right.

The parchment itself is unadorned, but seven letters (*shin*, *ayin*, *tet*, *nun*, *zayin*, *gimel*, *tzadi*) are embellished with decorative crowns (*ketarim*) or flourishes (*tagin*, Aramaic for "daggers") whenever they occur. According to the Talmud, God affixed the *tagin* to the letters of the Torah before Moses ascended Mount Sinai to receive it (Men. 29b). However, some modern scholars believe that these calligraphic flourishes were introduced by early scribes to enhance the beauty of the Torah lettering. Although Maimonides considered the inclusion of *tagin* an "exceptionally beautiful fulfillment of the mitzvah," but maintain that a scroll without them was still valid if all the letters and words were written clearly,[8] Ashkenazic authorities disagree and would consider such a scroll *pasul*. Kabbalah places great stress on the mystical meaning of the *tagin*, viewing every additional stroke or sign as a symbol revealing extraordinary secrets of the universe and Creation.

According to the Talmud, it is proper and not a sign of disrespect for a scribe to turn a newly written sheet of parchment face down to prevent it from being smudged while the ink is drying (Er. 98a; Sof. 3:16). The Rabbis envisioned a scenario in which, while the ink was still wet, a fly perched on the *tagin* of the letter "*dalet*" in the word "*echad*" at the end of the *Shema*, causing the letter to become smudged so that it looked like a *resh* (Er. 13a). This would have the disastrous effect of the "*echad*" being read as "*acher*" (other), so that instead of the end of the verse reading "the Lord is One," it would be "the Lord is [an]other!"[9]

Detailed regulations were established regarding the layout of the Torah so that the words are beautiful to view. To ensure that the letters are written straight and that there is equal space between the lines, the parchment is first ruled horizontally with a stylus or awl and a ruler (a pencil is forbidden). Two vertical lines are drawn on either side of the column to make certain that all lines of text begin and end evenly.[10] The text is set out in columns of 42 lines, the numerical value of the Hebrew word *bam* (ב = 2, מ = 40) in the phrase "*ve-dibarta bam*" (and you shall speak of them) in the first paragraph of the *Shema*. The Talmud notes that this is also the number of stops made by the Israelites during their journey through the wilderness from Egypt to the Promised Land (Sof. 2:6). The selection of 42 lines per column also has the practical advantage of allowing the scroll to have a script size that can be read easily yet not be too large or too heavy to carry. Traditionally, each sheet of parchment contains three columns of script. The width of the column should not be so long that Torah readers are confused as their eyes move to the next line (Sof. 2:9). As a simple guide, the Rabbis recommended that the length of a Torah line be such that it can accom-modate the longest word in the Torah three times—לְמִשְׁפְּחוֹתֵיהֶם, *le-mishpechoteihem*, "to their families" (Gen. 8:19). In talmudic times, this word contained 10 Hebrew letters, but in modern texts is spelled without a *vav* and has only nine. There must be two inches between each column of script—plus an extra inch where sheets are to be sewn together—and margins of three inches on the top and four inches on the bottom (which is subject to more wear). A space of four inches is required between each of the Five Books of Moses.[11] The last word of the Torah, "*Yisrael*," must end in the middle of the line. This teaches that even though we have reached the conclusion of the text, we are still in the middle of studying the Torah, for its wisdom is endless and we have not yet plumbed its depths.[12]

It is traditional for each column of a Torah scroll to begin with the letter *vav*. To accomplish this, the scribe must write some letters wider than normal, usually a *tav, resh, hei, dalet, lamed,* or final *mem* at the end of a word. The obvious exception to this rule is the first column of the Torah, which begins with a *bet* (*B'reishit*). It has become customary for scribes to start four other columns with words that do not begin with a *vav*: "*Yehudah*" (Gen. 49:8), the tribe from which David and the Messiah would emerge; "*ha-ba'im*" (Exod. 14:28); "*sh'mar*" (Exod. 34:11); and "*mah*" (Num. 24:5), the first word of *Mah Tovu*, which begins the morning service (see p. 401). The first letters in these five columns (ביהשמ) make up the phrase (בְּיָהּ שְׁמוֹ) (*Be Ya H She Mo*), which means "His name is *Yah*."[13]

The format of the Torah was designed by the Masoretes (see p. 493), who deemed certain parts of the text to be so significant that they must have a unique appearance in the scroll. *Shirat ha-Yam* (Song at the Sea; Exod. 15:1–19; see p. 409), the victory hymn praising God for the miraculous parting of the Sea of Reeds, is written in three sections with intervening white space that produces the visual effect of a brick wall. This symbolizes the two walls of water in between which the Israelites passed to safety on a dry path. A similar style is used for two other hymns of deliverance—the Song of Deborah (Judg. 6:1–31), which is part of the haftarah when the Song at the Sea is read, and the Song of Deliverance from the haftarah portion for the seventh day of Passover (2 Sam. 22:1–51). Other sections of the Bible that are written to have a special visual effect include both versions of the Ten Commandments (Exod. 20:1–14; Deut. 5:6-18); the Song of Moses (*Ha-azinu*; Deut. 32:1–43); the poem beginning "a time for being born" (Eccles. 3:2–8)[14]; and the listing of the 10 sons of Haman who were hanged (Esther 9:7–9).[15]

"Therefore, write down this poem" (Deut. 31:19)[16] was originally a divine command to Moses and Joshua to write down the final farewell hymn of joy that Moses spoke to the Children of Israel just before his death (Deut. 32:1–43). The Rabbis derived from this verse that every Jew is commanded to write a Torah scroll. Based on the talmudic statement, "Even if he corrected but one letter [in a *sefer Torah*] he is regarded as if he had written it [the entire Torah]" (Men. 30a), in recent centuries the custom has developed for the scribe who completes the writing of a Torah scroll to merely trace the outline of the letters of the first verses in Genesis and the last verses in Deuteronomy. At a festive celebration, various members of the congregation, often selected by auction, fill in each letter and thus symbolically participate in the writing of a Torah scroll.

Torah Ornaments

The beginning and end of the parchment scroll are attached to two carved wooden rollers, called *atzei hayim* (trees of life). This phrase (in the singular) is a symbol of the Torah itself, as in the verse, "It is a tree of life (*etz hayim*) to those who hold fast to it" (Prov. 3:18).[17] Like a bountiful tree, the Torah constantly replenishes its inspirational fruit. The *atzei hayim* allow the Torah to be opened, closed, and rolled to any part of the scroll without the hands needing to touch the parchment. They were modeled on the twin pillars of the Temple (termed Jachin and Boaz; 1 Kings 7:21), whose capitals were adorned with designs of pomegranates and lilies.

Atop the *atzei hayim* is either a crown (*keter*) or a pair of silver finials called *rimonim* (lit., "pomegranates"). The *rimonim* are often adorned with bells, which tinkle during the procession and are reminiscent of the robe of the *Kohen Gadol*, which was hemmed with golden bells and blue, purple, and scarlet balls shaped like pomegranates. An alternative is a silver crown, which fits completely over the two rollers and also is frequently encircled with silver bells. Originally, the crown may have been used only on special occasions, such as when the scroll was officially consecrated and on Simchat Torah.[18] The use of Torah ornaments with bells enables those seated in the back of the congregation to realize that a Torah is in procession so that they can stand up to fulfill the requirement of rising with reverential respect whenever the Torah is removed from the ark. Some modern scholars state that this custom originated in Middle Eastern Jewish communities, based on the belief that the noise of bells warded off evil spirits.[19]

In the East and in the Sephardic tradition, the Torah is enclosed in a cylindrical or octagonal case (*tik*), which is divided into two pieces and hinged in the back. The *tik* originated in 10th-century Iraq and is usually elaborately decorated and inscribed. It opens like a book to reveal the scroll, which is not removed and is read in an upright position.

In the Ashkenazic tradition, the Torah scroll is covered by a cloth mantle. This sheath of silk or velvet is usually embroidered with gold or silver threads and may be richly decorated with images of lions, crowns, pomegranates, the columns of Jachin and Boaz, and various implements of the Temple service. The mantle is open at the bottom and closed at the top, except for two circular openings through which protrude the two staves on which the scroll is rolled. On the High Holy Days, it is traditional to use a white mantle (and ark curtain). According to the Jerusalem Talmud: "Ordinarily, when a man has to face judgment, he wears black garments [to be humble in the presence of a stern judge], but [on Rosh Hashanah and Yom Kippur] we wear white garments in joyous confidence that God will perform a miracle for us" (RH 7b). Another often-cited reason is the verse, "Be your sins like crimson, they can turn white as snow (Isa. 1:18).[20]

Overlying the mantle, there is often a silver breastplate or shield, which probably originated as a plaque with changeable inserts that was hung from the staves on a heavy chain to indicate which scroll was to be taken out to be read for a particular service. Eventually, the changeable plates were left off and the breastplate became solely ornamental.[21] The breastplate of the Torah is derived from one of the most important items of ritual apparel worn by the *Kohen Gadol*, on which there were 12 precious stones arranged in four equal rows, with each engraved with the name of one of the tribes of Israel (Exod. 28:15–21). Into the breastplate were fixed the *Urim* and *Tummim*, which were used to discover what course God desired the Israelites to pursue on matters of vital significance to the entire community. As such, the breastplate is an ideal ornament for the Torah, which represents the revealed will of God.[22]

Before being read, the scroll is unwrapped and laid down on a reading stand. After the Torah reading, the scroll is rolled together on its *atzei hayim* and kept tight. Since antiquity, this has been accomplished by kerchiefs (*mitpachot*) in the East and by a long, wide ribbon in Europe. This latter Torah binder, called a *wimpel* (pennant) in German and a *gartl* (belt) in Yiddish, dates back to talmudic times. In some congregations, especially in southern Germany, it was customary to cut the linen cloth on which a boy was circumcised and sew it into an elaborately embroidered or painted *wimpel*, which was presented to the congregation on the child's first visit to the synagogue and was used to secure the Torah from which the boy read when he became bar mitzvah and before he married, symbolizing his "binding" himself to the Torah and to the Jewish community.[23]

One should not touch the parchment of the scroll with bare hands. Therefore, initially, the Torah reader merely pointed with the index finger to the words being read. However, this often made it difficult for the person who was called up to the Torah to see the script and follow the reading. This problem was solved with the development of the *yad* (hand), a wand shaped like a human hand with one finger pointing forward. The *yad* is made of wood or metal, and sometimes even of silver or gold.[24]

After the destruction of the Temple, the Torah replaced the sacrificial cult as the focus of the spirituality of the Jewish people and the mechanism to atone for Israel's sins. The Torah scroll itself inherited the vestments of the *Kohen Gadol* (Exod. 28:4–43):

> The mantle (*me-il*) replaced the robe of the ephod; the binder (*wimpel*), the girdle of the robe; the crown (*keter*) or *rimonim* (silver handle-covers), the mitre and gold plate; the shield (*tas*), the breastplate (*hoshen mishpat*). Many of the ornaments and customs surrounding the Torah derive from the symbolism of royalty and power: the crown and shield, the *yad* (pointer) resembling a scepter, the Torah procession, and the gesture of kissing the hem of the Torah's robe. Other rituals and customs emphasize the holiness of the scroll: not touching the parchment with one's bare hand, fasting if the scroll is dropped, draping the scroll in white vestments on the High Holy Days, burying a burned or torn scroll.[25]

Ark (אָרוֹן/אֲרוֹן קֹדֶשׁ)

The Holy Ark (*Aron Kodesh*) is the repository in the synagogue in which the Torah scrolls are kept. It hearkens back to the biblical Ark of the Covenant, which housed both the broken first tablets (BB 14b) and the intact second tablets of the Ten Commandments (Deut.10:1–5) as well as an omer of manna (Exod. 16:32) and the rod of Aaron (Num. 17:25). The Hebrew term "*aron*" was also applied to the coffin or sarcophagus containing the mummified body of Joseph (Gen. 50:26) and to the Temple charity box (2 Kings 12:10–11). The Ark of the Covenant was carried by the Children of Israel on their trek through the wilderness as a visible reminder of the covenant between God and the people, providing assurance that the Divine Presence was always with them on their journey. Originally, the ark was an acacia wood cabinet, "overlaid with pure gold, inside and out" (Exod. 37:1–5), which was housed in the Tabernacle (*mishkan*), the portable tent that served as the sacred hub of the community. Above the ark was the mercy seat (*kapporet*), a slab of gold representing the throne of God, which was covered with the wings of two golden cherubim that flanked it on both sides (Exod. 37:6–9).[1]

In the First Temple, the ark was kept in the Holy of Holies. A perfect cube of 20 cubits (30 feet), the Holy of Holies was entered only once a year—by the *Kohen Gadol* on Yom Kippur. A veil separated the Holy of Holies from the outer sanctuary, known as the *heichal* (palace), the term used today by Sephardim to refer to the ark in the synagogue. The *aggadah* indicates that the site of the ark marked the exact center of the world, the "footstool of God." Before the destruction of the First Temple in 586 B.C.E., the ark disappeared. Although according to legend it was hidden by King Josiah (Shek. 6:1–2), no trace of the ark has ever been found.[2]

With the development of synagogues, the ark became symbolized by a cabinet housing the Torah scrolls. At first, this ark was a movable chest containing several shelves on which the scrolls were kept in a lying position. Situated in a side room, the chest was separated from the congregation by a curtain. Later, the chest was moved to the center of the eastern wall, becoming a permanent part of the synagogue structure.[3]

Over the centuries, the ark has been the focus of design and decoration, heavily influenced by the artistic trends of the particular host culture. The early medieval ark was relatively modest, usually just a tall niche or cabinet in which the scrolls stood upright. However, with the rise of baroque art in the 16th and 17th centuries, European arks became more elaborate and even gaudy. Some were framed by marble columns, recalling the two pillars in the Temple court (Jachin and Boaz). In Dutch synagogues of the 17th century, a model of the twin tablets of the Ten Commandments was set on top of the ark, a style that soon became widely accepted. Sometimes the tablets were embellished with a lion on each side and a crown on top. Moorish arks, with domes and arches and decorated with geometric patterns, were popular in 19th-century America. Today, arks are made in a wide variety of designs and are still the most extravagant part of the synagogue.[4]

Despite the wide variation in design, most arks have several features in common. From ancient times, synagogues oriented the ark toward Jerusalem; in Jerusalem, the ark was oriented toward the Temple Mount. In front of the ark is the *ner tamid* (eternal light; see p. 336), a lamp that is kept continually burning and represents the perpetual presence of God.[5] A curtain (*parochet*), usually elaborately decorated, is hung in front of the doors of the ark (inside the doors in the Sephardic tradition). This is in imitation of the curtain of "blue, purple, and crimson yarns, and fine twisted linen" (Exod. 26:31–33) that separated the Holy of Holies, in which the ark was housed, from the rest of the Tabernacle (Exod. 40:21) and later the two Temples. On the High Holy Days, virtually all synagogues change the *parochet* (and Torah mantles and lectern covers) to white, a symbol of purity and forgiveness of sins. On Tisha b'Av (see p. 304), the *parochet* is removed from the ark to heighten the somber atmosphere of the day. Many contemporary synagogues have eliminated ark coverings, replacing them with ark doors that are ornately ornamented.[6] Among the most popular designs are the Ten Commandments, crowns, rampant lions of Judah (symbolizing the sovereignty of God), and representations of the Tree of Life.[7]

In addition to *An'im Zemirot* (see p. 472) and taking out and returning the Torah, the ark is opened for specific prayers such as *Avinu Malkeinu* (see p. 196) on fast days and during the Ten Days of Repentance, the *Ne'ilah* service on Yom Kippur (see p. 220), and for many of the *piyyutim* recited at the High Holy Day services. The custom is to stand while the ark is open, but this is not obligatory. Except for the Torah scrolls, the ark is considered the holiest part of the synagogue. Consequently, one may not use it for any secular purpose and it is even customary not to turn one's back toward it.

Jews have long considered the ark as having a special aura that could enhance one's prayers in times of trouble. For example, women would cling to the ark curtain while praying for children or for the cure of a sick relative. Today, both men and women may be seen opening the ark to offer private prayers through this "direct channel to heaven."[8]

Bimah (בִּימָה)

The *bimah* (elevated place) is the raised platform that contains the table on which the Torah scroll is placed when it is read. It is traditionally located in the center of the synagogue, emphasizing the central role of the Torah in synagogue worship. In many communities, the shofar (see p. 186) is sounded on the *bimah* on Rosh Hashanah, reminiscent of the blowing of trumpets that accompanied the sacrificial offerings on the altar.[1] In Sephardic synagogues, the prayer leader conducts most of the service from the *bimah*, which is known as *teivah* (box), the biblical term for both Noah's ark (Gen. 6:14) and Moses' basket (Exod. 2:5), and the talmudic word denoting the Ark of the Covenant.[2] In Ashkenazic synagogues, the *hazzan* leads the service from a separate reading stand that is situated immediately in front of the *bimah* and facing the ark.

The use of the *bimah* for reading the Torah in public was known as early as Nehemiah (8:4), and raised platforms were also documented in Second Temple times (Sot. 7:8) and in the synagogue of Alexandria in Egypt (Suk. 51b). In traditional Ashkenazic synagogues, there are often some intervening seats between the *bimah* and the ark (based on an opinion of Maimonides[3]), but this is not the practice in Sephardic and Middle Eastern synagogues.[4] Contrary to its name, at times the *bimah* has been constructed lower than the main floor of the sanctuary. One explanation for this design is to symbolize the humility of the worshiper, as in the verse, "Out of the depths I call You, O Lord" (Ps. 130:1).[5] Because medieval church regulations often restricted the height of synagogues, lowering the *bimah* added to the illusion of height. The traditional combination of the *bimah* in the center and the ark situated on the eastern wall, oriented toward Jerusalem, has exerted a profound effect on synagogue design throughout the ages.[6]

The Reform movement in the 19th century introduced the radical innovation of setting the *bimah* in front of the ark, a layout modeled on the church pulpit. Although Yosef Karo had ruled three centuries earlier that it was not essential to place the *bimah* in the center of the synagogue, the Reform decision was met with intense hostility. Some major traditional rabbis even issued proclamations prohibiting their followers from worshiping in a synagogue that did not have a central *bimah*. Nevertheless, locating the *bimah* in front of the ark is now the dominant architectural style in North America among liberal and even in many Orthodox congregations.

Moving the *bimah* to the front of the sanctuary has greatly affected Jewish prayer. In this configuration, the *bimah* has come to resemble a theater stage (indeed, "*Habimah*" is the name of the national theater of Israel). Rather than being full participants in the service, congregants tend to become spectators watching a drama enfold in front of them (strikingly similar to Temple times). Placing the *bimah* in front of the sanctuary also requires that the prayer leader, *hazzan*, or rabbi stand with his (or her) back to the ark. This is contrary to the traditional custom of respectfully facing the ark and praying eastward toward Jerusalem. To solve this dilemma, some contemporary synagogues have either eliminated the *bimah* or returned to earlier architectural models by focusing prayer toward the center of the worship space.[7]

Ner Tamid (נֵר תָּמִיד)

The *ner tamid* (perpetual or eternal lamp) in the synagogue is a continuously burning light, which usually hangs in front of the ark. The original eternal light is thought to have been the central or westernmost arm of the menorah in the Temple, which was constantly supplied with oil so that it burned at all times (Exod. 27:20; Lev. 24:2). Acting as a pilot light, it was used to kindle the other six branches that were extinguished daily to be cleaned.[8] According to the Rabbis, the *ner tamid* symbolizes the Divine Presence, which dwells among the congregation of Israel (Shab. 22b). It may also refer to the Torah, which rests in the ark below the *ner tamid*, and is associated with light: "The commandment is a lamp, the teaching [Torah] is a light" (Prov. 6:23).

After the Temple was destroyed, an oil lamp was put by the western wall of the synagogue as a symbolic reminder of the menorah (see p. 578). Eventually, however, the *ner tamid* was moved above the ark, despite the objection of some authorities that this was a gentile custom (in churches, there is a perpetual light above the altar). Those who contribute to its maintenance are specifically mentioned in the *Mi She*

Berakh prayer recited after the Torah reading on Saturday morning (see p. 462). In modern times, an electric light is used in place of an oil lamp. The *ner tamid* is usually made of glass and placed in a circular metal container.

Mechitzah (מְחִיצָה)

Mechitzah (partition) is the term for the physical separation in synagogues between the space reserved for men and the space, generally in the rear or upstairs, for women. Contrary to popular belief, the separation of the sexes in the synagogue is not an ancient tradition. There was a special women's court (*ezrat nashim*) in the Jerusalem Temple, but this generally was open to both men and women. The sole exception was the water-drawing ceremony on Sukkot (see p. 236), when the sexes were separated lest the ecstasy of the occasion lead to promiscuity (Suk. 51b–52a). The early synagogues had no formal rules regarding the place of women at the service. This was in contrast to the churches, in which women were strictly segregated at worship, probably reflecting the doctrine of original sin that is a fundamental tenet in Christian theology. The few references in the Mishnah imply that women participated in the service and even in the public reading of the Torah (see p. 452), though there already was a bias against this activity "out of respect for the congregation" (Meg. 23a)—because it might prove embarrassing or sexually distracting to the men.[1]

Midrash suggests that a reason for the separation of the sexes is that it reflects how the Israelites stood while at Mount Sinai receiving the Ten Commandments (PdRE 41). In excavations of ancient synagogues, there is clear evidence of a separate section, usually with a separate entrance, for those women who attended the public prayer services.[2] In talmudic times, attempts were made to formally segregate the sexes, especially during crowded festivals, and one sage is reported to have set up rows of pottery to separate the men and women, while another erected a "partition of canes" (Kid. 81a). However, the actual setting aside of a section of the synagogue for women developed at a later period. Some scholars explain that since men are obligated to worship and women are not, those with the obligation sit together and those without the obligation sit together—separately. Others suggest that men were concerned that seeing attractive women and hearing their voices during worship might distract them from the sacred task of prayer.[3] By the 13th century, separate sections for women in synagogues were widespread, and this practice soon became the universally accepted rule.[4]

Medieval European synagogues had a section for women either in the rear of the synagogue or in a separate balcony. The men's and women's sections were usually separated by a curtain or grill. In Eastern lands, women were relegated to a room adjacent to the synagogue that had connecting windows to enable them to hear the prayers.[5]

In the early part of the 19th century, the Reform movement abolished the *mechitzah*, arguing that the Bible does not command the separation of men and women during public worship. The outraged traditional authorities ruled that one could pray only in a synagogue with a *mechitzah*. Indeed, the *mechitzah* has come to represent so essential an aspect of the Orthodox synagogue that court orders have been issued in the United States prohibiting synagogue boards from instituting mixed seating if there is opposition. In Conservative and Reform synagogues, there is no *mechitzah* and men and women sit together.

Rabbi (רַב)

The title "rabbi" (lit., "my master" or "my teacher") was first applied to the talmudic sages who interpreted the Bible and developed the Oral Law. The first scholar referred to as "rabbi" was the *tanna* Rabban Gamaliel, the grandson of Hillel. The title was later applied to Shimon ben Gamaliel and Yochanan ben Zakkai, two other presidents of the Sanhedrin, the Jewish high court. Eventually, all Torah scholars who had been properly ordained as graduates of the talmudic academies in the Land of Israel were identified as "rabbi." This may have been designed to counter the growing expansion of Christian missionary activity by the early disciples, to prevent them from confusing the gullible masses who otherwise may not have been able to distinguish an authentic Torah sage from one preaching adherence to the new faith. Because they were not ordained in the Land of Israel, the Babylonian sages (the *amoraim*) were not called rabbi; instead, they were identified with the related title "*rav.*"

The major role of the early medieval rabbi was not to provide pastoral care, but rather to exercise scholarly wisdom in judging matters related to Jewish law. Initially, the Babylonian academies and their leaders, the *Ge'onim*, appointed the various scholars who would carry out this function. However, as the Babylonian academies declined and Jewish communities developed in far-flung regions, the significance of the rabbi and the autonomy of the local community in selecting him increased. The local community itself—and not the Babylonian academies—became the center of Jewish life in the Diaspora. Thus the authority and responsibilities of the local rabbi were augmented. The rabbi of a community became known as the *mara de-atra*, literally, "the master of the place."

In talmudic and early medieval times, the rabbinate was not a profession, partly because it was deemed inappropriate for someone to receive money for teaching Torah. Eventually, however, it became necessary for a community to support its rabbi. The development of a professional rabbinate was bolstered by Christian persecutions in Spain in the late 14th century, which forced distinguished rabbis—many of whom had earned their livings as physicians—to flee to countries where they had no opportunity to pursue their professions. To avoid the problem of paying a rabbi for teaching Torah, a legal fiction was instituted whereby a rabbi was paid for the time he was forced to take away from Torah study in order to fulfill his rabbinic duties. This is still the legal justification for paying rabbinic salaries. In addition, medieval communities adopted various other ways to compensate their rabbis indirectly. Rabbis were given tax privileges, and those who were merchants were usually given priority in the sale of their wares so that they would have more time for their studies. Nevertheless, despite their salaries and professional fees for performing marriages and judging court cases, most medieval rabbis provided their families with only the bare necessities of life.

Modern Period

The role of the rabbi continued to evolve over time. In the late medieval period, particularly in Poland and Lithuania, a rabbi's authority was often tied to his role as a *rosh yeshivah* (head of a talmudic academy) in addition to, or as an alternative to, his role as a community leader.

In the modern era, changes in the political and social situation of the

Jews have also affected the role of the rabbi. Judicial responsibilities decreased as civil courts came under government control. In addition, Jews influenced by Enlightenment culture demanded that their rabbis have broader knowledge in both Jewish subjects and in secular disciplines. However, most traditional *yeshivot* adamantly opposed such changes and continued to offer a curriculum virtually limited to Talmud and codes. This led to the development of rabbinical seminaries that provided a comprehensive program of Jewish studies, usually coupled with a university education. Almost every modern rabbi of all denominations, except the ultra-Orthodox, has been trained in one of these institutions.

Today, rabbis have a multitude of responsibilities. They preach—almost always in the vernacular—teach, and often lead the worship service. Rabbis also spend much of their time counseling, officiating at life-cycle events, and even engaging in fund-raising.

Women Rabbis

The Reform movement started ordaining women as rabbis during the early 1970s. Within a decade of Rabbi Sally Priesand's 1972 ordination by the Hebrew Union College, women made up more than one third of the students at the Reform seminary. The Reconstructionist Rabbinical College in Philadelphia likewise decided early on to admit women, ordaining its first female rabbi in 1974. The 1983 decision of the Conservative movement's Jewish Theological Seminary to ordain women provoked fierce attacks, not only from the Orthodox but from many traditional figures in the Conservative movement as well, particularly among the seminary's Talmud faculty. Two years later, Amy Eilberg was ordained the first Conservative woman rabbi. Currently, women constitute about half the graduates of non-Orthodox rabbinical seminaries in the United States.

***Semikhah* (סְמִיכָה)**

Semikhah is the traditional ordination required before a rabbi can decide practical questions of Jewish law. Literally meaning "laying (of hands)," the practice derives from the divine command to Moses to ordain Joshua by placing his hands on his successor, thus "investing him with some of his authority" (Num. 27:18–20; Deut. 34:9). The Torah implies that Moses ordained the 70 elders as well (Num. 11:16–17, 24–25), though the actual laying of hands is not mentioned. According to tradition, the elders ordained their successors, who ordained their successors, and so on.

Talmudic Period

Ordination was required to be a judge in ancient Israel, whether a member of the Sanhedrin, one of the lower courts, or any decider of Jewish law. According to the Talmud, "three rows of scholars sat in front of them [the Sanhedrin], each knowing his own place [according to rank]. Whenever it was necessary to ordain [a new member], one from the first row was chosen [and ordained]" (Sanh. 37a). There were various levels of ordination, which allowed the recipient to perform different functions, ranging from the lowest level of deciding only religious questions to the highest degree, which permitted one to judge criminal cases (Sanh. 5a). The complete formula of ordination was "*Yoreh Yoreh. Yaddin Yaddin. Yattir Yattir*" (May he decide? He may decide. May he judge? He may judge. May he permit? He may permit).

During Hadrian's persecution of the Jews, in the second century C.E., the Romans prohibited *semikhah* in the hopes of destroying Jewish authority. (A Roman soldier stabbed Judah ben Bava, one of the famous Ten Martyrs, while the rabbi was ordaining five of his students; Sanh. 14a.) Soon after, ordination through the laying of hands was abandoned, coinciding with a change whereby ordination became the domain of the patriarch (religious leader) instead of the individual teacher. Because the laying of hands was no longer an integral part of the ordination ceremony, the term *semikhah* fell out of favor, and ordination became known as *minui* (appointment). Instead of the laying of hands, ordination was bestowed merely by referring to the ordained as "rabbi." However, the laying of hands was retained by the Christians as a way of symbolically passing on authority.

To ensure that the Land of Israel remained the center of Jewish life, the Rabbis permitted ordination only there, based on the verse, "For out of Zion shall go forth the Torah, the word of the Lord from Jerusalem" (Isa. 2:3). Thus the Babylonian *amoraim* were referred to as "*rav*." Because the power of the Babylonian sages was not solidified by ordination, they were allowed to impose fines only "on the authority of, and as agents for, the Palestinian judges" (BK 84b; Git. 88b).[1] With the death of the last patriarch in the Land of Israel in the fifth century, the original *semikhah* was discontinued.

Medieval Period

In Babylonia during the gaonic period, the exilarch (political leader) awarded licenses to those qualified to judge legal disputes, while the *Ge'onim* appointed the judges in religious matters. Eventually, the word "*semikhah*" was reintroduced, though it did not have the same authority as the ancient institution. Instead, it was a degree—much like those given at Christian universities—awarded to a student who had mastered sufficient learning and possessed the qualifications of character and piety to such an extent that he had the right to serve as a judge and teacher.

This new form of *semikhah* was associated with a revival of the title "rabbi" but did not involve the traditional laying of hands. Those receiving documents of certification were empowered to judge in matters of ritual, and more advanced students were also permitted to issue decisions in all areas of Jewish law. Sephardim retained the title "rabbi" for extremely learned men, calling ordinary rabbinic scholars "*hakham.*"

In the 16th century, Jacob Berab of Safed tried to reinstitute the ancient *semikhah*, by relying on Maimonides' opinion that this could be accomplished if all the rabbis of the Land of Israel agreed. Berab ordained four rabbis, including Yosef Karo, the author of the Shulchan Arukh. However, the rabbis of Jerusalem vehemently objected, and the movement to reinstate traditional *semikhah* ended when its leader died.

Modern Period

After the Emancipation, there was a striking change in the position, requirements, and training of rabbis under the influence of the emerging Reform movement and the scientific study of Judaism. To meet community needs, rabbinical seminaries developed that placed less emphasis on Talmud and related subjects and increasingly stressed a well-rounded education, including Bible, homiletics, theology, and history. In the 20th century, pastoral skills and synagogue administration also became important facets of the training program. Today, the requirements of rabbinical seminaries differ widely. Although rabbinic ordination is still known as *semikhah*, the title "rabbi" has become merely the conventional term for the leaders of all Jewish denominations

Sermon (דְרָשָׁה)

Soon after the return from Babylonian exile, Ezra assembled the whole people and read the Torah "so they understood the reading" (Neh. 8:8), presumably through explanations and homilies.[2] By the end of the Second Temple period, a *derash* (religious discourse) was regularly delivered in synagogues after the Torah reading on Sabbaths and festivals. Coming from a Hebrew root meaning "to search," the *derash* was offered by a *darshan* (preacher) who searched the Torah portion for novel insights and fresh approaches to the problems of the day. The *derash* was delivered in the vernacular, and its general construction was governed by strict rules. It typically opened with a verse from the Writings section of the Bible, which related to the Torah and haftarah readings for the day. This was followed by the body of the homily, which dealt with either halakhic (legal) matters or aggadic (ethical, moral, or theological) issues, in which the preacher brought in additional biblical quotations, parables, allegories, or fables. The conclusion of the *derash* summarized the major ideas drawn from the text, and it ended with the familiar words of the *Kaddish*: "May His great name be praised for ever and ever." By skillfully linking biblical verses of the Written Torah with the rabbinic teachings constituting the Oral Torah, the formula of the *derash* demonstrated the unity and common divine authority of the Law.

The Pharisees and their rabbinic descendants were masters of the art of preaching, though they had no formal training in composing and delivering sermons. As the scholars and teachers of the day, many were capable of presenting both learned (halakhic) lectures in the academies as well as crowd-pleasing (aggadic) sermons in the synagogues. Their superb preaching won them the loyalty and respect of the people, who consequently turned to the rabbis for effective leadership in periods of national emergency. The sermons were a valuable educational tool, providing the people with an awareness of the basic beliefs of Judaism and guiding them in the observance of both the ethical and ritual laws of their faith. They gave rise to the vast literature of Midrash, which is devoted almost exclusively to the homilies preached by the rabbis of the talmudic and post-talmudic periods and contains many captivating parables and anecdotes illustrating their underlying moral lessons. As late as the early 10th century, the bishop of Lyons complained bitterly, "many Christians openly declare that the sermons of the Jewish preachers please them better than those of the Christian clergy."

Medieval Period

During the persecutions of the sixth and seventh centuries designed to suppress Jewish practice, the Church prohibited the expounding of Scripture during synagogue services. To combat these restrictions, the prayer leader began to take over the function of the preacher, reciting religious poems (*piyyutim*) that indirectly contained some of the rabbinic teachings that had been generally presented in the homily. Even after the Arab conquest of the Land of Israel, when the Jews again were permitted to worship freely, many of these *piyyutim* persisted as part of the service. In the post-gaonic period, the writing of *piyyutim* flourished, and the synagogue services became so filled with them that there was little time available for delivery of the sermon. During the same period, the increasing popularity of the *hazzanim* and their ever-longer cantorial renditions also prolonged the service. Due to time constraints, the sermon became optional and was slowly squeezed out of the service.

Another major factor in the temporary demise of the sermon was the decreasing competence of the medieval rabbis as preachers. Indeed, if the medieval rabbis had maintained the charisma and preaching mastery of the talmudic rabbis, it is doubtful whether the homilies would have yielded to the pressure of the *piyyutim* and the musical embellishments of the *hazzanim*. As the rabbis were forced to devote more of their time and energy to mastering the highly technical law so as to serve as judges in both religious and civil disputes, they were less able to gain proficiency in the art of preaching. Furthermore, they were so focused on their scholarly activities that they had difficulty dealing with issues that both were relevant to the daily life of the people and would hold their interest. For these rabbis, cultivating the art of preaching meant neglecting time devoted to Torah study. Consequently, when speaking to the congregation, the medieval rabbi preferred to demonstrate his scholarly grasp of Jewish law to impress his peers, rather than delivering a sermon that would both enlighten and captivate the people at large.

Another significant problem for the medieval rabbi was the need to earn a living. The office of rabbi was purely honorary; it was considered improper and even sinful for a rabbi to accept payment for the performance of his religious duties, since his reward would come from God in the world to come. The preoccupation with earning a livelihood tended to seriously restrict his preaching and other rabbinic activities. Consequently, rabbis generally delivered only two annual addresses to the congregation—one on the Sabbath before Passover (Shabbat ha-Gadol), which dealt with the technical legalities of the Passover observance, and another on the Sabbath before Yom Kippur (Shabbat Shuvah), which focused on issues of repentance and greater piety. As persecutions continued to restrict the economic activities of the Jews, it became impossible for medieval rabbis to serve their communities and at the same time support their families. By the 14th century, this led to the transition of the rabbinate from honorary status to salaried profession.

This dismal scenario generally applied only to Ashkenazic communities. Among the Sephardim, preaching continued to be an important rabbinic duty. The Sephardic services were not overfilled with *piyyutim*, and their prayer leaders did not consume excessive time in musical flourishes during the services. Thus the homily continued to thrive in medieval Sephardic synagogues.

Maggid

"The semi-annual lectures delivered by the [Ashkenazic] rabbis did not quench the popular thirst for moral instruction. On holy days, the people craved soul-stirring sermons, and on fast days they yearned for words of comfort." In Northern, Central, and Eastern Europe, this spiritual void was eventually filled by the *maggid*. Neither an ordained rabbi nor a trained preacher, the *maggid* had a natural flair for the poetic and dramatic, an innate talent for preaching coupled with a fervent desire to teach the will of God and to raise the moral tone of life.

The *maggid* was typically an itinerant preacher, who wandered from town to town attempting to attract an audience through a combination of the parables, folk tales, and quotations from biblical and rabbinic sources that he wove into his text and the oratorical flourishes of his delivery. The *maggid* generally was forced to subsist on the meager collections from those who attended his sermon on a weekday evening or on a Saturday afternoon (of course, paid after the Sabbath ended).

The most famous of these preachers was Jacob Kranz, popularly known as the Dubno Maggid, who served for 18 years as the official *maggid* of this Polish city. He was an extraordinary orator, and his parables have become legendary; his eloquence was said to move people to tears or to raise their spirits to great religious exaltation.

Modern Period

In 19th-century Germany, the traditional *derash* was replaced by a new type of sermon, which became a regular feature of the service and sought to express Jewish values in a contemporary idiom. The early Reform preachers consciously modeled their sermons on those of the Protestant clergy, focusing on a single central theme that they developed in an orderly fashion, without the academic digressions characteristic of earlier periods. Today, especially in the United States, the sermon has returned to its original place in the synagogue service and is generally regarded as an integral part of Jewish worship. The rabbi has resumed the initial role of teacher, responsible for conveying moral, ethical, and religious values to the congregation. In some liberal synagogues, however, the sermon has become a discussion session in which the rabbi briefly introduces a topic and members of the congregation volunteer their views. In most American synagogues, a Sabbath or festival service without a sermon is as inconceivable as one without a Torah reading.

Hazzan (חַזָּן)

In the days of the First Temple, when the sacrificial ritual was the focus of worship, both choral singing and instrumental music were constant elements of the service. When the Jews returned from Babylonian exile and resumed the Temple service, the Levites and *Kohanim* participated in the thanksgiving prayers with choirs and instrumental music. By the first century C.E., some of the Temple melodies were transferred to the synagogue by the *Kohanim* and Levites, who participated in both services. After the destruction of the Second Temple, music was banned as a sign of mourning. However, this apparently applied only to instruments and not to vocal music.[1]

In the Talmud, the term "*hazzan*" denotes a communal official who performed certain duties in the synagogue. He served as a professional superintendent of the house of prayer, bringing out the Torah scrolls for readings (Sot. 7:7–8) and blowing three blasts of a trumpet to announce the time to stop work at the approach of the Sabbath and festivals (Shab. 35b). The *hazzan* also recited the blessings at marriages (Ket. 5b), presided at funerals, blessed and consoled those in mourning, and recited *Kaddish* for their dead (Sof. 19:12).[2] Like the contemporary *shammash*, the *hazzan* was a minor functionary who was in charge of the synagogue building and its furnishings. At times, he led the services and read the Torah, like other knowledgeable members of the congregation, but these functions were incidental to his other duties and there was no permanent cantor in the modern sense.

As the liturgy became more complex and the general knowledge of Hebrew decreased during the gaonic period, the role of the *hazzan* transformed into that of permanent *shaliach tzibbur* (emissary of the congregation). He also was selected to recite and provide suitable melodies for the *piyyutim* (religious poems) that were becoming increasingly popular. Although frequently called the "*shaliach tzibbur*," the *hazzan* was to lead the congregation in prayer rather than praying on their behalf. The worshipers generally read the prayers silently, with the *hazzan* chanting the concluding verse(s) aloud. The major exception was the *Amidah*, which the *hazzan* repeated in full for the benefit of those who could not read the prayers but were able to respond with the traditional "amen."[3]

During the Middle Ages, the *hazzanim* were given better salaries, longer tenure of office, and more communal tax exemptions. In return, they were required to meet fixed qualifications. "He was required to have a pleasant voice and appearance, to be married, to have a beard, to be fully familiar with the liturgy, to be of blameless character, and to be acceptable in all other respects to the members of the community" (S.A. OH 53:4 *ff.*). These strict requirements were modified occasionally but were rigorously enforced on public fast days.[4] For such occasions, the Talmud had mandated centuries before that the person deemed most suitable to serve as *shaliach tzibbur* be "one having a large family, but who has no means of support, who draws his subsistence from [the produce of] the field, and whose house is empty, whose youth was unblemished, who is meek and acceptable to the people; who is skilled in chanting, has a pleasant voice, and possesses a thorough knowledge of the Torah, the Prophets, and the Writings, of Midrash, *halakhot* and *aggadot*, and of all the benedictions" (Taan. 16a). As the representative of the people, it was necessary that the *hazzan* have a close rapport with the worshipers. Therefore, some communities required a unanimous vote for the election of the *hazzan*, especially for the High Holy Day services.[5]

Despite their popularity, the *hazzanim* usually had neither formal musical education nor the time to fully develop their musical talent. An aspiring *hazzan* was born with a fine voice and generally learned the traditional melodies by ear from the local *hazzan*. In most cases, the *hazzan* could not earn a living from his musical activities and was required to supplement his salary by working as a ritual slaughterer, teacher, or scribe.[6]

Criticism of *hazzanim* escalated with their increasing popularity. Traditionally, a *shaliach tzibbur* was supposed to be a learned individual and a model of piety. However, with the rise of cantorial services, this requirement was often considered secondary to musical capabilities. This bothered those who believed that a *hazzan* should be, first and foremost, a religious representative. Rabbis were among the harshest critics of *hazzanim*, accusing them of needlessly repeating words and prolonging their chanting of the prayers merely to display the brilliant quality and range of their voices. Some cantors began to violate good musical taste, indulging in vocal gymnastics and even employing incongruous tunes that corrupted the sense of the prayers. A florid style of *hazzanut* (cantorial singing) became the characteristic style of the Ashkenazic synagogue, especially in Eastern Europe. The Sephardim were saved from cantorial excesses because they emphasized reading the prayers in unison, which limited the opportunity for solo singing. Moreover, the Sephardic service included relatively few of the *piyyutim* that provided the Ashkenazic *hazzan* a fertile source for extensive musical self-expression.[7]

Modern musical styles greatly influenced post-Emancipation synagogue services, particularly in Reform temples in Germany. Harmonies, choirs, and organ music were all integrated into the new service. Prayers were chanted in German, in addition to the traditional Hebrew, and German melodies replaced many of the traditional liturgical tunes. At around the same time, the Hasidic movement was also making changes in synagogue services and music. The Hasidic *nigun* (tune), a mainstay of Hasidic prayer, ultimately became ubiquitous in many traditional communities.

The first half of the 20th century has been described as the "Golden Age of *Hazzanut*." This was the era of massive immigration into the United States from Russia and Poland. Even if their level of religious observance declined, most immigrants preserved their love for classic Eastern European *hazzanut*, which thus became firmly transplanted in America. Large congregations competed to secure one of the big names among the *hazzanim*—who became major celebrities, filled their own synagogues to overflowing, and even made regular guest appearances at other synagogues and in concert halls. Improvements in transportation enabled *hazzanim* to travel to far-flung Jewish communities. Combined with the development of sound recordings, this allowed some cantors to develop international reputations of legendary proportions. *Hazzanim* became equated with the great operatic tenors—and some gained great success on the stage—and they were able to command substantial salaries and fees for concerts and High Holy Day services.[8]

The last half century has seen the virtual demise of classic *hazzanut*. The strong trend toward individual spiritual fulfillment has fostered active congregational singing of the prayers and a growing distaste for listening to a "performance." Many traditional synagogue melodies have been replaced by music developed in the modern State of Israel, especially the lively songs, set to verses from the prayer book, that were first introduced at the annual Hasidic Song Festival in Jerusalem. Economic considerations have also played a role, since only the largest and most wealthy congregations believe that they can afford to maintain two full-time officials.[9] Ironically, the role of the cantor is now far more important in the Conservative and Reform movements, both of which have admitted women to the profession despite the traditional prohibition against hearing the singing voice of a woman (*kol ishah*), which was considered too provocative for male worshipers.

Prayer (תְּפִלָּה)

Overview

Prayer is a way for mortal humans beings to communicate with a personal deity, a God who exists, hears, and answers. It can take the form of praise, petition, thanksgiving, and confession. All of this is encompassed in the most common Hebrew word for prayer, "*tefillah*" (Isa. 1:15), and the corresponding verb "*hit'pallel*" (1 Kings 8:42), which come from the root "פלל," meaning "to judge." When praying we often present our needs and desires to God with the hope that these requests will be deemed worthy of receiving favorable divine judgment.[1] An alternate possibility is that the word "*tefillah*" comes from the Hebrew root "נפל," meaning "to fall" (with the opening *nun* often dropped). When the Israelites threatened, "Let us head back for Egypt" (Num. 14:4–5),[2] Moses and Aaron "fell on their faces" without uttering any words. Moses repeated this action in the face of Korach's rebellion (Num. 16:4), praying for deliverance from the rebels by falling on his face—the original, wordless method of prayer among ancient peoples.[3]

In prayer we recognize our dependency on God and realize that every blessing, even life itself, is not earned but rather a generous divine gift. Prayers express our deepest feelings, the proper response to a world of what Abraham Joshua Heschel termed "radical amazement." As Heschel wrote, "to pray is to take notice of the wonder, to regain a sense of the mystery that animates all beings, the divine margin in all attainments."[4]

Biblical Period

Biblical prayers are simple and spontaneous human reactions to personal events or experiences. They range in length from the brief five-word plea of Moses to heal his sister, Miriam (Num. 12:13), to the extended prayer of Solomon at the inauguration of the Temple (1 Kings 8:15–21,23–53). Biblical figures prayed for a variety of reasons. Abraham prayed for Sodom to be spared if 10 righteous men could be found in this depraved city (Gen. 18:23–33). Jacob prayed for protection on his flight from Esau's wrath (Gen. 28:20). The barren Hannah, who became a model of Jewish prayer, beseeched God for a son (1 Sam. 1:11). The tortured Samson prayed for the strength to tear down the pillars to which the Philistines tied him (Judg. 16:28). The Prophets begged for divine forgiveness of the sins of the people (Jer. 14; Amos 7:2), and Daniel (9:3–19) asked for the restoration of Israel. Praise, a common element of prayer, is exemplified in the prayer of the Levites (Neh. 9).

The only formal prayers during the biblical era were the confessions to be recited when bringing the first fruits and the tithe (Deut. 26:5–15) and that of the *Kohen Gadol* on Yom Kippur, which had no prescribed formula (Lev. 16:21). In the Temple, the *Kohanim* recited a short liturgy consisting of a blessing, the *Shema* (see p. 413), the Ten Commandments (see p. 489), three additional benedictions, and the Priestly Blessing (see p. 432). However, there was no communal prayer, and those laymen present for the sacrifices participated in the ritual merely by prostrating themselves and, at appropriate pauses, chanting such responses as, "Praise the Lord, for He is good" (Ps. 136:1).

Some prayers were offered indirectly through a priest (1 Sam. 14:36–37) or prophet (2 Kings 19:2). However, it was clear that no intercessor was required, for as the Psalmist wrote: "The Lord is near to all who call upon Him, to all who call upon him in truth" (Ps. 145:18).

Formalizing Prayer

Personal prayers could be offered at any time, but the need for regular congregational worship led to the development of three specific times for prayer (see below)—morning and afternoon, to correspond with the sacrificial services, and then in the evening. Although not official Jewish law until the rabbinic period, this practice had biblical antecedents. The Psalmist wrote, "As for me, I call to God, and the Lord will deliver me. Evening, morning, and noon I complain and moan, and He hears my voice" (Ps. 55:17–18); and of Daniel it is written, "And three times a day he knelt down, prayed, and made confession to his God" (Dan. 6:11). This same verse indicates that Daniel prayed facing Jerusalem. Even though one could pray anywhere, holy places were preferred. When the Temple was built, it became the central site of Jewish worship; those who could not be present there turned toward Jerusalem while praying. The centrality of the Temple was eventually supplanted by the synagogue, which developed during the Babylonian exile as a place of assembly but later became the site of prayer and study. Nevertheless, synagogues are still built so that the worshiper faces Jerusalem. Congregational prayer in a minyan (a quorum of 10; see p. 372) was strongly encouraged, though private prayer was never eliminated.

Rabbinic Period

The Rabbis offered several reasons for the thrice-daily statutory prayers (Ber. 26b). According to one opinion, the three services correspond to the daily sacrifices in Temple times—the morning and afternoon prayers to the *Shacharit* and *Mincha* offerings; the evening (*Ma'ariv*) prayers to the nighttime burning on the altar of all the fat and organs of the daily offerings.[5]

The second opinion attributes the establishment of the three daily services to the Patriarchs, based on three biblical references (Ber. 26b): Abraham "[rose up early in the morning and] hurried to the place where he had stood before the Lord" (Gen. 19:27),[6] and "standing" always means "praying"; Isaac went out "to meditate in the field toward evening" (Gen. 24:63); and Jacob prayed before he went to sleep on his stone pillow and dreamt of angels ascending and descending the ladder connecting the earth to heaven (Gen. 28:11).

Even if the precedent of the Patriarchs was the source of the three services, the Rabbis understood prayer as a replacement for the sacrificial cult. Prayer became known as *"avodah she-b'lev"* (lit., "service of the heart"; Taan. 2a)—a reference to the original *avodah,* the sacrificial ritual. As Rabbi Eleazar observed, "prayer is more efficacious than good deeds ... [and] than sacrifices" (Ber. 32b).

The obligation to pray is considered a rabbinic commandment, even though it is supported by biblical verses. In addition to establishing the basic outlines of the three daily prayer services (Ber. 4:1), the Rabbis decreed that public prayers should be offered in times of peril, such as prayers for rain during a drought (Taan. 2:1–5).

The Rabbis stressed the need to pray with proper concentration *(kavanah)* on the words uttered in God's presence, not amid "laughter, or chatter, or frivolity, or idle talk" (Ber. 31a). The Hebrew word "*kavanah*" means "direction," implying a total concentration on the act of prayer with the intent toward coming ever closer to God. Achieving a state of *kavanah* is extremely difficult, because it is natural for the mind to be distracted and to wander. Thus the Rabbis warned Jews against walking within four cubits (six feet) of one who was reciting the *Amidah* (see p. 421) (Ber. 27a). Covering the head with the tallit (see p. 379) during prayer was one technique of eliminating distractions; praying facing a wall could achieve the same results.[7]

The Prophets strongly condemned mechanical worship, as did their successors, the Rabbis of the Talmud. They realized the danger that the rote recitation of established formulas of prayer could reduce them to mere outward performance of a religious duty. "If a man makes his prayer a 'fixed task,' it is not a [genuine] supplication" (Ber. 4:4). The term "fixed task" was defined as prayers that are like a "heavy burden," consisting of an established liturgy "without something fresh in it" (Ber. 29b). Canonization of the early synagogue prayers by Rabban Gamaliel II met with intense opposition because of the danger that strict regulation of prayer would severely limit spontaneity (Ber. 4:3). Nevertheless, most Rabbis recognized that fixed forms of prayer and regularity of worship were essential to a person's religious life. While waiting for the rare flash of inspiration conducive to prayers of self-expression, a person could forget the art of prayer, be incapable of praying even when that rare spiritual instant arrived, and end up never praying at all![8]

Nevertheless, the Rabbis did permit private prayers within the structure of the prescribed services. At the end of the silent *Amidah*, the worshiper was urged to add a personal prayer. Although the Talmud records several prayers that the sages composed for their private use, most ordinary worshipers were satisfied to recite the standard prayers with deep feeling.[9]

Though prayer was greatly esteemed by the Rabbis, studying Torah was considered to be a religiously superior activity (Ber. 6b). Some scholars who devoted their entire life to study prayed infrequently, with one reported to have "prayed only every thirty days" (RH 35a). A sage who was thought to spend too much time praying was chastised by his colleagues for ignoring the key to eternal life (the study of Torah) in favor of something more mundane (prayer) (Shab. 10a).

Post-Talmudic Period

The philosophers of the Middle Ages particularly stressed the need for adequate concentration in prayer. Maimonides defined "*kavanah*" as meaning "a man should empty his mind of all other thoughts and regard himself as if he were standing before the Divine Presence."[10] Bahya ibn Pakuda wrote that prayer without concentration is like a husk without a kernel or a body without a soul. Concerning the bedtime prayers, Jacob ben Asher said, "It is better to pray a little with *kavanah* than much without *kavanah*."[11]

In kabbalistic theology, God's self—known as the *Ein Sof* or "the Infinite"—cannot be comprehended by human beings. Instead, God can be understood only as manifested in the 10 *sefirot* (divine emanations). Because the *Ein Sof* is eternally unchangeable, prayer can affect only the *sefirot* (singular, *sefirah*), each of which represents an attribute of God, such as wisdom, lovingkindness, and power. Prayers are directed to the relevant *sefirah* in an attempt to engender the proliferation of that divine attribute. For the Hasidim, *kavanah* was transformed into an intense emotional experience in which the worshiper strove for an attachment to God *(deveikut)*. As a manifestation of this mystical encounter with the Divine, the body of one deeply in prayer often engaged in ecstatic movements.

A contrary belief is that the highest form of worship is simple silence. Prayer is pure and humble when the worshiper directs his or her entire being to God and utters no words of petition. This practice also precludes indulging in excessive praise or thanksgiving, which inevitably fails to adequately describe God's greatness and lovingkindness. As the Midrash noted, "For God is like a jewel without price; however high you appraise it, still you undervalue it."[12]

The Reform movement, in the early 19th century, modeled Jewish prayer on the patterns of Protestant worship, in an attempt to have the Jewish service be "respectable" to their gentile neighbors. To make the service more intelligible and appeal to the average worshiper, the use of Hebrew was limited and the services were shortened by omitting some of the lengthier prayers and study sections. For "aesthetic considerations," the Torah and haftarah portions and some of the prayers were simply read, rather than chanted in the traditional mode. New melodies, influenced by the musical tradition of the West, were introduced to the accompaniment of organ and choir. Many changes were based on theological grounds, such as deleting all references to the return to Zion and the restoration of the ancient sacrificial system. The Reformers believed that these references frustrated the universalistic aspect of Judaism, claiming that the dispersion of the Jews was neither exile nor punishment for Israel's sins. They emphasized the hope for the Messianic Age, rather than a personal messiah, and the prayers for the peace of Israel were extended to embrace all humankind. The Conservative movement subsequently took a less drastic approach, changing the petition for the restoration of animal sacrifice in a rebuilt Temple to a recollection of the way in which the Jewish ancestors worshiped.

Major Themes of Prayer

The predominant themes in the liturgy are blessing, petition, and thanksgiving. The blessing, opening with the word "*baruch*" in its various formulations, is the core of Jewish worship (see p. 386). Thus the preliminary service (*Pesukei de-Zimra*; see p. 407) begins with the poem *Baruch she-Amar* (see p. 408); the morning and evening services open with *Barchu* (see p. 411); the *Amidah* (see p. 421) begins with a blessing, and every paragraph concludes with one; and the Torah and haftarah readings are bracketed with blessings. Communal petitions form the central part of the *Amidah*, and the individual is allowed to ask for personal needs officially toward the end of the *Amidah* or whenever so moved. The ubiquitous request for peace concludes all of the major prayers (*Amidah*, *Kaddish*, Priestly Blessing, *Birkat ha-Mazon*). Giving thanks to God (which in Hebrew also often expresses a sense of acknowledgment) is a major element in such prayers as *Modeh Ani* (said upon waking; see p. 473), *Modim Anachnu Lach* (in the *Amidah*), *Hallel* (see p. 162), *Aleinu* (see p. 466), and the *Birkat ha-Mazon* (see p. 476).

God is repeatedly emphasized as the Creator of the world in such prayers as the first blessing before the *Shema*, the *Amidah*, and the

Aleinu. The divine role in the historical development of Israel is continually stressed, from the age of the Patriarchs (first blessing of the *Amidah*) to the kingship of David (in prayers for future redemption), the return from Babylonian exile, and the reaffirming of the Covenant (*Pesukei de-Zimra*). There are numerous references to the Exodus from Egypt—as in *Shirat ha-Yam* (Song at the Sea; see p. 409), which concludes the *Pesukei de-Zimra*—as well as in the third paragraph of the *Shema* and in the blessing that follows it. The recognition of divine redemption in the past leads to requests for similar intervention in the future, as in the middle blessings of the *Amidah* and the *Kaddish*, and the second paragraph of the *Aleinu*. The giving of the Torah at Mount Sinai is a recurrent theme, as in the second blessing before the *Shema* and in the blessings before and after the Torah readings. This is closely related to the idea of the election of Israel as God's "Chosen People" (see p. 592), "a kingdom of priests and a holy nation" (Exod. 19:6). Gratitude to God for making one a Jew and not a heathen is one of the morning benedictions in the Orthodox liturgy and a major theme in the first paragraph of the *Aleinu*.

Other themes that are stressed throughout the prayer service include the oneness and unity of God (*Shema*), the concept of God as eternal king (*Aleinu, Kaddish, Kedushah, U-va le-Zion Go'el*), the sanctification of God's name (*Kaddish*), and the hope for the speedy coming of the Messiah (*Amidah, Aleinu, Birkat ha-Mazon*, blessings after reading the haftarah, and especially the *Malkhuyot* section in the *Musaf Amidah* on Rosh Hashanah). The holiness of God is emphasized in two quotes from the Prophets in the *Kedushah* of the *Amidah*[1] (see p. 429): "Holy, holy, holy! The Lord of Hosts! His presence fills all the earth" (Isa. 6:3)[2] and "Praised is the presence of the Lord, in His place" (Ezek. 3:12).[3]

Language of Prayer

Hebrew has always been the preferred language of Jewish prayer.[1] "Rabbi Jonathan taught that there are four languages—the Roman is best for battle; the Greek best for song; the Persian best for lamentation; and the Hebrew best for prayer." According to the Talmud, "Secular matters may be uttered in the holy language, whereas sacred matters must not be uttered in secular language" (Shab. 40b). The Rabbis even opposed the use of Aramaic in prayer, despite the fact that this was considered a semi-holy tongue because several of the books of the Bible (Daniel, Ezra, Nehemiah) are largely written in this language. Rabbi Yochanan stated that "if anyone prays for his needs in Aramaic, the ministering angels do not pay attention to him, because they do not understand that language! [and thus cannot transmit these prayers to God]" (Sot. 33a). However, this extreme view did not prevail, and prayer in other languages was permitted. A number of Aramaic prayers were admitted into the liturgy (e.g., *Kaddish*, *Kol Nidrei*), and the Mishnah ruled that the *Shema* and the *Amidah*, which form the core of Jewish worship, "may be recited in any language" (Sot. 7:1).

Until modern times, the issue of using the vernacular in prayer posed little problem, because virtually all Jews could understand the prayers in Hebrew. Unfortunately, in most communities this is no longer the case. The argument is now made that if *kavanah* is essential, the prayers should be in the vernacular lest the words be merely "mysterious incantations." Defenders of the tradition maintain that Hebrew, the language of prayer for thousands of years, "contains sentiments and nuances that no other tongue can possibly reproduce." Translating prayers into the vernacular strips them of their historic significance and diminishes their powerful appeal to the collective heart of the people. "A Hebrew hymn, when recited by the congregation, evokes in the hearts of worshipers a feeling of oneness with the entire people of Israel throughout the world and across the ages."

According to Maimonides, the Rabbis mandated prayer in Hebrew because they foresaw the danger of Jews being dispersed throughout the world and speaking different languages. Formulating the prayers in pure Hebrew would allow all Israelites to worship together. Even today, the Jew who can pray in Hebrew is able to attend a synagogue anywhere in the world and feel at home in the worship service.

Proper Forms of Prayer

Some prayers are not appropriate and hence invalid. The Mishnah labels a supplication to God to change the past as a "vain prayer" (Ber. 9:3, 54a). It offers such examples as a husband praying that his pregnant wife will bear a male child, and a person returning from a journey who "hears cries of distress in the town and says, [God] grant that this is not in my house." Moreover, it is impossible for God to positively answer the conflicting prayers of various individuals. This is clearly indicated in the prayer of the *Kohen Gadol* on Yom Kippur, who before the rainy season that was so vital for the harvest in Israel, used to pray that God reject the supplications of travelers seeking fair weather (Yoma 53b).

Worshipers should not pray exclusively for themselves, but should always be concerned with the welfare of others, as indicated in the talmudic dictum, "A man should always associate himself with the congregation" (Ber 29b–30a). Consequently, one should use the plural form "grant us" rather than the singular "grant me." Congregational prayers in the plural always have been considered the ideal in Judaism, for the well-being of the individual is inextricably linked with that of the entire community of Israel. According to the Talmud, even one who is far removed from a congregation, praying on a lonely road for his or her personal safety, must pray for the group and not for oneself alone (Ber. 29b).[1]

Addressing Prayers Directly to God

Judaism has traditionally believed in a personal God who answers prayers. The Jerusalem Talmud records God as saying, "When a man is in trouble, do not cry out to the angel Michael or to the angel Gabriel but to Me, and I will answer immediately" (Ber. 9:1, 13a). Nevertheless, the Rabbis maintained, "a man must begin to pray only in a mood of humility—not in a mood of frivolity, nor in a mood of lightness, nor in a mood of banter—so that the Holy One, praised be He, will listen to his prayer."[2] When the disciples of Rabbi Eliezer asked how to attain the life of the world to come, part of his reply was: "When you pray, know before Whom you stand" (Ber. 28b). This advice is prominently inscribed on the ark of many synagogues, cautioning worshipers that although there is an element of intimacy in the relationship between the Jew and God, it must never be permitted to "degenerate into vulgar familiarity."[3]

Jewish tradition recognizes that worship may be difficult, and that the ability to pray is a divine gift. Therefore, special prayers were composed to help Jews direct their heart toward God—introductory supplications asking permission to recite the prayers that follow. The

Amidah, the central prayer of all services, is preceded by the words of the Psalmist: "O Lord, open my lips, and let my mouth declare your praise" (Ps. 51:17). The recitation of the *Ashrei* (see p. 408) in the afternoon service was designed to encourage worshipers to meditate a few moments before beginning the core prayers. When asked by one of his Hasidim, "What does the Rebbe do before praying?" the Tanzer Rebbe replied, "I pray that I may be able to pray properly."[4]

Attire

Maimonides stated that before praying one should dress appropriately, based on the verse, "Worship the Lord in the beauty of holiness" (Ps. 29:2).[5] He further noted that "one should not pray in sweaty clothes, nor bareheaded, nor barefoot in a society where it was deemed proper to wear shoes in the presence of important personages."[6] Proper attire was especially important when reciting the two major prayers of the liturgy; one must be clothed from the waist down to say the *Shema* and also cover the top of the body for the *Amidah* (Ber. 24b–25a).[7] According to legend, Rabbi Shimon bar Yochai and his son, under sentence of death by the Romans, hid in a cave for 12 years. "A miracle occurred and a carob tree and a water well were created for them. They would strip their garments and sit up to their necks in sand. The whole day they studied; when it was time for prayers they robed, covered themselves, prayed, and then put off their garments again, so that they should not wear out" (Shab. 33b).

Gestures

Body gestures are normal expressions of worship. The Bible does not mandate the use of any specific position, instead at various times it notes individuals who prayed standing, sitting, kneeling, prostrated on the earth, or with head bowed, and mentions the hands being uplifted or outstretched.

Today, standing is considered the formal posture for prayer. However, as the liturgy developed and the number of prayers progressively expanded, it became difficult for the average worshiper to stand for the entire service. Although there are variations among the different branches of Judaism as to when one sits and stands, as a general rule worshipers who are able to stand do so during *Baruch she-Amar* (see p. 408), *Shirat ha-Yam* (see p. 409), *Yishtabach* (see p. 411), *Barchu* (see p. 411), *Hallel* (see p. 162), the silent *Amidah* and its *Kedushah* portion during the reader's repetition (see p. 429), *Aleinu* (see p. 466), and when the Torah is taken out and returned to the ark.[8] Bowing the head and bending the knees are frequent gestures to demonstrate humility before the Divine Presence (e.g., *Barchu, Amidah, Aleinu*). The Talmud makes the important ethical point that the more elevated one's status in Jewish life, the more important it is to show humility. "The king was required to kneel throughout the *Amidah*; the high priest bowed at each benediction; an ordinary priest bowed only at the first and next to last benedictions" (Ber. 34a–b).

Taking steps backward and forward at the beginning and end of the *Amidah* symbolize the entrance into and departure from a royal court (see p. 425). Symbolically falling on one's face (*nefilat apayim*) by cradling one's face in the crook of the arm is limited to the recitation of *Tachanun* in the presence of the Torah (see p. 436). Kneeling and prostrating the whole body, which were closely associated with the ancient Temple service, have been abandoned almost entirely in modern times, possibly because some non-Jews have assumed these positions. Today, kneeling and prostration are restricted to short sections of the services on Rosh Hashanah and Yom Kippur (see p. 201).[9]

Ritual swaying (*shuckling*, from the Yiddish word meaning "to shake"), typically forward and back but also side to side, is a characteristic of male worshipers in traditional synagogues. Although many erroneously believe that these bodily movements originated with the Hasidim in the 17th century, early Hasidim merely accentuated a practice dating back to gaonic and even talmudic times to produce deeper concentration and more intense devotion in prayer. Indeed, the Talmud relates that when Rabbi Akiva prayed privately, his repeated "genuflexions and prostrations" were so vigorous that he would begin in one part of the room and finish in another (Ber. 31a).[10]

Many explanations have been offered for the development of this practice. When students were forced to share scarce books, one would bend or lean forward to read the text while another would move back out of the way and recite what he had just read. Over time, this continual forward and backward motion became so ingrained that students even used it during prayer. The Zohar quotes Rabbi Yose as indicating that this custom "describes the greatness of the soul as a ray of the divine light, which is God. Just as the light of a candle flickers when breathed upon, so does the soul of man tremble when pouring out its supplications to God who planted it within our mortal flame." For Yehudah ha-Levi, *shuckling* is a remnant of the trembling and shaking with fear that the Israelites experienced as they stood in awe at the foot of Mount Sinai to receive the Torah. Rashi observed, "If the stones, that are inanimate, tremble and sway when God's Name is pronounced, how much more should we tremble in prayer?" For the mystics, *shuckling* during prayer represented an erotic union with the Divine. Regardless of the underlying reason, this rhythmic motion tends to focus the worshiper's attention during prayer and increase the emotional intensity.[11]

Music

Music has long added to the beauty of prayer and enhanced its emotional fervor. "Sing to the Lord a song of praise, chant a hymn with a lyre to our God" (Ps. 147:7)[12] indicates the rich tradition of vocal and instrumental music among the ancient Israelites. In the Temple, a choir of Levites sang the appropriate psalms accompanied by musical instruments (Neh. 12:27–29,34). There was also an orchestra of Levites (1 Chron. 25:7), and the offering of first fruits featured the sound of the flute (Bik. 3:3–4). The final psalm (150) details the numerous instruments[13] that were used to enhance the beauty and spiritual impact of the Temple service.

After the Temple was destroyed, the use of musical instruments on the Sabbath and festivals was banned as a sign of mourning. The sages believed that no Jewish prayer service should approximate the glory of worship in the ancient sanctuary. Musical instruments were also prohibited because they might lead to work, such as the repair of a broken string on a violin.[14] In later times, certain instruments—especially the organ—were so closely associated with worship in the Christian churches that it would be a case of the prohibited "imitating of gentile customs" to play it in the synagogue. The sole exception to the sounding of a musical instrument in synagogue was the shofar (see p. 190), since it was used for the express purpose of fulfilling a mitzvah and thus did not fall within the ban. Nevertheless, it was not sounded on the Sabbath, because it might be inadvertently carried to the synagogue and thus violate one of the 39 prohibited labors on that day.

Today, Reform and some Conservative synagogues do permit the playing of instrumental music on the Sabbath and festivals. Several justifications have been offered for this practice. The prohibition of music as a sign of mourning for the destruction of Jerusalem included vocal no less than instrumental music. Nevertheless, the tradition obviously has accepted vocal music for religious purposes, and the use of musical instruments merely extends the compromise. Furthermore, the use of instrumental music in church is itself a borrowing from the Temple, and thus there is no reason to prohibit something as a "Christian" custom that was originally adapted from Jewish practice.

Vocal music has continued to be a fundamental aspect of prayer and the reading of the Torah and haftarah. In his 12th-century classic, *The Book of the Pious,* Rabbi Judah he-Hasid wrote: "Say your prayers in a melody that is most pleasant and sweet to you. Then you shall pray with proper *kavanah,* because the melody will draw your heart after the words that come from your mouth. Supplicate in a melody that makes the heart weep, praise in a melody that makes the heart glad" (*Sefer Hasidim* 11). The Talmud goes so far as saying that one of the qualifications of a prayer leader is to be "skilled in chanting and have a pleasant voice" (Taan. 16a).[15]

Although there are no musical notations in the printed siddur, a collection of musical motifs (*nusach*) that differentiate one service from another have been handed down throughout the generations. Thus specific modes and melodies characterize the weekday, Sabbath, festival, and High Holy Day services. For example, on the Sabbath the melodies create the mood and reflect the appropriate feeling that should accompany the words at different times of the day—from the joy and spiritual elevation that begin the Sabbath to the mournful sorrow as it departs. The musical tradition also differs from one ethnic division of Judaism to another, reflecting the secular music of the place where each group lived. The Hasidim emphasize song as an integral element of true prayer. For them, the wordless melody (*nigun*) can capture the heights of overwhelming ecstasy or the depths of grief.[16] The Hasidic emphasis on song as a way of joyously serving God has had a profound effect across the religious spectrum, leading to the return of congregational singing as a central component in contemporary synagogue services, especially on Sabbaths and festivals. In this way, modern Jews are increasingly heeding the words of the ancient Psalmist,

"Serve the Lord with gladness, come before His Presence with singing" (Ps. 100:2)[17]

There are two fundamental approaches in Judaism to the use of melody in prayer. In the Ashkenazic tradition, most of the service is recited individually in a singsong fashion. The leader keeps a steady pace, beginning and concluding each section and leading the chanting of those passages that are sung in unison. In contrast, in the Sephardic ritual the congregation chants most prayers aloud together, word by word, with only specific sections chanted by individuals.[18]

The Torah and haftarah are also traditionally chanted during the synagogue service. As the Talmud (Meg. 32a) teaches, "If one reads [Scripture] without chant or studies [Mishnah] without melody, of him it is written, 'I gave them laws that were not good'" (Ezek. 20:25). Even today, learning in traditional *yeshivot* is done to a type of singsong melody. The precise musical phrases for chanting the Torah are indicated by special signs called "trope" (from a Greek word meaning "turn" or "figure of speech"), which were developed by the 10th-century Masoretes (see p. 493). As with the nusach, the melody for chanting the Torah varies among Jews from different locations. Since the Torah has no punctuation marks, the trope indicates the beginning and end of phrases and even helps interpret the meaning of the text. The other books of the Bible also have trope markings, but with different and varied musical values.[19]

Answer to Prayer

"The premodern Jew fully believed that God hears and answers prayer. Thus Moses prayed on behalf of his sister, Miriam, and her 'leprosy' (*tzara'at*) was cured (Num. 12:13–14). The prophet Elijah prayed on behalf of a lifeless child, who was restored to life (1 Kings 17:20–22). The people of Nineveh repented and 'cried mightily unto God' and were saved from their impending doom (Jon. 3:5–10)." The talmudic Rabbis also accepted the concept that repeated prayer leads to a positive divine response, using as a proof text a verse from Psalms (27:14): "Wait for the Lord; be strong, and let your heart take courage; yea, wait for the Lord."[1]

Nonetheless, in the Bible not all prayers are answered. Abraham bargained with God to spare the city of Sodom; but because it did not contain 10 righteous men, it was destroyed (Gen. 18:17–33). Isaiah (29:13–15) observed that insincere prayers are not answered: "Because that people has approached [Me] with its mouth and honored Me with its lips, but has kept its heart far from Me, and its worship has been a commandment of men, learned by rote—truly I shall further baffle that people ... Ha! Those who would hide their plans deep from the Lord! Who do their work in dark places and say, 'Who sees us, who takes note of us?'"

Petitionary prayers must not be a substitute for human effort. When the Israelites at the shore of the Sea of Reeds cowered before the approaching army of Egypt, they and their leader, Moses, cried out to God for salvation. However, the sea was divided for them only after the people had stepped into it and the waters reached their noses (Exod. R. 21:10). The Rabbis concluded that human beings must first do whatever is in their power before properly calling for help from the power that transcends their own. Moreover, the Rabbis condemned those who expect a divine response to a petition as one's due: "He who prays long and relies on an answer ends disappointed" (Ber. 55a) and "To three sins man is daily susceptible—thoughts of evil, reliance on prayer, and slander" (BB 164b). On the other hand, the Midrash teaches, "Whoever does the will of Heaven and directs his heart sincerely to his prayer will be answered" (Exod. R. 21). Therefore, the Rabbis apparently believed that although sincere prayer is answered, one must never feel confident of receiving a favorable response or grumble and complain if it does not come.[2]

The medieval mystics, especially those of the Lurianic school, believed that prayer recited by the right person, at the right time, and with the proper concentration can exert a profound influence on the divine realm of the *sefirot*. Not only can proper prayer result in God granting the basic needs of daily life but it also can lead to the ultimate return of the Jews from exile. When confronted with the historical fact that many prior mystical attempts at such prayers seemed to have ended only in disaster, the response was that "some indispensable conditions of the perfect mystical prayer must have been absent."[3]

Devout Jews realize that God does not grant their every request. In his *Sefer ha-Ikkarim*, Joseph Albo explained that one reason prayer may not be accepted is that God knows that what a person is seeking is not what is best for that individual. Petitionary prayers are designed to show that human beings depend on God; rather than seeking a specific answer, we should pray that God grant whatever is good for us.[4]

The very act of prayer tends to spiritualize people's lives, increasing their ability to "listen more attentively to the inner voice of conscience" and thus act in a more moral and ethical way. "Prayer does not by itself make one godly, but it does tend to bring one a little nearer to God; prayer does not automatically make one a saintly person, but it does expose one to saintly ideals."[5] As Abraham Joshua Heschel observed, "Prayer may not save us, but it makes us worthy of being saved." By sharing their apparently insurmountable difficulties with God, worshipers can find untapped sources of strength to confront and even overcome their problems. For centuries, when Jews on Saturday evening prepared to deal with the seemingly unendurable burdens and uncertainties of the upcoming week, they gained immense comfort from reciting *Havdalah* (see p. 147), which begins with the words of Isaiah (12:2)[6]: "Behold the God who gives me triumph! I am confident, unafraid; for Yah the Lord is my strength and song, and He has been my deliverance."[7]

Congregational Prayer

Communal worship has always been a distinctive feature of Jewish prayer. Although an individual Jew can fulfill the mitzvah of prayer privately, joining others as part of a congregation is a particular virtue. Indeed, a person who cannot be present at a service should try to pray privately *at the same time* as the congregation. The Rabbis interpreted the phrase "*eit ratzon*" (favorable time [for prayer]; see Ps. 69:14) as meaning that God is most receptive to prayer "when the congregation is praying" (Ber. 8a). Consequently, many of the major parts of the worship service (*Barchu*, repetition of the *Amidah* with *Kedushah*, Torah reading, Priestly Benediction, and *Kaddish*) require the presence of a minyan (see p. 372). The person leading the communal worship is known as the *shaliach tzibbur* (emissary of the congregation).[1] The prayer leader does not have to be a professional cantor (*hazzan*; see p. 346) or an ordained rabbi; any adult male (or female, in Reform and most Conservative congregations) may assume this role. The Talmud stresses that the *shaliach tzibbur* is not an intermediary between the congregation and God, but simply an agent who recites the prayers on behalf of the worshipers[2] (Ber. 5:5).

Prayer as Polemic

In addition to being a means of expression for worship, prayer is also a statement of belief. As such, it not only is designed to articulate one's own principles of faith but also is an attempt by the normative majority "to counter dissidents and sectarian minorities."[1] Liturgical examples in Judaism include the following:

- *Yigdal* (see p. 470), a poetic rendition of Maimonides' "13 Principles of Faith" (see p. 509).
- *Elohai Neshamah* (see p. 403), which emphasizes the purity of the soul that God directly breathes into a person and, by implication, refutes the Christian doctrine of original sin.
- The second blessing of the *Amidah,* which repeats six times the doctrine of resurrection (denied by the Samaritans and Sadducees).
- The verse, "Who forms light and creates darkness, makes peace and creates all things" (Isa. 45:7), attacking the dualist Persian (Zoroastrian) religion that believed that "the world was created and preserved by two opposing forces, light and darkness, which manifest their existence in good and evil, respectively."[2]
- Removing the Ten Commandments from the daily service (see p. 489), in opposition to the Pauline Christians, who accepted them but rejected the authority of other Torah laws.

Several polemics were introduced against the Karaites, who followed the literal meaning of the Bible and denied rabbinic interpretation of the text. The Rabbis introduced a special blessing over the Sabbath lights (see p. 136), and the *Ge'onim* inserted into the Friday evening service a recitation of *Ba-meh Madlikin* (With what may we light), a mishnah that discusses which types of wick and oil should be used to provide the home with light on the Sabbath (Shab. 2:1, 20b). These practices, in direct opposition to the Karaite ritual of extinguishing all lights before the Sabbath and spending the day without heat or light, were designed to indicate unequivocally that having lights burning in one's dwelling was not merely permitted but a positive commandment.[3]

Siddur (סִדּוּר)

The siddur, also known as *seder tefillot* (order of prayers), is the collection of all the prayers for public and private worship on weekdays, Sabbaths, festivals, and fast days.[1] However, the development and maturation of the siddur was hardly an orderly process. Rather than appearing as a completed text that was logically organized by a committee of scholars, the siddur is the culmination of centuries of liturgical additions, each reflecting the theology, culture, and history of its period. Therefore, "the siddur is not only a handbook of Jewish prayer, but also a faithful record of Jewish thoughts, ideals, hopes, and anxieties during the many centuries of its growth ... the Jewish book of common prayer and the spiritual history of the Jewish people."

Unlike the Bible and Talmud, which once completed were permanently closed and could be enhanced only through commentaries and glosses, the siddur has always remained open to new prayers to respond to the ever-changing needs of the Jewish people.

Solomon Schechter noted that while the Bible is the record of the divine revelation to Israel, the siddur is the record of Israel's self-revelation to God. Within its pages, "Jews open their innermost souls to reveal their deepest yearnings and highest aspirations." Unlike scholars who pored over the massive tomes of the Talmud in their search for wisdom in making judicial decisions, the Jewish masses repeatedly read the siddur to seek words of consolation, healing, and hope in times of need.

History

For many centuries, the liturgy of the synagogue was solely an oral tradition and the prayers were recited from memory. Indeed, the Rabbis prohibited writing down the prayers (and the Oral Law), probably because of the fear that this might enable Christians or other anti-Jewish sectarians to maliciously alter them or permit informers to provide falsified versions to the authorities as evidence that the Jews were making subversive statements.[2] The Talmud declared that "those who write down benedictions [commit as grave a sin] as though they burned a Torah" (Shab. 115b). The person who led the congregation needed to know the prayers by heart; the worshipers either knew the prayers by memory or repeated them after the reader. This practice explains why the *Amidah* is recited twice during both the morning and afternoon services. Those who knew the prayers by heart recited them silently, while the reader repeated the *Amidah* for those who were less knowledgeable and could respond only with the traditional "amen" (see p. 392).

Toward the end of the second century C.E., the sages feared that centuries of learning would vanish forever in the wake of the poverty and persecutions afflicting the Jews of the Land of Israel. Consequently, Rabbi Judah ha-Nasi decided to edit the oral learning and organize it for publication as the Mishnah (see p. 499). Several centuries later, Rav Ashi, the head of the Sura Academy in Babylonia, took similar action by beginning the task of gathering the extensive rabbinic discussions of the Mishnah, which eventually became the Talmud.

The liturgy, nevertheless, remained a purely oral tradition for many more years. Initially, there was little danger of the prayers being forgotten, because they were repeated every day. As long as the Jews were concentrated in the Land of Israel and Babylonia, their respective traditions were unchanging and accepted by all. Any attempts to "improve" on the prayer service by additions or deletions were immediately quashed by the diligent heads of the major academies. However, as the Diaspora expanded throughout Europe and into Asia and Africa, the previous sources of authority gradually lost sway, and it became inevitable that local influences would result in different liturgical practices in these dispersed communities.

Earliest *Siddurim*

By the eighth century, privately compiled collections of prayers were in use. Written as aids to memory and without the approval of any recognized authority, they were often riddled with errors due to faulty copying or mistaken local practices. Each person recorded the service in his own way, adding or omitting as he thought best. The multiplicity of texts and customs eventually made it difficult to determine exactly what was correct practice. There was a pressing need for one or more authoritative leaders to formulate a single, standard liturgy. The obvious candidates for this task were the *Ge'onim*, the illustrious heads of the major Babylonian academies, who exerted profound influence over law and practice throughout the entire Jewish world.

In about 850, the community of Lucena in Spain wrote to Natronai Gaon of Sura, asking him to clarify the precise "100 blessings" (see p. 388) that Rabbi Meir insisted every person was obligated to recite each day. His four-page responsum, which was the first officially sanctioned written compilation of prayers, constituted the nucleus of the first prayer book.[3]

Natronai's successor as head of the academy at Sura, Amram Gaon, was asked by community leaders of Spanish Jewry for guidance in determining "the prayers and benedictions for the entire year." His responsum was the first authoritatively produced Jewish prayer book, which became the basis of the Sephardic rite.[4] This prayer book contained all the prayers for weekdays, Sabbath, Rosh Hodesh, fast days, and festivals, with each section beginning with a review of the applicable legal regulations. Blessings and prayers for special occasions, such as marriage and circumcision, were included at the end.

A century later, the great philosopher Saadiah Gaon produced the first authoritative prayer book for use by the ordinary worshiper. In the preface to his siddur, Saadiah related that on his travels to many Jewish communities in different lands, he saw so many variations in the religious services that he feared that relatively soon Jews would no longer have a common liturgy, and that the traditional order of prayers would be confused and forgotten. Therefore, he decided to "collect and arrange the established prayers, praises, and benedictions so that the original form should be restored."[5] Built on the work of his predecessor, Saadiah's siddur was more logically organized and enabled the average worshiper to follow the service. Instead of Amram Gaon's arrangement of the prayers across the festival cycle, which made it necessary for many of them to be repeated—such as the virtually identical *Amidahs* for the three major festivals—Saadiah arranged the prayers in coherent groups, such as those for festivals and fast days. Thus the worshiper could easily locate the appropriate prayers for every occasion.

Although later collections have improved some of Saadiah's groupings of the prayers, his overall approach remains the basis of the traditional siddur. The rules that Saadiah recorded in his commentary, written in the Arabic vernacular for popular use, are essentially those of traditional synagogues today.[6]

After the 10th century, Ashkenazic scholars in Central Europe supplanted the Babylonian *Ge'onim* as the pre-eminent Jewish authorities. The major exception was Maimonides, a Sephardic scholar whose authority was acknowledged throughout the Jewish world. In his monumental code, *Mishneh Torah,* Maimonides included a section on the liturgy, titled "The Order of the Prayers of the Whole Year." Rather than an actual siddur, it was a collection of alternative versions of prayers from which one could develop a comprehensive prayer book. Maimonides' work became authoritative for Jews in the Muslim world (particularly those in Egypt and the Land of Israel), and a fusion of his version and the existing tradition based on Saadiah's siddur was adopted in Yemen. With the exception of Maimonides, however, the fame and prestige of Sephardic scholars was generally limited to their own communities. Moreover, the renown of Spanish Jewry was founded less on talmudic scholarship than on other creative disciplines, especially philosophy, poetry, and linguistics, in such figures as Yehudah ha-Levi, Solomon ibn Gabirol, and the Ibn Ezras.[7]

By the 11th century, Ashkenazim were ready for their own siddur, which was provided by Rabbi Simchah ben Samuel, a pupil of Rashi, who lived in Vitry, France. Known as the *Machzor Vitry*, this work contained the text of all the regular prayers in accordance with the rite of northern France, which was close to that of Germany. In addition, there was a running commentary that included both notes on the prayers and the laws pertaining to every occasion. The *Machzor Vitry* was essentially a "comprehensive religious manual built around the liturgy" and contained virtually everything needed to lead a devout Jewish life. It even included material not previously considered components of the liturgy, such as the mishnaic tractate *Pirkei Avot* (Ethics of the Fathers) and the Passover haggadah, along with commentaries for each.[8]

Printed *Siddurim*

The siddur was revolutionized by Gutenberg's invention of the printing press with movable type in 1440. Before then, books were scarce and expensive; many synagogues possessed only a single siddur for the prayer leader. With the advent of the printing press, which medieval Jewish writers appropriately termed "a scribe with many quills,"[9] thousands of volumes could be produced at a single printing. The sharp reduction in the price of books allowed copies of the siddur to be placed in the hands of many, and eventually all, worshipers. In earlier times, there was no way for congregants to read the numerous prayers and *piyyutim* (prayer poems) that had accumulated over the centuries. Now it was no longer necessary for the reader to recite each *piyyut* aloud, for the worshipers could simply read them rapidly in an undertone. Nevertheless, this did not substantially shorten the services, for the *hazzan* simply used the time saved to perform more complex and virtuoso renditions of their concluding verses.

The best known of the early Hebrew printers was Nathan Soncino. A physician by profession, Soncino established a publishing house in Italy in 1483 and produced the first Hebrew prayer book (based on the Roman rite) three years later, a quarter century before the first Ashkenazic siddur was printed in Prague in 1512. As the number of printed editions increased rapidly, each publisher tried to attract buyers by increasing the value of his version. If one added *Pirkei Avot*, which was studied on summer Sabbath afternoons, in his siddur, a competitor would include the Book of Psalms, which many Jews read every day. To gain a competitive edge, various *siddurim* added commentaries on the prayers, kabbalistic explanations, short treatises on the laws of prayer, and even translations into the vernacular. Publishers also enhanced the layout of the siddur by printing the most important prayers in bold type. Prayer books of various sizes were produced, ranging from large volumes for the reader's desk in the synagogue to miniatures intended for merchants required to travel to fairs and other trading centers.

Over the generations, numerous additions to the basic prayers had been composed by poets, mystics, and ordinary pious Jews. At first optional, many eventually became obligatory, resulting in a siddur that was overly thick and bulky. This was exacerbated in the age of printing, when several biblical books and commentaries became included as integral parts of the prayer book. Consequently, in the early 16th century, the siddur was first published in two volumes—one containing the daily and Sabbath services, which retained the original name, and a second consisting of the prayers for the festivals, which among

Ashkenazim was called the *machzor* (cycle [of festival prayers]). Later, the *machzor* (see p. 163) was further subdivided into one for the High Holy Days and another for the festivals.

Minyan (מִנְיָן)

A minyan (lit., "number") is the term for a quorum, traditionally composed of 10 adult males (13 years of age or older), which is necessary for congregational worship and certain other religious ceremonies. A minyan is required for the following sections of the public synagogue service: *Barchu*, repetition of the *Amidah* with *Kedushah*, Torah and haftarah readings, Priestly Blessing, and *Kaddish*. If any of these recitations begin with a minyan, but some individuals leave so that a minyan is no longer present, the recitation may continue as long as at least six individuals remain.[1] A minyan is also necessary for the rites of comforting the mourners, the recital of the *Sheva Brachot* at wedding ceremonies, and the special invitation (*zimmun*) including the word "*Eloheinu*" preceding the *Birkat ha-Mazon* (Grace after Meals).

The Talmud derives the number "10" as constituting a congregation from the word "*edah*" (community), which in the Torah is applied to the 10 spies (termed a "wicked community") who gave a negative report on the land of Canaan (Num. 14:27) and thus condemned the people to 40 years of wandering in the wilderness (Meg. 23b). Others have related the requirement for a quorum of 10 to Abraham's plea to God to save Sodom if at least 10 righteous men were found there (Gen. 18:32); to the 10 elders mentioned in the Book of Ruth (4:2); or to the verse "Praise God in congregations" (Ps. 68:27), in which the Hebrew word "*b'machalot*" (congregations) has the same numerical value as "*b'asarah*" (with 10). On the basis of the first verse in Psalm 82—"God stands in the congregation of divine beings"— the Talmud concluded that if 10 men pray together, the Divine Presence is with them (Ber. 6a).

The definition of a minyan was less rigid in the Land of Israel during late gaonic times, when some sages considered seven or even six to be sufficient (Sof. 10:8). However, this practice was not accepted in Babylonia and did not survive.[2] To solve the frequent problem in small communities in which one person was needed to complete a minyan, some authorities permitted a minor who held a Torah, or merely the

Torah in the ark, to be the 10th person (JT Ber. 7:2). Rav Huna was quoted as saying that if nine adults are present, the ark may be counted as the 10th person so that a full service may be held, though he later qualified this to mean "if nine look like ten, they may be joined together" (so that the absence of one is not so noticeable) (Ber. 47b).[3] However, these ingenious innovations have never received widespread support. To be sanctified by the Divine Presence and to deserve the official designation of a "holy congregation," a quorum of 10 mature worshipers remains the rule.[4]

In larger communities, the requirement for a minyan did not pose a problem because there were always at least "10 men of leisure" (*batlanim*) who constituted the core of the permanent congregation and were highly respected for their piety and learning. The presence of these 10 men was one of the identifying features of a big city, as opposed to a town or village.[5] In later centuries, these men became paid functionaries ("minyan men") and were frequently old or idle individuals who received a dole from the community in exchange for always being available to make the required quorum.[6]

Ten male adults constitute a quorum in any setting. In Judaism, there is no need for a synagogue building or a rabbi to hold religious services. Indeed, the term "minyan" is also used to describe a group that regularly prays together, typically in a space other than a formal sanctuary. Orthodox congregations do not count women as part of the minyan, because they are not required to attend public prayer services—an exemption related to their important time-dependent responsibilities toward home and family. In Reform and many Conservative synagogues today, in which women have full religious equality with men, the requirement is merely for 10 *persons* to constitute the minyan needed for a public prayer service.

Rather than a mere technicality, the requirement of a minyan for congregational services had a significant effect on the organization and maintenance of Jewish communal life throughout the centuries. The need for a minimum of 10 families (not counting children) to settle together to establish a synagogue prevented the scattering of Jews in isolated areas, where they might easily have fallen victim to the lure of assimilation.[7]

There is a long tradition of not using actual numbers when counting to see if there are enough people to make a minyan. The Talmud understood Hosea's (2:1) prophesy—"The number of the people of Israel shall be like that of the sands of the sea, which cannot be measured or counted"—as both a blessing and a prohibition (Yoma 22b). The Bible records that God twice commanded Moses to take a census of the Israelites to determine the number who were age 20 and older and thus eligible for military service (Num. 1, 26). However, when David ordered an unauthorized census merely "so that I may know the size of the population" (2 Sam. 24:2), a severe plague befell the Israelites and 70,000 perished.[8] Based on this episode, the Talmud decrees: "Israel must not be counted [using numbers], even for religious purposes" (Yoma 22b). This privilege belongs only to God, and its performance without divine sanction can have catastrophic consequences. Therefore, several different counting customs developed to determine whether a minyan was present. Some use verses from Psalms that consist of 10 Hebrew words.

- הוֹשִׁיעָה אֶת עַמֶּךָ וּבָרֵךְ אֶת נַחֲלָתֶךָ וּרְעֵם וְנַשְּׂאֵם עַד הָעוֹלָם.
  Hoshia et amecha u-varech et nachalatechah u-r'eim v'nas'eim ha olam (Save Your people and bless Your inheritance, tend them and elevate them forever; Ps. 28:9).
- עֵינֵי כֹל אֵלֶיךָ יְשַׂבֵּרוּ וְאַתָּה נוֹתֵן לָהֶם אֶת אָכְלָם בְּעִתּוֹ.
  Einay chol eilecha y'sabeiru, v'ata notein la-hem et ochlam b'ito (The eyes of all look to You with hope, and You give them their food in its proper time; Ps. 145:15).
- וַאֲנִי בְּרֹב חַסְדְּךָ אָבוֹא בֵיתֶךָ, אֶשְׁתַּחֲוֶה אֶל הֵיכַל קָדְשְׁךָ בְּיִרְאָתֶךָ.
  Va'ani b'rov chasdechah avo veitechah, eshtachaveh el heichal kodshechah b'yiratechah (As for me, through Your abundant kindness I will enter Your house, and bow low toward Your holy Temple in awe of You; Ps. 5:8)

A different approach is to say "not one, not two ...," thus pretending that one is not actually counting.

Kippah (כִּפָּה)

"*Kippah*" (plural, *kippot*) comes from the Hebrew word "*kaf*" (palm), which describes the shape of the typical head covering worn by Jews in modern times. Also known by its Yiddish equivalent "yarmulke" (skullcap), the *kippah* has become a universally recognized symbol of Jewish identity.

Although the custom of covering the head at home, outdoors, and in the synagogue extends back several thousand years, there is no explicit biblical commandment to cover one's head for prayer or other religious functions. In Temple times, the *Kohen Gadol* wore a special head covering (*mitznefet;* miter), and regular *Kohanim* donned a turban (*migba'at*) (Exod. 28:4,37,40). However, ordinary Israelites were not commanded to cover their heads.

During the talmudic era, covering the head and face was regarded as a sign of reverence before God, especially while praying. Scholars covered their heads to indicate their elevated position, but the donning of a head covering by a person of lesser status was considered arrogant.[1]

In ancient Rome, free men went bareheaded; the wearing of a head covering stigmatized a person as a servant. To stress that they were the loyal servants of the Lord, Jews adopted the practice of covering the head in a House of God, while reciting prayers, and during any activity when blessings that included the divine name were said (such as eating). Eventually, Jews began to cover their heads at all times to demonstrate their awesome respect for God.[2] One sage is reported to have never walked more than four paces (six feet) with his head uncovered, because he recognized that the *Shekhinah* (Divine Presence) was above him (Kid. 31a).

Nevertheless, the sages of ancient Israel ruled that it was optional for men to cover their heads and only a matter of custom to do so for prayer (Ned. 30b). Medieval French and Spanish rabbinical authorities took a similar approach, but the Rabbis of Babylonia disagreed, viewing the covering of the head as an expression of the fear of God (*yirat Shamayim,* lit., "fear of Heaven") (Shab. 156b; Kid. 31a). According to the Shulchan Arukh, one should not mention the name of God or enter a synagogue bareheaded (OH 91:3).[3] Covering the head during prayer became more prevalent but not required by the Ashkenazic rabbis. Therefore, the current requirement among traditional Jews that all men cover their head during prayer and Torah study (and while eating meals) is comparatively recent. Indeed, some have argued that the custom was based on the verse "Nor shall you follow their laws" (Lev.

18:3) and essentially represented a reaction to the Christian practice of immediately taking off their hats when entering a church or other building. Therefore, it became the normative Jewish tradition to worship (and even walk around) with the head covered; being bareheaded became equated with showing insolent disrespect for God.[4]

In modern times, some observant Jewish men wear a *kippah* or other head covering at all times as a symbol of their piety and allegiance to tradition. To prevent being without a head covering for even a brief moment, some ultra-Orthodox men wear a *kippah* under their hat. This tradition began in 17th-century Germany, where it was customary to take off one's hat when in the presence of a government official as a mark of respect.[5] Others wear *kippot* only on formal religious occasions, primarily at synagogue services and while studying Torah.

Kippot come in various forms, from simple cloth to satin, velvet, and leather. They may be black or brightly colored, decorated or plain, lined or unlined. Some sport the wearer's Hebrew name or are decorated with a wide array of traditional or whimsical designs.[6] The style of head covering often provides a clue as to the type of religious observance—from the stringent black hat of the ultra-Orthodox to the knitted *kippah* of the modern Orthodox. The early Reform movement virtually eliminated the practice of covering the head during services, but now the wearing of a *kippah* is increasingly encouraged.[7]

Women's Head Coverings

In the Talmud, Rabbi Ishmael cites the Torah's description of the *sotah* (a woman accused of adultery) as the source for the obligation for women to cover their hair (Ket. 72a). As part of the ceremony to determine the suspected woman's guilt or innocence, the Torah records that "after he has made the woman stand before the Lord, and the priest shall bare the woman's head" (Num. 5:18). Although there are no explicit biblical references to the tradition of women wearing head coverings, by talmudic times it was accepted practice. A married woman who dared to walk bareheaded in the street could be summarily divorced by her husband without paying her *ketubah* (Ket. 7:6). Explaining why this violation was so serious, the Talmud compared a woman's hair to her private parts ("the hair of a woman is nakedness"; Ber. 24a). Because of this, it was prohibited to recite the *Shema* in the presence of a bareheaded woman. Nevertheless, despite the concept that a woman's hair was sexually exciting, head coverings were required only for married women (Ket. 2:1).

Talmudic and post-talmudic sources extol the woman who is conscientious about covering her hair. The Talmud relates the story of Kimchit, the mother of seven sons, each of whom became a *Kohen Gadol*. When asked why she was blessed to have so many eminent sons, she replied: "Because the beams (posts) of my house never saw my hair" (Yoma 47a). The Zohar says of the woman who is careful in covering her hair: "Her children will enjoy increased stature over other children; moreover, her husband shall be blessed with all blessings, blessings of above and blessings of below, with wealth, with children and grandchildren."

Toward the end of the 18th century, some women began wearing a wig (*sheitel*), a "radical innovation" that was vehemently opposed by some ultratraditional rabbis. Currently, only strictly Orthodox women cover their hair at all times. Nevertheless, many married women still cover their heads in synagogue. In egalitarian liberal congregations, some Jewish women—single as well as married—have opted to wear a *kippah* as a manifestation of their religious equality. Moreover, some of these synagogues require that a woman wear a *kippah* (and tallit) when leading services or being called for an *aliyah*.

Tallit (טַלִּית)

The tallit (plural, *tallitot*) is the traditional prayer shawl worn during daily morning prayers and all services on Yom Kippur. (On Tisha b'Av, it is worn only during the afternoon service.) A tallit is also worn by the prayer leader at the afternoon service; in some congregations, the prayer leader also wears a tallit for the evening service on Sabbaths and festivals. Ritual fringes (צִיצִית; tzitzit) are attached to each of the four corners of the tallit in accordance with biblical law (Num. 15:38). Because the explicit purpose of the tzitzit is "that you may *see* them [and recall all the commandments of the Lord and obey them, so that you do not go astray after your own heart and eyes]" (Num. 15:39), the tallit is worn only during the day. The sole exception is Yom Kippur, when the *Kol Nidrei* service (see p. 210) starts just before evening and the tallit adds sanctity to the occasion.

Wearing a tallit is obligatory for Jewish males 13 or older, though some Orthodox synagogues follow the Eastern European tradition in which a tallit is worn only by married men. This is based on the fact that the phrase "if a man marries a wife" immediately follows the repetition of the commandment concerning tzitzit (Deut. 22:12). However, all men wear a tallit whenever they are leading the congregation in prayer or are called up for an *aliyah* to the Torah.

When reciting the phrase "O bring us in peace from the four corners of the earth" in the second blessing before the *Shema* (*Ahavah Rabbah*; see p. 412), the worshiper gathers the four fringes of the tallit together in the left hand. During the third paragraph of the *Shema* (Num. 15:37–41), the fringes are kissed on the three occasions when the word "tzitzit" is read, again at the word *"emet,"* and finally kissed and released at *"nech'madim la-ad"* (and desirable forever) in the following paragraph. When reciting "and you shall look upon them," the fringes are held up to view or pressed to the eyes. When called to the Torah, the custom is to touch the tzitzit to the first word of the passage to be read, and then kiss them before reciting the Torah blessing. After the Torah reading, one touches the tzitzit to the last word read and kisses them before reciting the second blessing.

The tallit is usually white, based on the talmudic description that God wraps Himself in a tallit (RH 17b) and "His garment was like white snow" (Dan. 7:9).[1] It is typically made of wool, though cotton or silk may be used. Some have black or blue stripes, the number and pattern of which have mystical significance. As a color of mourning, the black stripes may serve as a visual reminder of the loss of the Temple. Today, some *tallitot* are made of various colors, inspired by kabbalistic symbolism or aesthetic preference.[2] Most Jews wear only a small, scarf-like tallit, since the biblical commandment specifically refers to the wearing of the tzitzit, not the tallit itself. However, others prefer large *tallitot* that cover most of the body, so as to qualify as a "garment" on which the fringes may be hung (Deut. 22:12).

An essential part of the mitzvah of wearing a tallit is being enwrapped in it. This entails covering the head with the tallit, at least when donning it, in accordance with this blessing: "… Who has commanded us to wrap ourselves in the fringed garment (*lehitatef ba-tzitzit*)" (Ber. 60b). Traditionally, the worshiper places the folded tallit on the right shoulder, recites the blessing, and then opens the tallit and places it on the head. After gathering together the four corners and throwing them over the left shoulder ("manner of the Ishmaelites"), the worshiper removes the part of the tallit covering the head and places it on the shoulders.[3]

Most people pray with the tallit resting on the shoulders. However, some prefer to have the tallit covering their head—especially during the *Shema*, *Amidah*, and *Kedushah*, and when called up to the Torah—to eliminate distractions and increase their concentration at these major portions of the service.[4] Being enfolded by the tallit is regarded as being surrounded by the holiness of the commandments of the Torah, symbolically indicating total obedience to the divine will. A mystical explanation for this practice is offered by the Zohar: "When a man stands at prayer, he should keep his feet together and cover his head as one who stands before a king, and he should also cover his eyes so as not to look at the *Shekhinah*" (a practice the Zohar considered disrespectful).[5] *Kohanim* always cover their heads with their *tallitot* when bestowing the Priestly Blessing (see p. 432) upon the congregation.

The collar of the tallit has a reinforced band of cloth called an *atarah* (crown), which is usually decoratively embroidered or inscribed with the blessing for putting on the garment. The *atarah* may have developed to mark the top of the completely symmetric tallit, since as a religious act it should be put on the same way every time. Another explanation is that the weight of the *atarah* helps keep the tallit on the wearer's shoulder, preventing it from slipping (though this still occurs all too often during the prayer service).

On days when tefillin (see p. 382) are worn, one puts on the tallit first. This is consistent with the general principle that when two mitzvot are to be performed at the same time, the more frequent one takes precedence. The tallit has priority because it is also worn on Sabbaths and festivals (when tefillin are not worn). Another reason for giving priority to the tallit is that the commandment of tzitzit is equal to all the mitzvot of the Torah, since it reminds the wearer of them (Men. 43a).[6]

History

The exact etymology of the word "tallit" is unclear, but it originally meant a "robe" or "cloak." In ancient times, most garments (tunics, capes) were rectangular, because they were woven on looms. In accordance with the biblical command, Jews merely attached fringes to the four corners of the clothing they wore every day. Thus the tallit was not a prayer shawl; it was a regular article of clothing whose religious significance lay solely in the fringes attached to it. After their exile from the Land of Israel, Jews throughout the Diaspora generally assumed the styles of clothing worn by their gentile neighbors, who did not wear four-cornered garments. Consequently, the tallit was no longer worn as part of the daily apparel and was used only for prayer.

The last half of the Torah verse commanding the wearing of tzitzit adds "and they shall put with the fringe of each corner a thread of blue (*tekheilet*)" (i.e., one blue thread and seven white ones). This blue was made from an expensive dye that was extracted from a sea snail (*chilazon*) by a few families on the Mediterranean coast (Men. 42b). After the destruction of the Second Temple, the secret of obtaining this exact shade was lost, and the use of the blue thread in the fringes was discontinued. Recently, some claim to have discovered a close relative of the snail, and *tallitot* with blue fringes are now available. The blue stripes now woven into many *tallitot* symbolize this ancient *tekheilet*.

Various commentators have suggested reasons for the blue threads. The Rabbis maintained that they help the wearer focus on his duty to God, since blue resembles the color of the sea, the sea resembles the heavens, and the heavens resemble the throne of glory (Sot. 17a). For the Kli Yakar, the blue threads of the fringes also symbolize the waters of the sea. Just as the ocean must be kept within defined boundaries lest flooding and disaster occur, so must each Jew live within the defined bounds of the commandments.[7]

There are eight threads (four doubled over as they are drawn through the perforation in the garment) on each of the four corners of the tallit. Thus the total number of threads is 32, the numerical value of the Hebrew word "*lev*" (heart). Since the Pentateuch respectively ends with a *lamed* (l) and begins with a *bet* (b), the mitzvah of tzitzit can be compared to the entire Torah.[8]

In each collection of eight threads, one is longer than the rest and is wound around the remaining seven threads in either of two different ways. Among Ashkenazic Jews, there are four series of rings of 7, 8, 11, and 13 windings, respectively. The sum of these numbers equals 39, the numerical value of the Hebrew words "*YHVH echad*" (God is one).

Thus when looking at the fringes, one is constantly reminded of the fundamental Jewish principle of monotheism. Among Sephardic Jews, the pattern of windings is 10, 6, 5, 6, numbers that, respectively, represent the letters in "YHVH."

The Rabbis noted that the numerical value of the Hebrew word "tzitzit" (fringes) is 600. When combined with the eight threads and five knots on each fringe, this adds up to 613—the precise number of mitzvot in the Torah. Thus by looking at the fringes we are to "recall all the commandments of the Lord and observe them" (Num. 15:39).[9]

Customs

At weddings, a large tallit supported by four poles is often used as a *huppah*. It is customary for the bridegroom to dress in a tallit during the ceremony. Sephardic and German Jews traditionally wrap a tallit around the bride and groom under the *huppah* to symbolize their marital bond. An observant Jew is usually buried in his tallit, from which the *atarah* has been removed and the fringes taken off or torn so as to render it ritually invalid. This symbolizes that the obligations of Jewish law are no longer required of the person who is now deceased.

On Simchat Torah, all the children are called up to the Torah and sheltered under a large tallit. The reader recites the biblical blessing of Jacob over Joseph's sons Ephraim and Manasseh: "The angel who has redeemed me from all harm—bless the lads" (Gen. 48:16).[10]

Women have traditionally been exempt from the commandment to wear tzitzit. According to the Talmud, women are not required to observe laws that must be performed at a specific time of day (time-bound mitzvot), since their primary obligation is considered to be to their home and family. Because the tzitzit must be worn at a specific time—during daylight hours—the wearing of the tallit is not incumbent on women. Another explanation is that garments with four corners on which fringes were hung were originally considered to be male attire, and the Bible forbids a woman from wearing a man's clothing, and vice versa (Deut. 22:5). Nevertheless, some women are known to have worn *tallitot* during talmudic and later times. For example, Rabbi Judah ha-Nasi is described as having personally attached fringes to his wife's apron (Men. 43a). Maimonides maintained that a woman may wear tzitzit, but should not recite the blessing.[11] In Conservative and

Reform synagogues, some women have begun wearing *tallitot* for worship, either at their bat mitzvah or later as adults. Although *tallitot* for women are not specifically prohibited by Jewish law, many women feel uncomfortable wearing one.[12]

Tallit Katan

In addition to the tallit worn during morning prayer services, some traditional Jews also wear fringes on a *tallit katan* (little tallit), a light undergarment that is fitted over the neck and shoulders so that the tzitzit hang down and are visible throughout the daylight hours. Use of the *tallit katan*, also called *arba kanfot* (four corners), developed when it became awkward and inconvenient to wear an outer garment with fringes throughout the day, especially when changes in fashion or local custom dictated that clothes no longer always had four distinct corners.[13] Furthermore, wearing fringes on an inner garment shielded from view (i.e., not hanging down far enough to be seen) was a safer alternative in communities in which Jews were singled out for persecution.[14]

It is customary to put a *tallit katan* on a child only at age three, based on the verse, "man is like the tree of the field" (Deut. 20:19). Just as the fruit of a tree may not be eaten during its first three years (Lev. 19:23), so the child is considered too immature to wear a *tallit katan* until reaching that age.[15]

Tefillin (תְּפִלִּין)

Tefillin are two small black leather boxes that are bound by black leather straps to the forehead and arm. They contain parchments on which are written the four sets of biblical verses that mention the commandment to wear them as "a sign [*ot*] upon your hand and as frontlets [*totafot*] between your eyes"—Exodus 13:1–10 and 11–16, which speak of the redemption of the Children of Israel from Egypt; and Deuteronomy 6:4–9 and 11:13–21, the first two passages of the *Shema*, which express the Jewish belief in one God, the acceptance of divine kingship, the concept of reward and punishment, and the responsibility to observe all the commandments. The box on the forehead (*tefillin shel rosh*) contains four separate compartments, each with a parchment on which is written one passage; that on the arm (*tefillin shel yad*) has a single compartment containing a single piece of parchment on which all four passages are written.

The box on the forehead is known as *totafot*, which, according to Cassuto,[1] refers to mnemonic devices, aids to memory that were worn between the eyes so that a person might see them and remember something.[2] The Israelites were commanded to wear *totafot*, inscribed with words of the Torah, to constantly remind them of the Exodus from Egypt and the divine commandments. Kaufmann[3] suggested an earlier and more primitive origin, that the word "*totafot*" actually means "drops" (derived from the verb "*taftef*," to drip). He offered evidence that in ancient times, worshipers would put drops of blood from the Passover sacrifice (or other sacrifice) on their foreheads, on their hands, and on the doorposts of their houses as protection against plague and other ills. He contended that this was the origin of the Israelites sprinkling blood on the doorposts of their houses on the night the firstborn of Egypt were slain during the 10th plague.[4]

Originally worn all day and removed at night, tefillin now are worn only during each weekday morning service. They are not worn on the Sabbath or on festivals because, like the Sabbath (Exod. 31:17) and circumcision (Gen. 17:11), tefillin are a sign of the covenant between God and Israel, the divinely chosen people. Therefore, wearing tefillin would be considered superfluous because these days are also symbols of holiness. Moreover, just as Jewish law requires the testimony of two witnesses to convict someone of any offense, so a man requires two witnesses to attest to his Jewishness. On weekdays, the tefillin and circumcision fulfill that role. On the Sabbath, however, the day itself is the second witness, so that it is not necessary to wear tefillin (Abudraham).[5] The Talmud offers another explanation for not wearing tefillin at night or on Sabbaths and festivals, based on the verse, "And you shall therefore keep this ordinance (tefillin) in its season from day to day" (Men. 36b on Exod. 13:10). The word "day" excludes night, and the expression "from day to day" means not all days.[6] Tefillin also are not worn on the morning of Tisha b'Av (postponed to the afternoon service), by a bereaved person before burial, by a bridegroom on his wedding day (since he would not be able to concentrate properly on their meaning), in a cemetery (or other ritually unclean place), or while asleep. Although worn every day, tefillin have great sanctity and are respectfully kissed when put on and taken off. If the tefillin are dropped, some maintain that one should fast the whole day.[7]

Tefillin are put on after the tallit. First, the tefillin of the arm is wrapped in seven rings, coiled in a descending spiral around the person's weaker forearm (for most people, the left arm closest to the heart). These rings may symbolize the seven branches of the menorah, the seven Hebrew words in Psalm 145:16 (*Poteach et yadechah u-masbiah l'chol chai ratzon*; You open Your hand and satisfy the desire of every living thing), the seven benedictions recited at the marriage ceremony, the seven angels,[8] or the seven handmaidens selected from the household of Ahasuerus to serve Queen Esther (Esther 2:9).[9] One reason for wearing the tefillin on the weaker arm is that this commandment is immediately followed in the Torah by the one to "write them on the doorposts of your house (mezuzah)." This led the Rabbis to conclude that the hand that writes must be the same hand that wraps—the stronger hand. (Thus left-handed people wear the tefillin on their weaker right arm; Men. 37a.)

After the tefillin of the head is put on, three rings are wound around the middle finger and then around the back and palm of the hand, while reciting the verses from Hosea (2:21–22), in which the word "betrothal" is used three times in the description of Israel's spiritual engagement to God. Jews who follow the Sephardic and Hasidic practice wind the tefillin around the arm in an overhand (clockwise) fashion, whereas Ashkenazim use a counterclockwise motion.

The kabbalists added the practice of representing the word "שַׁדַּי" (*Shaddai*; Almighty) on both tefillin. The first letter "שׁ" (*shin*) is inscribed on the head tefillin as well as woven with the arm straps through the fingers of the hand. This letter is written on two sides of the tefillin of the head—one in the usual way with three strokes, and the other with four prongs. Some explanations for this practice are that it symbolizes the three Patriarchs (Abraham, Isaac, and Jacob) and the four Matriarchs (Sarah, Rebecca, Rachel, and Leah) and that the total number of prongs (seven) equals the windings of the arm strap (for other symbolic uses of seven, see p. 636).[10] The second letter "ד" (*dalet*) is represented by the knot at the back of the head strap and is woven on the hand; the third letter "י" (*yud*) is indicated by the end of the head strap and the knot near the tefillin of the arm.[11]

As an indication of the great importance of tefillin, the Talmud reported that even God wears them (Ber. 6a). The kabbalists believe that these divine tefillin are composed of the prayers (*tefillot*) of the Jewish people. "Whoever has the tefillin on his head, the tefillin on his arm, tzitzit on his garment, and the mezuzah on his doorpost is in absolute security against sinning" (Men. 43b), based on the verse, "A threefold cord [referring to the three precepts enumerated] is not readily broken" (Eccl. 4:12). According to Nachmanides, the tefillin on the arm is a symbol of God's power, as well as our determination to devote our hearts and might to the divine will. The tefillin on the head reflects our resolve to also dedicate our thoughts to God.[12] Maimonides noted that the presence of tefillin on one's head and arms ensures that "a man is modest and God-fearing, being drawn neither into laughter nor into idle talk—shunning all thoughts of evil and rather directing his heart to words of truth and righteousness."[13] For Abravanel, tefillin are visual reminders of the need to bind ourselves in dedication to God, so that we obey the divine commandments rather than follow our evil inclination.[14] Lau observes that tefillin relate to the three parts of the body that most characterize the individual—the head (intellect), arm (physical strength), and heart (opposite the tefillin of the arm and the seat of the emotions)—all of which must be used to fulfill God's wishes.[15]

The Hebrew word "*tefillah*" (the rarely used singular of "tefillin") is identical to the word for "prayer." Some commentators maintain that it derives from a root meaning "to separate," because the wearing of tefillin as part of their regular daily attire made Jewish men easily distinguishable from their non-Jewish neighbors. The Christian Bible disparagingly refers to them by the Greek word "phylacteries" (amulets), and some scholars have suggested that tefillin may originally have developed from some form of magical talisman or amulet.[16] Today, both Jews and gentiles use the word "phylacteries" as the English translation of tefillin, because the word has lost its historical associations with magic.

Boys have the obligation to put on ("lay") tefillin when they reach the age of bar mitzvah. Traditionally, this mitzvah has not been obligatory for women, based on the verse "so that the Teaching of the Lord may be in your mouth" (Exod. 13:9), in which tefillin are associated with the study of Torah, which the Rabbis did not consider a woman's obligation. However, according to a *baraita*, Michal, the daughter of Saul and wife of King David, "wore tefillin and the sages did not protest" (Er. 96a). Moreover, the daughters of the great medieval scholar Rashi also wore tefillin. In modern times, some women have begun to wear traditional tefillin or those of their own design.

Blessings and Benedictions (בְּרָכוֹת)

Brachot (blessings, benedictions) are the fundamental components of prayer. The word "*brachot*" (singular, *bracha*) comes from a verb meaning to "bow" or bend the "knee" (*berech*) and thus indicates an act of submission to God. The men of the Great Assembly—the leaders of the Jews during the Second Temple period—are traditionally considered the authors of the liturgical *brachot* (Ber. 33a). Under their influence, *brachot* such as the original 18 benedictions of the *Amidah* (see p. 421), the blessings before and after the *Shema* (see p. 419), and the first three blessings of the *Birkat ha-Mazon* (Grace after Meals; see p. 476) became the norm in most Jewish communities. The sequence of prayers and blessings was standardized under Rabban Gamaliel II at Yavneh at the end of the first century C.E. However, the precise wording of individual *brachot* and their basic requirements were fixed only during the talmudic period. Rav stated that a benediction must contain the name of God, and Rabbi Yochanan declared that a benediction must proclaim God's kingship (Ber. 40b).

Types of Blessings and Basic Formulas

Maimonides classified the blessings into three categories: (1) those recited before "experiences of enjoyment," such as food and drink; (2) those recited for the privilege of performing religious commandments, such as hearing the shofar, wearing the tallit, and kindling the Sabbath lights; and (3) those that "express petition, thanksgiving, or praise" in public or private worship, such as Grace after Meals.[1] Each of these types of blessing has its own formula and structure.

All *brachot* open with the words "בָּרוּךְ אַתָּה יהוה" (*Baruch ata Adonai*; Praised are You, O Lord). When the blessing occurs at the beginning of a prayer, the words "אֱלֹהֵינוּ מֶלֶךְ הָעוֹלָם" (*Eloheinu melekh ha-olam*; our God, King of the Universe) are added. There are four basic formulas of *brachot*. The simplest is the "short" blessing for experiences of enjoyment, which opens "*Baruch ata Adonai, Eloheinu melekh ha-olam*" and concludes with a reference to the experience that called for the blessing. Thus in the blessing over bread one adds *"ha-motzi lechem min ha-aretz"* (Who brings forth bread from the earth); for wine, the blessing concludes *"borei peri ha-gafen"* (Who creates the fruit of the vine).

Blessings for the privilege of performing religious commandments open with an expanded formula: *"Baruch ata Adonai, Eloheinu melekh ha-olam, asher kid'shanu b'mitzvotav v'tzivanu"* (אֲשֶׁר קִדְּשָׁנוּ בְּמִצְוֹתָיו וְצִוָּנוּ; Who has sanctified us with His commandments and commanded us to ...). They conclude with the specific mitzvah that is about to be performed. Thus when lighting the candles on Friday night one adds *"le-hadlik ner shel Shabbat"* (to kindle the Sabbath lights). When a mitzvah is performed for the first time in the year, one adds the *Shehecheyanu* blessing ("Who has kept us alive and preserved us and enabled us to reach this season"; see p. 479).

Not every mitzvah requires a preceding blessing. As a general rule, no blessing is recited before mitzvot that:

- Do not involve an action (e.g., the negative commandments).
- May be refused by the intended recipient (and thus the blessing would have been recited in vain).[2]
- May be observed only in unfortunate situations (e.g., divorce) or involve a violation of the law (e.g., eating forbidden foods, returning stolen property).
- Involve the misfortune and suffering of others and are expected to be performed even by non-Jews (e.g., giving charity, visiting the sick, and comforting the mourner).[3]

The two forms of blessings expressing petition, thanksgiving, or praise are the essential prayers of public and private worship. If there is a single blessing, the body of the prayer is framed by the two benediction formulas—*"Baruch ata Adonai, Eloheinu melekh ha-olam"* at the start of the blessing and *"Baruch ata Adonai..."* at the end. When there is a series of blessings, however, the opening formula is used only for the first blessing, though the conclusion of each blessing has the usual benediction style. For example, the evening service opens with two blessings preceding the *Shema*. The first blessing begins with the standard "Praised are You, O Lord our God, King of the Universe (Who at Your word brings on the evening twilight)" and ends with the usual formula, "Praised are You, O Lord (Who brings on the evening twilight)."

However, the second blessing starts immediately "With everlasting love," without any benediction formula, though it ends in the conventional manner, "Praised are You, O Lord (Who loves Your people Israel)." In the siddur, most of the obligatory prayers—such as the *Amidah* and the benedictions preceding and following the *Shema*—consist of a series of blessings, in which the benediction formula is used only as a conclusion.

Brachot are essentially statements of thanksgiving for all that God has provided us, the opportunity to experience the manifestations of the Divine in nature, and the privilege of performing the mitzvot.[4] In view of the myriad examples of the workings of God around us, the pious Jew recites numerous blessings. Indeed, Rabbi Meir declared that it is the duty of every Jew to recite 100 benedictions daily (Men. 43b). He supported his statement with the verse, "And now, O Israel, what (*mah*) does the Lord your God demand of you?" (Deut. 10:12). Rabbi Meir offered this verse as a mnemonic, since the word "*mah*" is close in pronunciation to the word "*me'ah*," meaning "100." Another tradition relates Rabbi Meir's assertion to the legend that by uttering exactly 100 blessings daily, King David was able to end the mysterious epidemic that was killing 100 of his men every day. As a proof text for this otherwise unknown episode, Natronai Gaon suggested the verse, "The utterance of David son of Jesse, [and] the utterance of the man set on high" (2 Sam. 23:1). The last three words in Hebrew are "*hukam ol*," and *ol* (עֹל) has the numerical value of 100 (ע = 70; ל = 30). Therefore, the meaning of the biblical phrase is that 100 men were "saved" (lit., "were raised up") from the grave.[5] Rokeach[6] maintained that the 100 blessings counteract the same number of curses in Deuteronomy (28:15–61; *tochechah*), the divine punishment for failing to faithfully obey the commandments.[7]

The Midrash emphasizes the presence of an apparently superfluous pronoun in the verse "When any of you (*mi-kem*) presents an offering of cattle to the Lord" (Lev. 1:2). It concludes that the biblical text includes the word "*mi-kem*" to teach that whoever fulfills the obligation to recite 100 blessings each day is considered as if he or she offered a sacrifice, based on the fact that the numerical equivalent of the word "מִכֶּם" is 100 (מ = 40; כ = 20; ם = 40).[8] On weekdays, when the *Amidah* and its 18 (or 19) blessings are recited three times, there is no problem achieving this goal. However, this does present a problem on Sabbaths and festivals, when the *Amidah* contains only seven blessings. Rabbi Chiya ben Rav was reported to have succeeded in reciting 100 blessings on these days by using an ingenious technique—smelling various spices and eating different types of food (and reciting the appropriate blessing for each).[9]

Max Kadushin coined the term "normal mysticism" to describe the Jewish preoccupation with reciting blessings as part of everyday existence. Unlike those few individuals generally labeled as "mystics," who attempt to achieve an intimate sensory experience of God, most people cannot dream of ever reaching such lofty spiritual heights, let alone sustaining it on a regular basis. Therefore, the Rabbis wisely developed myriad blessings to accompany the ordinary moments of daily life, enabling average Jews to transform both usual and unusual activities into experiences of the Divine Presence.[10]

The Rabbis formulated blessings for practically every aspect of human existence from common experiences of daily life (rising from sleep, dressing, eating, drinking) to unusual occurrences (escaping from danger, recovering from illness, seeing some marvelous natural event such as lightning or a comet).[11]

Examples of Blessings Recited in Specific Situations

Fragrant scents

- Smelling spices—*borei minei vesamim* (Who creates various kinds of fragrant spices).
- Smelling trees, shrubs, or flowers—*borei atzei vesamim* (Who creates fragrant trees).
- Smelling herbs or grasses—*borei isvei vesamim* (Who creates fragrant herbs).
- Smelling fruits or nuts—*ha-notein rei'ach tov ba-peirot* (Who gives a good scent to fruits).

Natural phenomena

- Seeing lightning, a comet, high mountains, a volcano, a great desert, a waterfall, a glacier, or a massive canyon (events that engender a feeling of awe and amazement)—*oseh ma-aseh vereishit* (Who makes the works of Creation).
- Hearing thunder, witnessing a hurricane, or experiencing an earthquake—*she-kocho u-gevurato malei olam* (Whose strength and power fill the universe).

Seeing a rainbow—*zocheir ha-brit, v'ne'eman bivrito, v'kayam b'-ma'amaro* (Who remembers the covenant, is faithful to His covenant, and fulfills His word).

Seeing an ocean (after an interval of a month)—*she-asah et ha-yam ha-gadol* (Who made the great sea).

Seeing an exceptionally beautiful person, tree, or field—*she-kacha lo ba-olamo* (Who has such in His universe).

Seeing an exceptionally strange-looking person or animal—*mi-shaneh ha-bri'ot* (Who makes the creatures different).

Seeing an outstanding Torah scholar—*she-chalak mei-chochmato lirei'av* (Who has shared His knowledge with those who fear Him).

Seeing an outstanding secular scholar—*she-natan mei-chochmato l'vasar va-dam* (Who has given of His wisdom to flesh and blood).

Passing by a place where oneself (or parents, ancestors, Torah teacher, or the nation as a whole) was miraculously saved from imminent danger—*she-asah ... nes b'makom hazeh* (Who has performed a miracle for ... in this place).[13]

Escaping grave danger or illness (see p. 480)—*ha-gomel la-chayavim tovot, she-gemalani kol tov* (Who grants favor to the unworthy; Who has granted me everything good).

Putting on a new garment of significant value—*malbish arumim* (Who clothes the naked).

For a variety of "new things" (see p. 479)—*shehecheyanu v'kiy'-manu v'higiyanu laz'man hazeh* (Who has kept us alive, sustained us, and brought us to this season).[12]

The Talmud observed that "it is incumbent on man to bless [God] for the evil in the same way as for the good" (Ber. 54a). The blessing "*ha-tov v'ha-meitiv*" (Who is good and does good) is recited upon hearing good news that benefits both oneself and others, whereas the pious Jew praises God as "*dayyan emet*" (the true judge) even when receiving unusually bad news. As Rabbi Akiva noted (Ber. 60b), a person should always say, "Whatever the All-Merciful does is for good." Once Rabbi Akiva came to a certain town and looked for lodgings but was everywhere refused. Consequently, "he went and spent the night in the open field. He had with him a cock, an ass, and a lamp. A gust of wind came and blew out the lamp, a weasel came and ate the cock, a lion came and ate the ass. He said: 'Whatever the All-Merciful does is for good.'" Later Rabbi Akiva learned that on the same night some robbers came and carried off the inhabitants of the town!

The repeated blessings make the Jew continually aware of what God has graciously provided, turning the routine actions and occurrences of daily life into religious experiences. Life becomes a "spiritual adventure" or, as described by the Rabbis, "a partnership with God in the achievement of the divine goal of turning the world of men into the kingdom of God."[14]

The word *"baruch"* is translated as "blessed" or "praised," though this can give the mistaken impression that we mortals are somehow blessing or praising God for having brought about that which is mentioned in the remainder of the blessing. According to *Sefer ha-Hinnukh*, since all honor, wisdom, and blessing exist only within God, it is the height of human arrogance to think that these divine qualities are somehow increased by our prayers. Therefore, the word *"baruch"* should be considered as merely describing the manifestations of God. When we extol God as *"El rachum v'chanun"* (a merciful and compassionate God), in effect we are only referring to God as *El baruch*—a blessed God (i.e., from Whom all blessings [of mercy and compassion] flow). Thus the underlying meaning of *"Baruch ata Adonai"* is that God is the source of all blessings. This concept is supported by a midrash, in which the word *"bracha"* (blessing) is related to *"bereichah,"* a "spring" or a "natural pool" (Ber. R. 39).[15]

The way in which God is addressed and described in *brachot* was the subject of a rabbinic controversy that resulted in a grammatical inconsistency. In the third century C.E., Rav maintained that a blessing should begin with the words *"Baruch ata,"* speaking of God in the second person as "You." His contemporary, Samuel, thought this too familiar for the relationship between mere mortals and the Divine. The sages ruled in favor of Rav, but decided to combine both opinions in what became the approved formula. The opening of every blessing stresses the nearness of God to each worshiper by addressing God as "You," and as God is similarly referred to in other prayers as "our Father," who is merciful and compassionate toward His creations. However, as soon as the blessing refers to God as the more distant and unapproachable *"melekh ha-olam"* (king of the universe), we become more formal and respectful. The remainder of the every blessing switches into the third person, as in "Who has sanctified us by His commandments" and "Who creates the fruit of the vine."[16]

This seeming paradox is a typical example of the Jewish use of complementary polar opposites, two statements that would be mutually exclusive when applied to human beings or to the natural world but are perfectly reasonable when describing the attributes of God. According to Abudarham, the use of both the second- and third-person forms alludes to the revealed and hidden aspects of God. We use the more familiar second person to relate to the God who is revealed to humans by the many divine creations and wondrous deeds as well as to the God who provides continuing care and concern for the affairs of individuals and nations. The more formal third person is used when we attempt, however unsuccessfully, to describe the essential nature of God, which must by definition remain hidden and unattainable to mortal beings.[17]

Amen (אָמֵן)

Amen is an ancient response of affirmation that originated in the Torah and has now become a word in almost every language. As early as Deuteronomy (27:15–26), the Levites pronounced a series of solemn dooms for extreme transgressions to which the people responded "amen." When King David brought the ark to Jerusalem, "all the people said 'Amen' and 'Praise the Lord' when hearing the blessing, 'Blessed is the Lord, God of Israel, from eternity to eternity' (1 Chron.16:36)."[1] Amen was also the response to the songs chanted by the Levites during Second Temple times and to all prayers and blessings in the liturgy of the early synagogues.

Saying "amen" affirms agreement that what another has said is the truth. Maimonides observed that by saying "amen," the worshiper is considered as having actually recited the prayer or blessing.[2] When said after a petitionary prayer, "amen" is the equivalent of "so may it be."[3]

According to the Talmud (Shab. 119b), "amen" is an acronym for "אֵל מֶלֶךְ נֶאֱמָן" (*El melekh ne'eman*; God, the faithful king), the same phrase that precedes the reading of the *Shema* when recited in the absence of a minyan (see p. 372). As such, "amen" acknowledges acceptance of the yoke of the divine kingdom (*ol malkhut shaddai*).

Since most congregants were unfamiliar with the text of the prayers during Temple and talmudic times, responding "amen" was the primary way for them to participate in the service. Moreover, the format of public worship at the time generally consisted of a prayer leader who spoke the words while the others merely offered the response. Indeed, the Rabbis deemed that saying "amen" was equivalent or even superior to the blessing that it was affirming (Ber. 53b). Even when printed prayer books became widely available, enabling most worshipers to recite the prayers for themselves, synagogues retained the spiritually powerful congregational responses of "amen" during the repetition of the *Amidah*.[4]

According to *halakhah*, an individual who hears another recite a blessing is required to respond "amen." When the person reciting the blessing mentions the name of God, it is customary to say "*Baruch Hu, u-varuch Shemo*" (Praised is He, and praised is His name; see p. 408). However, a person should not say "amen" after a blessing that he or she has personally recited (Ber. 45b). This prohibition may have been a reaction to the Christian custom of concluding every prayer with the word "amen." Nevertheless, Sephardim permit the prayer leader to say "amen" at the end of major sections of the service—after *Yishtabach* (the close of *Pesukei de-Zimra*; see p. 411) and the *Amidah* (Who blesses His people with peace)—and after the third blessing of the Grace after Meals (Who rebuilds Jerusalem), which in early times was the conclusion of the *Birkat ha-Mazon*. Only the last of these is allowed in the Ashkenazic ritual.[5] During certain prayers, including the *Kaddish*, the leader introduces the communal response with "*v'imru* [and say] amen" or "*v'nomar* [and let us say] amen."

Numerous rules are given concerning how "amen" should be recited. The Talmud indicates that it must be said with a strong clear voice, but not in a louder tone than the blessing itself (Ber. 45a), based on the verse "Exalt the Lord with me, let us extol His Name together" (Ps. 34:4). The word should be pronounced only after the preceding blessing has been completed. It is forbidden to respond "amen" to a blessing that is unnecessary and thus takes the name of the Lord in vain, but it may be said when hearing a blessing recited by a non-Jew. A person should not say "amen" if he or she did not actually hear the blessing or know what it was, lest it be an "orphaned amen" without a "parent" blessing (Ber. 47a). However, it is permitted to join the congregation in saying "amen" if one knows the blessing to which the worshipers are responding. According to contemporary authorities, one should not say "amen" after hearing a blessing on radio, television, or a recording.[6]

Kaddish (קַדִּישׁ)

The *Kaddish*, which now closes every public service as well as the individual sections within it, was originally not even a part of the synagogue ritual. Instead, it was the formal dismissal that was recited by the preacher or teacher at the conclusion of a discourse on the Torah. Addressed to the assembly in the Aramaic vernacular, the *Kaddish* proclaimed God's greatness and holiness and expressed the hope for the speedy establishment of the divine kingdom on earth. The congregation enthusiastically replied with the words *"Y'hei shmei rabba mevorach, l'olam u-l'olmei almaya"* (May the great name of God be praised forever and unto all eternity). This response, similar to one that had been used in the Temple ritual, became viewed as the essential element of the prayer.[1]

The ancient custom of dismissing the assembly with the words of the *Kaddish* is still preserved in the *Kaddish de-Rabbanan* (*Kaddish* of the Rabbis), which is recited in the synagogue after communal study. However, instead of being uttered by the teacher, the *Kaddish de-Rabbanan* is now recited by those mourners who are in attendance. This custom developed out of the practice of honoring a deceased scholar, at the close of the seven-day shivah period (see p. 95), with a learned discourse delivered at the house of mourning. However, the absence of such an event at the end of the mourning period could be popularly interpreted as a denigration of the intellectual abilities of the deceased. To prevent the possibility of public embarrassment, the Rabbis ruled that a discourse be delivered, or a religious text studied, during the mourning period of every deceased Jew.[2]

Many Jews think of the *Kaddish* as the mourner's prayer, even though it contains no mention of death. Indeed, the practice of mourners reciting the *Kaddish* probably began during the 13th century, a time when Jews in Germany were suffering severe persecutions at the hands of the Crusaders. Scholars believe its origin may be related to a late aggadic legend that Rabbi Akiva rescued a soul from eternal punishment in hell by teaching the son of the departed to recite the *Kaddish* at a congregational service. Widespread belief in the efficacy of this practice led to children reciting the *Kaddish* for their parents during the year after burial (and later on the yahrzeit, the anniversary of the death). In actuality, mourners recite the *Kaddish* for only 11 months, based on a talmudic statement implying that only the wicked are judged in purgatory for a full 12 months—and no child would want to designate his or her parents as wicked (Shab. 152b). Initially, the *Mourner's Kaddish* was recited only in the house of mourning after a study period. However, since Torah study is regarded as divine worship in Judaism, it became traditional to also recite the *Mourner's Kaddish* after every section of public prayer in the synagogue, and eventually at several other designated places in the service.[3]

The mystical belief in the value of the *Kaddish* for redeeming the deceased at the time of divine judgment has been attacked by the rationalists of the modern age. Thus the current justification for reciting the *Kaddish* is that mourners rise to bear public witness to their faith in God, as did Job (1:21) who, after the loss of his loved ones, declared, "The Lord has given, and the Lord has taken away; blessed be the name of the Lord."[4] As the Talmud noted, "it is incumbent on man to bless [God] for the evil in the same way as for the good" (Ber. 54a).

The *Kaddish* is first mentioned as part of the prescribed synagogue daily prayers in about the sixth century C.E. (Sof. 10:7). Subsequently, two Hebrew verses were added for those who did not speak Aramaic—the explanatory passage "*Yitbarach v'yishtabach*" (blessed and praised) following the congregational response, and the concluding passage "*Oseh shalom bim'romav*" (He who creates peace above).

There are four main types of *Kaddish* in the synagogue ritual. The simplest is the so-called "half" *Kaddish* (*Hatzi Kaddish*), which is recited by the prayer leader after each subdivision of the service. In the morning, it is said after the introductory psalms (*Pesukei de-Zimra*), the *Amidah* (or *Tachanun*, when that is said), and the Torah reading. The "full" *Kaddish* (*Kaddish Shalem*) is recited by the prayer leader after the *Amidah* and virtually concludes each service. It contains a special verse beginning with the word "*titkabeil*" (let be accepted [the prayers and supplications of the whole house of Israel by their father in Heaven; and let us say "amen"]) as well as two prayers for peace. In the *Kaddish de-Rabbanan*, the *titkabeil* verse is replaced by several lines praying for the teachers of Israel, their disciples, and all who study the Torah. The *Mourner's Kaddish* (*Kaddish Yatom*; lit.,"orphan's *Kaddish*"), which contains the full text except for the *titkabeil* verse, is recited after the *Aleinu* at the end of each service and may be repeated after the reading of additional psalms. It is also said in the morning service at the beginning of *Pesukei de-Zimra*, just before *Baruch she-Amar*.

The congregational response, *Y'hei shmei rabba mevorach*, is the fundamental core of the *Kaddish*. The Talmud reports the declaration of a third-century sage: "He who responds, 'Amen! May His great name be praised' with all his might [absolute devotion], his decreed sentence [if Heaven has decreed evil for him] is torn up" (Shab. 119b). Another Rabbi stated: "If one answers [in a dream] *Y'hei shmei rabba mevorach*, he is assured of a share in the world to come" (Ber. 57a).[5] As the Talmud further notes, "Whenever the Israelites go into the synagogues and schoolhouses and respond, 'May His great name be praised!' the Holy One, blessed be He, shakes His head and says, 'Happy is the king who is thus praised in this house!'" (Ber. 3a).

According to the mystics, the Talmud attaches such great importance to the utterance of the congregational response in the *Kaddish* because, in Aramaic, it contains seven words composed of 28 letters—corresponding to the number of words and letters in the first verse in Genesis. Therefore, one who responds to the *Kaddish* with these words effectively becomes the partner of God in the Creation of the world.[6]

The *Machzor Vitry* has a striking interpretation of the congregational response to the *Kaddish* based on the phrase "*kes YH*" (throne of the Lord) used in the Torah portion dealing with the ongoing struggle between God and Amalek (Exod. 17:16). The Rabbis had observed that these words were "defective," with letters missing (it should read *kisei YHVH*), implying that God's sovereignty is not complete as long as the forces of evil (Amalek) are still at work in the world (Tanh. Ki Tetse). According to the *Machzor Vitry*, instead of the first three words of the congregational response to the *Kaddish* (*Y'hei shmei rabba*) being translated as "May the great name of the Lord," it should be "May the name of God be made great," indicating the fervent wish of Jews that their actions can overcome earthly evil and hasten the time when all the inhabitants of the globe will recognize the divine sovereignty so that, as said in the *Aleinu* prayer, "in that day shall the Lord be One and His Name One" (Zech. 14:9).[7]

Early versions of the *Kaddish*, such as those by Maimonides and Abudraham, add the phrase "*v'yatzmach purkanei v'kareiv m'shichei*" (and cause His salvation to sprout and bring near His Messiah) after the words *"v'yamlich malchutei"* (and may He establish His kingship). This continuation of the prayer for God's kingship, which is generally included by Sephardim and many Hasidic groups, has been omitted by Ashkenazim, who feel that both salvation and the Messiah are indispensable elements of the future kingdom of God and thus need not be explicitly noted.[8]

The *Kaddish* contains 10 expressions of praise—the first two words (*yitgadal v'yitkadash*) and the eight words from *"yitbarach"* to *"v'yithalal."* These may allude to the "10 utterances" with which God created the universe (Avot 5:1) and the Ten Commandments, implying that the world was fashioned as a place for human beings to perform mitzvot and thus give meaning to the divine Creation. The praises of the *Kaddish* are divided into sets of two and eight just as were the Ten Commandments—the first two given directly by God to Israel, the last eight proclaimed by Moses. The 10 praises also may relate to the *sefirot*, the mystical emanations of the Divine.[9]

As a public sanctification of the name of God (*kiddush ha-Shem*), the *Kaddish* is recited only in the presence of a minyan (Ber. 21b; Meg. 23b). The person saying *Kaddish* always stands, though traditions vary as to what other worshipers do. Formerly, only one person at a time recited the *Kaddish*. If there were several mourners, each said the prayer in turn. Today, in virtually all congregations all mourners rise and recite the *Kaddish* in unison.[10]

Daily and Sabbath Prayers

Daily Order of Prayers

Daily Jewish worship consists of three services—*Shacharit* (morning), *Mincha* (afternoon), and *Ma'ariv* (evening)—based on the biblical verse, "Evening and morning and at noon will I pray and cry aloud, and He shall hear my voice" (Ps. 55:18). They also correspond to the daily offerings (*Tamid*) brought in the morning and toward dusk, as well as the flesh of sacrifices burnt on the altar during the night hours. On the Sabbath and holy days (including Rosh Hodesh), a *Musaf* (additional) service immediately follows *Shacharit*. On Friday evening, the *Kabbalat Shabbat* (welcoming the Sabbath) precedes *Ma'ariv*. The core of every service is the *Amidah*, which is read silently by each individual and then repeated out loud by the *shaliach tzibbur* (leader of the service; lit., "representative of the community"). Because there was a controversy among the Rabbis as to the status of the *Ma'ariv* service, since there were no evening sacrifices in the Temple, the *Amidah* is not recited aloud at that time. During the *Ma'ariv* and *Shacharit* services, the *Shema* with its preceding and concluding blessings is recited immediately before the *Amidah*.[1]

The *Shacharit* service is the longest and most complex of the daily prayers. It is preceded by two preliminary services—*Birchot ha-Shachar* (Morning Blessings) and *Pesukei de-Zimra* (Verses of Song). The former contains blessings of thanksgiving relating to everyday matters, the gift of life, and the privilege of serving God as Jews. The latter is a collection of biblical prayers, many from the Book of Psalms, in which the worshiper praises God as the Creator of the world and everything within it and acknowledges the lovingkindness and redemptive acts that God has shown to our ancestors throughout history. The *Mincha* service has a very brief introduction, composed primarily of the *Ashrei*, which is also recited twice during the morning service. *Tachanun* (prayers of supplication) is recited on weekdays following the *Amidah* of the *Shacharit* and *Mincha* services. The *Kaddish* separates the different sections of the service. In the morning, it is recited at the end of *Pesukei de-Zimra* and after the *Shacharit* service; on Sabbath and holiday mornings, the *Kaddish* is also recited after the Torah reading and following the *Musaf* service. The Torah is read after the *Shacharit Amidah* on Mondays, Thursdays, Sabbaths, and festivals. This is followed by the reading of the haftarah on Sabbaths and festivals. On certain festivals, *Hallel* (Psalms of praise) is inserted between the *Shacharit Amidah* and the Torah reading. Every service concludes with *Aleinu* and the *Mourner's Kaddish*.[2]

Each component or service is discussed separately in subsequent sections.

General Outline of the Services

Shacharit (Morning service; שַׁחֲרִית)
- *Birchot ha-Shachar*
- *Pesukei de-Zimra*
- *Shema* (with two blessings before and one after)
- *Amidah*
- *Tachanun* (not on Sabbath, festivals, fast days, and other occasions)
- Torah reading (only on Monday, Thursday, Sabbath, festivals, and Rosh Hodesh)
- Haftarah (only on Sabbath and festivals)
- *Musaf* (only on Sabbath, festivals, and Rosh Hodesh)
- *Aleinu*
- *Mourner's Kaddish*
- Closing hymn

Mincha (afternoon service; מִנְחָה)
- *Ashrei*
- *U'va le-Zion Goel* (only on Sabbath and festivals)
- *Amidah*
- *Tachanun* (not on Sabbath, festivals, fast days, and other occasions)
- Torah reading (only on Sabbath and fast days)
- *Aleinu*
- *Mourner's Kaddish*

Ma'ariv (Evening service; מַעֲרִיב)
- Short reading from Psalms
- *Shema* (with two blessings before and two after)
- *Amidah*
- *Aleinu*
- *Mourner's Kaddish*

Morning Blessings (*Birchot ha-Shachar*; בִּרְכּוֹת הַשַּׁחַר)

Birchot ha-Shachar (Morning blessings) is the initial prayer section of the morning service. It contains a greater variety of prayers, blessings, and Torah study than any other part of the siddur. Many of the prayers and blessings were intended to be said privately at home before one attends the synagogue service; they were recited with each act of rising and getting ready for the day's work. However, they became widely neglected because many Jews did not know the blessings by heart and, as part of the Oral Law, it was forbidden to write them down. Therefore, the Rabbis decided to transfer these morning blessings to the beginning of the synagogue service; the prayer leader recited them aloud to provide an opportunity for the less knowledgeable to hear them and respond with the traditional "amen".[1]

Ashkenazim recite a special prayer, *Mah Tovu* (see p. 406), upon entering the synagogue in the morning. Its name derives from the initial words of the verse, "How fair [are your tents, O Jacob, your dwellings, O Israel"] (Num. 24:5)[2]; the sages interpreted the "tents" as referring to synagogues and schools, thus making this verse an appropriate opening to the public worship service. The remainder of the prayer consists of four verses from Psalms (5:8, 26:8, 95:6, 69:14). Sephardic Jews recite Psalm 5:8 on entering the synagogue and Psalm 5:9 on leaving.

The first of the morning blessings—after the *Modeh Ani*, which is said immediately upon waking up (see p. 473)—is for washing the hands (*al netilat yadayim*). This rabbinic commandment applies both when arising in the morning and before eating a meal. Washing the hands is not merely for sanitary purposes but also symbolizes the removal of ritual impurity to produce spiritual cleanliness, as with the requirement that the *Kohanim* wash their hands (and feet) before beginning the daily ritual in the ancient Temple service (Exod. 30:20). This blessing is not recited aloud by the prayer leader in the synagogue.[3]

After putting on the tallit (see p. 377) and donning the tefillin (see p. 382) on weekdays, the hymn *Adon Olam* (Master of the universe; see p. 471) is recited to reassert our faith in an omnipotent God who we unequivocally believe will provide for us and safeguard us from danger, both when we sleep and while we are awake.[4] The following blessing, *Asher yatzar* (Who fashioned [humans with wisdom]), extols God for creating human beings and is said privately by each worshiper before the start of the service. This blessing may be understood as praising God both for giving human beings the gift of wisdom and for using wisdom when creating men and women to produce the incredibly intricate and delicately balanced mechanism that is the human body and the house of the human soul.[5]

Every Jew is obliged to study Torah each day. According to the Rabbis, this study should be divided into three parts: Bible, Mishnah, and Gemara (Kid. 30a). However, observing the divine commandment to study Torah was a difficult task for those who were either extremely busy or unlearned. The solution to this problem was to integrate study passages from the Torah and Talmud into the synagogue service.[6] Customs varied in the Land of Israel and in Babylonia regarding which sections were incorporated into the prayer service, and as is generally the case, the rabbinic decision was to include both.

The first set of readings is short and consists of the Priestly Blessing (Num. 6:24–26; see p. 432) and selections from the Mishnah (Pe'ah 1:1) and the Gemara (Shab. 127a). The talmudic passages deal with various ethical duties, including obligations to the poor, honoring parents, visiting the sick, dowering the bride, accompanying the dead to the grave, and above all, studying the Torah (which is said to be equal to all of them).

Because the study of Torah is a religious obligation, it must be preceded by an appropriate blessing. Consequently, three blessings, corresponding to the three areas of study, are pronounced at the beginning of the daily morning prayer. The first praises God for granting Israel the privilege and obligation of studying Torah, the second is a prayer that the study of Torah be pleasant and eagerly pursued by one's children and the entire House of Israel, and the third is identical to the blessing recited before the Torah reading in the synagogue service (see p. 448). The daily recitation of these blessings and the appropriate selections from Scripture and the Talmud, though hardly qualifying as

"Torah study," was sufficient to satisfy the conscience and religious obligation of those who had neither the time nor the ability to engage in intensive textual analysis.[7]

The blessings and brief study of the Torah are followed by *Elohai neshamah* (My God, the soul [You placed within me is pure]). This prayer expresses gratitude to God for graciously restoring our souls when we awake. The Rabbis had drawn a parallel between death and sleep—"sleep constitutes 1/60 of death" (Ber. 57b)—observing that the human soul is not functional when asleep and becomes reactivated only upon wakening. *Elohai neshamah* boldly asserts that our daily reawakening anticipates the return of our souls in the world to come. In stark contrast to the Christian concept of human beings being born in original sin, this prayer stresses the Jewish belief that "just as God is pure, so the soul [of man] is pure" (Ber. 10a).[8]

Although not read in all congregations, most prayer books include the biblical narrative of *Akedat Yitzhak* (Binding of Isaac; Gen. 22:1–19). The command to sacrifice his beloved son and sole heir was the 10th trial of Abraham's faith in God, the final proof of his worthiness to be the founder of the Jewish people. As the Zohar observed, reciting the willingness of Abraham and Isaac to put their devotion to God ahead of life itself can elicit divine compassion whenever Jewish lives are in danger.[9]

The second Torah study unit is far longer and is now found toward the end of *Birchot ha-Shachar*. It is preceded by an abbreviated *Shema*, which originally was said privately at home so as to circumvent the effect of a fifth-century Persian decree proscribing its recitation in the morning service in the synagogue (see p. 417). The Torah and Mishnah selections in Orthodox *siddurim* consist of lengthy excerpts that describe the daily sacrificial ritual at the Temple in Jerusalem; these passages do not appear in prayer books of the Conservative movement.

Because the Rabbis considered reading about the Temple ritual as equivalent to actual participation in the sacrificial worship (Meg. 31b), this enabled the pious Jew to fulfill the duty of Temple worship before beginning the main morning prayer service of the *Shema* and the *Amidah*.[10] Beit Yosef maintains that chapter 5 of *Zevakhim* is read to symbolize the worshiper's desire for peace, since it is the only chapter of the Mishnah that does not record any controversy or differences of opinion among the sages. For the Gemara passage, there is a midrash (whose analysis is equivalent to Gemara) that begins "Rabbi Ishmael says" and summarizes the 13 rules of exegesis used by the oral tradition to explicate the Torah.[11] This passage is actually a *baraita* (see p. 500) that introduces the *Sifra*, a midrashic work interpreting the Book of Leviticus that primarily relates to the Temple ritual. As such, it is most appropriate for this concluding portion of the preliminary service.[12] These interpretive rules were added to the prayer service during the time of Saadiah Gaon (10th century) to counteract the contentions of the Karaites, who denied the authority of the Oral Law.[13]

Preliminary Morning Blessings

The Talmud lists a series of 15 preliminary morning blessings that one should say upon arising (Ber. 60b):

Who has given the rooster intelligence [i.e., given the heart understanding] to distinguish between day and night
(*asher natan la'sechvi vinah l'havchin bein yom u-vein lailah*).
Who did not make me a gentile (*she-lo asani goy*).
Who did not make me a slave (*she-lo asani aved*).
[Men] Who did not make me a woman (*she-lo asani ishah*).
[Women] Who made me according to His will (*she-asani kirtzono*).
Who gives sight to the blind (*poke'ach ivrim*).
Who clothes the naked (*malbish arumim*).
Who releases the bound (*matir asurim*).
Who straightens the bent (*zokeif k'fufim*).
Who spreads out the earth upon the waters (*roka ha-aretz al ha-mayim*).
Who has provided me my every need (*she-asah li kol tzorki*).
Who firms man's footsteps (*ha-meichin mitzadei gaver*).
Who girds Israel with strength (*ozeir Yisrael big'vurah*).
Who crowns Israel with splendor (*oteir Yisrael b'tifarah*).
Who gives strength to the weary (*ha-notein la-ya'eif ko'ach*).
Who removes sleep from my eyes and slumber from my eyelids
(*ha-ma'avir sheinah mei-einai u-tenumah mei-afapai*).

Each begins with the standard formula for a blessing—"Praised are You, Lord our God, King of the universe"—and concludes with a specific instance of the divine role of God in all one does in life and in the satisfaction of every human need. For example, thanking God for giving "the rooster intelligence to distinguish between day and night" (Job 38:36) not only refers to awakening the person from sleep (from the crowing of the rooster) but also is an indirect expression of gratitude for the daily "restoration" of our hearing. Giving "sight to the blind" (Ps. 146:8) relates both to the physical act of opening our eyes when we awake and to God granting us the gift of intelligence to properly utilize the knowledge we have acquired. God is praised for "releasing the bound" (Ps. 146:7) and "raising up those who are bowed down" (Ps. 146:8), which, respectively, refer to our ability to stretch limbs that were motionless while asleep (restrained, if not bound) and to rise and stand erect on the solid earth that God created for the dominion of human beings. "Clothing the naked" not only relates to getting dressed but also alludes to God having mercifully clothed Adam and Eve (Gen. 3:7) and the mitzvah of providing clothing for the needy (Sot. 14a). "Firms man's footsteps" (Ps. 37:23) and "has provided me with every need" refer to donning shoes and giving people the ability to earn a livelihood. "Girds Israel with strength" not only refers to the physical waist belt, in which weapons were placed for protection, but also is a symbol of the preservation of moral discipline that requires dividing the upper part of the body (spirit) from the lower (lust). "Crowns Israel with splendor" could refer to wearing a head covering (see p. 374), symbolizing the humble recognition of God "above," or be an allusion to the tefillin (see p. 382). Finally, "gives strength to the weary" (Isa. 40:29) and "removes sleep from my eyes and slumber from my eyelids" are concluding references to the passing of nighttime exhaustion and the ability to face the new day with a refreshed body and spirit.[14]

The other traditional blessings in this section thank God for not making the person a gentile, a slave, and a woman. The common denominator of these conditions is that all three are halakhically exempt from observing some or all of the mitzvot. The list originally included "an ignorant person," but this was rejected by the Rabbis and never was adopted into the prayer service. According to Rashi, the reason for this decision was that even an unlearned individual is still required to observe all the commandments. Therefore, the blessing that thanks God for not making one a slave was substituted.[15] The Conservative movement has revised these three blessings into affirmative statements—"Who has made me an Israelite ... a free person ... and in His image."[16]

A Jewish woman is not required to observe most religious duties that must be carried out at fixed times. Therefore, the intent of this blessing was not to imply any inferiority on the part of women, but rather for a man to express his thanks for the obligation to perform all the religious rituals that are incumbent on a free male Jew.[17] The general talmudic consensus is that an obligatory performance of a commandment is superior to a voluntary one, because of the natural tendency of human beings to refuse to accept responsibilities. According to the Rabbis, women by nature are the guardians of tradition, responsible for shaping the moral and ethical values of their families. Furthermore, women have guarded the basic ideals of Judaism when the innate rashness of men impelled them to make poor choices. For ex-

MAH TOVU (מַה טֹּבוּ)

Mah Tovu (How fair [are your tents, O Jacob, your dwellings, O Israel]) is the opening prayer of the morning service and is recited upon entering the synagogue. This biblical verse (Num. 24:5) was initially uttered by the gentile prophet Balaam, who was hired by Balak to curse the Israelites but blessed them instead. According to tradition, Jacob's tents refer to the houses of prayer, whereas Israel's dwellings represent houses of study. Balaam also was amazed at how the Israelite encampment (*ohel*) was constructed so that everyone's privacy was respected, and no one could see into a neighbor's home (BB 60a).[1]

The opening verse is followed by *va'ani* (As for me [through Your abundant kindness I will enter Your house; I will bow in awe toward your Holy Sanctuary]) (Ps. 5:8), a verse that conveniently contains 10 Hebrew words and is used to determine whether a minyan is present (see p. 374). Jewish tradition does not count people by numbers, and using the words of a verse instead of numbers is an acceptable alternative.

ample, during the wandering of the Israelites in the wilderness, it was the men (not the women) who worshiped the Golden Calf. Thus the general Orthodox perspective (not shared by all aspects of Judaism) is that although women are not required to observe all the mitzvot assigned to men, they are created closer to God's ideal.[18]

After the gaonic period, the tradition developed of having women replace the "male" blessing with *she-asani kirtzono* (Who has made me according to His will). Rather than a reluctant acknowledgment of their lower status, it can be construed as testimony to their inherent superiority. Aaron Soloveitchik, a leading modern talmudic scholar, maintained that women are inherently closer to God's desire that human beings attain the divine qualities of compassion and mercy. To prove this, he noted that God is termed "*Rachum*" (the Compassionate One), from the same root as the Hebrew word "*rechem*" (womb), the body part that clearly differentiates woman from man. Consequently, a woman can proudly declare that she was formed "according to His will." Conversely, although men are innately more powerful than women and can "fill the earth and subdue it," they are born with a coarser nature and must perform more mitzvot to refine their character. The Zohar endorsed this view by asserting that the ideal person is one who has the strength of a man and the compassion of a woman.[19]

Pesukei de-Zimra (פְּסוּקֵי דְזִמְרָה)

Pesukei de-Zimra (Verses of praise) is a collection of psalms and biblical passages that are recited immediately after *Birchot ha-Shachar* (morning blessings). It contains a description of the divine revelation in nature and history and is designed to permit the worshiper to achieve the required state of mind to recite the *Shema* and the *Amidah*, the core sections of the service.

The origin of *Pesukei de-Zimra* can be traced back to "the pious men of old" who, according to the Mishnah, "used to wait an hour before praying in order that they might concentrate their thoughts upon their father in Heaven" (Ber. 5:1). Moreover, they would not respond even if a king greeted them, nor would they stop their prayers if a serpent were coiled at their heels. Another source is the ancient practice among the sages of reading the entire Book of Psalms each day. Since this was obviously impractical for most people, reciting the last several psalms allowed every worshiper to "finish" the book daily.[1] The *Pesukei de-Zimra* remained optional for a long time and did not become an important portion of the synagogue service until the gaonic period.

As a separate section of the morning service with a purpose all its own, the *Pesukei de-Zimra* is introduced and concluded with blessings, the *Baruch she-Amar* (see below) and *Yishtabach* (see p. 411) respectively. It contains a variety of biblical prayers and passages (including *Shirat ha-Yam*; "Song at the Sea"; see next page); the last six psalms (Ps. 145–150); and Psalm 100, which was recited in the Temple whenever a thanksgiving offering was brought to the altar. On Sabbath morning, Psalm 100 is eliminated since no thanksgiving offerings were brought on that day, but nine additional psalms[2] and *Nishmat kol chai* (see p. 410) is included. The use of the word "*pesukei*" (verses) rather than "*pirkei*" (chapters) implies that originally only selections from the psalms (not whole chapters) were recited.

Baruch she-Amar (בָּרוּךְ שֶׁאָמַר)

Baruch she-Amar (Praised is He who spoke [and the world come into being]) is the prayer that opens the *Pesukei de-Zimra* section of the morning service in the Ashkenazic rite. (In the Sephardic and other traditions, some verses and psalms are recited before it.) It praises God as the Creator of the world and stresses the concept of divine mercy. Combining the second line (*baruch Hu*; "praised is He") and the final line (*baruch shemo*; "praised is His name") of this prayer results in "*baruch Hu u-varuch shemo*" (praised is He and praised is His name), the traditional congregational response whenever the name of God is recited in any blessing.[3]

Ashrei (אַשְׁרֵי)

The *Ashrei* (Happy are they) consists of Psalm 145 with two introductory verses (Ps. 84:5, 144:15) and one concluding verse (Ps. 115:18). The Talmud states that "Whoever recites the [psalm] Praise of David [i.e, *Ashrei*] three times a day" (Ber. 4b) is ensured a share in the world to come. This is supported by the threefold repetition of the word "*ashrei*" in the introductory verses, which conveys the idea that those who dwell in God's house of prayer and service are deserving of praise,[4] and the final verse, "We will bless the Lord from this time and forever [i.e., in the world to come]."[5] The *Ashrei* is read twice in the morning service (in the *Pesukei de-Zimra* and toward the end of the service) and at the beginning of the afternoon service.

Psalm 145 is the only psalm to bear the title "*tehillah*" (praise), from which the entire book of Psalms takes its Hebrew name (*Tehillim*). It is written in an alphabetical acrostic, starting with "*aromimcha*" (I will extol You), the first substantive word. It also contains the verse, "You open Your hand and satisfy the desire of every living thing," the inspiring and reassuring testimony to God's mercy as the ultimate source maintaining life.

Midrash records that especially important material was written in alphabetical acrostic style so that it was easier to memorize.[6] However, the *Ashrei* has no verse that begins with the letter *nun*. According to the Talmud (Ber. 4b), this is because that letter may suggest the Hebrew word "*naflah*" (fallen) and thus imply a reference to a prophetic verse that speaks of the destruction of Israel (Amos 5:2). However, one of the Dead Sea Scrolls has a verse beginning with *nun—ne'eman Elohim bid'varav ve-chasid be-chol ma'asav* (God is faithful in His words, and gracious in all His works).

When reciting the verse, "You open Your hand ...," Sephardim literally perform this gesture. In Reform synagogues, *Ashrei* is recited in the vernacular; in many Conservative synagogues, it is chanted responsively in Hebrew.

Song at the Sea (*Shirat ha-Yam;* שִׁירַת הַיָּם)

Shirat ha-Yam (Song at the Sea) is the victory hymn that Moses and the Israelites sang after crossing the Sea of Reeds (*Yam Suf*) to escape the pursuing Egyptians (Exod. 15:1–18). It is also known as *Az Yashir*, the first two words of the song, which is generally translated as "Then *sang* [Moses]," although the verb "sing" is in the future tense. According to Rashi, this grammatical construction is used to imply that the dead will be brought back to life in messianic times so that they will sing God's praises once again.[7]

During Temple days, *Shirat ha-Yam* was sung by the Levites on Sabbath afternoon, in conjunction with the *Mincha* offering (RH 31a). After the destruction of the Temple, when communities in the Land of

Israel wanted to retain as much of the Temple worship as possible, the recitation of the song was incorporated into the daily *Pesukei de-Zimra*. Today, *Shirat ha-Yam* is now said immediately after the six basic psalms and just before the concluding blessing, *Yishtabach*.[8]

Shirat ha-Yam is both a celebration of victory and an unequivocal declaration of the paramount role of God in history. While the psalms of *Pesukei de-Zimra* glorify the wonders of God in creating and sustaining the natural world, *Shirat ha-Yam* emphasizes the divine power in controlling the fate of nations.[9] Vast numbers of Israelites witnessed the Exodus and its climactic event—the splitting of the sea. So obvious was God's presence that our ancestors exclaimed, "This is my God and I will glorify Him." In referring to this incomparable event, the Rabbis observed that a maidservant at the sea saw more than Ezekiel in his heavenly prophecy. Today, we rise and repeat the words of our ancestors, expressing the faith in God that resulted from our people's witnessing the divine miracles.

Nishmat Kol Chai (נִשְׁמַת כָּל חַי)

Nishmat kol chai (The soul of every living being [shall bless Your name]) is the poetic glorification of God that is recited during Sabbath and festival morning services at the end of *Pesukei de-Zimra*, just before *Yishtabach*. It also is said at the Passover seder, after *Hallel* and just before the fourth cup of wine. The Talmud calls this prayer *Birkat ha-Shir* (Blessing of the song), because it concludes the preliminary psalms and songs and continues the theme of the preceding *Shirat ha-Yam* (Song at the Sea) (Pes. 118a). Initially, *Nishmat* was the concluding benediction of the Great *Hallel* (Ps. 136). However, when this psalm was included in the *Pesukei de-Zimra* for the Sabbath, its accompanying *Nishmat* was displaced to its current position.[10]

Nishmat consists of three major sections. The first recognizes that the Jews are totally dependent on God and divine mercy, noting that "without You we have no king, redeemer, or savior." This is followed by a passage similar to the formula of thanksgiving for abundant rain recited in the talmudic period. The final section ("From Egypt You have redeemed us") is thought to have originated during the gaonic period. In most prayer books, the words "הַמֶּלֶךְ" (*ha-melekh*; "the king"), "שׁוֹכֵן עַד" (*Shochein Ad*; "He who abides forever"), and "הָאֵל"

(*ha-El*; "the God) are printed in large type, since the prayer leader starts the central part of the morning service at these places on the High Holy Days, Sabbaths, and festivals, respectively.

The initial letters of the second words of the four verses starting with "*Be-fi yesharim*" (By the mouth of the upright) spell out the Hebrew word "*Yitzkhak*," suggesting that Isaac was the name of the composer of the prayer. In addition, the third letters of each of the verbs in these verses (if rearranged, as in the Ashkenazic High Holy Day liturgy) form the word "Rivkah" (Rebecca). This has led some to speculate that the author was none other than the Patriarch Isaac. In the Sephardic ritual, the verbs are rearranged and the words "Isaac" and "Rebecca" are printed in bold type so that everyone can see the name of the presumed author. Other scholars have discovered acrostics of the name "Shimon" (Simon) in previous verses, giving rise to speculation that *Nishmat* might have been written by Rabbi Shimon ben Shetach (about 100 B.C.E.) or even by the apostle Peter, whose Hebrew name was "Shimon."[11]

Yishtabach (יִשְׁתַּבַּח)

Yishtabach (praised) is the final prayer of *Pesukei de-Zimra*. The number "15" is fundamental in the structure of the *Yishtabach* prayer. The first half contains 15 expressions of praise, and there are 15 words after the phrase "*Baruch ata Adonai*." This number alludes to the 15 Songs of Ascents (Ps. 120–134) and the numerical value of the Divine Name "*yah*" (י = 10; ה = 5), which God used to create heaven and earth. Therefore, the prayer emphasizes the concept that everything on earth, as well as in the entire universe, belongs to God the Creator.[12] The first letters of the second, third, fourth, and fifth words of *Yishtabach* spell the name "Shlomo" (Solomon), giving rise to speculation that this was the name of the unknown author or that the prayer was written in honor of King Solomon.

Barchu (בָּרְכוּ)

Barchu (Let us praise) is the ceremonial call to worship by the prayer leader at the formal beginning of the daily morning and evening services. The morning service in the synagogue initially consisted only of the *Shema* (and its blessings) and the *Amidah*. Each worshiper recited the preliminary sections privately at home or in the synagogue before the beginning of the service, which formally began with the *Barchu*.[1] *Barchu* is not included in the afternoon service, since the *Shema* is not recited.

After the prayer leader recites the invocation *"Barchu et Adonai ha-mevorach"* (Praise the Lord, who is [to be] praised), the congregation responds *"Baruch Adonai ha-mevorach l'olam va-ed"* (Praised is the Lord, who is [to be] praised for ever and ever). Having summoned the congregation to praise God, the prayer leader repeats the response to indicate that this obligation is equally incumbent on him (or her).[2]

Although literally meaning "bless," in context the word *"barchu"* is the equivalent of "praise," for it would be the height of presumption to think that mere mortals could somehow confer anything on God. Instead the *Barchu* recognizes that God is the source of all blessings and is an assertion of the worshiper's dedication to fulfill God's will by performing the divine commandments.[3]

Barchu is recited while standing and only in the presence of a minyan. The prayer leader bows at the word "praise" and straightens at "Lord," while both the prayer leader and the congregation bow at the word "praised" and straighten at "Lord" in the response. The recitation of *Barchu* and the practice of standing during it may have originated at the time of Ezra, based on the verse in Nehemiah (9:5), "Rise, bless the Lord your God who is from eternity to eternity: 'May Your glorious name be blessed, exalted though it is above every blessing and praise!'"

Barchu is also recited by each person who is called up for an *aliyah* during the reading of the Torah, and it is followed by the same congregational response. Some communities have the paradoxical custom of also reciting *Barchu* at the conclusion of the daily morning and evening services when there is no Torah reading, for the benefit of those worshipers who arrived too late to hear it at the opening of the service.[4]

Ahavah Rabbah (אַהֲבָה רַבָּה)/ *Ahavat Olam* (אַהֲבַת עוֹלָם)

Ahavah Rabbah (With great love) and *Ahavat Olam* (With everlasting love) are different versions of the second of the two blessings preceding the recitation of the *Shema* in the morning and evening services. The

Talmud records divergent views as to which should be said (Ber. 11b), with the *Ge'onim* finally arriving at a compromise—both should be recited, *Ahavah Rabbah* (the longer and more complex) in the morning and *Ahavat Olam* in the evening. This practice persists in the Ashkenazic ritual, but in the Sephardic liturgy, *Ahavat Olam* is said during both services.

Both prayers are paeans to the divine love that forms the basis for the relationship between God and the Jewish people, which is solidified by the Torah. They contain a commitment to study the Torah and obey its laws, and thus are appropriate introductions to the *Shema,* which contains selection from the Torah (see next section).

The morning *Ahavah Rabbah* also contains the hope that God will redeem the Jewish people from exile, returning them from dispersion in the Diaspora to the Land of Israel. When saying the phrase "Bring us in peace from the four corners of the world," one symbolically draws the four corners of the tallit together and continues to hold them throughout the recitation of the *Shema,* kissing the fringes each time the word "tzitzit" is mentioned during the third paragraph.[1]

Shema (שְׁמַע)

Shema Yisrael Adonai Eloheinu Adonai Echad (Hear, O Israel: the Lord [is] our God, the Lord [is] one; Deut. 6:4)[1] is the basic declaration of faith of the Jewish people in the unity and oneness of God and their acceptance of the yoke of the kingdom of heaven. A midrash traces the origin of this verse to the last moments of the life of Jacob (Deut. R. 2:35). The Patriarch was concerned that his children and grandchildren, living in Egypt, would depart from the traditions of Abraham and serve the local gods. However, they put his mind at ease by assuring him: "Hear, O Israel (i.e., Jacob): 'We accept the one God as our God.'"

The word *"Shema"* also refers to the prayer composed of three biblical passages—Deuteronomy 6:5–9 (*Ve-ahavta*) and 11:13–21 and Numbers 15:37–41. The Talmud recounts that, during Second Temple times, these three paragraphs were recited with the Ten Commandments in a service that was held by the *Kohanim* in the Chamber of Hewn Stones after they had performed the initial act of the morning sacrifice (Tam. 5:1; Ber. 11b).[2] The people assembled in the Temple courtyard did not join in this reading, but on hearing the first line of the *Shema* they responded *"Baruch Shem k'vod malkhuto l'olam va-ed"* (Praised is the name of His glorious kingdom forever and ever) (Taan. 16b).

According to the commentators, the first line of the *Shema* contains many layers of profound meanings. Rashi maintains that although now the Lord is only our God and not yet acknowledged universally, eventually all humanity will recognize the Lord as the one and only God.[3] The word "one" has two major connotations. In opposition to polytheism, the *Shema* emphasizes that there is only a single God and not many gods. Yet God is also unique, totally different from what paganism means by "gods" and beyond all human understanding. Indeed, God is truly a supreme being, entirely different from anything in the divinely created universe.

The first word of the *Shema* emphasizes the need to listen, stressing that prayer encompasses not merely talking to God but also includes hearing what God has to say to us. According to Abraham Joshua Heschel, "Jewish prayer is an act of listening. We do not bring forth our own words. The self is silent; the spirit of the people Israel speaks. In prayer we listen to what the words convey."[4]

In the Torah scroll, the *ayin* (ע) of the word *"Shema"* and the *dalet* (ד) of the word *"echad"* are written larger than the other letters. Together they form the word *"eid"* (עֵד; "witness"), indicating that the Jew who pronounces the *Shema* bears witness to the unity of God and declares it to all the world.

After the first verse of the *Shema* is recited in the synagogue, it has been customary from rabbinic times to recite the Temple response ("Praised is the name") silently. The Rabbis offered two reasons for this practice. When Jacob (Israel) lay on his deathbed, his 12 sons declared their loyalty to God by reciting the *Shema*. Jacob responded "Praised is the name," but he was so weak that his words could barely be heard (Pes. 56a). The other explanation (Deut. R. 2:36) is that Moses heard this phrase recited by the ministering angels and brought it down to earth to teach to the Children of Israel. The sages compared this to a man who stole a valuable ornament from the palace of the king and gave it to his wife, on the condition that she wear it only at home and never in public. As sinful humans, we dare not say aloud an angelic formula. The sole exception is on Yom Kippur, when Israel elevates itself to the pure and sin-free level of angels.[5] Consequently, today the Temple response is said aloud several times on the Day of Atonement, after the first verse of the *Shema* and during the *Avodah* service in response to the three confessions of the *Kohen Gadol* and his utterance of the holy name of God (Tetragrammaton).

The first paragraph of the *Shema* is known as the *Ve-ahavta* (You shall love [the Lord your God]). It stresses that one not observe the commandments because of the fear of punishment or as an attempt to gain divine favor, but rather out of the pure love that represents the highest level in which a human being can relate with God.[6] The Mishnah explains that a person should serve God with passionate love ("with all your heart"), even if this means giving up your life ("with all your soul") and wealth ("with all your resources") (Ber. 9:5).[7] The Rabbis interpreted the phrase "with all your heart" to mean that Jews must obey God's will "with your two impulses," the evil as well as the good. Therefore, we must "learn to turn to God's service our appetites, our physical lusts, and our egocentricity ... [by] sanctifying the way we eat, the way we act sexually, and the way we earn and spend money."[8] This paragraph also contains the commandments to teach Torah to the children, to learn Torah on every possible occasion, to put tefillin on one's arms and head (see p. 382), and to and place a mezuzah on the doorpost of the house (see p. 580).

The second paragraph of the *Shema* emphasizes the study of Torah and the observance of the mitzvot, indicating some of the rewards for following the teachings of the Torah and the punishments for disobedience. Nachmanides observed that the first paragraph is in the singular and directed to each person, who succeeds or fails in becoming a worthy human being based on individual merit. In contrast, the second paragraph is in the plural and addressed to the entire community, whose collective action determines whether there will be sufficient rain and a bountiful harvest.[9]

The third paragraph of the *Shema* is primarily concerned with the commandment of putting tzitzit (fringes) on the corner of one's garments (see p. 377) as a reminder to observe the commandments so that Israel may become a holy people. It also mentions the Exodus from Egypt, fulfilling the daily duty to read a Torah passage referring to this seminal event in the history of the Jewish people (Ber. 12b; Men. 43b).[10] Before reciting the morning *Shema*, worshipers wearing a tallit traditionally gather the fringes from the four corners and hold them in the left hand (on which the tefillin is bound) while saying the prayer. On the three occasions when the word "tzitzit" is said, as well as when the *Shema* is concluded with the word "*emet*," we touch the fringes to the lips and kiss them as a sign of our desire to fulfill all of the divine commandments.[11]

The Rabbis considered these three selections to represent the entire Torah. They taught that reciting them twice daily during prayer services fulfilled the command to study Torah "day and night" (Men. 99b). However, they never told this to the people, lest it decrease their commitment to study. The *Shema* was also viewed as representing the acceptance of the yoke of both the kingship of Heaven (*kabbalat ol malkhut shamayim*) and the commandments (*kabbalat ol ha-mitzvot*). It effectively became a "pledge of allegiance" and a repetition of the ceremony at Mount Sinai, where the Israelites took an oath of loyalty to God the king and pledged to obey the royal laws.[12]

The Rabbis taught that the 248 positive commandments equal the number of organs in the human body, symbolizing that it is essential to dedicate one's entire body to servicing God and fulfilling the mitzvot. Because the total number of words of the *Shema* (together with "Praised is the name") is 245, in public worship it is customary for the prayer leader to repeat the last two words of the *Shema* (*Adonai Elohaichem*; "The Lord, your God") and the first word of the following benediction (*emet*; "true"). This brings the total number of words up to 248, echoing the parallel phrase in Jeremiah (10:10): "The Lord God is true" (Ber. 2:2). When the *Shema* is recited in private, or if there is no minyan, the total of 248 is achieved by first reciting "אֵל מֶלֶךְ נֶאֱמָן" (*El melekh ne'eman*; "God, faithful king"). These three words were chosen because their initial Hebrew letters spell "אָמֵן" (amen; lit., "it is true"), thus testifying that the worshiper is firmly convinced that the words about to be recited are completely true.[13]

In rabbinic times, the affirmation of God's unity was a revolutionary challenge to the accepted doctrines of the gentiles. It boldly denied the pagan deities, who constituted whole dynasties of male and female gods. In Babylonia, the doctrine of God's unity challenged the concept of Zoroastrian dualism—two deities, one of whom created light and the other darkness, representing opposing forces that are in eternal conflict. To negate this doctrine unequivocally, the Rabbis composed the first benediction before the *Shema*, which describes God as "Who forms light and creates darkness, makes peace and creates all" (see below). The proclamation of the absolute and indivisible oneness of God was also a challenge to the Christian concept of the Trinity.[14]

In the middle of the fifth century, a fanatical Persian king was offended by the Jewish emphasis on the unity of God and proscribed the recitation of the *Shema* at synagogue services. To ensure that the Jews would not disobey his decree, guards were stationed in the synagogue for the first quarter of the day, when the *Shema* must be read. As a countermeasure, the Rabbis ruled that the first verse of the *Shema* be recited on two occasions, which fulfills the obligation when there is an extreme emergency (Ber. 13b). They composed a short prayer unit, with the first verse of the *Shema* at the center, which was to be read privately at home before coming to the public services. The other recitation was inserted into the *Kedushah* of the *Amidah* for the *Musaf* (additional) service on the Sabbath, at a time when the government inspectors sent to enforce the prohibition had already left the synagogue, satisfied that the *Shema* had not been recited. Even after the king was killed, his decree lifted, and the *Shema* with its blessings restored to its traditional place in the service, the extra two abbreviated recitations of the *Shema* were retained as part of the regular ritual to commemorate this event. The home recitation became part of the introductory prayers, where it has remained to this day.[15]

The first verse of the *Shema* is also recited when the Torah scroll is taken from the ark on Sabbaths and festivals, during the *Kedushah* in the *Musaf Amidah* on these days, and on the deathbed (see p. 76). At the conclusion of the Yom Kippur service, the first verse of the *Shema* is recited once and "Praised is the name" is repeated three times (see p. 221). The *Shema* climaxes the seventh and last circling of the *bimah* (platform) during the *hoshanot* prayers on Hoshana Rabbah. Portions of the *Shema* are also included in the parchments enclosed in the mezuzah and tefillin. The first section of the *Shema* is recited at bedtime, based on the talmudic saying, "Though a man has recited the *Shema* in the synagogue, it is a religious act [meritorious] to recite it again on his bed" (Ber. 4b).

The *Shema* should be recited with full concentration on the meaning of the words. To prevent distractions, it is customary to follow the practice of Judah the Prince and place the right hand over the eyes while saying the first verse (Ber. 13b).[16] The *Shema* should be recited loud enough to be heard by the ear, since it is written "*Hear*, O Israel" (Ber.

15a). Any language can be used—because it is crucial that the worshiper understand what he or she is affirming—as long as one enunciates the words clearly (Sot. 32b). In the Talmud, there is a debate concerning how the *Shema* should be read (Ber. 1:3). Beit Shammai took the words "when you lie down and when you rise up" literally, ruling that the evening *Shema* should be recited while reclining whereas in the morning it should be said standing upright. Beit Hillel argued persuasively that the verse merely referred to the times of the readings, and that no special posture was required.

Unlike the *Amidah*, which must be said while standing, the *Shema* may be recited while standing or sitting, or even while traveling (stopping only to recite the first verse). According to Maimonides, "Everyone may read the *Shema* in the ordinary postures—standing, walking, lying down, or riding on an animal. It is forbidden to recite the Shema in a prone position (with one's face to the ground) or in a supine position (on one's back looking straight up), but one may read it while lying turned to one side."[17] For a long time, the Jews in Israel stood up for the *Shema*, both because of its importance and because it was an act of witnessing God (and testimony in a Jewish court is always given while standing). In ninth-century Babylonia, however, the Karaites argued that standing for the *Shema* meant that that the Jews considered only these three passages (and the Ten Commandments) to be fundamental tenets of the faith and of divine origin. To counteract such views, the Rabbis ruled that the *Shema* be recited while seated, and this remains the prevailing custom today.[18]

According to a midrash, when God visited Abraham as he was recovering from his circumcision, He did not permit the Patriarch to rise from his seat (Gen. R. 48). Abraham complained that it was improper for him to remain seated in the presence of the Lord, but God replied: "Just as you are now sitting and I am standing above you, so shall it be when your children will enter their synagogues and read the *Shema* in My honor—they will be sitting while I reside there, as it is written, 'God stands in the assembly of God [interpreted as pious scholars]'" (Ps. 82:1).[19]

There also was much debate during the tannaitic period as to the times for reciting the *Shema*. The Rabbis eventually ruled that the evening *Shema* can be recited from nightfall until dawn, though ideally it should be said before midnight (Ber. 1:1–2). The morning *Shema* can be recited from the first traces of the dawn until the end of the third hour after sunrise (i.e., one-fourth of the day).[20]

Blessings of the *Shema*

The Talmud mandates: "The morning [*Shema*] is preceded by two blessings and followed by one. The evening [*Shema*] is preceded by two blessings and followed by two" (Ber. 1:4). The reason for this decree was the rabbinic requirement that blessings be said both before and after the ritual recitation of any biblical passage (Torah, haftarah, *megillot* for festivals), and the *Shema* is essentially a collection of three such scriptural sections. The Rabbis fixed the opening and closing formulas for these blessings, but they allowed prayer leaders substantial latitude in developing the intermediate words. Therefore, even today there are differences in the text between the Ashkenazic and Sephardic rituals and among various traditions within them.[21]

The first blessing of the *Shema* is prefaced by *Barchu* (see p. 411), a call to the congregation to praise the Lord. In the morning, the first blessing focuses on the concept of light. Since the morning service was usually held at sunrise, it was natural to start with *Yotzer or* (He who creates light), a blessing thanking God for the sunrise as well as for the other miracles of Creation. Based on the verse from Isaiah (45:7), "I form light and create darkness, I make peace and create woe," the blessing was put in the third person and the last word changed to "everything."[22] Not only did the Rabbis deem this a euphemism or "more appropriate language" (Ber. 11b), but the new wording also emphasized that God is the sole source of Creation, serving as a polemic against the once-prevailing dualistic doctrine that day and night, and good and evil, were created and ruled by different deities. The first blessing before the evening *Shema* is similar, but praises God as the Creator of the night.[23] The first blessing before the *Shema* is substantially longer in the morning because it also contains the *Kedushah* (see p. 429), which is based on prophetic visions of Isaiah and Ezekiel in which ministering angels exalt and extol God. This blessing stressed that even the heavenly angels praise God and proclaim divine rule over the world.[24]

The second blessing before the *Shema*—*Ahavah Rabbah* (With great love) in the morning and *Ahavat Olam* (With everlasting love) in the evening (see p. 412)—thanks God for His love of Israel, which was made evident through the giving of the commandments and laws of the Torah at Mount Sinai. The blessing following the *Shema* is also found in two versions—*Emet* v'*yatziv* (True and certain) in the morning and *Emet* v'*emunah* (True and faithful) in the evening (Ber. 12a). In these blessings, the worshiper affirms a belief in the teachings of the Torah and thanks God for redeeming Israel from Egyptian bondage. They include three verses from the victorious *Shirat ha-Yam* (Song at the Sea; see p. 409): "Who is like You among the gods, O Lord" (*Mi-chamocha ba-eilim Adonai*), "This is my God," and "The Lord shall reign forever and ever." Facing persecution and humiliation in exile, the *Shema* and its blessings gave Jews the courage to resist the temptations of the dominant faiths in the lands where they lived as well as the strength to endure the constant trials of life. Twice each day these words reassured Jews that ultimately the God who rescued their ancestors from slavery in Egypt would also redeem them.[25]

In the evening service, there is an additional blessing after the *Shema*—*Hashkiveinu* (Let us lie down [to sleep in peace])—in which the Jew prays for divine protection against the terrors of the darkness and the evil forces of the night. It is based on the verse in Psalms (121:4), "God, the Guardian of Israel, neither slumbers nor sleeps." In isolated communities in Babylonia during the talmudic period, nighttime violence was common and such phrases as "guard our going forth and our coming in" and "remove our adversary from before us and from behind us" were most appropriate at this time of day. The latter supplication also could be interpreted as a plea to be spared from the inclination toward evil, which might prevent a person from following his good intentions. In the morning, the fears of physical danger were minimal, and thus there was no parallel prayer.[26]

The weekday evening service in Ashkenazic congregations contains one more prayer before the *Amidah*, a set of 18 scriptural verses beginning with the words "*Baruch Adonai l'olam*" (Praised be the Lord forever and ever). During the talmudic period when synagogues were permitted only in open fields and not within residential areas, the men who gathered in the synagogues at the end of a day's work to say the *Shema* wanted a shorter service that could be completed before dark. Since the Babylonian sages had ruled that the evening *Amidah* was optional, they compiled the 18 short blessings (in which the name of God is mentioned 18 times) to substitute for the full 18 blessings, which each individual could always recite later in the safety of his home. A short concluding blessing (*Yiru Eineinu*; "May our eyes see") and *Kaddish* ended the brief service. This prayer of 18 verses was never recited on Friday nights, for the full *Amidah* is not said on the Sabbath. Similarly, it was not said on Saturdays or on festivals, since the men were not in the fields on those nights. In the Land of Israel, the sages ruled that the evening *Amidah* was obligatory and could not be separated from the *Shema* and its blessings. Because they never permitted this intervening prayer into the evening service, it is not found in the Sephardic ritual or in Ashkenazic synagogues in Israel.[27]

Amidah (עֲמִידָה)

The *Amidah* ("Standing" prayer) is the highlight of the Jewish prayer service. Referred to by the talmudic rabbis as simply *Ha-Tefillah* (The Prayer), the *Amidah* is the paradigmatic prayer, containing the primary elements of praise, petition, and thanksgiving. It is made up of 19 blessings, though it originally had one less and thus is often known as the *Shemoneh Esrei* (18). As implied by its name, the *Amidah* is recited while standing. It should be recited with quiet devotion and without any interruption, loud enough to hear it oneself but not so that it is audible to others and disturbs their concentration. This requirement is based on the famous prayer of Hannah (the haftarah for the second day of Rosh Hashanah), in which she "spoke in her heart; only her lips moved, but her voice could not be heard" (1 Sam. 1:13). "One who says the *Tefillah* [*Amidah*] so that it can be heard is of the small of faith" (Ber. 24a), as though he or she were insinuating that God cannot hear the soft voice that barely escapes the lips. The *Amidah* is said with feet together, based on emulating either Ezekiel's (1:7) description of the ministering angels, "the legs of each were [fused into] a single rigid leg"[1] or the position of the *Kohanim* when ascending the altar, who respectfully shuffled along so slowly that their legs were hardly separated as they placed one foot in front of the other.[2] Another reason is that the numerical value of "*Tefillah*" (*Amidah*) equals that of "*yesharah*" (straight).[3]

In congregational worship, during the morning and afternoon service, the prayer leader repeats the *Amidah* out loud following the personal *Amidah*. This practice was devised to allow illiterate people to fulfill their prayer duty by answering "amen" to each of the blessings. Various additions are made to the *Amidah* when it is recited aloud in the congregational service. The most significant is the *Kedushah* (see p. 429), a prayer in which the community of Israel joins with the heavenly hosts to proclaim the holiness of God. While the reader intones the 18th benediction (*Modim anachnu lach*; "We give thanks to You"), the congregation recites a different prayer of thanksgiving in an undertone (see p. 431).

The *Amidah* is an ancient prayer whose origin is shrouded in mystery.[4] The Rabbis offered multiple mutually contradictory suggestions about its authorship and periods of origin, including the Patriarchs (Ber. 26b), Moses (JT Ber. 7), the 120 elders (Meg. 18a), the men of the Great Assembly (Ber. 33a), and the early sages (*Sifrei Devarim*, sec. 343).[5] Fixed community prayers gradually developed during the Second Temple period. Although the structure of the prayers initially differed widely among various groups, by the end of the Temple period the 18 benedictions of the weekday *Amidah* had become the general custom. Nevertheless, the exact sequence and the content of the individual sections probably still varied. After the destruction of the Temple, the Rabbis decreed that the recitation of the *Amidah* every morning and afternoon allowed Jews to fulfill the commandment of "serving the Lord" (Exod. 23:25), which previously had been interpreted as referring to the daily Temple offerings (Ber. 26b). In effect, the Jew substituted the "service of the heart" for the sacrificial ritual of the "service of the altar."[6]

The *Amidah* was put into its final form by Rabban Gamaliel II and his colleagues at Yavneh after the destruction of the Second Temple. It has been generally agreed that Gamaliel added a 19th benediction designed to attack the *minim*—sectarians such as the Sadducees, Essenes, and especially the early Christians, who posed a threat to the precarious existence of the Jewish people. Any reader who failed to recite this benediction, or any worshiper who failed to respond to it with the customary "amen," was immediately recognized as a heretic; in this way the sectarians were effectively eliminated from the synagogue.[7] However, fragments from the Cairo Genizah have confirmed that Gamaliel's *Amidah* consisted of only 18 benedictions, which included a pre-existing attack against separatists and heretics. The expansion to 19 blessings appears to be a third-century Babylonian creation, in which the single combined blessing in the Land of Israel for "David, builder of Jerusalem" was expanded into the current pair of separate blessings of David as builder of Jerusalem and as forerunner of the Messiah.[8] Although the specific sects against whom it was addressed no longer existed, the Rabbis retained the benediction against *minim* in the *Amidah* because the danger of nonbelievers and heretics persists in every generation.[9]

Even once the order, substance, and blessing formula of the *Amidah* were codified in the talmudic period, the individual worshiper or prayer leader was permitted to select the precise words to use. A definitive version of the *Amidah* was not written down until the early gaonic period, though even then there were substantial differences in the Babylonian and Palestinian versions. Today, the texts of the *Amidah* used in different communities have only minor variations.

The *Amidah* is recited individually during each of the daily services. Although it has long been the general custom to recite the *Amidah* during the evening service, the *halakhah* considers it optional since there was no corresponding Temple sacrifice at that time. However, the evening *Amidah* is not repeated aloud, except for an abbreviated version on the Sabbath. Known as *Magen Avot* (or "Shield of the forefathers" after its first two words), this was formulated as a synopsis of the seven blessings of the Sabbath *Amidah*. The *Amidah* is also included in the *Musaf* (Additional) service for the Sabbath and festivals; on Yom Kippur it is repeated a fifth time during the concluding *Ne'ilah* service.

Structure

Since talmudic times, the recitation of the *Amidah* has been prefaced by the verse from Psalms (51:17), "O Lord, open my lips, and my mouth will utter Your praises," in which the worshipers ask for divine assistance in articulating their prayers. In the afternoon and evening services, this verse is preceded by "For the name of the Lord will I proclaim; Give glory to our God" (Deut. 32:3).[10]

The various forms of the *Amidah* have in common three introductory and three concluding benedictions.[11] The first three blessings (*shevach*; "praise of God") are devoted to: (1) praising God for establishing the covenant with the ancestors of the Jewish people (*avot*; "forefathers") and requesting that our prayers be answered not on the basis of our own unworthy accomplishments but on "the merits of the fathers" (*zechut avot*); (2) revelation of the miraculous powers of God through nature, including the Prayer for Rain (see p. 239) from Shemini Atzeret to Passover and the Prayer for Dew during the rest of the year, concluding with the promise of the resurrection of the dead (*gevurot*; "powers"); and (3) divine holiness (*kedushat ha-Shem*; "holiness of God").[12] Thus the first two benedictions praise God for material and physical gifts and the third elevates prayer to a spiritual level. The Talmud (RH 32a) offers a rationale for this sequence, based on the first two verses of Psalm 29, "Ascribe to the Lord, O you mighty [Patriarchs]; give to the Lord glory and strength [God's powers]; give to the Lord ... worship the Lord in the beauty of holiness [sanctification blessing]".[13] During the reader's repetition of the *Amidah*, the short third blessing is replaced by the *Kedushah* (see p. 429). The last three blessings (*hoda'ah*; "thanksgiving") open with an expression of the hope that God will accept the prayers of the congregation (*avodah*, worship). Initially, the *Kohanim* prayed that their sacrificial offerings would gain divine acceptance (Yoma 7:1, 68b; Tamid 5:1), but after the destruction of the Temple the prayer was altered to a petition for the acceptance of Israel and its worship and for restoration of the sacrificial service. The other two concluding blessings are (1) thanksgiving for God's past, present, and future kindness and the miracles of daily living (*birkat hoda'ah*), which also was recited in Temple times (Yoma 7:1, 68b), and (2) a prayer for peace (*birkat shalom*), which comes in two versions (see p. 435). During the thanksgiving blessing (*Modim anachnu lach*), one bows while reciting the first word and at the end, at the word "*baruch*" (praised). The Talmud states that whoever does not bow during this blessing will be punished by having his spine twisted like a curled serpent (BK 16a).[14]

On weekdays, there are 13 intermediate benedictions (*bakashah*, "petition") that are essentially requests related to the needs of both the individual and the nation. The six petitions for personal needs are further subdivided into those of a spiritual nature—wisdom and understanding (*binah*), repentance (*teshuvah*), and forgiveness of sins (*selichah*)—and those of a physical, material or emotional character—redemption and security (*ge'ulah*), health (*refu'ah*), and economic prosperity (*birkat hashanim*, "who blesses the years"). The six petitions for specific Jewish national aspirations related to various aspects of messianic redemption are ingathering of the dispersed exiles (*kibbutz galuyot*), restoration of justice (*mishpat*), destruction of Israel's enemies (*minim*), prayer for the righteous (*tzadikim*), restoration of Jerusalem (*Yerushalayim*), and the coming of the Messiah (*birkat David*). The final intermediate benediction requests God to hear the prayers of all Israel (*tefillah*).

At the end of the silent recitation of the formal *Amidah*, it has become customary for the individual to add a personal prayer. The Talmud specifically mentions the supplications added by 11 prominent sages (Ber. 16b–17a). The petition of Mar ben Rabina (a fourth-century rabbi) became a favorite and found its way into the prayer book. Opening with the verse from Psalms (34:14), "May God guard your tongue from evil, and your lips from speaking guile," it beseeches God to keep one from spreading falsehoods and gossiping (*lashon hara*; see p. 550), a sin that the Talmud regarded as especially serious. Just as worshipers have purified their speech to recite the *Amidah*, so shall they continue on that high level in their daily communications with other human beings. In addition to asking for divine assistance in acting properly toward others, we pray that God frustrate the evil intentions of others against us.[15]

The *Amidah* ends with a recitation of *Oseh shalom* (He who makes peace [in His high heavens]), the beginning of which is part of a verse from Job (25:2). Before beginning this verse, the worshiper takes three steps back (starting with the left foot), and then bows to the left, right, and center, as though leaving one's teacher (Yoma 53b) or departing from the presence of royalty.[16] Another interpretation is that as we bow to the left we face the angel Michael, who symbolizes God's spirit of mercy and stands at the right of the divine throne. The bow to our right is toward the angel Gabriel, who stands at the left of the throne and represents the divine quality of strict justice. Finally, we bow forward, directly toward God, who alone can harmonize these two disparate divine manifestations and establish lasting peace, both on earth and in heaven.[17]

The Talmud (Ber. 34a) describes the overall structure of the *Amidah* as reflecting the actions of "a servant making requests of a master." Thus the Jewish supplicant first approaches God with words of praise; then presents a series of petitions; and finally takes leave, expressing gratitude and confidence in the graciousness and mercy of the Master.

Before beginning the *Amidah*, one humbly takes three steps backward and then moves three paces forward to symbolically draw nearer to God, just as Moses rose through three levels of holiness when ascending Mount Sinai.[18] Some maintain that Moses had to overcome three barriers (darkness, cloud, and thick cloud) when approaching God on the mountain, and thus the worshiper makes the symbolic gesture of "breaking down the barriers" to be able to open the *Amidah* by addressing God in the second person ("praised are You").[19] Another interpretation is that it reflects the three ancestors whom the Bible records as having "stepped forward—Abraham, when bargaining with God for the lives of the inhabitants of Sodom (Gen. 18:23); Judah, when he pleaded with the Joseph to allow him to be kept hostage instead of his brother Benjamin, fearing that otherwise it would lead to the death of their father, Jacob (Gen. 44:18); and Elijah, when he asked for divine help in defeating the prophets of Baal (1 Kings 18:36).[20] At the conclusion of the *Amidah*, the worshiper takes three paces backward so as to not turn his or her back on the divine king.[21]

At four points in the *Amidah* one is supposed to bow down. The first three are at the opening of the first blessing, at the end of that same blessing (concluding with *magen Avraham*; "shield of Abraham"), and at the opening of the next to last blessing (ending with "*ha-tov shim'cha u-lecha na'eh l'hodot*"; "Whose name is good and Whom it is fitting to thank"). In these three instances, one bends at the knee when saying the word "*baruch*," bows the top part of the body forward for the word "*ata*," and then assumes an upright posture before the word "*Adonai*" (the name of God). The fourth time is while reciting "*modim anachnu lach*" (we give thanks to You), when one bows forward at "*modim*" and remains in this position until standing straight up just before reaching the word "*Adonai*."[22]

An abbreviated version of the *Amidah* can be used when there is not enough time to recite the full text. Known as *Havineinu* (Grant us understanding), the initial word of the middle section, it consists of the first and last three paragraphs plus a brief restatement of the main ideas of the other paragraphs (Ber. 29a). In a talmudic discussion, Rabbi Joshua maintained that only this short version of the *Amidah* was required, but Rabbi Akiva held that it should be used only by one who did not know the entire prayer (Ber. 4:3–4). Rabbi Eliezer disagreed, arguing that reciting a fixed text of the *Amidah* is not equivalent to the sincere supplication before God that is the fundamental concept of the prayer.[23]

Sabbaths and Festivals

On Sabbaths and festivals, petitions are generally avoided because one should have a mood of contentment, appreciating what God has created rather than seeking ways to change it. This was also the practice in the Temple, where personal offerings were not accepted on those days. Therefore, the *Amidah* for the Sabbath and festivals consists only of the three introductory benedictions of praise, the three concluding benedictions, and a single, lengthy central benediction that expresses the special sanctity of the day. Unlike the weekday *Amidah*, in which the middle blessings are identical for all three daily services, on the Sabbath there is a different blessing for each of the four services. In all but the afternoon service, the intermediate blessing contains three sections—a reading from the Torah bracketed by an introduction and a uniform concluding portion, which probably was the early, original Sabbath blessing that was later elaborated in a different way in each of the four services. In the evening service, the biblical portion is *Va-y'chulu* ([The heaven and the earth] were finished; Gen. 2:1–3), the first mention of the Sabbath in the Torah. On Sabbath morning, the biblical portion is *Ve-shomru* ([The Children of Israel] shall keep [the Sabbath]; Exod. 31:16–17); the biblical passage in the *Musaf Amidah* describes the special additional sacrifices offered on that day (Num. 28:9–10) and adds a request that they be restored. The Conservative prayer book calls for the return of the dispersed Jews to the land where their ancestors sacrificed the various offerings but not for a resumption of the sacrificial service. The biblical verses detailing the specific sacrifice for the day are included in small print, with the instructions "some congregations add." The Reform prayer book makes no mention of the ancient sacrificial system.[24]

Although there is not a full repetition of the *Amidah* on Friday evening, the prayer leader recites aloud an abridged version known as *Magen Avot* (Shield of our fathers), which summarizes the seven blessings said quietly by each congregant. In talmudic times, when synagogues were generally outside the town limits, it was dangerous to walk home alone after dark. Reciting this extra prayer gave latecomers time to complete their prayers so that all the worshipers could return to town together (Shab. 24b).

The pattern of the intermediate blessing of the *Amidah* for the pilgrimage festivals of Passover, Shavuot, and Sukkot is less complex than that for the Sabbath, since it is the same for the evening, morning, and afternoon services. It begins with thanking God for choosing Israel from all the nations and having "granted us, O Lord our God, festivals for joy, holidays and seasons for rejoicing." The unique feature of the specific festival is noted—Passover as "the season of our freedom"; Shavuot as "the season of giving the Torah"; and Sukkot, Shemini Atzeret, and Simchat Torah as "the season of our rejoicing"—followed by the phrase, "a holy convocation, a memorial to the Exodus from Egypt." The second section of the festival blessing asks that God favorably remember our ancestors, Jerusalem, and the Messiah and provide the Jews with "deliverance, goodness, grace, kindness, and peace." It ends with a request that Israel be permitted to celebrate the festivals with joy and gladness. The central benediction of the *Musaf Amidah* for festivals describes the special Temple offering of the day and contains a prayer for the restoration of the Temple and its ritual.[25]

On Rosh Hashanah, the *Musaf Amidah* (see p. 197) contains three long intermediate benedictions that deal with the divine kingship over the entire universe (*Malkhuyot*), God's remembering Israel (*Zichronot*), and the sounding of the shofar on that day (*Shofarot*). The shofar is blown during the reader's repetition of the *Amidah* at the conclusion of each of these benedictions. In Sephardic congregations, this is also done during the silent *Amidah* (see p. 194).

On the New Moon (Rosh Hodesh), intermediate days of festivals, Hanukkah, and Purim, the regular weekday *Amidah* is recited at all three services, with the addition of a special prayer. On Rosh Hodesh and the intermediate days of festivals, *Ya'aleh v'yavo* (see p. 431), with reference to the appropriate occasion, is inserted into the 17th blessing. On these days there is also a *Musaf Amidah*, with a recitation of the appropriate additional sacrifices for the day. The miracles that God performed for the Jewish people on Hanukkah and Purim are described in *al ha-nissim* (for the miracles), which is added to the 18th benediction on these festivals.[26] In the Conservative liturgy, *al ha-nissim* is also recited for Yom ha-Atzmaut (see p. 296).

Kedushah (קְדוּשָּׁה)

The *Kedushah* (holiness or sanctification) refers to the proclamation of God's holiness and glory in the third benediction during the repetition of the *Amidah* when a minyan is present. This prayer has its origins during the rabbinic period in Babylonia, where mystics were engrossed in speculations concerning the nature, appearance, and functions of the heavenly chariot (*Merkavah*) and the angelic sanctification of God, as described in Isaiah (6) and Ezekiel (1, 3).[27]

The nucleus of the *Kedushah* consists of three biblical verses. The first is *Kadosh, Kadosh, Kadosh* (Holy, holy, holy! [The Lord of hosts! His presence fills all the earth!]) (Isa. 6:3),[28] which is taken from the prophet Isaiah's vision of the angels surrounding the divine throne and proclaiming the holiness of God. The second verse is taken from Ezekiel's (3:12) vision of Heaven, in which the rushing winds carry the angelic praise of God: "Praised is the glory of the Lord from His place." The third verse, "The Lord shall reign forever, Your God, O Zion, from generation to generation, Halleluyah" (Ps. 146:10), was declaimed by human beings and not by angels, but was considered to be a fitting climax for the proclamation of God's holiness and eternal sovereignty. In this way, the worshiper travels emotionally from the celestial realms where the hosts on high, in awe and trembling, declare God's holiness to the earthly realities of Israel's yearning for redemption and eternal faith in God as redeemer. The mystics then provided appropriate introductions and connecting sentences for these three verses in an effort to recapture the spirit and ecstasy reflected in their biblical contexts. They placed the entire *Kedushah* in its logical position immediately before the third benediction of the *Amidah*, which deals with God's holiness and concludes with the blessing, "Praised are You, O Lord, the holy God."[29]

The angelic quality of the *Kedushah* is dramatically emphasized during the recitation of "*Kadosh, Kadosh, Kadosh*." Worshipers rise up on their toes and lift their heels off the ground to symbolize their desire to escape the fetters of the material world on earth and ascend to Heaven to join the angelic choir praising God.[30]

The *Kedushah* begins in a different way depending on the service and communal custom. *Nekadesh* (We will sanctify [Your name in the world]) is used in Ashkenazic congregations in both the morning and afternoon services. *Na'aritzcha v'nakdishcha* (We will revere You and sanctify You [according to the mystic utterance of the holy seraphim]), based on Isaiah 29:23, is the introduction to the *Kedushah* for all morning and afternoon services in Sephardic and Middle Eastern congregations. It is also used by Ashkenazim for the *Musaf* service on Sabbaths and festivals. The Sephardic, Yemenite, and most Hasidic traditions use *Keter yitnu* (A crown shall be ascribed to you [the heavenly angels above, with Your people Israel assembled beneath]) for the *Kedushah* in the *Musaf Amidah* for Sabbaths and festivals.

During the fifth century C.E., religious persecution in Persia that prohibited Jews from publicly reciting the *Shema* led the sages in that country to insert its first verse and last few words (*ani Adonai eloheichem*) regularly into the *Kedushah*. Convinced that the *Shema* had not been recited, government inspectors who were to enforce the prohibition would leave the synagogue before the repetition of the *Amidah*. Even after these persecutions ceased,[31] the *Shema* was so intricately woven into the fabric of the original text that it was retained in the *Musaf Kedushah* on the Sabbath and festivals to commemorate these events.[32] In the Land of Israel, there was considerable resistance to including the *Kedushah* in the daily prayers, and for centuries it did not become part of the liturgy. However, as the Church intensified its persecution and the degradation and poverty of the Jews worsened, the influence of Babylonian Jewry increased, and those in the Land of Israel eventually yielded and accepted this innovation,[33] which has become the established usage everywhere to this day.

The verse, "Holy, holy, holy, is the Lord of hosts," became a source of conflict with the Christians, who realized that the Jews failed to perceive it as a reference to the Trinity. Instead, the Jews employed the verse to proclaim the absolute unity of God by using the Aramaic translation of Onkelos, who interpreted it to mean: "God is holy in the heavens above; God is holy on the earth below; and God is holy to all eternity." In effect, the recitation of the *Kedushah* became both an assertion of God's unity and an implied repudiation of core Christian doctrine. When the Christians prohibited the recitation of the *Kedushah*, the Jews simply inserted it into another prayer, *Uva le-Zion Go'el* (A redeemer shall come to Zion; see below). This had the advantage of being recited at a time when the government censors were not in attendance—at the conclusion of the homily when the congregation reassembled for the afternoon service. Not only was the *Kedushah* inserted but its polemical Aramaic translation was included as well. This practice has persisted, and the prayer continues to appear just before the Torah reading in the afternoon service. Later, this prayer was taken over by the Babylonian Jews, who included it in the daily service, where it still remains.[34]

The *Kedushah* has also found its way into the long first blessing before the morning *Shema*. Unlike the practice during the repetition of the *Amidah*, here the *Kedushah* is said while seated. The explanation is that at this point in the service one is merely reading a scriptural passage describing the actions of the angels, rather than making a fundamental assertion of God's holiness, for which it would be required to stand. For the same reason, it is permitted to say this *Kedushah* even when praying alone. Lest there be any confusion, the third major verse of the standard *Kedushah* ("The Lord shall reign forever") is omitted, because these words were not said by the angels in the prophetic vision.[35]

Ya'aleh v'Yavo (יַעֲלֶה וְיָבֹא)

Ya'aleh v'Yavo ([Our God and God of our forefathers, may our remembrance] rise up and come ... [before You]) is a request that on this day God "remember us for good [well-being], be mindful of us for blessing, and save us for life." After each of these supplications, the congregation responds "amen." *Ya'aleh v'Yavo* is added to the *Amidah* on Rosh Hodesh and on the pilgrimage festivals of Passover, Shavuot, and Sukkot (and is also said in the Grace after Meals on these holidays). The prayer is incorporated into the blessing that asks for a return to the Temple service and makes allusion to the special offerings that were brought on these days.

Since the destruction of the Temple, Jews no longer can bring tangible gifts to offer God on the festivals. Nevertheless, just as Jews remember the historical events relating to each of these occasions and perform the prescribed rituals, we pray that God will remember the people of Israel and grant them both material benefits and ultimate redemption.[36]

Modim of the Rabbis

The 18th blessing of the *Amidah*, beginning with "*Modim Anachnu Lach*" (We give thanks to You), is a grateful acknowledgment of all the "miracles, wonders, and favors" that God has bestowed upon us. Each member of the congregation accepts God's sovereignty by bowing during these three words, like a slave acknowledging the complete authority of the master. However, what should the congregation say while the prayer leader bows and recites this section during the repetition of the *Amidah*? The Rabbis argued that each member of the congregation must make his or her own assertion of submission. After quoting the personal declarations of four prominent sages, the Talmud concludes that the worshiper should recite them all (Sot. 40a). This composite of short thanksgiving prayers was thus given the name *Modim* of the Rabbis.[37]

Abudarham suggested that the *Modim* of the Rabbis was included in the service because, although one is permitted to *petition* God through a representative (prayer leader), it is not appropriate to *thank* God through one. Since each individual is obligated to personally thank God, the *Modim* of the Rabbis is said quietly when the *shaliach tzibbur* recites aloud the standard text of *Modim Anachnu Lach*.[38] This prayer of thanksgiving is included in all prayer books, usually printed in a column parallel to the *Modim Anachnu Lach* benediction and in smaller type.[39]

Priestly Blessing (*Birkat Kohanim;* בִּרְכַּת כֹּהֲנִים)

The verse, "You shall bless the Children of Israel, saying unto them: 'May God bless you and keep you; may God shine His face upon you and be gracious unto you; may God lift up His countenance upon you and give you peace'" (Num. 6:23–26) is the biblical source for the Priestly Blessing (*Birkat Kohanim*). According to Bahya ibn Pekuda, these short blessings of three, five, and seven words, respectively, are to remind us of the foundation of all blessings—the three Patriarchs, the Five Books of Moses, and the seven Heavens. The verses progress from a request for material blessing and protection to a petition for spiritual blessing, and finally to a plea for the highest of divine blessings, the gift of peace.[40]

Each morning and evening immediately after the daily offerings in the Temple, the *Kohanim* would ascend a special raised platform (*dukhan*), place their *tallitot* over their heads, raise their arms, spread out their fingers in a special fanlike gesture (forming the Hebrew letter *"shin,"* the first letter of *"Shaddai,"* one of the names of God), and pronounce these three blessings, which included the Tetragrammaton (name of God). During the Second Temple period, the Priestly Blessing was also recited outside the Temple in the synagogues, just before the last benediction of the *Amidah*, substituting *"Adonai"* for the sacred name (Sot. 38a). The Talmud stressed that this did not mean that the *Kohanim* had any independent power to confer or withhold blessings—only God can assure people of success, abundance, and happiness; instead, the *Kohanim* served only as the channel through which the blessing was conveyed.

After the destruction of the Second Temple, the *Birkat Kohanim* became the last significant remnant of the priestly cult. Originally, it was part of the morning service each weekday, but as the daily business of the people did not allow them to concentrate with proper devotion, in the Diaspora the *Birkat Kohanim* was reserved for Sabbaths and holidays.[41] Today, local customs differ as to the place (morning or additional service) and time of the recital of the Priestly Blessing, which requires a minyan. The general Ashkenazic custom is to recite it only during the *Musaf Amidah* on the High Holy Days and the three pilgrimage festivals of Passover, Shavuot, and Sukkot (exclusive of *hol ha-mo'ed*). In Israel and among Sephardic Jews everywhere, the *Kohanim* go up to recite the Priestly Blessing every day in accordance with the ancient Temple practice. They do this during the *Amidah* of the morning service and, whenever there is an additional service, during the *Musaf Amidah*. On Yom Kippur, they also recite the Priestly Blessing during the *Ne'ilah* service.[42]

In all communities, if the *Kohanim* do not recite the Priestly Blessing, the prayer leader recites the text during the repetition of the *Amidah*, just before the final benediction.

After the *Kedushah* is recited, the *Kohanim* prepare themselves by removing their shoes and washing their hands (as before participating in the Temple service) with the assistance of the Levites. Standing before the ark and facing the congregation and with their *tallitot* covering their faces, the *Kohanim* repeat the Priestly Blessing in a haunting and mysterious tone, word for word after the prayer leader. While chanting the Priestly Blessing, the *Kohanim* stretch both arms out at shoulder height with their hands touching at the thumbs and their palms forward. The first two fingers of each hand should be separated from the other two to produce a fanlike appearance. This custom appears to derive from a commentary on the verse, "My beloved [Israel] is like a gazelle or a young deer who stands behind our wall, gazing in at the windows, looking through the lattice" (Song 2:9). The Rabbis considered this to be an allusion to the Kohen as he blessed the people, with the "windows" representing the Kohen's shoulders and arms and the "latticework" his fingers. In a later period, outstretched hands became symbolic of the *Kohanim*, and it is common to find this representation engraved on tombstones of members of the priestly family.

According to *halakhah*, every adult Kohen is required to perform the Priestly Blessing unless disqualified by certain physical or spiritual defects. As gleaned from various sources, a Kohen may not participate in the ritual if he has committed one of the three cardinal sins (idolatry, forbidden sexual intercourse, murder), is intoxicated, suffers from certain physical deformities, or is unable to articulate the words properly.

The congregation stands quietly, with head bowed and eyes cast down as a sign of respect and humility, carefully listening to every word spoken by the *Kohanim*. The Talmud forbids a person from looking at the hands of the *Kohanim* while they are pronouncing the Priestly Blessing, lest their "eyes become dimmed" (Hag. 16a). Rashi explains that this is due to the glow of the Divine Presence in the synagogue radiating from the fingers of the *Kohanim*.[43] In many communities a father draws his children to himself and covers them with his tallit. Congregants initially listened silently while the prayer leader recited the Priestly Blessing, but then began to say appropriate biblical quotations to themselves (Sot. 40a). Today, it is customary to respond with "amen" after each of the three sections when said by the *Kohanim*, but with "*kein yehi ratzon*" (so may it be Your will) when recited by the prayer leader.

In many synagogues, the Priestly Blessing is now often read by the rabbi or cantor, not necessarily a Kohen, as a closing benediction at the end of the service. It also is recited as a special blessing by the officiating rabbi on other occasions, such as bar and bat mitzvah ceremonies, weddings, and circumcisions.

On Sabbath eve, it is a custom for parents to bless their children with the Priestly Blessing, after saying either "May God make you like Ephraim and Manasseh" (for sons) or "May God make you like Sarah, Rebecca, Rachel, and Leah" (for daughters).

Prayer for Peace

The final benediction of the *Amidah* appears in two versions: **שִׂים שָׁלוֹם** (*Sim Shalom*; "Grant Peace"), which among Ashkenazim is said in the morning service, and **שָׁלוֹם רָב** (*Shalom Rav*; "Abundant Peace"), which is used in the afternoon and evening services. Sephardic Jews use the first version (*Sim Shalom*) in all services.[44]

For a long time, the two equally valid versions of the prayer for peace co-existed in different localities. Instead of choosing one and rejecting the other, the Rabbis made a compromise and retained both.[45] *Sim Shalom* is recited only at the morning and *Musaf* services, in which the Priestly Blessing is pronounced. The rationale of Etz Yosef is that the six forms of divine favor for which *Sim Shalom* prays—peace, goodness, blessing, graciousness, kindness, and compassion—allude to the six blessings of the Priestly Blessing, which immediately precedes it in the service.[46] Another explanation is that *Sim Shalom* contains words and phrases from the Priestly Blessing, such as "peace," "blessing," and "the light of Your countenance."[47] The *Kohanim* were not permitted to bless the people at the afternoon service, lest they had drunk some intoxicating liquor that would have disqualified them. The sole exception was on fast days, when there was no danger that the *Kohanim* would have had any alcohol to drink (Taan. 26b).[48]

***Tachanun* (תַּחֲנוּן)**

Tachanun (Supplication) is a prayer unit containing confessions of sins and petitions for God's grace and mercy that is recited immediately after the reader's repetition of the *Amidah* in the morning and afternoon services on weekdays. The talmudic sages added personal appeals to God after the prescribed prayers (Ber. 16b–17a), a custom that gradually was adopted by most worshipers, who added their own prayers after the formal service concluded (Ber. 31a). These prayers were optional for centuries and, when offered, were a spontaneous outpouring from the heart in which worshipers expressed their innermost thoughts and concerns. A standardized text for *Tachanun* became part of the congregational service only in the 16th century.[1]

When the prophet Gad offered King David the choice of who should punish the monarch for the grave sin of taking a census of the people in a manner contrary to that prescribed in the Torah (Exod. 30:12), David replied: "Let us fall, I pray you, into the hand of the Lord, for His mercies are many, but let me not fall into the hand of men" (2 Sam. 24:14). Except on Monday and Thursday, *Tachanun* begins with these words of David. The central penitential psalm is Psalm 6 in the Ashkenazic ritual and Psalm 25 in the Sephardic rite.[2]

A major feature of *Tachanun* is the act of *nefilat apayim* (lit., "falling on the face"). This submissive posture is based on the actions of Moses and Aaron in response to the Korach rebellion (Num. 16:22) and Joshua after the disastrous defeat at Ai (Josh. 7:6). In the Temple, the people knelt and prostrated themselves until their faces touched the ground, a gesture of absolute humility and total self-effacement, indicating complete submission to God. In modern times, however, the prayer is recited in a seated position with head lowered and the face buried in the bend of the left forearm. (Worshipers who wear tefillin on the left arm rest the head on the right arm out of respect for the tefillin.) This posture indicates the feelings of desolation and guilt that threaten to overwhelm the worshiper but that are mitigated by the unquenchable hope that God's mercy will provide salvation from even the most desperate situation.[3] Because the Bible records that Joshua (7:6) "lay with his face on the ground in front of the Ark of the Lord,"[4] the traditional posture of *Tachanun* is assumed only in the presence of a Torah scroll (in the ark) to designate the sanctity of the place; otherwise, it is recited with the head erect.[5]

The last paragraph of *Tachanun* stresses that we have tried everything "and do not know what is left for us to do" (2 Chron. 20:12). As did Moses, we have prayed in every possible manner—sitting (*Shema*), standing (*Amidah*), and figuratively falling on our faces in abject supplication (*Tachanun*). All that is left is to appeal to God's mercy and kindness to save us from our plight. The prayer leader concludes these prayers of supplication with the plea, "Help us, O God of our salvation, for the sake of Your Name's glory; rescue us and pardon our sins for Your Name's sake" (Ps. 79:9).[6]

On Monday and Thursday mornings, *Tachanun* is augmented by a lengthy opening section of supplications beginning with the words "*ve-Hu rachum*" (He, the merciful one [is forgiving of iniquity and does not destroy]). It describes the unending sufferings of the Jewish people throughout the ages, especially during the medieval period when these heartrending elegies were written. Rather than blaming God or a specific oppressor for the disasters that have befallen the people, these prayers admit that Israel has only received just punishment for its failure to faithfully fulfill the terms of the covenant. Pleading for divine mercy and forgiveness, the worshipers pray that the "living and everlasting God" will not forsake His people.[7]

The reason for the expanded *Tachanun* on Mondays and Thursdays is based on a seminal event in Israel's national history. According to the midrashic tradition, after the shameful episode of the Golden Calf, Moses ascended Mount Sinai on a Thursday (First of Elul) to receive the second set of the Ten Commandments. He descended 40 days later on a Monday, Yom Kippur, carrying with him not only the tablets of the Law but also God's forgiveness for Israel's sin. Ezra established the custom of rabbinical courts convening on Monday and Thursday, the traditional market days in ancient Israel. According to the kabbalistic literature, on these days the heavenly court judges human beings. Consequently, extra supplications were introduced into the *Tachanun* recited on these days with the hope that God will show mercy to those who humbly seek forgiveness for their transgressions.[8]

Tachanun is not recited on festive occasions and other joyous days when expressions of tragedy and grief would detract from the celebration. Similarly, it is also omitted on days of sadness, when there is no need to add to the sorrow. Therefore, *Tachanun* is not recited on Sabbaths, festivals (Passover, Shavuot, Sukkot, Rosh Hodesh, Purim, Hanukkah, Tu b'Shevat, Yom ha-Atzmaut, Lag ba-Omer, Yom Yerushalayim), between Yom Kippur and Sukkot,[9] and during the entire month of Nisan.[10] It is not said on Tisha b'Av, which according to tradition will be transformed from a day of sorrow to one of rejoicing in the Messianic Era. *Tachanun* is also omitted at services conducted in a house of mourning during shivah, in the presence of a bridegroom on the day of his wedding or for seven days thereafter (only three days if a remarriage for *both* parties), in the synagogue where a circumcision will take place later that day, and in the presence of a primary participant (father, *mohel, sandek*) in a *brit milah* that will take place elsewhere. In Hasidic congregations, *Tachanun* is not said on the yahrzeit of a rebbe, since this is regarded as an uplifting day that provides an opportunity for spiritual renewal rather than one of abject sadness.[11]

Torah Service

History of Reading the Torah

The Torah is the inheritance of the entire Jewish people. Unlike the sacred literature of other ancient religious communities, which was available only to a select few, study and knowledge of the Law is incumbent on every Jew. Rather than having exclusive access to these religious texts, priests, prophets, elders, and rabbis were responsible for teaching the Torah to all the people, so that they would clearly understand the laws and precepts required to lead a fully Jewish life.[1]

The Ten Commandments were not given just to Moses but rather to the whole Israelite nation encamped at the base of Mount Sinai (Exod. 20:15). According to the Talmud, Moses instituted the custom of publicly reading portions of the Torah on Sabbaths, festivals, and Rosh Hodesh (a semifestival in ancient times) (JT Meg. 4:1). On the second day of Sukkot during a sabbatical year, the king was commanded to "Assemble the people, the men and the women and the children" (Deut. 31:12) to listen to specific readings from the Book of Deuteronomy: from the beginning of the book to the end of the first paragraph of the *Shema* (1:1–6:9); the second paragraph of the *Shema* (11:13–21), and passages dealing with allegiance to God, the covenant between God and the Jewish people, and reward and punishment (14:22–28:69).[2]

The Talmud states that after the return from Babylonian exile, Ezra the Scribe introduced the practice of also publicly reading the Torah on the market days of Monday and Thursday (BK 82a). This was established for the convenience of those living in isolated areas, who were unable to attend a local prayer meeting on the Sabbath. Because farmers came to town to do their shopping and trading, the market days were a perfect time to gather the people to teach them Torah. This eventually became the custom even in larger towns where a regular Sabbath reading of the Torah took place. For the sake of the town merchants, who had to protect their wares and thus could not leave their stalls when the Torah was being read on Mondays and Thursdays, Ezra instituted an extra reading of the Torah on Sabbath afternoon (which also became common practice).[3] Another explanation for this custom was to accommodate those who lived far from the center of town and could not attend the Saturday morning service early enough to hear the Torah read.[4]

The Rabbis suggested that Ezra may have merely formalized a preexisting practice (BK 82a). The Israelites in the wilderness were described as becoming weary because they "walked for three days ... and did not find water" (Exod. 15:22). Deeming water to be a symbol of Torah, the Rabbis developed the metaphor that just as water provides life-sustaining refreshment to the body, so is Torah indispensable sustenance for the soul. Therefore, they understood the biblical verse to imply that the weariness of the people resulted from having gone three days without the sacred nourishment of Torah. The practice of reading the Torah on Monday and Thursday, in addition to the Sabbath, ensured that there would never be a three-day period without a public Torah reading that was so essential to the soul of Israel.[5] Another theory is that the Torah is read on Mondays and Thursdays because these are especially propitious days for supplication. According to tradition, it was on a Thursday that Moses ascended Mount Sinai to receive the Ten Commandments, and he returned with them on a Monday.

Annual Versus Triennial Cycle

Initially, the biblical passages read were chosen by the head of the congregation or the Torah reader, either as suitable for the occasion or appropriate for the planned homily. Thus there was no systematic order for the substance and length of the public Torah readings until the Rabbis established the practice of consecutive readings.

In the Land of Israel, the text was divided into 155 portions, which were read on each Sabbath in the synagogue so as to cover the entire Torah in three years (Meg. 29b). In effect, what now is considered the weekly Torah portion—called parashah by Ashkenazim and *sidrah* by Sephardim—was read over three successive weeks. This practice probably originated because of the necessity of accommodating an Aramaic translation and exposition of the biblical verses during the reading. However, it did ensure that the Torah reading often corresponded thematically or was at least appropriate for the festivals and other special occasions. The triennial cycle in the Land of Israel began on the First of Nisan, so that the reading about the Creation of the world was heard at the start of the first month of the biblical calendar (Exod. 12:2), which was the date of the event according to Rabbi Joshua (RH 11a). In the second year of the cycle, the reading describing the Exodus from Egypt and the laws of Passover (Exod. 12) coincided with the time of the festival; the Ten Commandments (Exod. 20:1–14) were read on Shavuot, when the giving of the Torah is commemorated; and the sacrificial ritual for Yom Kippur (Lev. 16) was read on or close to the Day of Atonement. During the third year of the cycle, the dedication of the Sanctuary (Num. 6:22) was read in early Nisan, when the biblical event took place, whereas the last section of Deuteronomy, which describes the death of Moses, was always read at the beginning of Adar, the month in which the Lawgiver died according to rabbinic tradition.[6]

The large and influential community of Jews in Babylonia developed the custom of completing the entire Torah in a single year, and this rule eventually became the generally accepted practice throughout the world. The Babylonian tradition divided the Torah into 54 sections, making it inevitable that two portions be read on some occasions to complete the entire Torah during the year (especially since the regularly scheduled weekly portion is postponed for a week when a major festival falls on a Sabbath).[7] The relatively lengthy Torah portions from Genesis are never combined, because this would extend the service unduly and violate the Jewish legal principle against imposing unnecessary inconvenience on the congregation (*tircha de-tzibbura*).

Some American Conservative synagogues have returned to a triennial cycle, though they read only one-third of each parashah every year. Thus the initial third of a given portion is read in the first year, the middle third in the second year, and the final third in the third year—resulting in the entire Torah being read every three years. This practice has become increasingly popular, though it has the distinct disadvantage that the Torah is no longer read consecutively, so that narratives and bodies of biblical legislation are interrupted.

The Ark: Removing and Returning the Scroll

The most ceremonial ritual of the synagogue service, especially on the Sabbath and festivals, is the removal of the Torah from the ark and the return of the scroll after the reading has been completed. It clearly demonstrates the centrality of the Torah and its teachings in the Jewish tradition. The Torah must be carried with the right arm and received on the right when handed from one person to another, probably reflecting the fact that most people are right-handed and have a stronger right arm. This practice has also been linked to two biblical verses, "From

CHAPTERS AND VERSES

Although the Torah scroll has no punctuation, in the printed Five Books of Moses the text is subdivided into chapters and verses. This division was a 13th-century Christian innovation designed to aid missionaries and those engaged in public theological disputations with the Jews to quickly find numerous quotations to support their specious arguments. Thus it became necessary for rabbis to use the same system of chapters and verses so as to quickly find the references used by their enemies and offer effective rebuttals to the Christian version of the Jewish text.[1]

His right hand He presented the fiery Torah to them"[8] (Deut 33:2) and "His right hand embraces me" (Song 2:6), an allegory of the love of God for Israel.[9] The prominence of the right hand in ritual actions is also found in a description of the installation of the *Kohanim*, when Moses dabbed the blood of the sacrificial ram "on the ridge of Aaron's right ear, and on the thumb of his right hand, and on the big toe of his right foot" (Lev. 8:23–24).[10] Because the right side symbolizes the majesty and power of God, before being read the Torah is always taken first to the right side (i.e., proceeding counterclockwise when leaving the *bimah*, or "platform") when carried in procession around the synagogue.[11]

Just as one is commanded to rise before elders (Lev. 19:32), which the Rabbis extended to Torah scholars, how much more so should one rise before "a scroll of the Law" (Kid. 33b) when it is taken out of the ark and remain standing until it is laid down on the reading stand. The Torah is carried in a procession around the synagogue before and after the reading to emulate the pious men of Jerusalem who "followed it as a mark of respect" (Sof. 14:14). During the procession, members of the congregation honor the passing scroll by touching the covering mantle with the fingers, a tallit, or a prayer book and then kissing that object.[12]

Whenever the Torah is read in the synagogue, two biblical verses (Num. 10:35–36) are recited when opening and closing the ark, respectively. These are the invocation prayers recited by the Israelites in the wilderness when the Ark of the Covenant went forward or rested. In the Torah scroll, these verses are set off from the rest of the text by inverted "*nuns*". This indicates either that the verses are not in their original place or that they were taken from another source—such as the Book of the Wars of the Lord, which apparently contained an anthology of poems describing the divine victories over the enemies of Israel—and form a distinct section, scroll, or even "book" of the Torah. According to the last of these theories, the Book of Numbers was once divided into three parts, bringing the total number of books in the Torah to seven. Support for this view is the verse, "Wisdom has built her house, she has hewn out her seven pillars" (Prov. 9:1), which was interpreted as meaning that the Torah, the repository of the supreme wisdom, must also consist of seven parts.[13]

The first of these verses, *Va-yehi binso'a ha-aron* (When the ark would journey, [Moses said, "Arise, God, and let Your foes be scattered, let those who hate You flee from before You"]), describes the ark going forward at the head of the tribes of Israel, symbolizing God protecting the people and leading them on to final victory. The second verse opens with "*U-v'nucho yomar*" (When it rested, he [Moses] said) and continues, "Return, O Lord, unto the ten thousands of the families of Israel" (or, in an alternative translation, "Reside tranquilly, O God, among the many thousands of Israel"), an appropriate salutation to God as the ark returned in triumph.

Another verse recited when the Torah is removed from the ark is *Ki mi-Zion* (For out of Zion shall go forth the Torah, the word of the Lord from Jerusalem; Isa. 2:3), a prophecy of the ultimate Messianic Age. Most congregations add *Berich shemei* (Praised is the name), an Aramaic prayer from the Zohar that asks for divine favor, redemption, long life, and sustenance, and closes with the supplication, "May it be Your will to open my heart to the Torah, and to fulfill the wishes of my heart and of the hearts of all Your people Israel, for good, for life, and for peace."

On the three pilgrimage festivals (Passover, Shavuot, Sukkot), in the Ashkenazic tradition it is customary to add several additional prayers before *Berich shemei* (though like all personal supplications, they are omitted when the festival falls on the Sabbath). The Thirteen Attributes (see p. 180) are recited three times, as are two verses, "May the words of my mouth and the meditation of my heart be acceptable before You" (Ps. 19:15), and "As for me, may my prayer come to You, O Lord, at a favorable moment; O God, in Your abundant mercy, answer me with Your sure deliverance" (Ps. 69:14).[14]

When the scroll has been returned to the ark, the Torah is compared to an *etz hayim* (tree of life), and the ritual concludes with the verse, "Take us back, O Lord, to Yourself and let us come back; renew our days as of old" (Lam. 5:21).

After the Torah has been removed from the ark, on Sabbaths and festivals the prayer leader chants the *Shema* and the verse *Echad Eloheinu, gadol Adoneinu, kadosh shemo* (One is our God, great is our master, holy is His name), both of which are repeated by the congregation. On weekdays, these verses are omitted. In Ashkenazic congregations, those on the *bimah* turn and face the ark, and the entire congregation bows while the prayer leader chants, "Declare the greatness of the Lord with me, and let us exalt His name together" (Ps. 34:4).

Separate Scrolls for Each Reading

It is traditional to use a different scroll for every extra Torah reading that is required on special occasions. When Rosh Hodesh or a festival falls on the Sabbath, a description of the appropriate sacrifices is read as the *maftir* portion (see p. 459) from the second scroll. Occasionally, readings are made from three separate scrolls, as when the Sabbath of Hanukkah coincides with the new moon of the month of Tevet (Meg. 29b).[15] When this occurs, the ordinary weekly portion is read from the first scroll, the special portion for Rosh Hodesh from the second, and the section for Hanukkah from the third. Employing a separate scroll for each special reading, rather than using a single scroll and simply rolling it to the next passage to be read, is based on the principle of *k'vod ha-tzibbur* (regard for the honor of the congregation) (Yoma 70a). Noting that some congregants stand throughout the Torah reading, Maimonides explained that having two scrolls was consistent with the principle of not imposing an unnecessary burden on the community.[16] For similar reasons, the Torah scroll is always prepared in advance by being rolled to the proper place before the service begins.

Aliyot

The honor of reciting the blessings over the Torah is called an *aliyah* (plural, *aliyot*), which means "going up." This refers both to the physical ascent of the person to the *bimah* where the Torah is read and to the spiritual uplifting associated with participation in this hallowed ritual.[17]

The number of *aliyot* varies widely (Meg. 4:1–2). Three people are called to the Torah on Monday and Thursday mornings, on Sabbath afternoons, during the *Mincha* service on Yom Kippur, on the festivals of Hanukkah and Purim, and on all fast days. Among the reasons offered for this ruling are the three classes of Jews (*Kohanim*, Levites, Israelites) that must be represented; the threefold division of the Bible (Torah, Prophets, Writings); and the threefold Priestly Blessing, the first of which contains three Hebrew words (Meg. 21b). On Monday and Thursday mornings, when congregants have to go to work, calling up more than three people would overly lengthen the service. If there were more than three *aliyot* at *Mincha* on Saturday afternoon, the service would not be completed before dark (Rashi, Meg. 21a).[18] Each *aliyah* must consist of a minimum of three verses (Meg. 4:4), and a public Torah reading must have a minimum of 10 verses (Meg. 21b)—a practice traditionally related to the number of commandments in the Decalogue. The only exceptions to this practice are the reading for Purim morning (Exod. 17:8–16) and the weekday reading for the section of Va-yelekh (Deut. 31:1–9), when a total of nine verses are read.[19]

There are four *aliyot* on Rosh Hodesh and on the intermediate days (*hol ha-mo'ed*) of Passover and Sukkot; five on Rosh Hashanah and on the festival days of Passover, Shavuot, and Sukkot; six on the morning of Yom Kippur; and seven on Sabbath morning.

On Sabbath mornings, some congregations take advantage of a provision in Jewish law that permits dividing the Torah portion into more (but not less) than the required number of *aliyot* (Meg. 23a). This is not permitted on Mondays or Thursdays or when Rosh Hodesh, Hanukkah, and fast days fall during the midweek, lest it waste the time of people who must go to work (*bittul melakhah*). These extra *aliyot* (*hosafot*) allow one or more additional persons to have the honor of being called up to the Torah.[20] Other congregations reject this practice because it lengthens the service, insisting on limiting the number to the prescribed seven *aliyot*.[21]

There are two traditions concerning the proper way to approach the *bimah* when called for an *aliyah*. One custom is to ascend on the right and descend from the left, in accordance with the practice of approaching the altar in the Temple (Zev. 63a–b). In addition, the entrance to the

Temple Mount was from the right (Mid. 2:2). The other tradition is to ascend to the *bimah* by the shortest route and descend by the longest, thus demonstrating that one is eager to be called for an *aliyah* and reluctant to leave. According to the Shulchan Arukh, if it is necessary to choose between these two traditions, one should take the shorter route, even if this requires going up from the left (OH 141:7).[22]

It is a dishonor to the Torah to leave the *bimah* immediately after reciting the final blessing that concludes the *aliyah*. Among Ashkenazim, it is customary to remain until the entire subsequent Torah portion has been read and the final blessing recited. In the Spanish-Portuguese tradition, one waits only until the person honored with the next *aliyah* has recited the first Torah blessing, returning to one's seat while the Torah is being read.

In Ashkenazic synagogues, other worshipers typically congratulate the person returning from having an *aliyah* with the Yiddish phrase "*Yasher ko'ach*" (Hebrew: *Yishar koa'ch*; "May you grow in strength" or "May your strength be directed in the right path"). This custom may reflect the belief in talmudic times that intense study of the Torah, symbolized by the Torah reading, "weakens the strength of man" (Sanh. 26b). Among Sephardim, the expression used is "*Hazak u-varuch*" (Be strong and be blessed) or "*Baruch tihiyeh*" (May you be blessed), to which the person returning from having an *aliyah* responds "*Hazak ve-ematz*" (Be strong and of good courage). Sephardic women, primarily those from Syria, Iran, and Iraq, make an ululating sound after the Torah honoree (especially a bar mitzvah or bridegroom) has concluded the final blessing or has left the *bimah* to take his seat. This practice is thought to avert the evil designs of malevolent spirits determined to cast a pall on all joyous events, similar to the original rationale for breaking a glass at the end of the wedding ceremony (see p. 45).[23]

Traditionally, two people are not called up for the same *aliyah*. Jewish law requires that congregants hear every word of the Torah reading distinctly, which is difficult if two persons chant the portion simultaneously. This ruling was extended to prohibit two people from being called up to the Torah together, even if only to recite the blessings, since worshipers unable to hear the words clearly would not be permitted to respond "amen." In some Conservative and Reform congregations, two or more people are frequently called up for the same *aliyah*, especially when there is a bar or bat mitzvah. They may either recite the blessings in unison or have one person recite the blessing before the Torah reading and the other the blessing after it.[24]

Traditionally, two blood relatives may not be called consecutively to the Torah, either because of fear that the evil eye will cast a spell upon a family receiving too many blessings or because Jewish law forbids near relatives from testifying together—and those pronouncing the Torah blessings are effectively giving testimony to the truth of the sacred text. However, it is permitted to have one read the seventh *aliyah* and the other the *maftir* portion.

Allocation

The Talmud notes that the precise system for allocating *aliyot* was developed "for the sake of preserving peace in the congregation" (Git. 5:8). The privilege of the first *aliyah* is given to a Kohen. These members of the priestly caste and descendants of Aaron were to be shown honor and deference because they were consecrated to God and offered the sacrifices to the Lord (Lev. 21:8). The second person to be called to the Torah is a Levite, a descendant of the family that also played a major role in the Temple service. The remaining *aliyot* are distributed among the rest of the congregation, who are classified as "Israelites." Nevertheless, a Kohen or Levite may be called for the seventh *aliyah* on the Sabbath or for *maftir*, which is given to the person who reads the haftarah (see below) (Git. 60a). If there is no Kohen, a Levite has the next priority. If there is no Levite, an Israelite is called first. In either of these cases, an announcement is made that the individual is being awarded the *aliyah* "in place of the Kohen" (*bim'kom Kohen*). If there is no Levite, the Kohen who received the first *aliyah* is awarded the second one as well. Reform and some liberal Conservative synagogues have abolished the distinction between Kohen, Levite, and Israelite, both because it is difficult to be certain of the lineage of any Jew (though a genetic characteristic of *Kohanim* has been reported) and because of a belief in equality for all their members.

On the Sabbath the third and sixth *aliyot* are particularly esteemed, and it is customary to give them to learned individuals or to the person who sponsors the refreshments after services. It is an even greater honor to receive the final *aliyah* for each of the five books of the Torah.

This is based on the midrashic phrase, "the last [one] is most beloved" (Gen. R. 78:8), which relates to Genesis 33:2, in which Jacob, fearing a conflict with his brother, Esau, placed his adored Rachel and her son Joseph in the safest position at the rear. Other especially honored *aliyot* are *Shirat ha-Yam* (Song at the Sea; Exod. 15:1–21) and the Ten Commandments (Exod. 20:2–14; Deut. 5:6–18), for which the congregation stands while the Torah is being read.

According to an old tradition, those commemorating specific events in their lives are given precedence in receiving the honor of being called to the Torah. Because of the limited number of *aliyot* available, it has become necessary to develop guidelines concerning those who should receive them. In this way, "the potential for bias among synagogue leaders is eliminated, resentment among worshippers is reduced, and dissension is avoided."[25] In general, priority in the distribution of the third *aliyah* onward is as follows:[26]

1. A bridegroom on the Sabbath before his wedding.
2. A boy who has turned 13 years of age (bar mitzvah).
3. The father of a newborn infant, male or female, on the first Sabbath that the mother appears in the synagogue.
4. A bridegroom on the Sabbath after his wedding.
5. The father of a baby girl who is to be named.
6. One observing yahrzeit for a parent on that day.
7. The father of a baby to be circumcised on that day or during the coming week.
8. One observing yahrzeit for a parent during the coming week
9. One required to recite the blessing of *gomel* (see p. 480).
10. One who is about to leave on a long journey or has just returned from one.
11. A distinguished guest in the community.

When two or more people are observing the same occasion, priority is generally given to a regular worshiper over one who comes infrequently and to a member of the congregation over a nonmember.[27] Some congregations try to provide *aliyot* for those who are or will be observing yahrzeit for someone other than a parent, often in the format of a "group" *aliyah*.

Torah Blessings

According to Jewish law, the recitation of a blessing is required before performing most positive commandments, which includes the study of Torah (Meg. 21b). Since it is considered a form of study, the reading of the Torah in the synagogue must be preceded by a blessing. The recitation of a blessing at the completion of the Torah reading is derived from the custom of saying a form of the *Kaddish* (*Kaddish de-Rabbanan*; see p. 394) after completing Torah study sessions in the academies of learning.[28]

Originally, only two Torah blessings were recited—one by the first person before he began to read and the second by the last person after he had completed his reading (Meg. 21a). Those in between read their Torah portions without reciting any blessings at all. The first blessing, which opened the Torah service, was introduced by the *Barchu* (see p. 411), just as this traditional call to worship was recited before the *Shema*, which marked the beginning of the public worship service. The current practice, in which each person called to the reading of the Torah recites both blessings (and the preliminary *Barchu*), is a later rabbinic innovation. The stated rationale for this change was "to avoid error on the part of people entering and leaving the synagogue" (Meg. 21b). Otherwise, a person who came in after the reading had begun and saw a new person starting to read the Torah without saying a blessing, might think that no preliminary blessing is necessary. Similarly, those who leave before the reading is concluded might think that no blessing at all is necessary after reading the Torah. Another explanation for this practice is that those members of the congregation who arrive after the beginning of the Torah reading or leave before its end would not be deprived of the chance of hearing both blessings and responding "amen." The additional blessings also helped satisfy the tradition of the pious to recite a minimum of 100 benedictions daily (see p. 388).[29] Among Sephardim, the person called for an *aliyah* prefaces the preliminary *Barchu* with "*Adonai imachem*" (May the Lord be with you), to which the congregation responds, "*Yevarechecha Adonai*" (May the Lord bless you).[30]

Each Torah blessing contains 20 words, and the total of 40 symbolizes the number of days that Moses spent on Mount Sinai to receive the Law. The first blessing emphasizes that God chose Israel to receive the

Torah. It contains a grammatical inconsistency that has been invested with great theological significance. The first portion of the blessing describes God as *natan ha-Torah* (Who gave us the Torah), whereas the second changes this to *notein ha-Torah* (Who gives us the Torah). According to the Rabbis, structuring the second part of the blessing in the present tense indicates that the Torah is not merely a static and lifeless text. Instead, it was considered conclusive proof that Revelation is a continuing process, with subsequent interpretations of the Torah (Oral Law) also being divine and thus binding.[31]

The second blessing thanks God for giving us *Torat emet* (Torah of truth; interpreted as the Written Law) and having "planted everlasting life in our midst." This latter phrase parallels the verse, "The words of the sages are planted " (Eccles. 12:11), thus also thanking God for the Oral Law.[32] It also serves as an affirmation of the rabbinic concept of the existence of *olam ha-ba* (the world to come; see p. 114), promising that Israel will be an eternal people as long as it studies the Torah and lives according to its teachings.[33]

Each person called up for an *aliyah* traditionally touches the fringes (tzitzit) of the tallit to the scroll at the place where the reading is to begin and then kisses them before reciting the first Torah blessing. This sign of love and respect for the Torah is then repeated at the place where the reading ended and before reciting the final Torah blessing.

The Talmud describes two different procedures regarding whether the Torah scroll should be rolled closed while the Torah blessings are being recited (Meg. 32a). According to Rabbi Meir, a person called up for an *aliyah* should open the scroll, look at the place where the reading is to begin, roll the scroll closed, recite the first Torah blessing, and then unroll the scroll for reading. His rationale was that if the scroll were left open, an uninformed person might mistakenly think that the blessings are being read from the scroll itself. Rabbi Judah disagreed, arguing that there was no need to close the scroll because no one would be foolish enough to imagine that the blessings were written in it. Ashkenazic Jews generally follow the ruling of Rabbi Meir and close the scroll while the Torah blessings are recited (or cover it with the mantle or a special cloth). Sephardic Jews usually neither roll the Torah scroll closed nor cover it when reciting the blessings.[34]

Another custom is for the person reciting the Torah blessings to grasp the wooden rollers (*atzei hayim*; trees of life), based on the verse,

"It [the Torah] is a Tree of Life to those who take hold of it" (Prov. 3:18). Some raise the base of the *atzei hayim* when they pronounce any form of the word "Torah" in the blessings, indicating that it is the identical Torah that Moses received on Mount Sinai.

Reading the Torah

Originally, each person called to the Torah read his own portion (Meg. 3:11). Indeed, the Tosefta states that if only one person was competent to read from the Torah, he was to be given all the *aliyot*. This tradition continued through the medieval period and was codified as the norm in the Shulchan Arukh (OH 139:1–2). This passage, however, made an allowance for the situation in which a person who was unable to read his own portion might be needed because he was the only Kohen or Levite present. Therefore, it permitted one who was properly prepared to read the Torah portion for the person having an *aliyah*, who in turn was required to repeat the passage word for word.

As Torah learning among the laypeople declined, there were many communities where not all Jews knew how to read from the Torah scroll. As a result, some individuals were prevented from ever having an *aliyah*. An apparently simple solution was to allow such a person to merely recite the appropriate blessings, while a knowledgeable official of the synagogue read the Torah selection. However, this served only to publicly humiliate some members of the congregation by showing that they were so unlearned that they required a substitute to read for them. To solve this dilemma, the Rabbis found an ancient precedent relating to some farmers bringing their first fruits to the Temple in Jerusalem who were embarrassed by their ignorance of the proper prayers to recite. As the Mishnah relates, at first those who knew the prayers would recite them, while those who did not would simply repeat them after the *Kohen* (Bik. 3:7). However, when this led to some unlearned individuals not bringing their offerings because they were ashamed by this public display of their ignorance, the decision was to have everyone repeat the words after the *Kohen*. Following this example, the Rabbis ruled that an official Torah reader (*baal korei*, or more grammatically correct, *baal keriah*, meaning "master of the reading") would read for everyone—scholar and ignorant alike. With the person called to the Torah required only to recite the prescribed blessings, the privilege of having an *aliyah* is available to everyone.[35]

The person having an *aliyah* always stands to the right of the *baal korei*, just as one always holds the Torah with the right arm (see p. 440). This has the practical advantage that the Torah reader (standing on the left) can hold the pointer in the right hand (the stronger in most) while reading from the scroll. Because Hebrew is read from right to left, the person having the *aliyah* can clearly follow along in the text as the Torah pointer is moved from word to word.[36]

The *baal korei* must look at the actual words of the scroll when reading the Torah. This decreases the possibility that the Torah reader will make any mistakes (adding, omitting, or mispronouncing words) that would alter the meaning. Moreover, this also enables the *baal korei* to identify any indistinct letters or scribal errors. If a major error is discovered, the reading is immediately halted and the defective scroll is replaced with another one from the ark. For minor errors, such as faded letters, the reading is completed and the scroll is then taken out of service to be repaired. An intriguing custom for determining the severity of faded letters, rarely employed today, is to call up a child to view them. If the letters are sufficiently clear that the child is able to read the words correctly, the reading from that scroll is permitted to continue.[37]

The *baal korei* chants the Torah reading using a special trope—a series of musical notations used as early as talmudic times, when Rabbi Yochanan noted that the Bible should be read and studied with a pleasant melody (Meg. 32a). However, this system was not perfected until the work of the Masoretes (see p. 493), primarily members of the ben Asher family of Tiberias in the ninth and tenth centuries, who devised universally accepted accents that over the years were developed into distinctive musical notes by various Jewish communities. There are currently five musical modes: Yemenite, Ashkenazic, Middle Eastern and North African, Jerusalem Sephardic, and northern Mediterranean. "The Ashkenazic style can be divided into western and eastern substyles. The former is still preserved by Jewish communities from Frankfurt and Hanover and is popular in Great Britain. The eastern Ashkenazic style developed in the Polish-Lithuanian communities, and it remains [with variations] the most common system of musical motifs in North American Ashkenazic synagogues today."[38]

The Torah reader must memorize the cantillation, since there are no trope markings in the scroll. In some congregations, an official standing next to the *baal korei* uses hand movements to cue the reader regarding vocal modulations, the length of specific notes, and the word that ends each verse.[39]

Although the law explicitly states that a woman may not *write* a Torah scroll for public use (see p. 325), it is quite clear that she may *read* the Torah at a public service. The Talmud states, "All are qualified to be among the seven [who read the Torah before the congregation on a Sabbath], even a minor and a woman" (Meg. 23a). However, the text continues, "the sages said that a woman should not read the Torah because of *k'vod ha-tzibbur*." This is usually translated as "honor of the congregation" and interpreted to mean that if a woman were to read from the Torah, it would give the impression that there was no man qualified to do so. Support for this opinion is a similar rabbinic ruling with respect to the Grace after Meals (Ber. 20b). Although a woman is permitted to recite the *Birkat ha-Mazon* on behalf of her husband in certain circumstances, it was considered demeaning in that it would imply that he was incapable of doing so and thus would cast doubt on his education and piety. Another view is that *k'vod ha-tzibbur* may refer to proper etiquette among the sexes, with the Rabbis fearing that a woman reading the Torah could cause sexual distraction during the most significant service of the week. Indeed, they considered sexual distraction such a grave problem that they instituted the strict separation of men and women at worship services (*mechitzah*; see p. 337) and prohibited a woman from reading or reciting before men.[40]

A spurious argument for prohibiting women from publicly reading the Torah is that they may be menstruating and somehow render the scroll ritually impure and unfit for use by touching it. However, the Talmud unequivocally states that "the words of the Torah are not susceptible to ritual impurity" (Ber. 22a). Therefore, a menstruating woman is permitted to hold or kiss a Torah, just as she may touch and kiss a mezuzah, which encases a parchment scroll of passages from the Torah.[41] Today, women routinely read the Torah in egalitarian Conservative and Reform congregations as well as in Orthodox all-women minyanim.

Certain parts of the Torah are traditionally deemed so important that they must be read without being subdivided into more than one *aliyah*. These include *Shirat ha-Yam* (Song at the Sea; Exod. 15:1–19), both versions of the Ten Commandments (Exod. 20:2–14; Deut. 5:6–18), the listing of the 42 places in the desert where the Israelites stopped during their trek in the wilderness (Num. 33:1–49), and the *Tochachah* (Lev. 26:14–39; Deut 28:15–68)—the catalog of curses that the Israelites will suffer if they fail to properly observe the divine commandments.

Although it is customary to stand up when the Torah is removed from or returned to the ark, members of the congregation are seated while the Torah is read. A practical reason for this tradition in that it would be difficult for many worshipers to remain standing for the entire Torah reading. Moreover, reading the Torah in the synagogue is considered a form of study, for which students usually are seated. However, congregants do stand when certain especially significant passages are read—the Ten Commandments, *Shirat ha-Yam*, and the last verse of each of the Five Books of Moses.[42]

Certain Torah verses that depict disastrous scenarios are traditionally read softly and rapidly, based on the superstitious belief that their mere mention may cause them to occur or recur. These sections include the horrendous curses (*Tochachah*) that will befall the Israelites if they do not follow the divine commandments and the blasphemy of the Golden Calf (Exod. 32).

Translation and Exposition of the Torah

When the Jews returned from exile in Babylonia, where the vernacular was Aramaic, Hebrew was no longer the spoken tongue of the masses. The custom developed of having a special synagogue official (*meturgeman*) provide a verse-by-verse translation of the Torah reading. This was a challenging task because the translator was prohibited from having any written material in front him, since the translation was regarded as part of the Oral Law (which could not be written down). The *meturgeman* was "not permitted to translate word by word, lest he distort the sense of the text, nor was he permitted to elaborate on the text. His was to be a free, though exact translation. If he took any liberties with the translation, he was to be 'silenced and admonished.'" As the Tosefta observed, "He who translates a verse with strict literalness is a falsifier, and he who makes additions to it is a blasphemer." (Meg. 4:9)[43] Many centuries later, this gave rise to the *Targum Onkelos*, the official Aramaic version, which was officially accepted by first-century sages in the Land of Israel and today is printed next to the Torah text in most rabbinic Bibles.[44] Eventually, the practice of translating into the vernacular was discontinued because it unduly lengthened the service.

During the talmudic period, the custom developed of having a Rabbi expound at length on the text immediately after the reading from the Torah. This was the origin of the *derash* (lit., "searching"), a sermon or homily that interpreted the Torah reading and applied its teachings to the daily life of the people.

Other Functionaries Related to the Torah Reading

Gabbaim

The *gabbaim* (sing., *gabbai*) serve as an "honor guard" on either side of the Torah scroll as it lies on the reading table. The term originally referred to a pair of individuals who aided in the collection of taxes and charitable contributions for the community but eventually was applied only to those who supervise the synagogue services. According to the Jerusalem Talmud, just as the Torah was transmitted at Sinai through an intermediary (Moses), so there must be at least three persons standing on the *bimah*—the Torah reader (representing Moses, the "agent" through whom the Torah was given) and the two synagogue officials (symbolizing God and Israel) (Meg. 4:1). In capital cases before a Jewish court, two witnesses must attest that the accused had been forewarned about the consequences of the crime he was about to commit. Based on the verse, "I call heaven and earth this day to witness against you" (Deut. 4:26), the Vilna Gaon concluded that "two witnesses" must flank the person who reads to the congregation the warnings contained in the Torah, so that these admonitions comport with Jewish legal practice.[45]

One *gabbai* is responsible for calling people up to the Torah and reciting the special *Mi She Berakh*[46] prayer (see p. 462) after each *aliyah*. The other typically covers the Torah scroll after the second Torah blessing of one *aliyah* is completed and then removes the covering when the next person called for an *aliyah* is ready to begin the first blessing. However, the major duty of the *gabbaim* is to closely follow the Torah reading from a printed text and quietly correct any mistakes. Such errors are easy to make, since the scroll has neither punctuation nor vowel signs.[47]

Hagbah and *Gelilah*

The verse "And Ezra opened the book in the sight of all the people" (Neh. 8:5) is the biblical precedent for raising an open scroll so that the entire congregation can view the Torah script. The person who lifts the Torah traditionally opens at least three columns of the scroll before raising it up as high as possible, and then slowly turns to show the script to all assembled. This allows everyone in the congregation to see the text and proclaim *v'zot ha-Torah* (this is the Torah [that Moses placed before the Children of Israel]; Deut. 4:44). Some worshipers raise the edges of the tallit toward the script and then kiss the tzitzit, though the halakhic requirement is merely to bow toward the open Torah.[48]

Ashkenazim and Sephardim have developed different traditions for the timing and wording of this dramatic ceremony. In Ashkenazic congregations, the Torah scroll is raised after the reading is completed, whereas Sephardim raise the Torah scroll before the reading begins. In addition, in the Ashkenazic rite there is the addition of a second verse, "at the Lord's bidding through Moses" (Num. 9:23). Although now everyone at an Ashkenazic service says both verses together, at one time only the person who raised the Torah may have recited the first line, while the second was the congregational response.[49]

"*Hagbah*" is the term for raising the Torah, which is performed by the *magbi'ah*; "*gelilah*" is the word for rolling up and tying the Torah scroll and replacing its cover and ornaments, which is done by the *goleil*. The Talmud does not appear to separate these two functions, referring primarily to the latter (Meg. 32a). Indeed, at one time, the person who received the last *aliyah* may have performed both of these duties. However, having one person responsible for both holding the Torah and tying the binder around the scroll could be fraught with hazard and presumably led to the decision to share the honor between two people. Although these activities do not require the recitation of a blessing, *hagbah* and *gelilah* are considered religiously significant roles. Some Rabbis viewed the honor of *gelilah* as having the spiritual reward of all the *aliyot* combined, and thus this task was traditionally reserved for the most distinguished members of the congregation. Over time, *hagbah* became the more coveted task. In Western Sephardic congregations there were special groups of individuals—*levantadores* ("master lifters" of the scroll)—who were exclusively honored with the role of *hagbah* so as to minimize the danger of dropping the scroll or handling it in a degrading way.[50] In modern Sephardic congregations, *gelilah* is generally performed by one of the *gabbaim* standing on either side of the Torah reader.[51]

Completion of One of the Five Books

According to Jewish custom, the completion of any of the Five Books of Moses is marked in the synagogue by the congregation rising and exclaiming "*Hazak, hazak, ve-nitchazek*" (Be strong! be strong! And let us be strengthened [in our efforts]). This phrase may relate to the talmudic statement, "Four things must be done with energy [strength]: [study of] Torah, good deeds, praying, and one's worldly occupation (*derekh eretz*)" (Ber. 32b). Three biblical verses containing the word "*hazak*" address these issues. The exhortation of Joab, King David's general, before battle, "Be of good courage, and let us prove strong for our people" (2 Sam. 10:12), is viewed as a plea to be strengthened in good deeds and *derekh eretz*. "Be strong and let your heart be brave, and hope in the Lord" (Ps. 27:14) relates to being strengthened in prayer, and "But you must be very strong and resolute to observe faithfully all the Teaching that My servant Moses enjoined upon you" (Josh. 1:7)[52] encourages a person to be strengthened in Torah.[53]

Some communities emphasize the close relation between Moses and the Torah by repeating the word "*hazak*" three times after the completion of each of the five books. Since the numerical value of the Hebrew letters in the name "Moshe" (345) equals precisely three times the value of the word "*hazak*" (115), this threefold repetition of "*hazak*" honors the Lawgiver through whom Israel received the Torah.[54]

Haftarah (הַפְטָרָה)

The haftarah (plural, *haftarot*) is a selection from the books of the Prophets that is read after the Torah reading on Sabbaths, major festivals, and fast days. On Sabbaths and festivals, it is read during the morning service; on fast days, the haftarah is read at the afternoon service only (with the exception of Yom Kippur and Tisha b'Av, when it follows the Torah reading at both the morning and afternoon services). The haftarah is not read on a weekday, even if it is Rosh Hodesh or *hol ha-mo'ed*, nor is it read on Hanukkah or Purim. Because work is permitted on these days, the Rabbis did not want to unduly lengthen the morning service.[1]

The word "haftarah" means "concluding portion." Most scholars believe that the custom of adding a prophetic section after the Torah reading dates back to the days before the Hasmonean revolt of 167 B.C.E., when Antiochus Epiphanes issued a decree banning the public reading of the Torah. Since other public readings in the synagogue were still permitted, the Rabbis added the reading of prophetic verses that related directly or indirectly to the topic of the Torah reading scheduled for that week. Just as it had been traditional to read a minimum of three Torah verses for each of the seven *aliyot* at Sabbath morning services, the Rabbis ruled that a minimum of 21 verses be divided among the seven called up to read from the Prophets (Meg. 23b). After the Hasmonean victory, the weekly Torah readings resumed. Nevertheless, the custom of reading the haftarah persisted, though with only one person (rather than seven) called to read the entire prophetic portion.[2]

At times, the haftarah consisted of as few as three verses. According to the Talmud, the full 21 verses were recited only in those synagogues where there was no translation of the Torah into the vernacular (Meg. 23b). In the Sephardic tradition today, several *haftarot* consist of less than 21 verses. Brief prophetic readings also occur occasionally among Ashkenazim, because an entirely new theme is discussed in succeeding verses—as in the haftarah for the parashah Ki Tetze' (Isa. 54:1–10), which has only 10 verses.[3]

The earliest references to the actual reading of a haftarah are found in the Christian Bible. After reading the Torah at a Sabbath service in Nazareth, Jesus is described as being handed a scroll of the Book of Isaiah, from which he found and then read a specific portion. He then rolled up the scroll and handed it to the attendant, before sitting down and expounding on the reading (Luke 4:16–21). Similarly, Paul is described as being invited to deliver a talk "after the reading of the law and the prophets" (Acts 13:15). As with the readings from the Torah, the Talmud lists specific *haftarot* only for the festivals and special Sabbaths (Meg. 31a–b). The prophetic readings for ordinary Sabbaths (just as the Torah readings) were not predetermined until after the talmudic period (see p. 439). Instead, the choice was usually left to the reader, especially when he was the one designated to deliver the homily.[4]

Unlike the Sabbath Torah readings, which consist of successive portions of the Five Books of Moses without any omission (see p. 439), the *haftarot* are generally scattered prophetic sections. Only two prophetic books are read completely as *haftarot*—the Book of Obadiah, which consists of just 21 verses, is read for the the parashah Va-yishlach (Gen. 32:4–36:43) according to the Sephardic custom (and followed by many Ashkenazic congregations); and the Book of Jonah, which is the haftarah for the afternoon service on Yom Kippur.

There apparently were two major criteria for the selection of a particular haftarah. Whenever possible, the choice was determined by a thematic connection between the contents of the prophetic portion and the weekly Torah reading. As an example, for the parashah Be-shallah (Exod. 13:17–17:16), which contains *Shirat ha-Yam* (Song at the Sea; see p. 409), the haftarah reading includes the Song of Deborah (Judg. 4:4–5:31). Similarly, the haftarah for the parashah Shelach-Lekha (Num. 13:1–15:41), which describes the incident of the 12 spies sent by Moses, is an account of the spies sent by Joshua (Josh. 2:1–24). However, about one-third of the Sabbath *haftarot* are determined either by the calendar or by historical circumstances. For 10 successive weeks from the Sabbath before the 17th of Tammuz until the Sabbath before Rosh Hashanah, there are three *haftarot* of tribulation and then seven of consolation. There are also special *haftarot* read on Sabbaths that fall either on or the day before Rosh Hodesh (New Moon) and on the Sabbath during the Ten Days of Repentance (Shabbat Shuvah). Finally, there are specific *haftarot* for the four special Sabbaths that precede Passover (Shekalim, Zakhor, Parah, and ha-Hodesh), which relate to the special additional Torah portions read on these days (see p. 152). For festivals and fasts, there are designated *haftarot* appropriate to the day. As late as gaonic times, different *haftarot* were in vogue in various localities. To this day there are certain variations, primarily between the Sephardic and Ashkenazic rites (see Appendix).[5]

There is a long-standing tradition against ending a Torah or haftarah portion on a sad or despairing note. Consequently, in several prophetic readings the next to last verse is repeated after the last verse has been recited. This applies to the last verse of four books read for special Sabbaths and festivals—Isaiah (Rosh Hodesh), Malachi (Shabbat ha-Gadol), Lamentations (Tisha b'Av), and Ecclesiastes (Sabbath of Sukkot). In some instances, the Rabbis added one or more verses from a following chapter of the same prophetic book to end the reading on an optimistic note. On Yom Kippur afternoon, the complete Book of Jonah is followed by three verses from Micah (7:18–20), which includes the phrase "cast[ing] all our sins into the depths of the sea," which is also recited during the *Tashlikh* ceremony on Rosh Hashanah (see p. 203).

Originally, the haftarah was read from a handwritten scroll like the Torah. Some authorities, including the renowned Vilna Gaon, refused to read the haftarah from a printed book. However, this custom never became popular, both because of the high cost of such scrolls and because in most synagogues few, if any, congregants could read the unvoweled script of a handwritten scroll. Nevertheless, a few Eastern Sephardic and ultra-Orthodox congregations still read the haftarah from a handwritten *navi* (prophet) scroll.[6]

Maftir

The person who reads the haftarah is known as the *maftir* (lit., "one who concludes"), since this individual also is called up for the last part of the Torah portion. On the Sabbath, the *maftir* is not included in the minimum obligatory number of seven persons who must be called up for *aliyot* (Meg. 23a). This is emphasized by the fact that the half *Kaddish*, which traditionally follows the required Torah reading, is recited even before the person is called up for the *maftir aliyah*. Thus the custom arose for the *maftir* reading to consist of the repetition of a few verses from the end of the seventh portion. On festivals, Rosh Hodesh, and the four special Sabbaths that precede Passover, the *maftir* portion consists of a special reading from a second Torah scroll.

The rabbinic explanation for having the person who is to chant the haftarah being first called to the Torah for an *aliyah* is "out of respect for the Torah," for otherwise, it would appear that the books of the Prophets were considered equal to the Law of Moses (Meg. 23a). Having the *maftir* first read several verses from the Torah emphasizes that the teachings of the prophets were derived from the moral and ethical values expressed in the Torah, which has superior authority and holiness. Another indication of the lower halakhic status of the haftarah is that it (and the *maftir* portion) can be read by a minor. The only exception to this is the parashah Zakhor, when the special *maftir* portion dealing with the commandment to "remember Amalek" is regarded as a biblical requirement. Nevertheless, reading the haftarah has remained an important honor, which is frequently given to a congregant who is celebrating a special occasion.[7]

Haftarah Blessings

The *maftir* recites five blessings for the haftarah reading, one before and four after it, which symbolize the Five Books of Moses, whose ethical and moral teachings were stressed by the prophets. The single blessing before the haftarah notes that God has chosen "prophets of truth and righteousness" to continually guide Israel. The four blessings after the haftarah deal with a variety of praises, supplications, and thanksgivings, including prayers for a return of the Jewish people to Zion (Jerusalem) and the restoration of the House of David at the time of messianic redemption. They conclude with a blessing for God having sanctified the Sabbath or festival on which the haftarah is being read.[8]

In view of the determination of the Rabbis to maintain a lesser halakhic status for the haftarah, why was it given so many more blessings than the Torah reading? Issachar Jacobson suggested that the multiple blessings were originally a polemical attack against the Samaritans, a sect that revered the Five Books of Moses but rejected the sacredness of the prophetic writings and the authority of the Oral Law. The blessings declare the belief of the reader that just as God chose the written Torah, Moses, and Israel, so the prophets and their teachings were divinely inspired. The haftarah blessings stress that the Jews chose Jerusalem as their religious center and Mount Zion as the site for their holy Temple (rather than Shechem and Mount Gerizim, which were selected by the Samaritans). The blessings stress that the Messiah will be a descendant of the House of David of the tribe of Judah, adding the prayer that "no stranger will sit on his throne," unlike the Samaritans who believed in a messianic figure from the tribe of Ephraim.[9]

Another explanation for the extensive blessings accompanying the reading of the haftarah is that they once constituted a complete prayer unit similar to the Sabbath *Amidah*. Those who hold this view have concluded that these blessings go back to the time before the canonization of the prayers at Yavneh, following the destruction of the Second Temple. Although these blessings were not selected as the official *Amidah* for the Sabbath service, they were retained for use at the end of the prophetic reading. This rabbinic decision to preserve two worthwhile traditions is relatively common—as in the parallel versions of the blessings immediately before the *Shema* in the morning and evening services (see p. 412).[10]

Av ha-Rachamim (אַב הָרַחֲמִים)

Av ha-Rachamim (Father of Mercy) is a memorial prayer for Jewish martyrs and martyred communities. It was composed during the First Crusade at the end of the 11th century by an anonymous author, who left it on the reader's desk in the synagogue of Worms. The mysterious origin of the prayer no doubt added to its prestige and helped it become part of the official liturgy. *Av ha-Rachamim* is a mixture of tender recollection of the martyred victims and bitter denunciations of those who perpetrated the massacres. Rather than a prayer for sufficient strength to avenge the fallen martyrs, it requests that God choose how and when to exact punishment upon those who forced Jews to die for *kiddush ha-Shem* (sanctification of God's name).[1]

Av ha-Rachamim initially was recited only on the Sabbaths preceding Shavuot and Tisha b'Av, and at the conclusion of the *Yizkor* memorial service. In the Orthodox Ashkenazic ritual, the prayer has become a regular part of the Sabbath morning service and is recited after the Torah reading, before the scroll is returned to the ark. It is rarely read in Conservative synagogues, although it appears in the prayer books.

Yekum Purkan (יְקוּם פֻּרְקָן); *Mi She Berakh* (מִי שֶׁבֵּרַךְ)

Yekum Purkan (May salvation arise) is the collective name for a set of three prayers that immediately follow the reading of the haftarah on Sabbath morning in the Ashkenazic ritual. They ask divine favor for those who uphold the Torah—by teaching, study, and support, and especially by undertaking the difficult responsibilities of communal leadership.

The first two of these prayers open with the words *"Yekum purkan"* and were composed in Babylonia in the 10th or 11th century, when its famed academies were in decline and European scholars were increasingly assuming the spiritual leadership of world Jewry. As the prestige of the Babylonian academies decreased, so did their funding, forcing them to send emissaries throughout the Jewish world to seek additional contributions. With the survival of the academies, the *Ge'onim*, and the exilarch (political leader of the Jewish community) in real jeopardy, the *Yekum Purkan* was composed on their behalf. In addition to pleading for God's mercy, it was designed to make the people acutely aware of the immense value and critical financial needs of the academies so that they would give generously for their support. Since the prayers were addressed to the worshipers as much as to God, they were composed in the Aramaic vernacular and recited at every Sabbath morning service.[1]

The first *Yekum Purkan* prayer is primarily concerned with the major Babylonian institutions of the gaonic period, invoking divine blessing on the "heads of the academies" (*Ge'onim*), the "chiefs of the captivity" (exilarchs), and the judges "at the gates." Even though none of these positions exist and Jews no longer speak Aramaic, this prayer has remained part of the Sabbath liturgy. Modern worshipers may omit or reinterpret the prayer to call for God's blessings on the spiritual and lay leaders of their own communities.[2] The second *Yekum Purkan* prayer was probably written in postgaonic times and is also in Aramaic. Similar to the first, it requests God's blessings for fellow members of the congregation and their families.[3]

The third of these prayers is the *Mi She Berakh* (May He Who blessed [our forefathers, Abraham, Isaac, and Jacob]), which invokes God's blessings on those individuals who provide funds for the general welfare. It calls for special blessings to those "who give lamps for illumination and wine for *Kiddush* and *Havdalah*, bread for guests and charity to the poor; and all who involve themselves faithfully in the needs of the community."[4] The most popular of the three prayers, the *Mi She Berakh* is written in Hebrew but is often read in the vernacular because it clearly enunciates the fiscal and ethical responsibilities incumbent on members of the congregation.[5]

Because these prayers were written specifically for the Sabbath, in the Ashkenazic tradition they are not recited on festivals unless they fall on the Sabbath.

Additional *Mi She Berakh* Prayers

"*Mi She Berakh*" also are the initial words of a prayer formula that invokes God's blessings on the community and on individuals. For example, each person called for an *aliyah* generally receives a personal *Mi She Berakh*, though in some congregations a collective blessing is recited after completion of the entire Torah portion. Those celebrating a special occasion, such as a bar or bat mitzvah, forthcoming marriage, or birth of a child, receive a special version of the prayer that makes reference to the event.

The *Mi She Berakh* formula is also used as the introduction to the prayer for those who are ill. Unlike the blessing for a person who has been called to the Torah, which traditionally mentions the name of the honoree and the father's first name, the blessing recited on behalf of a sick person uses the name of the mother. According to the kabbalists, God shows more compassion if the plea for healing is addressed through the mother, based on the verse, "Turn to me and have mercy on me; ... and deliver the son of Your maidservant" (Ps. 86:16).[6] Another explanation is that the name of the mother is used to confound the Angel of Death, since an individual is more commonly identified by his or her father's name.

Prayer for the Government

A prayer for the welfare of the government is recited during the morning service, immediately after the prayers for the congregation (*Yekum Purkan*; see p. 461), which are said before returning the Torah scroll to the ark. Contrary to common belief, this prayer is not a modern innovation but dates back to biblical times. In his letter to the Jewish captives in Babylonia, Jeremiah (29:7) advised, "Seek the welfare of the city to which I have exiled you and pray to the Lord on its behalf; for in its prosperity you shall prosper." Similarly, in the Book of Ezra (6:10) it is written that the Jews "prayed for the life of the king and his sons." The Talmud relates that when Alexander the Great arrived in the Land of Israel with his army, he was met at the gates of Jerusalem by Simon the Just, who asked the conqueror whether he would "destroy the House wherein prayers are said for you and your kingdom that it be never destroyed?" (Yoma 69a). Josephus describes a similar incident of Jews pleading that Caligula not desecrate the Temple, stressing that they displayed their loyalty to the Roman emperor by offering sacrifices morning and evening "for Caesar and the Roman people."[1]

The inclusion of the prayer for the government in the service is based on the prudent teaching of Rabbi Hanina in the Mishnah, who urged the Jews to "pray for the welfare of the government, for were it not for the fear of the government, men would swallow each other up alive" (Avot 3:2). This view of the potentially anarchic law of the jungle is reinforced by a commentary on a verse in Habakkuk (1:14), which compares human beings to fish in the sea. The Talmud observes that, just as in the sea the big fish swallows up the small fish, so among human beings, people would swallow each other up alive if not for fear of the rulers (Av. Zar. 4a).[2] An indispensable basis for continued Jewish survival in the Diaspora was the establishment of the talmudic principle of *dina d'malkhuta dina* (the law of the state is the law) (BK 113b).

The prayer for the government used today appeared for the first time in a popular 14th-century commentary on the prayer book written by David Abudarham.[3] In most congregations, a prayer composed by the chief rabbinate for the welfare of the State of Israel is also recited after the Torah reading. Jews in Israel add a prayer for soldiers serving in the Israel Defense Forces.[4]

U-va le-Zion Go'el (וּבָא לְצִיּוֹן גּוֹאֵל)

U-va le-Zion Go'el (And a redeemer shall come to Zion; Isa. 59:20) are the first words of verses of comfort (not recited in the Sabbath or festival morning service) in which God promises to send a Messiah to redeem Jerusalem and the people of Israel. Salvation will be granted not only to those who remained righteous throughout the tribulations of exile but even "to those of Jacob who repent from willful sin."[1]

This prayer originated during the talmudic period, when worshipers usually remained after the weekday morning *Amidah* to hear prophetic selections read, translated into the Aramaic vernacular, and interpreted by the Rabbis. After this period of study, congregants read verses of consolation dealing with the divine promise of redemption. In difficult economic times, these additions made the service far too long for those who had to devote many hours to earning a living. Consequently, the daily prophetic reading was discontinued, but *U-va le-Zion Go'el* remained in the service, especially because it had assumed additional significance. During a period of harsh oppression when Jews were prohibited from saying the *Kedushah* during the reader's repetition of the *Amidah*, the Rabbis inserted this mystical prayer into *U-va le-Zion Go'el*, because it was recited after the government censors had already left the synagogue.[2] The Rabbis also included the polemical Aramaic translation of *Kadosh, Kadosh, Kadosh* against the Christian Trinity (see p. 430).

According to another opinion, the *Kedushah* was inserted toward the end of the synagogue service for the sake of those who arrived too late to hear the prayer during the regular repetition of the *Amidah*. Because these latecomers often were poorly educated and did not understand Hebrew, after the three biblical verses of the *Kedushah* were recited in their original language, they were repeated in an Aramaic translation, the vernacular of Babylonian Jews during the talmudic period. This also would explain why it never became customary to recite *U-va le-Zion Go'el* during the morning services on Sabbaths and festivals. Since these services started later, even those worshipers who generally came to synagogue late would still arrive early enough for the regular *Kedushah*.[3]

U-va le-Zion Go'el is also recited at the afternoon service on the Sabbath and following the Saturday evening service. "This practice goes back to the ancient custom of reading selections from the Prophets on Saturday afternoons and selections from the Writings after the Saturday evening service. These readings were discontinued long ago, but the prayer *U-va le-Zion Go'el* has remained in the ritual."[4]

Ein Keloheinu (אֵין כֵּאלֹהֵינוּ)

Ein Keloheinu (There is none like our God) is the popular hymn of praise recited at the end of the *Musaf* (additional) service on Sabbaths and festivals in the Ashkenazic ritual and on weekdays after the morning service in the Sephardic rite. The declaration of faith in *Ein Keloheinu* was formulated in response to a particular need for an additional source of blessings for Sabbaths and festivals. The Rabbis taught that it is meritorious to recite 100 blessings each day (see p. 388). On weekdays, the bulk of this total is accounted for by the thrice-daily recitation of the *Amidah*, which contains 19 blessings. On Sabbaths and festivals, however, the *Amidah* contains only seven blessings. The first three stanzas of *Ein Keloheinu* contain an acrostic that spells out the word "amen" four times in 12 lines; since "amen" is a response to a blessing, these 12 "blessings" added to the seven in the *Musaf Amidah* results in a total of 19 blessings to help reach the quota.[1]

A talmudic discussion (Ber. 10a) about the uniqueness of God suggests that the opening line of *Ein Keloheinu* may have been inspired by the prayer of Hannah: "There is no holy one like the Lord, truly there is none beside You; there is no rock like our God" (1 Sam. 2:2). It is possible that the hymn may initially have posed the question, "Who is like our God?" (the second verse) followed by the reply, "There is none like our God!" Today this order is reversed, so that the line beginning with "Who" has become an affirmative statement rather than a question. Moreover, in the current sequence the initial letters of the first three verses are an acrostic for "amen," a further allusion to the concept of blessing.[2]

In *Ein Keloheinu*, God is designated by four different names, which are arranged in the order in which they appear in the Torah:

- *Elohim* (God), from the first verse describing the Creation in Genesis.
- *Adon* (Master), first used by Abraham (Gen. 15:2).
- *Melekh* (King), implied in the phrase "the Lord will *reign* for ever and ever" (Exod. 15:18) and first used directly later (Num. 23:21).
- *Moshi'ah* (Deliverer), which is implied when Israel is termed "a people *delivered* by the Lord" (Deut. 33:29).[3]

Aleinu (עָלֵינוּ)

The *Aleinu* prayer combines the idea of Israel as a Chosen People (see p. 592) with the challenge that this status demands—that Jews exert all possible efforts to perfect humankind under the kingdom of God (*l'-takein olam b'malkhut Shaddai*). *Aleinu* was originally used as the introduction to the *Malkhuyot* (Kingship) section of the *Musaf Amidah* on Rosh Hashanah (see p. 201), which proclaims God's universal sovereignty and stresses the belief in the coming of the day when all human beings will acknowledge divine rule over the world. Since the 13th century, *Aleinu* has been recited at the conclusion of every prayer service.

The first paragraph of *Aleinu* praises God for having chosen the people of Israel from the other nations, teaching them to worship the one God while others bow down to idols. The second paragraph expresses the ardent desire for the time when the world will be perfected under the kingship of the Almighty, idolatry will vanish, and all humankind will recognize the only true God. *Aleinu* closes with two biblical verses, "The Lord will reign for ever and ever" (Exod. 15:18), and "the Lord shall be King over all the earth; on that day the Lord be one and His name one" (Zech. 14:9).

Although *Aleinu* has been ascribed to Rav, one of the greatest of the talmudic sages, who lived in Babylon during the early third century C.E., some have maintained that this declaration of faith and dedication was composed by Joshua after he led the Israelites across the Jordan. However, *Aleinu* probably was written by the men of the Great Assembly during the Second Temple period. Evidence for this view is the reference to the Temple practice of prostration and the absence of any expression of hope for the restoration of the Temple. The phrase "*Melekh malkhei ha-melakhim*" (King of the king of kings) to refer to God may reflect the influence of the Persians, who referred to their monarch as the "king of kings."

In the Ashkenazic tradition, congregants bow when reciting the words "*va-anachnu korim*" (we bend the knee). During the *Musaf Amidah* on Rosh Hashanah and the *Avodah* service on Yom Kippur (see p. 220), it is customary in traditional synagogues for prayer leaders to actually kneel down and touch their heads to the floor when reciting this portion. In some synagogues, all members of the congregation prostrate themselves before God at these times.

The original version of *Aleinu* contained a sentence that was censored during the Inquisition as an implied insult to Christianity. The verse, "For they bow to vanity and emptiness and pray to a god which helps not" (Isa. 45:20), appeared just before "but we bend the knee" and was claimed to be a slanderous reference to the Christian Trinity. The Jews countered that the objectionable line could not possibly refer to Christianity, since the biblical phrase was pre-Christian and *Aleinu* was composed either well before the time of Jesus or in a non-Christian country. This defense might have succeeded were it not for a Jewish apostate, who "proved" the anti-Christian sentiment of the prayer by demonstrating the coincidental equivalence of the numerical value (316) of the Hebrew words "*va-rik*" (emptiness) and "*Yeshu*" (Jesus).[1]

Eventually, the offending line was eliminated from Ashkenazic prayer books. The Sephardim, especially in Middle Eastern countries under Moslem rule, retained the full text, despite the tradition that the numerical value of "*la-hevel va-rik*" (vanity and emptiness) equals that of "*Yeshu u-Muhammad*" (Jesus and Muhammad).[2] Even in countries where censorship of Jewish prayers no longer exists, the expurgated sentence of *Aleinu* has generally not been restored in the Ashkenazic text, though it does appear in parentheses in the *ArtScroll Siddur* and some Israeli *siddurim*.

Aleinu has also been associated with martyrdom, especially of the Jews of Blois, who in 1171 were accused of ritual murder and were offered their lives in exchange for baptism. The Jews heroically refused, affirming their faith in God while fervently reciting this prayer as they were burned at the stake. Some authorities maintain that it was this act of defiance that led to *Aleinu* being included in every worship service.[3]

The early Reform movement made substantial cuts in the first paragraph of *Aleinu*, eliminating the lines "for God has not made us like the nations of the lands and has not emplaced us like the families of the earth; for God has not assigned our portion like theirs nor our lot like all their multitudes." This was a conscious attempt to deny the existence of a special "Jewish peoplehood" and to stress that Jews, except for their religious practices, were like all the other citizens of the countries in which they lived (e.g., "Germans of the Mosaic persuasion"). More recent Reform prayer books have offered the full *Aleinu* as an option.

Prayers Recited before Leaving the Synagogue

In some congregations, three short verses are read after *Aleinu* that indicate the worshiper's confidence in divine protection and the hope for redemption. The verse, "You will not fear sudden terror, or the disaster that comes upon the wicked" (Prov. 3:25)[1] urges one to remain steadfast regardless of what appears to be the dangerous intentions of an evildoer. The verse "Hatch a plot—it shall be foiled; agree on action—it shall not succeed. For with us is God!" (Isa. 8:10) assures Jews that the wicked plans of their enemies are ultimately doomed to failure. And the verse "Even in your old age ... I will carry [you to safety] and rescue [you]" (Isa. 46:4)[2] is a divine promise that God will always protect the people of Israel, even though they have sinned. According to a midrash, when the wicked Haman triumphantly left King Ahasuerus with the decree authorizing the destruction of the Jews, he met three Jewish children returning home from Hebrew school and asked what they had studied that day. When each quoted one of the above verses, Haman realized that his evil scheme would fail. Mordecai, overhearing the exchange, was assured that he had no reason to fear this mortal enemy of the Jews, for God would protect the people. Consequently, the Rabbis declared that these three verses should be recited before leaving the synagogue, both to remind God of His abiding love for Israel and to pray that divine mercy will soon deliver them from their oppressors.[3]

Psalm of the Day

Each morning in the Temple, the Levites chanted a psalm appropriate to that day of the week. As a memorial to the destroyed Temple, the Rabbis added these psalms to the daily morning service in the synagogue. As Nachmanides observed, unlike the non-Jewish custom of naming the days for events or pagan gods (e.g., Sunday for the sun, Monday for the moon), Jews count the days of the week with reference to the upcoming Sabbath. This is exemplified in the introductory sentence to each psalm—"Today is the first [second, third, etc.] day of the Sabbath"—which allows the worshiper to observe the biblical commandment to remember the Sabbath always.[1]

The Talmud explains how each psalm was related to its respective day (RH 31a). The psalm for the *first* day begins, "The earth is the Lord's and and all that it holds ..." (Ps. 24),[2] for on this initial day of Creation God took possession as sovereign of the entire universe and determined that everything on earth would be put under the dominion of human beings. The psalm for the *second* day begins, "The Lord is great and much acclaimed" (Ps. 48),[3] for God separated the heaven and the earth while ruling over both. It extols the incomparable beauty of Mount Zion in Jerusalem, the earthly center of divine holiness. The psalm for the *third* day stresses the need to maintain justice and equity (Ps. 82), which are necessary for the flourishing of human life that was made possible when God caused the dry land and the first vegetation to appear on this day. The psalm for the *fourth* day begins, "God of retribution" (Ps. 94–95:3),[4] because "He created the sun and the moon and will one day punish those who serve them [i.e., those idolators who failed to realize that these heavenly bodies were merely the servants of God and instead regarded them as independent deities to be worshiped]."[5] The psalm for the *fifth* day begins, "Sing joyously to God, our strength" (Ps. 81); the Talmud explains that it was selected because God created fishes and birds to praise His name. The psalm for the *sixth* day begins, "The Lord is king, he is robed in grandeur [at the completion of Creation]" (Ps. 93),[6] just as Jews dress in their finest apparel at the end of the workweek to greet the Sabbath.[7]

Mizmor shir l'yom ha-Shabbat (Psalm for the Sabbath day; Ps. 92) is a thanksgiving hymn of praises to God. In answer to the ancient theodicy problem of the apparent prosperity of evildoers and misery of those who are virtuous and honorable, it unequivocally asserts that the wicked are doomed to destruction, while God will cause the righteous to "flourish like a date palm and grow mighty like a cedar in Lebanon."[8] Although this psalm makes no mention of the Sabbath except in its title, Rashi taught that it refers not to the weekly Sabbath but to the world to come, when humanity will achieve the spiritual perfection that can now only be hinted on the seventh day.[9]

On special occasions, additional psalms are recited after the psalm of the day. These include Psalm 27 from Rosh Hodesh Elul until Shemini Atzeret, Psalm 104 on Rosh Hodesh, Psalm 30 on Hanukkah, and Psalm 49 or Psalm 16 in a house of mourning.

Sephardim recite the psalm of the day before *Aleinu*, which ends the service. When there is a *Musaf Amidah*, the psalm of the day is said after the *Amidah* of the morning service, just before the Torah reading. Ashkenazim always recite the psalm of the day (and all other special psalms) following *Aleinu*.[10]

Yigdal (יִגְדַּל)

Yigdal (Exalted [be the living God]) is a hymn ascribed to Daniel ben Judah, a judge in the rabbinical court in Rome during the first half of the 14th century. It is based on the "Thirteen Principles of Faith" expounded by Maimonides in his *Commentary to the Mishnah* (see p. 505).

Yigdal is an example of a prayer that not only was composed to assert a specific belief but also served as a polemic against dissidents and sectarian minorities. The phrase, "He is one, and there is no oneness like His," clearly aimed at Christianity and its doctrine of the Trinity, was intensified by the following line, "He has no bodily form or physicality." The verse, "He granted His rich gift of prophecy to the men of His choice, in whom He gloried," declares the exclusive inspiration of the classical biblical prophets of Israel, thus attacking as false any claims of Muhammad and Islam. The line, "God will never alter or change His law for any other," opposes the Christian Bible and Koran, both of which were claimed to have supplanted the Torah. The avowal of belief in the resurrection of the dead was directed at the Karaites, who rejected this fundamental doctrine of rabbinic Judaism as not being specifically stated in the Five Books of Moses. The firm belief in the future coming of the Messiah was an attack on the Christians, who asserted that Jesus had ushered in the Messianic Era. (When the early Christians became painfully aware that his "coming" had not had a salutary effect on the condition of their world, they developed the expedient concept of a "Second Coming.")[1]

In the Ashkenazic siddur, *Yigdal* can be found at the start of the daily morning service. However, it is usually recited only at the conclusion of the Friday and festival evening services, as in the Sephardic and Middle Eastern traditions. The Ashkenazic version is composed of 13 lines, one for each principle of faith. The Sephardic prayer contains 14 lines, the last of which is "These are the 'Thirteen Principles of Faith'; these are the foundation of the divine faith and of God's law."[2]

Adon Olam (אֲדוֹן עוֹלָם)

Adon Olam (Lord of the World, or Eternal Lord) is an inspiring song of praise attributed to Solomon ibn Gabirol, an 11th-century Spanish philosopher who was one of the most renowned of the literary poets (*paytanim*). One of the most popular hymns, *Adon Olam* was introduced into the initial part of the morning synagogue service in the 14th century to recall the merit of Abraham, who instituted the *Shacharit* service (Ber. 26b) and was the first person to address God with the title "Adon[ai]" (Gen. 15:2).[1] However, its next to last line ("Into God's hand I shall entrust my spirit when I sleep—and I shall awaken!") suggests that the hymn originally formed the conclusion of the bedtime (night) prayers (see p. 473), where it still appears.[2] Today, *Adon Olam* is generally sung at the conclusion of the Sabbath and festival *Musaf* services, in a variety of musical settings.

Adon Olam speaks of God as timeless, infinite, and omnipotent, the sole Creator and Sovereign of the universe. Nevertheless, it stresses that God is also the ultimate source of comfort in times of grief and misery, as exemplified by the final line, "God is with me, I shall not fear."[3]

An'im Zemirot (אַנְעִים זְמִירוֹת)

An'im Zemirot (Let me chant sweet hymns), also known as *Shir ha-Kavod* (Hymn of Glory), exalts the power and glory of God. It was written by Judah the Pious, a 12th-century German mystic who was the central figure of the Hasidei Ashkenaz. This movement stressed the immanence of God, and its followers concentrated their energies on praying with their entire heart and soul to achieve the goal of *deveikut*, a type of spiritual self-transfiguration that induced a feeling of God's closeness.[1]

An'im Zemirot is an alphabetic acrostic of 31 lines, each of which consists of two half-lines that rhyme. The first and last four lines are a prologue and epilogue, respectively. The hymn contains a series of striking anthropomorphic metaphors that draw on biblical and midrashic sources. Although in many prayer books *An'im Zemirot* appears at the end of the daily morning service, some rabbis considered it to possess such holiness that they objected to its daily recital lest it become too familiar. Therefore, in most Ashkenazic synagogues, *An'im Zemirot* is only recited in front of the open ark at the conclusion of the *Musaf* (additional) service on the Sabbath and festivals. A child often leads the congregational singing of *An'im Zemirot*.

Personal Prayers

Modeh Ani (מוֹדֶה אֲנִי)

Modeh Ani (I gratefully thank) are the initial words of a short prayer said immediately upon waking up in the morning. The full prayer—"I gratefully thank You, O living and eternal King, for You have returned my soul within me with compassion; great is Your faithfulness!"—does not mention any of the divine names and thus may be said while still in bed before washing. Short and simple, *Modeh Ani* is a favorite morning prayer for children who are too young to recite the ordinary daily morning service.

Bedtime Prayers

Before going to bed, the traditional Jew recites a prayer unit that is built around the *Shema* and was considered as protection against the dangers of the night ("the demons keep away from him"; Ber. 5a). For busy scholars, the Talmud prescribed adding a verse of supplication (Ber. 4b–5a), such as, "Into Your hand I entrust my spirit. You redeem me, O Lord, faithful God" (Ps. 31:6). However, this brief formula was not considered sufficient for normal use, and the Rabbis developed a more elaborate set of psalms and prayers that, with some additions, has become the standard ritual (Ber. 60b).[1] It includes Psalm 91 ("You need not fear the terror by night") and Psalm 3 ("I lie down and sleep and wake again, for the Lord sustains me"). Some precede the *Shema* with a prayer beseeching God to forgive one's sins, as well as a statement formally forgiving anyone who had "angered, antagonized, or sinned" against him, "whether accidentally, willfully, carelessly, or purposely, through speech, deed, thought, or notion."[2] The final prayer is *Adon Olam* (see p. 471), the last verse of which is, "Into God's hand I shall entrust my spirit when I go to sleep—and I shall awaken! With my spirit shall my body remain, God is with me, I shall not fear."

After reciting the bedtime prayers, the Jew could sleep peacefully. Should he not awaken from slumber, "the Jew had the comforting assurance of having finished his mortal existence with the traditional affirmation of the unity of God."[3]

Blessings before Eating

Based on the biblical verse, "the earth and all it contains is the Lord's" (Ps. 24:1), the Rabbis taught, "to enjoy [the pleasures of] this world without reciting a blessing is like robbing the Holy One" [i.e., stealing from God] (Ber. 35b).[1] Thus the blessings before eating and drinking are the equivalent of asking for (and receiving) official authorization to partake of divine property. Rather than thanking God, as in the Grace *after* Meals, the blessings *before* eating and drinking acknowledge God as the one who "creates the fruit of the vine" or "brings forth bread from the earth," thus effectively requesting permission to use these divine gifts. For the Rabbis (Ber. 35 a–b), this approach resolved the apparent conflict in the verse, "The heavens belong to the Lord, but the earth He gave over to man" (Ps. 115:16). Before one says a blessing, the bounty of the earth is the Lord's; however, after reciting the appropriate blessing, human beings are free to enjoy everything that the earth produces.

All of the blessings before eating or drinking begin with the same classic benediction formula—"*Baruch ata Adonai Eloheinu melekh haolam*"—and differ only in their description of the actions of God relative to the specific item to be consumed.

The blessing before eating bread baked from the flour of wheat, barley, oats, rye, and spelt—the five grains mentioned or alluded to in the Torah as indigenous to the Land of Israel—concludes "*ha-motzi lechem min ha-aretz*" (Who brings forth bread from the earth). Reciting the single blessing for bread at the beginning of a meal "suffices for all kinds of food [eaten during the meal]," except for wine and fresh fruit, which require separate blessings (Ber. 41b). When pronouncing this blessing, it is customary to place both hands on the loaf of bread (both loaves on the Sabbath). The 10 fingers of the two hands correspond to the number of Hebrew words in the blessing itself, in the verse that describes the abundant produce of the Land of Israel ("A land of wheat and barley, of vines and figs, and pomegranates; of olive trees and honey"; Deut. 8:8), and in the account of Isaac's blessing to Jacob ("May God give you of the dew of the heaven and the fat of the earth, abundance of new grain and wine"; Gen. 27:28).[2]

For foods *other than bread* made from the flour of these grains, including bread-type products made with fruit juice, milk, or other liquids (rather than with water exclusively), the proper blessing concludes *"borei minei mezonot"* (Who creates various kinds of nourishment). This blessing is appropriate for most cookies, cakes, cereals, noodle products, and dough filled with fruit, meat, or cheese. It also is said for rice, even though it is not one of the five major grains.

The blessing for vegetables concludes *"borei peri ha-adamah"* (Who creates the fruit of the earth), while that for fruit concludes *"borei peri ha-etz"* (Who creates the fruit of the tree). The criterion for distinguishing one category from the other is not the height of the plant, but rather whether it is an annual or perennial. Thus apples, cherries, peaches, nuts, and avocados are considered fruits for the purpose of selecting the proper blessing, whereas bananas, melons, strawberries, pineapples, and tomatoes (technically a fruit) are not. Dried fruit has the same status as ordinary fruit.

The sole fruit with its own special blessing is the grape—in the form of juice or wine—for which the blessing concludes *"borei peri ha-gafen"* (Who creates the fruit of the vine). It does not apply to the fermented juice of other fruits or vegetables, even if it is called wine, or to grapes themselves, which are considered a fruit for which the blessing *borei peri ha-etz* is appropriate.

For all food that does *not* grow from the soil, the blessing concludes with *"she-hakol nih'yeh bid'varo"* (through Whose word all things were called into being). This broad category includes water, milk and other dairy products, poultry and eggs, meat, fish, and honey. It also applies to food that comes from the earth or was grown on a tree, but which has undergone such extensive processing that it is impossible to identify its original appearance. This category includes coffee, tea, sugar, fruit juices and jams, candy, and alcoholic beverages (other than grape wine). Indeed, this "generic" blessing is always appropriate if one does not know the proper blessing to make for any specific food.

Which blessing should be recited if a product contains two or more components? According to the general hierarchical formula, the order of priority (from highest down) is *mezonot, peri ha-etz, peri ha-adamah,* and *she-hakol*. For example, although chocolate requires the *she-hakol* blessing, one should say *mezonot* for a chocolate cookie and *peri ha-etz* for a chocolate-coated nut. However, if one eats a separate piece of nut and chocolate, each item would require its own individual blessing. The blessing over wine or grape juice (*peri ha-gafen*) takes precedence over that for any other drink (*she-hakol*).

Grace after Meals (*Birkat ha-Mazon;* בִּרְכַּת הַמָּזוֹן)

The commandment to thank God after a meal is based on the verse, "When you have eaten your fill [lit., "have eaten and are satisfied"], give thanks to the Lord your God." (Deut. 8:10). Among Ashkenazim, the Grace after Meals is known by the Yiddish term "*Bentschen*" (Blessing).

The full *Birkat ha-Mazon*, consisting of four blessings, is recited only after a meal at which one has eaten bread of an amount at least equivalent to the size of an olive (*ke-zayit*), approximately one ounce by volume. The first blessing praises God for providing food for all creatures; the second expresses thanks for the good land (of Israel) that God has given us, the redemption from Egypt, the covenant of circumcision, and the Revelation of the Torah; the third is a plea for God's mercy, the rebuilding of Jerusalem, and the restoration of the ancient Temple and the Davidic kingdom; and the fourth offers thanks for God's eternal goodness to us and includes a request for sending Elijah the Prophet, as well as for blessings upon the house in which one has eaten and upon all who shared the meal. The last blessing also includes a number of general supplications beginning with the word "*ha-Rachaman*" (May the Merciful One) and ends with the same prayer for peace (*Oseh Shalom*) that concludes the full *Kaddish*—for only when at peace is it possible to truly enjoy all the other divine blessings.

According to the Talmud, the four blessings arose from different sources (Ber. 48b). The first is attributed to Moses upon receiving manna from Heaven, the second was composed by Joshua when he conquered the land of Canaan, and the third was written by David and Solomon because of their respective roles in making Jerusalem the capital of the Israelite state and building the Temple. The core of the fourth blessing (*ha-Tov v'ha-Meitiv*; "Who is good and Who does good") was added by the Rabbis after the unsuccessful rebellion led by Bar Kokhba in the second century C.E., in gratitude both for the corpses at Betar not decaying and spreading disease and for the Romans finally granting the Jews permission to bury them. The word "amen" is said only after the third blessing, to separate those based on biblical law from the final blessing that was instituted later by rabbinic authority.[1]

Some Jews do not recite the Grace after Meals until all utensils (especially knives) have been removed from the table. This reflects the comparison of the dining table to the Temple altar, which was constructed of stones that were not hewn with tools that also could be used as weapons.

On weekdays, it has been a custom to recite *Al Naharot Bavel* (By the rivers of Babylon; Ps. 137), in memory of the destruction of the Temple, before *Birkat ha-Mazon*. However, on Sabbaths and festivals and at the meals celebrating a wedding, circumcision, or *pidyon ha-ben* (when joy should not be constrained by remembering catastrophic events), the Grace after Meals is preceded by the singing of *Shir ha-Ma'alot* (Ps. 126), a prophetic description of the return of the Israelites from Babylonian captivity and the ultimate restoration of Zion (see p. 478).[2]

Near the end of the *Birkat ha-Mazon*, after praying that God will "make us worthy of the days of the Messiah and of life in the world to come," there is a section with two possible initial words. On weekdays, one says "*Magdil*" (He who makes great [the salvation to His King]; Ps. 18:51); on Sabbaths and festivals, the first word becomes "*Migdol*" (He who is a tower [of victory to His king]; 2 Sam. 22:51). In both of these verses, which were written by David, the word "king" refers to the Messiah.

The Grace after Meals may be recited in any language, but must be said at the table from which one has eaten. Whenever three or more have eaten bread together, one of them must summon the others to say *Birkat ha-Mazon*, according to a formula known as *zimmun* (invitation) (Ber. 49b).[3]

When bread is not eaten, there are two other forms of the Grace after Meals, depending on the type of food consumed. After eating food prepared from the five species of grain (wheat, barley, rye, oats, and spelt) not in the form of bread, wine, or fruits (grapes, figs, olives, pomegranates, and dates) that are indigenous to the Land of Israel, one recites a short summary of the *Birkat ha-Mazon* in a single benediction with insertions for the type of food eaten and for special occasions such as the Sabbath or festival. For any other food, the Grace after Meals consists of a brief benediction generally known by its first two words, "*Borei nefashot*" (Who creates living things).

Over time, the *Birkat ha-Mazon* grew from four brief blessings into a lengthy, time-consuming prayer. Therefore, an abbreviated Grace after Meals was provided in talmudic times for farm laborers during the weekdays. This short *Birkat ha-Mazon* generally includes the entire first blessing and summarizes the major points of the others.[4] In North America, the Conservative movement has developed a condensed version of the *Birkat ha-Mazon* for use at public events and summer camps, though on the Sabbath the traditional long form is often recited.

Maimonides accused those who enjoy a meal, or other divine gift, without offering a blessing of committing a sacrilege by failing to express their gratefulness to God for food as well as for past favors bestowed on the Jewish people. He decried those who take their blessings for granted and emulate Esau, of whom the Bible says, "He ate and drank, and he rose and went away. Thus did Esau spurn the birthright" (Gen. 25:34).[5]

Shir ha-Ma'alot (שִׁיר הַמַּעֲלוֹת)

Shir ha-Ma'alot (Song of Ascents) refers to the 15 psalms (Ps. 120–134) that were sung by pilgrims as they went up to Jerusalem for the festival celebrations in the Temple. They were also chanted by the Levites in the Temple on the festival of Sukkot, during the joyous water-drawing ceremony (see p. 236).[1]

Ashkenazim recite these psalms, along with Psalm 104, on winter Sabbath afternoons and on Tu b'Shevat. They serve both to commemorate the Temple rituals and to pray for restoration of the Land of Israel to the Jewish people, so that pilgrims and Levites will once again sing these psalms in Jerusalem.[2]

During the 16th century, the custom developed of chanting Psalm 126 in the home before the Grace after Meals on Sabbaths and festivals. It prophetically describes the return to Zion from Babylonian exile (about 500 years before the event took place, if one accepts the traditional belief that it was composed by King David) and contains the famous line, "those who sow with tears will reap with joy." When sung on the Sabbath, it relates to the tradition that on this day one experiences a foretaste of the redemption and of the world to come.

Shehecheyanu (שֶׁהֶחֱיָנוּ)

Shehecheyanu, one of the best-known blessings, is recited on a variety of joyous occasions and thanks God for having "kept us in life, sustained us, and permitted us to reach this time." It is recited at the candlelighting and *Kiddush* ceremonies on Jewish holidays, before reading the *Megillah* on Purim, on first hearing the shofar on Rosh Hashanah, and when initially taking the *lulav* and *etrog* on Sukkot. The *Shehecheyanu* prayer is also said whenever one does something "new" in a given year, such as eating a fruit for the first time in the season, moving into a new house, acquiring new clothes or household effects, or having a reunion with a dear friend whom one has not seen for some time.

Shehecheyanu is a joyous expression of thanksgiving for being alive. However, it was regarded as inappropriate to recite this blessing if one's pleasure resulted from harm to animals (whose welfare is an important Jewish principle). Consequently, a *shochet* does not recite *Shehecheyanu* the first time he performs the mitzvah of ritual slaughter, since this act requires taking the life of an animal. Similarly, it is customary not to say this blessing when wearing any article made of leather for the first time.[1]

Tefillat ha-Derech (תְּפִלַּת הַדֶּרֶךְ)

The recitation of *Tefillat ha-Derech* (Prayer for a Journey, or Wayfarer's Prayer) is based on the talmudic dictum that a person who "passes through a place infested with beasts or bands of robbers" must say a short prayer to complete the journey safely (Ber. 29b). It indicates that this practice began with the Prophet Elijah, who cautioned a scholar that "when you go forth on a journey, seek counsel of your maker and then go forth."

Medieval Jews were frequently forced to travel, either in search of a new home (due to expulsions or intolerable living conditions) or to seek a livelihood to provide for their families. Those engaged in international trade might be required to journey for months or even years and be exposed to grave dangers from highwaymen and pirates.[1] Thus recitation of the talmudic *Tefillat ha-Derech*, with appropriate added biblical selections and psalms, became a widespread practice.

The Wayfarer's Prayer is recited at the start of each day's travels. It is always said in the first person plural, both as a reflection of the talmudic statement that "a man should always associate himself with the congregation" (Ber. 29b–30a) and since it applies not only to the Jewish traveler who recites it but to all those who are making the trip. The *Tefillat ha-Derech* is still widely used in modern travel, especially by plane, where appropriate additions have been made to the text. In Israel, Shlomo Goren composed alternative versions of this prayer for various military units when he was chief rabbi of the Israel Defense Forces.

One custom designed to protect travelers is to give a small sum of money to any person setting out on a journey. In this way, the traveler becomes a *shaliach l'dvar mitzvah*, an agent responsible for carrying out the mitzvah of delivering funds to a charity upon arriving at his or her destination. As the Talmud promises, "Those sent to perform a mitzvah are not harmed on their way to do a mitzvah nor on their return" (Pes. 8b).[2]

Thanksgiving Blessing (*Birkat ha-Gomel;* בִּרְכַּת הַגּוֹמֵל)

Birkat ha-Gomel (He who bestows [good]) is a thanksgiving blessing recited by a person who has been saved from a life-threatening situation. According to the Talmud, it must be said by anyone who has completed a sea voyage or a hazardous land journey, has recovered from a major illness, or has been released from prison or captivity (Ber. 54b). It can also be said by an entire community that has been delivered from a potential calamity. The duty to recite *Birkat ha-Gomel* is derived from Psalm 107, which describes deliverance from four dangers common in biblical times. After being saved from any of these perils, the Psalmist says, "Let them give thanks unto the Lord for His mercy, and for His wonderful works to human beings" (Ps. 107:8,15,21,31).[1]

In modern times, there is a debate as to whether one should recite *Birkat ha-Gomel* after every airplane flight. Proponents of this view argue that air travel, like a sea voyage, entails separation from the earth (with its increased inherent dangers), so that it is appropriate to offer a prayer of thanksgiving for arriving safely. Other authorities object to everyday use of this blessing, preferring to reserve *Birkat ha-Gomel* for when a person wants to thank God for being saved from a dangerous situation. In Israel, *Birkat ha-Gomel* is recited by military reservists after returning home safely from a period of active duty.

Birkat ha-Gomel is ideally said in the presence of a minyan, within three days of the event, as public acknowledgment of God having saved the individual from a perilous situation. Whenever possible, the blessing is recited when the person is called to the Torah for an *aliyah*. However, it also is permissible to come up to the *bimah* at the end of the Torah reading to recite *Birkat ha-Gomel*.

The accepted text for *Birkat ha-Gomel* is, "Praised are You ... who bestows good things upon the undeserving, and who has bestowed every goodness upon me." The congregation responds, "Amen. May He who has bestowed goodness upon you continue to bestow every goodness upon you forever."[2]

Although in traditional communities women usually do not recite *Birkat ha-Gomel*, it is appropriate for them to do so, especially after childbirth.

Jewish Literature

Bible (תַּנַ"ךְ)

The English word "Bible" derives from the Greek "*biblos*," the vernacular translation by the Greek-speaking Hellenistic Jews of the Hebrew term "*ha-Sefarim*" (The Books). Used by Daniel (9:2) to refer to the writings of the prophets, *ha-Sefarim* was the earliest Hebrew designation for Scripture and was widely used for the sacred writings in the early talmudic literature. Nevertheless, no single designation for Scripture has been universally employed by all Jews and in all periods. *Kitvei ha-Kodesh* (Holy Writings) emphasizes the written nature of the text, as distinguished from the oral form in which the rabbinic teachings were transmitted. In contrast, the popular term "*Mikrah*" (lit., "reading") stresses the central role of the public reading of Scripture in synagogue services. In medieval times, the designation "*Sifrei ha-Kodesh*" (Holy Books) was often used. Today, the most frequently employed Hebrew term for the Bible is the acronym "*Ta-Na-Kh*" (TANAKH), derived from the initial letters of the names of its three major divisions: **T**orah (Five Books of Moses), **N**evi'im (Prophets), and **K**ethuvim (Writings). The Christian term "Old Testament" is not accepted in Jewish tradition because it expresses the belief that there is a "New Testament" that has somehow superseded the special divine relationship with the Jewish people.

Books of the Bible

The first five books of the Bible were originally known as *Torat Moshe* (Torah of Moses). Although combined on a single scroll for reading in synagogue services, for nonliturgical purposes, such as individual study, it was more convenient to transcribe the work on five separate scrolls. This led to the Greek name "the five-volume [book]," which in English became "Pentateuch." The Rabbis referred to these books as *Hamishah Humshei Torah* (lit., "The Five Fifth-Parts of the Torah"), from which derived the popular abbreviation *Humash*. In Hebrew, the name of each individual book reflects its initial (or first significant) word: B'reishit (in the beginning), Shemot (names), Va-yikra (and He [God] called), Be-midbar (in the wilderness), and Devarim (words). The English titles for these five books—Genesis, Exodus, Leviticus, Numbers, Deuteronomy—have their origins in the titles prevailing among the Greek-speaking Jews, who translated the Hebrew designations in use among their coreligionists in the Land of Israel. These titles (and their Hebrew correlates), which describe the overall content or major themes of the respective books, are as follows:

- Genesis: *Sefer ha-Yetzirah* or *Sefer Beri'at ha-Olam* (Book of the Creation of the world).
- Exodus: *Sefer Yetziat Mitzrayim* (Book of the Exodus from Egypt).
- Leviticus: *Torat Kohanim* (Book of the priestly code).
- Numbers: *Humash ha-Pekudim* (Book of the census).
- Deuteronomy: *Mishneh Torah* (Repetition of the Torah).

The second division of the Bible is known as Nevi'im (Prophets). It includes narrative historical works (Joshua, Judges, Samuel, Kings) and the more poetic orations and writings of the three "major" prophets (Isaiah, Jeremiah, Ezekiel) and the 12 "minor" prophets (Hosea, Joel, Amos, Obadiah, Jonah, Micah, Nahum, Habakkuk, Zephaniah, Haggai, Zechariah, Malachi). The popular epithet "minor" has solely a quantitative connotation and is no indication of relative importance. The Rabbis divided the prophets into "former" (up to the destruction of the First Temple) and "latter" (the final three post-exilic prophets).

The third division of the Bible, Kethuvim[1] (Writings or Hagiographa), is a varied collection that includes liturgical poetry (Psalms, Lamentations), love poetry (Song of Songs), wisdom literature (Proverbs, Job, Ecclesiastes), historical works (Ruth, Esther, Ezra, Nehemiah, Chronicles), and a blend of history and prophecy (Daniel).

The traditional Jewish Bible contains 24 books. However, most English Bibles list 39 books, a number obtained by dividing Samuel, Kings, and Chronicles into two books each, separating Ezra and Nehemiah, and counting each of the 12 "minor" prophets individually (though they initially were written on a single scroll and considered as

Current Order of the Books of the Jewish Bible

Torah
- Genesis
- Exodus
- Leviticus
- Numbers
- Deuteronomy

Nevi'im (Prophets)
- Joshua
- Judges
- Samuel (1 and 2)
- Kings (1 and 2)
- Isaiah
- Jeremiah
- Ezekiel
- Hosea
- Joel
- Amos
- Obadiah
- Jonah
- Micah
- Nahum
- Habakkuk
- Zephaniah
- Haggai
- Zechariah
- Malachi

Kethuvim (Writings)
- Psalms
- Proverbs
- Job
- The Song of Songs
- Ruth
- Lamentations
- Ecclesiastes
- Esther
- Daniel
- Ezra
- Nehemiah
- Chronicles (1 and 2)

only one book). The arrangement of the books also is different in the Christian Bible.

The five *megillot* are often grouped together because of the custom of reading these books on festivals: The Song of Songs on Passover, Ruth on Shavuot, Lamentations on Tisha b'Av, Ecclesiastes on Sukkot, and Esther on Purim.

Canonization

The books that constitute the Bible represent only a portion of the literary production of ancient Israel. Consequently, it was necessary to select those books that were deemed divinely inspired so as to constitute an authoritative body of sacred writings. This process of "canonization," which applied to both individual books and the entire Bible, derives from a Hebrew root meaning "measuring rod" (Ezek. 40:5) and later became a Greek word for "rule" or "standard of excellence." Scholars generally agree that the Pentateuch assumed its final form during the Babylonian exile. The prophetic canon probably closed during the Persian era (about 323 B.C.E.). Indeed, the Rabbis considered the post-exilic Haggai, Zechariah, and Malachi as the last of the prophets, for when they died "the Holy Spirit [divine inspiration] departed from Israel" (Sot. 48b).

The Kethuvim section may not have been finally canonized until the second century C.E.. Although some of the books (Psalms, Proverbs) were certainly written while the Prophets were still active (and canonized early), they were excluded from the Nevi'im because they seemed to be the product of human (rather than divine) inspiration. Ezra, Chronicles, and Daniel were written too late for inclusion among the Prophets, though they (and Job) were definitely canonized before the destruction of the Second Temple. Support for this view is a talmudic passage stating that these lesser-known books would be read to the high priest on Yom Kippur eve to arouse his interest and keep him awake, lest he become ritually impure (by a seminal emission during sleep) and thus unable to fulfill his essential duties on the Day of Atonement (Yoma 18b).

The Jews of Alexandria and the Greek-speaking Diaspora developed a canon different from that in the Land of Israel, both in the grouping and sequencing of the biblical books. The Greek Bible, which became the basis of the Christian Bible, also included a spectrum of books (collectively known as the Apocrypha, or "hidden books") that were not accepted into the normative Hebrew canon. These include 1–2 Esdras (Ezra), Wisdom of Solomon, Wisdom of Ben Sira, Judith, Tobit, Baruch (Letter of Jeremiah), 1–4 Maccabees, and the Psalms of Solomon.

Text

There probably was a fixed text of the Torah at a relatively early stage before its canonization. Deuteronomy (17:18–19) mandates that the king have a copy of the Law transcribed for him for daily study, so that he "may learn to fear the Lord his God" and "keep all the words of this law and these statutes." There was also a commandment to periodically give a public reading of the Law from an official copy deposited in the central Sanctuary (Deut. 31:9–13). However, as discovered in the Dead Sea Scrolls, there were various different texts for many of the books in the second and third portions of the Hebrew Bible. The talmudic reference to official "book readers" in Jerusalem, who were paid from Temple funds to check scribal errors on scrolls brought by members of the public (Ket. 106a), indicates that at some point during the Second Temple period there was a single authoritative text that was used as the standard against which the accuracy of other scrolls was measured. With the destruction of the Temple, it became essential to have a uniform Hebrew version of the Holy Scripture that could be used by all Jews throughout their lands of dispersion.

Printed Editions

The first complete printed version of the Hebrew Bible was by Soncino in 1488, though an edition of the Pentateuch had appeared six years earlier in Bologna. In 1516, Daniel Bomberg, a Christian merchant from Amsterdam who established a printing office in Venice, published the first Great Rabbinic Bible, edited by Felix Pratensis, who was born a Jew but was later baptized. This four-volume work, which included *Targums* and commentaries, was followed in 1524–1525 by the second Great Rabbinic Bible, which became the standard masoretic text for four centuries.

Ten Commandments (עֲשֶׂרֶת הַדִּבְּרוֹת)

The Ten Commandments (Exod. 20:2–14; Deut. 5:6–18) have formed the fundamental moral and ethical principles of the Western tradition. In Hebrew they are known as *Aseret ha-Dibrot* (lit., "Ten Words" or "Ten Utterances"), because the introductory verse begins, "And God spoke these *words*, saying" (Exod. 20:1).[1] A linguistically accurate term often used for the Ten Commandments is the Decalogue, a Greek word meaning "ten words." According to the Torah, God revealed the Ten Commandments to the Israelites as they encamped at the foot of Mount Sinai, seven weeks after being liberated from bondage in Egypt. After the Revelation, Moses ascended Mount Sinai and remained there fasting for 40 days before receiving the two stone "tablets of the covenant" (*luchot ha-brit*), which were engraved "by the finger of God" and included the conditions of the covenant between God and Israel (Deut. 4:13). Outraged over the blasphemy of the Golden Calf, Moses smashed the first pair of tablets (Exod. 32:19; Deut. 9:17) and again ascended the mountain, remaining another 40 days pleading with God on behalf of the people. After God forgave the Israelites, Moses was ordered to prepare a second pair of stone tablets identical to the first. God commanded that these be placed inside the Ark of the Covenant, which was housed first in the *mishkan* (tent sanctuary; Exod. 25:16; Deut. 10:2–5), later in the Tabernacle at Shiloh (1 Sam. 4:3), and ultimately in the Temple in Jerusalem (1 Kings 8).

The medieval philosopher Yehudah ha-Levi wrote that the divine purpose in proclaiming the Ten Commandments was to convince the people that Moses communicated directly with God and thus the remaining mitzvot contained in the Torah were not merely creations of his own mind. However, the people were so frightened by the thunder, smoke, and blaring shofar that they fell back, pleading with Moses to be their intermediary: "You speak to us ... and we will obey; but let not God speak to us, lest we die" (Exod. 20:16). Moses reassured the people that God wanted only to teach them so that the fear of God would always be with them and keep them from sin (Exod. 20:17). This sequence has given rise to the popular tradition that God revealed only the first two commandments (which are in the first person), while the remaining eight (in the third person) were transmitted by Moses (Mak. 24a). Nevertheless, each Israelite standing at the foot of the mountain believed that God was proclaiming the commandments directly to him or her.

Some maintain that God spoke only the first letter, the silent *alef*, while others claim that hearing God's voice caused the people to die of fright and they had to be revived by the dew of resurrection (Hag. 12b).[2] According to the Rabbis, the two alternate versions of the Ten Commandments were recited simultaneously, although it was "something that transcends the capacity of the human mouth to utter and of the human ear to hear" (RH 27a). This concept is illustrated in the Sabbath eve hymn *Lekhah Dodi* (see p. 146), the opening stanza of which begins "*shamor v'zachor b'dibur echad*" (observe and remember [the Sabbath] in a single utterance), indicating that both versions of the Fourth Commandment dealing with the Sabbath were spoken at the same time.

Structure

Various authorities have proposed different ways of counting the Ten Commandments. The generally accepted version is the following:

1. I am YHVH your God.
2. You shall have no other gods besides me (or make any graven image).
3. You shall not take the name of YHVH in vain.
4. Remember the Sabbath day.
5. Honor your father and mother.
6. You shall not murder.
7. You shall not commit adultery.
8. You shall not steal.
9. You shall not bear false witness.
10. You shall not covet.

According to Philo, the first four commandments deal with the relationship between man and God (*bein adam la-Makom*), whereas the last five focus on the interactions among fellow human beings (*bein adam la-chaveiro*). The Fifth Commandment, describing the relation of children to parents, forms a bridge between the two. The first five commandments appear to be addressed specifically to the Israelites, since each contains an additional phrase that provides a reason for observing the commandment and refers to "YHVH your God." In contrast, the last five commandments, which consist entirely of prohibitions, are universal ethical requirements incumbent on all human beings.

While the biblical text gives no indication of how the commandments were distributed on the two tablets, it is commonly assumed that they were arranged vertically, five on each. An ingenious homily based on this assumption correlates each commandment with the one directly opposite it: "(a) Murder is an injury to God, in whose image human beings were created; (b) apostasy is equivalent to marital infidelity; (c) stealing will lead to a false oath; (d) one who breaks the Sabbath attests falsely that God did not create the world in six days and rest on the seventh; and (e) one who covets his fellow's wife will end up fathering a child who rejects his true parent and honors another" (Mek. Yitro 8). Some commentators suggest that the two tablets symbolize the Written and Oral Law, both of which were transmitted to Moses by God at Mount Sinai.

Representations of the two tablets containing the Ten Commandments are popular decorations in synagogues. Wood or stone sculptures of the tablets are often mounted above the ark or on the outside of the synagogue building, and images of them are frequently embroidered on the ark curtain or Torah mantle.[3] The usual appearance of the tablets as two attached rectangular slabs with rounded tops probably was the creation of early Christian artists. In ancient Jewish descriptions, the tablets appear as rectangles or even two joined hands; the rounded-top design was first used in a synagogue in 17th-century Amsterdam. Instead of including the full text of the Ten Commandments, most representations portray only the initial letters of the Hebrew alphabet (representing the numbers one through 10) inscribed on the two tablets. Another approach is to simply use the first Hebrew word of each commandment.[4]

Use in the Liturgy

In ancient times, the *Kohanim* recited the Ten Commandments daily as part of the Temple service (Tam. 5:1). Israelites outside the Temple were forbidden to recite them, so as to disprove the insinuations by heretical sects *(minim)* that only the Ten Commandments and not the entire Torah were divinely revealed at Mount Sinai (Ber. 12a). Therefore, the Ten Commandments were excluded from the liturgy, though Rabbi Levi in the Jerusalem Talmud insisted that they were alluded to in the three paragraphs of the *Shema* (Ber. 1:8, 3c).[5]

The only extra importance given to the Decalogue during the service is that the congregation rises when it is read in synagogue as part of the regular weekly Torah portions—twice a year, in sections Yitro and Va-etchannan—and on the festival of Shavuot, the anniversary of the Revelation at Sinai.

Two sets of cantillations (musical notations for reading the Torah) appear in the first paragraph as well as for the brief commandments six through nine. The "upper" set treats the whole paragraph as one long verse and breaks the four "You shall not's" into individual verses; conversely, the "lower" set breaks the first paragraph into four verses and unites the "You shall not's" into a single verse. The upper cantillation, which is regarded as representing the traditional manner in which Israel heard the Ten Commandments at Sinai, is used for the public reading of the Decalogue in the synagogue (in some communities, only on Shavuot). The lower set is used on all other occasions, such as when reading the commandments in private.

Masoretic Text (מְסוֹרָה)

According to tradition, God dictated the entire Torah, not only the Ten Commandments, to Moses on Mount Sinai. This was the Torah that was transmitted to Joshua, and then to the elders, the Prophets, and the men of the Great Assembly (Avot 1:1). Thus the Torah that was read and studied in later generations is believed to be the same as the original Torah of Moses.

The whereabouts of this original scroll is not mentioned in the Five Books of Moses or the historical works for the next six centuries. Only during the reign of King Josiah (622 B.C.E.) is there a report of the discovery of a scroll of the Torah by Hilkiah, the *Kohen Gadol*. As part of his religious revival, Josiah gathered "all the people, both small and great; and he read in their hearing all the words of the book of the covenant [probably the Book of Deuteronomy] which had been found in the house of the Lord" (2 Kings 23:2). The next recorded public reading from a Torah scroll is by Ezra two centuries later, after the return from Babylonian exile (Neh. 8).[1]

Over the centuries, countless scribes wrote thousands of manuscripts, and it was inevitable that many variations appeared. In post-talmudic times, the need for a uniform text became evident. The scribes who assumed this task were called Masoretes, derived from the word "*masorah*" meaning "tradition" or "that which has been transmitted." Sorting through the numerous scrolls, they identified disagreements and generally adopted the text of the majority. However, determining and preserving the authentic text of the Torah was only part of the role of the Masoretes. From earliest times to this day, Torah scrolls have contained only the consonants of the text. The proper vowels, accentuation, and melody to be used when chanting the text were handed down orally to each generation. The Masoretes developed a system of vowel points designed to ensure the correct pronunciation of the individual words. They introduced cantillation marks to indicate the proper way of accenting and chanting the words; since the Torah contains no punctuation, they also show where sentences begin and end.[2] Because the Masoretes believed that the Torah had been dictated to Moses by God, they were unwilling to change the sacred text and made all changes as marginal notes in small type around the body of the text. To correct spelling errors that might alter the meaning, the Masoretes introduced the notation system of *ketiv* (writing) and *keri* (reading), in which they left the original text but indicated in the margin how the word should properly be spelled. According to Jewish law, the Torah reader must follow the *keri,* not the *ketiv,* when reading the Torah and thus must study the masoretic notes in printed texts before reading from the scroll. Occasionally, the Masoretes provided euphemistic substitutes for "indelicate expressions" (especially relating to sexual intercourse) when the Torah is read in the synagogue. This desire to spare the listener the sordid details was carried to an extreme with the insertion of an empty space in the middle of the verse, "and Israel [Jacob] heard" (Gen. 35:22), which refers to the shameful actions of Reuben, Jacob's eldest son, who had sexual intercourse with Bilhah, his father's concubine.[3]

The Masoretes identified 20 times when words should be read as written but understood differently (*severin,* meaning "suppose" in Aramaic)[4] as well as words that contain a superfluous letter (*malei,* meaning "full") or in which a letter is missing (*chaser,* meaning "absent"). They also developed the system of adding white spaces that break up the otherwise continuous text of the scroll. The Masoretes cataloged changes that scribes had traditionally made in the Torah scroll itself, such as larger letters; smaller letters; and 10 times where one or more dots appear over words or phrases, which indicate that they either convey an often-hidden ethical or moral teaching lesson or were of questionable authenticity.[5] Masoretic notes detailing the number of verses, chapters, and weekly portions in the book are found at the end of each of the five books in many printed Hebrew editions of the Torah.[6]

Manuscripts with masoretic notations were designed only for study and could not be used for public reading of the Torah in a synagogue service. Known as codices (singular, codex), they were handwritten on both sides of single sheets of parchment, which were bound between two pieces of wood. The oldest extant text containing masoretic notations is the St. Petersburg Codex of 916. The first complete Hebrew Bible with vowel points, accents, and masoretic notes in the margins of the text was produced by Moses ben Asher of Tiberias and is known as the Aleppo Codex, since it came into the possession of that Syrian Jewish community. The version generally considered the "official" masoretic text of the Hebrew Bible, and the model for all future editions, was the Great Rabbinic Bible (*Mikra'ot Gedolot*), which was published in 1524–1525 in Venice by the Christian printer Daniel Bomberg.

Biblical Commentary (פֵּרוּשׁ)

At the end of the 13th century, the Bible scholar Bahya ben Asher noted that there are four ways of interpreting Scripture, which came to be known by the acronym "*pardes*" (פַּרְדֵּס; *prds*, a Hebrew word meaning "orchard" or "Paradise"). This is a mnemonic for the initial letters of the following words:

***P**eshat* (plain, literal meaning of the verse in its context).
***R**emez* (allegorical or symbolic meaning only hinted at in the text).
***D**erash* (homiletic interpretation to uncover an ethical or moral lesson thought to be implicit in the text).
***S**od* (secret, esoteric, or mystical interpretation, emphasized by the kabbalists).

Peshat and *derash* are the more popular methods of exegesis, since they are comprehensible to most students. In essence, *peshat* is an objective method that attempts to understand the meaning of a passage based on its intrinsic language and historical context. In contrast, *derash* (from a Hebrew word meaning "seek") is a subjective method that strives to make the text applicable to the time of the interpreter by exploring its hidden meaning. During the rabbinic period, *derash* was the major form of biblical interpretation. By a detailed and often ingenious analysis of unusual spelling, vocabulary, and other elements in the sparse biblical text, as well as through extensive cross-references among various parts of the TANAKH, the Rabbis "filled in the details" and developed a detailed scheme of how the various mitzvot were to be fulfilled (*halakhah*). Using parables and anecdotes to elucidate the text, they also were able to reveal its moral and ethical teachings (*ag-*

gadah). The Rabbis developed the principles of hermeneutics, the science of biblical interpretation. Initially, Hillel (first century B.C.E.) formulated seven hermeneutical principles, and these were subsequently expanded by Rabbi Ishmael into the 13 principles that are found in modern prayer books.

Although it would seem that *peshat* preceded *derash*, it did not become the primary Jewish method of biblical interpretation until the rise of Islam, when Jewish scholars became exposed to Greek rational modes of thought and historical perspective, as well as the scientific study of language, which enabled them to understand what the biblical verses meant at the time they were written. The spread of this technique was aided immeasurably by the work of Saadiah Gaon, who in the 10th century published the first Arabic translation of the Bible as well as a grammar and lexicon of biblical Hebrew. For example, Hebrew verbs are constructed on roots of three consonants. Certain "weak" letters (*alef*, *vav*, and *yod*) are often dropped in some verb forms, but they are always present in Arabic. Thus a scholar conversant in Arabic grammar might understand a difficult biblical text by realizing that a weak consonant was part of the Hebrew verb even when it was not evident, whereas a Jewish commentator who did not read Arabic might become hopelessly confused about the identity of both the underlying verb and the meaning of the verse.[1]

Ironically, the most renowned exponent of the *peshat* method was an 11th-century French scholar with little linguistic or scientific training—Rashi, who wrote a running commentary to the Bible (and Talmud) that persists to this day in traditional circles as the key version of what the Torah means. (Rashi's Torah commentary was the first Hebrew book to be printed mechanically, even before the Bible itself.) Rashi was unequaled in his ability to explain difficult words and phrases, enabling the student to understand the basic meaning of the text.[2]

As Jews in the later Middle Ages became increasingly isolated and endangered, they again embraced *derash* as the preferred way of interpreting the Bible, turning away from *peshat* (which was little used until the 19th century). During the Enlightenment, Jewish scholars began to delve into the new historical–critical study of the Bible, and when these studies were combined with discoveries in archaeology and Semitic philology, there was a revitalization of the *peshat* approach to biblical interpretation.[3]

The allegorical or philosophical interpretation of the Bible (*remez*) reached its height during the 14th to 16th centuries, with such commentators as Ralbag, Arama, Sforno, and Abravanel. A basic example of this approach is the talmudic concept that the Song of Songs is not simply a secular love song but is actually an allegory for the relationship between God and Israel.

Sod posits that truth is beyond human sensory perception and cognition, and thus it cannot be expressed solely in words. Therefore, the true meaning of the divinely inspired language of the Bible cannot be understood by merely analyzing the connotations and denotations of the words themselves. Instead, it requires an entirely different approach for, as the mystics observed, "many lights shine forth from each word and each letter."[4] Among the many techniques used to reveal the hidden meaning of the words of the biblical text are *gematria* (numerology; see p. 646) and two types of *notarikon* (from a Greek word meaning "shorthand writer"). In the first of these, a word is understood as an acronym for its real meaning (i.e., each letter of the word represents an entirely new word). For example, *Anochi*, meaning "I" (the first word of the Ten Commandments), is actually an abbreviation for "*Ana Nafshi Ketavit Yahavit*" (I, Myself, wrote and gave [them]), so that there can be no doubt that the Decalogue is the word of God (Shab. 105a). The second and later type of *notarikon* consists of breaking up a word into two or more components that have meanings of their own—so that the name Reuben becomes *re'u ben* (see the son).[5] The kabbalists used these techniques to show the hidden meaning in the word "*b'reishit*" (in the beginning), the first word of the Torah. The six Hebrew letters could be read as an acronym for "*barah rakiah eretz shamayim yam tehom*" (He created the firmament, the earth, the heavens, the sea, and the abyss), which outlines the cosmogenic order, or could be split into the two words "*bara sheet*" ([the world was] created in six [primordial days]). *Remez* and *sod* were often deemed too dangerous for those without extensive talmudic knowledge, lest such students mistakenly stumble on a misinterpretation that could lead them into heresy.

Rabbinic Literature

Following the devastating defeat by the Romans and destruction of the Temple, the Rabbis were convinced that the very survival of the Jewish people could be achieved only through intensified dedication to Torah. This included not only the Five Books of Moses (Written Law), but also a complete understanding of the divine plan for how the Chosen People of Israel should live. This meant the Oral Law, which the Rabbis maintained had been part of the Revelation granted to Moses and subsequently transmitted faithfully by the leaders of each generation to their successors—from Moses to Joshua, and then to the elders, the Prophets, the men of the Great Assembly, the leaders of the Pharisees, and eventually to the earliest Rabbis. The Rabbis used the Oral Law in two ways. First, they attempted to take the "holiness" associated with the Temple and extend it to the entire spectrum of everyday existence. The levitical purity that had formerly been required only for sacrificial foods was now applied to all meals. The detailed laws relating to the Temple were transformed to affect the routine activities of daily life, thus producing numerous opportunities for average Jews to perform the dictates of divine law and sanctify their lives. The Rabbis also assumed the role of the scribes, studying and teaching the Scripture and developing new ways for uncovering its meaning.[1]

The Oral Law consists of two major divisions: *halakhah* and *aggadah*. *Halakhah* ("path," derived from the Hebrew verb "to go") is usually translated as "Jewish law," though it encompasses all life activities. In their roles as judges and community officials, the early Rabbis and their disciples immersed themselves in often-intricate analyses to determine precisely what the Torah commanded so that they could apply its teachings to practical situations. *Aggadah* refers to all nonhalakhic teachings, such as statements of major moral and ethical principles, stories about biblical heroes and the great Rabbis, and Jewish folklore.[2]

The study of the Oral Law was essentially a matter of memorization and repetition, unlike the Written Law that could be read (Avot 3:8). The term "*mishnah*" (from the Hebrew verb "*shanah*," meaning "to repeat") was initially used as a synonym for each specific *halakhah* (law). These *halakhot* developed from multiple sources, including local laws and customs, historical traditions, priestly rituals, judgments by the courts in cases that came before them, and rabbinic pronouncements and decrees. However, the true meaning of the early *halakhot* was often in doubt. This led various Rabbis and academies to form contradictory opinions and teach the *halakhot* according to their own particular approaches. Among the early scholars of the first century B.C.E., the two giants were Hillel and Shammai, who continually clashed in their interpretations of Torah law. Shammai generally was extremely rigorous, whereas Hillel took a more liberal and sympathetic approach. The multiplicity of divergent opinions led several Rabbis to arrange their own collections of *mishnayot* (plural of mishnah).

Mishnah (מִשְׁנָה)

Early in the third century, Judah ha-Nasi (Judah the Prince, known simply as "Rabbi") sifted through, evaluated, and edited the vast number of legal opinions that had been expressed over the centuries in the academies of learning, primarily in the Land of Israel. Around 220, he finished compiling his magnum opus—the Mishnah—the earliest major rabbinic book. Rather than being organized as a running commentary on specific biblical verses, the Mishnah is an independent text, written in Hebrew, that has a compact and precise style and an internal logic all its own. It records disagreements among the various sages and schools, but frequently does not conclusively determine the *halakhah*. Nevertheless, there often is a hint as to which is the authoritative view. Anonymous opinions are generally accepted as the normative principle that should govern one's behavior. When an opinion is attributed to a particular rabbi, but is followed by an opposing view introduced by the phrase "but the sages say" or "in the view of the sages," the latter opinion should be followed in practice.[1] For centuries, the Mishnah provided a uniformly recognized starting point for subsequent deliberations of scholars and commentators.

The Mishnah is divided into six orders (*shishah sidrei mishnah*, abbreviated *shas*).[2] A mnemonic for the sequence of the orders was provided by Resh Lakish (Shab. 31a), based on the verse, "And there shall be faith in your times, strength, salvation, wisdom, and knowledge" (Isa. 33:6).[3] "Faith" refers to the order *Zera'im* (Seeds), since a farmer sowing his crop must have faith that God will provide a bountiful harvest. "Your times" relates to the order *Mo'ed* (Festivals, which are also termed "appointed times"). "Strength" refers the order *Nashim* (Women), because the word used here for "strength" (according to Rashi) derives from a root meaning "to inherit," and heirs are created through women. "Salvation" relates to the order *Nezikin* (Damages), since knowledge of civil law "saves" people from infringing on the rights of their neighbors or permitting their own to be taken away. "Wisdom" refers to the order *Kodashim* (Holy Things) and "knowledge" relates to the order *Tohorot* (Purities), because these are extremely complicated to understand. (A popular mnemonic is the acronym "Z'MaN NaKaT.") Each order is divided into *massekhtot* ("tractates"; see appendix), which are generally arranged within each order according to their length. The first order, though primarily dealing with agricultural tithes, first fruits, and similar topics, opens with tractate *Berachot* (Blessings), presumably because this seemed to be the most fitting way to begin this compendium of the divine will.[4]

The Mishnah originally was taught orally because of the prior prohibition against writing down the Oral Law. Its initial teachers were the *tannaim*, the authorities whose work was assembled in the collection. From an Aramaic word meaning "repeater," the *tannaim* acted as "living books" in teaching the Mishnah to their disciples.

Baraita (בָּרַיְתָא) and Tosefta (תּוֹסֶפְתָּא)

A *baraita* (Aramaic for "outside") is a piece of legal, historic, or aggadic tradition that was not included in the Mishnah of Judah ha-Nasi. They are attributed to rabbinic teachers who lived in the Land of Israel at or before the time of the Mishnah. The *amoraim* in the Babylonian Talmud (see below) employed *baraitot* to clarify an issue, raise or resolve questions, or merely provide additional information on a specific topic. They generally are introduced by technical terms that indicate their function in a given passage. Thus "our sages taught" is the sign of a *baraita* quoted for the sake of information, "as it is taught" means that the *baraita* supports the most recent statement, and "but it is taught" indicates that the *baraita* challenges it. "He taught" introduces a brief *baraita* that merely has been brought to explain a passage in the Mishnah or add to it.[1] A *baraita* occasionally is preferred, but usually the latter was considered more authoritative. When they conflicted or contradicted each other, the Rabbis preferred to term the *baraita* a "faulty tradition" rather than alter the Mishnah.

The Tosefta (Hebrew, *tosafah*) is a collection of *baraitot* arranged according to the order of the Mishnah. About four times larger than the Mishnah itself, the Tosefta (meaning "supplement") is an independent work that contains versions of *halakhot* that support or even contradict the Mishnah and sometimes appear to be completely unrelated to it.

Talmud (תַּלְמוּד)

The Talmud is a compendium of the extensive discussions and interpretations of the Mishnah by scholars known as *amoraim* (Aramaic for "those who discuss") in the great academies of learning. In general use, the term "Talmud" refers to the Babylonian Talmud, which tradition dates from the first half of the third century (Rav and Samuel) to the editing by Rav Ashi and Ravina around 500 (though the final editing was probably completed by the middle of the sixth century by the *Savora'im*, the disciples of the last *amoraim* and their immediate successors). There is also a much smaller Jerusalem Talmud, actually produced in the Galilee, which was completed in the early fifth century.

After initially focusing their attention on clarifying obscure passages in the Mishnah, the *amoraim* concentrated on gaining a more profound understanding of the subject matter. By analyzing specific rules in the Mishnah, they attempted to deduce general principles of action. Moreover, they developed a collection of legal precedents illustrating how the laws of the Mishnah were applied in the rabbinic courts of the time. As this mass of material increased dramatically, it also became the basis of rabbinic learning, known as "Talmud" in Hebrew and "Gemara" in Aramaic (both words meaning "study").[1]

The Babylonian Talmud contains about 2.5 million words on 5,894 folio pages. This monumental work, aptly termed the "sea of Talmud," details the discussions of approximately 2,000 scholars spanning six generations, with no attempt to transform the vast amount of material into a concise or systematic form. In addition to interpretations of the biblical commandments and legal issues, the Talmud is a treasure trove of historical facts and traditions; scientific speculations in medicine, astronomy, and biology; moral and ethical teachings; folklore, proverbs, and legends; and profound observations on all phases of human experience.

Although all six orders of the Mishnah were studied in the academies, several have only a small amount of Gemara, presumably because the final editing of the Talmud included only those sections that had contemporary significance. The only exception is the order *Kodashim*, which deals mainly with the Temple service in Jerusalem. This is explained by the talmudic teaching that "whosoever occupies himself with the study of the Torah needs neither burnt offering, nor meal offering, nor sin offering, nor guilt offering" (i.e., study of the Temple service is equal to its actual performance) (Men. 110a).

Like the fine print in a legal contract, the Rabbis of the Talmud painstakingly dissected every word or phrase of the Mishnah to search for its underlying meaning. Using a "case history approach," they developed the *halakhah* by applying the mishnaic teachings to novel situations, often engaging in hotly disputed arguments before the problem was resolved. Occasionally, however, the discussion ends with the word "*teiku*" ("the problem remains unresolved"). This is an acronym for the Hebrew phrase "*Tishbi yetaretz kushi'ot va-abayot*" (the Tishbite [Elijah] will answer difficulties and problems), implying that the ultimate resolution of the issue will have to wait until the Messianic Age.

A controversial issue was the relative standing and authority of preceding scholars in relation to those of later Rabbis in terms of their halakhic rulings and interpretation of the Torah. The Talmud stressed that the worth of the generations had decreased as they progressively became further removed in time from Sinai: "If the early authorities were as angels, we are as men; and if they were as men, we are as donkeys" (Shab. 112b). The later gaonic literature challenged this view, emphasizing the halakhic rule that "the law is in accordance with the later authority." They argued that this was either because those who came later were "more painstaking in clarifying the *halakhah*" (Tosefta to Kid. 45b), or because they had already seen and taken into consideration the reasoning of their predecessors and were, therefore, in the words of the well-known proverb, like "a dwarf sitting on the back of a giant."

Babylonian and Jerusalem Talmuds

There are numerous fundamental differences between the Babylonian and the Jerusalem Talmuds. Although both are primarily written in Aramaic, the vernacular of the time, the Babylonian Talmud contains a substantial number of words in Hebrew, whereas the Jerusalem Talmud contains words from the Greek dialect prevalent at that time in Syria and the Land of Israel. Although barely half the size of the Babylonian, the Jerusalem Talmud has Gemara to all the tractates of the first order (*Zera'im*), which deals with agricultural laws that largely applied only to the Land of Israel. Unlike the numerous tangents and extraneous material in the Babylonian Talmud, which frequently delves into topics in great depth, the discussions in the Jerusalem Talmud are shorter but often obscure. The Jerusalem Talmud, completed almost a century and a half before the Babylonian, shows signs of insufficient editing, with numerous repetitions and contradictions and a general lack of continuity. The Jerusalem Talmud contains much less aggadic material than the Babylonian (about one-sixth versus one-third), reflecting the fact that in the Land of Israel the aggadic element was assembled in special collections out of which later evolved the Midrash (see p. 507).

Initially, each Talmud was authoritative in its own sphere. However, the spread of Islam and the presence of the caliphate at Baghdad in the eighth century allowed the *Ge'onim* to establish the authority of the Babylonian Talmud throughout Europe. Students from all parts of the Diaspora flocked to the prestigious academies at Sura and Pumbedita, where the supremacy of the Babylonian tradition was reinforced. The final death blow to the acceptance of the Jerusalem Talmud came from Isaac Alfasi,[2] who noted that, when the two works were in disagreement, one should follow the Babylonian Talmud, because it is later in time and is thus more authoritative than the Jerusalem Talmud.

Layout of the Talmud

On every page of the Talmud, the Mishnah and Gemara are situated in the center and set in larger type. Surrounding the text are the two most famous medieval commentaries (see below). Toward the binding is that of Rashi, and in the outside column are the subsequent discussions of the Tosafists ("the Men of the Additions," from the Hebrew "*Tosafot*"). Beyond these commentaries, at the margins of the page, are found a potpourri of cross-references to other talmudic sources, quotations from the Bible and the great codes of Jewish law, and short commentaries from the medieval and more recent periods. In the upper outer corner is the Hebrew letter(s) indicating the number of the page (*daf*). No talmudic tractate has a page one. A homiletic explanation for starting on page two is that the prospective student immediately realizes that it is impossible to know everything. A more practical reason relates to the custom of early printers, who devoted page one to a highly decorated title page at the beginning of each volume and routinely began the text with page two. Hebrew books numbered "leaves," rather than "pages"; thus references to a source in the Talmud should indicate whether they fall on the "a" or "b" side of the page.[3]

Commentaries and Codes

Once the Talmud was completed, it became the authoritative text taught in the Babylonian academies and then in Jewish communities throughout the world. However, it soon became apparent that there was a need to explain its meaning. During the gaonic period, this primarily took the form of responsa, answers by illustrious rabbis to queries from abroad. Each responsum (Hebrew, "*teshuvah*") was preceded by a question that described the facts of the case and the specific legal issue for which a ruling was needed. Citations of all relevant talmudic passages were often included, like a legal brief to a modern court that notes the rulings in prior relevant cases. In this way, the mass of responsa issued through the centuries from the gaonic and medieval periods to modern times provides an intriguing insight into the development of Jewish law in terms of case-based precedents, as well as a broad understanding of key talmudic passages.[4] The major limitation of responsa is that they are poorly collected and organized, so that it may be difficult to determine whether there are relevant responsa on a specific subject. However, this problem has decreased in recent years with the development of computer databases in which numerous medieval and early modern responsa have been cataloged.[5]

The first extensive commentaries on the Babylonian Talmud appeared in the early 11th century. The most popular and influential was by Rashi, who wrote a clear and concise summary of the traditional interpretations prevalent in the principal French and German schools, where he had studied for many years. By carefully reading Rashi's commentary, those who followed him were able to acquire for the first time a profound comprehension of the Talmud. From the 12th to the 14th centuries, Rashi's commentary also served as the point of departure for the Tosafists, whose most illustrious scholars were Rashi's sons-in-law and grandsons. The Tosafists sought to answer questions by pointing to differences and distinctions between cases and sources to produce new halakhic deductions and conclusions. Their extensive writings were essentially records of the lively oral discussions of *halakhah* between the heads of the *yeshivot* and their pupils on selected talmudic passages, mainly when they disagreed with the views of Rashi.

Unlike the commentators who studied the text for its own sake and to provide understanding of a given subject (*mefarshim*), one group of scholars concentrated on determining the practical *halakhah* to decide specific legal cases (*posekim*, or decisors). Most *posekim* were heads of *yeshivot* and members of rabbinic courts, but their decisions were binding only on those communities that accepted their authority. Since the Talmud is a huge work without an index, knowing what it says about a given subject effectively requires one to read it completely through. This prohibitive task led some rabbis to prepare extensive summaries of specific legal topics and eventually to develop comprehensive codes.

In the Middle Ages, by far the greatest of these legal codes was the *Mishneh Torah* of Maimonides. In this massive 14-volume work—also known as the *Yad*, since the numerical value of the letters "*yud*" (10) and "*dalet*" (4) equals 14—Maimonides discussed every conceivable topic of Jewish law in an immensely logical sequence. He collected and digested all talmudic sources relevant to any given subject and then wrote down a simple statement of the law in the clearest possible language, without any summary of the ancient discussions. Maimonides wrote that the purpose of his code was to make the study of the Talmud unnecessary for those who merely wanted to know the law and how to live their lives as observant Jews. For this perceived arrogance, Maimonides was actually condemned and denounced as a threat to traditional Judaism.

The most influential code in modern Jewish life—and the last comprehensive one to be written—is the Shulchan Arukh (Set Table) of Yosef Karo. Actually a digest of Karo's own commentary to an earlier, more elaborate code, the Shulchan Arukh (first printed in Venice in 1565) provides a simple statement of the law as it affects the life of the ordinary Jew. Unlike Maimonides, Karo simply ignored all areas of the law that were no longer applicable; like his great predecessor, Karo tended to omit all references to earlier sources or to opinions he had decided to reject. Similar to the earlier *Arba'ah Turim* (Four Rows) of Jacob ben Asher, the Shulchan Arukh is divided into four major sections: Orach Hayim, concerning the daily commandments, Sabbaths, and festivals; Yoreh De'ah, dealing with various subjects such as dietary laws, interest, purity, and mourning; Even Ha-Ezer, on marriage, divorce, and related topics; and Hoshen Mishpat, dealing with civil and criminal law. In his decisions, Karo relied on three major authorities: Isaac Alfasi (11th century; known as the "Rif"), Maimonides, and Asher ben Jehiel (late 13th to early 14th century; known as "the Rosh"). When they disagreed, Karo generally followed the majority.

The Shulchan Arukh reflected Karo's Sephardic background and was initially not accepted as an authoritative code by Ashkenazic Jews, since it completely ignored the halakhic decisions and customs that had developed among the Jews of Germany and Poland in the almost 250 years since ben Jehiel's time. The Shulchan Arukh gained universal acceptance through the work of Moses Isserles (mid-16th century; known as "the Rema"), a renowned Polish rabbi who wrote a "Tablecloth" (*Mappah*) for the Set Table that included the distinctive customs of the Jews of Eastern Europe. This composite work has become the functioning code for observant Jews to the present day.[6]

Some prominent authorities voiced strenuous opposition to any code that purported to lay down a definitive version of Jewish law. They objected to the arbitrariness of the form, which presented Jewish law the way one particular codifier understood it, with no mention of the sources or reasoning that led him to his conclusions or any mention of alternate opinion and practices. Moreover, these objectors argued that every code gives rise to commentaries and super-commentaries—which have just the opposite effect intended by the authors of the original code—and thus the only source for determining the *halakhah* should be the Talmud.

Another problem in understanding the meaning of the Talmud was its language, primarily Aramaic, which was unknown to the Jews of Europe. Even in Babylonia, Aramaic had been supplanted by Arabic as the vernacular after the Muslim conquest. The first talmudic lexicon, the Arukh of Nathan ben Jehiel of Rome (a contemporary of Rashi), provided invaluable explanations of difficult words and entire subjects in the Talmud as well as Babylonian Jewish customs of the period. Thus the combination of the Arukh, Rashi's commentary, and the Shulchan Arukh allows Jews to study the meaning of individual words and the overall text to determine the binding *halakhah*.

Midrash (מִדְרָשׁ)

The term "midrash," which derives from a Hebrew root meaning "to search out," can refer to either the process of interpreting the Bible or to the genre of rabbinic literature that has collected these interpretations. One reason for the development of the Midrash is to fill in the gaps of the terse biblical narrative, which provides little information as to the thoughts and feelings of the characters or the motivations behind their actions. For example, the Midrash discusses the height of Adam in the Garden of Eden, why Cain killed Abel, and what Isaac thought when his father Abraham took him to be sacrificed. Similarly, the Bible often states matters of law without clarification or detail. Thus halakhic Midrash helps us understand what it means to love one's neighbor as oneself, how to observe the Sabbath, and the source for requiring separate dishes for meat and milk.[1]

The Bible is an ancient document that reflects its time of origin. By the time of the Rabbis, the social and political situation had dramatically changed and was heavily influenced by Hellenistic culture. Thus the Midrash provided an opportunity for the Rabbis to reread the biblical text based on the values and beliefs current in their own era. A quintessential example is the talmudic reinterpretation of the frequently misunderstood biblical concept of "an eye for an eye" (Exod. 21:23–24); the Rabbis indicate that the verse should not be taken literally but as a reference to monetary compensation (BK 83b–84a). The Midrash also was a vehicle for allowing "external" ideas in contemporary culture, such as the soul and afterlife, to influence rabbinic theology. The profound questions relating to the destruction of the Temple forced the Midrash to attempt to make sense out of the recent tragic historical events. With sacrifice no longer available for the expiation of sin, the Midrash radically reinterpreted the law by stating that the performing of deeds of human kindness was an equivalent way of making atonement. In response to the desolation of the people, the Midrash developed the comparison of the Torah to a marriage contract (*ketubah*) between God and Israel. In a series of parables, it assures the Jews that if they continue to obey the divine commandments expressed in the Torah, God will eventually fulfill the covenantal promises made to the Chosen People.[2]

Many midrashim are based on variant spellings, puns, and other allusions that cannot be fully appreciated unless one can understand the original Hebrew of the biblical text. Because the Rabbis were convinced that nothing is superfluous in the Bible, the basis of a midrash may be only an apparently extra word or even a single letter. For example, in one midrash a close reading of the biblical account of Creation allowed the Rabbis to gain a profound insight into human nature. In the verse, "The Lord God formed man" (Gen 2:7), the verb is written וַיִּיצֶר, with a double *yud* that is not necessary for proper spelling. The Talmud explains that this was done "to show that God created [human beings with] two inclinations, one good and the other evil," (Ber. 61a) consistent with the rabbinic notion that within each person there are two opposing natures continually in conflict.[3]

There are three basic types of Midrash: exegetical, homiletic, and narrative. An exegetical midrash contains short comments on each chapter, every verse, and even every word of an entire book of the Bible (e.g., *Genesis Rabbah*, *Exodus Rabbah*, and *Lamentations Rabbah*; *Mekhilta*; *Sifra*; *Sifrei*). A homiletic midrash (*Leviticus Rabbah* and *Deuteronomy Rabbah*; *Tanchuma*; *Pesikta de-Rav Kahana*) is more discursive and is structured around sermons expounding on verses from the weekly Torah portion or the readings for special Sabbaths and festivals. In the most common type, the author begins with a biblical quotation from the Writings (such as Psalms or Job) and then through a string of often-intricate relationships links this "verse from afar" to the opening verse of the Torah reading for that day. Each chapter or section of these midrashim constitutes a collection of homilies and sayings on one specific topic that seem to combine into one long homily. A narrative midrash (e.g., *Pirkei de-Rabbi Eliezer*) does not attempt to explicate the Bible in a direct or orderly manner but instead is a collection of stories and legends about individual rabbis or biblical characters. Some of these texts are known as "rewritten Bible," since they embellish the original biblical narrative.[4]

Probably the best-known collection of midrashic literature is the Passover haggadah (see p. 273). Although the haggadah contains prayers, Passover rituals, and biblical verses, most of the seder before the festive meal consists of pure Midrash—the long *maggid* (telling) section and its introductory Four Questions (see p. 276). This includes the story of the five rabbis in the town of Bnei Brak discussing the Exodus from Egypt (because if these learned sages studied the Exodus all evening, so should we), the four children (see p. 277), the detailed explanations of the 10 plagues (see p. 280), and even the imaginative reasoning behind holding the seder at night.[5]

Thirteen Principles of Faith

Historically, Judaism has never separated creed from deed. In Maimonides' list of the biblically based commandments, belief in the existence of God is only one (albeit the first) of the 248 positive mitzvot. The concept of "dogma," a concise formula expressing a fundamental system of beliefs, is popular in Christianity but not a basic idea in Judaism. According to the Rabbis, every Jew is born into God's covenant with the people of Israel; therefore, no official declaration of faith is necessary to secure membership in the community. Nevertheless, the Talmud does contain several short statements regarding specific requirements of belief for those who adhere to traditional Judaism. For example, in an attempt to combat sectarian heresy, the Mishnah states that all Israelites have a share in the world to come, but this does not apply to those who "maintain that resurrection is not a biblical doctrine" or who believe that "the Torah was not divinely revealed," or who is an *apikoros* (an adherent of the Epicurean philosophy) (Sanh. 10:1).

For years, the closest thing to a statement of creed in Judaism was the emphatic declaration of faith immediately following the *Shema*. Now incorporated in the morning prayer *Emet v'Yatziv* (True and Certain) and the evening prayer *Emet v'Emunah* (True and Faithful), in its original form it may have read: "True and firm ... is the word unto us forever and ever ... It is true that You are indeed the Lord our God and the God of our fathers; our King, the King of our fathers; our Redeemer and the Redeemer of our fathers; our Maker, the Rock of our salvation; our Deliverer and Rescuer, from everlasting, such is Your Name; there is no God beside You."[1]

This confession of faith, a clear statement of rabbinic beliefs that reflected deep conviction and was composed in a powerful idiom, satisfied the needs of the synagogue for centuries. However, it lacks the precise, logical presentation of a philosophical thesis. During the medieval period, Jews were confronted with other faiths (especially Islam) and the challenge of Greek philosophy, which had become popular among the intelligentsia and was beginning to influence a number of Jews. To counteract this trend, the rabbinic authorities recognized a need to respond by defining the core principles of Judaism. This "led to the composition of multiple philosophical formulations of the basic doctrines of the Jewish faith."[2] The one that eventually secured virtually universal acceptance was the Thirteen Principles of Faith, which Maimonides set down in his commentary to the Mishnah as an introduction to his discussion on Sanhedrin 10.

The Thirteen Principles of Faith fall into three general categories: the nature of belief in God; the authenticity, validity, and immutability of the Torah; and the responsibility of human beings and their ultimate reward. The specific principles are as follows:

- Existence of God (Who "creates and guides all creatures" and the entire universe, which continues to exist only because God wills it so).
- Complete and total unity and uniqueness of God (as in the *Shema*).
- Incorporeality of God (anthropomorphic expressions applied to God in Scripture are only metaphorical).
- God is eternal ("the very first and the very last," who transcends time).
- God alone is to be worshiped and obeyed (prayers must only be said directly to God and not to any intermediary).
- Prophecy ("all the words of the prophets are true," for they are direct communications from God).
- Moses is unsurpassed by any other prophet.

- The entire Torah was given to Moses by God (both Written and Oral Law).
- The Torah is unchangeable (nothing can be added or subtracted from it, "nor will there be another Torah from the Creator").
- God knows the thoughts and deeds of human beings.
- Reward and punishment (God rewards with good those who observe the commandments and punishes those who violate them).
- The coming of the Messiah ("even though he may delay [a Jew must] anticipate every day that he will come").
- The resurrection of the dead (in the Messianic Era of spiritual and physical perfection).[3]

Several of these principles are of a polemical nature, especially the statement that no later prophet could ever claim to have received a Torah superior to that of Moses. This clearly was designed to refute both the Christian argument that the New Testament superseded the Torah and the Moslem assertion that the Koran supplanted both the Jewish and Christian Bibles.[4]

The Thirteen Principles of Faith were incorporated into the prayer book as *Ani Ma'amin* (I believe [with complete faith]), which is found at the conclusion of the morning service as one of the optional selections available to the pious for daily review. They also are the basis for *Yigdal*, which was included in the prayer book as an opening or closing hymn (see p. 470).

Mitzvot

Overview

The term "mitzvah" (plural, mitzvot) comes from a Hebrew root meaning "to command" and applies to a religious obligation. In common usage, mitzvah has also come to mean a "good deed." The Torah uses several other terms to indicate laws—"*torah*" (teaching; Lev. 6:2), "*chukah*" (statute; Num. 19:2), "*mishpat*" (ordinance; Num. 9:14), "*eidut*" (testimony; Deut. 4:45), and "*mishmeret*" (observance; Lev. 8:35)—but only the word "mitzvah" is generally used to include all the commandments.

The mitzvot have been divided into 248 positive requirements and 365 negative prohibitions (see below). As the Rabbis imposed additional ritual obligations, the mitzvot were also separated into the two major categories: *mitzvot de-oraita* (biblical commandments) and *mitzvot de-rabbanan* (rabbinic precepts). Some of the commandments were classified as *mitzvot kallot* (less important; lit., "light") or *mitzvot chamurot* (more important), but the Rabbis stressed that Jews should "be as scrupulous in performing a 'minor' mitzvah as in a 'major' one, for you do not know the reward given for the respective mitzvot" (Avot 2:1). Medieval Jewish philosophers distinguished between mitzvot that were "rational" (*sichliyot*) and those that were "revealed" (*shimiyot*).

Enumeration of the Mitzvot

The Torah is the source of all the commandments, though it does not specifically enumerate them. The first mention of a precise number of commandments appears in a talmudic statement by Rabbi Simlai, a fourth-century sage in the Land of Israel, who observed that "613 commandments were communicated to Moses; 365 negative commandments [*mitzvot lo ta'aseh*], corresponding to the number of days [in the solar year], and 248 positive commandments [*mitzvot aseh*], corresponding to the number of parts of the human body" (Mak. 23b). In Hebrew, the commandments are termed the *taryag* (תרי״ג) *mitzvot*, since the numerical value of these letters equals 613: ת = 400, ר = 200, י = 10, ג = 3. These 613 mitzvot can also be viewed as the sum of the 611 scriptural commandments that were announced to the people directly by Moses—the word "Torah" (תורה) in Hebrew has a numerical value of 611 (ת = 400, ו = 6, ר = 200, ה = 5)—plus the first two of the Ten Commandments, which were spoken directly to the people by God (Mak. 23b–24a).

During the talmudic period, there was no attempt to precisely enumerate each individual commandment. The first effort in this direction was made in the gaonic period, during the second half of the eighth century by Simon Kayara (or Kairo) in his *Halakhot Gedolot* (Great Laws). However, he cited a different division of commandments—265 positive and 348 negative—and included some mitzvot that were established only by rabbinic decree.

The major monumental work listing and elucidating the meaning of the commandments was the *Sefer ha-Mitzvot* (Book of the Commandments) of Maimonides. *Sefer ha-Hinnukh* (Book of Education), which is attributed to Aaron ha-Levi of Barcelona (13th century), arranged the commandments according to the order in which they appear in the Torah, so that they could be studied along with the weekly reading in the synagogue. In the 19th century, the Chafetz Chaim (Israel Meir ha-Cohen) wrote the *Sefer ha-Mitzvot ha-Katzar* (Short Book of the Commandments), which includes a listing of those positive and negative commandments that are still applicable today.

Rabbinic Commandments

The Rabbis established seven mitzvot that were not based on any verses in the Torah:

- Washing hands before eating (Eduy. 5:6; see p. 553).
- Lighting Sabbath candles (Shab. 20b; see p. 136).
- Reciting the *Hallel* psalms of praise on festival days (Ber. 14a; Pes. 117a; see p. 162).
- Lighting Hanukkah candles (Shab. 23a; see p. 248).

- Reading the Scroll of Esther on Purim (Meg. 7a; see p. 257).
- Making an *eruv* (to alleviate some Sabbath restrictions concerning the limitation of movement and transfer of objects) (Er. 21b; see p. 134).
- Saying a blessing of thanksgiving before experiencing pleasure in worldly items (such as for specific foods) (Ber. 35a; see p. 474).

Like the performance of mitzvot based on Torah verses (*de-oraita*), the observance of rabbinic (*de-rabbanan*) commandments is preceded by reciting a blessing of sanctification. Nevertheless, there are substantial differences in the manner in which these two types of commandments are observed. Commandments based on Torah verses must be observed with the greatest possible strictness; the mitzvah must be repeated if there is any doubt whether it has already been performed. Thus, if uncertain whether one has recited the *Shema*, a person must recite it, on the assumption that he had not already previously said it. In contrast, a similar uncertainty as to whether one has fulfilled a rabbinic commandment would not obligate the individual to repeat the mitzvah. According to Jewish law, conscious purpose (*kavanah*) is an unequivocal requirement for discharging most scriptural commandments, but is not strictly necessary (though strongly recommended) in the case of rabbinic mitzvot.[1]

Reasons for Observance of the Mitzvot (*Ta'amei ha-Mitzvot*)

Why should Jews observe the commandments?[1] Are they to be obeyed merely because they represent the will of God or because they possess some intrinsic meaning designed to spiritually improve the person who performs them, or for both reasons? Throughout the centuries, the answers to these questions have varied among the classical Jewish texts. Some have argued that we should not search for reasons for the mitzvot since they transcend our understanding, while others have maintained that every effort should be made to discover their underlying meanings. Abraham Joshua Heschel[2] observed that "in doing more than we understand, we come to understand more than we do"—of ourselves, the tradition, and the world.

Biblical Period

The Torah offers specific reasons for relatively few of the commandments. A classic example is the prohibition against oppressing a stranger, which is repeated 36 times in the Torah and is based on the verse, "for you were strangers in the land of Egypt" (Exod. 22:20). This implies that the Israelites had learned firsthand the need to be sensitive to the plight of strangers in their midst. Broad reasons given for observing the entire gamut of positive and negative commandments include ensuring the holiness of the nation, upholding the everlasting legal covenant, sustaining the love relationship between God and Israel, the concept of reward and punishment, sanctifying the name of God, and leading a wise and moral life.

As the Israelites stood at the foot of Mount Sinai, God offered them the opportunity to be "a kingdom of priests, and a holy nation" (Exod. 19:6). The root of the Hebrew word for "holy" is "*kadosh*" (lit., "separate"). Therefore, by observing the commandments the Israelites would become a unique nation, God's "treasured possession among all the peoples" (Exod. 19:5).The relationship between God and the Jewish people can be seen as both an everlasting legal covenant (*brit*) and a passionate love affair. In exchange for strict observance of the divine commandments, God promised the Israelites physical prosperity, a homeland, and a unique spiritual relationship. The Israelites formally ratified this agreement when they stated as one, "All that the Lord has spoken we will do and obey" (Exod. 24:7). This covenant was understood to continue through the generations, for as Moses declared almost 40 years later: "It was not with our fathers that the Lord made this covenant, but with us, the living, every one of us who is here today" (Deut. 5:3). Thus all Jews are obligated to fulfill the terms of the covenant just as if they had personally stood at the foot of Mount Sinai. Similarly, in every generation all Jews are to regard themselves as having been personally redeemed from bondage in Egypt.

The relationship between God and Israel can also be seen as a marriage contract, signifying intense, unquenchable love. Israel is described as a "beloved people," divinely selected not because of its size but rather "because the Lord your God chose you to be His treasured people" (Deut. 7:6–8). Describing the divine love for Israel, Hosea

(2:23) relates God as saying: "And I will betroth you forever; and I will betroth you with righteousness and justice, and with goodness and mercy, and I will betroth you with faithfulness. Then you shall be devoted to God."[3] These prophetic words of consecration are recited each morning by traditional Jews as they wrap the tefillin around their hands (see p. 382), symbolizing the daily renewal of the eternal relationship established between God and the Israelites at Mount Sinai.

A constant theme in the Torah is that one receives a reward for observing the commandments and suffers punishment (either divine or human) for disobeying them. The second paragraph of the *Shema* stresses that the prosperity of the Israelite nation depends on its faithfully obeying the divine mitzvot (Deut. 11:13–21). If the Israelites heed the commandments, God will "grant the rain for your land in [its proper] season ... [so that] you shall gather in your new grain and wine and oil. I will also provide grass in the fields for your cattle—and thus you shall eat your fill." Conversely, in response to forsaking the commandments, God will "shut up the skies so that there will be no rain and the ground will not yield its produce; and you will soon perish from the good land that the Lord is giving you."

The quintessential descriptions of reward and punishment based on whether the Israelites followed or disobeyed the commandments are the two elaborate lists of blessings and curses (Lev. 26:3–39; Deut. 28:1–68). Following a recital of the blessings that the nation will receive for fulfilling the commandments, there is a chilling prophecy detailing an extensive list of dire consequences that will befall the people (termed the *Tochachah*, "admonition") if they spurn God and the mitzvot in the Torah.

Observing the commandments serves to sanctify God's name (*kiddush ha-Shem*), enhancing God's reputation and honor among the nations. Conversely, disobeying the mitzvot, especially those prohibiting the maltreatment of non-Jews, can bring shame on the entire House of Israel and profane the name of God (*hillul ha-Shem*).

The Bible considered the performance of the commandments to be essential for leading a life of wisdom and morality. Observing the mitzvot results in an incomparable personal satisfaction and sense of well-being, which would inspire other peoples to exclaim, "Surely this great nation is a wise and understanding people!" (Deut. 4:6). Similarly, the mitzvot are the true standard of how to lead an ethical life, since they are the commandments of a completely moral God. "The teaching of the Lord is perfect, renewing life; the decrees of the Lord are enduring, making the simple wise; the precepts of the Lord are just, rejoicing the heart; the instruction of the Lord is lucid, making the eyes light up. The fear of the Lord is pure, abiding forever; the judgments of the Lord are true, righteous altogether … " (Ps. 19:7–9). Human beings are created in the image of God, who embodies virtues such as holiness, compassion, and justice. Jews are commanded to walk in God's ways and to imitate the divine pattern of actions as much as can be done by mere mortals.

Talmudic Period

The predominant view of the talmudic Rabbis is that one should obey the commandments because they come directly from God and reflect the divine will. This view maintains that God the Creator has a certain plan for the universe and human beings. God's will has been revealed in Scripture, the meaning of which is interpreted by the tradition. Because of the supranatural origin of the commandments, it is pointless to try to find rational or natural reasons to justify them. Therefore, the duty of the Jew is simply to obey them.

Ironically, attempting to discover the underlying reasons for the commandments might actually lead to people *not* observing them. A person might decide that the reason is valid but that the commandment does did not apply in his or her specific case. Similarly, the reason may have been valid when the commandment was decreed but is no longer applicable because of changes in social, economic, or other conditions. One who is a true believer does not need reasons to observe the mitzvot; conversely, one who does not observe the commandments will not necessarily be convinced if a reason is given.

Nevertheless, the Rabbis offered several specific reasons for observing the mitzvot in addition to affirming those given in the Bible. The commandments were given "only to refine God's creatures." God is quoted as saying, "If you read the Law, you do a kindness, for you help to preserve My world, since if it were not for the Law, the world would again become without form and void" (Deut. R. 8:5). In addition to purifying humanity and preserving the world, the Rabbis considered obeying the commandments a mechanism for maintaining the identity of the Jewish people despite their dispersion among the nations. "If it were not for My Law which you accepted, I should not recognize you, and I would not regard you more than any of the idolatrous nations of the world" (Exod. R. 47:3). In summary, the reason offered by the Rabbis for observing the commandments was to help the Jewish people transform themselves (and the world) into the kind of community that God wanted them to become.

Medieval Period

The dominant medieval view (philosophers, mystics, Musar movement) was that the commandments are not ends in themselves but rather the means to the end of human self-development and perfection. The talmudic Rabbis were primarily concerned with what actions were required to perform the commandments detailed and explicated in the Written and Oral Law, viewing the mitzvot as a way of fulfilling God's will—the purpose of human existence. In contrast, the medieval mind focused on why and how the mitzvot should be observed.

According to the Jewish philosophers of the Middle Ages, unreflective faith in observance of the commandments is necessary but not sufficient. To have complete faith, one must reflect on the reasons for the mitzvot and the proper way in which to perform them, based on the intense text study that scholars viewed as a major religious obligation for Jews. However, this effort was to be limited to an intellectual and spiritual elite and not available to the unlettered masses. If certain knowledge were given to those who were not prepared for it, they would misunderstand and misuse it, ending up observing the commandments even less than before.

Saadiah Gaon, the first of the great medieval Jewish philosophers, argued that unless one really understood the ideological, conceptual, and theological underpinnings of one's beliefs, religious observances have no foundation, are meaningless, and are simply mechanical. He divided the commandments into those that are rational, such as the prohibitions against murder and stealing, and those that are irrational and could be given only through Revelation—such as *sha'atnez* (see p. 562) and the red heifer. Maimonides argued that all of the commandments had rationales and useful purposes, even if these could not yet be understood by the human mind. The general explanation for the mitzvot was that they were a means for improving human character—the development of correct thinking and behavior, as well as the instilling of moral virtue and the dispelling of moral vice. Theologically, the essence of the commandments was to affirm the oneness of God and to polemicize against idolatry. For example, Maimonides maintained that the prohibition against combining milk and meat was an attack against the idolatrous practice of a fertility cult during the biblical period. A problem not addressed by Maimonides was that, if a commandment was based on what was done long ago, why should it still be observed when that reason no longer exists? In essence, he viewed the commandments as a means of moving people from a state of moral, intellectual, and spiritual potentiality to actualizing their human perfection. Indeed, living a moral life and developing the virtues were ways to make the transition from a human being to being human. According to Maimonides, the only truly happy individuals were not those who attained pleasure but rather those who fulfilled their potential.

For the Jewish mystics and practitioners of Kabbalah, the goal of life was communion with the divine (*deveikut*, or cleaving to God). Observance of the commandments and the development of a proper moral and ethical character were prerequisites for such communion, for God does not want to enter into an intimate relationship with an immoral person. The Zohar developed the concept that what we do on earth has an effect not only on ourselves, our society, and the cosmos but also on the inner life of God. Fulfilling the mitzvot restores union and harmony in the spiritual realm of the *sefirot*; in turn, this ultimately channels positive divine energy into our material world. According to this theurgical approach, not only does God redeem humans but we redeem God.

The Musar movement, founded by Israel Salanter in mid-19th-century Lithuania, stressed the proper motivation that a person should have when observing the commandments. Efforts were made to identify and inculcate the right attitude that would strengthen observance, so that one did not do the right thing for the wrong reasons. Centuries earlier, in his discussion of the meaning of "holiness," Nachmanides had argued that there must be more than merely observing the commandments—a person can observe all the laws but, if done for the wrong motivation, can still be a moral degenerate ("a scoundrel with the permission of the Torah"). Bahya ibn Pekuda had stressed the distinction between the "duties of the limbs" (actions) and the "duties of the heart" (internal spiritual motivation). One who physically fulfills the commandments without the right intention and attitude misses the entire point of performing the mitzvot.

The mystical Nachmanides played with the similarity between the Hebrew words "*mitzvot*" and "*midot*" (moral values). He argued that the purpose of a human being is to become a *baal midot* (virtuous person) by fulfilling the mitzvot, which can be understood as vehicles for the formation of proper character.

Performance of the Mitzvot

The Rabbis stressed that performance of the commandments (*sh'mirat ha-mitzvot*) is not merely a mechanical ritual or the discharge of a burdensome obligation but rather an infinitely rich and rewarding experience within the reach of every individual.[1] Instead of a thoughtless matter of routine, religious observance requires constant and careful consideration, since the greater the devotion with which the mitzvot are carried out, the greater the reward and spiritual satisfaction.

Glorifying the Mitzvah (*Hiddur Mitzvah*)

Going beyond the call of duty in fulfilling a mitzvah allows one to reflect glory upon the One who commanded its observance. Based on the verse, "This is my God and I will glorify Him" (Exod. 15:2), the Talmud suggests that one should spend up to an extra third of the cost of a mitzvah on its adornment (BK 9b). Thus on Sukkot one should buy the best *etrog* possible and bedeck the sukkah with the most beautiful decorations. Other examples of glorifying the mitzvah include purchasing the most beautiful tefillin, shofar, and tallit as well as employing the finest clear ink, best quality pen, and most skilled scribe with superb script for the writing of a Torah scroll. However, one must always be wary of focusing too much concentration on the means for performing a commandment and not paying sufficient attention to the meaning of the mitzvah itself. Closely related to the idea of glorifying the mitzvah is the requirement to make a sincere effort to perform a mitzvah as fully and completely as possible, even though a lesser degree of performance would suffice to merely fulfill one's obligation.

Love of the Mitzvah (*Hivuv Mitzvah*)

The classic example of manifesting love of the mitzvah is to not bargain over the price when buying something pertaining to a mitzvah, but rather to immediately agree to whatever the seller asks. This is done to show that the love of God is greater than any attachment to material goods. Similarly, one demonstrates love of the mitzvah by performing a commandment personally, even when it is permitted to delegate the task to others. When departing Egypt, the Israelites carried the unleavened bread "wrapped in their cloaks upon their shoulders" (Exod. 12:34), rather than placing them on their beasts of burden. Similarly, in preparing for the Sabbath, distinguished talmudic sages showed their love of the mitzvah by performing such menial tasks as plaiting the wicks, cutting up beetroots, chopping wood, kindling the fire, and carrying heavy loads in and out of the house (Shab. 119a).[2]

Joy in the Mitzvah (*Simcha shel Mitzvah*)

Rather than regard the commandments as burdens, each Jew should feel joy in having the privilege of such opportunities to serve God. The mitzvot should be performed with enthusiasm and an uplifted heart; absence of these sentiments detracts from the perfection of fulfilling a commandment. As the Rabbis observed, "One should not stand up to say *Tefillah* [the *Amidah*, and by extension all the prayers] while immersed in sorrow, or idleness, or laughter, or chatter, or frivolity, or idle talk, but only while still rejoicing in the performance of some religious act" (Ber. 31a). Related to this is the eager and excited anticipation one should feel for an approaching festival, treating it as an honored guest that will soon arrive.

Although difficult to accomplish, "It is incumbent on a man to bless God for the evil in the same way [with joy] as for the good" (Ber. 54a). The verse "I will sing of faithfulness and justice" (Ps. 101:1) was interpreted to mean that one must praise God equally whether the recipient of divine mercy or of punishment in strict accordance with divine justice. For the Rabbis, the ultimate experience was achieved by Rabbi Akiva, who submitted to execution rather than betray his faith. As his martyred soul was departing his body, Akiva had such profound belief in the perfect goodness of God that he was able to perform with a joyful heart *kiddush ha-Shem* (sanctification of God's name), the highest mitzvah in Judaism.[3]

Alertness (*Zerizut*)

A mitzvah should never be postponed, but rather always performed at the earliest possible moment, based on the verse, "I have hurried and not delayed to keep Your commandments" (Ps. 119:60). When commanded to sacrifice his beloved son, rather than hesitating Abraham "woke up early in the morning" to accomplish this grim divine command (Gen. 22:3).[4] Similarly, Jews traditionally fulfill the mitzvah of circumcision in the morning. Although it could be performed at any time on the eighth day, the Talmud notes that "the zealous are early [to perform] their religious duties" (Pes. 4a).

The Rabbis based the requirement of alertness on the verse, "you shall observe the [Feast of] Unleavened Bread" (Exod. 12:17), which literally means "you shall watch the matzot". Playing on the fact that the consonants of the words "mitzvot" and "matzot" are identical when written in Hebrew (as in the unvoweled Torah), the *Mekhilta* observed: "Just as one should not be slow when making unleavened bread, lest it leaven, so one should not be slow to perform a mitzvah. If a mitzvah comes your way, perform it immediately."[5]

Conscious Purpose (*Kavanah*)

When a mitzvah requires a specific act, such as giving charity or eating matzah at the seder, conscious purpose is usually not needed to discharge the duty. However, if no specific act is required, a person must be definitely aware of the desire to fulfill his or her religious responsibility. The Talmud notes, "If one was passing behind a synagogue, or if his house adjoins the synagogue, and he heard the sound of the shofar or of the reading of the Scroll of Esther, then if he listens with attention [lit., "if he applies his heart"], he performs the religious precept; but otherwise he does not" (RH 27b). The blessing recited before performing a mitzvah not only offers praise to God but also reminds the individual of the importance of the sanctified act.

For some mitzvot, it is essential that the person be mindful of what he or she is doing. For example, when reciting the *Shema* it is necessary not only to understand the words but to be sincerely willing to assume "the yoke of the kingdom of Heaven." Mitzvot should be performed for their own sake (*lishmah*), without any ulterior motive or expectation of a reward. In the performance of mitzvot, one must strive for the highest perfection through body and soul, completely subjugating one's personal desires to the service of God. As written in the Psalms (40:9), "To do what pleases You, my God, is my desire; Your teaching is in my inmost parts."[6]

What to Avoid When Performing Mitzvot

A commandment may not be treated with disrespect (*bizui mitzvah*). The talmudic phrase, "One must not count money by the Hanukkah light" (Shab. 22a), refers to the use of a sacred object for a secular purpose. If one beautifies the sukkah "by suspending in it nuts, peaches, almonds, pomegranates, grape clusters, garlands of ears of corn, wines, oils and flours, he may not use them until the conclusion of the last day of the Feast" (Shab. 22a). Similarly, one is forbidden to remove a mezuzah from a house when moving if the next occupant is Jewish. Because taking care of one's own concerns before performing a mitzvah is also a form of disrespect, a person should not eat before reciting the morning prayers (Ber. 10b). Any object that has been used to perform a mitzvah—such as tzitzit, tefillin, prayer book, and Torah scroll—must be treated with proper respect. When these religious items are too old or torn to be used, they are buried rather than merely discarded. (In past centuries, they were placed in a *genizah*, a sacred storeroom such as the famed one in Cairo.)[7]

A mitzvah must never be performed with the fruits of sin (*mitzvah ha-ba'ah b'averah*). One does not discharge the obligation of taking up the Four Species on Sukkot (see p. 231) through a stolen *lulav* (Suk. 30a). Similarly, "If one has stolen a *se'ah* [measure] of wheat and has ground, kneaded and baked it, and set apart the challah [see p. 141], how can he recite a blessing over it? It would not be a blessing, but rather a blasphemy!" (Sanh. 6b).[8]

Obligation of Women to Perform the Commandments

As Rachel Biale observed, the great majority of mitzvot apply equally to men and women—from the universal prohibition "You shall not murder" to the exacting details of the laws of kashrut and the observance of the Sabbath.[1] Obvious exceptions are those mitzvot that are gender based, such as circumcision and the laws regarding menstruation. Others are not directly related to biological differences, yet are still gender based.

The Mishnah states that women are obligated to observe virtually all the negative commandments (Kid. 33b). The exceptions are trimming the locks and the beard, from which women are exempt for biological reasons, and avoiding contact with a corpse, which applies only to male *Kohanim,* since women do not have any priestly functions. With respect to the positive commandments, both men and women are required to perform all that are independent of time. However, for those that are time bound, "men are obligated and women are exempt."

The most common explanation for this distinction is that it reflects the traditional domestic role of women in society. Occupied with the responsibilities of a housewife and mother, the imposition of time-bound mitzvot would be an unreasonable burden. Some Rabbis argued that women have greater innate spirituality and thus they need to fulfill fewer mitzvot to achieve spiritual perfection. According to the medieval commentator Abudarham, women were exempted from time-bound positive mitzvot because of a basic conflict between the commands of God and the demands of a husband. As the servant of two masters, a woman might be caught in the crossfire of jealousies between the requirements of each. Perhaps surprisingly, it is God who gives in and graciously allows the demands of the husband to be preeminent by exempting women from the time-bound positive commandments and thus preserving *shalom bayit* (peace in the home).

The Talmud lists five specific time-bound positive commandments for which women are not obligated: dwelling in the sukkah (see p. 228) and taking up the *lulav* (Four Species; see p. 231) on Sukkot; hearing the shofar (see p. 190) on Rosh Hashanah and Yom Kippur; wearing tzitzit (fringes; p. 377), and putting on tefillin (see p. 382). (Elsewhere, women are also exempted from counting the Omer (see p. 292) and from reciting the *Shema* (see p. 413); nevertheless, they still have an obligation to pray at their own time and in private.) The Rabbis question whether there is truly a general principle by noting that some time-bound positive commandments are obligatory for women, such as observing the Sabbath, rejoicing on festivals, eating matzah on Passover, fasting on Yom Kippur, lighting the Hanukkah lights, and assembling to hear the reading of the Torah. Conversely, women are exempt from some positive commandments that are not time bound, such as the study of Torah, procreation, and the redemption of the firstborn son (see p. 20). According to Biale, these various exemptions reflected a gradual evolution of daily practice and communal customs that allowed women not to perform certain mitzvot. These later acquired the force of law, and the general principle that women were exempt from all time-bound mitzvot and obligated in all others was an after-the-fact attempt to explain and systematize the reality that women did not perform all the same mitzvot as men. She argues that the common thread uniting the exemptions is that they all relate to obligations outside the realm of women's domestic role, representing instead the central duties of public religious life that was focused on men.

In describing the time-bound positive commandments that were not obligatory for women, the Mishnah uses the term "exemption." This raises the question whether women "may" perform these mitzvot if they so choose. In practice, women have voluntarily assumed most of the time-dependent mitzvot as if they were obligatory, and most rabbinic authorities have not only sanctioned this but have considered it praiseworthy. The only exceptions among Orthodox women are the mitzvot of tallit and tefillin; they are permitted in liberal, egalitarian communities.

Authorities are divided regarding whether women observing an optional mitzvah may recite the appropriate blessing that usually accompanies the performance of that commandment. Maimonides maintained that a woman cannot recite a blessing including the phrase, "Who has sanctified us with His commandments and commanded us to" in conjunction with a mitzvah that she is not obligated to perform. However, the custom among Ashkenazic Jews is that she may do so.[2]

Maimonides also ruled that while a woman may perform these actions, it is not equal to the mitzvah performed by a man, because fulfilling a mitzvah that one has been commanded to perform has greater merit than assuming obligations that are not required. "Those who perform a precept which they were not commanded to execute [are rewarded, but] are not rewarded to the same degree as those who are commanded to perform the precept, but to a lesser degree."[3]

The opposing view was championed by Rabbenu Tam,[4] who held that the mitzvot referred to the collective obligation of the Jewish people and thus could be performed by women. In essence, once a woman takes on a mitzvah by assuming the obligation, she is just as accountable as a man for all aspects and implications of the new duty. If this point of view is accepted, it raises the highly controversial issue of whether a woman assuming a given mitzvah as her duty—such as reading the Torah—can now perform this commandment on behalf of the congregation. Except for a few recent opinions, the general consensus in traditional circles has been that women may not discharge men's obligations for mitzvot they have taken upon themselves, because they are fulfilling them voluntarily rather than as a divinely mandated responsibility. One concept underlying this decision is *k'vod ha-tzibbur*. Literally translated as "honor of the community," the precise meaning of this term is not provided by either the Talmud or the medieval commentators. Some have suggested that it refers to *kol ishah*—the sexual distraction that the voice or even the mere presence of a woman would produce in male worshipers. The majority view, however, is that *k'vod ha-tzibbur* refers to the fact that having a woman discharge a mitzvah for men would cast doubt on the education and piety of the male members of the congregation, putting them to shame by implying that none of them was capable of performing this function. This would be similar to a talmudic teaching that permits a woman to recite the Grace after Meals on behalf of her husband under certain circumstances (Ber. 20b), though the Rabbis add: "A curse light on the man whose wife and children have to say the grace for him" (since he would appear insufficiently knowledgeable or pious to do it for himself). In egalitarian Conservative and Reform synagogues, women can read the Torah and lead prayer services, thus discharging mitzvot for men.

Proper Behavior and Ethical Living

Gemilut Hasadim (גְּמִילוּת חֲסָדִים)

As Shimon the Just declared in the opening lines of *Pirkei Avot* (1:2), "On three things does the [continued] existence of the world depend: Torah [study], *avodah* [initially the temple service, later prayer], and *gemilut hasadim*." Thus *gemilut hasadim* (lit., "the giving of lovingkindness") is a core social value, which the Rabbis considered a quintessential and distinctive attribute of the Jew. "Whoever denies the duty of *gemilut hasadim* denies the fundamental of Judaism" (Eccles. R. 7:1). *Gemilut hasadim* was one of the three characteristics required to be "fit to join this nation [i.e., be a true member of the Jewish people]" (Yev. 79a). Those failing to cultivate this virtue were even suspected of not being of Jewish descent.

Gemilut hasadim is enumerated among the things "that have no fixed measure," for which "man enjoys the fruits in this world, while the principal remains for him in the world to come" (Pe'ah 1:1). More comprehensive a virtue than *tzedakah* (charity; see p. 531), the Talmud states that *gemilut hasadim* is superior to charity in three respects: "Charity can be given only with one's money; *gemilut hasadim*, both by personal service and with money. Charity can be given only to the poor; *gemilut hasadim*, both to rich and poor. Charity can be given only to the living; *gemilut hasadim*, both to the living and the dead [by attending the funeral and the burial]" (Suk. 49b). Thus helping a blind person across the street is an act of *gemilut hasadim*, though not of charity. A grudging gift to a poor person may qualify as charity; but by adding a sincere smile and a kind word, the same amount is transformed into *gemilut hasadim*. Indeed, the ultimate example of *gemilut hasadim* (termed *hesed shel emet*; the "true" lovingkindness) is giving honor to the dead, since there is no chance that the deceased will ever return the favor. There is no maximum limit on acts of personal service ("with his body") that one can do for another, whereas donations of money and other material goods are restricted to one-fifth of one's possessions (JT Pe'ah 1:1, 15b).

During the Middle Ages, the broad concept of *gemilut hasadim* became restricted to the granting of interest-free loans to the needy. At a time when money lending (to non-Jews) was the major Jewish occupation, making a loan to a fellow Jew without interest essentially precluded the opportunity to use that money for a profitable business transaction. In the modern period, the term "*gemilut hasadim*" has again been expanded to refer not only to free-loan societies but also to a wide variety of communal welfare organizations.

Ismar Schorsch[1] observes that the Torah begins and ends with God performing the supreme Jewish value of *gemilut hasadim*.[2] As Adam and Eve are about to be exiled from the Garden of Eden, God Himself sewed the first couple their "garments of skin ... and clothed them" (Gen. 3:21). When Moses dies alone on Mount Nebo after viewing the Promised Land that he was forbidden from entering, the Bible states, "He buried him in the valley in the land of Moab ... and no one knows his burial place to this day" (Deut. 34:6). According to Rabbi Simlai, this means that it was God who took responsibility for attending to the funeral of the Lawgiver of Israel (Sot. 14a). In the same discussion, the Talmud figuratively interprets the verse, "Follow none but the Lord Your God" (Deut. 13:5), as indicating that the essence of morality is to act in a "God-like" manner toward other human beings. In emulation of God's actions of *gemilut hasadim*, we also should clothe the naked, visit the sick, comfort the mourners, and bury the dead. Similarly, in interpreting the verse in *Shirat ha-Yam* (Song at the Sea; see p. 409), "This is my God and I will glorify Him" (Exod. 15:2), the Jew can do justice to the glory of God only by "aspiring to the divine level of mercy and compassion."

Tzedakah (צְדָקָה)

The Bible repeatedly stresses the obligation to aid those in need, but never designates a special term for this requirement. The Rabbis adopted the word "*tzedakah*" to apply to charity, primarily in the form of giving gifts to the poor, which they deemed one of the essential mitzvot of Judaism. *Tzedakah* literally means "righteousness" or "justice," as in the famous biblical phrase, "*tzedek, tzedek, tirdof*" ("Justice, justice, shall you pursue"; Deut. 16:20). For the Rabbis, charity is not merely a generous or magnanimous act. Rather, it is the performance of a religiously mandated duty to provide something to which the needy have a right. By providing the chance to carry out an important mitzvah, "the poor man does more for the householder [in accepting alms] than the householder does for the poor man [by giving him the charity]" (Lev. R. 34:8). Both wealth and poverty are determined by God, who is the ultimate owner of all human possessions—"Give unto God of what is His, seeing that you and what you have are God's" (Avot 3:8)—and therefore a person should be willing to give whatever he or she has to fulfill the divine will.

There is a critical distinction between the Jewish ideal of "*tzedakah*" and the Christian concept of "charity," which has dominated the connotation of the English word. Charity comes from the Latin "*caritas*" (love), as does the Greek term "philanthropy," which literally means "love of human beings." Christianity focuses on charity as motivated by love for our fellow human beings—though many of those in need of assistance are dirty, diseased, and even dangerous and are difficult for most people to love. Judaism takes a more realistic view, requiring us to provide assistance not because we love the people in need of help but simply because it is right—we have resources and they have need. This does not mean that Jewish ethics has no concept of love or philanthropy; instead it uses the term "*gemilut hasadim*" (see p. 530), which implies going above the requirements of the law (i.e., the *tzedakah* that one is obliged to provide), as an act of lovingkindness.[1]

Biblical Period

Several biblical commandments require the Israelite to leave some of the produce of the fields and vineyards for the poor. When reaping the harvest, the farmer was commanded to leave a corner (*pe'ah*) of the field (Lev. 19:9). Although the precise size of this section was not prescribed in the Torah, the Rabbis declared that it should be not less than one-sixtieth of the crop and always proportional to the size of the field, the number of the poor, and the yield of the harvest (Pe'ah 1:2).

Similarly, the farmer was required to leave the "gleanings" of the harvest (Lev. 19:9), single ears of corn that fell to the ground at the time of reaping. The Rabbis decreed that if two ears dropped they belonged to the poor, but if three or more ears fell together the farmer could retrieve them (Pe'ah 4:10). This same principle applied to the forgotten sheaf of grain in the fields (Deut. 24:19) and to single grapes that fell to the ground in the vineyard (Lev. 19:10). The Rabbis took these laws seriously: "If a man puts a basket beneath the vine while he is gathering the grapes (so no single grapes fall to the ground), he is a robber of the poor" (Pe'ah 7:3). In contrast, Rashi said, "He who leaves the gleanings, the forgotten sheaf, and the *pe'ah* for the poor in due manner is regarded as though he had built the Temple and offered his sacrifices therein."

A special tithe for the poor was due in the third and sixth years of the sabbatical cycle (Deut. 14:28). This was the equivalent of the *ma'aser sheni* (second tithe) that the owner was required to separate from his harvested crop during the first, second, fourth, and fifth years and bring to Jerusalem, where he was to eat it with members of his family (Deut. 14:22). If this were impossible due to the distance, the owner was to redeem the second tithe and bring its monetary value (plus one-fifth extra) to the Temple, where he was required to spend it exclusively on food and drink.

However, the biblical concept of tithing dates back to a much earlier time. After rescuing his nephew Lot and defeating the alliance of five cities, Abram (Abraham) gave Melchizedek, the priest-king of Shalem, a tenth of all the spoils of war (Gen. 14:20). While fleeing from his brother and after the dream of the angels ascending and descending on a ladder stretching between earth and Heaven, Jacob vowed that if God would protect him and permit him to return safely to his father's house, "the Lord shall be my God … [and] I will set aside a tithe for You" (Gen. 28:21–22).

During the sabbatical year, there was no harvesting; whatever grew from the land was considered ownerless. Thus the owner, the servants, the poor, the stranger, and even wild and domesticated animals had equal rights to the produce (Lev. 25:6–7), so that "the needy among [the] people [may] eat of it" (Exod. 23:11). In addition, all debts outstanding at the end of the sixth year of the seven-year cycle were canceled, although this rule applied only to fellow Jews and not to gentiles living in the Land of Israel. While the law of release of the sabbatical year canceled the right of creditors to claim their debts, debtors nevertheless remained under a moral obligation to pay.

The Torah warned against letting the approach of the sabbatical year prevent one from helping a needy fellow Jew (Deut. 15:7–11). But, as the Israelites moved from an economy based on agriculture to one founded on business and commerce, the release of debts contracted in trading became onerous. People refrained from making loans to one another as the sabbatical year approached. Consequently, in the first century C.E., Hillel enacted the *prosbul*, in which a creditor declared before a court of law (attested by witnesses) that all debts due to him were given over to the court for collection (Shev. 10:4). Since remission of loans during the seventh year applied only to individuals and not to public loans, the effect was to render the individual's loan public and therefore not nullified (and thus collectable after the sabbatical year).

Charity was considered a divine attribute, since "[God] upholds the cause of the fatherless and the widow, and befriends the stranger, providing him with food and clothing" (Deut. 10:18). Giving to the poor was also regarded as an essential element of the righteous life. Referring to Yom Kippur, Isaiah (58:5–7) castigated those whose fast consisted of merely afflicting their souls and wearing sackcloth and ashes. Instead, in the next verses, the prophet declared that an "acceptable day to the Lord" and "the fast I [God] desire" is that Jews "share your bread with the hungry ... and take the wretched poor into your home," and clothe the naked. According to Ezekiel (16:49), the destruction of Sodom resulted from its lack of charity: they had "had plenty of bread and untroubled tranquility; yet ... did not support the poor and the needy." One quality manifested by "a woman of valor" (see p. 129) is that "she gives generously to the poor; her hands are stretched out to the needy" (Prov. 31:20). "He who is generous to the poor makes a loan to the Lord," who will "repay him his due" (Prov. 19:17). When inaugurating the new festival of Purim, the Book of Esther (9:12) included the custom of sending gifts to the poor (*mishloach manot*; see p. 258).

Talmudic and Rabbinic Period

The Rabbis continually stressed the importance of *tzedakah*. Rabbi Assi observed that "*tzedakah* is equivalent to all the other religious precepts combined" (BB 9a). Rabbi Eleazar interpreted the verse, "To do what is right [*tzedakah*] and just is more desired by the Lord than sacrifice" (Prov. 21:3), as meaning that "greater is he who performs charity than [he who offers] all the sacrifices" (Suk. 49b). The Rabbis believed that *tzedakah* "brings the redemption nearer" (BB 10a), atones for sins (BB 9a), "delivers from death" (BB 10a), and ensures that the giver "will have sons wise, wealthy, and versed in the *aggadah* [i.e., learned]" (BB 19b). "Anyone who shuts his eye against charity is like one who worships idols" (Ket. 68a). Based on the verse, "and I, in righteousness [*tzedek*], will see Your face" (Ps. 17:1),[2] it is customary to give charity just before praying. Along with *teshuvah* (repentance) and *tefillah* (prayer), *tzedakah* can "avert the severity of the decree" (RH 16b) when God judges all on Rosh Hashanah (*U-netaneh Tokef,* see p. 185).

Since the Rabbis deemed *tzedakah* a biblical commandment, they defined its parameters in precise detail—who is required to give, who is permitted to receive, how much one should give, and in what manner. These laws were codified by Maimonides in his *Mishneh Torah*[3] and later in the *Tur* and the Shulchan Arukh (YD 247–259).

Who Must Give

Every person has a duty to give charity. "Even a poor man who himself subsists on charity should give charity" (Git. 7b). The rabbinic court has the power to compel a person to give an amount of charity commensurate with his or her economic situation (Ket. 49b).

Based on the verse, "If you lend money to My people, to the poor among you" (Exod. 22:24), the Rabbis drew several inferences: "Between a Jew and a gentile, My people come first; ... between your poor [members of your family] and the [general] poor of your town, your poor come first; between the poor of your city and of another city, the 'poor among you' [of your city] come first" (BM 71a). Nevertheless, according to the Shulchan Arukh, this rule does not apply to the poor of the Land of Israel, who have priority over all. The Rabbis maintained that charity should be given to the non-Jewish poor "to preserve good relations," though they strongly urged Jews not to accept financial assistance from non-Jews unless absolutely necessary.

Who May Receive

A Jew should do everything possible to avoid having to take charity. As Rabbi Akiva said, "Treat your Sabbath like a weekday [not buying special food and drink] rather than be dependent on man [i.e., take from charity]" (Pes. 112a). Individuals should take any work that is available, even if they think it is beneath their dignity, rather than depending on community charity. The greatest of the sages adhered to this principle, performing physical labor to support themselves and remain independent. "Flay carcasses [skin unclean animals] in the market place and earn wages and do not say, 'I am a priest and a great man and it is beneath my dignity'" (Pes. 113a). According to Maimonides, "a person who is really entitled to take charity but delays doing so and thus suffers rather than be a burden to the community will surely be rewarded and not die before he reaches a position in which he will be able to support others. About such a person was it written: 'Blessed is he who trusts in the Lord' (Jer. 17:7)."[4]

Nevertheless, a person should not feel embarrassed to accept charity when unable to obtain money and support in any other way. Indeed, refusing charity when needed is a sin, and any suffering this entails is equivalent to shedding one's own blood. If a poor person has too much pride to accept charity, he or she can be misled into believing that a gift is really a loan. However, if a person "has the means and does not wish to maintain himself [at his own expense], no one need feel any concern about him" (Ket. 67b).

How Much One Should Give

The general rabbinic principle is that one is required to give a tenth of one's wealth to charity. "If a man desires to spend liberally [in charity] he should not spend more than a fifth, [since by spending more] he might himself come to be in need [of the help] of people [i.e., dependent on charity]" (Ket. 50a). Charity is not meant to merely provide the essentials of life; the psychological needs and social status of the recipient should be taken into consideration. Reflecting on the biblical phrase "you must open your hand and lend him sufficient for whatever he needs" (Deut. 15:8) (in the context of lending money before the sabbatical year cancels all private debts), the Rabbis state that one must "maintain him but not make him rich" (Ket. 67b). The story is related that a formerly wealthy man of good family who had become impoverished asked Hillel to provide him funds for a horse and a slave to run before him, so that the man could preserve his image in the community. "On one occasion he [Hillel] could not find a slave to run before him, so he himself ran before him for three miles."

How to Give

When giving charity, it is essential that the recipient not be shamed in any way. Consideration for the sensibilities of the poor led the Rabbis to observe that the best form of giving charity is when neither the donor nor the recipient know the identity of the other (BB 10b). Indeed, the Talmud relates some of the clever schemes that the sages invented so that they could remain anonymous when giving charity (Ket. 67b; Taan. 21b–22a).

Maimonides offered a list of eight degrees of charity.[5] The highest is giving money to prevent others from ever becoming poor, such as by offering a loan or employment or investing in someone's business. It is much harder for people to emerge from bankruptcy than for them to be helped before their business fails. Rashi noted that when a donkey's load begins to slip from its back, a single man is capable of adjusting it and keeping the donkey from falling. Once the animal has fallen, however, even five people cannot get it back on its feet. The second highest level of charity is the rabbinic ideal of giving to the poor in such a way that neither the donor nor the recipient knows the identity of the other. In descending order, the next levels of charity are the donor knows the recipient, but the recipient does not know the donor; the recipient knows the donor, but the donor does not know the recipient; giving directly to a poor person without being asked; giving only after being asked; giving cheerfully but less than one should; and giving grudgingly.

Charity not only is required of the individual Jew but also is an obligation of the entire community. Indeed, Maimonides observed that "in every town where there are Jews they must appoint 'charity wardens' (*gabba'ei tzedakah*), men who are well-known and honest, who should collect money from the people before every Sabbath and distribute it to the poor ... We have never seen or heard of a Jewish community which does not have a charity fund."[6] To ensure scrupulous honesty, a minimum of two wardens was required to collect charitable contributions (food and clothing as well as money), and at least three were needed to decide how much should be given to whom. In addition to maintaining the poor, the charitable fund was also used to redeem captives, dower poor brides, and establish communal soup kitchens to provide food for those who did not have sufficient funds for two meals each day.[7]

The Rabbis debated how long a person had to be a resident of a town before being required to contribute to the community charitable funds (BB 8a). Although the general conclusion was 12 months, this was reduced to "30 days [to be liable for contributing] to the soup kitchen, three months for the charity box, six months for the clothing fund, nine months for the burial fund, and 12 months for contributing to the repair of the town walls." (Rabbis, however, did not have to donate to the repair of the walls, because they "do not require protection!")

Medieval and Modern Periods

Institutions for providing charitable assistance developed at an early period in medieval Jewish communities. The major method of relief was the donation of money through the charity box (*kuppah*). Collections were made in private homes, in the synagogue just before the start of major festivals (including gifts to the poor on Purim), and even in the cemetery. To alleviate the burden on the less affluent, the community was empowered to impose taxes on its wealthier members for charitable activities. Among Ashkenazic Jews, a special communal representative randomly drew from a container of tickets supplied by each householder to determine where poor men could eat (and even sleep) for that day.

Charitable associations (*hevra*) dedicated to specific purposes developed in all substantial Jewish communities. Among these were societies for visiting the sick (*bikur holim;* see p. 542) and preparing the dead for burial (*hevra kadisha;* see p. 78). The community provided accommodations for the transient sick or travelers at the *hekdesh* (hospital, hospice, or poor house). Larger Jewish communities employed a physician to give medical care to the indigent. Provision was made for dowerless brides by the *hakhnasat kallah*, no-interest loans were granted, and a Talmud Torah was maintained to educate the children of the poor.

Today, there are a host of local, national, and international philanthropic enterprises. Jews have long been in the forefront in providing funds both to care of their coreligionists and for other charitable causes. In America, every sizable Jewish community conducts a single fund-raising campaign each year to support a broad range of activities, including bureaus of Jewish education; vocational, family, and medical services; and community centers. Charitable agencies have evolved on a national scale, often coordinating the activities of local units. There are also a large number of international charitable organizations that are specifically concerned with the welfare of Jews living in the State of Israel.

Hospitality (*Hakhnasat Orchim;* הַכְנָסַת אוֹרְחִים)

Welcoming the stranger (*ger*) is a major ethical value in Jewish tradition, ultimately related to the historical experience of the Israelites as being "strangers in the land of Egypt" (Lev. 19:34). The Bible recounts numerous incidents of hospitality. When Abraham saw the three men of Mamre "from afar," he raced to bring them to his house and provide for their physical needs: "Let a little water be brought; bathe your feet and recline under the tree. And let me fetch a morsel of bread that you may refresh yourselves; then go on."(Gen. 18:1–5). Just before the *Akedah* (binding of Isaac), Abraham "planted a tamarisk tree in Beer-sheba" (Gen. 21:33). According to the Talmud, the Hebrew name for this tree (*eshel*) is an acronym for eating (*achilah*), drinking (*sh'tiyah*), and lodging (*linah*)—three integral components of Abraham's devotion to the mitzvah of welcoming the stranger (Sot. 10a).

When Abraham sent his servant to find a wife for Isaac, Laban warmly welcomed the emissary (Gen. 24:28–32), while Rebecca graciously watered the traveler's thirsty camels (Gen. 24:19–20). Jethro the Midianite chastised his daughters ("Where is he then? Why did you leave the man? Ask him in to break bread"; Exod. 2:20) for failing to invite home the stranger (Moses) who had rescued them from the shepherds (Exod. 2:20). When the angel came to announce the upcoming birth of his son Samson, Manoah would not permit the celestial being to depart before sharing in his hospitality ("Let us detain you and prepare a kid for you"; Judg. 13:15). The Shunamite woman prepared a "small enclosed upper chamber" with a "bed, a table, and chair, and a lampstand" for the prophet Elisha "so that he can stop there whenever he comes to [visit] us" (2 Kings 4:8–11). However, protection of guests could be taken to a horrendous extent. Because of the sacred duty of providing asylum to those who "have come under the shelter of my roof," Lot was willing to allow the men of Sodom to take his daughters and "do to them as you please" so that he could safeguard his male guests (who were complete strangers) from homosexual rape (Gen. 19:4–8).

Some acts of hospitality are specifically rewarded. After hiding Joshua's two spies, Rahab (and her family) was protected from harm when the Israelites conquered and utterly destroyed Jericho (Josh. 2). Conversely, the shameful violation of this virtue by the Benjamites led to the Israelites waging war on them (Judg. 19:22, 20:17). The only "breach of hospitality" praised in the Bible was Yael's killing of Sisera, the Canaanite general, when he sought refuge in her home after fleeing from the Israelites under Barak (Judg. 4:18–24, 5:24–27).

According to the Talmud, a lack of hospitality led directly to the destruction of the Second Temple (Git. 55b–56a). A certain unnamed man had a friend named Kamtza and an enemy named Bar Kamtza. When hosting a large banquet, his servant was instructed to invite Kamtza; but the servant mistakenly asked Bar Kamtza instead. When the host saw his adversary, he furiously demanded that Bar Kamtza leave immediately. The abashed guest pleaded to be allowed to remain, even offering to pay for the cost of his dinner. When the host refused, Bar Kamtza raised his offer, first to half and then to the entire expense of the banquet. Eventually, the host ordered his servants to throw Bar Kamtza out of his house. The mortified guest was determined to exact revenge, not merely on his host, but against all of Jerusalem, since many of the leading rabbis of the city had been present at the banquet but none had done anything to prevent his disgrace. Bar Kamtza convinced the Roman emperor that the Jews of Jerusalem were plotting against his rule—thus precipitating the destruction of the Temple due to the lack of hospitality of a nameless host.[1]

For the Rabbis, *hakhnasat orchim* (lit., "bringing in of guests") was regarded as an important element of *gemilut hasadim* (the giving of lovingkindness; see p. 530), one of the mitzvot "which man performs and enjoys their fruits in this world, while the principal remains for him for the world to come" (Shab. 127a). They believed that "hospitality to wayfarers is greater than welcoming the presence of the *Shekhinah* [Divine Presence]," based on Abraham having turned away from God (who was visiting the Patriarch to distract him from the pain of his recent circumcision) to attend to the needs of the three strangers (Gen. 18:1–2). One who "entertains a scholar in his house and lets him enjoy his possessions ... [was regarded] as if he had sacrificed the daily burnt offering" (Ber. 10b).

Extolling the virtue of hospitality, the Rabbis related that Abraham and Job kept the doors of their homes open on all four sides, so that strangers would feel welcome and easily enter them. Whenever he had a meal, Rabbi Huna "would open the door wide [as an invitation to strangers] and declare, 'Whosoever is in need let him come and eat'" (Taan. 20b); this Aramaic saying, "*Kol dich'fin yeitei v'yeichul,*" is still recited at the Passover seder.

Conversely, the Rabbis condemned the insensitive guest (especially a scholar) who took advantage of hospitality. To make *hakhnasat orchim* a mutually rewarding experience, they attempted to clearly define the duties of both parties. A host must not make guests uncomfortable, whether by appearing depressed, tending to their needs too assiduously, or failing to personally serve them. In return, the Talmud states that a guest was required to appreciate all the efforts of the host ("How much trouble my host has taken for me! How much meat, wine, and cakes he has set before me!" [Ber. 58a]), and to recite a special blessing for the host in the Grace after Meals (Ber. 46a), which in the Shulchan Arukh appears as: "May it be God's will that this host should not be shamed nor humiliated in this world or the world to come. May he be successful in all his dealings and they be conveniently close at hand. May no evil impediment reign over his handiwork, and may no semblance of sin or iniquitous thought attach itself to him from this time and forever." Today, the accepted text is: "May the compassionate One bless the man and woman of this house, them, this house, their family, and all that is theirs."[2] This is contrasted with the thoughts of a bad guest: "How much effort did my host make for me? I have eaten [only] one piece of bread, I have eaten [only] one slice of meat, and I have drunk [only] one cup of wine! Whatever trouble my host has taken was only for the sake of his wife and his children!" (Ber. 58a).

The proper guest also leaves some food on the plate (Er. 53b) and obeys the requests of his or her host ("Whatever your host tells you, do"; Pes. 86b). A morbid story illustrates the concept that a guest should not give food to others unless the host approves (Hul. 94a). During a time of scarcity, a man invited three guests to his house and set before them his only three eggs. The host's child wandered in and each guest gave him his egg. When the father returned and saw the child stuffing one egg in his mouth and holding two in his hands, he was so enraged by this apparent breach of hospitality that he struck and accidentally killed the child. Stricken with grief, the father threw himself off the roof to his death, as did the mother when she came upon this grisly sight. As the Talmud concluded, "Because of this, three souls in Israel perished."

A midrash indicates that guests who remain for more than three days are overstaying their welcome (Tehillim R. 23:3). "On the day a guest arrives, a calf is slaughtered in his honor; the next day, a sheep; the third day, a fowl; and on the fourth day, he is served just beans!"[3]

Visiting the Sick (*Bikur Holim;* בִּקּוּר חוֹלִים)

Visiting the sick is another aspect of righteous living that constitutes the fundamental Jewish concept of *gemilut hasadim* (see p. 530). Just as God observed this mitzvah by visiting Abraham when the Patriarch was recovering from his circumcision (Gen. 18:1), so human beings are required to emulate this divine example (Sot. 14a). *Bikur holim* is listed as one of the deeds for which "a man enjoys the fruits in this world while the principal remains for him in the world to come" (Shab. 127a). Recognizing the psychological value of convincing a sick person that he or she has not been abandoned to suffer alone, the Rabbis observed that one who visits the sick "takes away a sixtieth of his pain" (Ned. 39b). Conversely, Rabbi Akiva maintained that "he who does not visit the sick is like a shedder of blood" (Ned. 40a). Those who visit the sick merit blessings: they are saved from the evil impulse and from suffering, and they will receive honor and be blessed with faithful friends (Ned. 40a).[1] The mitzvah of visiting the sick does not merely apply to Jews who are ill; one should also "visit the sick of the non-Jew ... in the interests of peace" (Git. 61a).

One should not visit too early in the morning (when a sick person is often being attended by a physician) or too late at night (when the patient is tired). According to the Talmud, coming at these times may cause the visitor to "omit to pray for him; during the first three hours of the day his [the invalid's] illness is alleviated [and thus the visitor may think him on the road to recovery]; in the last three hours his sickness is most virulent [and the visitor may feel that prayer is hopeless]" (Ned. 40a). According to the Shulchan Arukh, "It is a religious duty to visit the sick. Relatives and friends are to visit a sick person as soon as he falls ill, while casual acquaintances wait three days. If the malady takes a turn for the worse, all enter immediately" (YD 335).[2] Long visits can be too taxing for the patients. As Eliezer ben Isaac of Worms advised, "Do not fatigue him by staying too long, for his malady is heavy enough already. Enter cheerfully, for his heart and his eyes are on those who come in" (i.e., a shocked look on the face of a visitor will demoralize even the most stoic patient).[3] According to Judah the Pious, "Even the great should visit the humble. If a poor man and a rich man fall ill at the same time, and many go to the rich man to pay him honor, you go to the poor man, even if the rich man is learned in Torah."[4]

Merely visiting the sick is not sufficient to completely fulfill this mitzvah. The Talmud uses the expression, "He gave him his hand and he raised him," explaining that "the prisoner cannot free himself from jail" (i.e., the patient cannot cure himself) (Ber. 5b). One who visits the sick must offer spiritual comfort and be attentive to the patient's material needs. Prayers for the sick are vital (see below) and may be said in any language. Multiple visits to a patient are permitted as long as they are not too tiring. The Talmud recommends not visiting those "suffering with bowel [trouble]," so that they do not become embarrassed, or patients for whom the effort of speaking is too tiring; instead, it is preferable to remain in an adjacent room and ask whether one can help in any way (Ned. 41a). Sick persons should be spared from hearing of the death of a relative or any other bad news, to avoid delaying their recovery because of being "distracted in mind" (MK 26b).

The Rabbis disagreed as to whether one was permitted to visit the sick on the Sabbath, the day of joy on which sorrow should not intrude. Beit Shammai prohibited the practice, but the *halakhah* agrees with Beit Hillel, which permitted such visits. "If one enters [a house] to visit a sick person [on the Sabbath], he should say, 'It is the Sabbath, when one must not cry out, and recovery will soon come.' Rabbi Meir said, '[One should say] it [the Sabbath] may have compassion [i.e., proper observance of the Sabbath will bring recovery in its wake]'" (Shab. 12a).

Indeed, in medieval synagogues congregants generally visited the sick after Saturday morning services.

Prayer for the Sick

When his sister, Miriam, was afflicted with *tzara'at* (a skin disorder usually mistranslated as "leprosy"), Moses uttered a simple five-word prayer: *El na, rifah na la* ("God, please heal her";[5] Num. 12:13). The Rabbis included a prayer for healing the sick as the eighth blessing in the daily *Amidah*, which praises God as the "faithful, merciful Physician ... Who heals the sick of His people Israel." Those who visit the sick should pray for his or her recovery. The custom of invoking a get-well blessing for the sick (*Mi She Berakh*; "May He who blessed") in conjunction with the reading of the Torah developed in the Middle Ages. On the Sabbath, the prayer concludes, "It is the Sabbath, when one must not cry out, and recovery will come soon" (Shab. 12a). When reciting the prayer for the sick, the person who is ill is called by his or her first name (and middle name) followed by *ben* (son of) or *bat* (daughter of) and then the first (and middle) names of the mother—not that of the father, which is always used on other occasions, especially in traditional circles. A precedent for use of the mother's name in a prayer for mercy may be David's expression in Psalms (116:16), "I am Your servant, the son of Your maidservant." The name of an extremely ill person is often changed during this prayer, in accordance with a talmudic statement that this practice (along with charity, supplication, and change of conduct) "cancels the doom" (RH 16b). In addition to saying specific psalms on behalf of a person who is seriously ill, one recites those verses in Psalm 119 (which has 176 verses, eight starting with one each of the 22 letters of the Hebrew alphabet) that begin with the letters of the sick person's name, followed by those verses with the initial letters of the words קְרַע שָׂטָן (*kera Satan*; "destroy Satan").

Prevention of Sickness and Sanctity of the Body

In Jewish thought, the concept of "health" entails both physical and emotional or spiritual well-being—health of both the body and the soul.[6] This holistic view is evident in the word "*shleimut*" (completeness), one of the Hebrew terms for health. Another word for health is *"beri'ut"* (from the root "to create"), which identifies health with creating one's life as a work of art. This implies that one can have a disability, such as an amputation or deafness, and yet be considered healthy in terms of productivity and the ability to contribute to society. Even the word for physician (*rofeh*) comes from a root meaning "to ease," indicating that the doctor treating a "dis-ease" is effectively removing some impediment that is preventing the patient from proceeding further in the creation of a whole and fulfilling life.

Judaism teaches that each person is responsible for taking those steps necessary to preserve health and for seeking qualified medical care when needed. The Bible commands Jews to "take good care of yourself" (Deut. 4:9),[7] requiring that they not endanger themselves through lifestyle choices. Because the body is viewed as a vessel for the soul and the instrument through which one worships God and carries out the divine will, taking proper care of the body is a mitzvah, for only a healthy body is capable of sustaining a holy soul. As the caretaker of a body on loan from God, it is incumbent on each person to keep the divine vessel clean (Lev. R. 34:3). Indeed, the Talmud states that a Jew may not live in a town without a bathhouse (BK 46a). Similarly, a Jew is forbidden to mark his or her body by tattoos and prohibited from the ancient pagan mourning custom of mutilating the flesh (Lev. 19:28).

Maimonides, the most illustrious medieval Jewish physician and philosopher, offered a six-point plan for preventing disease and preserving health in his *Treatise on Asthma.* Stressing the Aristotelian ideal of moderation, Maimonides cited the importance of clean air (antipollution), diet (high-fiber, low-fat), exercise (a sedentary existence leads to constipation, aches and pains, and decreased strength), regular excretion, ample sleep, and regulation of emotions (direct link between body and soul). Although not specifically mentioned in this treatise, elsewhere Maimonides emphasizes the critical role of developing good health habits so that they become routine.

Healing the Body and Treating Illness

Based solely on the literal meaning of the biblical text, it is unclear whether human beings are even permitted to treat illness.[8] Sickness is often described as a divine punishment for sin—either as a specific statement ("King X did ... and he became sick") or in nonspecific terms ("If you do ..., you will be punished by a certain sickness"). Thus medical care could be interpreted as a human attempt to intervene in divine actions, a rejection of God's prerogative. Jeremiah (17:14) exclaims, "Heal me, O Lord, and let me be healed,"[9] and the eighth benediction in the *Amidah* describes God as "Who heals the sick of His people Israel"—implying that only God cures those who are to get well and suggesting that humans should not interfere. One talmudic-era tract states that the physician is counted among the seven professions whose members have no share in eternal bliss, because he or she is the accomplice of the patient who should leave his or her destiny to the decree of the Lord (ARN 36:5).[10]

The Talmud suggests various proof texts permitting the physician to attempt to heal. The most quoted citation refers to the situation in which one person strikes and injures another; the batterer is required to ensure that the victim is "thoroughly healed" (*rapo y'rapei;* Exod. 21:19).[11] A later verse notes that if a person loses something that you know is his or hers, "you shall give it back to him" (Deut. 22:2). Maimonides interpreted this phrase as referring to one's health, implying that it is permissible to provide medical care. Commenting on the well-known phrase, "You should love your neighbor as yourself" (Lev. 19:18),[12] the Rabbis argued that this even permits curative measures that require inflicting a wound in the process. The concept of *pikuach nefesh* (see p. 135) associates medical care with the religious requirement of saving a life, implying that the delivery of medical care is legally required. Similarly, one is obliged to "not stand idly by the blood of your neighbor" (Lev. 19:16).[13] The Talmud concludes that human beings and God are partners, not antagonists, in aiding the sick, each playing an important role in the process of health care. Rabbi Akiva noted that just as a farmer works the soil rather than leaving the growing of crops solely to God, so physicians are required to treat the sick—in order to "cultivate" health.

The Talmud observes that "no Jew may live in a town without a physician," and if a Jew feels ill, he or she must immediately consult a doctor (BK 46a). According to Maimonides, the physician should also see the patient when well, not only when ill, so as to be aware of the patient's normal state, such as a higher-than-normal temperature when healthy. Drugs should be employed only as a final remedy; in mild cases, the physician should first try to find a natural cure so that the body can heal itself. Maimonides argued that using drugs in mild cases may be counterproductive. If a mistake is made, the therapy may prove to be contradictory to the course of nature, impeding cure while aggravating pain. Even if the correct drug is given, the inner nature of the patient learns lazy ways rather than exerting itself to heal in the absence of external help. Maimonides also maintained that the physician should not merely treat the disease but rather the person suffering from it, for successfully treating the disease often does not mean that one has cured the patient.

In a bizarre text, the Mishnah states that "the best of doctors go to hell" (Kid. 82a). Taking a cynical or playful view of medical care, the Hasidic Rebbe Nachman of Bratslav maintained that when God created the Angel of Death, the latter protested that he was being given too much work for one angel; immediately God assured him, "Don't worry, I've given you helpers called physicians!" In *The Book of Delight*, Joseph ibn Zabara[14] relates that a philosopher went to a physician, who said that the philosopher was so sick there was no reason to treat him; the philosopher recovered and later met the physician in the street. "Have you returned from the next world?" asked the physician. After an affirmative response, the physician continued, "What did you see there?" When the philosopher described the terrible punishments visited on physicians because "they kill their patients," the physician was horrified. "Do not feel alarmed," reassured the philosopher, "because I swore to them there that you are no physician!"

In a less satiric vein, Rashi argued that the statement refers to the physician who arrogantly believes that the recovery of a patient was due to his or her own skill, with God playing no role in the process. Some have suggested that "hell" is the fate of those physicians who are convinced they know everything and never seek the advice of their colleagues. The Maharal of Prague said it referred to those doctors who deal only with the physical dimension of medical care and deny the spiritual aspect.

Commentators have noted that the prayer for healing in the *Amidah*, "which designates God as the Ultimate Healer, is repugnant to the haughty doctor and so he deletes it, or recites its without sincere intent." For such a doctor, the original 18 blessings are reduced to 17—the numerical value of the Hebrew word "*tov*" (good)—which is why "the Talmud sarcastically refers to him as 'the best.'"[15]

In essence, the Jewish view is that physicians are agents or partners of God. Although given permission to treat patients, physicians should never feel that their power and skill alone has resulted in a cure. The major duty of physicians is to educate their patients in ways to prevent illness and attain health. They must serve as role models for their patients because, as expressed in the ethical will of Judah Tibbon[16] to his wayward physician son, doctors cannot expect their patients to listen unless they themselves practice what they advise.

Pikuach Nefesh (פִּקּוּחַ נֶפֶשׁ)

"*Pikuach nefesh*" is the rabbinic term applied to the obligation to save an endangered human life. It applies both to an immediate threat—such as a severe illness—and to a less acute or serious condition that has the potential to rapidly become life threatening. The concept of *pikuach nefesh* developed from the biblical command, "Neither shall you stand idly by the blood of your neighbor" (Lev. 19:16). Even desecration of the Sabbath is permitted for *pikuach nefesh*. The Talmud justifies this by arguing, "If circumcision, which attaches to one only of the 248 members of the human body, suspends the Sabbath, how much more shall [the saving of] the whole body suspend the Sabbath!" (Yoma 85a). This ruling ultimately reflects the rabbinic interpretation of the verse, "You shall keep My laws and My rules, by the pursuit of which man shall *live*" (Lev. 18:5), mandating that, "he shall live by [observing] them [the commandments], but he shall not die because of [observing] them" (Yoma 85b).

Based on the verse "The Israelite people shall keep the Sabbath, observing the Sabbath throughout the ages" (Exod. 31:16), the Rabbis justified the violation of one Sabbath to save a person's life since it would enable him or her to observe many others in the future (Yoma 85b). Therefore, a seriously ill person must be given any required medical treatment on the Sabbath (and festivals), even such supportive measures as extinguishing a light to allow the patient to sleep. The laws of the Sabbath are suspended even when there is only "a possibility of danger to life ... If debris falls on someone and it is doubtful whether or not he is there or whether he is alive or dead, or whether he is an

Israelite or a heathen, one should open [even on the Sabbath] the heap of debris for his sake. If one finds him alive, one should remove the debris, and if he is dead, one should leave him there [until the Sabbath day is over]" (Yoma 83a). As examples of rapid action that should be performed to save a life on the Sabbath, "without need to obtain permission from the *beit din*," the Talmud includes spreading a net to bring up a child who has fallen into the sea (even though violating the Sabbath by catching fish in it), breaking loose segments of the wall of a pit to save a child who has fallen into it (even though thereby making a forbidden step [stairs]), breaking a door about to close on an infant (though thereby consciously making chips of wood), and dousing a fire (even though one is forbidden to extinguish on the Sabbath) (Yoma 84b).

The Shulchan Arukh speaks of the care to be provided to patients on the Sabbath (OH 328:12–17). A Jew should administer any necessary medical treatment for those who are seriously ill. However, if a patient has only a minor illness or physical discomfort, any violation of the Sabbath should be kept to a minimum and, when possible, be done by a non-Jew. If a gravely ill person requires meat on the Sabbath, it is better to ritually slaughter an animal than give the patient nonkosher food. However, a patient is permitted to eat forbidden food if a physician determines that this is required to make a full recovery. For three days after giving birth, when a woman is considered in a weakened and vulnerable condition, all efforts must be made to make her comfortable, even lighting a fire on the Sabbath to warm her. On Yom Kippur, a sick person is forbidden to fast if a doctor is convinced that this would impair the patient's chance of being healed. Conversely, according to the Mishnah, "if one [a healthy person] is seized by a ravenous hunger, he may be fed even unclean things [nonkosher food]" (Yoma 8:6; 83a).

What is the proper course of action when faced with the choice of saving one's own life or that of a companion? The Talmud discusses the hypothetical situation of two men "traveling on a journey [in a desert far from civilization] with a single pitcher of water. If both drink, they will [both] die, but if one only drinks, he can reach civilization" (BM 62a). Ben Peturah taught that "it is better that both should drink and die, rather than that one should behold his companion's death" (i.e., save his own life at the expense of the other). However, the prevailing opinion of Rabbi Akiva was that the person in possession of the water should save his own life and not share the water. This ruling was justified by reference to the biblical phrase, "Let him live by your side as your kinsman" (Lev. 25:36). In context, it commands one not to exact interest from a fellow Jew, but Akiva interpreted the phrase as implying that "your life takes precedence over his life." Similarly, the injunction to "love your neighbor as yourself" (Lev. 19:18) does not require that one love another *more* than oneself.

Martyrdom is preferred only if the choice is between death and committing idolatry, unlawful sexual intercourse, or murder (Sanh. 74a–b). In addition, one must sacrifice one's life rather than be forced to publicly violate any religious law, if a reasonable onlooker would deem such an action as meaning that one was renouncing Judaism. The Talmud distinguishes between a Jew being compelled to light a fire in a church (permitted, since the motivation was merely to provide warmth, rather than force him to be associated with idolatrous worship) and one ordered to cut grass to feed cattle on the Sabbath (forbidden, because the intention was to force the Jew to violate his religion) (Sanh. 74b). In all other situations, the general rule of *pikuach nefesh* applies.

Lashon ha-Ra (לָשׁוֹן הָרָע)

The prohibition against *lashon ha-ra* (lit., "evil speech," often translated as "gossip") refers to any derogatory or damaging statements against an individual, even when the slanderous or defaming remarks are true, which if publicized to others would cause the subject physical or monetary damage, anguish, or fear.

The Rabbis offered numerous biblical commandments emphasizing the seriousness of this injunction. They interpreted the verse, "Reprove your kinsman but incur no guilt because of him" (Lev. 19:17), as meaning that one may reprove but not insult a neighbor—for if you make your neighbor blush or turn pale from shame or fury, then you have incurred guilt. Other biblical exhortations supporting the forbidding of *lashon ha-ra* include "Do not go about as a talebearer" (Lev. 19:16), "You must not carry false rumors" (Exod. 23:1), "You shall not hate your kinsfolk in your heart" (Lev. 19:17), "You shall not take vengeance or bear a grudge" (Lev. 19:18), and "Love your neighbor as yourself" (Lev.

19:18). Among the verses that prohibit specific types of insulting speech are "You shall not insult the deaf" (Lev. 19:14) and "You shall not ... put a curse upon a chieftain among your people" (Exod. 22:27).

Lashon ha-ra destroys three people—"he who relates [the slander], he who accepts it, and he about whom it is told" (Ar. 15b). Ibn Ezra noted that the same verse that forbids "bearing tales" also includes a warning against "standing idly by the blood of your neighbor", indicating that slander is considered tantamount to murder. The Talmud agreed, noting that both "shed blood" (BM 58b). As the apochrypal book *Ecclesiasticus* (28:18) observed, "Many have been killed by the sword, but not so many as by the tongue."

The most vicious form of slander is false accusations made to a ruling authority (*malshinut*) with the intent of endangering a person's livelihood and even his or her life. Through their slanderous allegations, informers sometimes jeopardized entire Jewish communities. The Talmud even declared that the destruction of Jerusalem resulted from false charges brought to the Roman authorities by a disgruntled individual who was insulted by his neighbor (Git. 55b–56a). These especially vicious slanderers were placed in the category of persons who commit assault with intent to kill, and putting them to death was authorized. If their intention to slander was clear, death was sanctioned even before the crime was committed. The extent to which Jewish communities were harassed by slander led to the inclusion in the daily *Amidah* of the prayer, "And for slanderers (*malshinim*), let there be no hope."

In the Bible, Miriam was stricken with the skin disease *tzara'at* for slandering her brother Moses "because of the Cushite woman he had married" (Num. 12:1–15). The 10 spies were punished for their false report that the Israelites would be unable to conquer the land that had been divinely promised (Num. 14:36–37), which led to the Israelites being forced to wander for 40 years in the wilderness. According to the Talmud, "had David not paid heed to slander, the kingdom of the House of David would not have been divided" (Shab. 56b).

"Although one should not believe slander, one should take note of it" (Nid. 61a). This means that on some occasions it is permissible for a person to listen to *lashon ha-ra* when the information might be used for self-protection or the benefit of another (e.g., potential business partner, roommate). However, one is forbidden to accept the material as true and may only suspect and investigate its accuracy. If someone starts speaking *lashon ha-ra*, one should attempt to respectfully and privately tell the individual that this is forbidden speech. (The best way to prevent others from speaking *lashon ha-ra* is to set a good example and not do so yourself.) If caught among people who are engaging in *lashon ha-ra* and unable to leave or change the topic, it is necessary to consciously not accept the material as true, not enjoy it (even if it is a funny story, because the subject is being shamed), and not pretend by facial expressions or eye contact that one agrees with the import of what is being said.[1]

Those who engage in *lashon ha-ra* merit and will receive severe punishment. "Whoever relates or accepts slander shall be cast to the dogs" (Pes. 118a). Elsewhere it is stated that they will be stoned (Ar. 15b), suffer from croup (Shab. 33a–b), and be afflicted with plagues (Taan. 7b). Slanderers are one of four classes that will not receive the *Shekhinah* (Divine Presence), based on the verse from Psalms (5:5), "For You are not a God who desires wickedness; evil cannot abide with You" (Sot. 42a). "He who makes another's face turn pale [humiliates his fellow] in public ... has no share in the world to come" (Avot 3:15). *Lashon ha-ra* also has national repercussions, because rain is withheld from the land because of those who engage in "evil speech" (Taan. 7b).

The Talmud specified that scholars committing *lashon ha-ra* should atone for this sin by engaging in Torah study (Ar. 15b), based on the verse, "A healing tongue is a tree of life" (Prov. 15:4, which is usually translated as "A soothing tongue is the tree of life"). However, "if he be an ignorant [simple] person, let him humble himself." To make amends for the sin of *lashon ha-ra*, it is necessary for the speaker to inform everyone who heard the evil words that what was said was incorrect. The speaker also must apologize to the subject of the slander and beg forgiveness. However, if the subject would be hearing the slander for the first time or if rehashing the material would only provoke added distress, the speaker must merely tell the subject that he or she had committed an "unspecified" sin against him or her.[2]

When he finished the prescribed daily prayer, Mar ben Ravina (Ber. 17a) added the following phrase from Psalms (34:14), "Guard your tongue from evil, your lips from deceitful speech," words that today are added to the end of the *Amidah* (see p. 421).

In modern times, the Chafetz Chaim (Israel Meir ha-Kohen) gained wide recognition for his writings that stressed the gravity of the sin of *lashon ha-ra*. One day, a *maggid* (itinerant preacher) delivered a long-winded sermon in the Chafetz Chaim's synagogue. Although the sermon was rather insipid, the Chafetz Chaim complimented the *maggid* lavishly, whereupon the latter humbly admitted that he did not think his talk was that good. "My dear friend," replied the Chafetz Chaim, "the entire time that you delivered your address, no one in the audience had an opportunity to speak *lashon ha-ra*. Thus your lengthy sermon prevented a grievous sin." Abraham Twerski[3] made an analogy between this tale and the statement in the haggadah, "The more one relates the story of the Exodus, the more praiseworthy one becomes." At the seder, when family members gather, often after not seeing each other for months, it is highly likely that the conversation will turn to talk about relatives and friends, unfortunately leading to much gossip. Therefore, the more one relates about the Exodus at the seder the more praiseworthy, because this prevents words of *lashon ha-ra*![4]

Washing the Hands (נְטִילַת יָדַיִם)

Washing the hands in Judaism is performed in relation to meals, synagogue services, and other daily activities. This practice is primarily a religious, not a hygienic, act and was instituted by the Rabbis to correct the condition of *tumat yadayim*, their concept of "impurity of the hands." The detailed regulations dealing with this subject, which constitute one of the few times that the *halakhah* sides with Beit Shammai rather than Beit Hillel, initially met with considerable opposition. The Rabbis countered by warning of dire consequences for those who disregarded them, including poverty and even premature death (Shab. 62b; Sot. 4b). Rabbi Akiva, who personally disapproved of the ordinance, nevertheless used the limited water allowed him in prison for this ablution rather than for drinking (Er. 21b).

The method of ritual washing is either by immersion up to the wrist or by pouring one-quarter *log* (about one-half pint) of water over both hands from a receptacle with a wide mouth and an undamaged lip. Ideally, the water should be poured over the entire hand up to the wrist, but the procedure is effective as long as the fingers are washed up to the third joint (where the fingers meet the palm of the hand). Before ritual washing, the hands must be thoroughly cleaned and any rings must be removed so that the water can reach the entire surface area. The water should be neither hot nor discolored, and it is customary to perform the act by alternately pouring water over each hand three times (first washing the right hand by pouring water from a vessel held in the left hand). Holding one's hands under an open faucet with the water already running is to be avoided.

The ritual of washing the hands, along with the appropriate blessing, is *netilat yadayim*. The precise source of this term is unclear, though the Rabbis interpreted it as "lifting of the hands," based on the verse in Psalms (134:2), "Lift up your hands in holiness and praise the Lord" (even though a different Hebrew verb is used in the verse).[1]

Before entering the sanctuary to perform the divine service, the *Kohanim* were commanded to wash their hands and feet (Exod. 30:19). Failure to comply with this mitzvah desecrated the holiness of the sanctuary and invalidated the service of any ministering *Kohen*. Today, the Levites wash the hands of the *Kohanim* before they perform the ceremony of the Priestly Blessing during public prayer services (see p. 432). Consequently, the laver has become the heraldic symbol for the Levites and often appears on their tombstones. Even in the absence of the Temple, observant Jews ceremonially wash their hands before beginning any prayer service, which the Rabbis declared to be the current equivalent of the ritual sacrifices in the Temple.

Traditional Jews ritually wash their hands (with recitation of the appropriate blessing) before meals, since the dining table is compared to the altar upon which the sacrificial service was performed. This custom apparently spread from the *Kohanim*, who washed their hands before eating consecrated food, to the pious among the laity, before finally becoming universal. Although the most commonly observed ritual washing of the hands occurs before eating bread, the Rabbis deemed it to be of at least equal importance to wash the hands after the meal, before saying *Birkat ha-Mazon* (Grace after Meals). This was to remove any traces of "a certain salt of Sodom [adhering to the fingers] that makes the eyes blind [could cause serious injury to the eyes]" (Hul. 105b). However, since this hand washing is done as a precautionary health measure rather than as a religious obligation, no blessing is recited.

Washing the hands is required on many other occasions, some of which are motivated by hygienic considerations and others by superstitious beliefs. In many traditional homes, a pitcher and basin are placed next to the bed for immediate washing of the hands after awakening; many recite the blessing *al netilat yadayim* at this time, whereas others do so when washing their hands before the morning prayer service. The Kitzur Shulchan Arukh states that "one is not allowed to walk four cubits [six feet] without having washed one's hands, except in cases of extreme necessity." While asleep, "man's hands are constantly in motion" (Shab. 14a) and must be purified in case they inadvertently touched areas that are normally concealed. Because "sleep is one-sixtieth of death" (Ber. 57b), it is necessary to wash one's hands on awakening to remove the small amount of impurity resulting from such "mini-death." A person waking from sleep is like a newborn and must wash his or her hands before serving God, just as did the *Kohanim* in the Temple.[2] Some believe that during sleep the soul is replaced by an unclean spirit; on wakening, this interloper disappears from all but the fingers, where it remains until the hands have been washed. Washing the hands is also required before eating the *karpas* (greens) at the Passover seder and after the following activities: going to the toilet; cutting nails; taking off shoes with bare hands; combing the hair; sexual intercourse; touching hairy parts of the body that are usually covered by clothing; bloodletting; touching vermin (or searching clothes for them); and attending a funeral, leaving a cemetery, or departing from a house where a corpse is present.[3]

Mikveh (Ritual Bath; מִקְוֶה)

In biblical times, a number of conditions resulted in a person becoming "ritually impure" and unable to participate fully in cultic observances, including bringing sacrifices to the Sanctuary. All relate to some type of *loss*—"of bodily fluid, potential life, or life itself" —and include people with the skin disease *tzara'at* or a bodily discharge, considered signs of some "spiritual defect"; men with a seminal discharge or menstruating women, both of which were deemed as a loss of the potential to create life; women after childbirth, since for some period afterward they cannot conceive; and people who came in contact with a corpse, which is no longer able to perform mitzvot. Regaining a state of ritual purity required a symbolic act of immersion known as *tevilah*. Ritual immersion also was performed by the *Kohanim* during their consecration ceremony (Exod. 29:4; Lev. 8:6) and by the *Kohen Gadol* before the Yom

Kippur rituals (Lev. 16:4). The Rabbis and commentators emphasized that the purpose of immersion was not to remove any physical uncleanness; instead, the purifying waters were designed to symbolically remove ritual impurity so that the individual could fully engage in the ceremonial life of the community.[1]

Initially, ritual immersion took place in a natural, flowing body of water (*mayim hayim*; lit., "living water")—a river, stream, lake, pond, or ocean. However, these venues are not available for Jews living in all locations, and in some climates bodies of water freeze for part of the year. This led to the development of an alternative place to perform ritual immersion, the *mikveh*.[2]

A *mikveh* (lit., "a collection [of water]") is a pool or bath that must contain 40 *se'ah* (about 200 gallons) of clear water and must be deep enough to cover the entire body of the person undergoing immersion. Traditionally, there are seven steps (representing the six days of Creation and the Sabbath) leading down into the pool.[3] The water must be taken directly either from a river or a spring or from rainwater or snow melt that is channeled into the bath. A *mikveh* can be hewn out of rock or built permanently into the ground, making it an integral part of the earth; a portable receptacle may not be used, since it could potentially contract impurity. The *mikveh* must be watertight, since any leakage invalidates it. The minimum 40 *se'ah* of water required for a *mikveh* must come from a natural source; the bath must not be artificially filled with drawn water via a bucket or tubing that brings water stored above the ground. However, if the *mikveh* already contains the requisite 40 *se'ah* of natural water, the addition of any amount of drawn water does not disqualify it.[4] The pipes through which the water passes on its way to the *mikveh* must be free of recesses where water can collect; they must be made of earthenware, stone, concrete, asbestos, or plastic, materials that would not attract sources of impurity in the biblical sense.[5]

Before entering the *mikveh*, it is essential to wash thoroughly. This indicates, both literally and symbolically, that the purpose of immersion is ritual purity rather than physical cleanliness. No object can be interposed between the body and the water of the ritual bath. Therefore, before entering the *mikveh* it is necessary to remove all jewelry, makeup, and even nail polish.[6]

Today, the *mikveh* is most frequently used by a woman before resuming sexual relations with her husband after completing the period of separation related to her menstrual cycle. According to *halakhah*, the purification attained by immersion in a *mikveh* is not in itself a mitzvah but is required only when the resumption of sexual relations depends on it. For example, a woman does not observe the purification ritual after every menstruation if her husband is out of town. Similarly, an unmarried woman does not go to the *mikveh* for purification and typically performs *tevilah* for the first time before her wedding (rather than after her first menses).

A woman is not permitted to purposely defer ritual purification to "annoy her husband" (i.e., to prevent the resumption of sexual activity). By not immersing herself in the *mikveh* after her menstruation ends, a woman persistently remains in a state of *niddah* (see below) and, according to *halakhah*, is forbidden to her husband. Numerous responsa detail bitter cases of recriminations between spouses in which the wife claims that her husband attempted to have sex during her *niddah* period, while he counters that this only occurred because she continually postponed going to the *mikveh* and thus was always unavailable for sexual relations.[7]

Immersion in the *mikveh* is also indispensable in the conversion of non-Jews to Judaism (see p. 600). It is the only ritual act required of female converts; men who convert are also required to undergo circumcision (or for those already circumcised, a symbolic drop of blood is taken from the penis). Some Orthodox Jewish men immerse themselves in the *mikveh* on Fridays and before Jewish holidays (especially Yom Kippur), to stress the transition between regular days and, respectively, the Sabbath and festivals.[7] Scribes (*sofrim*; see p. 325) immerse themselves in the *mikveh* before embarking on the sacred task of writing a Torah scroll. There also is the ancient custom (based on Num. 31:22–23) of immersing in a *mikveh* all new cooking pots and dishes purchased from non-Jews.

Niddah (Menstruating Woman; נִדָּה)

Judaism prohibits contact with a menstruating woman. In Hebrew, she is termed a "*niddah*," a word meaning "separated" or "excluded." The complex laws that define the status of a *niddah* are based on the two different contexts in which the menstruating woman appears in biblical law: the sexual prohibitions (Lev. 18:19) and the laws of purity and impurity (Lev. 15:19–33), which also include other causes of ritual contamination such as contact with a corpse, *tzara'at* (a skin disease), and seminal discharge. Initially designed to exclude ritually impure persons from the Temple, laws pertaining to ritual purity were no longer necessary after its destruction; only the sexual prohibitions related to the *niddah* remained relevant.[1]

According to the Bible, both men and women have two kinds of discharges that cause ritual impurity: a normal discharge, and an abnormal one that results in a longer period of impurity. For a man, the normal discharge is the emission of semen, which renders him ritually impure "until evening" (Lev. 15:16–18). For a woman, the normal discharge is the monthly flow of blood. Because the normal menstrual period was regarded as lasting seven days, a woman was deemed ritually impure for one week from the time blood first appeared (Lev. 15:19). After this time, she bathed herself, washed her clothes, and regained her ritual purity.[2] Prolonged bleeding resulted in a woman becoming a *zavah* (one who has a discharge), who was unclean until her discharge of blood ceased. Unlike the menstruating woman, the *zavah* had to wait a further seven "clean" days from the day her bleeding stopped to regain her state of ritual purity, after offering "two turtledoves or two pigeons" as a sacrifice (Lev. 15:25–30).

Although the distinction between *niddah* and *zavah* was eliminated as a practical issue during the talmudic period, the *niddah* was subjected to more stringent regulations. Her period of impurity was extended from the biblical maximum of seven days to up to 14 days—as many as seven days of menstrual flow followed by a mandatory period of seven "white days" (free of bleeding).[3] Therefore, during the time of her menstrual bleeding and for a full week thereafter, a woman was prohibited from having sexual relations with her husband.

In ancient Israel, a menstruating woman was excluded from her home and forced to stay in a special residence known as "a house for uncleanness" (Nid. 7:4). Men did not eat with a menstruating woman, and she did not attend to her household duties. This custom continued even after the destruction of the Second Temple, because of the rabbinic decision to prepare and eat ordinary meals according to the levitical rules originally required for sacred food. The situation was substantially different in Babylonia, where the menstruating woman attended to almost all the needs of her household except for "filling his [her husband's] cup [of wine]; making ready his bed; and washing his face, hands, and feet" (Ket. 61a), acts that were deemed to be so provocative that they could lead to forbidden intimacy between them. Even these restrictions were eliminated by some creative reasoning. For example, one sage allowed a menstruating wife to prepare her husband's bed as long as he was not there at the time. To indicate that things were not "normal," the wives of other Rabbis developed ways of filling their husbands' cups in an unusual way ("with her left hand"), or by placing them in an unusual spot (on the edge of a wine cask, at the head-side of his couch, or on his footstool) (Ket. 61a).[4]

A major talmudic issue was whether a menstruating woman could use makeup and wear jewelry and colorful clothes (Shab. 64b). This reflects an inherent conflict between eliminating anything that might result in sexual arousal during the *niddah* period and the need to prevent any long-term harm to the marital relationship due to the enforced period of separation. The strict approach of the early sages was overturned by the more permissive statement of Rabbi Akiva: "If so, you make her repulsive to her husband, with the result that he will divorce her."[5] Maimonides went even further, claiming that it is a halakhic obligation for a woman to make an effort to dress attractively and adorn herself during her period of separation from her husband.

Rashi noted that some of the biblical requirements of separation were still observed in his day, not because of any concern for impurity but simply to prevent any contact between husband and wife. This motivation was evident from the fact that a stranger was permitted to transfer objects between them. If the underlying issue were ritual purity, the stranger would be just as at risk as the husband by contact with the *niddah*.[6] The *halakhah* does not forbid the *niddah* from participation in public life and ritual. Nevertheless, custom dictated that her activities be substantially restricted, especially those related to public worship and the synagogue (because of its symbolic identity with the Temple).[7]

The consequences of a man who has intercourse with a *niddah* are strikingly different in the two biblical passages dealing with the issue. In one, he merely contracts the same ritual impurity that affects the menstruating woman and is unclean for seven days (Lev. 15:24). This state of impurity in and of itself was no transgression, as long as the man did not try to approach the Temple in such a condition. However, in the other biblical section, intercourse with a *niddah* is an unequivocal taboo that is listed among the sexual transgressions and is punishable by *karet* (premature death) (Lev. 20:18). The traditional reason for this difference is that the former refers to accidental intercourse, whereas the latter applies to intentional relations. Some scholars suggest a historical explanation for the discrepancy, based on one text preceding the other. According to this view, including intercourse with a *niddah* among the sexual transgressions may have been a reaction to the destruction of the First Temple in 586 B.C.E. This catastrophic event effectively eliminated the need for preserving ritual impurity, and thus the laws of *niddah* were transformed into a mechanism for ensuring the continuity of the Jewish family.[8]

Current Status

The laws of sexual separation are known as *taharat ha-mishpachah* (purity of the family). Although, as noted above, the Bible forbids only intercourse during a woman's menstrual period, subsequent rabbinic rulings have also precluded any physical contact that could conceivably be sexually stimulating. This includes kissing, hugging, or otherwise touching one's spouse during the forbidden days, during which husband and wife sleep in separate beds. Rather than handing something directly to their wife, some Orthodox men place the object on a table for her to pick up.[9] The rule forbidding touching a *niddah* has led many Orthodox men to protect the privacy and modesty of their wives by never touching them in public (so no one knows whether or not they are in a state of *niddah* at the time). Similarly, they do not shake hands with any woman (not knowing whether or not she is a *niddah*). For the same reason, Orthodox men and women generally do not dance together in public; when doing so, they grasp a handkerchief between them rather than holding hands.[10]

On the evening of the completion of the 12th day—assuming there has been no bleeding during any of the seven days following the five days of menstrual flow, which would require the count of seven days to begin again from that time—the woman immerses herself in the *mikveh* (see p. 555) as an act of symbolic ritual purification. Only then can marital relations be resumed.

Rabbi Meir[11] considered the period of separation to be of great benefit to the conjugal relations between man and wife. "Being in constant contact with his wife, [a husband might] develop a loathing towards her. The Torah, therefore, ordained that she be unclean for seven days in order that she shall be beloved by her husband as at the time of her first entry into the bridal chamber" (Nid. 31b). Indeed, many couples renew their sexual relationship each month with an eagerness and passion that is reminiscent of their honeymoon. In addition, the resumption of sexual relations between husband and wife generally occurs near the time when she is most fertile, thus increasing the chance of her becoming pregnant and ensuring the continuity of the Jewish people.

IMPURITY AFTER CHILDBIRTH

A special case of ritual impurity for a woman is after giving birth (Lev. 12:1–8). Although she is still termed a *niddah,* her period of impurity depends on the gender of the baby. According to the Torah, a woman who gives birth to a son is a *niddah* for seven days (like a menstruating woman), but she must wait for an additional 33-day period of purification before being permitted to bring a sacrifice to the Temple and regain her ritual purity. Following the birth of a girl, the mother is a *niddah* for 14 days and then must wait an additional 66 days before she is purified. In sum, a woman is deemed ritually impure for 40 days after the birth of a son and twice that (80 days) after the birth of a daughter.

The prolonged postpartum period of ritual impurity is related to the fact that bleeding often continues for four to six weeks after giving birth. However, the reason for doubling the impure period after the birth of a girl is unclear. One possibility is that the newborn daughter will one day herself menstruate and give birth. Another is that the normal period of ritual impurity following childbirth is two weeks, but is reduced after the birth of a son "to allow the mother to attend the *brit* [circumcision] in a state of ritual purity, or because the *brit milah* on the eighth day is a purifying rite."[1]

Sha'atnez (Mingling of Fabrics)

The Torah prohibits several types of mixed species (*kilayim*) in the verse, "You shall not let your cattle mate with a different kind; you shall not sow your field with two kinds of seed; you shall not put on cloth from a mixture of two kinds of material [fibers]" (Lev. 19:19). The precise prohibited mixture of fibers (*sha'atnez*) is later defined: "you shall not wear cloth combining wool and linen" (Deut. 22:11). The Rabbis ruled that the law of *sha'atnez* refers only to the weaving together of these two specific animal and vegetable fibers in the same garment (Kil. 8:1). Thus a linen tie worn with a wool suit is permitted, but a wool suit with linen-threaded buttons is prohibited. The combination of wool and linen may be mixed with cotton, silk, and other fibers in the manufacture of products other than clothing.[1] Based on the general principle that a positive commandment overrides a negative one, it is permitted to attach woolen tzizit (fringes) to a linen garment (Men. 40a). Similarly, *Kohanim* were permitted to wear garments of mixed texture when performing the Torah-mandated priestly service in the Sanctuary (Yoma 69a).

While in practice many garments do not have any *sha'atnez* and may be assumed to have none, the particulars vary by garment type. The padding in many garments, such as suits, or the embroidery thread, such as designs on sweaters (men's and women's), may cause *sha'atnez* problems. The padding filler in many suits is made of various fabrics, which may be mixed linen and wool in themselves—so it is not just a worry of linen-threaded padding in a wool-shell suit. Today, the usual way of observing the prohibition against *sha'atnez* is to first check the fabric list. If the fabric list shows a forbidden mixture, it probably cannot be fixed. Since the fabric list on suits usually refers only to the shell, ignoring padding or ornamental threads, the label can be used to identify only garments that definitely have *sha'atnez*. If the label suggests that the garment may be permitted, it can be taken for testing at a special *sha'atnez* laboratory, which can be found in most cities with at least a medium-size Orthodox community.[2]

Although Rashi observed that the law of *sha'atnez* defies logic and must be obeyed without question like a royal command, many commentators have offered explanations. Maimonides maintained that wearing such a combination of fibers was the custom of idolatrous priests at the time the Torah was given.[3] This is a somewhat puzzling explanation, since the *Kohanim* wore various garments of interwoven linen and colored wool when they served in the Temple (Kil. 9:1). One commentary related this prohibition to the fact that the curtain in the Temple was woven from wool and linen, and it was forbidden to duplicate the furnishings of the Temple for nonsacred use. Nachmanides suggested that a person mixing diverse kinds of materials was guilty of defiance by attempting to improve upon the species created by God (tampering with the divinely ordained order of Creation). Recanati[4] related this prohibition to the story of Cain and Abel. Linen comes from a plant and represents the "fruit of the ground" offered up by Cain; wool is derived from sheep and symbolizes the "firstlings of the flock" brought by Abel. God's acceptance of Abel's offering and rejection of Cain's resulted in the first fratricide in human history, indicating that linen and wool symbolize two incompatible elements.[5]

Despite these various rationales, the prohibition of *sha'atnez* remains one of the quintessential *hukim*—commandments for which there is no convincing explanation but that loyal Jews obey simply as a manifestation of the divine will.[6]

Jewish Courts (בֵּית־דִּין) and Judges (שׁוֹפְטִים)

"Tzedek, tzedek tirdof" ("Justice, justice, shall you pursue"; Deut. 16:20) is a major ethical cornerstone of Judaism. Establishing fair and impartial courts of justice is one of the seven Noahide laws—along with the prohibition of blasphemy, idolatry, incest, bloodshed, robbery, and the eating of flesh cut from a living animal (based on Gen. 9:7)—which constitute the basic requirements for any civilized society. The Torah strictly prohibits anything that perverts justice or even gives the appearance of injustice.

During the wanderings of the Israelites after the Exodus from Egypt, Moses exercised judicial power over the people (Exod. 18:13). When the task became too overwhelming, he delegated some of this authority to appointed "chiefs of thousands, hundreds, fifties, and tens ... the difficult matters they would bring to Moses, and all the minor matters they would decide themselves" (Exod. 18:25–26). According to the

Torah, judges were to be "capable men who fear God, trustworthy men who spurn ill-gotten gain" (Exod. 18:21) and were "wise, discerning, and experienced" (Deut. 1:13). Warned not to be "partial in judgment," judges were required to "hear out low and high alike [and] fear no man, for judgment is God's" (Deut. 1:17). After the conquest of the Promised Land and its division among the various tribes, judges were appointed in every settlement (Deut. 16:18).

The *beit din* (rabbinic term for a Jewish court of law) was essentially a creation of the Second Temple period. Its establishment is attributed to Ezra, who decreed that local courts were to sit on Mondays and Thursdays in all populated centers (BK 82a), with a supreme court (Great Sanhedrin) in Jerusalem.

Types of Jewish Courts

There were three levels of courts in Temple times. The highest court in Israel was the Great Sanhedrin, which was composed of 71 judges who sat in the Temple in Jerusalem. This corresponded to the 70 elders and officers who assisted Moses in dispensing justice during biblical times (Num. 11:16–17). Headed by the *nasi* (president), the Great Sanhedrin exercised sweeping judicial, legislative, and executive powers and was the only court that could try "a tribe, a false prophet, and a *Kohen Gadol*" (Sanh. 1:5). In addition to being the sole venue for adjudicating such crimes as an entire town that had turned toward idol worship (Sanh. 1:5) and rebellious teaching by an elder (Sanh. 11:2), the Great Sanhedrin was the site where a woman suspected of adultery (*sotah*) underwent her ordeal (Sot. 1:4). Judges of the Great Sanhedrin were required to affirm the death penalty of persons convicted of specific crimes (such as being false witnesses or rebellious sons, or of enticing others to commit idolatry) before they could be executed.

However, by far the most important role of the Great Sanhedrin was its development and interpretation of the Oral Law, which became the binding authority on all Jews. Any violation of its edicts was liable to the death penalty (Deut. 17:12). This was true even when it appeared that the court may have been in error: "You shall act in accordance with ... the ruling handed down to you; you must not deviate from the verdict that they [the judges] announce to you either to the right or to the left" (Deut. 17:11).

Communities with more than 120 people had a Lesser Sanhedrin, which was composed of 23 judges (Sanh. 1:6) and had jurisdiction over most criminal matters, including capital cases (Sanh. 1:4). In smaller villages, a court of three judges (to ensure a majority) was appointed to decide minor cases (civil law) and to remit the important ones to the superior court. They also had jurisdiction in matters of divorce, conversion, absolution from vows, and the power to condemn to a period of involuntary servitude a person convicted of theft who did not have sufficient funds to repay the victim (Exod. 22:2).

Judges

According to Maimonides,

> [J]udges must be wise and understanding, learned in the law, and versed in many other branches of learning ... such as medicine, mathematics, astronomy and astrology; and the ways of sorcerers and magicians and the superstitious practices of idolaters [so as to be competent to judge them]; ... [a judge must be] neither a very aged man nor a eunuch ... or childless; ... just as he must be free from all suspicion with respect to conduct, so must he be free from all physical defects, ... a man of mature age, imposing stature, and good appearance, and able to express his views in clear and well-chosen words and be conversant with most of the spoken languages ... [so there is no need] of the services of an interpreter.[1]

The seven fundamental qualities of a judge are "wisdom, humility, fear of God, disdain of gain [money], love of truth, love of people, and a good reputation."[2] A judge must have "a good eye, a lowly [humble] spirit, must be friendly in intercourse [pleasant in company], and gentle in speech and dealings with others; he must be very strict with himself and control his passions; he must have a courageous heart to rescue the oppressed from the hand of the oppressor, cruelty, and persecution, and eschew wrong and injustice."[3] According to the Talmud, those who "are ineligible [to be witnesses or judges include] a gambler with dice [i.e., any type of gambler], a usurer [one who loans money at interest], a pigeon trainer [who races birds], and traders [in the produce] of the sabbatical year" (Sanh. 3:3).

Judges must be scrupulously fair and honorable to preserve the integrity of the judicial system, not departing from the Torah-mandated principles of guilt and innocence. "He who does not deliver judgments in perfect truth causes the Divine Presence to depart from the midst of Israel" (Sanh. 7a). A judge is forbidden to handle a case if he is related to one of the litigants or has any other personal relationship (Sanh. 3:4–5). A judge may not favor one of the litigants in a trial (Lev. 19:15) and must maintain absolute equality before the law. If one litigant is a man of high rank and distinction, the judge is must not afford him any special honor or treat him with more deference and respect (Shev. 30a–31a). Accepting gifts (bribes) from litigants is expressly forbidden (Exod. 23:8), even if the judge renders a judgment that "acquits the innocent and condemns the guilty." However, according to *Sefer ha-Hinnukh*, a judge who was not paid by the community for his services and was forced to take time off from his usual occupation to preside over a court was permitted to accept a fee, as long as it was paid equally by both parties in the litigation (i.e., considered as just compensation rather than a bribe).[4]

A judge must not decide in favor of poor people because of pity and compassion for them (Exod. 23:3; Lev. 19:15). Despite the temptation to render a verdict that would allow the poor to receive money from the rich (who would not miss it), one cannot pervert the law regardless of how admirable the purpose. Justice must be rendered with complete impartiality, whether the person is "rich or poor, sinner or saint."[5] Similarly, a judge must not allow his decision to be influenced by the past criminal record of the defendant. The defendant must be judged for the crime for which he or she is now being tried, not for any past transgressions. Only God may judge all the actions of people, both past and present.[6]

A judge is forbidden to have compassion in sentencing a person convicted of committing murder or causing a victim the loss of a limb: "You must show him no pity. Thus you will purge Israel of the blood of the innocent" (Deut. 19:13). The law of *lex talionis*—"life for life, eye for eye, tooth for tooth, hand for hand, foot for foot" (Deut. 19:21)—was designed to prevent the Mesopotamian practice of allowing wealthy perpetrators who intentionally caused bodily injury to someone from the lower class to escape with only a fine. In the Bible, punishment in kind applied to all classes of victims (except for slaves; Exod. 21:26–27).

This policy was changed in the Talmud, which ruled that monetary fines are to be levied for all crimes except murder.[7] Rashi observed that a judge should not say, "One person was already killed, what is the point of killing a second—so that two Jews will be killed?"[8] According to Nachmanides, compassion for a murderer only leads to further bloodshed, both because it frees the person to commit more crimes and because it encourages others who may be tempted to follow the murderer's example.[9]

A judge may not listen to one litigant in the absence of the other. Such a private conference generally results in the litigant presenting false evidence that, since the other party is not present to contradict it, will lead the judge to form an inaccurate or untrue view of the case.[10] A judge must deliberate with care before finally pronouncing his verdict, but may not unduly delay justice. Rather than relying on the opinion of a fellow judge in convicting the guilty or acquitting the innocent, each judge must come to his own conclusion based on an independent understanding of the evidence and the law. According to Rashi, a judge must not alter his opinion merely to agree with the majority of his colleagues if he thinks they either are in error or are intentionally misinterpreting the law.[11] Indeed, a judge who cannot justify his decision on the basis of his own learning and reasoning ability is guilty of rendering a "false judgment" (Sanh. 4:6).[12]

Under rabbinic law, 10 types of witnesses were disqualified from testifying in court: (1) women (who were thought to be too emotional to render a reasoned judgment), (2) slaves, (3) minors, (4) the mentally retarded, (5) deaf-mutes (who could not hear questions nor speak in response to them), (6) the blind (who clearly could not be "eyewitnesses"), (7) relatives of the parties involved in the case, (8) those personally involved in the case, (9) a "shameless" person, and (10) a wicked person (such as a compulsive gambler, pigeon racer, thief, or userer).[13]

Post-Temple Period

After the fall of Jerusalem, the legal, political, academic, and cultural center of the Jewish world became the *beit din* established by Rabbi Yochanan ben Zakkai at Yavneh. The prestige and authority of this central institution increased under his successor, Gamaliel II, and attained its greatest influence under Judah ha-Nasi, the compiler of the

Mishnah (see p. 499). In the third century, however, leadership of the Jewish world gradually passed from the *beit din* of the *nasi* in the Land of Israel to the scholars of Babylonia, where no single *beit din* ever attained unquestioned authority (even for Babylonia alone) because of the intense rivalry between the two major talmudic academies at Sura and Pumbedita.

During the Middle Ages, the *beit din* was the judicial branch of the self-governing *kahal* (community), and Jews were strictly prohibited from litigating cases among themselves in gentile courts. However, with the disintegration of the autonomous Jewish community as a result of the Emancipation in the modern era, Jews increasingly brought their disputes to the general civil courts. Today, the *beit din* in most countries deals with a variety of religious matters (such as divorce and supervision of the dietary laws) and serves as a court of arbitration (provided that all concerned agree to its jurisdiction), with its decisions upheld by the secular law of the land. The major exception is the State of Israel, where an extensive network of *beit din* courts (under the Supreme Rabbinical Court in Jerusalem) exercises complete jurisdiction over the Jewish population in all matters of personal status (such as marriage, divorce, and conversion).

Business Ethics

Traditional Judaism does not condemn the pursuit and acquisition of wealth, as long as it operates within the parameters established by Jewish law, morality, and custom and does not detract excessively from the time that a Jew should dedicate to Torah study. All wealth is a gift from God; therefore, one has an obligation to conduct business affairs in accordance with the divine will. Consequently, dishonesty in business is not merely a legal crime but, more important, a religious transgression. Judaism rejects the concept of "let the buyer beware," instead placing the full responsibility for disclosing defects and other shortcomings on the seller, even in the absence of a written guarantee. Based on the biblical injunction against "[placing] a stumbling block before the blind" (Lev. 19:14), the Rabbis required that all customers be fully informed about the quality of merchandise (no false advertising) as well as the dangers in such inherently harmful products as cigarettes, liquor, drugs, and weapons not used solely for self-defense.

The Torah expressly prohibits the use of false weights and measures (Lev. 19:35). On Rosh Hashanah, God decides each individual's income for the year. By using false weights, a person unfairly increases his or her income and thus interferes with the divine plan.[1] A grain merchant was required to wipe the measuring vessels clean at least once every 30 days, so that he or she always sold the exact measure and not less (BB 88a). Jews were prohibited from keeping false weights in their pockets or home (Deut. 25:14), even though they did not use them for purposes of trade. As Sforno observed, "God abhors not only the actual practice of dishonesty, but also the instruments that enable one to commit it."[2] Rashi noted that the verses regarding weights and measures immediately precede the commandment to wipe out the memory of Amalek, the archenemy of Israel. He concluded that it was because the Jews failed to be scrupulously honest in their business dealings that God sent enemies against them.

The Torah demands that employers treat their workers with dignity and respect: "You must pay him his wages on the same day, before the sun sets, for he is needy and urgently depends on it; else he will cry to the Lord against you and you will incur guilt" (Deut. 24:15). The Talmud concurs: "He who withholds an employee's wages is as though he had taken his life" (BM 112a).

An example of ideal business ethics reported in the Jerusalem Talmud is the response of Shimon ben Shetah when informed that the donkey his students had bought for him carried a hidden pearl that the seller had overlooked (BM 2:5). Although according to the strict letter of the law Shimon could have kept the pearl, since the seller was a heathen, the sage ordered his students to immediately return it, stating that he would rather have the heathen say "Praised be the God of the Jews" than receive any reward the world has to offer.[3]

Louis Jacobs[4] relates several tales of the extraordinary business integrity of the famed talmudist the Chafetz Chaim (Israel Meir ha-Kohen).[5] As a young man, the Chafetz Chaim and his wife opened a small general store that dealt only in goods that were fresh and in excellent condition. He always added a little to everything he sold, thus making certain that the customer was receiving good value. Lest too many customers patronize his store and not buy enough at other establishments, the Chafetz Chain closed his store at midday. On one occasion, an unidentified non-Jewish customer forgot to take a herring he had bought. Rather than inadvertently be guilty of theft, the Chafetz Chaim gave a fresh herring to each of his non-Jewish customers when they came to his store on the next market day. When as a renowned author he began publishing and selling his own books, the Chafetz Chaim spent months at the printers in distant Warsaw to ensure that each copy sold was in perfect condition. Whenever he arranged for the hand delivery of books that had been ordered by mail, he would purchase and then destroy stamps equivalent to the value of the postage, lest he be guilty of cheating the post office.

Although few can match the righteousness of the Chafetz Chaim, all Jews should do their utmost to conduct their business (and all other) activities in a highly ethical fashion. Such actions constitute a powerful form of *kiddush ha-Shem*—for gentiles impressed by the exemplary business ethics of their Jewish neighbors will echo the words of the Saracen seller, "Praised be the God of the Jews."

Prohibition against Lending at Interest (רִיבִּית)

Biblical Period

The Torah strictly forbids Jews from lending at interest, even though such payments might be regarded as no more than a "rental charge" for use of the money (Exod. 22:24; Lev. 25:35–37). This biblical prohibition is not against usury (excessive rate of interest), but against any interest, however minimal. Nevertheless, the Bible states that "you may lend at interest to foreigners" (Deut. 23:21).[1] Although Maimonides interpreted this as a command to exact interest from non-Jews to whom one lends money,[2] virtually all other commentators prefer the literal translation, arguing that a Jew is permitted (but not required) to charge interest to a non-Jew for a loan. The permission to exact interest from a non-Jew applied only to money borrowed for commercial purposes. If a non-Jew needed money for his or her subsistence, no interest could be charged.[3]

Giving a loan without any expectation of profit was considered one of the highest forms of charity, because it preserved the self-respect of the borrowers and allowed them to rebuild their own financial stability, so that they would no longer depend on others. Kli Yakar observed that the lender actually gains more from his or her generosity than the borrower does from the loan. The borrower is helped only in this world, whereas the lender who assists a poor person receives a reward in the world to come.[4] This is derived from the verse, "If you lend money to My people, to the poor among you" (Exod. 22:24). The borrowers are "My people" (God's nation), whose livelihood is a divine responsibility. Therefore, Jews who aid the poor can be sure that God will recompense them. In addition, the poor provide the wealthy with a priceless opportunity, for God richly rewards those who give charity. However, the prohibition against lending at interest appears to have been an ideal that often was not achieved in biblical times. For example, Ezekiel (22:12) castigates those who have "taken advance and accrued interest ... [and] have forgotten Me."

Talmudic Period

The Talmud extended the biblical prohibition against lending at interest to include, in addition to the creditor, "the borrower, the surety [who guarantees an interest-bearing debt], the witnesses ... and the notary [scribe who writes out the legal document]" (BM 5:11, 75b). In addition to direct and fixed interest payments (lending three coins and receiving four in return), the Talmud prohibited a broad spectrum of "indirect benefits" that could be offered in lieu of interest. These included offering a gift when asking for a loan or giving a gift when repaying it (prepaid and postpaid interest, respectively; BM 5:11, 75b), allowing the lender to live on the borrower's premises rent free or at a reduced rent (BM 64b), and giving the lender valuable information or even "extending a greeting to him if that is not his usual practice" (BM 75b). If two people agreed to do work for each other in turn, they had to make certain that the values were identical (since in different seasons the work may be of unequal difficulty), lest the more valuable work be construed as containing a component of forbidden interest (BM 5:10).

Moneylenders who took interest were considered morally reprehensible and without any share in the world to come. Regarded as "shedders of blood" for whom "death is prescribed" (BM 61b), they were disqualified as witnesses (Sanh. 3:3) and fated to fall into bankruptcy ("he who lends on interest, his wealth [possessions] dissolves") (BM 71a).

Techniques for Avoiding the Prohibition

As the agrarian society of the biblical Land of Israel was transformed into a more urban economy, lending money at interest became necessary to preserve the financial well-being of the Jewish community. Consequently, the Rabbis developed a variety of techniques for circumventing the prohibition against lending at interest. The simplest method was to lend money at interest to a non-Jew, who in turn would lend the money to a Jew (BM 61b). A more ingenious approach was the *heter iskah* (permission to form a partnership). Using a standardized and witnessed legal form, the "lender" would agree to provide a specified amount of money to the "borrower" as a "joint venture." The borrower alone would operate the business, pledging to pay a fixed minimum profit (i.e., interest) and guaranteeing the lender's capital against all loss. At the agreed time of maturity, the lender would recover the initial investment (loan) plus the promised minimum profit as stipulated in the deed. Today, making an interest-bearing business transaction comply with Jewish law merely requires adding the words *al-pi heter iskah* to the legal document.

Miscellany

Symbols of Jews and of Israel

Magen David (Star or Shield of David; מָגֵן דָּוִד)

The Magen David (lit., "Shield of David") has become the most distinctive and universally recognized sign of Judaism and Jewish identity. It is a six-pointed star (hexagram) formed by two interlocking equilateral triangles, one pointing upward and one pointing downward. A popular symbol in Europe and the Middle East since ancient days because of its geometric symmetry, the earliest known Jewish use of the hexagram was on a seal from about the sixth century B.C.E. In the synagogue of Capernaum in Israel (second or third century C.E.), the hexagram appears as a decorative design on a stone frieze, which also features the pentagram (five-pointed star) and the swastika (another ancient symbol). During the Middle Ages, hexagrams appeared frequently on seals and in churches but rarely in synagogues or on Jewish ritual objects. Indeed, from antiquity until after the Renaissance, the menorah (see p. 578) rather than the hexagram was the primary symbol of Judaism.

In Arab sources, the hexagram, called the "Seal of Solomon," was widely used. Legends connect this symbol with the magical signet ring used by King Solomon to overcome demons and evil spirits (Git. 68a). The notion of a magical shield of David that protected David from enemies was originally unconnected with this sign. From 1300 to 1700, Jewish mystics (kabbalists) used the terms "Shield of David" and "Seal of Solomon" interchangeably. They considered the two triangles to represent the reciprocal relationship between the heavenly realm of the *sefirot* and the earthly abode of the Jewish people. The triangle pointing up symbolized the good deeds of mortals that ascend to Heaven to activate the flow of divine goodness back to earth (the triangle pointing down). Another mystical concept was that a six-pointed star, which symbolizes the divine rule over the universe in all directions (north, south, east, west, up, down), receives form and substance from its solid center (the spiritual dimension), an idea that is similar to the Sabbath providing balance and perspective to the six other days of the week.[1] By transforming the Shield of David into the Shield of the Son of David (i.e., the Messiah), the six-pointed star became popularly viewed as a messianic symbol.

When Charles IV became Holy Roman Emperor, he made his capital in Prague and issued writs of protection for Jews, who had been recently subjected to particularly vicious persecutions. As a token of his royal benevolence, in 1354 Charles granted the Prague Jewish community the privilege of displaying its own distinctive red flag with a six-pointed star.[2] Consequently, this symbol became widely used in Prague (where it was always called "Magen David") in synagogues, on printed books, and on the official seal of the community. In Vienna three centuries later (1656), a marker was set up to demarcate the boundary between the city and the Jewish ghetto. A cross identified the Christian section and a six-pointed star indicated the Jewish area.[3] This was the first time that the Magen David was used as a religious-cultural symbol of the Jewish community. Following the French Revolution, the politically emancipated Jews searched for an object to be the identifying symbol of Judaism, similar to the cross that represented Christianity. They selected the six-pointed star, which already was in widespread use on kabbalistic amulets, even though it had no real biblical source or religious meaning. In the late 19th century, the Rothschild banking family adopted the Magen David on its coat of arms.

Theodor Herzl selected the Star of David to be the symbol for the new Zionist movement, probably because it had achieved wide circulation among Jewish communities yet did not evoke any definite religious associations.[4] In the classic *The Star of Redemption*, Franz Rosenzweig constructed his philosophy of Judaism around the image of the Jewish star, two triads (triangles) of critical relationships underlying his concept of Jewish belief—God, Israel, and the world; Creation, Revelation, and Redemption. During the Holocaust, the

Nazis selected the yellow star as a symbol of Jewish identification to be worn on the garments of all Jews. After the war, Jews turned this badge of humiliation and death into a major symbol of the newly established State of Israel. Searching for a time-honored image of Judaism, the Magen David was retained as the central figure on the national flag. It is also the emblem of the Magen David Adom, the Israeli equivalent of the Red Cross.

Today, the Star of David is widely used on religious articles and in the decor of many synagogues, as well as on necklaces and other jewelry as a secular symbol of Jewish identity.

Israeli Flag (דֶגֶל עִבְרִי)

During their wanderings in the wilderness after the Exodus from bondage in Egypt, the Jewish people raised banners and flags (*degel*) in their camps to signify their tribal identities (Num 2:2). According to the Midrash, each tribal prince had a flag (*mappah*) of a unique color, corresponding to one of the 12 precious stones of the breastplate of Aaron, the *Kohen Gadol* (Num. R. 2:7).

Theodor Herzl's first design for a Zionist flag, as written in his diary in 1895 and proposed in *The Jewish State* one year later, was seven gold stars (representing the "seven working hours" of the day) on a white background (standing for "our new and pure life"). Although other Zionist leaders convinced him to accept the Star of David (see p. 575), Herzl insisted that six stars appear opposite the six points of the Magen David, with a seventh star above it. This design, with the inscription "*Aryeh Yehudah*" (Lion of Judah) embroidered in the center, became the first Zionist flag. The combination of blue and white as the colors of the Jewish flag was derived from an 1860 poem ("Judah's Colors") by Austrian Ludwig August Frankl, which explained that the blue symbolized "the splendors of the firmament," and the white represented "the radiance of the priesthood." The blue stripes on the Zionist flag were also inspired by the stripes on the tallit (see p. 378). They provided a religious and ritual symbolism of Jewish life guided by precepts of the Torah, while the Star of David reflected the unity of the Jewish people. The dark blue stripes in the original flag were later lightened to enhance visibility at sea. Soon after the establishment of the State of Israel, the Zionist flag became the official national flag—"a white rectangle with two blue stripes along its entire length and a Star of David in the center made up of six dark blue stripes forming two equilateral triangles."[1]

Hatikvah (הַתִּקְוָה)

Hatikvah (The Hope) is the national anthem of the State of Israel. The words come from the poem *Tikvateinu* (Our Hope), written in 1887 by Naphtali Herz Imber, who had moved from Galicia to the Land of Israel in 1882. The music was arranged by Samuel Cohen, an immigrant from Moldavia, based on an Eastern European folk song *Carul cu Bo* (Cart and Ox). The same melody had previously been used by the classic Czech composer Bedrich Smetana in *The Moldau*. Sung at successive Zionist conferences, *Hatikvah* was adopted as the official anthem of the movement in 1933. Fifteen years later, *Hatikvah* was played and sung at the moment Israel was declared a state, and it has been the national anthem ever since. The simple text of *Hatikvah* is a stirring expression of the age-old Zionist dream, to which the Jewish people clung during their almost two millennia of dispersion in the far-flung Diaspora: "As long as deep in the heart, the soul of a Jew yearns, so long as the eye looks eastward toward Zion, our hope is not lost—the 2,000-year hope, to be a free people in our land, the land of Zion and Jerusalem."[1]

Menorah (מְנוֹרָה)

The menorah, the seven-branched candelabrum that once stood in the Jerusalem Temple, is one of the most beloved and enduring symbols of Judaism and the emblem of the State of Israel. In two parallel passages, the Bible specifies exactly how the menorah was to be made. Rising from its base, six branches (three on each side) curved upward from a central shaft (Exod. 25:31–40, 37:17–24). The shaft and each of the branches were ornamented with various cups, knops, and flowers of almond blossoms, and the entire menorah was carved from a single ingot of gold. The measurements of the menorah are not given in the Bible, but the Talmud states that its height was "18 handbreadths" (Men. 28b).

In the portable Tabernacle (*mishkan*), the menorah was placed in front of the curtain (*parochet*) on the south side against the table. The lamps (*nerot*) were lit at dusk; and in the morning, it was the duty of the *Kohanim* to remove the burnt wicks, replace them with fresh ones, and fill the lamps with absolutely pure olive oil (Exod. 30:7–8). The lights of the menorah had to be kindled even on the Sabbath, when lighting other fire is forbidden, just as burnt offerings also were brought on that day.

In Solomon's Temple, the original menorah was lit daily by the *Kohen Gadol*. Ten other golden menorahs were made for ornamental purposes, "five on the right and five on the left" (2 Chron. 4:7; Men. 98b). When the Babylonians destroyed the First Temple, these menorahs were destroyed, though there is a legend that the original was hidden away and brought back by the exiles.[1] After the destruction of the Second Temple, the menorah was taken to Rome. On the inside of the Arch of Titus, which commemorates the Roman victory over Judah, is a carved replica of a menorah being carried in a triumphal procession by defeated Jewish slaves. Although most scholars believe that this was not the original menorah because of its base, observant Jews refuse to walk under the Arch of Titus because it symbolizes the end of Jewish self-rule and the beginning of almost two millennia of exile.

After the destruction of the Temple, a tradition developed of Jews not making a precise duplicate of the Temple menorah. As the Talmud states, "He may, however, make one [menorah] with five, six, or eight [branches], but with seven he may not make one, even though it be of other metal [i.e., not gold]" (Men. 28b). The menorah was a common symbol during the rabbinic period, especially in synagogue mosaics and in various amulets, seals, and rings. It also appears on medieval illuminated manuscripts and bookplates, and today it is a popular design in decorations for Torah mantles and the ark.

The Rabbis interpreted the menorah as a symbol of Israel and its mission to be "a light unto the nations" (Isa. 42:6).[2] Maimonides and *Sefer ha-Hinnukh* considered the menorah as enhancing the glory of the sanctuary through its illumination. Abravanel took a more symbolic approach to the menorah, seeing the lamp of God as the soul of man (Prov. 20:27), with its seven branches representing the seven degrees of wisdom found in the divine law. The lamps all turned inward toward the Holy of Holies, indicating that true wisdom must be consistent with the fundamentals of the Torah, which was housed in the Ark of the Covenant. The pure gold of the menorah implied that wisdom must not be polluted by alien ideas. Sforno noted that the unity of the People of Israel was stressed by the fact that the entire seven-branched menorah was fashioned from a single block of gold.[3] The kabbalists focused on the menorah as a major symbol of the seven lower *sefirot* (divine emanations).

Some botanists believe that the shape of the menorah may have been inspired by the moriah plant (*Salvia palaestinae*), which grows wild in the Sinai desert and Israel. When pressed flat, the branches of this fragrant plant resemble six arms with a central stem.[4]

The emblem of the State of Israel combines the menorah, the symbol of light, with two olive branches, the symbol of peace.[5] The menorah is frequently reproduced on stamps, coins, and souvenirs. A large sculptured menorah portraying significant incidents in Jewish history stands outside the Knesset (parliament) building in Jerusalem, a symbol of the miraculous rebirth of the Jewish people after almost 2,000 years of exile.

Mezuzah (מְזוּזָה)

A mezuzah is the distinctive mark of a Jewish home. It consists of a piece of parchment, made from the skin of a kosher animal, on which a scribe has written the first two paragraphs of the *Shema,* both of which include the commandment, "Inscribe them on the doorposts [*mezuzot*] of your house and on your gates" (Deut. 6:4–9, 11:13–21). These biblical passages are traditionally written on 22 lines, equal to the number of letters in the Hebrew alphabet. The parchment is rolled up and enclosed in a wood or metal case, since it has the status of a Torah scroll and cannot be touched directly. The case is fastened to the upper third of the doorpost on the right side of the outside door, as well as to the doorpost of every living room in the house (excluding bathrooms, storerooms, and the kitchen).

When the medieval sages could not decide whether the mezuzah should be affixed vertically (Rashi) or horizontally (Rabbenu Tam, Rashi's grandson), they compromised on an angled tilt with the upper end of the case pointed inward. One commentator suggested that this compromise position is a constant reminder to husband and wife of the necessity to be flexible and meet one's spouse halfway to preserve *shalom bayit* (peace in the house). If the doorpost is not wide enough to hold the mezuzah on a diagonal, it may be affixed in a vertical position. The mezuzah is placed at eye level as a reminder to always be aware of and reach up toward God. *Mezuzot* must be inspected periodically (twice in seven years) to ensure that the writing is still readable. The Hebrew word "*Shaddai*" (Almighty) is written on the back of the parchment, which is inserted into the case in such a way that the word can be seen through a small opening near the top of the container. According to the Zohar, this divine name is used in the mezuzah because its three Hebrew letters (שדי) are an acronym for *Shomer daltot Yisrael* (Guardian of the Doors of Israel).

Some scholars believe that the mezuzah may relate to the ancient custom of marking the doorposts of the house to protect against evil spirits. Indeed, this practice appears to be reflected in the Passover story, when the Israelites daubed blood on their doorposts to keep away the Angel of Death, which was to kill all the firstborn of Egypt in the 10th plague (Exod. 12:7,22). The earliest evidence of the use of the mezuzah dates back to the Second Temple period (fourth century B.C.E.).[1] The Talmud observes that a person who has tefillin on his head and arm (see p. 382), tzitzit (fringes) on his garments (see p. 377), and a mezuzah on his doorpost "is in absolute security against sinning, for it is written, 'And a threefold cord is not quickly broken' (Eccles. 4:12)" (Men. 43b). It also compared these three religious objects to "the angel of the Lord [that] is on guard around those that fear Him and rescues them" (Ps. 34:8)[2] from transgressions.

During the Middle Ages, the mezuzah became increasingly viewed as a protective device to prevent evil spirits from entering the house. Under kabbalistic influence, additional passages with the names of angels and symbols such as the pentagram and the Star of David were added to the text inscribed on the parchment. Indeed, it was stated that the word "mezuzah" was a combination of two Hebrew words, "*mavet*" and "*zaz*," meaning "Death, go away." Maimonides attacked those who believed the mezuzah to be a mere amulet to ward off evil spirits as ignorant people who failed to appreciate that its true purpose was to keep Jews constantly aware of the unity of God and the need to fulfill their moral duties. Maimonides' rationalist argument won out, and today the mezuzah contains only the traditional two biblical passages. Nevertheless, since at least the 13th century, written upside down at the bottom of the back of the mezuzah is a seemingly meaningless combination of Hebrew letters: כוזו במוכסז כוזו (*Kozu be'Mochsaz Kozu*). This is a cryptogram formed by substituting the next letter of the alphabet for יהוה אלהינו יהוה (YHVH *Eloheinu* YHVH; the Lord, God, the Lord).

A Jew who moves into a new home is expected to put a mezuzah on the outer door immediately, or at least within the first 30 days. A Jew who sells or rents a home to a fellow Jew is required to leave the *mezuzot* in place, but must remove them if the purchaser or lessee is a non-Jew.

A mezuzah is generally placed at the entrance to a synagogue or other Jewish community building, though this is not strictly required unless it contains an apartment and thus qualifies as a dwelling (Yoma 11b). The commandment to affix a mezuzah applies only to permanent structures and not to temporary or casual places, such as a sukkah (see p. 228), a camping tent, or an automobile.

Despite Maimonides' attack on the use of a mezuzah as a protective amulet, even the Rabbis shared this belief. As the Talmud relates about the mezuzah: "According to universal custom, the mortal king dwells within, and his servants keep guard on him without; but [in the case of] the Holy One, blessed be He, it is His servants who dwell within while He keeps guard on them from without; as it is said: 'The Lord shall guard your going out and your coming in from this time forth and for evermore' [Ps. 121:8]" (Av. Zar. 11a). Traditional Jews observe the custom of kissing the mezuzah (either by touching it with a fingertip and then kissing the finger or by kissing the finger before touching the mezuzah) both on entering and leaving the house. This may relate to the talmudic passage just quoted. When the convert Onkelos was being taken by the Romans to their emperor, he passed by a door where he saw the mezuzah and placed his hand on it, as a symbol of the constant watchfulness and protection of God.[3] Some modern Jews wear a mezuzah (lacking the inner parchment) around the neck as a good luck charm or as an affirmation of Jewish identity. Beautifully designed and decorated mezuzah cases have become superb examples of Jewish art.

Magic and Superstition

Amulet (קָמֵיעַ)

Fearing injury from unseen evil forces, all ancient cultures turned to the protective magical powers of a variety of amulets, charms, and talismans. Despite rabbinic contention that tefillin (Deut. 6:8–9) and the mezuzah (Deut. 11:18–21) were only reminders of the divine commandments and the duty to bear witness to their God, many Jews probably viewed these objects as good luck charms to counteract the power of evil spirits.

In the Talmud, an amulet is called *kame'ah* (plural, *kemi'ot*). This word probably derives from either the Hebrew root "to bind" or from the Arabic "to hang," since amulets are usually either attached to clothing or hung as a necklace or bracelet. Most were designed to protect the wearer against a specific danger (the evil eye, miscarriage) or to promote good health or fertility. Depending on their specific purpose, amulets could be inscribed with various biblical verses, prayers (especially the Priestly Blessing; see p. 432), and combinations of the letters of the multiple names of God.

The efficacy of an amulet was deemed to depend not only on the inscription but also on the piety of the person who wrote it. In addition to praying, fasting, and undergoing ritual purification, before writing an amulet the scribe should say: "Praised are You, Lord our God, King of the universe, who has sanctified Your great and revered name, and revealed it to the pious ones, who invoke Your power and Your might by means of Your name and Your word and the words of Your mouth, oral and written. Praised are You, Lord, King, Holy One; may Your name be extolled."[1] According to the Talmud an effective amulet—one that had cured a sick person on three different occasions or had cured three different sick people—could even be carried into the public domain on the Sabbath (Shab. 61a).

In the Middle Ages, the use of amulets inspired intense controversy. The rationalist Maimonides vehemently opposed their use, deriding the "folly of amulet writers."[2] Studying Torah and performing mitzvot were all that a Jew needed to combat evil. As Judah the Pious wrote, "Do not wear an amulet as a charm against evil, but put your implicit trust in God alone, for He will watch over you."[3] However, the more mystical Nachmanides permitted the use of amulets.

Although belief in the protective power of amulets has greatly decreased in the West since the Emancipation of European Jewry, they remained in common use in Eastern Europe until the Holocaust. Amulets are still popular among Jews of Middle Eastern and North African descent, especially in Israel, where they have aroused controversy during political campaigns when distributed by certain ultra-Orthodox parties under the auspices of prominent rabbis.

Hamsa (חַמְסָה)

The *hamsa*—from a Semitic root meaning "five" (*hamesh* in Hebrew, and used in this context to refer to fingers)—is a hand-shaped amulet worn as a superstitious practice to ward off the evil eye. Symbolically representing the protective hand of God and long popular in Mediterranean cultures, in Muslim lands it has also been termed the "hand of Fatima" (after the daughter of Muhammad) or even the "hand of Miriam." A *hamsa* frequently has a single eye set in the middle of the palm, either symbolic of the ever-vigilant eye of God or as a means to repel the evil eye. Magical hand-shaped amulets are still commonly used by Jews originating in Muslim countries and, through the influence of Sephardim in Israel, *hamsas* also have become popular among Jews in the West.[4]

Evil Eye (עַיִן הָרָע)

In many folk traditions there is belief in the Evil Eye (*Ayin ha-Ra*) to injure or cast a spell on another person. Deeming the Evil Eye the cause of all sickness, Rav" went to a cemetery, performed certain charms, and then said, 'Ninety-nine [have died] through an evil eye, and one through natural causes'" (BM 107b). At times, pious individuals could employ the magical power of the eye for good. The Talmud relates that, when confronting an evil man, Shimon bar Yochai "cast his eyes upon him and he became a heap of bones" (Shab. 34a). Some of the Rabbis deemed Jews to be immune from the harmful effects of the Evil Eye: "Just as the fishes in the sea are covered by water and the Evil Eye has no power over them, so the Evil Eye has no power over the seed of Joseph" (Ber. 20a).

Many practices have evolved for preventing or counteracting the Evil Eye. Believing that the most frequent cause of the Evil Eye was jealousy, the Rabbis offered several practical measures to avoid engendering envy in others. They warned against excessive praise, especially of children, and ostentatious displays of riches. To temper celebrations, blood relatives traditionally are not called consecutively to the Torah, and double weddings are not permitted. As the Talmud observes, "Blessing comes only on those things that are hidden from sight" (Taan. 8b).

Nothing is exempt from the damaging effects of the Evil Eye. According to Rashi, because the first tablets of the Ten Commandments were given to Moses accompanied by a spectacular display of thunder, lightning, and the sound of the shofar (Exod. 19:16), they came under the spell of the Evil Eye and thus were shattered by Moses when he saw the abomination of the Israelites dancing around the Golden Calf. Consequently, the second tablets were given privately; not even the elders were permitted to ascend the mountain with Moses, nor were the people allowed to gather at its base (Exod. 34:3). If an event so sacred as the giving of the Ten Commandments could be adversely affected by the ravages of the Evil Eye, how much more should one exercise modesty and self-restraint when engaged in everyday activities.[1]

Once the Evil Eye has been triggered and its harmful effects are imminent, preventive measures are no longer of value and counter-magic is required. Mirrors and red or blue objects may be powerful enough to reflect the evil glance, while an obscene gesture or a holy verse in an amulet may frighten it. Another technique is to divert the glance from the intended target by distracting it with an attractive decoy, such as a precious stone hung between the eyes of the endangered person. Other rituals that have developed to counteract the effects of the Evil Eye include putting a spot of dirt or ash on the forehead of a child who has been praised, spitting three times onto the fingers, throwing salt into the corners of a room, piercing a lemon with iron nails, and combining prayer with dripping olive oil or wax into water or dropping coal or match heads into water (see below).[2] Fumigation was a popular remedy against the Evil Eye, based on the belief that demons could not tolerate the smoke of acrid incense. Dirt (in which evil spirits lived) taken from the four corners of the room, incense, and a piece of the garment of one suspected of having employed the Evil Eye were mixed together and placed on glowing coals, which were positioned so that the curative smoke blew into the face of the afflicted person.[3]

Although many consider belief in the power of the Evil Eye and various ways to combat it as ancient myths, even modern rationalist Jews in the Western world pay heed to this superstition. Among Yiddish-speaking Ashkenazic Jews, any praise is typically tempered with the phrase *"keyn ayen horeh"* (without the Evil Eye), which is generally shortened to *"keynahora."* Indeed, a prominent charitable organization sends out small laminated cards labeled *"shemira neged Ayin ha-Ra"* (protection against the Evil Eye), which contains a red ribbon "wound seven times around the tomb of our Matriarch Rachel" as a protection against evil, illness, and misfortune.

Popular Superstitions

As have all cultures, Jews have developed numerous superstitious practices applicable to a variety of occasions.[1] The following are some of the most common.

Spitting Three Times

Whether done literally or figuratively (by saying "pooh, pooh, pooh"), spitting three times (a mystical number) is a classic response to something exceptionally evil or good. For centuries, Jews have performed this ritual in response to seeing, hearing, or learning of something terrible and as a prophylactic measure to prevent such a tragedy from happening or recurring. Ironically, it is traditional to perform the same action in response to something wonderful—such as good news or the birth of a beautiful and healthy child—to ward off the Evil Eye (see above).

Spitting was long considered a potent protector against magic and demons. Ancient and medieval physicians, including Maimonides, described the positive values of saliva and spittle. However, this popular Jewish superstition may well have originated from the Christian Bible, which mentions the miraculous power of the spittle of Jesus. "And they bring unto him one that was deaf, and had an impediment in his speech.... And he took him aside from the multitude, and put his fingers into his ears, and he spit, and touched his tongue; and looking up to heaven, he sighed, and saith unto him, Ephphatha, that is, Be opened. And straightway his ears were opened, and the string of his tongue was loosed, and he spake plain" (Mark 7:32–35). In a another reference, Jesus spat in the dirt and made "clay" and put it in the eyes of a blind man, who subsequently could see (John 9:1–7).

Because spitting eventually was viewed as a crude and messy practice, it was replaced by the more refined ritual of simply saying "pooh, pooh, pooh."

Chewing on Thread

A popular *bubbe meise* (old wives' tale) is chewing on a piece of thread whenever one is wearing a garment upon which someone is actively sewing—such as attaching a button or repairing a seam. This practice may relate to the Yiddish phrase "*mir zollen nit farnayen der saychel,*" meaning that one should not sew up the brains (or common sense). Another explanation is that burial shrouds are sewn around the remains of the deceased (see p. 80). Actively chewing while another is sewing on one's garments is a clear indication that one is quite alive and not yet a candidate for the grave.

Pulling or Tugging One's Ears When Sneezing

Especially common among Jews from Galicia and Lithuania, the practice of pulling on one's ears when sneezing has engendered heated arguments. Should one ear or both be pulled (or tugged) and should one pull up or down? The reason for this custom is unclear. Originally, it was performed if the sneeze occurred when speaking about one who was dead. However, tugging has long been extended to all sneezes and is usually accompanied by reciting the Yiddish phrase "*tzu langeh mazaldikker yohrn*" (to long, lucky years).

Sneezing on the Truth

Midrashic legend maintains that a sneeze used to announce impending death: "The story is told that until the time of Jacob, a person, at the close of his life, sneezed and instantly died." Some ancient peoples believed that the "little explosion in the head" ensured approaching eternity. Rather than a mere irritation of the nasal passages, a sneeze was deemed a grave omen. Indeed, this may be the underlying reason for the development of the custom of saying "long life" and "good health" to one who has sneezed.

A traditional belief is that when a person sneezes during a conversation, whatever has just been said will occur, based on the concept of "sneezing on the truth." While not as foolproof as direct prophecy, it is said to indicate that events that are rational and plausible will actually come to pass or that an event that has already occurred really happened just as the story related.

Closing Books That Have Been Left Open

Closing prayer books, Bibles, and talmudic tracts is a common practice in synagogues and study halls. The explanation appears to be related to the medieval fear of the evil power of devils and demons, who would take "holy knowledge" and somehow use it for their own nefarious purposes.

Placing Salt in Pockets and Corners of the Room

Demons and similar creatures were known to reside in new houses and cause such chaos that people were actually paid to live in them before the arrival of their intended occupants. Because salt was generally regarded as having superb powers against evil spirits, it was often placed in the corners of a room where these creatures hid. The same reasoning applied to new clothes, where smaller goblins and elves could secret themselves in pockets. By placing a small amount of salt in the pockets, the owner of the clothing hoped to drive these beings away and foil their evil designs.

Wearing a Metal Pin on Clothes When Embarking on a Trip

In some communities, a safety or straight pin is attached out of sight under a shirt collar or on a sleeve before taking a journey. Metal was thought to be a powerful protective substance. According to the renowned Eleazer of Worms (a leader of the pietistic Hasidei Ashkenaz of the medieval period), metals were the products of civilization and thus could successfully attack and repel the evil spirits of a less sophisticated society. The protective power of metal also can be derived from the biblical discussion of the first plague, in which God states that all water stored "in vessels of wood and stone" (Exod. 7:19) will turn to blood. According to this, metal receptacles are not mentioned because they must have protected the water from changing. Another explanation is that metal means luck, since *"barzel"* (the Hebrew word for "iron") is an acronym for the names of four of the mothers of the Children of Israel (Bilhah, Rachel, Zilpah, and Leah), who could ward off all dangers to their progeny.

Knocking on Wood

Knocking on wood to protect from evil is a non-Jewish practice, even though many Jews do it. Many connect this action to Christian beliefs that relate wood to slivers of the cross, which were believed to bring good luck. However, this practice has a more universal, pantheistic origin. Long before the time of Jesus, some cultures regarded trees as gods; believers were convinced that touching (or knocking on) wood could produce magical results.

Other Customs and Concepts

A number of topics relating to Jewish traditions, customs, and beliefs are difficult to categorize. Therefore, there are presented here in alphabetical order.

Beards (זָקָן)

The Torah expressly prohibits shaving the "side-growth of your beard" (Lev. 19:27, 21:5), which was interpreted to mean the hair between the head and the cheeks. The long and curly hair at the side of the head, known as *payot* (in Hebrew) and *payes* (in Yiddish), has become a sign of ultra-Orthodox and Hasidic Jews. The reason for the ban on shaving this area of the beard was presumably to distinguish the Israelites from the priests of pagan cults, who ritually shaved certain areas of their faces to designate their sacred status. Another interpretation is that leaving the corner of the head uncut serves as a visual reminder of the commandment to also leave unharvested the corner of the field (*pe'ah*) and designate it for the poor, thus emphasizing the ethical requirement to provide for the needy (Lev. 19:9).[1]

In biblical times, the beard was regarded as a symbol of male attractiveness and virility and a natural feature distinguishing men from women. Thus a shaved face was a sign of humiliation. When Hanun, the king of Ammon, accused the envoys of King David of being spies plotting to overthrow his government, he "clipped off one side of their beards and cut away half of their garments at the buttocks, and sent them off" (2 Sam. 10:4). Understanding their deep humiliation, David ordered the men to hide in Jericho until their beards had grown again. Similarly, shaving the head and beard was an indication of intense grief and bereavement. In Jeremiah's (48:37) prophecy about the demise of

Moab, he declared: "every head [will be] bald, and every beard [will be] shorn." Ezra (9:3) stated that when hearing about the assimilation and idolatry committed by the Israelites, "I rent my garment and robe, I tore hair out of my head and beard, and I sat desolate."

Tearing one's clothing is still a sign of mourning, but ironically, since many Jewish men are now clean shaven, growing a beard—as opposed to shaving—has become a sign of mourning. Shaving the head and body was mandated for those who had been stricken with the skin disease *tzara'at* (Lev. 14:8) as well as for the Nazirite contaminated through contact with the dead (Num. 6:9). Pulling a man by his beard may have been a show of affection (2 Sam. 20:9).

The Mishnah codified the biblical law not to "mar" the corners of the beard (Mak. 3:5), and the Talmud termed the beard "the glory of the face" (Shab. 152a), a sign of maturity and piety. Young priests in the Temple had to wait until their beards were "fully grown" to "act as the representative of the community and to descend before the ark [lead the congregation in prayer] and to pronounce the priestly benediction" (Hul. 24b). In general, though, clipping the beard was tolerated and only shaving with a razor prohibited. One person was permitted "to cut his hair in the gentile fashion as he was in close contact [had frequent dealings] with the government" (BK 83a).

During the early Middle Ages, Jews living in Islamic countries wore long beards; those living in Christian-dominated portions of Europe clipped them with scissors. As one of the main factors distinguishing men from women, shaving was effectively a violation of the commandment prohibiting men and women from adopting the clothing and other practices associated with the other sex (Deut. 22:5). Maimonides suggested that the reason for the biblical prohibition on shaving was that idolatrous priests were clean shaven. Still, the Shulchan Arukh ruled that as long as a razor is not used, it is acceptable to remove all facial hair (YD 181:10).

For the kabbalists, hair (including facial hair) possessed great mystical significance. In the radical imagery of the Kabbalah, a man's beard represents the beard of the Holy Ancient One, the point of Creation when divinity flows to the created world. The beard is also mystically associated with God's mercy. Thus the kabbalists prohibited even the shortening of one's beard. The Hasidim of Eastern Europe adopted this practice. However, Italian Jews (including kabbalists) always shaved, and this created a controversy when Italian Jews moved to Salonica, where the Jews wore beards and demanded that their Italian coreligionists follow the local custom and do the same. Some European rulers (such as Nicholas I of Russia) demanded that Jews shave off their beards and sidelocks, whereas others (for example, Maria Theresa of Austria) required that Jews keep their beards to be easily differentiated from Christians.

Today, some strictly observant Jews do not shave their beards, as a sign of their devotion to tradition. Many more Jews do not cut their beards (or shave) during the *Sefirah* period of counting the Omer (see p. 292) and for the three weeks preceding Tisha b'Av (see p. 304), in accordance with the mournful tone of these periods. Despite the rabbinic pronouncements against it, shaving the beard is halakhically permitted if one uses scissors, a chemical depilatory, or an electric shaver with two cutting edges. Only instruments with a single cutting edge are forbidden.

A Chosen People (עַם סְגוּלָּה)

The concept of the Children of Israel being a "Chosen People" with a unique relationship to God that imposes special responsibilities has been a central tenet in Jewish thought throughout the centuries. It derives from the series of divine choices underlying the biblical narrative—the selection of one man (Abraham) to spread the word of the One God, one family (the Children of Israel) to carry on that tradition, one High Priest (Aaron) and family of priests (Levites), one king (David, after the failure of Saul), one land (Israel), and one permanent site for the Sanctuary (Jerusalem). Each of the chosen individuals and groups are responsible for certain tasks and are required to assume particular roles. As Moses stated to the Israelites in his farewell address: "For you are a people consecrated to the Lord your God: of all the people on earth the Lord your God chose you to be His treasured people [or special possession]" (Deut. 7:6). Israel is to be "a light unto the nations" (Isa. 49:6),[1] spreading the idea of God's salvation to the ends of the earth. The selection of Israel, which was sealed by several covenants, was not motivated by its size and strength ("the smallest of peoples"), but rather solely by divine love (Deut. 7:7–8). However, there is no concept of a relationship between chosenness and national origin, since King David and ultimately the Messiah himself are descendants of Ruth, the Moabite princess who converted to Judaism.

The Bible emphasizes that the doctrine of election does not imply the conferring of special privileges but instead imposes extra obligations and responsibility. Israel is obligated to "keep His laws and observe His teachings" (Ps. 105:45). The most famous verse dealing with the chosenness of the Jewish people makes it clear that because "you alone have I singled out of all the families of the earth—that is why I will call you to account for all your iniquities" (Amos 3:2). Israel's election to spread the divine message even includes the burden of vicarious suffering for the other nations (Isa. 52:13–53:12) . Nevertheless, although the wickedness of the people may incur heavenly wrath and punishment, the divine love underlying the initial choice of Israel will preclude any absolute rejection by God. "Yet even then, when they are in the land of their enemies, I will not reject them or spurn them so as to destroy them, annulling My covenant with them: for I the Lord am their God" (Lev. 26:44).

For the Rabbis, the selection of Israel as the Chosen People was based on their voluntary acceptance of the Torah at Sinai (*ol malkhut shamayim*; "the yoke of the kingdom of Heaven"). They interpreted the verse, "If you will obey Me faithfully and keep My Covenant, you shall be My treasured possession among all the peoples" (Exod. 19:5), as implying that the Torah was offered first to the other nations of the world, which summarily rejected it because following its commandments would clash with their depraved lifestyles (Av. Zar. 2b–3a). According to legend, even the Jews were somewhat hesitant, agreeing to receive the Torah only when God "suspended the mountain over Israel like a vault," saying, "If you accept the Torah, it will be well with you, but if not, here you will find your grave" (Av. Zar. 2b–3a). A more positive approach to the election of the Israelites was the view that they eagerly accepted the Torah and promised to obey its commandments even before they were announced, declaring "*na-aseh v'nishma*" ([first] we will obey [the law, then] we will hear/understand it; Exod. 24:7).[2] The Rabbis interpreted the love poem of The Song of Songs (see p. 268) as an allegory of the special relationship between God and the Children of Israel, which cannot be severed even in times of deep distress: "How beloved is Israel before the Holy One, blessed be He; for wherever they were exiled [Egypt, Babylon], the *Shekhinah* [Divine Presence] was with them" (Meg. 29a).

Critical moments in the synagogue service reinforce the idea of God's choice of the Jewish people. In the festival *Amidah*, it is written: "You have chosen us from all peoples; You have loved us and taken pleasure in us, and have exalted us above all tongues; You have hallowed us by Your commandments, and brought us near to Your service." Each person honored with an *aliyah* expresses gratitude to God, "Who has chosen us from all peoples, and has given us Your Torah." The *Kiddush* (see p. 139) recited on the Sabbath and festivals praises God, "Who has chosen us from all the nations and sanctified us with His commandments." A similar view is expressed in the *Aleinu* (see p. 466), in which Jews thank God "for He has not made us like the nations of the lands nor placed us like the families of the earth; for He has not made our lot like that of the multitudes," and in the *Havdalah* ceremony at the end of the Sabbath (see p. 147), in which Jews praise God for making the distinction "between Israel and the (other) nations."

The early Christian Church maintained that the Jews, by their rejection of Jesus, had forfeited their favored position. It pointed to the desperate straits of the Jews in their midst as proof that the Church had inherited the role of the "true Israel," God's Chosen People. Jews totally rejected this claim, clinging to the biblical belief that even in times of persecution and despair, by steadfastly remaining loyal to the tradition, only they would always remain in a unique relationship with God.

The universalism of the modern era has led many Jews to advocate modifying or even completely dropping the traditional concept of being a Chosen People. The philosopher Moses Mendelssohn regarded Judaism as a "religion of reason," arguing that the Jews had been selected at Sinai to be continually responsible for preserving the divine Revelation. The Reform movement developed the concept that the Jews were chosen for a specific "mission"—to receive the word of God and then pass on its moral and ethical teachings to the other nations of the world. The idea of the Jews being a Chosen People has led to vicious charges of "religious racism" by anti-Semites, who assert that the Jewish claim of "superiority" has led them to devise an international conspiracy to rule the world, as expressed in the notorious forgery "The Protocols of the Elders of Zion." Realizing that the term had been misunderstood and too often taken as a sign of Jewish superiority, when instead it was conceived as an expression of Jewish obligation to God and humanity, Mordecai Kaplan eliminated this concept from the prayer book of the Reconstructionist movement that he founded, even using a different version of the Torah blessing to avoid the phrase "Who chose us from all the peoples."

For much of the non-Jewish world, the ironic notion that the despised Jews could conceive of themselves as the Chosen People was summed up in Hilaire Belloc's jingle, "How odd of God to choose the Jews," to which later was added the retort, "It was not odd—the Jews chose God!"

Conversion (גֵּרוּת)

Throughout its history, Judaism has always been open to accepting converts. However, there has been significant variation in the extent to which conversions took place and the response of the established Jewish community to Jews-by-Choice.

Historical Perspective

Biblical Period

The Hebrew word for a male convert is "*ger*," though in the Bible this term referred to a stranger or sojourner who lived in a land other than his homeland (resident alien). Thus on multiple occasions the Torah describes the Israelites as having been *gerim* in Egypt ("strangers in a strange land"), even though they had lived there for 400 years. The *ger* who chose to live among the Israelites in their land was expected to obey the same laws followed by native-born Israelites and in return was be treated with loving kindness and respect.[1]

The ancient Israelites were a nomadic people who struggled to keep their group identity. For example, Abraham insisted that Isaac marry a wife from his extended family in Mesopotamia, rather than a woman from the neighboring pagan tribes. When the Israelites entered the Promised Land, they were forbidden from marrying women from the seven Canaanite nations dwelling there, lest they "turn your children away from Me to worship other gods" (Deut. 7:4). However, this prohibition did not apply to other peoples. Moses married Zipporah (a daughter of Jethro, the priest of Midian; Exod. 2:21) and Joseph wedded Asenath (the daughter of an Egyptian priest of On; Gen. 41:45), without either incurring biblical disapproval for marrying an outsider. Indeed, the most famous non-Israelite biblical figure who embraced the God of Israel was Ruth, the Moabite princess who became the great-grandmother of King David. The acceptance of foreigners ceased abruptly after the Jews returned from their Babylonian exile. Ezra (9–10) demanded that the returnees immediately divorce their foreign wives and expel them and their children, precluding the possibility that they could ever become part of the Jewish people.[2]

Rabbinic Period

Toward the end of the Second Temple period, there was substantial conversion to Judaism and the word "*ger*" became synonymous with a proselyte or convert. The Talmud and the Midrash make multiple references to conversion, manifesting both positive and negative attitudes to the practice. The most famous nonjudgmental passage describes the pagan who offers to convert if someone can teach him all about Judaism "while standing on one foot" (Shab. 31a). Although Shammai was convinced that the pagan was merely mocking Judaism and angrily chased him away, Hillel responded: "What is hateful to you do not do to your neighbor. This is the entire Torah, the rest is commentary. Now, go and learn it."

Rabbi Eliezer stated, "When a person comes to you in sincerity to be converted, do not reject him, but on the contrary encourage him" (Mek. Amalek 3). As the Talmud notes, "the Holy One, Blessed be He, exiled Israel among the nations so that proselytes might join them" (Pes. 87b). It adds, "Beloved are the proselytes [by God], for [Scripture] everywhere uses the same epithet of them (*gerim*) as of Israel" (Ger. 4:3). One passage praises those who have converted to Judaism as "dearer to God than all of the Israelites who stood at Mount Sinai. Had the Israelites not witnessed the lightning, thunder, quaking mountain, and sounding trumpets, they would not have accepted the Torah. But the convert, who did not see or hear any of these things, came and surrendered to God and accepted the yoke of Heaven. Can anyone be dearer to God than such a person?" (Tanh. Lekh Lekha 6 f., 32a). A tendency to increase the honor of converts may be reflected in the tradition that traces the origins of great rabbinic personalities to wicked forebears. For example, Rabbi Meir was described as descending from Roman emperor Nero (Git. 56a) and the "descendants of Sisera [Canaanite general who fought against Deborah and Barak] taught children in Jerusalem; descendants of Sennacherib [king of Assyria who besieged Jerusalem during the time of Isaiah] gave public expositions of the Torah" (Git. 57b), and they were, respectively, the ancestors of Shemaiah and Avtalyon, who were the teachers of Hillel. And it is said that the descendants of Haman learned the Torah in B'nai Brak (Sanh. 96b). Another famous convert was Onkelos, the nephew of a Roman emperor, whose Aramaic translation of the Torah (*Targum Onkelos*) is close to the original Hebrew and is still used to explain obscure passages.[3]

Nevertheless, some authorities were extremely opposed to the concept of conversion. The Rabbis expressed concern about the true motivation of potential converts, indicating that none was accepted during the reigns of King David and King Solomon because it was suspected that such individuals might be converting only for financial gain (Yev. 24b). The bitter experience of Jews with proselytes in times of war and revolt influenced the negative attitude to conversion. Proselytes and their offspring became renegades and informers, often slandering their new religion and denouncing the Jewish community and its leaders to foreign rulers. "Do not trust a convert, even to the 24th generation, because the inherent evil is still within him" (Ruth Zutra 1:12). The Rabbis accused the proselytes who left Egypt with the Israelites as being responsible for the shameful episode of the Golden Calf (Exod. R. 42:6). At the time of the Bar Kokhba revolt, it was said that proselytes "impede the arrival of the Messiah" (Nid. 13b). The extent to which some of the sages despised converts is seen in the declarations that "converts are as hard for Israel [to endure] as a sore" (Yev. 47b) and "evil after evil comes upon those who receive proselytes" (Yev. 109b).[4]

Post-Talmudic Period

During the Middle Ages, most Jews resided in countries dominated by Islamic or Christian rule. Both of these monotheistic religions strongly condemned those who abandoned their faith, regarding it as a capital offense. Thus conversion to Judaism decreased substantially. Nevertheless, the upper classes of two peoples—the Himyars in southern

Arabia and the Khazars, a national group of Turkish origin—converted to Judaism. In Muslim countries, the adoption of Judaism by Christians was not forbidden and was even common.

With the Emancipation of the Jews at the dawn of the modern period, most Jewish communities were reluctant to accept converts, especially since the laws of many European countries prohibited this practice. In 20th-century North America, Jews (especially in the Reform movement) adopted a more tolerant attitude to those wishing to convert. A major factor in this increased acceptance of converts was the substantial rise in the rate of intermarriage among members of the Jewish community. Converts to Judaism are now commonly termed Jews-by-Choice, stressing that they freely elected to join the Jewish people and avoiding the words "convert" and "proselyte," which can be viewed as derogatory or as being associated with Christianity. Between 5,000 and 10,000 North Americans are estimated to convert to Judaism each year.[5]

Conversion Process

The process of conversion to Judaism, first described in the Talmud (Yev. 47a), has remained quite consistent over the centuries. When approached by persons who wish to convert to Judaism, most rabbis follow the tradition of discouraging them three times by pointing out the difficulties they might face as a Jew, the obstacles to be overcome in casting their lot with the Jewish people, and the new responsibilities they would have to assume (Yev. 47b; Ger. 1:1–2).[6] According to the Midrash, this threefold act of discouragement is based on the three times that Naomi tried to dissuade Ruth, the most famous biblical convert, from returning with her to the Land of Israel (Ruth R. 2:1). However, if the potential converts still persist, they are received, for one should "always discourage with the left hand and draw near with the right."[7] Other rabbis prefer to be more encouraging to a prospective Jew, while at the same time asking many questions to determine the person's sincerity.

Many of those wishing to convert do so to marry a Jew. Traditionally, this has been considered an invalid motive (Ger. 1:3). Rabbis permitted conversion only to those seeking admission to the Jewish people on the basis of sincere conviction, who pledged full and unreserved commitment to all the laws of Judaism.[8] Some rabbis still refuse to convert a person whose decision is based solely on an upcoming marriage to a Jew. However, today most rabbis will agree to work with such individuals if they are convinced that the potential convert has a strong desire to become Jewish.

The conversion process consists primarily of a period of study, ranging from several months to a few years, that includes private or group classes on Jewish history, beliefs and prayers, holidays, life-cycle ceremonies, and home rituals. Many rabbis require that a person wishing to convert to Judaism learn basic Hebrew; in Orthodox conversions

CONVERSION OF A CHILD

An adopted child under the age of bar or bat mitzvah requires a formal conversion to Judaism if his or her mother is not known to be Jewish. If an intermarriage, Orthodox and Conservative rabbis require that the child be converted if only the father is Jewish. In contrast, the Reform and Reconstructionist movements accept patrilineal descent as long as the child is raised solely as a Jew. A child also must be converted if his or her entire family joins the Jewish faith. As with adults, conversion consists of immersion in a *mikveh* and, for boys, circumcision or *hatafat dam brit* ("shedding the blood of the covenant"). Once these formalities have been completed, the child receives a Hebrew name.[1]

Conversion must be voluntary, but a young child obviously cannot act on his or her own. Therefore, the rabbis ruled that the child of a non-Jewish mother who is adopted by Jewish parents is converted *al da'at beit din* (by advice and consent of the court). The Shulchan Arukh allows this practice, deeming it a "privilege" for a child to be converted to Judaism (YD 268:7). However, at the age of bar or bat mitzvah, any child may choose to annul the conversion, though it must be done promptly (Ket. 11a).[2]

If a woman converts while pregnant, the child does not require conversion, even if it was conceived before the conversion (since at the time of birth its mother was already Jewish).[3]

there is an emphasis on the specific requirements of Jewish law. Prospective converts begin to adopt a Jewish lifestyle, such as attending synagogue services; observing the Sabbath, festivals, and dietary laws; and performing acts of *tzedakah* (see p. 531) and *gemilut hasadim* (see p. 530).[9]

Once satisfied that the person possesses the necessary knowledge and has shown the determination to live as a Jew, the rabbi arranges for the formal conversion. Traditionally, the prospective convert appears before a *beit din*, a court of three rabbis (or learned Jews, at least one of whom is a rabbi), which asks the candidate a variety of questions to test his or her basic Jewish knowledge and commitment to Jewish beliefs, ethics, ritual observances, and acceptance of the burden of *ol malkhut shamayim* (the yoke of the kingdom of Heaven).[10] In Orthodox and Conservative conversions, the next steps in the process are the rituals of circumcision for males (see p. 7) and immersion in the *mikveh* (ritual bath; see p. 555) for both men and women (Yev. 46). An uncircumcised male must be circumcised to join the Jewish community. If he has already been circumcised or cannot undergo the procedure for health reasons, a drop of blood is taken from the penis as a symbol of circumcision (*hatafat dam brit*; "shedding the blood of the covenant") (YD 268:1). Immersion in the *mikveh* symbolizes spiritual rebirth as a Jew. The Reform movement does not require either circumcision or immersion in the *mikveh*, though it recommends that the rabbi acquaint prospective converts with the halakhic background and rationale for these practices and offer them the opportunity, if they so desire, to observe these additional rites.[11] The conversion is completed with a short ceremony during which the convert receives the Hebrew name he or she has chosen. The name includes the phrase "*ben* (son of) or *bat* (daughter of) Avraham Avinu (our father)," the first Jew, to indicate that the person is a convert who has terminated all formal family ties and "is considered a newly born child" (Yev. 48b). Liberal communities that also include the name of the mother use *ben* or *bat* Sarah.

Attitude toward Converts

It is forbidden to taunt converts by reminding them of their non-Jewish past and suggesting that this makes them unfit to study God's Torah

(Rashi). As the *Sifra* states, "Do not say to him: 'Yesterday you worshiped idols, and now you have come under the wings of the *Shekhinah* (Divine Presence).' "[12] Jews by birth tempted to disparage converts because they are not direct descendants of the Patriarchs must remember that their Israelite ancestors, while slaves in Egypt, had sunk to the lowest level of spiritual depravity and thus were no better than a convert before his or her conversion.[13]

In a responsum, Maimonides wrote a glowing tribute to the proselyte in answer to the question of whether a convert could use the term "God of Our Fathers" in prayer. He replied that not only were they permitted to do so, seeing that Abraham was the father of all those who believe in the unity of God, but that the status of a convert as a Jew was even superior to that of an Israelite. Although Israel's lineal descent is from the Patriarchs, that of the proselyte is from God, based on the verse: "One shall say: 'I am the Lord's,' another shall use the name of 'Jacob' " (Isa. 44:5).[14]

A Jew-by-Choice has virtually the same rights as a Jew by birth. One exception is that a female convert traditionally may not marry a Kohen, unless she became Jewish at age three or younger (Yev. 60b).[15] In the talmudic period, a convert generally could not be appointed to any public office or serve as a judge in a criminal court.

Acceptance of Converts

Because rabbis of different movements in Judaism have various standards for conversions, not all conversions are recognized by all rabbis or by all denominations. In general, most Reform and Reconstructionist rabbis will accept a conversion by any other rabbi. Most Conservative rabbis will accept conversions by other Conservative and Orthodox rabbis and by Reform and Reconstructionist rabbis if the person has gone to the *mikveh* and, if a male, has been circumcised or undergone *hatafat dam brit*. Orthodox rabbis usually accept conversions performed only by other Orthodox rabbis, though some will accept other conversions if the requirements meet Orthodox standards of *halakhah*.

Obviously, this matter is a very controversial one, with deep roots on both sides of the issue.

Controversy over Who Is a Jew

"A vexing issue in Israel is the question, "Who is a Jew?" The chief rabbinate has consistently refused to recognize as Jews those who have converted under the auspices of non-Orthodox rabbis. However, according to the Law of Return as interpreted by the Supreme Court of Israel, all converts must be registered as Jews on their identity cards and in the population registry.

Secular Jews have argued that since the essence of religion is personal belief, how can the Orthodox presume to judge the sincerity of one who has had a non-Orthodox conversion? According to Evelyn Gordon, this view of religion is essentially Christian, not Jewish.[16] The basic requirement for being a Christian—belief in Jesus—is indeed a matter of personal faith, and it would be presumptuous for anyone to judge the sincerity of the belief of a self-proclaimed Christian. However, Judaism has never viewed itself as a religion in the Christian sense; indeed, the term "religion" is not found in the Bible. Instead, there are endless references to *Am Yisrael* or *B'nai Yisrael* (People or Children of Israel). Therefore, Gordon maintains that the most accurate paradigm for the Jewish "religion" is the modern nation-state. To become a citizen of the nation-state of Judaism, one must either be born a Jew or undergo the naturalization process prescribed by law and be formally awarded citizenship by an authorized court. It is immaterial how Jewish one feels, just as it makes no difference how much you wish to become an American (or French or German) citizen and identify with the philosophical tenets of the country.

If born a citizen of a country, you remain one even if you reject all of its principles. Similarly, a Jew remains a member of *Am Yisrael* even if he or she eats pork on Yom Kippur. Using this same analogy, every nation in the world sets standards for naturalization, generally including a residency requirement, basic knowledge of the country's institutions, and a commitment to obey its laws. Just as no American judge would ever tell applicants for citizenship that they are entitled to pick and choose which American laws they wish to obey, traditional Judaism has trouble accepting a non-Orthodox conversion process that tells applicants that they can select what parts of Jewish law they wish to follow. Gordon notes that the differences between the Orthodox and Conservative conceptions of what standards a convert must observe are relatively minor; the major problem is how these standards are applied in practice.[17] However, Reform Judaism opposes conversion standards on principle, arguing that each rabbi has the power to set his or her conversion requirements. Gordon compares the situation to American judges being given permission to draft their own citizenship requirements instead of using standard American law—which she sees as the road to anarchy. According to Gordon, those who oppose non-Orthodox conversions do not question the sincerity of a convert's faith, but rather are convinced that the Jewish people is like a nation-state, whose requirement for naturalization is not belief, but a commitment to its laws.

Dreams (חֲלוֹמוֹת)

Biblical Period

Most ancient peoples considered dreams as revelations of realms that were otherwise inaccessible to the conscious thought of a wakeful mind. They served as an insight to both Heaven and the world of evil spirits and were a means of foretelling the future.[1]

The first dream mentioned in the Bible occurred not to one of the Patriarchs, but to Abimelech, the heathen king of the land of Gerar, where Abraham and Sarah had settled. Fearing for his safety, Abraham had introduced Sarah as his sister, and she was abducted into the royal household. Instead of inflicting a severe plague on the king, as had been the punishment of Pharaoh as the result of a previous similar incident (Gen. 12:14–20), God "came to Abimelech in a dream by night and said to him, 'You are to die because of the woman that you have taken, for she is a married woman'" (Gen. 20:3). As the dream continued, Abimelech protested his innocence, arguing that he was unaware of the true situation. God accepted his contention, indicating that He had stopped Abimelech from sinning by preventing him from touching Sarah (Gen. 20:6).

The Bible reports several dreams of Jacob at critical junctures when he was either leaving or re-entering his homeland. The first occurred as the Patriarch was fleeing the Land of Israel to escape from the wrath of his brother, Esau, whose blessing Jacob had stolen. Jacob dreamed of a ladder reaching toward Heaven, with angels of God ascending and descending on it. God appeared to Jacob, assuring him of the same divine promise of the land and innumerable descendants that had been given to Abraham (Gen. 12:15). When Jacob awoke from his sleep he understood that his dream had been a divine prophecy: "Surely the Lord is present in this place, and I did not know it!" (Gen. 28:16). Twenty years later, an angel of the Lord appeared to Jacob in a dream, commanding him to "arise and leave this land and return to your native land" (Gen. 31:11–13). On the night before he was to meet Esau, Jacob had the mysterious wrestling match "until the break of dawn" (Gen. 32:25), which many commentators consider to be a dream sequence. Finally, God appeared to the elderly Jacob in a dream, telling the Patriarch as he was about to embark with his family to Egypt: "I will make you there into a great nation. I Myself will go down with you to Egypt, and I Myself will also bring you back; and Joseph's hand shall close your eyes" (Gen. 46:2–4).

The master biblical dreamer and interpreter of dreams was Joseph. This youngest and most beloved son of Jacob engendered the hatred of his brothers by relating his dreams of their sheaves bowing down to his sheaves (Gen. 37:7), and of the sun (Jacob), moon (Rachel), and 11 stars (the brothers) bowing down to him (Gen. 37:9). When the brothers exclaimed, "Would you then reign over us? Would you then dominate us?" little did they realize that this would be precisely the situation when they traveled to Egypt and unsuspectingly placed themselves at the mercy of Joseph, who had become the all-powerful viceroy of the country.

Next Joseph turned to dream interpretation. After being cast into prison on the basis of false charges by Potiphar's wife, Joseph successfully interpreted the dreams of his fellow inmates: Pharaoh's cupbearer and baker. Stressing that "interpretations belong to God," Joseph correctly explained that within three days the cupbearer would be restored to his former position but that the baker would be executed (Gen. 40:5–23). Two years later, Joseph was called upon to interpret Pharaoh's dreams of the seven robust cows eaten by seven scrawny ones and the seven full ears of corn swallowed up by seven withered ones (Gen. 41:17–24). According to Joseph, these were two versions of a single dream, in which God was revealing to Pharaoh that there would be seven years of abundance followed by seven years of famine (Gen. 41:25–32). Not only did Joseph provide an interpretation, he also urged Pharaoh to select someone to amass food during the years of plenty that could be used during the years of famine. Pharaoh selected Joseph himself for this task, noting that "since God has made all this known to you, there is none so discerning and wise as you" (Gen. 41:39).

During the period of the judges, a man is reported to have dreamed that "a loaf of barley bread was whirling through the Midianite camp. It came to a tent and struck it, and it fell; it turned it upside down, and the tent collapsed"—a sign that "God is delivering Midian and the entire camp" to be conquered by "the sword of the Israelite Gideon" (Judg. 7:13–14). On one occasion, "the Lord appeared to Solomon in a dream by night," asking what he would like to receive as a divine gift. Solomon merely asked for "an understanding mind to judge Your people, to distinguish between good and bad." Pleased that Solomon had not requested "long life ... riches, [or] ... the life of your enemies," God announced that He would reward Solomon with not only the "wise and discerning mind" he had requested, but also with riches, honor, and length of days (1 Kings 3:5–15).

Dreams are associated with prophecies, and these two types of visions are often presented as a pair (1 Sam. 28:6). Just as there are false prophecies, there are also false dreams (Jer. 23:25; Zech. 10:2).

Talmudic Period

The Rabbis of the Talmud asserted a spectrum of views about dreams, though most believed that they were significant. One rabbinic source regards dreams as "a variety of prophecy" (Gen. R. 17:5). After dreaming that his nephews would lose a large sum of money, Yochanan ben Zakkai acted upon this vision, urging his nephews to give charity in the hopes that their loss would be put to good use. The Talmud remarks that Rabbi Hanina refused to forgive Rav for insulting him because of a dream that he interpreted to mean that Rav was going to replace him as head of the talmudic academy (Yoma 87b).

Other Rabbis believed that dreams were only somewhat revealing. "While part of a dream may be fulfilled, the whole of it is never fulfilled" (Ber. 55a). Rabbi Yochanan attempted to determine which dreams would be realized: "Three kinds of dreams are fulfilled: an early morning dream, a dream which a friend has about one, and a dream which is interpreted in the midst of a dream." Others rejected the veracity of dreams outright. Rabbi Meir remarked that "dreams neither help, nor harm" (Hor. 13b). Rabbi Jonathan claimed that dreams derive from within, not from a prophetic source. "A man is shown in a dream only what is suggested by his own thoughts" (Ber. 55b). He deduced this from the statement of Daniel (2:29) to the

Babylonian king: "the thoughts that came to your mind in your bed." Rava also believed that internal temperament affects the content of dreams, suggesting that a good dream is caused by happiness, particularly the happiness that follows the fulfillment of a commandment (Shab. 30b).

Based on the statement, "fasting is potent against a dream," after a bad dream some sages observed a *ta'anit chalom* (dream fast), even on the Sabbath or a festival if the dream was especially troubling (Shab. 11a). An alternative was to recite a special prayer during the Priestly Blessing: "If they are good dreams, confirm and reinforce them like the dreams of Joseph, and if they require a remedy, heal them as the waters of Marah were healed by Moses, our teacher, and as Miriam was healed of her leprosy and Hezekiah of his sickness, and the waters of Jericho by Elisha. As You turned the curse of the wicked Balaam into a blessing, so turn all my dreams into something good for me" (Ber. 55b). An intriguing ritual based on talmudic teaching is *hatevet chalom* (remedying the dream), in which the dreamer asks three close friends to assemble on the morning after the dream to encourage the dreamer to interpret the dream for good (Ber. 55b). The three friends open the ritual by reciting in unison, "Do not interpretations belong to God?" This is followed by the responsive recitation of various verses, some of which are repeated three times. It is recommended (but not required) that the dreamer fast and repent on the day of the ritual.[2]

Medieval Period

Maimonides, the quintessential rationalist, deemed dreams a function of the "imaginative faculty" rather than the intellect. In contrast, the Zohar, the classic text of Jewish mysticism, considered dreams as having substantial import: "nothing takes place in the world except what has previously been made known, either by means of a dream or by means of a [divine] proclamation." In the past, prophets and wise sages were the intermediaries, but since they no longer exist, "that which is to come is revealed in dreams." Some medieval and even later thinkers depended on dreams when deciding on matters of religious law. However, other scholars vehemently attacked this practice.

Excommunication (חֵרֶם)

In the Bible, *herem* (the later Hebrew word for "excommunication") refers to any person or item that was separated from common use or contact, either because it was forbidden as an abomination or was consecrated to God. When the prophet Samuel relayed to King Saul the divine order to wage a war of extermination against Amalek for its cowardly ambush of the Israelites after the Exodus, Saul's failure to completely carry out this command resulted in his losing the kingship (1 Sam. 15; 1 Chron. 10:13). Earlier, Joshua (6:17–21) had ordered that his troops destroy all the inhabitants of Jericho, man and beast, and dedicate their objects of precious metal to the Sanctuary. When Achan defied the ban and "took some of the forbidden things" (Josh. 7:1),[1] he was stoned to death (Josh. 7:27).

Whatever one privately devoted to the Lord was deemed *herem* and considered sacred in the highest degree *(kodesh k'doshim)*. Once dedicated to God, this status was irrevocable. The object could be neither sold by the Sanctuary nor redeemed by the donor (Lev. 27:28); it belonged to the *Kohanim* (Num. 18:14).

The first indication of *herem* in the context of excommunication occurs in the period following the return from Babylonian exile, when loss of property and separation from the community was mentioned as a penalty to coerce individuals to obey communal authorities (Ezra 10:8). During talmudic times, compulsory isolation of varying length and severity was imposed on individuals who violated the rules of the community. In the Middle Ages, when Jewish communities were autonomous jurisdictions, it became particularly important to guard the integrity of the community and its laws. Thus someone who subverted community norms—such as by disobeying decisions of the court or by insulting authority figures—could be punished with the severe but appropriate measure of *herem*. The threat of excommunication was also used to ensure general acceptance of and obedience to new laws. Thus Rabbenu Gershom's bans on polygamy and divorcing a wife against her will were enforced by the threat of a *herem* against any person who violated them. Restrictions on the living conditions of the person under excommunication were intensified during this period. The Talmud prohibited coming within four cubits (six feet) of someone under *herem*; but in medieval times social, religious, and economic sanctions were sometimes extended to the family of the excommunicated person as well. Someone in *herem* could not have his sons circumcised, and his wife and children were barred from the synagogue. Symbolic measures, such as the cutting of the excommunicated person's tzitzit, were also introduced.

Excommunication was an awesome ritual, pronounced with the sounding of the shofar in front of the open ark while those in the congregation held black candles that were symbolically extinguished as the ritual was completed. Biblical curses were hurled at the person being excommunicated, and a public warning was issued forbidding all to associate with him.

Famous Excommunications

The threat of excommunication was a potent rabbinic tool to force individuals to conform their actions and beliefs to the norms of the community. One who was unwilling to alter his philosophy was Baruch Spinoza, who in the 17th century criticized what he perceived as the internal contradictions in the Pentateuch and rejected its Mosaic authorship as well as the concept of a transcendent God who related to human beings. Spinoza stopped attending synagogue and succeeded in persuading many of the youth of the community of the validity of his ideas, which were also considered blasphemous by the Christian Church. Fearful that Spinoza's activities could lead to the expulsion of the Jews from Amsterdam, the leaders of the community pleaded with him to repudiate his heretical beliefs. When he refused, Spinoza was excommunicated and completely isolated from all Jewish contact. However, this had little effect on Spinoza, who was able to earn a living by grinding optical lenses and never renounced his beliefs or returned to the Jewish community.[2]

At times, excommunication has been used to ban the writings of an individual. The classic example is Maimonides, the major medieval Jewish philosopher and author of an encyclopedic code of Jewish Law (*Mishneh Torah*) and a seminal philosophical work (*Guide of the Perplexed*). Despite almost universal praise for these books, some rabbis attacked Maimonides' unwillingness to accept everything in the Bible as literal truth—such as God having human form and attributes—as well as his attempt to find rational explanations for miracles.

However, these rabbis were particularly incensed by what they deemed Maimonides' arrogance in claiming that his systematization of the entire corpus of Jewish law would replace the Talmud, making it unnecessary to consult the classic compendium in the future. Shortly after Maimonides' death, the rabbis of northern France placed a *herem* on the philosopher's works, banning his books from their communities. Scholars and community leaders of southern France and Spain countered by issuing a *herem* of their own against these opponents of Maimonides, and it took almost two centuries for this acrimonious controversy to be resolved.[3]

Mutual excommunications characterized the bitter 18th-century dispute between the Vilna Gaon, the foremost talmudic scholar and halakhic authority of his age, and the new Hasidic movement. In his edict of excommunication, the Vilna Gaon condemned the practice of Hasidic worship: "In their recitation of the Eighteen Benedictions (*Amidah*) they roar in abominable words in the vernacular and they behave in a crazed manner and say that their thoughts wander in all the worlds. They belittle the study of Torah and repeatedly claim that one should not study much, nor deeply regret one's transgressions." In response to what was regarded as an "act of war," the Hasidim declared that the Vilna Gaon was excommunicated. After the latter's death, relations between the two groups worsened even further, with both the Hasidim and the *mitnagdim* (lit., "opponents"; those who supported the Vilna Gaon) viciously attacking each other in print and instituting severe economic sanctions against the other. Eventually, these antagonistic movements united in opposition to a new common enemy that threatened the very survival of traditional Judaism—the Enlightenment.[4]

A famous modern case of excommunication involved Mordecai Kaplan, controversial founder of the Reconstructionist movement. Highly critical of both the Orthodox and Reform movements, Kaplan's philosophical ideas and modified liturgy offended many in the Jewish world. In 1945, the Assembly of the Union of Orthodox Rabbis of the United States unanimously issued a proclamation of excommunication (the first in its 43-year history) against Kaplan and burned his *Sabbath Prayer Book*, which embodied his ideas.

The plethora of excommunications (and counter-excommunications) ultimately weakened the credibility of *herem*. Changes in the nature of Jewish authority also affected *herem*. When Jewish communities were self-ruled, excommunication was socially and economically crippling; but after the Emancipation, when Jews became citizens of the secular state, the ramifications of *herem* were less acute. Some European governments even outlawed *herem*. Although still sometimes declared by extreme Orthodox authorities, excommunication has ceased to be of any relevance for the vast majority of Jews.

Golem (גּוֹלֶם)

A golem is a legendary creature that is made of clay and dust by human hands in a magical, artificial way to serve its creator. The word appears only once in the Bible, where it refers to "unformed limbs" (Ps. 139:16). In describing the first 12 hours of Adam's existence, the Talmud calls him a golem, a "shapeless mass" fashioned into a body that did not yet possess a soul (Sanh. 38b). It also observes that "if the righteous desired it, they could [by living a life of absolute purity] be creators ... Rava created a man and sent him to Rabbi Zera, who spoke to him and, receiving no answer, said to the man: 'You are a creature of the magicians. Return to your dust'" (Sanh. 65b).

The legend of the golem became fully developed during the Middle Ages, under the influence of non-Jewish European folklore and the Kabbalah. According to *Sefer Yetzirah* and other mystical books, it is possible (using a detailed set of instructions) to create living beings out of earth by using secret combinations of the letters of the Hebrew alphabet, the names of the 10 *sefirot*, and the secret names of God. Legends maintain that a golem is incapable of speech and lacks a soul but has superb vision and superhuman strength and generally follows its master's orders without question.[1]

Making a golem could be a dangerous endeavor and should be attempted only by those who are extremely pious and deeply immersed in the divine mysteries. Some golems reportedly went out of control and began to destroy the villages (and their inhabitants) in which they were made. If the golem had been created by writing the Hebrew word "אמת" (*emet*; "truth") on its forehead, it could be destroyed by erasing the first letter to produce the word "מת" (*met*; "dead"). If one had created a golem by placing the name of God in its mouth, all that was needed was to remove the parchment. Another way to control a runaway golem and return it to dust was to recite in opposite order the words initially used to create it.[2]

The most famous golem legend involves Rabbi Judah Loew (16th century), known as the Maharal (acronym of *Moreinu* [our teacher] *ha-Rav Liva*) of Prague, who created one to protect the Jews of his city against a false charge of blood libel. One night, he and two disciples sculpted a giant body out of clay taken from the banks of the Moldau, bringing it to life through a series of mystical incantations, invocations of the four elements (fire, water, air, earth), and walking around the creature in a prescribed pattern. On Friday, the Maharal is said to have removed the spirit of life from his golem so that it would not desecrate the Sabbath. Once the Prague Jewish community had been saved, the Maharal reversed the spell and returned the golem into lifeless clay, which was hidden in the attic of the synagogue. In a variant of the legend, which is eerily similar to the story of Frankenstein's monster three centuries later, the Maharal created the golem to serve him, but was compelled to turn the creature back into dust when it got out of control and threatened the lives of members of the community.

Heavenly Bodies

Sun (שֶׁמֶשׁ)

God created the sun (*shemesh*) on the fourth day of Creation as "the greater light to dominate the day" (Gen. 1:16). Israel's pagan neighbors worshiped the sun as a god, so this was a particularly important articulation of the idea that God held dominion over the sun. Psalm 74:16 reiterated that God is the Creator of the sun, and Job (9:7) referred to God as the One "who commands the sun not to shine." The Torah expressly forbids sun worship (Deut. 4:19, 17:3), and one who violated this prohibition was to be stoned at the gates of the city (Deut. 17:2–5). Apparently, this did not dim the allure of sun worship, as evidenced by the fact that King Manasseh built altars in the Temple dedicated to the heavenly luminaries (2 Kings 21:3). Ezekiel (8:16) also testified to sun worship in the Temple. In 621 B.C.E., King Josiah destroyed Manasseh's altars as well as chariots that had been dedicated to sun worship.

Hellenized Jews renewed worship of the sun and even wore amulets, blasphemously referring to Helios (the Greek sun god) as

"God in the Heavens." Mosaic floors in some ancient synagogues, especially Beit Alpha in the Galilee, depicted Helios as a handsome youth riding in a chariot drawn by the four horses of the sun (placed in the center of the signs of the zodiac).[1]

To counteract this popular fascination with the sun and to prevent their straying from strict monotheism, the Rabbis developed an aggadic tale that personified the sun and the moon and was based on an apparent conflict in the Creation chapter of Genesis (1:16): "God made the two great lights, the greater light to dominate the day and the lesser light to dominate the night; and the stars," which implies that the two major heavenly bodies initially were of equal size. However, when mutual jealousy led each heavenly body to claim that it should be larger than the other, the moon was reduced in size because it had unlawfully intruded into the domain of the sun, by sometimes remaining visible while the sun was still above the horizon (Gen. R. 6:3; PdRE 6). In another version of the tale, the moon asked God: "Can two kings share a single crown?" When God responded that the moon should make itself smaller, the latter replied: "Because I presented a proper claim, must I be diminished?" Recognizing the justice of the moon's plea, God compensated the moon by decreeing that only it would be seen both day

BLESSING OF THE SUN (בִּרְכַּת הַחַמָּה)

Once every 28 years, at the vernal equinox early on the first Tuesday of the month of Nisan, the sun begins a new cycle. After the morning service on Wednesday (the day that the sun was created), Jews traditionally recite *Birkat ha-Hamah* (Blessing of the Sun), a service that thanks God for the sun and its continued blessings. At the conclusion of the ritual, worshipers express the hope that they will be privileged to live until the coming of the Messiah, to witness the fulfillment of the prophesy of Isaiah (30:26), "and the light of the sun shall become sevenfold, like the light of the seven days." The next occasion for the *Birkat ha-Hamah* service will be in 2009.

and night. God also gave the moon an honor guard of stars and assured it that the Jewish people would calculate months and years by its phases (Hul. 60b).[2]

The Bible relates two instances in which the position of the sun deviated from the normal course of nature. As night approached while the Israelites were defeating the Amorites, Joshua declared "in the presence of the Israelites, 'Stand still, O sun, at Gibeon, O moon, in the Valley of Aijalon!'" These heavenly bodies obeyed, "while a nation wreaked judgment on its foes," and the Bible describes this as a unique day "when the Lord acted on words spoken by a man" (Josh. 10:14). In the second instance, Isaiah asked God to make the shadow of the sun retreat 10 degrees as a sign that Hezekiah would be healed of his illness (2 Kings 20:8–11).

The Rabbis also concerned themselves with the intrinsic nature of the sun. The motes dancing in the sun's rays have healing powers (Ned. 8b), and sunshine (like the Sabbath) is considered a foretaste of the world to come (Ber. 57b). Determining the precise color of the sun stirred a rabbinic controversy (BB 84a). Some of the sages argued that its real color was red, as at sunrise and sunset, but that the sun appears white during the day because its powerful rays dim the sight of human beings. Others maintained that the true color of the sun is white, but that it appears red in the morning, "because it passes by the roses of the Garden of Eden [which is in the East; Gen. 2:8] and at sunset, because it passes the gate of Gehenna [and thus reflects the fires of Hell]."

As among most ancient peoples, eclipses were thought to be an evil portent, particularly for Jews, "because they are inured to blows" (Suk. 29a). Indeed, Rabbi Meir compared this "to a school teacher who comes to school with a strap in his hand. Who becomes apprehensive? He who is accustomed to be daily punished." According to another opinion, a solar eclipse was a bad omen for the idolaters (gentiles) and a lunar eclipse for the Jews, since the Jews base their calendar on the moon, while the idolaters base theirs on the sun.

The Talmud outlines specific meanings for eclipses, based on their location in the sky:

> If an eclipse occurs in the east, it is a bad omen for those who dwell in the east; if in the west, it is a bad omen for those who dwell in the west; if in the midst of Heaven [zenith of the sky], it is bad omen for

> the whole world. When the color of the ellipse is red, the sword is coming to the world [a sign of war]; if it is like sackcloth [dark and overcast], the arrows of famine are coming to the world; if it resembles both, the sword and the arrows of famine are coming to the world. If the eclipse occurs at sunset, calamity will be delayed; if at dawn, it hastens on its way [evil will come soon] (Suk. 29a).

However, Jews who are loyal to their faith need not be concerned about these dire premonitions. The Talmud observes that, unlike members of other nations, Jews should "not be awed by the signs in the heavens" (Suk. 29a on Jer. 10:2).

Moon (יָרֵחַ, לְבָנָה)

God created the moon (*yare'ach* or *levanah*) on the fourth day of Creation "to dominate the night" (Gen. 1:16). As with the sun, the Israelites were forbidden to worship the moon, and those who defied this ban were to be stoned at the gates of the city (Deut. 4:19, 17:2–5). Still moon worship, like sun worship, continued. King Manasseh set up altars to the celestial bodies (2 Kings 21:3); and during Jeremiah's (44:17) time, the Israelites worshiped the moon as the "Queen of Heaven." As noted previously, according to tradition, the moon and sun were originally created of equal size, but the moon was subsequently diminished. The Rabbis explained that the male goat offered on the day of New Moon represented a sin offering brought by God to atone for this arbitrary decision.

The moon represents Jacob and thus is a symbol of the Jewish people. Although the sun, a symbol of Esau, is the brighter of the two major luminaries, only the moon shines both day and night, an indication that only Israel has a portion both in this world and the world to come (Gen. R. 6:3).[3] "The countenance of Moses was like that of the sun; that of Joshua was like the moon" (BB 75a), since his glory was inferior to that of Moses. The waxing moon was deemed a favorable time for Israel, whereas a lunar eclipse was considered an evil omen, attributed in the Talmud to the four sins of "forgery, false witness, raising small cattle in the Land of Israel [which damaged the crops of the field], and cutting down fruit trees" (Suk. 29a).

The New Moon (Rosh Hodesh; see p. 166) was proclaimed by the

Sanhedrin, which sent word throughout the land first by mountaintop signal fires and later by special messengers. A minor holiday since Second Temple times, Rosh Hodesh has become the focus of particular celebration by Jewish women. Rosh Hashanah is the only major Jewish festival to begin on the new moon. Passover, Sukkot, and Purim begin at the full moon, as do the midwinter holiday of Tu b'Shevat (see p. 252) and the midsummer festival of Tu b'Av (see p. 307), which are precisely six months apart. Only Hanukkah begins during the waning moon, though it continues for several days after the appearance of the new moon.[4]

Stars (כּוֹכָבִים)

Stars are a biblical symbol of limitlessness, as in the divine promise to Abraham that his descendants would be "as numerous as the stars of Heaven and the sands on the seashore" (Gen. 22:17). This verse is sung at the *Havdalah* ceremony (see p. 147), when the presence of three stars in the sky on Saturday night indicates the conclusion of the Sabbath. Stars also are a symbol of prophecy. A midrash relates that a bright star appeared in the eastern sky marking the birth of Abraham (*Sefer Yashar Noah* 18a–19a), which is strikingly similar to the Christian description of the astral activity accompanying the birth of Jesus. When forced to bless Israel against his will, Balaam predicted that "a star rises from Jacob, a scepter [leader] comes forth from Israel; it smashes the brow of Moab" (Num. 24:17), an ironic conclusion to the prophecy of this pagan seer who had been hired by Balak, the king of Moab, to curse the Israelites. When the Jews revolted against Roman rule in 135 C.E., the rebel leader, Bar Koziba, was nicknamed "Bar Kokhba" (son of a star) because of the general belief that he was the Messiah of Balaam's prophecy. Christians were convinced that the biblical verse referred to Jesus, whose birth they asserted was heralded by the "star of Bethlehem."[5]

Astrology (אֲסטרוֹלֹגְיָה)

Astrology is the study of how the stars allegedly influence human events and the development of a systematic attempt to use this knowledge to predict the future.

Biblical and Talmudic Periods

Although astrology is not specifically mentioned in the Torah, the Rabbis interpreted the passages dealing with the diviner (Lev. 19:26) and the soothsayer (Deut. 18:10) as forbidding people from regulating their conduct by using an astrological forecast of good luck or success to decide whether the time was auspicious for a particular action. However, most talmudic sages appeared to believe that celestial bodies were powerful determinants of human affairs: "[Length of] life, children, and sustenance depend not on merit but [rather on] *mazal* [the stars]" (MK 28a); others deemed this to apply only to gentiles and argued that "Israel is immune from planetary influence" (Shab. 156a).

One page of Talmud goes into painstaking detail as to the effect of the day and month of birth on the character of the individual (Shab. 156a). There Rabbi Joshua ben Levi notes that a person born on Sunday will have one perfect attribute, "completely virtuous or completely wicked," since "light and darkness were created on that day" (and the person's nature will be one or the other). One born on Monday will be "bad-tempered" since "the waters were divided on that day" (division or disunity is caused by bad temper, making the individual estranged from others). A person born on Tuesday will be "wealthy and unchaste," since "herbs were created on that day" (they multiply rapidly and continually intermingle with each other). One born on Wednesday will be "wise and have a retentive memory," because "the luminaries [sun, moon, and stars] were suspended then." A person born on Thursday will "practice benevolence," because "the fishes and birds [which are fed by God's lovingkindness] were created then." One born on Friday will be "a seeker after good deeds" (just as one on the eve of the Sabbath seeks to complete every detail necessary for proper observance of that sacred day). Finally, a person born on the Sabbath "will die on the Sabbath, because the great day of the Sabbath was desecrated on his account" (though some say that this applies only to those who are very holy and pious).

Rabbi Hanina disagreed, maintaining that "not the constellation [sign] of the day but that of the hour is the determining influence." The Talmud (Shab. 156a) relates that a person born under the constellation of the sun (acting as one of the planets) will be a "distinguished [bright, handsome] man; he will eat and drink of his own and his secrets will lie uncovered; if a thief, he will have no success." One born under Venus will be "wealthy and unchaste [immoral]," because "fire was created therein." A person born under Mercury "will have a retentive memory and be wise," because "Mercury is the sun's scribe." One born under the moon will be "a man to suffer evil, building and demolishing, demolishing and building; eating and drinking that which is not his and his secrets will remain hidden: if a thief, he will be successful" (just like the moon, which waxes and wanes, has no light of its own but merely reflects the sun's light, and is basically dark). A person born under Saturn will "have his plans frustrated," though others assert that, "all [nefarious] designs against him will be frustrated." One born under Jupiter will be "righteous ... in good deeds." A person born under Mars will be "a shedder of blood—either a surgeon, a thief, a slaughterer, or a circumciser."

Post-Talmudic Period

Several medieval Jewish scholars, including Saadiah Gaon and Abraham ibn Ezra, were great students of astrology. Conversely, Maimonides utterly rejected astrology, attacking what he regarded as "the absurd ideas of astrologers, who falsely assert that the constellation at the time of one's birth determines whether one is to be virtuous or vicious, the individual being thus necessarily compelled to follow a certain line of conduct." Instead, "man's conduct is entirely in his own hands, no compulsion is exerted, and no external influence is brought to bear upon him that constrains him to be either virtuous or vicious."[6] However, despite Maimonides' august standing in the Jewish community, his criticism of astrology had virtually no effect.

Although such mystical texts as the *Sefer Yetzirah* (Book of Creation) and *Sefer Razi'el ha-Malach* (Book of the Angel Raziel) contain material relating to astrological topics, the Zohar generally downplays the significance of astrology. Indeed, it indicates that all creatures initially depended on the stars; however, after giving the Torah at Sinai, God exempted those Jews who studied and observed the Law from the rule of these astral bodies.

Mazel tov (good luck; lit., "good star") has become the most common congratulatory expression among Jews. A person who succeeds in all his endeavors is known as a *bar mazel* (son of luck), while one who fails at everything is scorned by the Yiddish term "*shlimazel.*"

Zodiac (The Wheel of Stars; גַּלְגַּל הַמַּזָּלִים)

Many ancient peoples believed that the character traits and ultimate fate of a person depended on the astrological sign under which he or she was born. The 12 constellations of astrology were represented by symbols arranged in a circular pattern known as the zodiac, from a Greek word meaning "little animals." The 12 signs and their relation to the months of the Hebrew year are as follows: Aries (Nisan), Taurus (Iyar), Gemini (Sivan), Cancer (Tammuz), Leo (Av), Virgo (Elul), Libra (Tishrei), Scorpio (Heshvan), Sagittarius (Kislev), Capricorn (Tevet), Aquarius (Shevat), and Pisces (Adar). These symbols were frequently incorporated in early Jewish art, especially on the mosaic floors of ancient synagogues such as Beit Alpha, and later in *ketubot* (marriage contracts). Some images of the zodiac were even inserted into prayer books flanking the special prayers for dew on Passover (see p. 292) and rain on Shemini Atzeret (see p. 239).[7] Although popular, the zodiac is not part of contemporary normative Judaism.

Kissing Holy Objects

Kissing holy objects is a widespread custom. Though not a religious duty, it expresses a depth of reverence and spiritual devotion. The following practices are commonly observed:[1]

- The two ends of the *atarah* of the tallit are kissed just before putting on the prayer shawl (see p. 379).
- The tefillin are kissed when taken out and returned to their bag (see p. 382).
- The tzitzit (fringes) are kissed at the end of *Baruch she-Amar* and during the recitation of the *Shema* (see p. 378).
- The curtain on the ark (*parochet*) is kissed before opening and after closing (when the Torah is taken out and then returned).
- The Torah mantle is kissed when it passes by in procession in the synagogue (see p. 441).
- The Torah scroll is kissed before one recites the blessings over it, either with the intermediary of the edge of the tallit or the sash used to tie the scroll together, but never with the bare hand (see p. 449).
- A siddur (prayer book) and *Humash* (Five Books of Moses) are

kissed before being put away; they also are kissed if accidentally dropped on the floor.

- The mezuzah on the doorpost is kissed when entering or leaving a house (see p. 582).

Kitel (קִיטֶל)

A *kitel* (Yiddish for "gown") is a white robe (usually with a lace collar and belt) that was once worn every Sabbath and is now used in some Ashkenazic communities on special occasions and as a shroud. Its use as a shroud was mentioned as early as the 12th century by Rabbi Eleazar of Worms. The white color, traditionally representing purity and forgiveness of sin, makes the *kitel* appropriate for worshipers during prayer services on the High Holy Days (Rosh Hashanah and Yom Kippur). Wearing the *kitel* is similarly an attempt to mimic the angels who are "clothed in white," and it also hearkens back to temple times, when the *Kohen Gadol* entering the Holy of Holies on Yom Kippur was clad in simple white linen garments rather than his usual golden vestments. Because of its use as a shroud, the *kitel* is a reminder of death, which also befits the somberness of the High Holy Days. A wedding day is considered a "day of atonement" leading to the start of a new and pure life, so the bride and groom traditionally fast and the groom wears a *kitel*. In view of the ancient belief that rain and dew are withheld from the community because of the sins of the people, prayer leaders wear a white *kitel* during the solemn prayers for dew on Passover (see p. 292) and for rain on Shemini Atzeret (see p. 239). As the symbol of a new beginning, the white kitel is also worn by the person conducting the Passover seder (where all assembled symbolically leave the slavery of Egypt for newfound freedom) and by the father at the circumcision of his son (to initiate the newborn into the covenant). Although traditionally worn by men, some women have begun wearing them. [1]

The Messiah (מָשִׁיחַ)

The word "messiah" comes from the Hebrew word "*mashiach*" (anointed), reflecting the practice in ancient Israel (as elsewhere in the Near East) of anointing kings (and priests) with olive oil. In Judaism, "messiah" came to refer to a divinely appointed redeemer who would rule over a restored kingdom of Israel where the dispersed Jews would be gathered at the end of days. Absolute trust in the ultimate coming of the Messiah is a core belief in Judaism and one of Maimonides' Thirteen Principles of Faith (see p. 509): "I believe with perfect faith in the coming of the Messiah, and though he may tarry, still I await him every day."

With the establishment of the monarchy in Jerusalem around 1000 B.C.E. by King David, the Israelites believed his descendants would rule their people forever (2 Sam. 7:13). With the division of the kingdom after the death of his son Solomon, the people looked forward to the time when someone from the Davidic line would reign over a reunited Israel (Northern Kingdom) and Judah (Southern Kingdom). Isaiah and the other prophets wrote of a future Messianic Age, an ideal time of peace and justice (Isa. 11). In the Book of Zechariah, written during the Second Temple period, there is mention of two messianic figures, a king (Zech. 9:9) and a priest (Zech. 6:13). Gradually, the concept of Messiah developed into the vision of a single Davidic king (*Mashiach ben David*), who would conquer the enemies of Israel, return the Jewish people from exile, rebuild the Temple and reinstitute the sacrificial cult, and establish a kingdom of God in which peace would come to the entire earth. A second Messiah (*Mashiach ben Joseph*) would precede the messianic king and be killed in an epic battle with the enemies of God and Israel.[1]

The Jews denied the messianic claims made on behalf of Jesus on two basic grounds: he did not bring about political sovereignty for the Jews or protection from their enemies, and he did not usher in the era of world peace as described in the prophecy of Isaiah (2:4): "Nation shall not take up sword against nation, neither shall they learn war any more."[2] A century later in 135 C.E., many (including Rabbi Akiva) believed that the Messiah had come in the figure of Bar Kokhba, the charismatic leader of the disastrous Jewish rebellion against Rome, though he himself denied this role.

In Jewish tradition, the Messiah has always been depicted as a human agent of divine redemption. The concept of a divine or semidivine "savior," whose self-sacrifice will save mortals from the punishment merited by their sins, is a purely Christian idea that has no foundation in Jewish thought. The Messiah is imagined as riding into Jerusalem on a donkey (Zech. 9:9), a white horse (Sanh. 98a), or the clouds of Heaven (Dan. 7:13); sitting among the lepers (in Rome), untying and retying his bandages (Sanh. 98a); or ascending the Mount of Olives heralded by a shofar blast of the prophet Elijah.[3] According to various legends, the Messiah was born in Bethlehem on the day that the Temple was destroyed (Mic. 5:1), was present at the Creation of the world, or was here even before the world was created (PR 36:161).

Throughout the Middle Ages and early modern times, Jews speculated extensively on the apocalyptic end of days, attempting to determine precisely when the Messiah would appear. Among the dozens of dates proposed were several that coincided with major upheavals in the world and terrible persecutions of the Jews: the onset of the Crusades (1096), the years of the Black Death in Europe, the expulsion of Jews from Spain (1492), and the vicious pogroms in Poland and Ukraine (1648). As each date proved not to be accurate, the explanation was always that the Jews were not sufficiently righteous to accept the Messiah, and a new date was set. Many prominent rabbis attacked

WHEN WILL THE MESSIAH COME?

Normative Judaism teaches that one should work actively to bring the Messiah, by doing everything possible to perfect the world (*tikun olam*), rather than simply waiting passively for him to come. Even the advent of the Messiah will not relieve human beings of responsibility for taking care of the world. This is illustrated by the statement of Rabbi Yochanan ben Zakkai, "If you are planting a tree, and you hear that the Messiah has come, finish planting the tree and then go greet him" (ARN 31).

The Talmud teaches, "The Messiah will come if every Jew observes the Sabbath twice in a row" (Shab. 118b). Other scholars stress that the Messiah will come only when we are ready. The Talmud relates that Rabbi Joshua ben Levi found Elijah the Prophet, disguised as a filthy beggar, sitting at the gates of Rome. He asked, "When will you come and proclaim the Messiah?" Elijah replied, "Today, if you will only hear his voice" (Sanh. 98a).[1]

those predicting the date of the Messiah's coming, arguing that when this did not transpire the masses might lose faith in both the messianic concept and Judaism itself. Indeed, this actually occurred in the 17th century, when the infamous Shabbetai Zevi proclaimed himself the Messiah and attracted thousands of followers. When Zevi's messianic claims proved false and he converted to Islam under threat of death, many disillusioned Jews converted with him.[4]

In modern times, classical Reform Judaism replaced the concept of a personal Messiah with the belief in a future Messianic Age of universal justice, a utopian era that will result from the efforts of human beings in perfecting the world rather than via a messenger sent by God. This movement attacked as too particularistic the traditional association of a return of the exiles to Zion and the rebuilding of the Temple. Instead of regarding the destruction of the Temple and the exile of the Jewish people as catastrophic events, they were viewed as valuable opportunities to spread the moral and ethical values of Judaism throughout the world. In contrast, Orthodox Judaism still firmly believes in the doctrine of a personal Messiah, a descendant of the House of David. Many Orthodox rabbis initially opposed Zionism as a "secular messianic movement" in which human beings were brazenly attempting to abrogate the divine prerogative of determining when the Messiah would come. However, after the establishment of the State of Israel, the general Orthodox view (as found in most prayer books) is that Israel represents *reishit tz'michat g'ulateinu* (the dawn of our redemption). This was accentuated after the Six-Day War of 1967, in which Israel captured the Old City of Jerusalem and for the first time in more than two millennia achieved Jewish rule over all of their biblically ordained homeland. Nevertheless, some extreme Orthodox sects do not recognize the political existence of the Jewish state, because the Messiah has not yet come to redeem the people.[5]

The Messiah in Festivals and Imagery

Yearning for the coming of the Messiah plays a major role in the Jewish festivals and liturgy. The Sabbath has always been considered a foretaste of the Messianic Age and the world to come. Jews traditionally eat fish on the Sabbath as a symbol of Leviathan, the great sea monster (see p. 301), which will be the messianic meal for the righteous. According to tradition, the Messiah will come during *Havdalah* (see p. 150), when

Jews sing *Eliyahu ha-Navi* (Elijah the Prophet) in the fervent hope that the Messiah will come soon, "speedily in our days." Similarly, there is a chair for Elijah (see p. 11) at every circumcision, since this Jewish child may be the long-awaited Messiah, as well as a cup of Elijah (see p. 288) at the Passover seder.[6]

The *Musaf Kedushah* states, "He is our Savior, and He will let us hear, in His compassion, for a second time in the presence of all the living ... to be a God for you." The "second time" refers to the concept of a total redemption of the Jewish people in the Messianic Age, unlike the limited deliverance that ended the Babylonian exile and led to the building of the Second Temple.[7] There is also the tradition that the Messiah will be born on Tisha b'Av, the anniversary of the destruction of the Temples in Jerusalem (see p. 304). Jews pray for the redemption of the Holy Land and the rebuilding of the Temple at the close of both the seder and the *Ne'ilah* service on Yom Kippur (see p. 220), by exclaiming, "Next year in Jerusalem." The shofar of Rosh Hashanah will ultimately herald the arrival of the Messiah (see p. 191). Even the Hanukkah dreidel (see p. 251) has messianic overtones, for the numerical value of the letters on its four faces (358) is the same as the Hebrew word "*mashiach*."[8]

The Messianic Age of universal peace is described as a time when "the wolf shall live with the sheep, and the leopard lie down with the kid; the calf with the young lion shall grow up together, and a little child shall lead them" (Isa. 11:6). It will be a time when "every man shall sit under his grapevine or fig tree with no one to disturb him" (Mic. 4:4). Traditionally, the dead are buried with their feet facing Jerusalem, along with earth from the Holy Land, awaiting the final resurrection of the dead when the Messiah comes (see p. 619).

Mizrach (מִזְרָח)

"*Mizrach*" (east) is the term for a calligraphic design or ornamental plaque that hangs on the eastern wall in many Jewish homes and synagogues to indicate the direction in which to pray and to aid in meditation. The Hebrew word comes from a root meaning "to cast forth rays," as the sun does every morning when it rises in the east. In impoverished European homes where even a simple plaque was not affordable, Jews sometimes produced the same effect by skipping a brick or leaving a small portion of the eastern wall unplastered.[1]

From Temple times to the present, Jews have faced Jerusalem when they pray. According to the Talmud, a person praying in the Diaspora must turn toward the Land of Israel; in the Land of Israel, toward Jerusalem; in Jerusalem, toward the Temple; and in the Temple, toward the Holy of Holies (Ber. 30a). "In this way, all Israel will be turning their hearts [in prayer] towards one place." Consequently, the term "*mizrach*" really only applies to locations west of Jerusalem. Muslims also initially faced toward Jerusalem when praying, but Muhammad subsequently changed the direction of prayer to Mecca after the Jews rejected his teachings.

Traditionally, the *mizrach* on the eastern wall of the home contains this Hebrew word, as well as the verse from Psalms (113:3), "From the rising (*mi-mizrach*) of the sun until its going down, the name of the Lord is to be praised." Many include other biblical, liturgical, and kabbalistic verses, such as "from this direction comes the spirit of life," the first letters of which in Hebrew spell "*mizrach*." Often paper cuts in Eastern Europe, *mizrachim* are commonly adorned with pictures of animals or kabbalistic symbols.[2] As a device to orient the home on a symbolic axis toward the site of the Temple in Jerusalem, the *mizrach* often includes images of Temple implements, the Holy City, and prominent figures in Jewish history.[3]

Beginning in the 18th century, the eastern wall of some synagogues became identified by an ornamental plaque known as the *shivti*, a term derived from the verse, *Shiviti Adonai le-negdi tamid* ("I have set the Lord always before me"; Ps. 16:8).[4] Traditionally, the eastern wall was the site where seats were reserved for the rabbi and other dignitaries. *Hatikvah* (The Hope; see p. 578), the national anthem of the State of Israel, proclaims, "As long as the eye looks eastward, gazing toward Zion, our hope is not lost."[5]

Names of God

In the biblical view, a name describes the essential character of each creature and its function in the overall divine plan for the world. After indicating that it was not good for Adam to be alone and that the first human needed a companion, God brought him all the beasts of the field and birds of the sky: "Whatever the man called each living creature, that would be its name" (Gen. 2:19). Radak noted that Adam was able to perceive the fundamental nature of every animal and thus named each accordingly. However, when it soon became apparent that none was Adam's social, intellectual, or spiritual equal, God immediately created woman.[1]

The names of God reflect the various ways in which the divine manifestations are perceived by human beings. At the Burning Bush, when Moses inquires of God how he should reply to the Israelites asking, "What is His name?" (Exod. 3:13), he is not seeking merely an appellation but rather information about the essential nature of God that he can convey to the people. God's response—*Eh'yeh Asher Eh'yeh* (אֶהְיֶה אֲשֶׁר אֶהְיֶה; "I am Who I am" or "I will be What I will be")—indicates that God is timeless and eternal, the God of Creation and their ancestors (past) who is cognizant of their suffering in Egyptian slavery (present) and will soon redeem them from bondage (future). Another example of the expansive use of the Hebrew word "name" in Judaism are the concepts of *kiddush ha-Shem* (sanctification of God's name) and *hillul ha-Shem* (profanation of God's name), which refer, respectively, to any actions that increase or harm the reputation of God or Judaism, or the respect that other nations have for them.

Biblical Period

Over the centuries, Jews have coined many names for God. At first, these were borrowed from their pagan neighbors. The oldest of these names is "*El*," which is often incorporated as the first part of a biblical name (Elijah, Elisha) or, more commonly, as the last syllable (Israel, Ishmael, Samuel, Daniel). "*El*" (אֵל) often appears as the first element in compound names of the Divine, such as *El Elyon* (אֵל עֶלְיוֹן; "Most High God") and *El Shaddai* (אֵל שַׁדַּי; "God Almighty"). For the Canaanites, the term "*El Elyon*" referred to the supreme deity and ancestor of their other gods, whereas in Israel it expressed the absolute transcendence of the One True God (Gen. 14:22).

In the Bible, the full name "*El Shaddai*" is used only in connection with the Patriarchs (Exod. 6:3). According to a midrash, the name derives from a Hebrew root meaning "sufficient" (as in the Passover song, *Dayenu*; see p. 279) and refers to the fact that the newly created universe continued to expand until God declared *dai* (enough). Rashi interpreted "*Shaddai*" as implying either the omnipotence ("sufficient power") of God or that the divine mercy of God is enough to outweigh the divine justice in forgiving human beings for their sins. Some have noted the relationship of "*Shaddai*" to "*shadai'im*" (breasts) and the fact that the blessings containing the name "*Shaddai*" deal with fruitfulness and fertility (e.g., Gen. 7:1, 28:1, 35:11, 49:25) as indications that the term refers to the nurturing aspect of God.[2] The name "*Shaddai*" also is written on the back of the mezuzah scroll (see p. 580), because it is considered an acronym for *Shomer daltot Yisrael* (Guardian of the doors of Israel).

The first and one of the two major biblical names of God is *Elohim* (אֱלֹהִים), a plural word in Hebrew that is used more than 2,000 times and is often preceded by the definite article as *ha-Elohim* (the [true] God). This paradoxical use in Hebrew of a plural noun to designate the one God of Israel illustrates the many manifestations of the Deity. Similarly, another common biblical name for God, *Adonai* (אֲדוֹנָי; lit., "my Lords"), is also in the plural form. "*Elohim*" sometimes refers to princes, judges, and even other gods, and it is used when stressing God's might, creative power, and attributes of justice and sovereignty.

The holiest name of God, and the one that is most distinctly Jewish, is written in the Hebrew Bible with the four consonants YHVH—*yud, hei, vav, hei* (יהוה). Referred to as the "Tetragrammaton" (Greek for "four-letter word"), it occurs 6,823 times in the Bible[3] and probably reflects a form of the verb "to be." It may have derived from "*Eh'yeh Asher Eh'yeh,*" the name by which God was revealed to Moses at the Burning Bush (Exod. 3:14). In the Bible, YHVH is used when describing the relationship between God and human beings or when stressing the divine qualities of lovingkindness and mercy. The first two letters ("Y" and "H") are often added at the beginning or end of a Hebrew name, as in Yehoshua (Joshua, meaning "the Lord is my salvation") and Eliyahu (Elijah, meaning "My God is the Lord"), and in the familiar *Halleluyah* ("praise the Lord").[4]

YHVH is often combined with "*Tzeva'ot*" into a phrase that is usually translated as "Lord of Hosts." This latter Hebrew word refers to an army or other military group, and thus the name is a manifestation of divine sovereignty. YHVH *Tzeva'ot* does not occur in the Torah, but is common in the prophetic books and found extensively in the Psalms.[5]

According to tradition, YHVH was regularly pronounced with its proper vowels by all Israelites, at least until the destruction of the First Temple in 586 B.C.E. However, its use was eventually restricted to the *Kohen Gadol* in the Holy of Holies on Yom Kippur, and other *Kohanim* when reciting the Priestly Blessing during the daily services in the Temple. When the Temple was destroyed, the word lost its vocalization. By the time of the Talmud, the term "*Adonai*" was generally substituted for YHVH, as is still the custom in the standard prayer formula, "*Baruch ata Adonai.*" Indeed, some Rabbis went so far as to state that a person who pronounced "YHVH" according to its letters (the "Ineffable Name") should be put to death and would have no place in the world to come.

In the early Middle Ages, when vowel points were introduced into the purely consonantal text of the Bible to preserve the traditional reading, the four consonants of YHVH were vocalized with vowels borrowed from *Adonai*, resulting in the mistaken reading by Christian scholars of "YHVH" as "Jehovah." Another suggested pronunciation is "*Yahweh*" (from the alternate designation YHWH), in view of the fact that its first syllable (*yah* or *yahu*) frequently serves as the final syllable in many Hebrew names. To avoid pronouncing even the sacred name "*Adonai*" for YHVH, Jews began substituting "*ha-Shem*" (lit., "the Name"), thus emphasizing the strict prohibition against pronouncing the Tetragrammaton.[6]

Although the refusal to pronounce the name YHVH is generally ascribed to a sense of reverence, some argue that that it actually was caused by a misunderstanding of the Third Commandment (Exod. 20:7; Deut. 5:11). Although the plain meaning of the verse "You shall not take the name of YHVH, your God, in vain," seems to prohibit using God's name altogether, its true meaning is that "You shall not swear falsely by the name of YHVH your God." For the Mishnah, a vain oath is one that "is contrary to the facts known to man, saying a pillar of stone is of gold, or of a man that he is a woman, or if he swore concerning a thing that is impossible [a camel flying in the air]" (Shev. 29a). YHVH is now often abbreviated as a pair of *yuds* (יי). This practice probably evolved from the *Targumim* (Aramaic translations of the Hebrew Bible), which abbreviated this name of God as two *yuds* with a *vav* across the top.[7]

The prohibition against pronouncing the name of God applied only to the Tetragrammaton (YHVH). Nevertheless, it became the accepted custom among Orthodox Jews to use variations of most of the divine names in speech, particularly "*Elokim*" for "*Elohim*" and "*ha-Shem*" for "*Adonai*."

Several names of God used in the Apocrypha are still used in Hebrew prayers. These include "the Praiseworthy God" (אֵל הַתִּשְׁבָּחוֹת; *El ha-Tish'bachot*), "Shield of Abraham" (מָגֵן אַבְרָהָם; *Magen Avraham*), and "Supreme King of Kings" (lit., "King over the king of kings"; מֶלֶךְ מַלְכֵי הַמְּלָכִים; *Melekh malkhei ha-melakhim*). During this period, the word "Heaven" (God's abode) was substituted for "God" (Himself), a usage that still persists in such modern English expressions as "Heaven help us!"

Talmudic Period

The Rabbis developed a number of additional names for God that referred to the divine attributes and are found frequently in the liturgy. The most common is "*ha-Kadosh baruch Hu*" (הַקָּדוֹשׁ בָּרוּךְ הוּא; "the Holy One, praised be He"). Others are as follows:

- *Ribbono shel Olam* (רִבּוֹנוֹ שֶׁל עוֹלָם), "Sovereign of the Universe."
- *Ha-Makom* (הַמָּקוֹם; lit., "the place"), "the Omnipresent."
- *Ha-Rachaman* (הָרַחֲמָן; derived from "*rechem*" [womb]), "the All-Merciful," which is used particularly in the Grace after Meals.
- *Avinu Malkeinu* (אָבִינוּ מַלְכֵּנוּ), "Our Father, Our King," which especially occurs in prayers on the High Holy Days.
- *Avinu she-ba-Shamayim* (אָבִינוּ שֶׁבַּשָּׁמַיִם), "Our Father in Heaven," which opens the modern prayer for the State of Israel.
- *Melekh ha-Olam* (מֶלֶךְ הָעוֹלָם), "Ruler of the Universe," which concludes the opening formula of all blessings.
- *Shekhinah* (שְׁכִינָה), "Divine Presence," which is often depicted as the feminine aspect of God.

The Talmud makes reference to a 12-letter name of God that "used to be entrusted to all people, but when unruly men increased [who were not fit to pronounce it], it was confided to the pious of the priesthood, and they 'swallowed it' [pronounced it indistinctly] during the chanting [of the benediction] by their brother priests" (Kid. 71a). A 42-letter name of God was "entrusted only to him who is pious, meek, middle-aged, free from bad temper, sober, and not insistent on his rights."

The Rabbis prohibited writing the name of God, except in sacred texts (Shev. 35a–b). This specifically applied to seven biblical names: *El, Elohim* (also with suffixes), *Eh'yeh Asher Eh'yeh, Adonai,* the Tetra-grammaton, *Shaddai,* and *Tzeva'ot*. The reason for prohibiting the writing of the name of God for secular purposes was based on the fear that any paper on which it was casually written might later be defaced, obliterated, or destroyed accidentally by someone who did not know any better. The commandment not to erase the name of God is derived from the biblical verse in which the Israelites, after conquering the Promised Land, are to destroy everything connected with the idolatry of the Canaanites, including the order to "obliterate their name from that site" (Deut. 12:3). This is immediately followed by the verse, "Do not worship the Lord your God in like manner," which the Rabbis interpreted as meaning that it was forbidden to destroy any sacred object or erase a name of God. This prohibition even extends to the writing of the number "15" in Hebrew letters, which spell one of the names of God. Instead of the expected *yud hei* (10 + 5), it is written *tet vav* (9 + 6), since the former is a common abbreviation of the four-letter name of God.[8]

According to recent rabbinic decisions, this prohibition against writing the name of God applies only when it is in some "permanent" form and not to typing on a computer. Consequently, it is not a violation to backspace over the name of God or to use the "cut and paste" features of a word processor; nor is it forbidden to copy and delete computer files containing a divine name. However, once the document is printed, it becomes "permanent" and cannot be erased. Therefore, many traditionally observant Jews do not write the name of God on Internet websites, lest someone print it out and subsequently deface it.[9]

Another controversial issue is whether in correspondence it is permitted to use the names of God in the vernacular. Many traditional Jews never write the word "God" or any other divine name in full, even in the vernacular, preferring to use such designations as "G-d" and "L-rd."

Out of respect, documents containing the Hebrew name of God are buried rather than merely thrown away.

Post-Talmudic Period

The kabbalists articulated an intricate theology in which God's essential self was ineffable and the manifest attributes of the Divine were dynamic. They called God's essential self *"Ein Sof"* (אֵין סוֹף; the "Infinite" or "Eternal"; lit., "without end"), and God's 10 knowable attributes are called *"sefirot,"* usually translated as "emanations." The kabbalists had many other names for God, such as "the Hidden of the Hidden" and "Ancient of Ancients." Nachmanides suggested that the words of the Torah are a combination of God's names. Similarly, Abulafia believed that by mixing up and recombining words of the Torah one could form divine names and achieve prophecy. Kabbalistic sources also mention a 72-letter divine name—a combination of the number of Hebrew letters in the names of the 12 tribes and the Patriarchs, plus the nine Hebrew letters of the words *"shiv'tei Yisrael"* (the tribes of Israel)—and a 22-letter divine name.

The medieval philosophers used names for God that accorded with the Greek philosophy that influenced them. Thus God was often referred to as the "First Cause" or the "Prime Beginning." However, some of the medieval philosophers also went out of their way to stress that YHVH was the exclusive name of God, with all other appellations referring to the various divine attributes. This was an important distinction for thinkers who vehemently defended God's unity, both as a philosophical necessity and as a characteristic that distinguished Judaism from Christianity.

Since the Middle Ages, the various names of God have been increasingly associated with magic and inscribed on amulets to enhance their power to heal the sick and prevent the Evil Eye. In Eastern Europe during the 17th and 18th centuries, a miracle worker was known as *Baal Shem* or *Baal Shem Tov* (Master or Owner of the Good [Holy] Name). The most famous of these was the founder of the Hasidic movement, Israel ben Eliezer, who was popularly known as the Baal Shem Tov or the BeShT.[10]

Numbers (מִסְפָּרִים)

In the Bible, numbers are often more than just quantitative indicators and are replete with symbolic significance. Even when numbers are used to indicate quantity, they are not necessarily to be taken literally and may represent approximations or hyperboles. For example, the Book of Daniel (7:10) mentions the "thousands upon thousands" who served the "beast." The largest real biblical number is David's census of the northern tribes, which indicated 1,100,000 men capable of bearing arms compared to 470,000 from Judah (1 Chron. 21:5). The Bible also recognizes that some numbers are beyond human comprehension, as in the divine promise to Abraham, "I will make your offspring [as countless] as the dust of the earth" (Gen. 13:16). The following sections discuss numbers that are especially prominent in the biblical text and that have symbolic meaning.

One (אֶחָד)

The number "one" (*ehad*) is the quintessential number of Jewish monotheism, best expressed in the central affirmation of faith, *Shema Yisrael, Adonai Eloheinu, Adonai Ehad* (Hear O Israel, the Lord is our God, the Lord is One)[1] (Deut. 6:4; see p. 413). The commentators stress that "*ehad*" also means "unique" and that the numerical value of the Hebrew word equals 13, the traditional number of divine attributes (see p. 642). Other liturgical references to the oneness of God include *Adon Olam* ("He is One and there is no second to compare with Him"; see p. 471), *Yigdal* ("He is One, and there is no unity like His oneness"; see p. 470), the ceremony for taking out the Torah ("One is our God, great is our Master, Holy is His Name"), and the messianic conclusion of the *Aleinu* ("On that day, God will be One and His Name will be One"; see p. 466).

"One" is also a symbol of marriage, the joining of two human beings into a single entity. "Hence a man leaves his father and mother and clings to his wife, so that they become one flesh" (Gen. 2:24). After the wedding ceremony, the bride and groom spend a few quiet moments alone, a custom called "*yichud*" (solitude, from a root implying "together as one"). Originally an occasion for consummating the marriage, *yichud* is now simply a time for the couple to relax and break their fast before joining family and friends for the postnuptial festivities (see p. 40).[2]

Two (שְׁתַּיִם)

The number "two" (*sh'tayim*) is mentioned in many places in the Torah. The Ten Commandments (see p. 489) were inscribed on two tablets of stone, the Israelites collected a double portion of manna on Friday to last them through the Sabbath, when all work was forbidden (Exod. 16:22), and the unclean animals entered Noah's ark two by two (Gen. 6:19). Furthermore, pairs of contrasting siblings play major roles among the ancestors of the Jewish people—Isaac and Ishmael, Jacob and Esau, Rachel and Leah.

In Jewish tradition, two goats are featured in the Yom Kippur ritual (Lev. 6:8–10), one for a sin offering and the other "designated for Azazel" (see p. 224). This number is also noted in the two parts of the tefillin (see p. 382). Moreover, the testimony of two witnesses is required in capital and other criminal cases under Jewish law (Deut. 8:6).

The fraction "one-half" also occurs in the Bible, as in the half tribe of Manasseh (Num. 32:33) and the half shekel that was used for the first census of the Israelites and later annually for the upkeep of the Temple (Exod. 30:11–16).

Three (שָׁלוֹשׁ)

According to *Pirkei Avot* (1:2), the continued existence of the world depends on three things: Torah (study), *avodah* (initially the Temple service, later prayer), and *gemilut hasadim* (deeds of lovingkindness). The number "three" (*shalosh*) is a common biblical number. For example, there are three Patriarchs (Abraham, Isaac, and Jacob), three pilgrimage festivals (Passover, Shavuot, and Sukkot), and three major divisions of the Bible—Torah, Nevi'im (Prophets), and Kethuvim (Writings), which form the acronym "TANAKH."

"Three" is also important in Jewish liturgy. There are three major prayer services on weekdays—*Shacharit* (Morning), *Mincha* (Afternoon), and *Ma'ariv* (Evening)—and three formal meals on the Sabbath, the last of which is known simply as *seudah shelishit* (the third meal). The Sabbath (and festivals) conclude with the appearance of three stars in the evening sky. The Priestly Blessing (see p. 432) has three verses in which the Tetragrammaton occurs three times (Num. 6:24–26), and there are three declarations of God's holiness (*kadosh, kadosh, kadosh*; Isa. 6:3), echoing the angelic choir in the *Kedushah* of the *Amidah* (see p. 429). At the Passover seder, the three matzot represent the basic divisions of the Jewish people (Kohen, Levite, Israel), which are also recognized during the traditional Torah service. On Rosh Hashanah, the shofar is sounded three times in combinations of three different notes (see p. 192). Three people are called to the Torah on a regular Monday or Thursday morning, and there are three rabbinic commandments specifically for women: taking challah (see p. 141), going to the *mikveh* (see p. 555), and lighting Sabbath candles (see p. 136).

The Sanctuary had three divisions, a court, a holy place, and a Holy of Holies (Exod. 26:33, 27:9; 1 Kings 6:16–17), and a Jewish court (*beit din*) is composed of three judges.

Many biblical passages include the number "three." Genesis (10:1) notes that after the Flood the human race descended from the three sons of Noah (Shem, Ham, Japheth). Three "men" announced to Abraham that the aged Sarah would bear him a son (Gen. 18:14). Later, Abraham was commanded to sacrifice this son after a three-day journey to Mount Moriah (Gen. 22:4). The story of Joseph's interpretations of the dreams of his fellow prisoners, Pharaoh's butler and baker (Gen. 40), is replete with the number "three": three tendrils of grape vines, three wicker baskets containing bread, and three days (on Pharaoh's birthday) before each met his fate. Moses' mother hid her newborn baby at home for three months to protect him from Pharaoh's killers (Exod. 2:1). When the grown Moses later appeared before Pharaoh, he asked for permission to take the people on a three days' journey into the wilderness so that they might bring offerings to God (Exod. 3:18).

"Three" is also a classic number in folklore. Magical actions were performed three hours before sunrise, three days before the new moon, or three days in a row. Magical rituals required three objects, incantations were repeated three times, and any occurrence (especially dreams) that took place three times was deemed an omen.[3] The protective function of this number may be the basis of the custom of making three circles with the hands upon lighting the Sabbath candles and spitting three times to prevent the adverse effects of the Evil Eye (see p. 584).

In Kabbalah, the 10 *sefirot* are often grouped together into the three higher (representing the "hidden" or transcendent aspects of the Divine) and the seven lower emanations.[4]

Four (אַרְבַּע)

The number "four" (*arba*) plays an important role in both the Bible and Jewish tradition. There were four biblical Matriarchs (Sarah, Rebecca, Rachel, and Leah), and Jacob had four "wives" (Rachel, Leah, Bilhah, and Zilpah, although the last two are more generally termed "maid-servants" or "concubines"), who gave birth to the 12 tribes (three times four), the ancestors of the Jewish people. According to the Torah, four rivers flowed out from the Garden of Eden (Gen. 2:10), and the holiest name of God consists of the four letters YHVH (Tetragrammaton; see p. 626). In Ezekiel's vision of the divine chariot (Ezek.1:10), which symbolized the spirit of God and was the source of intense mystical speculation, there were four cherubim, each with four faces and four wheels.

The number "four" commonly appears in the observance of the festivals. At the Passover seder there are four questions (see p. 276), four cups of wine (see p. 274), and four kinds of children (see p. 277). The Tu b'Shevat seder also has four cups of wine that represent both the changing seasons and the four worlds, according to the Kabbalah (see p. 253 The four species on Sukkot have a variety of symbolic meanings and are waved during *Hallel* and carried in procession around the synagogue (see p. 233).

"Four" is also important in Jewish prayer. The tallit (prayer shawl; see p. 377) worn during the morning service is a four-sided garment, as is the *tallit kattan* (little tallit; see p. 382), an undergarment with fringes that is traditionally worn by Orthodox Jewish men and boys. Jews pray daily for the ingathering of the exiles from "the four corners of the earth" (*arba kanfot ha-aretz*).

Jewish literature contains many references to the number four. *Pirkei Avot* (Ethics of the Fathers) contains several lists of fours, including character types (5:13), temperaments (5:14), qualities of students (5:15, 18), charitable dispositions (5:16), and reasons for going (or not going) to the house of study (5:17).[6] Furthermore, the most authoritative code of Jewish law (the Shulchan Arukh of Yosef Karo; see p. 506) contains four sections: Orach Hayim, concerning the daily commandments, Sabbaths, and festivals; Yoreh De'ah, dealing with subjects such as dietary laws, interest, purity, and mourning; Even ha-Ezer, on marriage, divorce, and related topics; and Hoshen Mishpat, dealing with civil and criminal law.

Five (חָמֵשׁ)

"Five" (*hamesh*) has been a fundamental number since antiquity, based on the fingers of the hand used by early human beings in their simple calculations. In Judaism, the major use of the number "five" is the designation of the Torah as the *Humash*, the Five Books of Moses (Genesis, Exodus, Leviticus, Numbers, and Deuteronomy). There are five *megillot* (The Song of Songs, Ruth, Lamentations, Ecclesiastes, and Esther), five species of grain indigenous to the Land of Israel (wheat, barley, spelt, oats, and rye), and five Hebrew letters that have a final letter (*kaf*, ך; *mem*, ם; *nun*, ן; *peh*, ף; *tzadi*, ץ).

The connection between the number "five" and the human hand is found in many aspects of Jewish life. For example, the five-fingered hand, in the form of the *hamsa* (see p. 584), is a popular amulet in Mediterranean and North African communities to ward off the ill effects of the Evil Eye. The practice of the *Kohanim* spreading out their fingers when reciting the Priestly Blessing (see p. 432) may also have originated in the popular belief of the number "five" as a symbol of divine protection.[7]

Six (שֵׁשׁ)

The Bible mentions the number "six" (*sheish*) in connection with a variety of phenomena. For example, the Torah notes that there are six days of Creation (Gen. 2:2) and hence six working days of the week (Exod. 20:9). There were six cities of refuge where those who had committed accidental homicide could flee to escape the blood avenger (Num. 35:6), and the maximum time that a Hebrew slave could serve was six years (Exod. 21:2). The number "six" is reflected in traditional Jewish writings as well. For example, there are six orders of the Mishnah (see p. 499)—*Zera'im* (Seeds), *Mo'ed* (Festivals), *Nashim* (Women), *Nezikin* (Damages), *Kodashim* (Holy Things), and *Tohorot* (Purities)—as well as six chapters in *Pirkei Avot*.[8] A major symbol of Judaism is the Magen David (see p. 575), a six-pointed star.

"One-sixtieth," a fractional multiple of six, is commonly used in the Talmud. "Five things are a sixtieth part of something else: namely, fire, honey, Sabbath, sleep, and a dream. Fire is one-sixtieth part of *Geihinnom* (Hell). Honey is one-sixtieth part of manna. Sabbath is one-sixtieth part of the world to come. Sleep is one-sixtieth part of death. A dream is one-sixtieth part of prophecy" (Ber. 57b). Elsewhere it is written, "He who visits an invalid takes away a sixtieth of his pain" (Ned. 39b). In Jewish dietary laws, the prohibition of most forbidden food accidentally mixed with permitted food is nullified if it constitutes less than one-sixtieth of the total volume (though this does not apply to *hametz* on Passover, where even the most minute amount renders everything with which it has been mixed forbidden).

Seven (שֶׁבַע)

"Seven" (*sheva*) was a holy number for many early civilizations, which worshiped seven heavenly bodies (sun, moon, and the five visible planets of Mercury, Venus, Mars, Jupiter, and Saturn). There are many other universal occurrences of "seven." For example, there are seven days in the week, and the lunar month is divided into four quarters of a little more than seven days each. "Seven" is also the sum of the sacred numbers "three" and "four." There are seven colors of the rainbow, and seven notes in the Western musical scale.[9]

The Bible abounds in the number "seven." Most significant is that God rested on the seventh day after the six days of Creation. There were seven ritually clean animals in Noah's ark (Gen. 7:2), seven ancestors of Israel (three Patriarchs and four Matriarchs), and seven cows and ears of corn in Pharaoh's dreams that were interpreted by Joseph (Gen. 41:1–7).

The Torah notes that the period of ordination of the *Kohanim* and consecration of the altar was seven days (Exod. 29:35–37; Lev. 8:33–35), the *Kohen Gadol* sprinkled sacrificial blood seven times (Lev. 4:6,17; Num. 19:4), and there are seven species of foods indigenous to the Land of Israel (see p. 667). Seven Hebrew letters in the Torah are adorned with crowns (*tagin*; see p. 327): ג (*gimel*), ז (*zayin*), ט (*tet*), נ (*nun*), ע (*ayin*), צ (*tzadi*), and ש (*shin*).[10] The Israelites made seven circuits around Jericho on the seventh day before the walls of the city came tumbling down (Josh. 6:15–16). The Hebrew name "Bathsheba" (the wife of David and mother of Solomon) literally means "daughter of seven."

Other traditional Jewish works also mention the number "seven," as in the seven chords of David's harp (Num. R. 15:11) and the seven prophetesses (Sarah, Miriam, Deborah, Hannah, Abigail, Hulda, and Esther; Meg. 14a). According to tradition, Moses was born and died on the Seventh of Adar.

There are seven Noahide laws, which were deemed the basis of any civilized society:

- Do not murder.
- Do not steal.
- Do not worship false gods.
- Do not practice sexual immorality.
- Do not eat the limb of an animal before it is killed.
- Do not curse God.
- Establish courts and brings offenders to justice.

Similar to many cultures, Jews base their calendar on sevens. The Hebrew word for week is "*shavuah*," which is derived from the word "*sheva*" (seven). On the Sabbath, the seventh day, the Torah reading is divided into seven portions. There are seven leap years in the 19-year cycle of the Jewish calendar. The sabbatical year, when the land was to lay fallow, occurred every seven years, and there were 49 years ("seven cycles of seven years") between jubilee years (Lev. 25:2–8).

The number "seven" occurs frequently in Jewish practice and prayer. According to the Bible, Passover and Sukkot are seven-day holidays (see p. 264, 227) and the High Holy Days occur during the seventh month of Tishrei. There are 49 days (seven times seven, or seven weeks) of counting the Omer between Passover and Shavout (see p. 292). At the conclusion of the *Ne'ilah* service on Yom Kippur, the congregation affirms seven times: "The Lord, He is God"—the words of the Israelites who fell on their faces after witnessing Elijah miraculously defeat the priests of Baal (1 Kings 18:39).[11] There are seven processions with the *lulav* on Hoshana Rabbah and with the Torah on Simchat Torah.

Life-cycle events, festivities, and ritual objects in Jewish tradition often come in sevens as well. There are seven wedding blessings (*Sheva Brachot*) and seven days of wedding festivities, based on the example of Jacob when he married Leah (Gen. 29:27–28), for whom he had toiled for seven years. When his father-in-law Laban failed to offer Rachel as a bride, Jacob was forced to work for an additional seven years to gain her hand (Gen. 29:30), though these "seemed to him but a few days, for the love he had for her."[12] Among Ashkenazim, the bride typically circles the groom seven times under the *huppah*.

Other traditions incorporate the number "seven." There is a seven-day period of intense mourning after a funeral (shivah; lit., "seven"; see p. 95), and Sephardic Jews circle a coffin seven times. The menorah (see p. 578) in the Temple had seven branches (Exod. 25:31–37), and the tefillin (see p. 382) are wrapped around the arm seven times.

Eight (שְׁמוֹנֶה)

The most important use of "eight" (*shemoneh*) in Jewish tradition is in connection with circumcision (*brit milah*; see p. 7), the first life-cycle ritual that a Jewish male undergoes, which occurs on the eighth day of life and represents the covenantal relationship between God and Abraham (Gen. 17:11–12). Other biblical references to this number include the eight days that an animal had to remain with its mother before it could be sacrificed (Exod. 22:29) and the eight garments worn by the *Kohen Gadol* (Exod. 28); these include:

- Ephod, a short, close-fitting apron worn around the body under the arms, with straps over the shoulders to keep it in place.
- Breastplate, in which were set the 12 precious stones, each engraved with the name of one of the tribes of Israel.
- Golden head plate, inscribed "Holy to the Lord."
- Mitre, possibly a type of turban.
- Robe, a long garment worn under the ephod.
- Tunic.
- Girdle (sash).
- Breeches.

Additional uses of eight are the eight days of Hanukkah (see p. 244) and Maimonides' eight degrees of charity (see p. 537).[13]

Ten (עֶשֶׂר)

Both in biblical times and today, the basis of calculations is the decimal system, which is based on the number "10" (*eser*) and derived from the number of fingers that human beings use in counting. The sum of the sacred numbers "three" and "seven," "10" is also the sum of the first four numbers.

The most famous biblical use of the number is the Ten Commandments (see p. 489). In the bargaining between Abraham and God over the fate of the wicked cities of Sodom and Gomorrah, the final agreement was that they would be spared if 10 righteous souls could be found (Gen. 18:22–23). Before the Exodus, God brought 10 plagues upon Egypt (see p. 280). The Bible also mentions the 10 generations from Adam to Noah (Gen. 5) and from Noah to Abraham (Gen. 11:10–27),[14] 10 tests of faith by which God tried Abraham, and the 10 tests of faith by which the Israelites tried God in the wilderness.

Pirkei Avot offers a series of lists in which the number "10" plays a major role. Based on the biblical text, it recounts (5:1-6) 10 sayings by which the world was created (all but one introduced by the Hebrew word "*va-yomer*" [and God said]):

- Let there be light (Gen. 1:3).
- Let there be an expanse in the midst of the water (Gen. 1:6).
- Let the water below the sky be gathered into one area, that the dry land may appear (Gen. 1:9).
- Let the earth sprout vegetation (Gen. 1:11).
- Let there be lights in the expanse of the sky to separate day from night (Gen. 1:14).
- Let the waters bring forth swarms of living creatures (Gen. 1:20).
- Let the earth bring forth every kind of living creature (Gen. 1:24).
- Let us make man in our image, after our likeness (Gen. 1:26).
- See, I give your every seed-bearing plant ... and every tree [with fruit]; they shall be [yours] for food (Gen. 1:29).
- It is not good for man to be alone (Gen. 2:18).

Pirkei Avot (5:8) also lists 10 miraculous things that were created at twilight as the sixth day of Creation drew to a close:

- The mouth of the earth that swallowed up Korah and his fellow conspirators (Num. 16:32).
- The mouth of the well that supplied water for the Israelites in the wilderness.
- The mouth of the donkey that spoke to Balaam (Num. 22:28).
- The rainbow that was shown to Noah after the Flood.
- The manna that came from Heaven to feed the Israelites for 40 years in the wilderness.
- The staff on which was engraved the four-letter name of God, with which Moses performed the signs in Egypt (Exod. 4:17).

- The *shamir*, a worm that could split large stones by crawling on them and thus took the place of conventional tools in the construction of the Temple (for which no sword or iron, symbols of violence, could be used).
- The forms of the letters (Hebrew alphabet) engraved on the tablets of the Ten Commandments.
- The instrument used to engrave the tablets of the Decalogue.
- The first set of stone tablets of the Ten Commandments, which were miraculously written "on both their surfaces [sides]" (Exod. 32:15), unlike the second set, which was carved by Moses himself.

This work also describes 10 miracles attributed to the holiness of the Temple (5:7):

- No woman miscarried from the scent of the holy meat.
- The sacrificial meat never became putrid.
- No fly was seen in the slaughterhouse.
- No seminal emission occurred to the *Kohen Gadol* on Yom Kippur (rendering him ritually impure and unable to perform the atonement service).
- The rain never quenched the fire on the woodpile on the altar.
- The wind did not disperse the vertical column of smoke from the altar.
- There was never a disqualifying defect in the Omer, the two loaves, or the showbread.
- The people stood crowded together, yet had enough space to prostrate themselves.
- Neither a serpent nor a scorpion ever caused injury in Jerusalem.
- No one ever said to his fellow, "There is not enough space for me to stay overnight in Jerusalem."

The number "10" also is important in Jewish prayer. The Rabbis established 10 as the minimum number for a minyan (see p. 372), a quorum for a communal prayer service (Ber. 21b; Meg. 23b). There are the Ten Days of Repentance between Rosh Hashanah and Yom Kippur (see p. 204), 10 verses in each of the three special sections (*Malkhuyot*, *Zichronot*, *Shofarot*) recited in the *Musaf Amidah* on Rosh Hashanah (see p. 197), and 100 (10 times 10) blasts of the shofar on that day (see p. 193). On Yom Kippur, the 10th of Tishrei, the Martyrology service describes the 10 rabbis executed by the Romans, which one legend claims was punishment for the betrayal of Joseph by the other 10 sons of Jacob.[15] The *Megillah* on Purim recounts the 10 sons of Haman, who were slain after the death of their notorious father (Esther 9:7–10).

Historically, the conquest of the Northern Kingdom of Israel in 721 B.C.E. led to the Jews of this region being scattered throughout the Assyrian empire and disappearing—the "10 lost tribes."

In Kabbalah, there are 10 *sefirot* representing the emanations of God:[16]

- *Keter* (crown)
- *Hokhmah* (wisdom)
- *Binah* (understanding)
- *Hesed* (mercy)
- *Din* or *Gevurah* (judgment or power)
- *Tiferet* (beauty)
- *Netzach* (eternity)
- *Hod* (majesty)
- *Yesod* (foundation)
- *Malkhut* (kingdom)

Twelve (שְׁתֵּים–עֶשְׂרֵה)

"Twelve" (*shteim-esrei*) has magical qualities as the product of three and four, whose sum is seven. A common number in dealing with the heavenly bodies, there are (a little more than) 12 months in the lunar year, two 12-hour periods in the day, and 12 signs of the zodiac.

The major biblical use of the number is the 12 tribes of ancient Israel, which can be listed in two different ways. First, Jacob had 12 sons: Reuben, Simeon, Levi, Judah, Dan, Naphtali, Gad, Asher, Issachar, Zebulun, Joseph, and Benjamin (Gen. 29–30, 35:16–18). However, for purposes of settling the Promised Land, Joseph received a double share that was passed on to his sons, Ephraim and Manasseh (Gen. 48:5–6). The post-settlement listing of the 12 tribes of Israel excludes Levi, because this tribe inherited the priesthood rather than any of the tribal lands and was scattered among the people. Jews today are the descendants of the two southern tribes (Judah and Benjamin) plus the Levites, since the 10 northern tribes were lost after the Assyrian conquest (see above).

Other biblical uses of "12" and its multiples include the 12 tribes of Ishmael (Gen. 17:20), the 12 "minor" prophets,[17] the 12 loaves of showbread used in the Tabernacle (Exod. 25:30; Lev. 24:5–9), the 24 classes of *Kohanim* and Levites (1 Chron. 24:4–25:31), the 24 districts that each sent a delegation of eminent and pious Israelites to Jerusalem to represent it at the daily public offerings for one week every six months (*Anshei Ma'amad* [men of standing]; see p. 317), the 48 levitical cities (Num. 35:7), and the 24,000 men in the monthly courses that served King David (1 Chron. 27:1–15). At the age of 12, a Jewish girl first becomes obligated to fulfill the mitzvot (see p. 26).

Thirteen (שְׁלוֹשׁ-עֶשְׂרֵה)

Although "13" (*sh'alosh-esrei*) is an unlucky number in many cultures (as in Friday the 13th), it has many positive connotations in Judaism. Thirteen is the age of bar mitzvah (see p. 23), when a boy reaches his religious and legal maturity and becomes responsible for fulfilling all the mitzvot. After the disastrous episode with the Golden Calf, God revealed to Moses the Thirteen Attributes of Mercy (see p. 180), which are the answer to the final question in *Ehad Mi Yode'a*? ("Who knows one?"; see p. 289) in the Passover haggadah. In the opening lines of the mystical Zohar, the divine attributes are said to surround the Jewish people like a "13-petaled rose." In the talmudic period, Rabbi Ishmael developed 13 exegetical principles with which to explain the Torah (often included in traditional prayer books). The Thirteen Principles of Faith (see p. 509) compiled by Maimonides has been repeated for centuries in the form of the popular hymn, *Yigdal* (see p. 470). The fringes (tzitzit) of the tallit (prayer shawl) contain five knots binding eight threads for a total of 13, which is also the numerical value of the Hebrew letters in the word "אֶחָד" (*ehad*, "one") that is used in the *Shema* to indicate the unity of God (א = 1, ח = 8, ד = 4).[18]

Eighteen (שְׁמוֹנֶה-עֶשְׂרֵה)

The core of the weekday prayer services is the 18 blessings of the *Amidah* (see p. 421), which is also known as the *Shemoneh Esrei* (lit., "the

18," though now there are actually 19 blessings). According to the Rabbis, these blessings correspond to the 18 times the name of God is mentioned in the *Shema* and Psalm 29, and to the "18 vertebrae in the spinal column" (Ber. 28b). (Note that *Amidah* means "standing [prayer].") The name of God appears 18 times in *Shirat ha-Yam* (Song at the Sea; Exod. 15:1–21; see p. 409), which celebrates the divine miracle that enabled the Israelites to pass on dry land while the pursuing Egyptians drowned. On Passover, the entire process of preparing the matzah, from kneading to final baking, may not exceed 18 minutes. Sabbath candles are lit 18 minutes before sundown. "Eighteen" is the numerical value of *chai* (life), which consists of the letters "ח" (8) and "י" (10). Many Jews wear the Hebrew word "*chai*" as a pendant or good luck charm and give charity in multiples of 18.[19]

Multiples of 18 include the 36 righteous people (*tzadikim*), unknown to the world and even to themselves, who appear in every generation and for whom the world is sustained. They often are called the "*lamed-vavniks,*" since the numerical values of the Hebrew letters "*lamed*" and "*vav*" are 30 and 6, respectively. There is also a mystical 72-letter name of God (18 times the four-letter "YHVH").

Twenty (עֶשְׂרִים)

On two occasions in the Bible, "20" (*esrim*) denotes the age for assuming responsibility. During the second year after the Exodus from Egypt, God commanded Moses to take a census of the Israelite males 20 and older to determine the number "able to bear arms" (i.e., eligible for military service). Similarly, every male of this age became obliged to contribute a half shekel for the support of the Temple (Exod. 30:14). After 20 years of a barren marriage, Rebecca finally bore Isaac twin sons, Jacob and Esau (Gen. 25:20,26).

Forty (אַרְבָּעִים)

In the Bible, the number "40" (*arba'im*) is most commonly found as a measurement of substantial time. In the story of Noah and the ark (Gen. 7:4,12), it rained for 40 days and 40 nights. The Israelites were condemned to wander in the wilderness for 40 years after the Exodus from Egypt (Exod. 16:35; Deut. 2:7, 29:4)—one year for each of the 40 days that Joshua (who was 40 years old) and the other 11 spies spent reconnoitering the Promised Land before returning with the pessimistic majority conclusion that they would not be able to conquer it (Num. 13:25). At age 40, Isaac married Rebecca (Gen. 25:20) and Esau married his two foreign wives (Gen. 26:34). According to tradition, Moses was 40 when he killed the Egyptian taskmaster and fled Egypt (Exod. 2:12), 80 when he saw the Burning Bush (Exod. 3:2) and appeared before Pharaoh, and 120 when he died (Deut. 34:7). Moses remained on Mount Sinai twice for 40 days, while receiving the first and second tablets of the Ten Commandments (Exod. 24:18; Deut. 10:10). King David ruled for 40 years (2 Sam. 5:4), as did his son Solomon (1 Kings 11:42). Elijah fasted for 40 days in the wilderness (1 Kings 19:8), and Jonah's (3:4) prophecy was that in 40 days the wicked city of Nineveh would be overthrown.

The full human life is three times 40 (120) years, the age at which Moses died with "his eyes undimmed and his vigor unabated" (Deut. 34:7). Twice 40 (80 years) represents advanced old age (2 Sam. 19:33–36), to which one may survive if "given the strength" (Ps. 90:10).

The Rabbis, who valued the study of Torah more than anything else, considered 40 years a notable period for scholarship and study. Rabbi Akiva was a shepherd for 40 years, studied for 40 years, and was a teacher for 40 years (*Sif. Dev.* 34:7). The Mishnah states that at age 40, one achieves understanding (Avot 5:21), and according to Rabbah, "A man does not comprehend his teacher's full intention until he is 40" (Av. Zar. 5b). Rabbi Eliezer states that the Messianic Age will last for 40 years (Sanh. 99a).

Seventy (שִׁבְעִים)

As a multiple of the most important number—seven—and a product of the sacred numbers "seven" and "10," "70" (*shivim*) is a common round number. Terach was 70 years old when he sired Abraham (Gen. 11:26), Abraham was 70 years old when God made a covenant with him (Gen. R. 39:7), and there were 70 members of Jacob's family who went down to Egypt to join Joseph (Exod. 1:5). The 70 elders that Moses appointed to assist him in leading the Israelites through the wilderness (Exod. 24:9), with Moses at their head, became the prototype of the Great Sanhedrin—a panel of 71 judges (70 plus a chief judge) who acted as the supreme court of ancient Israel. The

70 vessels in the Tabernacle, which measured 70 cubits, corresponded to the 70 holy days celebrated in the Jewish year: 52 Sabbaths (Christian calendar); seven days of Passover; seven days of Sukkot; and one day each of Shavuot, Rosh Hashanah, Yom Kippur, and Shemini Atzeret.[20] The first Temple in Jerusalem was rebuilt 70 years after it was destroyed.

According to the Talmud, the 70 bulls sacrificed as offerings during Sukkot were offered to make atonement for the 70 nations, the traditional number of gentile peoples, based on the genealogical listing in Genesis 10 (Suk. 55a). Starting at 13 bulls on the first day, the number decreased by one on each of the succeeding six days. Similarly, there will be a progressive decline in those who resist the divine teachings, until in the Messianic Age all nations will accept God's law under the spiritual guidance of Israel.[21] On Shemini Atzeret (the day following Sukkot), only a single bull was sacrificed—for the nation of Israel. As the Talmud explains, "This may be compared to a mortal king who said to his servants, 'Prepare for me a great banquet'; but on the last day he said to his beloved friend, 'Prepare for me a simple meal that I may derive benefit from you.'"

Seventy years is described as "the span of our life" (Ps. 90:10).[22] A midrash indicates that Adam was originally supposed to live for 1,000 years but he donated 70 of them to David when he discovered that this future king of Israel had been fated to live only three hours (PdRE 10).

One Thousand (אֶלֶף)

"One thousand" (*elef*), and its multiples, is a common round number that designates a substantial quantity rather than a precise number, as when Moses assures the Israelites that obeying the divine commandments will enable them to easily defeat their enemies: "Five of you shall give chase to 100, and 100 of you shall give chase to 10,000" (Lev. 26:8). Other examples are the chant of the Israelite women—"Saul has slain his thousands, David his tens of thousands" (1 Sam. 18:7)—that drove King Saul mad with anger toward the younger and more powerful hero; the adoring claim in The Song of Songs (5:10), "My beloved is clear-skinned and ruddy, preeminent among 10,000;" the 70,000 men who died of pestilence after David disobeyed God and carried out an unsanctioned census of the people (2 Sam. 24:15); and the one million talents of silver prepared by David for his son Solomon to build the House of the Lord (1 Chron. 22:14). There are also the almost unimaginably large numbers, such as the "thousands of myriads" of offspring that was the blessing her parents gave Rebecca (Gen. 24:60), and the "thousands upon thousands" who stood before the "beast" in the night vision of Daniel (7:10).

Gematria

Gematria is an interpretative device whereby words are understood through the numerical value of their letters. The *tannaim* of the second century, following the Greek system, gave each of the 22 letters of the Hebrew alphabet a numerical value. The letters "א" to "ט" represent the digits one to nine, "י" to "צ" from 10 to 90, and "ק" to "ת" from 100 to 400. Thousands are expressed by placing two dots above the letters for units ("א" to "ט"). Rabbi Eliezer ben Yose made *gematria* the 29th of his 32 aggadic hermeneutical rules for interpreting the Torah. For example, the Talmud derives that there are 903 types of death from the phrase *la-mavet totza'ot* (lit., "avenues to death"; Ps. 68:21)[23] because the *gematria* of *totza'ot* is 903 (ת = 400, ו = 6, צ = 90, א =1, ו = 6, ת = 400) (Ber. 8a). An example of the relatively infrequent use of *gematria* in *halakhah* is the mishnah, "A Nazirite vow of unspecified duration [remains in force] 30 days" (Naz. 5a). According to Rabbi Mattena, this ruling is derived from the word "יִהְיֶה" (*y'hiyeh;* "he shall be [holy]"; (Num. 6:5),[24] whose numerical value is 30 (י = 10, ה = 5, י = 10, ה = 5). In addition to being used in the Talmud and Midrash, *gematria* is found in the Christian Bible calculation that 666 is the "number of the beast" (Revelation 13:18). (For some other instances of *gematria* see pp. 67, 328, 381, 516)

Other more complicated systems of *gematria* were later introduced. One of these is *atbash,* in which the last letter (ת) is substituted for the first (א), the penultimate (ש) for the second (ב), etc. A mnemonic using the first six couplets of this technique helps recall the day of the week on which the Jewish holidays fall in a given year. The first Hebrew letter of the couplet stands for the number of the day of Passover; the second is the initial of the holiday that falls on that day of the week (OH 428:3):

- ת ... א, the first day of Passover falls on the same day of the week as Tisha b'Av (תִּשְׁעָה בְּאָב).
- ש ... ב, the second day of Passover falls on the same day as Shavuot (שָׁבוּעוֹת).
- ר ... ג, the third day of Passover falls on the same day as Rosh Hashanah (רֹאשׁ הַשָּׁנָה).
- ק ... ד, the fourth day of Passover falls on the same day as Simchat Torah (קְרִיאַת הַתּוֹרָה).
- צ ... ה, the fifth day of Passover falls on the same day as Yom Kippur (צוֹם כִּפּוּר).
- פ ... ו, the sixth day of Passover falls on the same day as Purim (פּוּרִים).[25]

Other sophisticated systems of *gematria* include the following:

- *Atbah*, in which the ninth letter (ט) is substituted for the first (א), the eighth (ח) for the second (ב), etc.
- The *filling system*, in which the numerical value of each letter itself is not calculated but rather the numerical value of all the letters that make up the name of the letter are calculated. For example, the word "דָלֶת" (the first letter) is composed of the letters ד (4), ל (30), and ת (400), which add up to 434.
- The sum of the squares of the numerical value of each letter, so that יהוה (YHVH, the Tetragrammaton) would be $10^2 + 5^2 + 6^2 + 5^2 = 186$, the same as "Makom" (place), another name for the omnipresent God, who is in every place.
- The addition of the number of letters in the word (or just the number one) to the numerical value of the word itself, so that "יהוה" (YHVH) would equal either 30 (26 + 4) or 27 (26 + 1).
- The *great number system*, which counts the five final letters (*kaf*, ך; *mem*, ם; *nun*, ן; *peh*, ף; *tzadi*, ץ) as a continuation of the alphabet with values of 500 to 900.
- Adding up of the value of all the preceding letters in an arithmetical series, so that "d," the fourth letter, equals 1 + 2 + 3 + 4 = 10 (most useful in complicated *gematria* that reaches into the thousands).
- The interpretation of a word by taking the numerical equivalent of each letter separately to signify something specific.

An example of this last approach involves the Hebrew word "יִצְחָק" (Isaac). The "י" has a numerical value of 10, which refers to the 10 trials with which Abraham (Isaac's father) was tested, according to the Rabbis. The "צ" has a numerical value of 90, the age of Sarah when she gave birth to Isaac. The "ח" is equal to eight, referring to the eighth day on which Isaac was circumcised. Finally, the "ק" has a numerical value of 100, the age of Abraham when his son Isaac was born (Num. R. 18:21).[26]

The kabbalists went to fantastic lengths in applying *gematria* as an exegetical device. Although this practice was supposed to be employed in order to discover new hidden truths, in almost all cases the idea preceded the inventing of a supporting *gematria*. Eventually, even some major kabbalists tried to limit the arbitrary use of this technique, with Nachmanides arguing that there were only specific *gematria* that were transmitted to Moses to serve as mnemonics for other portions of the Oral Law.

Satan (שָׂטָן)

Rather than a demonic creature who is the personification of evil and the enemy of God, the biblical word "*satan*" is merely a common noun that means "adversary," "accuser," or "hinderer." The role of Satan is to make things difficult for human beings, so that they can overcome temptations and their evil inclinations and eventually succeed in accomplishing the tasks that God has prepared for them. Thus Satan convinces God to test the faithfulness of Job, whom God had described as "there is no one like [My servant Job] on earth, a blameless and upright man who fears God and shuns evil" (Job 1:8). Similarly, in a talmudic legend, it is Satan who challenged God to put Abraham to the test of the *Akedah* (binding of Isaac) to prove the Patriarch's allegiance (Sanh. 89b). Satan also is reported to have "arisen against Israel and incited David to number [an unauthorized census of] Israel" (1 Chron. 21:1), which led to a devastating plague.

Nevertheless, throughout the Bible, Satan is clearly subordinate to God and unable to act without divine permission. In later Jewish thought, Satan became viewed as the impersonal force of evil—strikingly different from the Christian concept of Satan as an autonomous being (Antichrist) who personifies evil. Only in the Talmud and the Midrash does Satan increasingly emerge as a distinct entity (often called "Samael"): "Satan, the evil prompter [*yetzer ha-ra*, the inclination toward evil], and the Angel of Death are all one" (BB 16a). According to the Midrash, Satan was responsible for all of the sins in the Bible, including the disobedience of Adam and Eve in the Garden of Eden and the worship of the Golden Calf (by telling the people that Moses would not return from Mount Sinai and even "showing them a vision of his bier"). Explaining the genesis of the sin of David with Bathsheba, the Talmud relates that when she was cleaning her hair behind a screen, Satan came to David "appearing in the shape of a bird. He shot an arrow at him, which broke the screen, thus she stood revealed, and he saw her" (Sanh. 107a).

According to the Rabbis, the purpose of sounding the shofar on Rosh Hashanah is "to confuse the Accuser [Satan]," so as to prevent him from bringing before God any charges against the Jews on the Day of Judgment (RH 16b). In line with this tradition, one of the verses from Psalms read before the blowing of the shofar (*Min ha-meitzar*; "From the depths") is composed of an acrostic that reads "*kera satan*" (destroy Satan). However, the Talmud notes that "Satan has no permission to act as accuser on the Day of Atonement"; the numerical equivalent of the Hebrew "*ha-Satan*" equals 364, meaning that on all these days Satan "has permission to act as the accuser" but is not allowed to do so on the Day of Atonement (Yoma 20a).

Shalom (שָׁלוֹם)

One of the most common words in the Hebrew language, "shalom" has a multiplicity of meanings in addition to the well-known "hello," "good-bye," and "peace."

There are several variants of "shalom" in the Bible, all of which describe a positive state of affairs, such as safety, prosperity, and well-being. Indeed, the word "shalom" derives from "*shalem*," which means "whole or complete" and is connected to the word for perfection (*shleimut*). In the Bible, shalom also can mean "peace" (Eccles. 3:8).

Virtually every major blessing or prayer in the liturgy—*Amidah*, *Kaddish*, Priestly Blessing, Grace after Meals—concludes with a prayer for peace. However, while Jews pray for peace every day, they realize that the ideal of true universal peace must await the Messianic Age, when "nation shall not lift up sword against nation, neither shall they learn war any more" (Isa. 2:4).[1] Until this utopian era, war may sometimes be justified and may even be obligatory.

In Rabbinic Judaism, shalom is one of the most important values. The Midrash states that "all that is written in the Torah was written for the sake of peace" (Tanh. Shoftim 19). In *Pirkei Avot* (1:18), Rabbi Shimon ben Gamaliel[2] asserts: "By three things the world is preserved—by truth, by justice, and by peace [shalom]." The Talmud interprets these three concepts as being effectively one, since "if justice has been accomplished, so has truth, and so has peace" (JT Taan. 4:2, 68a), but other sources suggest that peace is more important than truth. "It is permissible to deviate from the truth in order to preserve peace" (Yev. 65b), and *shalom bayit* (domestic harmony; lit., "peace in the house") is the cornerstone on which the Jewish home is built. As the Jerusalem Talmud observes concerning the biblical description of dipping a scroll containing curses that use the divine name into a potion to be drunk by a wife accused of unfaithfulness (*sotah*; Num. 5:23): "If in order to establish peace between husband and wife the Name of God, which was written in holiness, may be blotted out, how much more so to bring about peace for the world as a whole" (JT Sot. 1:4, 16d). Abaye frequently said: "A man should always strive to be on the best terms [increase peace] with his brethren and his relatives and with all men, even with the heathen in the marketplace, in order that he may be beloved above [by God] and well liked below [on earth] and be acceptable to his fellow creatures" (Ber. 17a). In *Pirkei Avot* (1:12), Hillel urges Jews to "be of the disciples of Aaron, loving and pursuing peace, who loves his fellow creatures and brings them near to Torah." This depiction of Aaron as the great peacemaker is in contrast to his brother, Moses, who was the exemplar of the ideal of justice.

Because of their relative impotence vis-à-vis the world community, the medieval Jewish philosophers tended to stress the future peace that would be ushered in by the Messiah. The kabbalists, on the other hand, believed that even the politically powerless Jew could help bring peace on earth. Human activities, particularly the fulfillment of commandments, affect the divine realm of the *sefirot*. The good deeds of the righteous on earth promote peace between the male and female elements of God, whose union results in the flow of divine blessing to our world.

The root of the word "shalom" remains a vital part of traditional Jewish life. It is used in the sense of "full" or "whole" in the term "*Kaddish Shalem*" (full *Kaddish*; see p. 395) and the wish for a sick person to have a *refu'ah shleimah* (complete healing). Furthermore, the focus of all Jewish prayers, *Yerushalayim* (Jerusalem), is based on the same root, meaning either "possession" or "foundation" of peace.[3] Jews often greet one another with "*shalom aleichem*" (peace be unto you), to which the response is "*aleichem shalom*" (to you, peace). *Shalom Aleichem* is also the name of the hymn traditionally recited before the Friday evening meal (see p. 143), when Jews wish each other a "*Shabbat shalom*" (peaceful Sabbath). In the Broadway show *Milk and Honey,* one of the major songs expresses the multiplicity of meanings of the word "shalom": "It means a million lovely things, like 'peace be yours,' 'welcome home'; and even when you say good-bye, if your heart has 'I don't want to go' in it, say goodbye with a little 'hello' in it, and say goodbye with *shalom*!"[4]

Food

Overview

Food plays a major role in the daily life of Jews as well as in their celebration of festive occasions (see p. 157).

During the biblical period, the Mediterranean diet generally consisted of grains, such as wheat (see p. 669) and barley (see p. 669), and legumes, such as lentils (see p. 686) and fava beans, which were cultivated in permanent settlements. Most vegetables were picked wild when needed and cooked for the daily meal. Grapes, figs, and dates (see p. 670, 671, and 673, respectively) were consumed fresh or dried. Almonds (see p. 674), walnuts, and pistachios were popular nuts. Olives (see p. 672) were a major source of oil and were also preserved. The eating of meat, primarily mutton and goat raised by nomads, was almost always limited to festive occasions. Milk (see p. 688) was consumed fresh and in the form of butter, cheese, and sour milk (*leben*). Wines (sweet, sparkling, or spiced) were made from grapes as well as from raisins, fermented dates, figs, and pomegranates. Wine vinegar was used for pickling and as a dressing. The most common seasoning was salt (see p. 689), which was used to enhance virtually every food as well as to accompany all sacrifices. Herbs and spices (used as flavoring, for medicinal purposes, and as incense) included coriander, cumin, pepper, ginger (imported from Arabia and India), fenugreek, dill, sesame seeds, and fennel.[1]

When speaking of the abundance of the Land of Israel, the Bible mentions three general types of food—*dagan* (grain), *tirosh* ([new] wine), and *yizhar* (oil)—the prime products of the Israelite agriculture (Deut. 7:13; 2 Kings 18:32).

The Torah prohibited the consumption of certain foods. An animal fit for eating must chew its cud and have split hooves; a fish must have fins and scales. The Torah explicitly lists which birds are forbidden. In addition, animals and birds (but not fish) can be eaten only if they are slaughtered in a ritually precise manner. The consumption of blood is also prohibited. Food that accords with the Jewish dietary laws came to be known as "kosher" (kasher), which literally means "fit" or "appropriate," though this word is never used in the Torah to describe food.

Dietary Laws (Kashrut; כַּשְׁרוּת)

According to the dietary laws, all fruits and vegetables are permitted, based on the verse, "See, I give you every seed-bearing plant that is upon all the earth, and every tree that has seed-bearing fruit; they shall be yours for food" (Gen. 1:29). In fact, this verse and the subsequent one imply that vegetarianism was the earliest biblical ideal. Only in the

CHARACTERISTICS OF JEWISH COOKING

The two main categories of Jewish cooking may be broadly classified as Sephardic (originating from around the Mediterranean in the Middle East and North Africa and extending to Asia) and Ashkenazic (of more Western and Northern European origin). A major dividing line was the mountains separating the north and south of Europe, extending from the Caucasus to the Pyrenees. Over the centuries, the significant Jewish migrations between east and west, rather than north and south, accentuated the differences between Sephardim (who for years tended to live a more cosmopolitan life under Islamic rule) and Ashkenazim (who had a more rural existence and suffered frequent persecutions under Christian domination). The differences in the two styles of cooking are closely related to the climate, soil, and locally available produce. In general, Ashkenazim inhabit a cold world of beef and bland vegetables (cabbage, carrots, potatoes), freshwater fish (especially carp), and salt herring, in which the flavor is brought out by fats, sugar, and onions. In contrast, the world of the Sephardim "is a warm one of peppers and eggplant, zucchini and tomatoes" and features a "sensual, aromatic, and colorful" cuisine that focuses on herbs and spices, olive oil, rice, cracked wheat, beans, lamb, and saltwater fish.[1]

time of Noah did God allow humans to be carnivorous (Gen. 9:3). God did give Noah one restriction—the consumption of blood was prohibited—but the full set of dietary laws was commanded to the Israelites after they left Egypt, and was further embellished and explicated by the Rabbis. The Jewish dietary laws (derived largely from Lev. 11:1–43) detail which animals, birds, and fish may be eaten; how they are to be slaughtered and prepared; and the rules concerning the separation of meat and milk.

Quadrupeds

The Bible divides the "beasts of the earth" into those animals that are permitted for consumption (*tahor*; clean) and those that are prohibited (*tamei*; unclean). This is based on God's command that Noah take seven pairs of every clean beast and two pairs of all unclean animals into the ark (Gen. 7:2), a difference that presumably related to the former group being suitable for sacrifice.

To qualify as kosher, a quadruped must both chew the cud (ruminant) and have completely cloven (divided) hooves (Lev. 11:3; Deut. 14:6), meaning that they cannot hold prey and thus are not carnivores. The Torah specifies 10 herbivorous animals (wild and domestic) that meet these criteria: ox, sheep (see p. 729), goat (see p. 718), deer, gazelle (see p. 714), roebuck, wild goat, ibex, antelope, and mountain sheep (Deut. 14:4–5). The camel (see p. 711), hare (see p. 719), and hyrax chew their cud but are forbidden because they have incompletely split hooves; the pig (see p. 726) has a completely cloven hoof but is prohibited because it does not chew its cud (Deut. 14:7–8).

Birds

Although kosher quadrupeds and fish are mentioned by characteristics so that their identities are clear, the Torah specifically names 20 non-kosher species of birds, thus implying that all others are kosher (Lev. 11:13–19; Deut 14:11–18). The forbidden birds include osprey, kite, vulture, raven, falcon, and hawk. Unfortunately, over time the precise identities of some of the biblically prohibited birds became unclear. Consequently, the Shulchan Arukh ruled that it is forbidden to eat any species of bird (or its eggs; see p. 707) unless there is a well-established tradition that it is kosher (YD 82:2).[1] These include chicken, capon, Cornish hen, domestic duck and goose, pigeon, partridge, and peacock. In general, all birds of prey and scavengers that eat carrion are prohibited (Hul. 59a). According to Nachmanides, all unclean birds are in some degree cruel, so that one who eats their flesh becomes exposed to the danger of acquiring the same characteristic.[2] The Mishnah states, "Every bird that has an extra toe [talon], a crop [pouched enlargement of the gullet that stores food], and a gizzard that can be peeled [inner lining that can easily be separated from the outside muscular portion] is clean" (Hul. 3:6; 59a). Nevertheless, in regard to certain birds, such as pheasant, quail, and even turkey, there is a difference of tradition, with some communities regarding them as permitted and others deeming them forbidden.

The Rabbis discussed whether the white stork (*hasidah*) was a kosher bird. According to the Talmud, its Hebrew name (lit., "pious bird") reflects that "it shows kindness [*hasidut*] to its companions [i.e., by sharing food with other members of its species]" (Hul. 63a). Nevertheless, the white stork is still considered a nonkosher bird because it shows such compassion only toward its own kind and not to other species, a behavior that was scorned by the sages.[3]

Fish

Of "all that live in water," only those that have fins (*snapir*) and scales (*kaskeset*) are "clean" and permitted as food (Lev. 11:9–12). The scales must be capable of being scraped off easily with a knife (Nachmanides), which excludes creatures with scales that are not clearly defined, such as shellfish, shark, catfish, and amphibians.[4] Nachmanides explained that fish with fins and scales can swim close to the surface, so that occasionally they come up for air. This warms their blood and enables them to rid their bodies of excess fluids and other impurities. In contrast, those lacking fins and scales keep close to the bottom of the sea, cannot purify their bodies, and thus would be harmful to human health if eaten.[5]

Jews are also forbidden to eat from "among all the swarming things of the water and among all the other living creatures that are in the water" (Lev. 11:10); this prohibits small aquatic creatures and large water animals that are not fish (such as seals, dolphins, sharks, and whales).[6] A major controversy concerns the status of swordfish, which has scales when young but then loses them as it gets older. Swordfish is permitted by the American Conservative movement but forbidden by most Orthodox authorities.

Insects

The Torah specifically permits the eating of four kinds of locusts (see p. 722; Lev. 11:21–22), but because none can be unequivocally identified, later rabbis declared all species of insects to be forbidden. The prohibition against "all winged swarming things" (Deut. 14:19) includes flies, bees (see p. 710), hornets, and similar insects. An exception is the product of an insect that is not part of its body, such as honey from bees (Bek. 7b). Unlike milk from a cow, honey is a product of the flower nectar that bees gather and then convert into honey. The ban on "all the things that swarm upon the earth" (Lev. 11:41) forbids the eating of worms, beetles, snakes, scorpions, and lizards, which Rashi defined as being low, having short legs, and appearing to creep along the ground.[7]

Shechitah (שְׁחִיטָה)

The law of ritual slaughtering is derived from the verse, "you may slaughter any of the cattle or sheep ... as I have instructed you" (Deut. 12:21). The Rabbis interpreted this to imply that Moses had previously taught the people a method of slaughtering animals. However, since the precise details are not mentioned in the Torah, it follows that the Jewish method of ritual slaughter must have been communicated as part of the Oral Law. Today, the complex and minute regulations dealing with ritual slaughtering must be carried out by a licensed *shochet*, who in addition to being a skilled professional must be a pious individual who is well trained in Jewish law.

Jewish ritual slaughtering strives to prevent unnecessary suffering to the animal. It requires one continuous deep horizontal cut with a perfectly sharp blade with no nicks or unevenness. This severs the windpipe and all of the great blood vessels of the neck so that the animal instantly loses all sensation. Because an animal may not be eaten if it has not been properly slaughtered, the technical requirements must be strictly observed.

In addition to slaughtering the animal, the *shochet* must also carry out a detailed examination (*bedikah*) of the carcass. Any defect of the major organs renders the animal *treif* and forbidden for consumption. Initially referring to the flesh of an animal torn by a wild beast or wild bird, the word "*terefah*" was later applied to the flesh of any injured or diseased animal that would not have lived for more than a year (Hul. 3:1). Eventually, *treif* became the generic term for any product that was not kosher, and thus not ritually fit for Jewish consumption. The *halakhah* permits certain abnormalities in the lungs that have been determined to be harmless. However, those Jews who are strictest in their observance of kashrut eat only *glatt kosher* meat—a term that is derived from the Yiddish word for "smooth" and refers to animals with smooth, lesion-free lungs.[8]

Shechitah and *bedikah* of poultry are carried out in the same careful manner, though only the intestines are examined. There are no specific regulations about how fish are to be killed. After *shechitah*, the animal is suspended head down to drain as much blood as possible from the body (see below).

Jewish law prohibits eating the flesh of any kosher animal that has died without kosher slaughter. Termed "*nevelah*," this includes not only an animal that died a natural death but also one that has been killed by hunting or was not correctly slaughtered. Unlike the nonkosher creatures that the Torah terms "abomination," *nevelah* is permitted to gentiles; according to Sforno,[9] it is forbidden to Jews only because it is not appropriate food for a holy people.[10] Although Abravanel[11] deemed *nevelah* to be reprehensible to God because it was a pagan custom to eat of this particular kind of meat,[12] Rabbi Meir[13] stated that the owner of the carcass had the right to benefit from it by selling it to a gentile, even though it could not be eaten by a Jew (Pes. 21b).[14]

Preparation of Meat (Kashering)

The unequivocal biblical prohibition against the consumption of blood is the basis for the process of kashering meat (Lev. 7:26–27, 17:10–14). This is the only dietary law for which the Torah provides a reason: "For the life of the flesh is in the blood, and I have assigned it to you for making expiation for your lives upon the altar." Therefore, before meat is cooked, it is necessary to remove all traces of blood—by soaking and salting the meat or by broiling or roasting it over an open flame.

After being washed to remove all externally visible blood, the meat is placed in a large container and covered completely in lukewarm water for a half hour so that it softens and will absorb salt. The meat is then placed on a flat slatted board through which blood can drip or on a sloped board so that the blood can drain off into a sink or empty container. It is salted thoroughly on all sides and left on the board for one hour. Coarse (kosher) salt is used because of its effectiveness in drawing out the blood from the meat. After being rinsed off several times, the meat is considered in proper condition for cooking. This entire process must be completed within 72 hours after ritual slaughter; otherwise, the blood is considered to have congealed inside the meat, which must them be broiled or roasted over an open flame before it can be eaten.[15]

Meat that is to be broiled does not need to be kashered, since the broiling process drains off at least as much blood as is removed by soaking and salting. Nevertheless, some people still sprinkle salt on meat before broiling. Salting is not considered effective enough to kasher the blood-saturated liver, which must first be broiled on a rack to allow the juices to drain before being further cooked in whatever way desired.[16]

Forbidden Portions of Kosher Animals

The sciatic nerve and its associated blood vessels must be removed before the hindquarters of any quadruped can be prepared for consumption. This nerve extends from the rear of the spinal column and runs down the inner side of the leg. Although some expert butchers can perform the difficult task of cutting out the sciatic nerve, in general the process is so time-consuming and costly that many kosher butchers do not handle the hindquarter at all. Packinghouses usually sell the hindquarters of kosher-slaughtered animals to the general market for nonkosher cuts of meat such as sirloin or T-bone steak and filet mignon.[17]

The prohibition against eating the sciatic nerve is an eternal reminder of the wrestling match between Jacob and the "stranger," which took place as the Patriarch was returning to the Land of Israel after dwelling 20 years with his father-in-law, Laban (Gen. 32:25–32). During this titanic struggle—which resulted in Jacob's name being changed to Israel, since he had "struggled with God"—the attacker injured Jacob's thigh, resulting in a residual limp. *Sefer ha-Hinnukh* maintained that this commandment is a symbol of Israel's survival; just as Jacob faced a daunting task yet emerged victorious, so Jews throughout the ages should have confidence in God's assistance in helping them overcome the fiercest attacks of their enemies. Sforno viewed the commandment as symbolically teaching Jews that physical handicaps should not discourage their fight for survival.[18]

The fat portions (*chelev*) surrounding the kidneys, liver, stomach, and intestines, which were sacrificed on the altar in biblical and Temple times, are also forbidden for consumption (Lev. 7:23). This prohibition applies to the abdominal fat of oxen, sheep, and goats, unless it is covered by flesh; however, it was permitted to eat the fat (*shemen*) of the deer, hart, and other kosher wild animals that could not be used for sacrificial offerings. Abravanel wrote that eating *chelev* could lead one to become fat and lose the ability to function physically or mentally. Recanati maintained that fats were forbidden as food because they were included in animal sacrifices and thus were considered sacred.[19]

Mixing Milk and Meat

The prohibition against mixing milk and meat derives from the verse, "You shall not boil a kid in its mother's milk" (Exod. 23:19, 34:26; Deut. 14:21). Since it became impossible to determine which baby goat and which mother's milk were related, the law was extended so that no animal (meat) could be cooked in any milk (dairy). The Rabbis interpreted the threefold repetition of this verse as defining three separate prohibitions: cooking meat and milk together, eating such a mixture, and deriving any benefit from it (such as savoring the aroma or feeding it to a pet) (Hul. 115b). The term "milk" was interpreted to mean all dairy products, such as butter, cheese, and fresh and sour cream. Because many commonly eaten processed foods contain unsuspected dairy ingredients—such as bread, cakes, and cookies made with buttermilk, nonfat dry milk, whey, or dairy-derived additives—kashrut observers always read the labels carefully and buy products only with a *hechsher* (kosher certification).

Those Jews who are strictest about their observance of kashrut have special requirements for the dairy products they eat, consuming only those labeled *chalav Yisrael* (milk of the Jewish people). In addition to making certain of the standard requirement that all milk and dairy products never come into contact with any meat or meat products, the most rigorous insist that cows be closely watched to ensure that they never eat any nonkosher food or have their milk mixed with any that is not kosher.

The production of cheese is also tightly regulated. Most hard cheeses require that the milk be curdled or coagulated in rennet, the inner lining of the stomach of a calf. To be strictly kosher, the rennet must come

KASHRUT CERTIFICATION

Keeping kosher has become much easier in recent years, since at least 75% of prepackaged products (and most major brands) now have some type of kosher certification indicated by a *hechsher*. Coming from the same Hebrew root as the word "kosher," a *hechsher* is effectively a symbol indicating that the product has been certified as kosher by a specific rabbi or organization. In addition to the kashrut symbol, many kosher certifying organizations add the letter "D" (or the word "dairy") or "M" (or the word "meat") as appropriate. For pareve (neither milk nor meat) products, the word itself is added, since the letter "P" is used to indicate that a product is kosher for Passover. In the absence of such clarifying words or letters, it is essential to read the list of ingredients carefully to determine whether the product is meat, dairy, or pareve.[1]

"Kosher-style" is a meaningless term, since a product is either kosher or not kosher. Indeed, the term is highly misleading since it "tends to confer credibility upon merchants doing business in the Jewish community by attaching a quasi-religious label to their wares, when in fact no kosher status exists." It is important to remember that so-called Jewish foods—such as challah, gefilte fish, blintzes, kugel, latkes, and even chicken soup—are not inherently kosher. Even though they are associated with Jewish traditions, these items must still be prepared from kosher ingredients according to the dietary laws.[2]

from a kosher animal that was slaughtered in a ritually correct manner and whose stomach was correctly prepared and thoroughly dried. Conservative halakhic interpretation permits all hard cheeses. Today, cheese can be made using vegetable enzymes.[20]

In order to create a "fence around the Torah," the Rabbis decreed that the separation of meat from milk must be as complete as possible. Thus it is necessary to use separate utensils (pots, pans, dishes, and flatware) for dairy foods and meat (known in Yiddish as milchig and fleishig, respectively). This entails storing the utensils in separate areas, washing them in separate bowls or sinks, and drying them with different dishcloths (ideally of distinct colors to prevent any mistake). When using a dishwasher, it is necessary to have separate dish racks; if these are not available, the dishwasher must be run through a cycle between meat and dairy loads.

Because meat takes a long time to digest, or due to residual meat particles or fatty residues caught in the teeth or their taste remaining on the palate, Jewish law rules that one must wait a designated period after eating a meat meal before ingesting milk products. Customs range from an hour for Jews of Dutch ancestry to three hours for German Jews and six hours for those from other European countries. The waiting time between milk and meat is much shorter. One is generally permitted to eat meat almost immediately after a milk meal, after thoroughly rinsing the mouth and eating a piece of bread or some other "neutral" solid. After hard cheese, however, it is customary to wait a longer period (up to six hours in some traditions) before eating meat.

Today, there is wide availability of imitation milk derived from soybeans, coconuts, almonds, rice, and oats that may be used with meat. Fruit, vegetables, grains, and eggs are all considered neutral (pareve) and may be eaten together with milk or meat dishes. Fish is also a neutral food, but the Rabbis traditionally prohibited cooking or eating fish and meat together because they were convinced that this mixture was dangerous for one's health. Today, there is a difference of opinion on the subject of eating meat and fish together.

Maimonides viewed the prohibition against mixing meat and milk as an attack on idolatry and superstition.[21] He argued that combining meat and milk was a pagan custom and thus not appropriate for Jews. Abravanel and Luzzatto maintained that it was a humanitarian ordinance to discourage a practice that would tend to harden the heart.[22]

Ibn Ezra argued that it would be the "act of a cruel heart" to take milk, a substance that the Creator made to nourish life, and use it in a manner designed to destroy that life.[23]

Rationales for the Dietary Laws

Many attempts have been made to explain the dietary laws. The Bible defines them as *hukim*, divine statutes that by definition are not explained in the text. However, the underlying rationale for the laws of kashrut is stated in the verse, "You shall sanctify yourselves and be holy, for I [your God] am holy" (Lev. 11:44). This commandment has two aspects: the positive aspect of imitating God by manifesting such divine traits as being merciful and loving, and the negative aspect of withdrawing from things that are impure and abominable. Thus Jews were required to avoid anything that could defile them, either physically or spiritually.[24] The consumption of nonkosher food impedes people's ability to elevate and sanctify themselves, dulling their spiritual potential and creating a barrier between Jews and their perceptions of holiness.

Maimonides noted that "the dietary laws train us in the mastery over our appetites; they accustom us to restrain both the growth of desire and the disposition to consider the pleasure of eating and drinking as the end of man's existence."[25] This concept is illustrated in the *Sifra* (11:22), a halakhic midrash on Leviticus, which states: "Let not a man say, 'I do not like the flesh of swine.' On the contrary, he should say, 'I like it but must abstain, seeing that the Torah has forbidden it.'"

Effects on the Soul

For Ezekiel (33:25), the eating of blood was equivalent to the sins of idolatry and murder. Conversely, abstaining from this practice decreases the innate human instinct for violence. The Zohar extended this to all forbidden food, noting that the consuming of blood and the worshiping of idols are both referred to as "abominations." The prohibition of birds of prey, which survive by their ability to kill other creatures, is a moral injunction against taking advantage of one another, for such predatory behavior is out of character with the Jewish attitudes of compassion and mercy.[26] For Ibn Ezra, the prohibition against aesthetically repulsive animals (such as eels, roaches, and ants) was simply that it would be impossible for one to have a pure, clean conscience with the knowledge that his own flesh is the product of a diet of insects, snakes, and other vermin. In his allegorical Torah commentary, *Akedat Yitzhak,*[27] Isaac ben Moses Arama (15th century) wrote: "The reason behind all the dietary prohibitions is not that any harm may be caused to the body, but that these foods defile and pollute the soul and blunt the intellectual powers, thus leading to confused opinions and a lust for perverse and brutish appetites that lead men to destruction, thus defeating the purpose of Creation."

Effects on the Body

As a physician, Maimonides observed, "All food that is forbidden by the Law is unwholesome."[28] *Sefer ha-Hinnukh* noted that "the injurious effect of some forbidden foods in not known to us, or even to physicians. The True Faithful Doctor who has commanded us in all these things is infinitely wiser than we. How petty and foolish is the man who thinks that only those things which his understanding grasps are true, and everything else, everything unknown to him, is not true."[29] Maimonides maintained that the reason for the injunction against the consumption of sacrificial fat (*chelev*) was that "it fattens and destroys the abdomen and creates cold and clammy blood."[30] Concerning the prohibition of milk and meat, he added, "Meat boiled in milk is undoubtedly gross food, and makes a person feel overfull."[31] Later authorities argued that certain animals (especially nonkosher ones) harbor parasites that spread disease. Indeed, medieval Jews suffered less than their gentile neighbors from the waves of epidemics that decimated the population.

Separation

The dietary laws preserved the distinction between the Jews and other neighboring peoples (Tob. 1:10–11), as is first told in the story of Joseph, when the Egyptians refuse to eat with their Hebrew visitors (Gen. 43:32). Later, the young Daniel in the Babylonian court "resolved not to defile himself with the king's food or the wine he drank"; he made do with a spare vegetarian diet (Dan. 1:8, 12). And Judith ate her own food when she dined with a Babylonian general (Judith 12:2). In the Maccabean period, obedience to the dietary laws became such a mark of Jewish loyalty that Jews chose martyrdom rather than eating pig meat.[32]

For the early Rabbis, the secret of Jewish survival was separatism—being a holy people required being a people apart. As expressed in the early Apocryphal Book of Jubilees (22:16): "Separate yourself from the nations, do not eat with them, do not act according to their deeds, and do not associate with them, because their work is uncleanness, all their ways are contamination, detestation and abomination. They slaughter their sacrifices to the dead and pray to demons."[33] By following the dietary laws, the observant Jew may have less opportunity to socialize with non-Jews (since this often entails eating together). According to this view, the observance of kashrut has been a critical factor in decreasing the rates of Jewish assimilation and intermarriage.[34]

Conclusion

The general consensus is that the Torah is not a medical textbook and the dietary laws are not primarily designed to preserve bodily health. Rather, as Samuel Dresner wrote:

> Kashrut demands sacrifice, self-discipline and determination—but what that is really worthwhile in life does not? It demands the courage to turn our face against the powerful current of conformity that almost overcomes us daily. The goal of kashrut is holiness, a holy man and a holy nation. It is part of Judaism's attempt to hallow the common act of eating, which is an aspect of our animal nature. It likewise sets us apart from the nations. Thus it achieves its objective—holiness—in these two ways, both of which are implied in the Hebrew word *kadosh*: inner hallowing and outer separateness."[35]

Seven Species (שִׁבְעַת הַמִּנִים)

The Torah lists seven species of agricultural produce that symbolize the fertility of the Land of Israel: wheat, barley, grapes, figs, pomegranates, olive oil, and honey from dates (Deut. 8:8). Once the Israelites settled in Canaan, they were commanded to bring their first fruits (*bikurim*) as offerings to the *Kohanim* in Jerusalem (Exod. 23:16, 34:22; Num. 28:26). Although no specific fruits or grains are mentioned in the biblical text, Rabbi Akiva declared that they were the seven species listed above (Bik. 3:9).

Each year, when Jews went out to their fields and saw that these crops were beginning to ripen, they would mark their "first fruits" by tying straw around them (Bik. 3:1). When the crops had ripened completely, the farmer would bring them to the Temple in Jerusalem, at any time between Shavuot (also known as Hag ha-Bikurim) and Sukkot.[1] "Those who lived near [to Jerusalem] brought fresh figs and grapes, but those from a distance brought dried figs and raisins [since fresh fruit would rot on the way]" (Bik. 3:3). Because the *bikurim* symbolized the readiness of Jews to devote the first fruits of their labors on earth to the service of God, the trip to Jerusalem was celebrated in every town and city along the way with music and parades.[2] "An ox with horns bedecked with gold and with an olive-crown on its head led the way, and a flute was played before them" (Bik. 3:3). "The rich brought their *bikurim* in baskets overlaid with silver or gold, while the poor used wicker baskets of peeled willow branches" (Bik. 3:8). When they reached the Temple Mount, those bringing their first fruits were greeted by Levites, who raised their voices in song.

After presenting their basket of first fruits to the Kohen, the farmers were commanded to recite a brief synopsis of Jewish history, humbly thanking God for treating Jacob mercifully in his hour of need, delivering the Israelites from slavery in Egypt, and bringing the Jewish people to their Promised Land flowing with milk and honey (Deut. 26:1–11). Beginning with words that can be translated either "my father (Jacob) was a fugitive Aramean" or "an Aramean (the deceitful Laban) tried to destroy my forefather (Jacob)," these verses became an important part of the Passover haggadah.

The thanksgiving offering of first fruits was visible proof of the fulfillment of the divine promise to the Patriarchs that their descendants would become a great nation dwelling in comfort in a rich and fertile land. The recitation had to be in Hebrew, and those that could not speak the language were required to repeat the words after the Kohen. When farmers not conversant in Hebrew began to refrain from bringing their first fruits out of shame, it was decided that everyone must repeat the words after the Kohen (Bik. 3:7).

Wheat (חִטָּה)

A valuable crop since ancient times, wheat (*chitah*, plural *chittim*) was sown in the Land of Israel, like barley, at the beginning of the winter, but it develops more slowly and ripens about two months later (Exod. 9:31–32). Therefore, the *omer* (first barley crop; see p. 293) is brought on Passover, but the "first fruits of the wheat harvest" are offered seven weeks later on Shavuot (Exod. 34:22).

During biblical times, an abundant wheat harvest ("the finest wheat") symbolized well-being and peace (Ps. 81:17, 147:14). The choicest wheat was used in meal offerings, and this grain was considered superior to barley. Although wheat was initially the food of the rich, as agriculture improved during mishnaic and talmudic times, wheat became the common food for all.

The prophets frequently used the metaphor of separating the kernels of wheat (righteous) from the useless chaff (sinners). Although wheat (with barley) was the essential raw material of bread, the staple of the Israelite diet, the Torah emphasizes that "man does not live on bread alone" (Deut. 8:3). For the Rabbis, flour (*kemach*) served as a metaphor for a person's earnings that provided sufficient funds for his or her bodily needs, which were essential for the more important task of study. A popular song derived from *Pirkei Avot* (3:21) recognizes the interrelationship of the physical and spiritual aspects of life, observing that "without flour, there is no Torah; without Torah, there is no flour." In a practical vein, the Rabbis observed that "one who grows wheat is sure of his bread, but one who buys wheat in the market, his future is doubtful" (Men. 103b).

Barley (שְׂעוֹרָה)

Barley (*se'orah*) was the grain used in the bread, cakes, and porridge that formed the staple of the Israelite diet during biblical times. One of the world's most ancient cultivated grains, its hardiness and ability to resist drought made it the foremost crop. The importance of barley in biblical times can be seen from the injunction that the valuation of a field was determined according to the amount of this grain that could be sown in it (Lev. 27:16). When wheat became more plentiful and the preferred source of flour in mishnaic times, barley was relegated to the poor and as food for livestock. Although still added to some soups and stews, in modern Israel barley is most commonly used as the primary ingredient in brewing locally produced beer.[3]

As the first grain to ripen, barley was a symbol of spring (Ruth 1:22). The first *omer* of barley was reaped on the second day of Passover (see p. 265), marking the beginning of the spring harvest season (Lev. 23:9–15). The end of the barley harvest (and the beginning of the wheat harvest) is associated with the festival of Shavuot, when the Book of Ruth (which takes place during the barley harvest) is read in synagogue.[4]

Grapes (עֲנָבִים)

Since ancient days, the grapevines of the Land of Israel were celebrated for their quality and abundance. The first cultivated plant mentioned in the Bible is the grapevine (Gen. 9:20–24), which was planted by Noah immediately after the flood, though "he drank of the wine and became drunk." When the 12 spies returned from Canaan, two of them were required to carry a single cluster of grapes on a pole (Num. 13:23)—an image used in advertisements promoting tourism in modern Israel. Along with the fig, the vine symbolizes the fertility and peace of the land (1 Kings 1:5) and evokes the image of messianic redemption (Mic. 4:4; see p. 619).

The drinking of wine has long been an essential element of Jewish ceremonial celebrations. The Sabbath and festivals are greeted and conclude with blessings over a cup of wine (*Kiddush*, see p. 138; *Havdalah*, see p. 149). Four cups of wine are drunk at the seders on Passover (see p. 274) and Tu b'Shevat (see p. 254), as well as at circumcisions and weddings. Throughout Europe, spilling wine on the ground was a folk custom believed to appease evil spirits. Although this may have been the genesis of the Jewish customs of spilling drops of wine at the recitation of the 10 plagues (see p. 282) and overfilling the *Kiddush* and *Havdalah* cups, these practices soon were transformed into symbols of thanks to God, as in the joyful declaration in Psalms (23:5), "my cup runneth over."[5]

Kosher wine must be produced under rabbinic supervision. Only Sabbath-observant Jews are permitted to handle the wine or operate the wine-making equipment from grape crushing to consumption. An exception is wine that is *mevushal* (pasteurized, lit. "boiled"). In this process, the wine is heated to the boiling point so that air bubbles are brought to the surface with some loss of the liquid due to evaporation. This is required according to the laws of kashrut for a wine to retain its kosher status once opened and poured by a non-Jew (such as a waiter). Thus a wine that is produced in this manner retains its religious purity, regardless of who opens or pours it. The prohibition against Jews drinking wine prepared by gentiles was initially instituted lest some of it may have been used as a libation in a pagan ceremony connected with idol worship. In rabbinic times, this decree remained in effect to prevent Jews from fraternizing with gentiles in social situations, which could lead to assimilation or intermarriage.[6]

Figs (תְּאֵנָה)

In ancient times, the fig (*t'einah*) was eaten fresh or as a seasoning as well as used to make honey and alcohol. With two crops, in early and midsummer, the fig is best eaten straight from the tree in the late afternoon after being baked naturally by the sun.[7] Dried figs were pressed into cakes for travelers (1 Sam. 25:18) and were used as a poultice for treating skin disorders (Isa. 38:21).[8]

The fig is the first fruit mentioned in the Bible (Gen. 3:7). Adam and Eve covered themselves with the broad leaves of a fig tree when they became ashamed of their nakedness after eating the forbidden fruit in the Garden of Eden. Throughout the Bible, the fig (and vine) symbolize the existence of peace and security in the Land of Israel (1 Kings 1:5; Zech. 3:10). In his vision of the future Messianic Age, the prophet Micah (4:4) promised that "each man will dwell under his own vine and fig tree, and none will be afraid."

Pomegranate (רִמּוֹן)

The pomegranate (*rimon*) has striking red flowers and decorative fruit, which have a tangy, yet delicate sweet flavor and huge clusters of seeds. According to tradition, the pomegranate has precisely 613 seeds, representing the number of mitzvot in the Torah. It was one of the fruits brought back by the spies as proof of the fertility of the Promised Land (Num. 13:23). In The Song of Songs (4:3, 6:7, 8:2), the "brow behind your veil" of the beloved is described as "like a pomegranate split open," and the lover offers to "let you [the beloved] drink of the spiced wine, of my pomegranate juice." Bells shaped like pomegranates adorned the pillars of the Temple (1 Kings 7:20) and the hem of the robe of the *Kohen Gadol* (Exod. 28:34–35). As a popular motif in Jewish art, the fruit of the pomegranate has appeared on coins in both the Hasmonean period and the modern State of Israel. The silver ornaments placed atop the two wooden rollers of the Torah scroll are known as *rimonim*, the Hebrew word for "pomegranates."[9]

Olive Oil (זַיִת)

Olive trees have always been the most prominent and extensively distributed in the landscape of Israel, growing on terraced hillsides throughout the land. Their hard and beautifully grained wood is ideal for making various articles and ornaments. Although the fruit of different varieties comes in different sizes, the olive was a common standard of measurement. Indeed, the phrase "*ke-zayit*" ([as large] as an olive) is often used to indicate the minimum amount required to fulfill a ritual obligation.

As the waters of the Flood abated, the dove brought an olive leaf back to the ark so that Noah realized that dry land had once more appeared (Gen. 8:11). According to legend, this olive branch came from the Mount of Olives, since Jerusalem was not affected by the Flood.[10] The image of a white dove bearing an olive branch in her mouth has become a universal symbol of peace, and a menorah flanked by two olive branches is the emblem of the State of Israel. Capable of bearing fruit even when more than 1,000 years old, the olive tree is a symbol of long life.

In ancient Israel, olive oil was used for cooking, as a fuel for lamps, and as a major element in the meal offering (*mincha*). The Bible frequently describes the bounty of the land in terms of "grain and wine and oil" (Deut. 7:13), the major products of the Israelite agricultural economy and among the blessings promised to the people by God as a reward for their faithful performance of the divine commandments (Deut. 11:14). Olive oil was used for anointing Israelite priests (Lev. 8:12,30), prophets (1 Kings 19:16 [Elisha]), kings (1 Sam. 10:1 [Saul]; 16:13 [David]; 1 Kings 1:39 [Solomon]), and holy places such as the site of Jacob's dream (Gen. 28:18) and the Tabernacle in the wilderness (Lev. 8:10–11). Eventually, the Hebrew word "*mashiach*" (anointed one) became synonymous with the descendant of the royal house of David who would usher in the Messianic Age.

Olive oil was the original source of light in the menorah of the Tabernacle (Exod. 27:20; see p. 578), the eternal light (*ner tamid*, see p. 336), and in the menorah kindled on Hanukkah, a holiday when it is traditional to eat foods fried in oil (see p. 244).

Honey from Dates (דְּבַשׁ)

In the description of Israel as "a land flowing with milk and honey" (*chalav u-devash*; Exod 3:8), the Bible is referring to a syrup made from dates (or figs or grapes), rather than bee's honey, which was much less common in the area.

In biblical times, honey was eaten by itself (1 Sam. 14:27) or as a sweetener in baked goods (Exod. 16:31). In this latter source, the taste of manna is compared to that of wafers made with honey. Honey was not allowed to be brought as part of a sacrificial burnt offering (Lev. 2:11) because the pagans considered it the food of their gods. Still, the first fruits of honey were brought to the Temple (2 Chron. 31:5). In the Bible, honey is used as a metaphor for a variety of entities, such as the words of God ("the judgments of the Lord are true, righteous altogether, more desirable than gold, ... sweeter than honey"; Ps. 19:10–11) and wisdom ("My son, eat honey, for it is good; let its sweet drops be on your palate. Know: such is wisdom for your soul"; Prov. 24:13–14).

During the talmudic period, honey came to refer specifically to bee's honey. Based on the principle, "that which goes forth [issues] from the unclean is unclean" (Bek. 1:2, 5b), the honey of a bee should be forbidden since the bee is considered an unclean insect. However, the Rabbis permitted its use on the grounds that honey is not produced by the bee but rather comes from the nectar of a flower and is merely stored in the insect's body (Bek. 7b).

At the festive meal on Rosh Hashanah, it is traditional to dip the piece of bread over which the blessing has been recited into honey (instead of the usual salt) as a token of the sweet year that we hope will come. For the same reason, many Jews also eat pieces of apple dipped in honey. Based on the verse, "How pleasing is Your word to my palate, sweeter than honey" (Ps. 119:103), it has been a custom since medieval times to smear honey over letters of the Hebrew alphabet written on a slate when children begin school. As soon as the children repeated the name of the letter after the rabbi, they were allowed to lick the honey covering it, so that they would always associate the letters of the Torah with sweetness.[11]

Specific Foods

Various foods are either mentioned in the Bible or Talmud or are especially associated with Jews. Some of these are discussed in the following sections, which are arranged in alphabetical order.

Almond (שָׁקֵד)

With its Hebrew name (*shaked*) coming from a root meaning "wakeful" or "to hasten," the almond is the first tree to flower in Israel, blooming as early as January or February, while other fruit trees are still bare. Accordingly, the period when almond trees flower was selected by the Rabbis as the time for the festival of Tu b'Shevat, the New Year of the Trees (see p. 252).[1]

When Joseph's brothers returned to Egypt with Benjamin, Jacob included the almond among the gifts ["choice products of the land"] he sent with them (Gen. 43:11). Earlier, Jacob had taken "fresh shoots of poplar, and of almond and plane, and peeled white stripes in them" in an effort to produce "streaked, speckled, and spotted" animals (believing that animals seeing striped rods would bear striped young), which he was entitled to keep according to the terms of the bargain he had made with his father-in-law, Laban (Gen. 30:31–43). On the six side branches of the menorah there were "three cups shaped like almond-blossoms, each with calyx and petals" (Exod. 25:33–34).

The Torah ascribes magical properties to the almond tree as a symbol of divine favor. At the time of the Korah rebellion in the wilderness (Num. 17), it was Aaron's rod that miraculously sprouted almond blossoms, unequivocally indicating that God had chosen him to lead the people as the *Kohen Gadol*. When Moses and his brother had their first audience with Pharaoh, this same rod of Aaron had miraculously transformed itself into a snake and swallowed all the similar serpentine rods of the magicians of Egypt (Exod. 7:11–12).

Apple (תַּפּוּחַ)

The apple (*tapuach*) is noted in the Bible for its sweet aroma and taste. In The Song of Songs (7:9), the lover is likened to the scent of apples. "Like an apple tree among the trees of the forest, so is my beloved among the youths. I delight to sit in his shade, and his fruit is sweet to my mouth" (Song 2:3). A well-spoken word is said to be like "gold apples in silver showpieces" (Prov. 25:11).

The apple figures prominently in several Jewish customs. On Rosh Hashanah, the eating of apples dipped in honey symbolizes the wish for a prosperous and sweet new year (see p. 189). Ashkenazic Jews eat apples at the Passover seder as part of the *haroset* (see p. 286). As one explanation, the Talmud recounts the legend that during the time when the Israelites were slaves in Egypt, they would go out into the apple orchards to give birth lest they be forced to give up their male children to be killed by the soldiers of Pharaoh (Sot. 11b).

Bagel

Once a characteristically Jewish food, in the United States the bagel has become equally popular in the general community. One explanation for the name of this yeasted roll is that it comes from a German word meaning "ring" or "bracelet," which describes its shape. The unique texture of a bagel comes from being boiled in water before baking, which produces a crisp crust and moist, chewy interior. In medieval Europe, bagels were given to women about to give birth, as well as to the midwives who attended them, to drive away evil spirits and demons. In the United States, bagels are commonly sliced and served with cream cheese and lox, toppings that were never combined with bagels in Europe.[2]

Blintz

Blintzes are thin pancakes that originated in the Ukraine and are relatively modern descendants of the ancient Russian buckwheat pancakes known as blinis. A perfect dish for stretching limited resources and transforming leftovers into a special meal, blintzes are commonly filled with cheese, mashed potatoes, kasha, ground meat, or fruit. In Ashkenazic communities, cheese blintzes topped with sour cream or fruit sauce are frequently served on days when it is customary to eat dairy dishes, such as on Shavuot and during the week before Tisha b'Av. They are especially appropriate on Shavuot, which commemorates the giving of the Torah, since two blintzes placed side by side resemble the two tablets of the commandments that Moses received at Mount Sinai.[3]

Bread (לֶחֶם)

Often called the "staff of life," bread is a chief ingredient of the Western diet. In addition to baked goods made from cereal flour, the Hebrew term "*lechem*" also is used in the Bible to refer to food in general, as when the brothers "sat down to eat bread" after throwing Joseph into the pit (Gen. 37:25).[4] In biblical times, bread was prepared from wheat or barley. Dough to which leaven was added was called *hametz*, to differentiate it from unleavened matzah.

From the earliest periods, the baking of bread was an essential daily household chore. Initially it was primarily women's work, for which the diligent housewife (*eshet chayil*; "woman of valor"; see p. 129) "rises while it is still night and provides food for her household" (Prov. 31:15).[5] Only in later periods was the task performed by experts in local bakeries.

During their wanderings in the wilderness, the Israelites were fed with manna, "bread … from the sky" (Exod. 16:4). The phrase "bread and water" referred to the level of minimal subsistence—Abraham sent away Hagar and Ishmael with "some bread and a skin of water" (Gen. 21:14), Obadiah fed the 100 prophets persecuted by Jezebel with "bread and water" (1 Kings 18:4),[6] and "cake baked on hot stones and a jar of water" was sufficient to maintain Elijah for 40 days (1 Kings 19:6). The righteous one feeds bread to the hungry (Ezek. 18:7), and conversely, it was considered a grievous sin to "deny bread to the hungry" (Job 22:7). Metaphorically, the ungodly were said to "eat the bread of wickedness [and drink the wine of lawlessness]" (Prov. 4:17), and the good wife "[oversees the activities of her household, and] never eats the bread of idleness" (Prov. 31:27).

For the Rabbis, bread was an essential element of every meal. Consequently, they introduced a special blessing to be recited before eating bread from one of the five species of cereals grown in the Land of Israel (wheat, barley, spelt, oats, rye). Popularly known as *ha-Motzi*, it thanks God, "Who has brought forth bread from the earth" (see p. 474). After eating bread at least the size of an olive, a full *Birkat ha-Mazon* (Grace after Meals) must be said (see p. 476). To decrease the possibility of assimilation that might result in intermarriage, Jews were prohibited from eating bread baked by a non-Jew, though this did not apply to bread sold by a professional non-Jewish baker using ingredients not otherwise forbidden by the dietary laws.

Whenever Rabbi Huna[7] ate ("wrapped bread," referring to the cus-

CHALLAH (חָלָּה)

Challah is the familiar braided bread baked for the Sabbath (see p. 141). It also is frequently baked in special shapes for the festivals. On Rosh Hashanah, the challah is typically round to symbolize the annual cycle and the hope for an abundant year of peace and goodness. For that festival, raisins are customarily included in the dough to emphasize the desire for a sweet year. In some communities, the challah is shaped like a crown, to suggest the King of kings who created the universe. On both Rosh Hashanah and Yom Kippur, the challah is sometimes formed into a bird's head, based on the verse in Isaiah (31:5) in which God is pictured as shielding Jerusalem "like a bird hovering over its young."[1] Another custom is to design a ladder atop the challah to signify the hope that our prayers for forgiveness will ascend swiftly to heaven. On Hoshana Rabbah, the top of the challah may be in the shape of a hand reaching up, symbolizing our receipt of the divine judgment that was decreed on Yom Kippur but not confirmed until this last day of Sukkot.[2] Some challot are shaped like a menorah on the Sabbath of Hanukkah, while on Purim the bread may be molded into a single giant braid representing the long rope used to hang Haman or into small triangular loaves to symbolize Haman's ears.[3]

tom of beginning a meal with herbs and salt placed between two pieces of bread), he first "would open the door wide and declare, 'Let everyone in need come and eat'" (Taan. 20b). These words in Aramaic are still repeated by Jews today at the beginning of the Passover seder. Even though they had manna to eat, the Israelites in the desert were described as "afflicted" because "there is no comparison between one who has bread in his basket and one who does not have bread in his basket" (Yoma 74b). The Israelites were in the latter category because the manna that fell daily was just the amount sufficient for that day. Rabbi Eliezer opined that "one who has bread in his basket and asks, 'What will I eat tomorrow?' is of those who have little faith" (Sot. 48b). According to the Talmud, the fare of a poor man is "bread with salt" (Ber. 2b). This is also all that is required for one who studies Torah: "A morsel of bread with salt you shall eat, and water by measure you shall drink, and upon the ground you shall sleep, and a life of privation you shall live, and in the Torah you shall labor" (Avot 6:4). One who can eat (less expensive) barley bread and eats wheat bread instead violates the prohibition on wasting food (Shab. 140b). As an indication of the high regard the Rabbis had for bread, the Talmud notes: "Raw meat should not be placed on bread; a full cup should not be passed along over bread [lest some wine spill on it], bread should not be thrown [across the table], and a dish should not be propped up [on it]" (Ber. 50b). Similarly, during an extensive discussion about demons and evil spirits, the Talmud mentions that it is inappropriate to hang bread (Pes. 11b).

Religious Requirements and Customs

In observant households and Jewish bakeries where bread is baked, an olive-sized piece of dough, termed "challah," is set aside and burned in the oven (Shab. 2:6) as a remembrance of the dough offering to the *Kohanim* in the Temple (Num. 15:20; see p. 141). Two loaves of a special bread (challah) are placed on the dinner table on Sabbaths and festivals, both as a symbol of the double portion of manna that the Israelites received each Friday (Exod. 16:5) and to recall the showbread that was displayed each Sabbath in the Temple and eaten by the *Kohanim* (Lev. 24:5–9; 1 Sam. 21:7; see p. 142). On Passover, Jews eat only unleavened bread (matzah), which reflects both the humble bread of poverty and the fact that the Israelites did not have time to allow their dough to rise as they hastened to escape from bondage in Egypt. Before the festival, bits of bread are hidden and ceremoniously "discovered" to rid the home of *hametz* (see p. 268). For the *Tashlikh* ceremony on Rosh Hashanah, Jews symbolically cast off their sins by throwing crumbs of bread into a lake or flowing stream (see p. 203).

Since the dinner table is compared to the Temple altar, salt is generally sprinkled over bread before each meal, especially on the Sabbath, as a symbol of the ancient sacrificial ritual. As a wish for wealth and good fortune, it is traditional to give a loaf of bread ("staff of life") and a jar of salt (an elemental substance and preservative) to newly married couples or to people moving into a new house.[8]

Carob (חָרוּב)

The carob (*charuv* in Hebrew; *bokser* in Yiddish) is an evergreen tree that grows wild in the Mediterranean regions of Israel and produces a sweet fruit. The tree has a rounded head that can grow bushy enough to cloak its small trunk.

The carob matures more slowly than most other fruit trees, requiring about 10 years for its rich, chocolate-like fruit to be edible. The Talmud extends the maturation period substantially in the popular legend in which the wonder-working Honi the Circle-Maker came across a man planting a carob tree (Taan. 23a). To his question, "How long does it take [for this tree] to bear fruit?" the man replied, "Seventy years." When Honi asked if he was certain that he would live that long, the man answered that just as he had found fully grown carob trees planted by his ancestors when he came into the world, so he was planting them for his children and grandchildren.

The Talmud suggests that the verse, "[God] fed him honey from the crag" (Deut. 32:13) may allude to the carob, since the tree grows among the rocks and the pod contains a type of honey when ripe (JT Pe'ah 7:4). Carob fruit was often preserved in wine (Shev. 7:7).

The carob tree is featured prominently in one of the most famous rabbinic disputes (BM 59b). When the Rabbis were arguing over a technical point of Jewish law, one scholar, Rabbi Eliezer, "brought forward every imaginable argument, but to no avail. He then said to the Rabbis: 'If the *halakhah* agrees with me, let this carob tree prove it!' Thereupon the carob-tree was torn 100 cubits out of its place. ... [But] the others retorted that 'No proof can be brought from a carob tree.'" After several similar demonstrations, Eliezer called on God to affirm the correctness of his position. In response, a heavenly voice cried out: "Why do you quarrel with Rabbi Eliezer, seeing that in all matters the *halakhah* agrees with him!" However, the other sages disagreed, citing the verse, "It is not in the heavens" (Deut 30:12), to prove that ever since the Torah was given at Mount Sinai, it is the responsibility of the majority of Rabbis to determine what the Law means. God clearly agreed with this decision, for "He laughed [with joy], saying, 'My sons have defeated Me, My sons have defeated Me!'"

Carob fruit was usually eaten only by the poor, but according to the Talmud, it was so nutritious that Hanina ben Dosa lived "from one Sabbath eve to another" on carobs alone (Taan. 24b). Similarly, for 12 years, carobs sustained Shimon bar Yochai and his son while they hid in a cave from the Romans (Shab. 33b). Because of the association between this reputed author of the mystical Zohar and Lag ba-Omer (see p. 294), carob is traditionally eaten on this holiday. Although not mentioned in the Bible as one of the eight agricultural products listed as indigenous to the Land of Israel, carob flourished there and was the most popular fruit used for celebrating the holiday of Tu b'Shevat since it could survive the long trip to Jewish communities in Europe, North Africa, and other distant sites.

Chickpea (חִמְצָה)

The chickpea (or garbanzo bean), one of the earliest-known cultivated plants, is actually not a pea but a legume that grows two to a pod. Most often tan, round, and with a nutty flavor, it has long been a staple in the Jewish diet. Hummus, a thick puree of chickpeas and sesame seed paste (tahini), is a popular dip in Israel and other Middle Eastern countries, and felafel (spicy chickpea croquettes) are sold by street vendors and kiosks as their equivalent of fast food.[9] Both are eaten with pita, a round, hollow, flat bread that is puffed up and separated into two layers by steam while it is baked in a very hot oven.

Chickpeas are traditionally eaten on the first Friday night after the birth of a son (*shalom zachar*; see p. 6) and at the *seudah shelishit*, the third Sabbath meal (see p. 142). They are also consumed on Purim, because of the legend that Queen Esther observed the laws of kashrut in the palace of King Ahashuerus by eating only vegetarian foods, specifically beans, peas, and grains (Meg. 13a). Daniel, another Jew in the Persian court, similarly limited his diet to "legumes to eat and water to drink" to avoid violating the dietary laws (Dan. 1:12).[10]

Some Middle Eastern Jews do not eat chickpeas on Passover because of the similarity between its Hebrew name (*himtza*) and *hametz*, which is forbidden during this festival. In some communities, chickpeas is a traditional dish on Rosh Hashanah, since another Hebrew name for this legume is "*kara*" (cold), symbolizing the "cooling down" of God's stern judgment for which Jews pray on this day.[11]

Cholent

Because cooking is one of the 39 categories of creative work forbidden on the Sabbath, it was necessary to develop an ingenious technique for preparing a warm meal that would enrich the enjoyment of the Sabbath lunch and still be consistent with the halakhic requirement that the food must be at least half cooked before the onset of the day of rest. Every Friday morning in medieval Ashkenazic European communities, the women of each household would fill a large pot with beans, potatoes, some type of meat, and various spices, seal it with a flour and water paste, and take it to a central communal oven, where the mixtures would slowly simmer unattended all night until retrieved after synagogue on Saturday. This Sabbath stew was known as *cholent*, a Yiddish word possibly derived from the Old French "*chald*," meaning "hot." Another etymological approach is that *cholent* comes from a combination of two Yiddish words—"*shul*" (synagogue) and "*ende*" (end)—a precise description of when this dish is served. Heinrich Heine was so enamored with *cholent* that he composed the poem "Princess Sabbath" extolling its virtues and calling it "the food of Heaven ... kosher ambrosia." Sephardim also have a traditional slow-simmered bean stew for the Sabbath lunch meal. It is known either as *chamin* or *chamim* (from "*cham*," the Hebrew word for "hot") or as *adafina* or *dafina* (from the Arabic word for "covered"). Sephardim generally use chickpeas and fava or large lima beans, while Ashkenazim prefer small beans, barley, and potatoes.[12]

These Sabbath stews have influenced non-Jewish cultures in Europe and the Americas. In Spain, bean and chickpea stews were such a characteristic Jewish dish that the Inquisition suspected anyone preparing them of practicing Judaism. Conversos wishing to secretly maintain their Jewish traditions while outwardly living as Catholics began adding pork (which no traditional Jew would eat) to the stew instead of the customary beef or lamb. This led to the development of a classic Spanish dish, *cocida madrileno* (lit., "boiled from Madrid"), which later was eaten in Central and South America as well. In the United States, the Pilgrims refrained from cooking on Sunday, their day of rest. After being exposed in Holland to the customs of the Sephardic Jews who settled in that country after being expelled from Spain, the Pilgrims adopted the idea of a slow-cooking Sabbath stew, substituting maple syrup and bacon for some of the traditional ingredients. Leaving the pot in the oven Saturday night, the Pilgrims had a warm lunch to eat after church; this became the classic American dish of Boston baked beans.[13]

Egg (בֵּיצָה)

Based on the talmudic dictum, "That which emerges from the clean [animal] is clean" (Bek 1:2, 5b), it is an established principle that the eggs of clean birds are permitted for food. Because the hard shell of the egg is formed even before it has been laid, the egg is regarded as "completed on its issue"—an entity independent from the fowl that laid it and thus not subject to the prohibition against eating a part of a living animal or the law forbidding the eating of meat (extended by the Rabbis to fowl) with milk (Betz. 6b). However, because "that which emerges from the unclean [animal] is unclean" (Bek. 1:2, 5b), the eggs of forbidden birds are prohibited. The Talmud attempts to describe the physical characteristics of eggs that determine whether they are clean or unclean: "All that are arched and rounded, with one end broad and the other end narrow, are clean. Those that are broad at both ends or narrow at both ends are unclean. Those with the white outside and the yolk in the center are clean, those with the yolk outside and the white in the center are unclean" (Hul. 64b).

Even the eggs of permitted birds are forbidden if they have been fertilized, which generally results in a dark spot in certain parts of the albumen. Although the Rabbis disagreed as to the significance of blood spots in various locations (Hul. 64b), the general rule is that any spot of blood in the egg renders it unfit for consumption. The sole exception is an egg that comes from a chicken in an area where there is no cock. Because it could not have been fertilized, the egg may be eaten if one removes the spot itself.

For Jews, the egg has long been a sign of mourning and consolation, consumed by mourners at the meal given to them when they return from the cemetery after the burial (*se'udat havra'ah*; see p. 94), as well as eaten by all at the meal before the fast of Tisha b'Av, which commemorates the day of national mourning for the destruction of the Temples in Jerusalem. Eggs play a major role at the Passover seder. The roasted egg that is placed on the seder plate, but not eaten, is a symbol of the special festival offering (*Hagigah*) for the holiday. A popular custom is eating an egg dipped in saltwater before beginning the festive meal. This may be a sign of mourning for the destruction of the Temple and the consequent inability of Jews to fulfill the commandment of sacrificing the paschal lamb. Eggs also are a symbol of rebirth and thus appropriate for this major spring festival.[14]

The egg was also an important standard of measurement, from which were calculated such larger volumes as the *log* (6 eggs), *kab* (24 eggs), and *se'ah* (144 eggs). The Talmud stressed that this referred to a hen's egg rather than to one of the *Bar Yokani*, a gigantic member of the ostrich family (Yoma 80a). According to legend, a huge egg once fell from this fabulous bird in mid-flight "and its contents swamped 16 cities and destroyed 300 cedar trees" (Bek. 57b).[15]

Fish (דָּג)

According to the laws of kashrut, only fish (*dag*) that have fins and scales are permitted for consumption (Lev. 11:9–11). Unlike meat, there is no requirement for fish to be slaughtered ritually (*shechitah*) and their blood is not prohibited. However, the Rabbis forbade eating or cooking fish and meat together based on the belief that this combination "is harmful to [one's] smell and in respect to 'something else' [euphemistic phrase, equivalent in context to making the body susceptible to leprosy]" (Pes. 76b). After eating fish it is not necessary to wait before eating meat; all that is required is to rinse the mouth or chew something else. Fish are considered pareve—neither milk nor meat—and may be cooked or eaten with milk products.

GEFILTE FISH

For a multitude of reasons, fish has been a favorite food at Sabbath meals since talmudic times. However, one of the forbidden forms of work on the Sabbath is removing the inedible part of food from the edible part, based on the prohibition of winnowing, the separation of wheat from the chaff. Although one is not allowed to remove the bones from a piece of fish on the Sabbath, one may eat around the bones of a non-filleted piece of fish. Lest this tedious task impinge on the joy of the Sabbath meal, the solution was to prepare in advance a boneless piece of fish that could be eaten without fear of violating the Sabbath laws (or choking on a bone). Rabbi Papa suggested a fish pie based on chopped boneless fish and flour as a delightful delicacy for the Sabbath eve (Shab. 118b; Er. 65a). However, he refused to pray in a house where it was being cooked because of its pungent odor, and he recommended that nursing mothers not eat this dish.[1]

Gefilte fish originated in Germany around the 14th century. It takes its name from the original technique of stuffing (*gefulte,* in German) the chopped and seasoned flesh of the fish into the skin, then sewing it up and baking it. Eventually, the complex stuffing step was eliminated and the fish was mixed with onions and matzah meal to produce what became the quintessential Sabbath dish in Eastern Europe. Gefilte fish was generally prepared from the most readily available type of fish—pike in Germany and carp in Poland—with other varieties of whitefish, sweeteners, and spices added in varying proportions, depending on regional preferences. Gefilte fish was originally eaten with vinegar and later mayonnaise in Germany, and with horseradish (*chrein*) in Eastern Europe.[2]

Fish has long been a favorite food for all three meals on the Sabbath. One reason for this custom is the fact that in the biblical account of Creation, three things are blessed after they are created—fish, humans, and the Sabbath. Another relationship between fish and the Sabbath is that the day is a foretaste of the world to come, in which the righteous will feast on Leviathan, the great legendary sea monster (see p. 724). Moreover, in Hebrew the numerical value of fish (4 = ד, 3 = ג) equals seven. The Kabbalists suggested that sometimes, when people die, they are reincarnated as fish; but when eaten by a righteous person on the Sabbath, the soul of such a person is returned to a nobler path.

In the 17th century, the fishermen of Moravia colluded to raise the price of fish before the Sabbath because they knew the Jews would pay exorbitant fees to continue their tradition. Rabbi Menachem Mendel Krochmal responded by forbidding the consumption of fish, proclaiming it as essentially nonkosher. The demand fell, and subsequently the price of fish did too.

Fish have numerous symbolic meanings. Because their eyes never close, fish are a symbol of the ever-observant protection of God. As a symbol of fertility, because of the large numbers of eggs they lay, fish were eaten by women desiring to conceive a child. Jacob used a term derived from the word for fish (*dag*) when he blessed Ephraim and Menasseh (the sons of Joseph): "May they be teeming multitudes [*v'yidgu*] upon the earth" (Gen. 48:16).[16] From this comparison of the grandsons of Israel to fish, the Rabbis deduced: "Just as the fish [*dagim*] in the sea are covered by water and the evil eye has no power over them, so the evil eye has no power over the seed of Joseph" (Ber. 20a).

Fish were thought to bring luck, based on the fact that Pisces (the zodiac sign for fish) usually falls during Adar, the month of Purim when "our joy greatly increases" (Taan. 29a). To stress this association, the plates used for sending gifts of food (*shalach manot*) during this festival often contain fish designs. A custom among Sephardic Jews is to eat fish heads on Rosh Hashanah so that they rise to the "head" of the community in righteousness and good deeds. In Eastern Europe, some parents named their sons Fishl as a good omen against the Evil Eye."[17]

Garlic (שׁוּם)

Garlic (*shum*) is listed, along with its relatives onion and leek, as one of the foods that the Israelites had eaten as slaves in Egypt and for which they were nostalgic while wandering through the wilderness (Num. 11:5). The Rabbis taught that garlic "satiates, keeps the body warm, brightens up the face, increases semen, and kills parasites in the bowels [intestinal worms]" (BK 82a). Considered an aphrodisiac, the Jerusalem Talmud recommends that garlic be eaten on Friday evenings since "it promotes love and arouses desire" (Meg. 4:1, 75a). The "Sabbath delight" for one Rabbi was "a dish of beets, large fish, and heads of garlic" (Shab. 118b). Because of their passion for this vegetable, the Jews referred to themselves as "garlic eaters" (Ned. 3:10), though some were less than enamored with its smell. Once while giving a lecture, Judah ha-Nasi asked those who had eaten garlic to leave the study hall. "Rabbi Hiyya arose and left; then all the other disciples rose in turn and went out" (Sanh. 11a).

Lentil (עֲדָשָׁה)

One of the first plants cultivated in the ancient Middle East, the lentil (*adashah*) was the stew of "red stuff" for which the famished Esau sold his birthright to Jacob (Gen. 25:29–34). According to a midrash, this event occurred "the day on which Abraham our father died, and Jacob our father made a potage [soup] of lentils to comfort his father Isaac" (BB 16b). He was preparing this traditional mourning dish, which his mother, Rebekah, could not do, since as a wife she was excluded from cooking the *seudat havra'ah* (meal of consolation). Later commentators explain that Jacob was so shocked by Esau's insensitivity upon entering the house of mourning, caring only about his own hunger and not showing the requisite sadness and respect, that the younger brother realized the need to acquire the birthright and its associated spiritual leadership of the family.

Lentils are traditionally eaten by Jewish mourners. The Talmud asks why this particular legume was an appropriate dish. One explanation is that "just as the lentil has no mouth [no cleft like other kinds of legumes], so the mourner has no mouth [for speech]" and should remain silent in the face of death and not speak of ordinary subjects (BB 16b). Another explanation is that "just as the lentil is round, so mourning comes round to all the inhabitants of this world [i.e., all are mortal]."

In mishnaic and talmudic times, lentils were a major food of the common people. They grow so close to the ground that the Rabbis coined the expression "as lowly as the lentil" (JT Sanh. 2:5, 20b). One reason for the antipathy shown by the upper classes to the lentil was that it caused bad breath (Ber. 40a), though the talmudic passage adds that it is a remedy for diphtheria.

Meat (בָּשָׂר)

According to the Torah, humans were meant to be vegetarians, for God gave them "all the green plants for food" (Gen. 1:30). The consumption of meat was first specifically permitted to Noah, with the proviso that "You must not … eat flesh with its lifeblood in it" (Gen. 9:3). Nevertheless, the diet of the Israelites consisted primarily of agricultural products, and soon after the Exodus they were condemned for lusting after the "fleshpots [of Egypt]" (Exod. 16:3).

According to the laws of kashrut, Jews may eat the flesh of only clean animals after proper slaughtering (*shechitah*) and the removal of forbidden blood and fat (see p. 659). On three occasions, the Torah expressly prohibits "boiling a kid in its mother's milk" (Exod. 23:19, 34:26; Deut. 14:21), which was interpreted as forbidding the cooking of milk and meat together, eating such a mixture, and deriving any benefit from it.

The Talmud states that those who "engage in [the study of] the Torah may eat the flesh of beast and fowl," while an "*am ha-aretz*" [common person] may not on a regular basis (Pes. 49b). The exception was the Sabbath and festivals, when eating meat was considered obligatory since "there is no joy without meat and wine" (Pes. 109a). Rabbi Judah ben Bathyra disagreed, arguing that this applied only "when the Temple was in existence" (Pes. 109a); following its destruction, one can rejoice with wine, based on the verse from Psalms (104:15), "wine … cheers the hearts of men." Numerous responsa have supported this view, and several modern chief rabbis have been strict vegetarians who did not eat meat even on Sabbaths and festivals.[18] Because eating meat is considered celebratory, Jews are expected to refrain from consuming meat during the first nine days of the month of Av, a time of national mourning for the destruction of the Temples. Similarly, during *aninut*, the period of mourning between death and burial (see p. 93), mourners do not eat meat.

The Rabbis considered poultry to be superior to meat, and meat better than fish (Num. R. 21:25). "The best of cattle is the ox; the best of birds is the fowl [chicken]" (BM 86b). However, those recovering from illnesses were to avoid "beef, fat meat, roast meat, poultry, and roasted egg," since they "bring a man's sickness on again in a severe form" (Ber. 57b).

Milk (חָלָב)

The quintessential biblical description of the Promised Land is "a land flowing with milk and honey" (Exod. 3:8; Num. 13:27; Deut. 6:3), symbolizing its rich fertility. When poetically depicting God's gracious generosity toward the Israelites in his farewell address, Moses included "curd of kine" [butter, cream, and yogurt] and "milk of flocks" (Deut. 32:14). In Song of Songs (4:11), the lover describes the sweetness of his beloved as having "honey and milk ... under your tongue." In his vision of the Messianic Age, the prophet Joel (4:18) stated that "the mountains shall drip with wine, the [Judean] hills shall flow with milk."

Most dairy products during the biblical period were produced from the milk of sheep or goats, since there were relatively few cattle. As an important source of dietary liquid in a region where water was scarce and often contaminated, milk and dairy products were popular offerings by pagan peoples to their gods or king. The prohibition against "boiling a kid in its mother's milk"—which is repeated three times in the Torah (Exod. 23:19, 34:26; Deut. 14:21) and is the basis for the separation of meat and milk (see p. 662)—may thus be the divine rejection of an ancient Canaanite religious practice.[19]

The milk of clean animals (cows, sheep, goats) is permitted for consumption, even though it comes "from the living" (Bek. 6b). However, the Talmud prohibited Jews from consuming "milk which a heathen milked without an Israelite watching him," because of the fear that the former may have inadvertently mixed it with milk from an unclean animal (Av. Zar. 2:6, 35b). Today, some strictly observant Jews drink only *chalav Yisrael* (milk obtained and bottled under the supervision of a Jew), though many authorities permit the consumption of milk even if Jews did not supervise the milking, since there are laws strictly forbidding the adulteration of milk.

Similarly, the Talmud prohibits eating cheese made by gentiles, because the rennet used to curdle the milk might come from the stomach of a nonkosher animal, a kosher animal that had not been slaughtered according to the requirements of the dietary laws, or one that was sacrificed as part of an idolatrous rite (Av. Zar. 2:5, 34b–35a). This prohibition did not extend to cottage cheese and other soft cheeses, for which rennet is not used.

The eating of dairy products is especially associated with the festivals of Shavuot (see p. 298) and Hanukkah (see p. 244).

Onion (בָּצָל) and Leek (חָצִיר)

Onions (*batzal*) and leeks (*chatzir*) are mentioned with garlic as among the vegetables of Egypt for which the Israelites yearned during their journey in the wilderness (Num. 11:5). The Talmud urges Jews to "eat *batzal* [onions] and sit *ba-tzeil* [in the shade of your house], and do not eat geese and fowl" (Pes. 144a). Implying that one who spends too much on food will not be able to afford a house, the expression was interpreted to mean that Jews should not wish for luxuries but rather be satisfied with very little. Leeks were so highly valued as a remedy for snakebite that it was permitted to cut one on the Sabbath for this purpose (Yoma 83b).

Salt (מֶלַח)

Present in huge quantities in the area of the Dead Sea, which is known in Hebrew as "*Yam ha-Melach*" (Salt Sea), salt is first mentioned in the Bible in reference to Lot's wife turning into a "pillar of salt" (Gen. 19:26).

According to the Torah, "You shall season your every offering of meal with salt" (Lev. 2:13), but the Talmud extended this requirement to all sacrifices (Men. 20a). In his *Mishneh Torah*, Maimonides stated that the commandments dealing with offerings were *hukim* (statutes), whose purpose must remain incomprehensible to the human mind.[20] In his later *Guide of the Perplexed*, Maimonides offered a rationalistic interpretation, arguing that the laws of sacrifices ordained by the Torah were concessions to the universal custom of bringing offerings to the various pagan deities.[21] However, the specific requirements in Jewish sacrifices were diametrically opposite to those of heathen cults. Idolaters offered only leavened bread, seasoned their sacrifices with honey (a favorite food of their gods), and never used salt. Therefore, the Torah forbade the Israelites from offering leavened bread and honey and commanded them to bring salt with every offering. With the destruction of the Temple and its sacrificial rites, the family dining table came to symbolize the Holy Altar. Therefore, the commandment to bring salt with every offering is recalled by sprinkling salt over the challah at Sabbath and festival meals.

As the best food preservative in antiquity and a symbol of permanence among ancient peoples, covenants were customarily sealed with bread and salt. Accordingly, the Bible describes both the right of the *Kohanim* to their share of the offerings (Num. 18:19) and the divine granting of the kingdom to the House of David (2 Chron. 13:5) as "a covenant of salt." Bread dipped in salt is a symbol of hospitality, and even today these items are brought as gifts to those moving into a new home. In Israel, the mayor of Jerusalem traditionally welcomes distinguished visitors with an offering of bread and salt at the entrance to the city.

As an effective cleansing agent, salt was rubbed on a newborn to remove the creamy white substance (vernix) covering it (Ezek. 16:4). Elisha purified the bad waters of Jericho by casting salt into the springs, "no longer shall death or bereavement come from it" (2 Kings 2:20–21). The ability of salt to absorb blood, which Jews are forbidden to consume, is the basis of its use in the kashering of meat (see p. 687). According to the Talmud, the custom of washing one's hands after a meal, in addition to the specific rabbinic commandment of washing the hands before meals (see p. 553), was related to the presence in common salt of the "salt of Sodom," which could be harmful to the eyes (Hul. 105b). At the Passover seder, Jews dip greens in saltwater to remember the bitter tears shed by their ancestors when they were slaves in Egypt. After being exiled from the Garden of Eden, Adam was condemned to earn his bread "by the [salty] sweat of [his] brow" (Gen. 3:19).[22]

Tzimmes

Tzimmes is a slow-simmered stew dating back to the late medieval German practice of sweetening meats or vegetables with fruits and honey or sugar. Initially coming from two Yiddish words "*zum*" and "*essen*," meaning "to eat," the term has entered the English language as a word denoting "making a fuss over something" or "making a big deal over nothing" (probably reflecting the intense labor of chopping, stirring, and stewing required to prepare the dish). In the Ashkenazic community, tzimmes has become a popular dish for Sabbath and festival meals, especially the celebration of the abundant harvest on Sukkot and as a symbolic wish for a sweet year on Rosh Hashanah.[23]

Tzimmes may contain meat or be vegetarian and is generally sweetened with fresh, or more frequently, dried fruits (especially prunes). All recipes include at least one root vegetable, primarily carrots or sweet potatoes. On Rosh Hashanah, Jews in Eastern Europe traditionally prepared tzimmes with carrots, based on that vegetable's Yiddish name "*mehren*" (many), expressing the hope for a productive year with many blessings; based on its Hebrew name "*gezer*" (tear), indicating a desire that any evil decrees be torn up; or simply because when sliced they appear like gold coins, symbolizing prosperity.[24]

Plants and Animals

Plants

Trees (עֵצִים)

In ancient Israel, trees were an important source of food and shelter. Their wood provided for the construction of houses, boats, the Tabernacle in the wilderness, and the Temple in Jerusalem. The shade of trees was especially valuable in the hot sun of the Land of Israel, and their fruit was a valuable commodity for nutrition and export.

Many primitive peoples in the ancient Near East congregated in sacred groves to worship the spirits inhabiting the trees. Solidly rooted in the ground and reaching upward toward the limitless sky, trees were viewed as representing the link connecting Heaven and earth. The Bible prohibited all sacred plantings (Deut. 16:21), so that the Israelites would not imitate the practice common among their Canaanite neighbors of planting beautiful, shapely trees to honor their idols in their houses of worship. Consequently, no trees were permitted for purposes of adornment and beautification within the courtyard of the Sanctuary (where the altar stood), even for the worship of God. However, images of trees have been used as religious symbols. The tree of life (*etz hayim*; see below), which tradition associates with the Torah, has long been a favorite decoration in synagogues. Trees were models for the two supporting pillars of the Temple (Jachin and Boaz), which in turn probably served as the basis for the wooden staves (*atzei hayim*) around which the Torah scroll is rolled (see p. 330).[1]

Jews are forbidden from destroying fruit trees during a military campaign so as not to cause distress and suffering to the inhabitants of a besieged city (Deut. 20:19–20). Unlike human beings, trees cannot protect themselves by taking refuge behind city walls.[2] Even during times of war, Jews must remain conscious of the need to maintain their concern for the general welfare, including of their enemies. Recognizing that fruit trees are vital to humankind, the Rabbis developed the general principle of *bal tashchit*—prohibiting the wanton destruction of anything valuable to human existence, including vessels, clothing, buildings, springs, and food. The Zionist movement went even further, stressing the planting of trees as a tangible manifestation of the rebirth of the Land of Israel. Today, many Jews plant a tree in Israel to memorialize special family occasions, such as a birth, bar or bat mitzvah, wedding, or death.[3]

The "New Year of the Trees," Tu b'Shevat, is celebrated with a "seder" that includes four cups of wine and the eating of fruits and nuts grown in the Land of Israel (see p. 253).

Tree of Knowledge of Good and Evil (עֵץ הַדַּעַת טוֹב וָרָע)

The first command given by God to Adam in the Garden of Eden was to not eat of the Tree of Knowledge of Good and Evil (Gen. 2:17). Legends variously identify this as the fig, apple, pomegranate, *etrog*, carob, palm, or nut tree.[4] Induced by the serpent to consume the forbidden fruit of the tree, Eve in turn gave some to her husband to eat (Gen. 3:6).

The punishment decreed for disobeying the divine commandment was explicitly stated: "For as soon as you eat of it, you shall die" (Gen. 2:17). This penalty cannot be understood literally, for Adam continued to live for 930 years. Instead, various commentators have suggested that the consequence of their sin was that Adam, Eve, and their progeny became both subject to death and the only creatures aware of their own mortality.[5]

All parties involved received additional punishment (Gen. 3:14–19). The snake was condemned to crawl on its belly and eat the dust of the earth, as well as to become the eternal enemy of human beings (see p. 730). Just as Eve had convinced her husband to eat at her command, so now she and all subsequent women would become obedient to the demands of their husbands ("he shall rule over you"; Gen. 3:16). Rather than conceive promptly and have an easy delivery, from this time on many women would have difficulty attempting to become pregnant (as with the experiences of Sarah, Rachel, and Hannah) and "in pain shall you bear children" (Gen 3:16). Adam would be forced to work hard to sustain himself: "By the sweat of your brow shall you get bread to eat" (Gen. 3:19). The ultimate punishment for the first couple was their expulsion from the Garden of Eden (Gen. 3:23–24).

Ibn Ezra and many modern scholars have argued that the "knowledge" imparted by eating of the fruit of the tree was carnal knowledge: "the eyes of both of them were opened and they perceived that they were naked; and they sewed together fig leaves and made themselves loincloths" (Gen. 3:7). The shame that this engendered was so intense that they "hid from the Lord God among the trees of the garden" (Gen. 3:8).

Tree of Life (עֵץ חַיִּים)

Planted in the middle of the Garden of Eden (Gen. 2:9), the Tree of Life has long been associated with the Torah. When the Torah scroll is returned to the ark, the congregation proclaims that "it is a tree of life (*etz hayim*) to all who hold fast to it, and all who uphold it are *me-ushar* [variously translated as "praiseworthy," "happy," "content," or "safe"]" (Prov. 3:18).[6] The blessing recited after each *aliyah* states that the Torah represents "eternal life planted within us." The wooden staves around which the parchment of the scroll is rolled are called *atzei hayim* (trees of life; see p. 330). Consequently, the image of the Tree of Life as a symbol of the Torah has become a popular synagogue decoration.

Specific Plants

A number of plants are mentioned in the Bible and Talmud and are involved in Jewish rituals. Some of these are discussed in the following sections, arranged in alphabetical order.

Acacia (שִׁטָּה)

Acacia (*shittah*) was the only wood used in the building of the Tabernacle and its accessories (ark, altar, table, staves) (Exod. 25–27). A hard but light and water-resistant wood, the acacia was used extensively for construction and shipbuilding during biblical times. However, because acacia trees are not native to the Sinai wilderness, where did the Israelites find them after the Exodus from Egypt? According to a midrash quoted by Rashi, while on his way to Egypt for his reunion with Joseph, the Patriarch Jacob foresaw that his descendants would someday need acacia trees and planted them in the wilderness, instructing his sons that their progeny should take the wood with them when they were freed from bondage centuries later. The huge planks for the Tabernacle are described as "acacia wood, upright" (Exod. 26:15), which the Rabbis interpreted as a guarantee of Jewish survival in the darkness of exile (Yoma 72a).[1]

Cedar (אֶרֶז)

The majestic cedar was renowned in biblical times for its strength, fragrance, and hardiness. Described as "the trees of the Lord ... His own planting" (Ps. 104:16) and famed for their longevity, the tall cedars were contrasted to the lowly hyssop (1 Kings 5:13). An indication of divine power was that "the voice of the Lord breaks the mighty cedars" (Ps. 29:5). The best-known biblical reference is: "The righteous bloom like a date palm; they thrive like a cedar in Lebanon" (Ps. 92:13).[2] Along with hyssop and some scarlet-dyed material, small pieces of cedar wood were used in the purification rites for the person afflicted with the skin disease *tzara'at* (Lev. 14:4) and in preparing the ashes of the red heifer (Num. 19:6) used to ritually purify a person who had been contaminated by contact with a corpse.

The fine-grained, reddish wood of the cedar is resistant to water and was used to construct royal palaces, the walls and ceilings of houses, and the masts of ships (Ezek. 27:5). King David thought it inappropriate that "I am dwelling in a house of cedar, while the Ark of the Lord abides in a tent!" (2 Sam. 7:2). Later his son Solomon used cedar wood in the construction of the First Temple, and it was also used in building the Second Temple after the return from Babylonian exile (Ezra 3:7).

The Talmud reports, "It was the custom when a boy was born to plant a cedar tree and when a girl was born to plant a pine tree, and when they married, the trees were cut down and a canopy [*huppah*] made of the branches" (Git. 57a).

Cypress (תְּאַשּׁוּר)

According to tradition, the cypress has been identified with both the gopher tree, from which Noah built his ark (Gen. 6:14), and the box tree (*te'ashur*, apparently derived from "*yashar*" [upright]), a tall, graceful evergreen widely used in the ancient world to build ships (Ezek. 27:6). "Meanwhile, David and all the House of Israel danced before the Lord to [the sound of] all kinds of cypress wood [instruments]" (2 Sam. 6:5), and Solomon used it in constructing the First Temple (1 Kings 6:15,34). While in exile, Isaiah (60:13) prophesied that eventually the cedar would be used to "to adorn the site of My Sanctuary, [i.e., the rebuilt Temple]."

Etrog (אֶתְרוֹג)

The *etrog* (citron) is traditionally identified as "the fruit of a goodly tree" (*peri etz hadar*; Lev. 23:40), which is one of the four species used as part of the celebration of the festival of Sukkot (see p. 232). This yellow citrus fruit, which is usually larger and more bitter than a lemon, has both a pleasant taste and smell. The *etrog* symbolically represents those Jews who possess both learning and good deeds to their credit. During Sukkot, it is customary to protect the *etrog* and its fragile stem (*pitam*) in an ornamental container. After the festival, the *etrog* is often made into jam or studded with cloves, its fragrant aroma mixing with the sweet spices used during the *Havdalah* service (see p. 151). During the Second Temple period, the *etrog* was a popular design on Israelite coins, synagogue walls, and mosaic floors.

Some legends suggest that the *etrog* was the forbidden fruit eaten by Adam and Eve in the Garden of Eden. Consequently, a folk tradition is for pregnant women to eat an *etrog* or place it under their pillow to ease the pain of childbirth, which was Eve's punishment for this transgression. The Talmud states, "One who eats an *etrog* [during pregnancy] will have fragrant children" (Ket. 61a); in a Hebrew play on words, it adds, "If one sees an *etrog* [*hadar*] in his dream, he is honored [*hadur*] in the sight of his Maker" (Ber. 57a).

Mandrake (דּוּדָאִים)

The mandrake is a member of the nightshade family and grows wild in many parts of the Land of Israel; it produces small, yellow tomato-like fruits that ripen during the early spring. Since ancient times, the mandrake has been the subject of numerous legends, based on its powerful fragrance (Song 7:14); its purgative, narcotic, and aphrodisiac properties; and its thick forked root, which is shaped like a miniature lower torso. Used incorrectly, however, the toxins in the mandrake can cause dizziness, insanity, and even death.

In Hebrew, the mandrake is termed "*duda'im*" (love apples, apparently connected with the word "*dod*," meaning "beloved"), suggestive of its alleged property as an aphrodisiac. The Talmud refers to the mandrake by its Aramaic name, *yav'rucha* (chaser), which relates to the popular belief that the plant wards off demons (Sanh. 99b).[3] In exchange for mandrakes found by Reuben, the childless Rachel agreed to allow Jacob to spend an extra night with the unloved Leah (Gen. 30:15). Soon thereafter, Rachel conceived her first child, Joseph. Consequently, in one corner of the flag of the tribe of Reuben is the small figure of a man symbolic of the mandrake.[4]

In some Middle Eastern communities, barren women ingested precious stones internally in the hope of becoming pregnant. Because of the association of Reuben with mandrakes and fertility, and the similarity between his name and the word "ruby" (in both Hebrew and English), it was believed that if a woman ground a ruby into dust, mixed it with food, and ate it, she would conceive, "since the ruby contains the charm of the mandrakes."[5]

Myrtle (הֲדַס)

The myrtle is an aromatic evergreen that grows wild on Mount Carmel and in Upper Galilee and is prized as an ornamental shrub. According to tradition, branches of myrtle (*hadas*) are identified as the "boughs of leafy trees" (Lev. 23:40) that constitute one of the Four Species used on Sukkot (see p. 232). With an exquisite sweet scent and leaves that are dried for their perfume (Suk. 37b), the myrtle symbolizes the Jew who is deficient in Torah (no taste) but possesses good deeds (aroma).

In ancient Israel, wreaths of myrtle branches were worn by bridegrooms (Sot. 15:8) and even juggled by sages on festive occasions (Ket. 17a). According to the Talmud, one who saw a myrtle in his dream would have "good luck with his property ... and if he has no property, he will inherit some from elsewhere" (Ber. 57a). For centuries, myrtle was a popular choice for the spice used in the *Havdalah* ceremony that concludes the Sabbath (see p. 147).

Queen Esther was also known as Hadassah (Esther 2:7), the feminine form of the Hebrew word for myrtle. In the 20th century, an organization of Jewish women dedicated to improving medical care in Israel and supporting other charitable activities, which has become the largest Zionist organization in America, adopted the name "Hadassah" in honor of the biblical heroine of the Purim story.

Special spiritual qualities have been attributed to the myrtle. Zechariah (1:8) had a prophetic vision of an angel of the Lord standing among the myrtles. In describing the messianic redemption, Isaiah prophesied, "Instead of the nettle, a myrtle shall rise ... [and] stand as a testimony to the Lord, as an everlasting sign that shall not perish" (Isa. 55:13).

Palm Tree (דֶקֶל ,תָמָר)

The date palm (*tamar* in Hebrew; *dekel* in the Mishnah) has been a valuable tree in the Middle East since ancient times. According to rabbinic tradition, the biblical description of Israel as a "land flowing with milk and honey" (Exod. 3:8) referred to date honey, one of the seven species (see p. 673) indicating the fertile abundance of the land (Deut. 8:8). The first biblical reference to the date palm occurs immediately after the Israelites escaped from the pursuing Egyptians at the Sea of Reeds, when they camped at Elim with its "12 springs of water and 70 palm trees" (Exod. 15:27). Jericho, the first town conquered by the Israelites in the Promised Land, is still known as "the city of palm trees" (Deut. 34:3), since it has the hot climate needed for the fruit of the tree to ripen.

The palm is a distinctive tree with a towering trunk topped with immense spreading leaves. In biblical poetry, the palm tree symbolized nobility, beauty, and fruitfulness. The psalmist compared the righteous to a flourishing palm (Ps. 92:13), as did the lover his beloved (Song 7:8). The prophetess Deborah judged the people in the shade of a palm tree (Judg. 4:5), and Tamar was the name of the daughter-in-law of Judah (Gen. 38:6) and the daughter of David (2 Sam. 13:1).

The palm tree with its flowing fronds was a popular ornamental design for the Temple (1 Kings 6:29) and ancient synagogues. The Maccabees selected the palm as their symbol of victory, and it appears on the coins of the Hasmonean period. After the Roman conquest, coins were minted that depicted the defeated Jews as a forlorn woman sitting in mourning beneath a palm with the inscription "*Judaea capta est*" (Judah is captured).

The palm branch (*lulav*) is one of the Four Species carried in the *hoshanot* processions in the synagogue during Sukkot (see p. 232). According to tradition, the date—a tasty fruit but devoid of fragrance—symbolizes the person who has extensive learning but a paucity of good deeds (Lev. R. 30:12). According to the Talmud, "If one sees palm trees in a dream, his sins will come to an end" (Ber. 57a).

The Midrash compared the Jewish people to the palm tree: "As no part of the palm has any waste—the dates are eaten, the branches used for *Hallel*, the twigs for covering [the sukkah], the bast [inner bark] for ropes, the leaves for brooms, and the planed boards for ceiling rooms—so are there none worthless in Israel" (Gen. R. 41:1).

Pine (אֹרֶן)

Various biblical trees have been identified as types of pine, including the "gopher wood" from which Noah made his ark (Gen. 6:14). The Talmud reports, "It was the custom when a boy was born to plant a cedar tree and when a girl was born to plant a pine tree, and when they married, the trees were cut down and a canopy [*huppah*] made of the branches" (Git. 57a). Traditional Jews are buried in simple coffins made of pine, an inexpensive wood, to symbolize the equality of all human beings in the eyes of God (see p. 81).[6]

Over the past century, the pine has been adopted as the most important forest tree in Israel. The Jewish National Fund has planted tens of thousands of acres with pine trees because of their rapid growth, abundant shade, and ability to grow on rocky ground.

Rose (שׁוֹשַׁנָּה, וֶרֶד)

Wild roses grew in biblical Israel, but the fragrant rose known in the West was not cultivated during this period and thus was not mentioned in the Bible. The term "*shoshanah*," the later Hebrew word for "rose" and mentioned as a paragon of beauty and fragrance in Song of Songs (2:1–2), probably refers to the white (Madonna) lily, which blooms in the Carmel and Galilee areas at the beginning of summer.

In rabbinic times, rose oil (*shemen vered*) was used as a medicinal anointment. Thus the Mishnah prohibited its use on the Sabbath, when medication is permitted only in emergencies. Aristocrats, however, also used rose oil for nonmedicinal purposes and were thus allowed to anoint themselves with it on the Sabbath (Shab. 14:4). Rose petals were also used to make jam, and the blossoms were soaked in water as a bath fragrance. According to the Talmud, "childhood is like a garland of roses" (Shab. 152a) and the sun is red during sunrise because it passes by the roses of the Garden of Eden (BB 84a). Roses were used for ornamental purposes, but the Rabbis decreed that in a city where idolatry is being practiced, it was forbidden to buy goods in shops "decorated with garlands of roses and myrtle" (Av. Zar. 12b), presumably since these flowers were strewn before idols as part of the worship service. The city of Jerusalem was subject to "10 special [zoning] regulations," including "that neither gardens nor orchards should be cultivated there," but an exception was made for the "garden of roses which existed from the days of the Prophets" (BK 82b).

The opening lines of the mystical Zohar interpret the expression "rose among thorns" (Song 2:1)[7] as a symbol for Israel, indicating that "there is a rose above and a rose below," and that the Thirteen Divine Attributes of Mercy (see p. 180) surround the Jewish people like a "13-petaled rose."[8]

Sabra (צַבָּר)

Originally imported from Mexico in the 1600s, the sabra (prickly pear cactus) now grows abundantly in the Land of Israel.[9] The fruit of the sabra is thorny on the outside with a thick peel that must be removed, to get to the sweet meaty inside.[10] "Sabra" has become the proud nickname of native-born Israelis, symbolic of their national character of being prickly and hard on the outside to withstand the dangers of living in an often-perilous part of the world, but soft and sweet on the inside.

Willow (עֲרָבָה)

Described in the Bible as a tree that grows rapidly near water (Isa. 44:4), the willow (*aravah*) plays a major role in the festival of Sukkot. One of the Four Species (see p. 232), the willow is characterized as having "neither taste nor fragrance," symbolizing those among Israel "who are neither learned nor possessed of good deeds" (Lev. R. 30:12). On Hoshana Rabbah, the seventh day of Sukkot, willow branches are beaten on the ground (Suk. 4:5) or against the seats of the synagogue until the leaves fall off their stems (see p. 237). This is a final opportunity to symbolically remove our sins, reminiscent of beating one's breast while reciting the confessional prayers on Yom Kippur. On the next day, Shemini Atzeret, a special Prayer for Rain is recited (see p. 239), since the Talmud states that this is the day on which "judgment is passed in respect to rain" (RH 1:2, 16b)—the coming winter rains that determine the yield of the spring harvest. Willows are an ideal symbol for Israel's dependence on these rains, because their leaves wilt rapidly without sufficient water.

After the fall of the First Temple, "by the rivers of Babylon, there we [the exiles] sat, sat and wept, as we thought of Zion. There on the willows [which grow in abundance on the riverbanks] we hung up our lyres, for our captors asked us there for songs, our tormentors, for amusement, 'Sing us one of the songs of Zion.' How can we sing a song of the Lord on alien soil?" (Ps. 137:1).[11] In Jewish art, this image is a powerful symbol of mourning over the destruction of the Temple. The drooping leaves of the tree, which continually sway back and forth in the breeze, has given rise to the English phrase "weeping willow," another indication of the relation between the willow and mourning.

Animals

Cruelty to Animals (צַעַר בַּעֲלֵי חַיִּים)

The prohibition against cruelty to animals (*tza'ar ba'alei hayim*; lit., "pain of living things") is a fundamental Jewish value, based on the concept that human beings are responsible for all God's creatures. Not only is cruelty to animals forbidden, it is a positive commandment for human beings to show compassion and mercy to them. The eating of meat was permitted only after the Flood (Gen. 9:3), and then only in moderation and tightly regulated by the dietary laws. One of the seven Noahide Laws, which apply to all humanity, is the prohibition against eating the flesh of a living animal, or blood drawn from it (Sanh. 56a–b).

Although the Rabbis agreed that human needs took priority, they opposed the cruelty inherent in the hunting of animals, even for a living. Indeed, the Talmud prohibits associating with hunters, based on the verse in Psalms (1:1), "Happy is the man who does not stand in the way of sinners, nor sit in the seat of the scornful"[1] (Av. Zar. 18b). In the 18th century, Rabbi Ezekiel Landau noted that the only biblical hunters were fierce characters such as Nimrod and Esau, and thus this activity is not appropriate for the children of the Patriarchs. He said that when animals are killed merely for the pleasure of hunting, it is cruelty. This antipathy toward cruelty to animals is strikingly illustrated in the rabbinic prohibition against reciting the festive benediction *Shehecheyanu* (see p. 479) before the act of ritual slaughter or before putting on new leather shoes, because human enjoyment is achieved only through the death of the animal.

As explicitly stated in the Ten Commandments, animals as well as human beings must be allowed to rest on the Sabbath (Exod. 20:10; Deut. 5:14). For Rashi, this meant that animals must be free to wander about, take in their surroundings, and enjoy the beauty of nature. Similarly, animals are to be provided for during the sabbatical year, when the fields lie fallow and whatever grows in them is to be enjoyed by "the poor of your people ... and the beast of the field" (Lev. 25:6–7).[2] The angel rebuked Balaam for smiting his donkey (Num. 22:32; see p. 716), which Maimonides considered as the proof text that forbids causing pain to any animal,[3] and God Himself admonished Jonah (4:11), "And should not I care about Nineveh, that great city, in which there are more than 120,000 persons ... and many beasts as well!" In the Book of Psalms, God is praised as the One whose "mercy is upon all His works" (Ps. 145:9),[4] "feeding every creature to its heart's content" (Ps. 145:16), and who "gives the beasts their food" (Ps. 147:9). Based on the verse, "I will also provide grass in the fields for your cattle, and [then] you shall eat and be satisfied" (Deut. 11:15),[5] the Rabbis decided that a person is forbidden to eat before feeding his animal because the animal is mentioned first (Ber. 40a).[6]

Many biblical leaders of Israel were trained for their tasks by being shepherds. Moses was "keeping the flock of Jethro, his father-in-law," when God appeared to him at the Burning Bush (Exod. 3:1–6). Similarly, David was considered worthy of leading the Jewish people by virtue of the tender love he showed to the sheep under his care.[7]

Several traditional stories record the compassion for animals demonstrated by major figures in Jewish history. When Rabbi Judah the Prince was studying Torah, a calf being taken to the slaughterhouse begged the sage to save him. "What can I do for you?" he shrugged. "For this you were created." As punishment for his insensitivity, Rabbi Judah suffered from a toothache for 13 years. One day, a weasel ran past the sage's daughter, who was about to kill it. Rabbi Judah admonished her to let the animal live, citing the verse from Psalms (145:9), "The Lord is good to all; and His mercy is upon all His works." Because Rabbi Judah's compassion prevented the suffering and death of the harmless animal, his toothache went away (BM 85a).[8]

One Yom Kippur evening, Rabbi Israel Salanter, the leader of the Musar movement in the 19th century, did not arrive at the synagogue in time to chant *Kol Nidrei*. Fearing that harm had come to their master, a search party was dispatched and eventually found the rabbi in the barn of a Christian neighbor. As Salanter explained to his relieved congregants, while walking to the synagogue he had seen one of his neighbor's calves, lost and tangled in the brush. Seeing that the animal was confused and in pain, the rabbi freed it, comforted it, and then led it home. This act of mercy and compassion sufficed for Salanter's prayers that evening.[9]

The Rabbis understood the following mitzvot as explicitly related to the prohibition against cruelty to animals.

Shechitah (Kosher Slaughtering)

Jewish ritual slaughtering strives to prevent unnecessary suffering to the animal. It must be performed by a skilled professional, with one continuous cut of a knife that is exceedingly sharp and without the slightest notch (Hul. 9a). This severs all of the great blood vessels of the neck so that the animal instantly loses all sensation. Because an animal may not be eaten unless it has been properly slaughtered, the technical requirements must be strictly observed.

Working with Two Different Kinds of Animals

The Bible explicitly states, " You shall not plow with an ox and a donkey together" (Deut. 22:10). According to Rashi, this prohibition applied to the coupling of any two different species and to any activity (not only plowing). The ox and donkey differ greatly in temperament, size, and strength, and it would be cruel to the weaker animal to yoke them together.[10]

Muzzling an Animal as It Threshes

The verse, "You shall not muzzle an ox while it is threshing" (Deut. 25:4), prohibits the farmer from preventing an animal from satisfying its appetite by eating of the produce with which it is working. This prohibition extends to all animals employed in any type of labor. As *Sefer Ha-Hinnukh* observes, this and other regulations forbidding cruelty to animals develop an attitude of kindness and compassion that human beings can use when interacting with each other.[11]

Mother and Its Young

The commandments relating to the humane treatment of a mother and her young derive from the verses, "If ... you chance upon a bird's nest ...

and the mother [bird is] sitting over the fledglings or on the eggs, do not take the mother together with her young. Let the mother go, and take only the young" (Deut. 22:6–7) and "[But an ox or a sheep or a goat], you may not slaughter it and its offspring on the same day" (Lev. 22:28).[12]

Maimonides explained that one may not kill an animal and its young on the same day so that "people should be restrained and prevented from killing the two together in such a manner that the young is slain in the sight of the mother; for the pain of the animals in such circumstances is very great. There is no difference in this case between the pain of man and the pain of other living beings, since the love and the tenderness of the mother for her young ones is not produced by reasoning but by feeling, and this faculty exists not only in man but in most living things."[13] He added, "If the Law provides that such grief should not be caused to cattle and birds, how much more careful must we be that we should not cause grief to our fellow man."[14] According to Nachmanides, the purpose of this commandment was directed not toward the animal but toward humans, to purge them of callousness, cruelty, and savagery. For Abravanel, allowing the mother bird to live would encourage her to lay more eggs and thus preserve bird species for the long-term benefit of humanity.[15]

The reward for sparing the mother bird is so "that you may fare well and have a long life" (Deut. 22:7). This is strikingly similar to the effect of observing the Fifth Commandment honoring parents—"that you may long endure on the land that the Lord your God is assigning to you" (Exod. 20:12)[16]—implying that God will treat human beings in accordance with how well they care for animals. Commenting on the Talmud, Rashi noted that if God gives long life and material success for fulfilling the simple mitzvah of sparing the mother bird, which requires neither intense physical effort nor financial loss, how much more is the divine reward for discharging commandments that are difficult to perform (Hul. 142a).[17]

Relieving an Animal of Its Burden

"When you see the donkey of your enemy lying under its burden and would refrain from raising it, you must nevertheless raise it with him" (Exod. 23:5) commands a person to help unload a beast that has fallen under its burden in the field, even if it belongs to his or her enemy.

Indeed, if two individuals who hate each other work together and demonstrate their compassion for the animal, they might even overcome their mutual animosity and become friends (Tanh. Mishpatim 1).[18] As previously noted, Maimonides maintained that not inflicting undue pain on an animal helps prevent a person from forming the habit of cruelty, thus decreasing the likelihood that he or she will inflict pain on others.[19] He noted that unloading the burden from a laboring animal is permitted even on the Sabbath.[20] Indeed, many acts otherwise forbidden on the Sabbath (such as asking a non-Jew to milk cows) are permitted when their purpose is to relieve an animal's suffering. According to the Shulchan Arukh, one is also permitted to tend an animal's painful wound, race animals around as a remedy for overeating, and help them escape from a pit or body of water into which they have fallen.[21]

Specific Animals

A number of animals are mentioned in the Bible and Talmud. Some of these are discussed in the following sections, arranged in alphabetical order.

Bear (דֹּב)

Although generally harmless to humans, the Bible portrays the bear as a dangerous animal, especially the female of the species when robbed of her young. When David tried to convince Saul that he was strong enough to fight Goliath, he boasted that he would kill the enemy giant just as he had once single-handedly slain a bear and a lion threatening his flock (1 Sam. 17:34–37). David himself was later described as a hardened warrior and "savage as a she-bear in the wild, robbed of her cubs" (2 Sam. 17:8).[1] Nevertheless, the author of Proverbs (17:12) deemed it better to "meet a bereaved she-bear [robbed of her cubs] than a fool with his nonsense" (Prov. 17:12).[2] Later, the acts of a "wicked man ruling a people" was compared to "a prowling bear" (Prov. 28:15). As a cruel punishment, the prophet Elisha called down two female bears to attack the 42 children who had mocked him (2 Kings 2:24). However, the Talmud castigated this behavior, noting that Elisha was punished with sickness for having "incited the bears against the children" (Sanh. 107b).[3]

The bear later became a symbol of the powerful Persian Empire, which Daniel (7:5) saw in a vision as "a beast, which was like a bear but raised on one side, and with three fangs in its mouth among its teeth." The Rabbis extended this image to describe the Persians themselves, "who eat and drink like a bear, are fleshy [fat] like the bear, overgrown with hair like the bear, and are restless like a bear" (Kid. 72a). In folklore, the image of a bear looking for a honey tree represented the Jewish people searching for the sweetness of Torah, the "Tree of Life."[4]

In Isaiah's (11:7) prophetic vision of the peace accompanying the Messianic Age, "the cow and the bear shall graze, their young shall lie down together."

Bee (דְּבוֹרָה)

Bees are plentiful in the Land of Israel, but during biblical times they were primarily wild insects that were especially noted for their ferocity in attack. The Psalmist (118:12) describes enemy nations that "beset me [Israel] like bees," but they are defeated because the Jews trust in the Lord. As the Israelites prepared to enter the Promised Land after 40 years of wandering, Moses recounted the shameful incident of the evil report brought by the princes sent to spy out the land. When they learned that the punishment for their lack of faith in God was that all the adults would perish in the wilderness, the chastened people made an abortive attempt to forcibly enter the land despite the divine decree (Num. 14:40–45). Forty years later, Moses recalled, "the Amorites who lived in those hills came out against you like so many bees and chased you" (Deut. 1:44). However, the sages noted, Moses indirectly added some consolation to his harsh words. Rashi observed that just as a bee dies after stinging its victim, so the victorious Amorites were destroyed after defeating the Jews. Moreover, the absence of any mention of casualties indicates that the Jews were like most people stung by bees, suffering intense pain but not a fatal injury.[5]

The only biblical mention of bees in connection with honey is the verse, "And he [Samson] turned aside to look at the carcass of the lion, and he saw a swarm of bees in it, and honey" (Judg. 14:9).[6] This refers to the fact that a few hours after the death of an animal, the scavengers (such as jackals and vultures) reduce the carcass to bone; after the skeleton has dried in the sun, bees find this an excellent place to start a new honeycomb.[7] According to the Rabbis, the famous description of the Land of Israel as "a land flowing with milk and honey" (Deut. 8:8) refers to date honey (see p. 673).

Although bees are "unclean" insects, honey was permitted as food since it is not produced by the bee but rather merely sucked from flowers and stored in its body (Bek. 7b)(see p. 710).

The Hebrew word for bee, "*devorah*," probably derived from the root "*daber*" (to speak), referring to the constant humming noise of the insect. Deborah was the name of the judge and prophetess who led the Israelites to victory against the Canaanites (Judg. 4), as well as the name of Rebecca's wet-nurse (Gen. 35:8).[8]

Camel (גָּמָל)

The camel is mentioned many times in the Bible. It served as a beast of burden and a mode of transportation. Camels were particularly common among desert people because the tough sponge-like substance covering their feet allows them to cross burning sand. This earned the camel the nickname "ship of the desert."[9] A hardy breed, camels can go for several days without food and water.

In the Bible, Rachel hid her father's idols in the saddle of her camel (Gen. 31:34). A caravan of Ishmaelites with camels bearing spices brought Joseph down to Egypt (Gen. 37:25). The Torah explicitly prohibits eating camel meat (Lev. 11:4; Deut. 14:7). A large herd of camels was a measure of wealth (Job 1:3) and military power (Judg. 7:12). The Midianites outfitted their camels with decorative chains (Judg. 8:26).

According to legend, a camel played a major role in selecting the burial place for Maimonides. The great medieval sage lived and died in Egypt but asked that he be buried in the Holy Land. His body was placed on a camel, which carried it on the long trek to the Land of Israel. Once it reached Tiberias, however, the camel stubbornly refused to go farther. Thus Maimonides was buried in a plot of ground chosen by the camel—which happened to be near the tomb of the revered talmudic scholar Yochanan ben Zakkai.[10]

Cattle (בָּקָר)

In ancient times, cattle were the most important possession of nomadic people, including the Patriarchs. They reared cattle, which provided them with milk, meat, and skins for clothing and shelter. Joseph told his brothers to inform Pharaoh that they "have been keepers of cattle from our youth even until now, both we, and our father" (Gen. 46:34).[11] Cattle were used to thresh grain (Deut. 25:4) and as beasts of burden (1 Chron. 12:41). Cattle were not to be yoked to a plow together with a donkey (Deut. 22:10).

In addition to the generic term "*bakar*," the Bible employs specific words for cattle, depending on their age, sex, physical characteristics, and work performed. Among the animals extensively used for sacrifices were the *par* or *ben-bakar* (young bull) and *shor* (ox or bull). The infamous incident of the *Egel ha-Zahav* (Golden Calf), which was fashioned by Aaron while his brother was on Mount Sinai, led Moses to smash the first set of Tablets of the Law (Exod. 32). After the division of the monarchy, Jeroboam, ruler of the Northern Kingdom, placed golden calves in the temples he built in Beit El and Dan (1 Kings 12:28–29). When the victim of an unwitnessed murder is found lying in the open, the elders of the nearest town must slay a young heifer, similarly termed "*eglah*," in an uncultivated valley with a stream (Deut. 21:1–4). The mysterious rite of the *parah adumah* (red heifer) produced the paradoxical situation in which its ashes purified people who had become ritually unclean through contact with a human corpse, yet made those who engaged in its preparation ritually impure (Num. 19:1–22). This is the quintessential example of a *hok*, a statute that has no obvious reason but is observed because of absolute obedience to a divine decree.

In a midrashic parable discussing why the righteous suffer, Rabbi Eleazar explained: "A man had two cows, one strong and the other weak. Upon which does he put a burden? Upon the strong. So God does not try the wicked, for they could not endure it, but he tries the righteous" (Song R. 2:1).[12]

Chicken (תַּרְנְגוֹל)

Archeological discoveries have demonstrated that chickens were raised in the Land of Israel in late biblical times, probably arriving from India or Persia. In the Mishnah, the chicken is called "*tarnegol*" (feminine, *tarnegolet*), derived from a Sumerian word meaning "king bird."

In modern times, the turkey is known as "*tarnegol hodu*" (lit., "chicken of India"). The rooster is called "*gever*" (also *sechvi*, see below), which is the modern Hebrew word for "man" and related to "*gevurah*" (strength).

Based on a reference in Job (38:36), the Rabbis developed the blessing in the morning service thanking God for giving "the rooster [*sechvi*] intelligence to distinguish between day and night" (see p. 404). Not only does this express our gratitude for this method of being awakened from sleep—from the crowing of the rooster—it also is an indirect expression of thanks for the daily "restoration" of one's hearing.

According to Josephus, the early Rabbis disagreed as to whether the chicken was kosher. It was considered a ritually clean bird and permitted as food in the Galilee, whereas in Jerusalem the chicken was deemed unclean and was kept only as an ornamental fowl (together with the peacock). Therefore, when Jesus spoke of a hen "gathering her chicks under her wings," he was referring to the barnyard fowl of his Nazareth childhood, while the cock that Peter heard crowing three times was probably a resident in someone's private zoo.[13]

The Talmud considered the hen as the "best of birds" and its egg was used as a basic unit of volume for halakhic purposes (BM 86b). "It was the custom that when a bride and bridegroom were being escorted [to the marriage ceremony] a cock [symbol of procreation] and a hen were carried before them, as if to say 'Be fruitful and multiply like chickens'" (Git. 57a). In answer to the perennial question—"Which came first, the chicken or the egg?"—the Talmud appears to side with the former: "All [the works] of Creation were brought into being with their full stature, their full capacities, and their full beauty" (RH 11a).[14]

On the day before Yom Kippur, a rooster (for a male) or a hen (for a female) was traditionally swung around the head three times in the ceremony of *kaparos* (lit., "atonements," but in the sense of "ransom"; see p. 223) and then donated to the poor. This practice of symbolically transferring a person's sins to the fowl was castigated as a superstitious pagan ritual by the Rabbis, but *kaparos* remained popular among the masses in Orthodox communities. Today, many people have substituted money for the rooster or hen and give the money to charity (see p. 537).

Deer (אַיָּל) and Gazelle (צְבִי)

The deer (*ayal*) and gazelle (*tzvi*) are included among the seven species of wild animals that both chew the cud and have cloven hooves and thus are permitted as food (Deut 14:5). Hunting for wild game plays an important role in the story of Jacob and Esau. "Isaac favored Esau because he had a taste for game; but Rebekah favored Jacob" (Gen. 25:28), and thus the Patriarch asked his elder son to take "your gear, your quiver and bow, and go out into the open and hunt me some game [venison]" (Gen. 27:3) before giving him the birthright—which was "stolen" by Jacob with the help of his mother.

The deer and gazelle are symbols of grace and speed. Jacob blessed his son Naphtali as a wild deer (*ayalah*) who "delivers beautiful sayings" (Gen. 49:21).[15] According to the Talmud, when Jacob died and his sons were preparing to bury him in the Cave of Machpelah, Esau tried to stop them by asserting that as the firstborn he had a prior claim to the last remaining gravesite. When Esau demanded, "Produce a document [of sale] for me!" the fleet Naphtali ran like a deer to Egypt and brought back the deed (Sot. 13a).[16]

In *Pirkei Avot* (5:23), the speed of the deer is invoked as one of the qualities needed "to do the will of your Father who is in Heaven." In the popular Sabbath hymn *Yedid Nefesh* (Beloved of My Soul), the soul "runs like a deer" (*ayal*) to be near to God, so intense is its yearning for an intimate relationship with the *Shekhinah*.[17] The Song of Songs depicts the gazelle as "he stands behind our wall, gazing through the window, peering through the lattice" (Song 2:9) and describes the lover with these words: "Your breasts are like two fawns, twins of a gazelle, browsing among the lilies" (Song 4:5). Although the epitome of speed (2 Sam. 2:18), the gazelle was hunted almost to extinction for its tasty meat.

In modern Israel, the gazelle (along with the ibex, the only wild kosher ruminant that has survived in the land) is the symbol of the postal service.[18]

Dog (כֶּלֶב)

In biblical times, the dog (*kelev*) was considered a potentially dangerous animal that was often trained to be vicious and might attack passersby (Ps. 22:17). As Proverbs (26:17) observed, "A passerby who gets embroiled in someone else's quarrel is like one who seizes a dog by its ears." Dogs were described as ownerless animals that howled at night and prowled in desolate areas (Ps. 59:7,15), carnivores that were both scavengers and predators. "The dogs shall devour Jezebel in the field of Jezreel" (1 Kings 21:23) was the predicted fate of Ahab's wicked queen.

Rather than eating "flesh torn by beast in the field [i.e., nonkosher]," the Israelites were commanded to "cast it to the dogs" (Exod. 22:30). According to Rashi, as a reward for their remaining quiet on the night of the Exodus from Egypt (rather than emitting loud barks or howls that might have terrified and intimidated the escaping Israelites), God ordained that any food unfit for human consumption (*treif*) be given to the dogs.[19]

In biblical times, "dog" was a derogatory term that apparently was applied to a male prostitute who practiced immoral conduct as a religious rite. "You shall not bring the fee of a whore or the pay of a dog into the House of the Lord ... for both are abhorrent to the Lord your God" (Deut. 23:19)[20] was interpreted to mean that no animal bought with money obtained in exchange for improper actions could be used for an offering on the altar, because it would be demeaning to God (Ibn Ezra).[21] Nachmanides observed that although sinners frequently attempt to justify illicit activities by contributing some of the profits to charitable causes, this commandment clearly states that a person cannot purify such unlawful gains by using them for sacred purposes.[22] The prohibition against gifts gained by immoral means also applies today to synagogues, houses of study, and other charitable Jewish institutions.

A number of rabbinic stories tell of dogs who saved their masters from violence and death. One such narrative tells of a snake that injected venom into milk being prepared by a group of shepherds. The shepherds' dog saw this happen and tried to warn them by barking. When they paid no attention to the barking, the dog drank the milk and died (PdRK 10:1). In another story, Rabbi Abbahu's friend seated him next to a dog as a show of honor, because the dog had saved his wife from rape by biting the assailant's testicles (PdRK 11:1). However, this same ferocity made the Rabbis wary of dogs. The Talmud ruled that, "one should not breed a dog unless it on a chain," but Rabbi

Eleazer opposed any raising of dogs in the Land of Israel, declaring that "he who breeds dogs is like one who breeds swine" (BK 83a). However, this practice was permitted in a frontier town as long as the owner agreed to "keep it chained during the daytime and loose it only at night." One early sage even stated that a person should not live in a town "in which no horses neigh or dogs bark" (Pes. 113a).

The Rabbis gave five criteria that indicated if a dog was rabid: "Its mouth is open, its saliva dripping, its ears flap, its tail is hanging between its thighs, [and] it walks on the edge of the road." Others stated that, "it also barks without its voice being heard." Proposed causes for rabies were "Witches are having their fun with it [the dog]" and "An evil spirit rests upon it" (Yoma 83b).

Donkey (חֲמוֹר)

Although Jewish folklore often considered the donkey (*hamor*) the epitome of foolish or stubborn behavior, ancient Jewish sources regarded the animal as a symbol of patience and understanding. Issachar, who chose the life of the modest farmer, is likened by Jacob to a "strong-boned donkey" who has "bent his shoulder to the burden and become a toiling serf" (Gen. 49:14–15).[23] Although the plain meaning of the text and the description of his "pleasant country" seem to refer to agricultural endeavors, Rashi preferred the traditional rabbinic interpretation that this alludes to Issachar being a dedicated and accomplished student of Torah (1 Chron. 12:33), many of whose descendants were spiritual leaders of the Jewish people.[24]

The most famous incident involving the animal is the story of the talking donkey of Balaam (Num 22:21–35). Three times the animal sees an angel standing in her path with drawn sword; at first she swerves off the road and then stops to save her master's life. Having neither perceived the presence of the angel nor realized the danger, Balaam strikes the donkey on all three occasions. Miraculously, the donkey has the power of speech to reprove Balaam for his own obstinacy and quick temper. As God uncovers his eyes, Balaam finally understands the situation, bows his head, and prostrates himself on the ground. The Rabbis observe that if God could allow a beast to talk intelligently, surely Balaam could speak only in accordance with the divine will and could not carry out Balak's plan to curse the Israelites.[25] According to legend, the talking donkey was one of the miracles created at twilight on the sixth day of Creation, just before the onset of the first Sabbath (Avot 5:8).

The donkey was a symbol of royalty—Saul, David, Solomon, and Absalom are described as riding donkeys, as will the Messiah at the end of days. Based on the prophesy of Zechariah (9:9) that the Messiah will ride into Jerusalem "triumphant and victorious, [yet] lowly [humble], and riding on a donkey,"[26] the Talmud states, "if one sees a donkey in a dream, he may hope for salvation" (Ber. 56b).[27]

Dove (יוֹנָה)

The white dove (*yonah*) is a universal symbol of peace, purity, beauty, vulnerability, and innocence. In The Song of Songs (5:2), the lover calls his beloved a "faultless dove." The dove has long been a herald of spring in Israel: "The blossoms have appeared in the land; the time of pruning has come; the song of the turtledove [*tor*] is heard in our land" (Song 2:12).[28] The Psalms refer to the graceful flight of the dove (Ps. 55:7) and to the beauty of the bird's feathers as they shimmer in the bright sunlight (Ps. 68:14).[29]

The first and most famous dove mentioned in the Bible was the one that Noah sent out from the ark. She returned to the ark with an olive leaf in her mouth (according to tradition, plucked from the Mount of Olives in Jerusalem), so that "Noah knew that the waters had decreased on the earth" (Gen. 8:8–11). The dove holding an olive branch in its mouth is a well-known symbol of peace.

During temple times, doves and turtledoves were brought as sacrificial offerings by the poor (Lev. 5:7) because they were the least expensive animal offering, by a Nazirite after the completion of his vow (Num. 6:10), by a woman after her days of purification following childbirth (Lev. 12:6; see p. 561), and as part of the purification ritual of a poor person who had been afflicted with the skin disease *tzara'at* (Lev. 14:22). These birds were included among those that Abraham offered at the "covenant between the pieces" (Gen. 15:9), when God promised that the Patriarch's descendants would be granted the Land of Israel as their eternal heritage.

In rabbinic literature, Israel is often likened to a dove, the gentlest of birds that is unable to fight either with its claws or beak. A tireless flier, the powerless and persecuted dove was an apt simile for the Jewish people, who have steadfastly persisted in exile despite almost constant suffering. Unlike other birds, which rest on the top of a tree or a rock when they grow weary from flying, the dove merely folds one of her wings and flies with the other. The *aggadah* (Gen. R. 39) interprets this behavior as meaning that the nations of the world need both wings (land and culture) to survive, whereas Israel (in the Diaspora) can soar to great heights even on one wing (i.e., its culture, which is the Torah) (Gen. R. 39). In another passage, the Rabbis note that just as the dove does not struggle when slaughtered, so the Israelites do not resist when they are killed for *kiddush ha-Shem* (sanctification of God's name) (Midrash Tehillim 159a).[30] The Talmud observes that just as feathers protect the dove, so the mitzvot protect Israel from danger (Shab. 49a).[31]

According to legend, above the throne of King Solomon perched a dove with a hawk in its talons, symbolizing the ultimate victory of Israel over its enemies.[32] The Talmud notes that among people ineligible to be witnesses are those who race pigeons or set up decoys to attract other birds from the dovecote of their neighbor (Sanh. 25a).

Goat (גְּדִי, שָׂעִיר, עֵז)

In biblical Israel, the goat was a vital part of the economy. In addition to serving as a valuable source of meat (Gen. 27:9, 38:20; Judg. 13:15) and milk (Prov. 27:27), its hide and hair were used for clothing, parchment, tents, water vessels, and the curtains of the Tabernacle. The goat was the most common sin offering (Lev. 4:23,28), possibly because its black hair was the antithesis of the white of purity. On Yom Kippur, the sins of Israel were symbolically transferred to a goat (scapegoat) in the rite of *Azazel* (Lev. 16:5–22; see p. 224).

The ancient practice of boiling a kid in milk as part of idolatrous fertility ceremonies may have been the underlying source of the prohibition against "boil[ing] a kid in its mother's milk" (Exod. 23:19, 34:26; Deut. 14:21). From the threefold repetition of this prohibition, the Rabbis deduced the general law against eating meat with milk and its associated laws (Kid. 57b).

In the popular *Had Gadya* (One little kid), sung at the conclusion of the Passover seder, the kid is the symbol of the Jewish people. This animal also is featured in a prophetic image of the Messianic Age of peace, when "the leopard [shall] lie down with the kid" (Isa. 11:6).

Hare (אַרְנֶבֶת)

The hare is one of the nonkosher animals that the Israelites are forbidden to eat (Lev. 11:6; Deut. 14:7). However, the Bible incorrectly categorizes the hare as a ruminant. This may be related to the constant movement of its jaw (it munches its food as it eats). An alternative explanation is the hare's habit of regurgitating previously eaten food to its mouth from its stomach.[33]

According to the Talmud, when the 70 Jewish elders were summoned to Alexandria to translate the Bible for Ptolemy (the Septuagint), they independently rendered the Hebrew word for "hare" as "the beast with small legs," lest they offend the king's wife—Lagos, whose Greek name meant "hare"—by mocking her as an unclean animal in the Torah (Meg. 9b).[34]

Horse (סוּס)

The relatively mountainous Land of Israel was not noted for breeding horses, and thus these animals were regarded as a luxury. As a mode of transportation, only the wealthy and the nobility rode horses. When raised to the position of viceroy of Egypt, Joseph was honored by riding in one of Pharaoh's horse-drawn chariots (Gen. 41:43). In Persia, Ahasuerus honored Mordecai by dressing him up in royal garments and allowing him to sit atop "the horse on which the king has ridden" while being led through the streets of the capital by Haman, his archenemy (Esther 6:7–11). The prophet Elijah was carried up to Heaven in a fiery chariot, drawn by "fiery horses" (2 Kings 2:11).

The Bible warned the king that, in addition to too many wives and excessive treasure, he should not amass too many horses or send people to Egypt to acquire more of them (Deut. 17:16). Ibn Ezra and *Sefer ha-Hinnukh* noted that, after leaving Egypt, the Israelites were forbidden to ever settle there again. Egypt was a major source of horses in ancient times. In the earliest biblical reference to the animal, it is related that in the time of famine "Joseph gave them bread in exchange for horses" (Gen. 47:17). If permitted to purchase horses without restriction, a king would send agents for this purpose to Egypt, thus setting up an Israelite settlement there.[35] Despite this admonition, Solomon realized that horses drawing iron chariots were formidable implements of war and began to purchase them (1 Kings 10:28–29). He felt no qualms about violating this (and the other) restrictions on the royal privileges, because he was certain that his incomparable wisdom would protect him from the consequences indicated in the biblical verses. However, Solomon was mistaken. Filling his large stables did bring the people back to Egypt, his foreign wives led the people to idol worship, and the heavy taxes he imposed let to a split of the kingdom after his death.[36]

In Babylonia, Rav cautioned his pupil, "Do not dwell in a town in which no horse neighs and no dog barks," for dogs raise the alarm and the robbers are pursued on horseback (Pes. 113a). The horse sleeps for a very brief period (only "sixty respirations" at night; Suk. 26b), and thus can serve as a model for the diligent scholar who should spend all his time studying Torah. "Six things were said of a horse: it loves promiscuity, it loves battle, it has a proud spirit, it needs little sleep, it eats much, and it excretes little. Some say it also seeks to slay its master in battle" (Pes. 113b).

The power of the warhorse is well illustrated by its vivid portrayal in Job (39:20–22): "The glory of his snorting is terrible. He paws in the valley and rejoices in his strength: he goes forth to meet the clash of arms. He mocks fear and is not afraid; nor does he turn back from the sword." Nevertheless, horse-drawn war chariots were not invincible. As Moses and the Israelites exclaimed after crossing the Sea of Reeds, "He [God] has triumphed gloriously; horse and driver He has hurled into the sea" (Exod. 15:1). The Psalmist (20:8) warns against overestimating the abilities of this animal: "They call on chariots, they [call] on horses,[37] but we call on the name of the Lord our God."[38]

Leopard (נָמֵר)

The leopard (*namer*), whose Hebrew name means "spotted coat," was once the strongest and most deadly carnivorous animal in the Middle East. In modern Israel, only a few remain in the Negev and Arava. The prophets describe the swiftness of the leopard (Hab. 1:8), possibly a reference to the cheetah, and to its habit of waiting motionless before leaping on its prey (Hos. 13:7). The strength of the leopard (along with the swiftness of the deer, the courage of the lion, and the lightness of the eagle) was one of the four qualities needed "to carry out the will of your Father in Heaven" (Avot 5:23). In a famous verse, Jeremiah (13:23) asked, "Can the Cushite [Ethiopian] change his skin, or the leopard his spots?"

In Isaiah's (11:6) vision of the Messianic Age, when carnivorous animals and their usual prey will live peacefully together, the prophet declares that "the leopard [shall] lie down with the kid."

Lion (אַרְי)

Termed "the king of the wild animals" (Hag. 13b) in the Talmud, the lion (with the bear) is mentioned in the Bible several times as the most powerful predator and a general symbol of strength (Prov. 28:15; Joel 1:6; Nah. 2:13). Only on rare occasions was a lion killed by a man of great personal courage, such as Samson (Judg. 14:5–6), David (1 Sam. 17:34–36), and Benaiah the son of Jehoiada (2 Sam. 23:20). In one of Daniel's (7:4) visions, the powerful kingdom of Babylonia is represented as a lion with eagle's wings.

The tribes of Gad (Deut. 33:20), Dan (Deut. 33:22), and Judah (Gen. 49:9) are compared to lions, although it was Judah whose name eventually became closely associated with this symbol. King David, the foremost descendant of Judah, first displayed his strength and courage as a lad when he killed a lion and a bear (1 Sam. 17:34–36). Consequently, the Davidic dynasty and the Messiah (who will spring from this royal house) have also been identified with the lion. Two lions stood on either side of King Solomon's throne, as well as on both sides of the six steps leading up to it (1 Kings 10:20). In Ezekiel's (1:4–21) incredible vision of the divine chariot (*merkavah*), there were four creatures, each with four faces (lion, ox, eagle, human being) and four wings fused together into a fiery four-wheeled vehicle whose rims were covered with eyes. In the Messianic Age, "the lion will lie down with the lamb" (Isa. 11:6).[39]

The "Lion of Judah" has long been a major symbol of the Jewish people. Today, the ark curtain and the mantle covering the Torah scroll are often embroidered with lions, especially "rampant lions"—a pair of the animals rearing on their hind legs. Based on this image, common

Jewish names have been Aryeh and Ari (lion), Ariel (lion of God), and their Yiddish equivalents Leib and Loeb.[40]

According to the Mishnah, the qualities required to perform God's will included the bravery of a lion combined with the strength of a leopard, the ability to soar like an eagle, and the swiftness of a deer (Avot 5:23). The lion also represented spiritual as well as physical prowess, and thus the term was used figuratively to refer to outstanding talmudic scholars. In the 16th century, Isaac Luria, the famed kabbalist, was known as the Ari (lion) in recognition of his extraordinary knowledge and spiritual energy.

Lions roamed the desert and mountainous regions of the Land of Israel throughout biblical times and the talmudic period. Hunted almost to extinction by the Crusaders, lions have virtually disappeared from the area.

Locust (אַרְבֶּה) and Grasshopper (חָגָב)

The locust (*arbeh*) and the grasshopper (*hagav*) are two of the four insects that have "above their feet, jointed [jumping] legs to leap with on the ground" and are permitted as food (Lev. 11:21–22). Although these insects were eaten in talmudic times, later rabbis declared that all species of locusts and grasshoppers are forbidden because the four types of permitted insects can no longer be unequivocally identified. Nevertheless, some Yemenite Jews still eat fried locusts and grasshoppers based on of their tradition of kashrut.

The locust was the eighth of the 10 plagues of Egypt (Exod. 10:4–19; see p. 280). The Midrash teaches that this was "measure for measure," just as the Egyptians forced their Jewish slaves to grow crops, so did the locusts devour them.[41] One of the curses that would befall the Israelites if they failed to obey the will of God was, "Though you take much seed out to the field, you shall gather in little, for the locust shall consume it" (Deut. 28:38). For centuries, periodic swarms of locusts have devastated the landscape. The description in Exodus (10:15) that these creatures "hid all the land from view, and the land was darkened" was not simply a literary device, for in some parts of Africa locusts have been known to blanket the ground for more than 2,000 square miles.[42] One of the most severe plagues occurred during the days of Joel, who devoted most of his prophecy to a precise description of the catastrophic damage they caused and the deafening roar they produce. "With a clatter as of chariots they bound on the hilltops, with a noise like a blazing fire consuming straw; like an enormous horde arrayed for battle" (Joel 2:5). There was little the people could do in the face of a locust invasion, other than "blow a horn in Zion,[43] solemnize a fast, proclaim an assembly [to pray for divine mercy]" (Joel 2:15).

The small grasshopper hiding in the grass is used figuratively in the Bible to depict the insignificance of human beings when seen from above, as in Isaiah's (40:22) observation that "He [God] is enthroned above the vault of the earth, so that its inhabitants seem as grasshoppers." The Israelite spies sent by Moses to scout out the land of Canaan reported that its inhabitants were of such gigantic size that "we looked like grasshoppers in our eyes, and so were we in their eyes" (Num. 13:33).[44] Because they had no confidence in their own strength or in the divine promise that they would take over the land, the cowardly spies assumed that others also saw them as small and powerless.[45]

Mouse (עַכְבָּר)

The mouse (*achbar*) is a small rodent listed among the "things that swarm on the earth" that are prohibited as food (Lev. 11:29). Isaiah (66:17) attacked those who eat "the flesh of the swine, the reptile, and the mouse" as part of idolatrous rites, warning that they will be "consumed together" as part of the divine judgment. A horde of these prolifically multiplying rodents was reported to have destroyed the crops and caused a plague to break out among the Philistines after they captured the Ark of the Covenant (1 Sam. 6:4–5).

The Rabbis believed that mice were "half flesh and half earth" (i.e., capable of spontaneous generation) (Hul. 9:6, 126b). A miserly person was called "a mouse lying on his money" (Sanh. 29b), a reference to the fact that these creatures often drag glittering objects, such as coins and rings, into their holes. People who ate food that had been nibbled by mice (or who ate a mouse itself) would lose their memory (forget their learning) (Hor. 13a). What would happen if a mouse fell into a large volume of liquid? If "a mouse fell into a cask of beer," the beer was prohibited. Although according to one opinion this was because it [the mouse] "imparts a worsened flavor," the general consensus was that this case "was an anomaly since it is something repugnant and people recoil from it." If a mouse fell into vinegar, so that the rodent would not affect its sharp and pungent taste, the vinegar would still be prohibited because the mouse "may have been dissolved into pieces," and there was the fear that one might swallow some of this forbidden animal (Av. Zar. 68b–69a). According to the Talmud, "originally the *terumah* [sacred food] was stored near the Scroll of the Law," (Shab. 14a) since both were holy, but this practice was discontinued because the food attracted mice and injured (imposed uncleanness on) the sacred books.[46]

Mythical Creatures

Leviathan (לִוְיָתָן)

In biblical and talmudic literature, the term "Leviathan" refers to various marine animals, some real and others legendary. Derived from a Hebrew root meaning "to coil or twist," Leviathan was a gigantic sea serpent that encircled itself around the seas of the world.[47] According to the Bible, on the fifth day God created the "great sea monsters" (*tanninim gedolim*) (Gen. 1:21). Although the term "*tannin*" may occasionally refer to crocodiles or whales, it most often denotes a mythical creature, one of which may have been the "huge fish" that swallowed Jonah (2:1). When these sea monsters rebelled against the divine authority, God utterly destroyed them (Ps. 74:13–14; Isa. 27:1). This scenario is similar to prebiblical myths of a primordial combat between the creator deity and the forces of the sea for control of the universe.[48]

Leviathan was originally created in a male and female form. "[But] had they mated with one another they would have destroyed the whole world [with their numerous progeny]. What [then] did the Holy One, blessed be He, do? He castrated the male and killed the female, preserving it in salt for the righteous in the world to come" (BB 74b). According to tradition, Leviathan and Behemoth (see below) will fight to their deaths at the end of days, and the righteous will feast on their flesh (Lev. R. 13:3). This epic struggle and the subsequent messianic banquet are vividly depicted in *Akdamut* (see p. 301), the 11th-century Aramaic liturgical poem that Ashkenazim chant in the synagogue on Shavuot.[49] The skin of Leviathan will be used to "make a tabernacle for the righteous," and God will spread the rest of the sea monster "upon the walls of Jerusalem, and its splendor will shine from one end of the world to the other" (BB 75a).

Behemoth (בְּהֵמוֹת)

According to tradition, this king of the land beasts (*behemot*) also was created on the fifth day and destined to feed the righteous at the messianic banquet after fighting the sea monster Leviathan to the death. Each day, this legendary monster was reputed to consume the grass of a thousand hills (BB 74b). In the Book of Job (40:15–24), Behemoth is depicted as an animal that "eats grass like an ox," lives in the marsh hidden in the reeds, eats vast amounts of food, and can "draw the [waters of the] Jordan into his mouth." Of astounding strength, "he stiffens his tail like a cedar; the sinews of his thighs are knit together; his bones are like tubes of bronze, his limbs like bars of iron rods."[50] This precise description suggests that Behemoth originally referred to an existing animal—the huge hippopotamus that once inhabited the Land of Israel—though in later Jewish literature it appears as a purely mythical creature.

Nesher (נֶשֶׁר; Eagle or Vulture)

Although the word "*nesher*" is usually translated as "eagle," in many biblical passages the bird possesses characteristics (bald head, feeding on carcasses) indicating that it actually is a griffon vulture. The *nesher* is one of the species of bird that is forbidden for food (Lev. 11:13; Deut. 14:12). The talmudic sages traditionally identified the *nesher* as an eagle, applying the term to this symbol of imperial Rome. During the reign of Herod, the golden eagle perched above the gates of the Temple was a constant source of friction with the Jews in the Land of Israel.[51]

Although the largest of Israel's carnivorous birds and a mighty predator, the eagle treats its slowly developing young with concern. This image is often used as a metaphor for divine protection, especially God's loving care of Israel when leading the people safely through the wilderness. Just as the *nesher* carries its young on its back, using its own body as a shield against arrows, so God protected the Israelites from the Egyptians at the Sea of Reeds by placing the pillar of cloud between the Jews and their pursuers.[52] Indeed the phrase "I bore you on eagles' wings and brought you to Me" (Exod. 19:4) was applied to the airlift of the Yemenite Jews to Israel after the establishment of the State in 1948.

In describing the qualities needed to perform God's will, *Pirkei Avot* (5:23) says one should be "swift as an eagle ... to do the will of your

Father in Heaven." The speed and ability of the eagle to soar higher than other birds has been a symbol of prayer. In the morning service, one says, "Were our hands outspread like eagle's wings," we still could not give sufficient thanks for all the divine blessings.[53] Proverbs (23:5) warns against coveting riches, for once attained "it [riches] grows wings and flies away, like an eagle, heavenward."[54]

Pig (חֲזִיר)

The pig (*chazir*) is one of the unclean animals prohibited as food; although it has a cloven foot, it does not chew its cud (Lev. 11:7; Deut. 14:8). In his *Guide of the Perplexed*, Maimonides observed that "pork contains more moisture than is necessary (for human food) and too much superfluous matter. The principal reason why the Law forbids swine's flesh is that the habits and food of the swine are very dirty and loathsome."[55] Rabbi Papa noted, "The mouth of a swine is as dirty as dung itself" (Ber. 25a). The pig is a symbol of everything repulsive, as in the verse, "like a gold ring in the snout of a pig is a beautiful woman bereft of sense" (Prov. 11:22). Nevertheless, the Rabbis noted that the refusal of a Jew to eat pig should be based not on personal revulsion but on the divine command. "A man should not say, 'I have no desire to eat swine's flesh'; rather should he say, 'I would like to eat it, but what can I do seeing that my Father in Heaven has decreed against it'" (Sifra Ked. 11:22). The Rabbis even offered a substitute—the "*shibuta*" (Hul. 109b), a fish whose brain reportedly had a taste similar to swine's flesh.

The pig was so despised by Jews that the Talmud often refused to mention it by name, referring to it only as "*davar acheir*" ("another thing"; Ber. 43b; Shab. 129a). Rashi noted that the swine eats anything and is also given much food, giving rise to the talmudic expression, "None is richer than a pig" (Shab. 155b). Nevertheless, the pig suffers from numerous illnesses: "Ten measures of sores [diseases] descended to the world; nine were taken by swine" (Kid. 49b).

Rabbinic law distinguished between items prohibited for food (*treif*) and those from which no benefit can be enjoyed (such as *hametz* on Passover). Therefore, although it is forbidden to eat the flesh of swine, it is permitted to wear pigskin shoes (even in the synagogue), carry a pigskin wallet, and even bind religious books in pigskin.[56]

The pig figures in a famous passage in which the Rabbis elucidate the dangers of drunkenness (Tanh. Noah 13:21b). One who drinks properly becomes strong as a lion, but those who drink more than they should become like a pig wallowing in the mire, and one who becomes drunk "dances like an ape and utters folly before all."[57]

In the days preceding the Maccabean revolt, Antiochus Epiphanes forced the Jews to offer pigs as religious sacrifices on their altars (1 Macc. 1:47) and then eat of their flesh (2 Macc. 6:18–7:42). The Greeks, to whom pork was a delicacy, wanted the Jews to eat swine flesh as part of the effort to Hellenize them. However, many Jews suffered martyrdom for refusing to violate the dietary laws (e.g., Hannah's seven sons; 2 Macc. 7:20).[58] After a subsequent occurrence during Titus's siege of Jerusalem, when a pig was sacrificed instead of a kosher animal, the Rabbis declared, "Cursed be a man who rears pigs [and cursed be a man who teaches his son Greek wisdom!]" (Sot. 49b).

The question of raising pigs in the modern State of Israel has engendered heated controversy. The religious parties fought for a national law forbidding pig breeding, but in the early years the matter was left to the local authorities. A 1962 law prohibited the breeding, keeping, or slaughtering of pigs, except in Nazareth and some other areas with substantial Christian populations. Nevertheless, there is a kibbutz in the Galilee that raises pigs and has a plant to produce pork sausage. Moreover, several Russian markets sell pork products in Jewish areas, arousing the ire of Orthodox Jews living in these communities.

Quail (שְׂלָו)

The smallest member of the pheasant family, the quail (*s'lav*) is featured in one of the biblical incidents in which the Israelites displayed their ingratitude for the divine miracle of freeing them from slavery in Egypt. The "mixed multitude" succeeded in influencing the rest of the nation to complain about their steady diet of manna: "If only we had meat to eat! We remember the fish that we used to eat free in Egypt, the cucumbers, the melons, the leeks, the onions, and the garlic. Now our gullets are shriveled. There is nothing at all! Nothing but this manna to look to!" (Num. 11:4–6). God instructed Moses to inform the people that they would eat meat for a full month, so much that it would "come out of your nostrils and become loathsome to you," and they would regret their arrogant declaration that they would prefer to be back in

Egypt (Num. 11:18–20).[59] Consequently, God caused a wind to blow large flocks of quail from the sea and spread them widely over the land, "about a day's journey on this side and about a day's journey on that side, all around the camp, and some two cubits deep on the ground" (Num. 11:31). Some of the birds were eaten fresh; the rest were spread out on the ground to dry in the sun. The Psalmist recalled this instance of the Lord's bounty to the wandering Israelites in the verses: "He rained meat on them like dust, winged birds like the sands of the sea" (Ps. 78:27) and "They asked and He brought them quail, and satisfied them with food from heaven" (Ps. 105:40).

However, this story had a tragic epilogue—"the meat was still between their teeth, not yet chewed, when the anger of the Lord blazed forth against the people and the Lord struck the people with a very severe plague" (Num. 11:33). According to Nachmanides, those who had incited the people to complain died immediately. Chizkuni added that before killing these instigators, God wanted to dramatically demonstrate the ability to supply sufficient meat to satisfy everyone.[60] Finally, God named the place *Kivrot-hatta'avah* "because the people who had the craving were buried there" (Num. 11:34).

The biblical narrative has its basis in a natural phenomenon. During their annual migrations, large flocks of quail used to cross over the Mediterranean Sea. Upon reaching the coast near Gaza and exhausted from their lengthy flight, the birds would land and could be easily caught in nets spread out on the ground.

Scorpion (עַקְרָב)

The scorpion (*akrav*) is described in the Bible as a dangerous creature of the wilderness (Deut. 8:15). Elsewhere, the scorpion is used symbolically, as in King Rehoboam's warning to the people: "My father chastised you with whips, but I will chastise you with scorpions" (1 Kings 12:11; 2 Chron.10:11,14).[61] In this context, scorpions are prickly thorns, whose sharp ends can sting just as scorpions inject a poison that causes severe pain. If a scorpion is wound around a man's foot, he is permitted to stop his prayer because the scorpion will sting (Ber. 33a). Indeed, these animals are so dangerous that if a man falls into a pit full of scorpions (and serpents), this can be used legally as evidence of his death to enable his wife to marry again (Yev. 121a). One of the minor miracles mentioned as occurring during the Second Temple period was that "no serpent or scorpion inflicted injury in Jerusalem" (Avot 5:7).[62]

Sheep (שֶׂה, כֶּבֶשׂ)

Sheep were important domestic animals in ancient Israel, providing meat, wool, and hides for shoes and clothing. Sheep were a valuable source of rich milk (Deut. 32:14), which was usually allowed to curdle before drinking to produce *leben*. In the Psalms (144:13), there is a prayer for the fertility of the flocks: "May our sheep bring forth thousands and ten thousands in our fields!"[63] Sheep were often used as sacrifices in the Temple, giving rise to the expression "sheep [or lamb] for the slaughter" (Ps. 44:23; Jer. 12:3; Isa. 53:7). This phrase describing weak and innocent animals being led to their deaths became allegorically applied to the martyrdom of Jews from biblical times to the Holocaust.

The curved horn of the ram, the male sheep, was the classic shofar (RH 3:4), the symbol of Rosh Hashanah that is sounded repeatedly to call the people to repentance (see p. 190). Although a shofar can be made from the horn of a variety animals, a ram's horn is preferred because it recalls the *Akedah* (sacrifice of Isaac), the quintessential example of utter obedience to the divine will that is a key aspect of the High Holy Day season. The fleece of the ram is used for the fringes of the tallit (tzitzit), and its hide provides the straps of the tefillin and the parchment of the Torah scroll.[64]

The shepherd tending his flock is a popular biblical metaphor for God caring for the Jewish people (Ezek. 34; Ps. 23:1). The *U-netaneh Tokef* recited on Rosh Hashanah (see p. 199) depicts all creatures passing before God, one by one, like a flock of sheep before the shepherd who decrees their fate. On Yom Kippur, the Jewish people are metaphorically described as the dutiful sheep of the divine shepherd in *Ki Anu Amecha* (see p. 218).

Before the 10th plague, God commanded the Israelites to sacrifice a lamb and smear its blood on their doorposts (Exod. 12:6–13) as a sign for the Angel of Death to pass over their houses when smiting the firstborn of Egypt. Since the destruction of the Temple, the ritual of sacrificing the paschal lamb has been symbolized by the roasted shank bone on the Passover seder plate (see p. 270).

Born in the spring and associated with Passover, the festival of national redemption, lambs symbolize rebirth and renewal. Indeed, in early Hebrew mosaics the lamb is the sign for the first month of spring, which the pagan zodiac depicts as Aries the Ram.[65]

Snake or Serpent (נָחָשׁ)

Since the beginning of biblical history, the snake has been considered the eternal enemy of human beings. According to legend, God originally made the serpent king of the beasts, standing erect and endowed with some ability to speak. However, the snake's intense jealousy toward human beings led to its downfall (Gen. R. 20:5).[66] After enticing Eve into disobeying the divine prohibition against eating from the Tree of Knowledge of Good and Evil (see p. 696), the snake received the severe punishment of having to crawl on its belly and eat the earth. The enmity between the snake and humans would be everlasting: "they shall strike at your head, and you shall strike at their heel" (Gen. 3:14–15). From this verse, the sages derived an approach that should be followed when human beings are confronted with the inclination to do evil, which is symbolized by the serpent. Because the wily serpent tempts the Jew to tread on the mitzvot with his *heel*, the Jew can overcome the evil inclination by using his or her *head*—the study of Torah.[67] In Egypt, the rod of Aaron turned into a snake and swallowed the serpentlike rods of the magicians of Pharaoh (Exod. 7:11–12). Jacob described his son Dan as "a serpent by the road, a viper by the path, that bites the horse's heels so that his rider is thrown backward" (Gen. 49:16–17). Rashi and Ramban noted that this was an apt depiction of Samson, a descendant of Dan, who repeatedly attacked the enemy Philistines in lightning raids and then disappeared from sight before they could retaliate. Just as a snake "bites the horse's heels" so that it throws and indirectly kills its rider, so the blind and chained Samson caused the collapse of the idolatrous temple of the Philistines by pulling down its massive pillars, killing himself and 3,000 of the enemies of Israel (Judg. 16:29).[68]

As punishment for their rebellion in the wilderness, God sent fiery serpents to bite the people. When the people repented, God heeded their prayers and ordered Moses to make a model of a serpent and place it on a pole, "and if anyone who is bitten looks at it, he shall recover" (Num. 21:6–10). Although God did not specify the material to be used, Moses chose copper (*nechoshet*), because in Hebrew it contains the letters of the *nachash* (serpent) that was attacking the sinners (Rashi).[69] According to the Mishnah, the copper serpent had no intrinsic power, but was effective because "when Israel turned their thoughts and subjected their hearts to their Father in Heaven, they were healed" (JT RH 3:8, 29a), just as Israel prevailed in the battle against Amalek (Exod. 17:11) when Moses raised his arms and focused the gaze and minds of the people toward Heaven.[70] This copper serpent eventually became an object of idol worship in the Temple until it was destroyed by King Hezekiah in the eighth century B.C.E. (2 Kings 18:4), an action that was praised by the Rabbis (Ber. 10b).[71]

The Psalmist (140:4) asked God for protection from violent men who have "sharpened their tongue like a serpent."[72] On the Sabbath, it was permitted to slay "the [poisonous] snake of Israel (Shab. 121b) and the Jerusalem Talmud (Kid. 4:11, 66c) maintained that "even with the best of snakes, crush its head". Appreciating that poisonous snakes generally do not attack human beings without provocation, the Rabbis ruled that a person should not interrupt the recitation of the *Amidah* "even if a snake is wound around his heel" (Ber. 5:1).

Wolf (זְאֵב)

The wolf is frequently mentioned in the Bible and rabbinic literature as a dangerous animal that attacks at night and poses a serious danger to flocks of sheep. When wolves attack in a pack, the shepherd cannot be held liable for the loss of the animals in his care (BM 7:9, 93b). When castigating the "evil princes" of Israel, Ezekiel (22:27) compares them to "wolves rending prey in her midst; they shed blood and destroy lives to win ill-gotten gain."

In Jacob's blessings for his sons, the youngest (Benjamin) is described as "a ravenous wolf; in the morning he consumes the foe [devours his prey], and in the evening he divides the spoil" (Gen. 49:27). Many of Benjamin's descendants were powerful and fearless warriors. According to Rashi, the "morning" refers to King Saul, who was the leader of the Israelites during the early successful years of their history. When the people were exiled to Babylonia and Persia in the national "evening" of decline, it will be the offspring of Benjamin who will defeat the enemies of Israel and "divide the spoils" of their victory. This is an allusion to Mordecai and Esther, of the tribe of Benjamin, who triumphed over Haman and, after the hanging of this epitome of wickedness, were granted all his worldly possessions.[73]

Notes

Life-Cycle Events
The Stages of Life

1. Rashi cites an opinion that the word "pursuit" refers to this being the age when the heavenly court *pursues* a person for his actions, holding him liable for Divine punishment for his sins (*ArtScroll Siddur,* 578).
2. Fifty was the age at which Levites were no longer considered fit for heavy work, but continued to act as guides and counselors to their younger colleagues (Num. 8:25). At this age, one can draw on his or her life experience and intellect to advise others (*ArtScroll Siddur,* 578).
3. This may refer either to a person's appearance or to intellectual maturity (ibid.).
4. Seventy was the age at which King David died, of whom it is said: "He died at a ripe old age" (1 Chron. 29:28; *ArtScroll Siddur,* 578).
5. This is based on the verse: "The span of our life is seventy years, or given the strength, eighty years" (Ps. 90:10). This implies that God has given one who lives to 80 special natural strength and vigor, both physical and spiritual (*ArtScroll Siddur,* 579).
6. A person who reaches the age of 100 has lost most of his or her natural faculties (ibid.).
7. Trepp, 214.
8. Blech, 202.

First 16 Years of Life
Birth

1. M. Klein, 148–152; Schauss, 53–54.
2. Gelbard, 125.
3. M. Klein, 205.
4. Lau, 356; Project Genesis.

Circumcision

1. Frankel and Teutsch, 26.
2. Ibid.
3. MT Milah 2:1.
4. M. Klein, 245–246.
5. Sperling, 271.
6. Ibid., 273–274.
7. Frankel and Teutsch, 26–27.
8. Dosick, 286–287
9. Alternate translation.
10. Alternate translation.
11. Rosen, 203.
12. Blech, 168.
13. Strassfeld and Strassfeld, 30–37.

Names

1. Tanḥ. Ha'azinu 7.
2. Frankel and Teutsch, 117.
3. Dosick, 289.
4. Gross, 566.

5. *Etz Hayim*, 323.
6. Frankel and Teutsch, 117.
7. Gross, 566.
8. Schauss, 13.
9. Ibid., 568.
10. Ibid., 566.
11. EJ, at "Names."
12. Gross, 568.
13. Ibid., 569–571.
14. Schauss, 47.
15. EJ, at "Names."
16. Gross, 571; Bloch, 7.
17. Frankel and Teutsch, 118.
18. Trepp, 323.

Pidyon ha-Ben

1. Trepp, 231.
2. Kadden and Kadden, 5.

Adoption

1. This article was adapted with permission from Dorff, 107–109.

Bar Mitzvah

1. Kadden and Kadden, 27.
2. Frankel and Teutsch, 16.
3. Kadden and Kadden, 28.
4. Strassfeld, 63.
5. Donin, *To Pray as a Jew,* 249.
6. Lau, 365.
7. Frankel and Teutsch, 16.

Bat Mitzvah

1. Dosick, 294.
2. Kadden and Kadden, 28.
3. Ibid.
4. Frankel and Teutsch, 16.

Marriage

Jewish Marriage

1. Alternate translation.
2. M. Lamm, *The Jewish Way in Love and Marriage,* 98–101.

Marriage Ceremony

1. Frankel and Teutsch, 188.
2. Biale, 53.
3. Ibid., 48–49.
4. Kadden and Kadden, 63.
5. Ibid.
6. Biale, 57.
7. M. Lamm, *The Jewish Way in Love and Marriage,* 148.
8. Kadden and Kadden, 63.
9. M. Lamm, *The Jewish Way in Love and Marriage,* 147.
10. Kolatch, *The Jewish Book of Why,* 34.
11. Trepp, 283.
12. M. Lamm, *The Jewish Way in Love and Marriage,* 148–152.
13. Kolatch, *The Jewish Book of Why,* 38.
14. Diamant, 98.
15. Ibid., 101.
16. M. Lamm, *The Jewish Way in Love and Marriage,* 210.
17. Kadden and Kadden, 66.
18. Greenberg, 226.
19. M. Lamm, *The Jewish Way in Love and Marriage,* 214–215.
20. Kolatch, *The Jewish Book of Why,* 39.
21. Kadden and Kadden, 68.
22. M. Lamm, *The Jewish Way in Love and Marriage,* 231.
23. Trepp, 288.
24. Witty and Witty, 410–411.
25. M. Lamm, *The Jewish Way in Love and Marriage,* 189.
26. Kolatch, *The Jewish Book of Why,* 31.
27. Witty and Witty, 403.
28. M. Lamm, *The Jewish Way in Love and Marriage,* 190.
29. Ibid., 221.
30. Diamant, 175.
31. Kolatch, *The Jewish Book of Why,* 42.
32. Greenberg, 228.
33. Kolatch, *The Jewish Book of Why,* 40.
34. M. Lamm, *The Jewish Way in Love and Marriage,* 198.
35. Biale, 80–83.
36. Frankel and Teutsch, 88.
37. EJ, at "Ketubbah."
38. Frankel and Teutsch, 88.

39. Kadden and Kadden, 65.
40. Kolatch, *The Jewish Book of Why*, 43–44.
41. Kadden and Kadden, 61.
42. Diamant, 28–29.
43. Schauss, 159.
44. Kolatch, *The Jewish Book of Why*, 28.
45. Witty and Witty, 399.
46. Ibid.

Huppah

1. Frankel and Teutsch, 77.
2. Kadden and Kadden, 64.
3. Frankel and Teutsch, 77.
4. Ibid.
5. Kolatch, *The Jewish Book of Why*, 35.
6. M. Lamm, *The Jewish Way in Love and Marriage*, 210.
7. Frankel and Teutsch, 77.

Bridal Veil

1. Greenberg, 224.
2. Alternate translation.
3. Kolatch, *The Jewish Book of Why*, 36–37.

Harmonious Married Life

1. This section was adopted with permission from Lewittes, 99–101.
2. MT Hilchot Ishut 15:20.
3. Quoted in Lewittes, 100–101.

Obligations and Rights of the Husband

1. MT Ishut 12:1–4.
2. Ibid.
3. Ibid.

Prohibited Marriages

1. Hertz, 490.
2. Chill, 478.
3. *Stone Chumash*, 673.
4. Ibid., 674.
5. Maimonides, *Guide of the Perplexed* 3:49.
6. Rabbenu Gershom (c. 960–1028), great German talmudic scholar, known as Me'or ha-Golah (Light of the Exile).

Levirate Marriage and *Halitzah*

1. Maimonides, *The Commandments*, 232.
2. M. Lamm, *The Jewish Way in Love and Marriage*, 72–73.
3. *Stone Chumash*, 1065.
4. MT Yibbum 1:2.
5. Biale, 116–118.
6. Ibid., 118–119.

Intermarriage

1. Lamm, *The Jewish Way in Love and Marriage*, 49–51.
2. Torah Tidbits, at www.ou.org/torah/tt/pinchas61/specialfeatures_mitzvot.htm; accessed in July 2003.

Sex

Premarital Sex

1. Biale, 190–192.
2. M. Lamm, *The Jewish Way in Love and Marriage*, 31.

Male Homosexuality

1. *Stone Chumash*, 653.
2. MT Issurei Bi'ah 22:2.
3. Yosef Karo (1488–1575), author of the Shulchan Arukh, the major authoritative code of Jewish law.
4. Joel Sirkes (1561–1640), Polish talmudic scholar.
5. M. Lamm, *The Jewish Way in Love and Marriage*, 66–67.
6. Kolatch, *The Second Jewish Book of Why*, 151.
7. Gross, 381.
8. Norman Lamm, former President of Yeshiva University.
9. "Judaism and the Modern Attitude to Homosexuality," EJ Yearbook, 1974.
10. Moses Tendler, expert on medical

ethics and professor of biology and of Talmud at Yeshiva College.
11. Tendler.
12. Quoted in Grossman, 56, 97.
13. Ibid., 58.
14. Ibid., 57.

Female Homosexuality
1. MT Issurei Bi'ah 21:8.
2. Biale, 195.

Divorce
Jewish Concepts of Divorce
1. Telushkin, 621.
2. Biale, 78.
3. Ibid., 81–82.

Divorce Other Than by Consent
1. Riskin, *Women and Jewish Divorce*, xi–xiii.
2. Ibid.
3. Biale, 86–88.
4. Alternate translation.

Consequences of Divorce
1. Haut, 43.
2. Haut, 44–45.
3. Dorff, 359.

Get
1. Kolatch, *The Jewish Book of Why*, 47–48.
2. Telushkin, 622.
3. Kolatch, *The Jewish Book of Why*, 48.
4. Telushkin, 622.
5. Biale, 97–98.
6. Haut, 23–24.
7. Biale, 98–100.
8. Haut, 28–29.
9. Lewittes, 200.

Agunah
1. Biale, 102.
2. Strassfeld and Strassfeld, 117–118.
3. Biale, 102–103.
4. Ibid., 106; Kaufman, 192
5. Biale, 105.
6. Ibid., 108.
7. Lewittes, 200.
8. Rabbenu Tam (Jacob ben Meir; c. 1100–1171), leading French talmudic scholar.
9. Biale, 108–109.
10. Ibid., 110.
11. A. Weiss at www.yerushalayim.net/organizations/oc/prenup/weiss.htm; accessed in December 2003.
12. Ibid.
13. S. Weiss, 55.
14. A. Weiss at www.yerushalayim.net/organizations/oc/prenup/weiss.htm; accessed in December 2003.
15. Biale, 110.
16. Kadden and Kadden, 69.
17. Riskin, "Breaking the Chains," 39.
18. Biale, 112.

Death
Death and Dying
1. *ArtScroll Siddur*, 797.
2. Witty and Witty, 463–464.
3. Trepp, 322.
4. M. Lamm, *The Jewish Way in Death and Mourning*, 4; T. Rabinowicz, 8; Sperling, 290–291; Schauss, 261–262.
5. M. Lamm, *The Jewish Way in Death and Mourning*, 5.

Angel of Death
1. Schauss, 281.
2. Ibid.
3. Ibid., 282.

Preparation for Burial
1. T. Rabinowicz, 28.
2. M. Lamm, *The Jewish Way in Death and Mourning*, 6.
3. Frankel and Teutsch, 157.
4. Kolatch, *The Jewish Book of Why*, 53.
5. Frankel and Teutsch, 157.

6. Ibid.
7. M. Lamm, *The Jewish Way in Death and Mourning*, 16.
8. Kolatch, *The Jewish Book of Why*, 54–55.
9. M. Lamm, *The Jewish Way in Death and Mourning*, 16.
10. Kolatch, *The Jewish Book of Why*, 54–55.
11. T. Rabinowicz, 31.

Funeral Service and Burial

1. Kadden and Kadden, 104.
2. Schauss, 226–227.
3. M. Lamm, *The Jewish Way in Death and Mourning*, 18.
4. Ibid., 19–20.
5. Kadden and Kadden, 104.
6. Kolatch, *The Jewish Book of Why*, 54.
7. Kadden and Kadden, 104–105.
8. M. Lamm, *The Jewish Way in Death and Mourning*, 52–53.
9. Schauss, 224, 235.
10. Kadden and Kadden, 105.
11. M. Lamm, *The Jewish Way in Death and Mourning*, 60–61.
12. Kadden and Kadden, 105.
13. M. Lamm, *The Jewish Way in Death and Mourning*, 65.
14. Kadden and Kadden, 105.
15. I. Klein, 281–282.
16. Ibid., 400.
17. *ArtScroll Siddur*, 815.
18. Ibid.
19. T. Rabinowicz, 101–102; Kadden and Kadden, 107.
20. Kolatch, *The Jewish Book of Why*, 76.
21. Schauss, 254.
22. Kadden and Kadden, 106.
23. Kolatch, *The Jewish Book of Why*, 75.
24. Kadden and Kadden, 107.
25. Ibid.

Mourning

1. M. Lamm, *The Jewish Way in Death and Mourning*, 39.
2. Kadden and Kadden, 104.
3. M. Lamm, *The Jewish Way in Death and Mourning*, 44.
4. Ibid.
5. Ibid., 23.
6. Ibid., 21.
7. Kadden and Kadden, 103.
8. Ibid., 105.
9. M. Lamm, *The Jewish Way in Death and Mourning*, 67.
10. Ibid., 98–99.
11. Ibid., 100.
12. T. Rabinowicz, 48.
13. Kadden and Kadden, 106.
14. T. Rabinowicz, 46–47.
15. Kolatch, *The Jewish Book of Why*, 64; M. Lamm, *The Jewish Way in Death and Mourning*, 112.
16. Kadden and Kadden, 106.
17. M. Lamm, *The Jewish Way in Death and Mourning*, 112.
18. M. Lamm, *The Jewish Way in Death and Mourning*, 109–122, 125–136.
19. Ibid., 102–104.
20. Ibid., 101–102.
21. Dosick, 309.
22. Kadden and Kadden, 106.
23. I. Klein, 290–291.
24. Dosick, 310.
25. T. Rabinowicz, 90–91; Millgram, *Jewish Worship*, 448.
26. Millgram, *Jewish Worship*, 448.
27. Dosick, 312.
28. Schauss, 299.
29. Sperling, 198.
30. Hammer, *Entering Jewish Prayer*, 286.

Suicide

1. Cited in Dorff, 180.
2. Oshry, 34.
3. Dorff, 182.
4. M. Lamm, *The Jewish Way in Death and Mourning*, 216.
5. Ibid., 217; T. Rabinowicz, 67–68.

Euthanasia and Assisted Suicide

1. MT Rotze'ach 2:7.
2. Bleich, 79, n. 12 (referring to BM 52a).
3. Ibid., 69–70.
4. Resnicoff, 289.
5. This section was adapted with permission from Dorff, 183–184.

Cremation

1. T. Rabinowicz, 15–18.
2. M. Lamm, *The Jewish Way in Death and Mourning*, 84.
3. Kadden and Kadden, 102.
4. Dorff, 223–224.

Modern Issues Concerning the Dead

1. Jakobovitz, 150.
2. Dorff, 225.
3. Ibid., 239–241.
4. This section was adapted with permission from Dorff, 225–239.
5. Moses Isserles (mid-16th century; known as Rema), renowned Polish rabbi who wrote *Mappah* (Tablecloth) for Karo's Shulchan Arukh (Table).
6. MT Avel 14:1.

Afterlife and the World to Come

1. This article was adapted with permission from the lectures of Byron Sherwin (Spertus Institute, Chicago).
2. Philo (c. 30 B.C.E.–c. 40 C.E.), Hellenistic Jewish philosopher and biblical interpreter.
3. Jacobs, 480.
4. At 2:27, 3:54.
5. MT Teshuvah 3:5.

Paradise (Gan Eden)

1. MT Teshuvah 8:1,5.
2. *Sefer ha-Ikkarim* 4:33

Gehenna

1. Jacobs, 480, 506.

Sabbath and Festivals

Sabbath

Overview

1. EJ, at "Sabbath."
2. MT Shab. 30:15; *Guide of the Perplexed* 2:31.
3. *Guide of the Perplexed* 2:31.
4. Hirsch, 2:21.
5. In *The Sabbath.*
6. Ha-Am, 3:30.
7. In Biale.
8. Frankel and Teutsch, 152.

Eshet Chayil

1. Witty and Witty, 167. "Grace is deceitful, beauty is vain; but a woman who fears the Lord, she shall be praised. Give her of the fruit of her hands, and let her works praise her in the gates." The Hebrew word "*hevel*" is traditionally translated as "vain" (as in Ecclesiastes) rather than "illusory"; in the second part of the sentence, the woman is the subject and the Hebrew word "*t'nu*" literally means "give" rather than "extol."
2. Ibid.; Lau, 167.

Restrictions

1. Lau, 194.
2. Witty and Witty, 187.
3. Ibid., 187–192.
4. Chill, 38.
5. Witty and Witty, 193.
6. Alternate translation.
7. Witty and Witty, 193, 194; Lau, 196.
8. Hazon Ish (Man of Vision), major work of Avraham Yeshayahu Karelitz (1878–1953), outstanding Polish-born talmudic scholar who became almost exclusively known by this name.
9. Kolatch, *The Jewish Book of Why*, 166.

10. Telushkin, 600.
11. Ibid.
12. Hertz, 277.
13. Menachem ha-Bavli (16th century), rabbi and kabbalist of the Safed school.
14. Maimonides, *The Commandments*, 296.
15. Telushkin, 484.
16. MT Shab. 1.
17. MT Shab. 27:17.
18. Law, 202.

Observances

1. Alternate translation.
2. Maimonides, *The Commandments*, 165.
3. Frankel and Teutsch, 152.
4. Donin, *To Pray as a Jew*, 334.
5. Siegel et al., 42.
6. Kolatch, *The Jewish Book of Why*, 170.
7. The standard prayer recited after kindling the Sabbath candles is as follows:

   May it be Your will, O Lord my God and God of my ancestors, that you be gracious to me [my husband, my sons, my daughters, my father, my mother] and all my relatives and grant us and all Israel a long and good life. Remember us for good and blessing and consider us for salvation and compassion. Bless us with your great blessings, grant us perfect peace in our homes, and cause Your Presence to dwell in our midst. Make us worthy to raise children and grandchildren who are wise and understanding, who love and fear God, are people of truth and holy deeds, and attached to God, who illuminate the world with Torah and good deeds, doing the work of our Creator. In the merit of our Sarah, Rebecca, Rachel, and Leah, our mothers, please hear my supplication at this time. May the light [of our candles] never be extinguished, and may Your countenance shine on us and let us be saved. Amen.

8. Witty and Witty, 157.
9. Garfiel, 127–128.
10. MT Shab. 5:3.
11. Gelbard, 226.
12. Donin, *To Pray as a Jew*, 319–320.
13. Ibid., 320.
14. Rashbam (1085–1174), acronym of French biblical scholar Rabbi Samuel ben Meir.
15. Sperling, 129.
16. *Kol Bo* (Everything Within), anonymous work from the late 13th or early 14th century containing both halakhic rulings and explanations, arranged in accordance with the subject matter.
17. Ibid., 124.
18. Millgram, *Jewish Worship*, 299.
19. Donin, *To Pray as a Jew*, 321.
20. Ibid., 322.
21. Ibid., 322–323.
22. *Etz Hayim*, 852.
23. Kolatch, *The Jewish Book of Why*, 172–174.
24. Ibid.
25. Gelbard, 225.
26. Sperling, 155.
27. Trepp, 77.
28. Kolatch, *The Jewish Book of Why*, 174–176.
29. Sperling, 146.
30. *Harvard Hillel Songbook*, 4.
31. Ibid., 48.
32. Witty and Witty, 183; *Harvard Hillel Songbook*, 86–87.
33. Millgram, *Jewish Worship*, 501.

Liturgy

1. Millgram, *Jewish Worship*, 502; Gelbard, 232.
2. Diament et al., 117; *Harvard Hillel Songbook*, 94,97.

3. Witty and Witty, 162.
4. Donin, *To Pray as a Jew*, 260.
5. *ArtScroll Siddur*, 318.
6. Sperling, 121.
7. Gelbard, 241–242.

Havdalah

1. Frankel and Teutsch, 73.
2. "God is my salvation." In traditional translations, the Hebrew word "*yeshu'ati*" is in the possessive case (rather than a direct object) and comes from the word "*yeshu'ah*," which is generally rendered as "salvation" (as in the opening phrase of the *Havdalah* ceremony) rather than "triumph."
3. Garfiel, 199–200.
4. Sperling, 162.
5. Frankel and Teutsch, 73.
6. Donin, *To Pray as a Jew*, 332.
7. Ibid., 329.
8. Frankel and Teutsch, 74.
9. Donin, *To Pray as a Jew*, 331.
10. Millgram, *Jewish Worship*, 300.
11. Millgram, *Sabbath*, 21.
12. Donin, *To Pray as a Jew*, 332.
13. Frankel and Teutsch, 29.
14. Gelbard, 307.
15. Millgram, *Sabbath*, 21.
16. Witty and Witty, 198.
17. Author's translation: "What is the end of my days" (literal translation).
18. Millgram, *Sabbath*, 21–22.
19. Donin, *To Pray as a Jew*, 333.

Spice Box

1. Frankel and Teutsch, 160.

Special Sabbaths

1. Toperoff, 30.

Festivals and Fasts

Overview

1. Donin, *To Be a Jew*, 208.
2. Maimonides, *The Commandments*, 62.
3. Ibid.
4. MT Yom Tov 6:18.
5. *Stone Chumash*, 783.
6. Ibid., 683.
7. Maimonides, *The Commandments*, 300.
8. Chill, 278.
9. MT Yom Tov 7:1-4
10. Donin, *To Be a Jew*, 210–211; Steinsaltz, *Guide to Jewish Prayer*, 148–149.
11. *ArtScroll Siddur*, 632.
12. Ibid.; Sperling, 133.
13. Millgram, *Jewish Worship*, 210–211.
14. Donin, *To Pray as a Jew*, 268–269.
15. Ibid., 267–268.
16. Riskin, *The Passover Haggadah*, 107.
17. Steinsaltz, *A Guide to Jewish Prayer*, 392.

Jewish Calendar

1. In the third, sixth, eighth, 11th, 14th, 17th, and 19th years of the cycle.

Rosh Hodesh

1. Millgram, *Jewish Worship*, 263.
2. Frankel and Teutsch, 141.
3. Millgram, *Jewish Worship*, 264
4. Steinsaltz, *A Guide to Jewish Prayer*, 214–215.
5. Millgram, *Jewish Worship*, 265.
6. Donin, *To Pray as a Jew*, 273.
7. *ArtScroll Siddur*, 612.
8. Donin, *To Pray as a Jew*, 276–277.
9. Ibid., 277.
10. Sperling, 172–173
11. *ArtScroll Siddur*, 612.

High Holy Days

Repentance

1. Much of this article was adapted from lectures given by Byron Sherwin at the Spertus Institute (Chicago).
2. Alternate translation.
3. *Etz Hayim*, 1493.
4. MT Teshuvah 1:1,3.

5. MT Teshuvah 2:1.
6. Alternate translation.

Selichot

1. Millgram, *Jewish Worship,* 227.
2. Ibid.
3. Sperling, 216–217.
4. Millgram, *Jewish Worship,* 228. "I arise at midnight to praise You for Your righteous judgments." The Hebrew word "*mishpetei*" is generally translated as "judgments" (rather than "rules"), which are rendered in a *beit mishpat* (court). The purpose of *Selichot* is to pray for God's mercy and a favorable judgment.
5. Hammer, *Entering the High Holy Days,* 40.
6. Steinsaltz, *A Guide to Jewish Prayer,* 246.
7. Sperling, 219.
8. *ArtScroll Siddur,* 434.
9. Hammer, *Entering the High Holy Days,* 126.
10. Abudraham (David ben Joseph; 14th century), Spanish liturgical commentator.
11. *ArtScroll Siddur,* 817–820; Sperling, 217–218.
12. *ArtScroll Siddur,* 434 using *ArtScroll Tanach.*

Elul

1. Strassfeld, 93.
2. Hammer, *Entering the High Holy Days,* 38.
3. Steinsaltz, *A Guide to Jewish Prayer,* 246.
4. "The Lord is my light and my salvation; whom should I fear?" The Hebrew word "*yeshu'ah*" is generally translated as "salvation" rather than "help."
5. Ibid.
6. Hammer, *Entering the High Holy Days,* 41.
7. Strassfeld, 98.
8. Ibid., 97.

Rosh Hashanah

1. This is similar to the Gregorian calendar, in which the numerical values of the names September, October, November, and December indicate that the calendar should begin in March, though the year is actually calculated from January (Steinsaltz, *A Guide to Jewish Prayer,* 178).
2. Strassfeld, 102–103; Sperling, 230.
3. Unlike other festival days, which commemorate historical events, the agricultural cycle, or instances of divine salvation, Rosh Hashanah (and Yom Kippur) relate to the private life of the individual. On the High Holy Days, the Jew stands alone, though within a congregation of other people, before the "King Lord of Hosts" (Isa. 6:5), "the great, the mighty, and the awesome" (Deut. 10:17) (Steinsaltz, *A Guide to Jewish Prayer,* 177).
4. Strassfeld, 100–101.
5. Alternate translation; Sperling, 220–221.
6. Kolatch, *The Jewish Book of Why,* 227–228.
7. *ArtScroll Yom Kippur Reader,* 47.
8. Witty and Witty, 237.
9. Reider, 14.
10. Kolatch, *The Jewish Book of Why,* 237–238.
11. Sperling, 224
12. Frankel and Teutsch, 140.
13. Sperling, 224.
14. Steinsaltz, *A Guide to Jewish Prayer,* 183.
15. Kitov, 1:55.
16. Frankel and Teutsch, 156–157.
17. Ibid., 157.
18. Ibid., 156–157.

19. Agnon, 68–69; I. Klein, 193.
20. Hammer, *Entering the High Holy Days*, 71–72.
21. Ibid., 72.
22. Strassfeld, 219.
23. Hammer, *Entering the High Holy Days*, 70.
24. Ibid., 70–71.
25. MT Teshuvah 3:4.
26. Donin, *To Pray as a Jew*, 279–280.
27. Martin, 194.
28. Hammer, *Entering the High Holy Days*, 68.
29. Millgram, *Jewish Worship*, 241.
30. Hammer, *Entering the High Holy Days*, 77.
31. *ArtScroll Machzor*, 480; and Witty and Witty, 221.
32. *ArtScroll Machzor*, 482–483.
33. Martin, 210.
34. *ArtScroll Machzor*, 483.
35. Martin, 210.
36. Hammer, *Entering the High Holy Days*, 80.
37. Witty and Witty, 225.
38. Millgram, *Jewish Worship*, 242.
39. Hammer, *Entering the High Holy Days*, 82–83.
40. Witty and Witty, 227.
41. Hammer, *Entering the High Holy Days*, 92.
42. Trepp, 108.
43. Hammer, *Entering the High Holy Days*, 93.
44. Waskow, *Seasons of Our Joy*, 19.

Hineni

1. Witty and Witty, 227.

Ten Days of Repentance

1. Siegel et al., 123.
2. Kolatch, *The Jewish Book of Why*, 80.

Yom Kippur

1. See www.torahtots.com/holidays/yomkipur/yomkstr.htm; accessed November 2003.
2. *ArtScroll Yom Kippur Reader*, 67.
3. Strassfeld, 220.
4. Sperling, 235.
5. Kitov, 1:87.
6. Strassfeld, 116–117.
7. Sperling, 237.
8. Trepp, 113.
9. Witty and Witty, 248–249; Kitov,1:98–99; Sperling, 238.
10. Author's translation: "For all the people have transgressed unwittingly." The Hebrew is in the active, not passive voice.
11. Hammer. *Entering the High Holy Days*, 115.
12. Witty and Witty, 248.
13. Trepp, 113.
14. Millgram. *Jewish Worship*, 246–247.
15. Ibid., 248.
16. Ibid.
17. Hammer. *Entering the High Holy Days*, 135
18. Ibid., 140–141; Sperling, 220.
19. Millgram. *Jewish Worship*, 249.
20. Hammer. *Entering the High Holy Days*, 157.
21. Millgram. *Jewish Worship*, 254.
22. Steinsaltz, 206.
23. Hammer. *Entering the High Holy Days*, 167.
24. Millgram. *Jewish Worship*, 258–260.
25. Hammer. *Entering the High Holy Days*, 168.
26. Witty and Witty, 271.
27. Millgram. *Jewish Worship*, 260.
28. Sperling, 243.
29. Steinsaltz, 210–211.
30. Hammer. *Entering the High Holy Days*, 176.
31. Trepp, 110.
32. Schauss, 66.
33. Hammer, *Entering the High Holy Days*, 104.
34. Ibid., 9–10.
35. Ibid., 15–16.

36. Witty and Witty, 266.
37. *Etz Hayim*, 681.
38. Ibid.
39. *ArtScroll Yom Kippur Reader*, 28–30.

Fall Festivals

Sukkot

1. Author's translation: "Joyfully shall you draw water from the fountains of salvation." The Hebrew word "yeshu'ah" generally means salvation or deliverance.
2. Frankel and Teutsch, 165.
3. Steinsaltz, 169.
4. Kolatch, *The Jewish Book of Why*, 248.
5. Gelbard, 408.
6. Frankel and Teutsch, 164.
7. Strassfeld, 222.
8. Lau, 252.
9. Sperling, 250.
10. Chill, 294.
11. Ibid., 293.
12. Author's translation: "Give thanks to the Lord for He is good; His mercy endures forever." The Hebrew word "Hodu" generally means to give thanks. The Hebrew "chasdo" derives from "chesed," and most often means "mercy" or "lovingkindness" rather than "love."
13. Author's translation: "Please, Lord, deliver us." The Hebrew word "ana" that begins the line literally means "please," as in Moses' prayer that God heal Miriam: "Ana Adonai, refah la" (Please God, heal her!).
14. Strassfeld, 223.
15. MT Lulav 7:23.
16. Witty and Witty, 347; *ArtScroll Siddur*, 726–733.
17. Frankel and Teutsch, 185.
18. Kitov, 2:158.
19. Strassfeld, 129.
20. Ibid., 222.

Hoshana Rabbah

1. MT Lulav 7:21–22.
2. Strassfeld, 135–136.
3. Ibid., 136.
4. Ibid., 136–137.
5. Gelbard, 425.

Shemini Atzeret

1. Strassfeld, 225.

Simchat Torah

1. Sperling, 82.
2. Author's translation: "The commandment is a lamp, the Torah [teaching] is a light."
3. Strassfeld, 152–153.
4. Siegel et al., 128–129.
5. Waskow, *Seasons of Our Joy*, 81.
6. Siegel et al., 129; Sperling, 257.
7. Frankel and Teutsch, 165.
8. Wiesel, 44–66.

Winter Festivals

Hanukkah

1. Strassfeld, 161–162.
2. Ibid., 162.
3. Kolatch, *The Jewish Book of Why*, 261; Sperling, 258–259.
4. Strassfeld, 163.
5. Frankel and Teutsch, 71.
6. Strassfeld, 169.
7. Roden, 33.
8. Kolatch, *The Jewish Book of Why*, 267.
9. MT Hanukkah 4:12.
10. *ArtScroll Siddur*, 783.
11. Ibid., 783–784.
12. Ibid., 784–785.
13. Lau, 275.
14. Groner.

Dreidel

1. Frankel and Teutsch, 42–43.

Tu B'Shevat

1. Frankel and Teutsch, 182.
2. Strassfeld, 180; Gale and Goodman.

3. Strassfeld, 181; Waskow, *Seasons of Our Joy*, 108; Gale and Goodman.
4. Waskow, *Seasons of Our Joy*, 108.
5. Strassfeld, 181.
6. Waskow, *Seasons of Our Joy*, 108.
7. Frankel and Teutsch, 182.

Purim

1. Strassfeld, 188.
2. www.bnaimoshe.org/littlepurim_2003.htm; accessed November 2003.
3. MT Meg. 2:18.
4. Witty and Witty, 371.
5. Strassfeld, 188.
6. Ibid., 191.
7. Waskow, *Seasons of Our Joy*, 118.
8. Strassfeld, 191.
9. Witty and Witty, 377.
10. Exod. 30:15.
11. Sperling, 265.
12. Frankel and Teutsch, 132.
13. Kolatch, *The Jewish Book of Why*, 277.
14. Pedagogic Center of the Department for Jewish Zionist Education, 2002.
15. Frankel and Teutsch, 49.
16. Strassfeld, 198.

Spring Festivals

Hamantashen

1. Frankel and Teutsch, 69.

Passover

1. Sperling, 198.
2. Torah and haftarah readings:
   - First day: Exodus 12:21–51; Numbers 28:16–25; Joshua 3:5–7, 5:2–6:1, 6:27.
   - Second day: Leviticus 22:26–23:44; Numbers 28:16–25; 2 Kings 23:1–9,21–25.
   - Third to sixth days: varying portions, depending on when a Sabbath intervenes.
   - Seventh day: Exodus 13:17–15:26; Numbers 28:19–25; 2 Samuel 22:1–51.
   - Eighth day: Deuteronomy 14:22–16:17 (Sabbath), 15:19–16:17 (weekday); Numbers 28:19–25; Isaiah 10:32–12:6.
3. Witty and Witty, 315.
4. Greenberg, 400–401.
5. *Etz Hayim*, 1081.
6. Berl Wein, *Jerusalem Post*, March 23, 2001.
7. Ibid.
8. Witty and Witty, 282–283.
9. Ibid., 288–289.
10. Rabbinical Assembly, 15.
11. Strassfeld, 12.
12. Frankel and Teutsch, 69.
13. Author's translation: "Your navel is a round goblet that shall never want for spiced wine; your belly is a heap of wheat fenced in by lilies; your breasts are like two fawns that are twins of a gazelle"
14. Dosick, 173.
15. Kol Dodi, 11.
16. Rabbinical Assembly, 18.
17. Strassfeld, 19–25.
18. Roden, 36.
19. Frankel and Teutsch, 145.
20. Ibid., 66.
21. Greenberg, 432.
22. Strassfeld, 19.
23. Kitov, 2:268–271.
24. Frankel and Teutsch, 59.
25. MT Hametz u-Matzah 8:2.
26. In the Talmud, the third question is, "On all other nights we eat meat roasted, stewed, or boiled; why on this night, roasted only?" The fourth and final question was the one currently recited third.
27. Strassfeld, 22.
28. *ArtScroll Haggadah Treasury*, 43.

29. Rabbinical Assembly , 38.
30. *ArtScroll Haggadah Treasury*, 55.
31. Ibid.
32. Rabbinical Assembly, 39.
33. Riskin, *The Passover Haggadah*, 56.
34. Ibid., 58–59.
35. Ibid., 59–60.
36. Ibid., 60–61
37. Ibid., 61–62.
38. Malbim is the acronym of Meir Loeb ben Yehiel Michael (1809–1879), Eastern European rabbi, preacher, and Bible commentator; ArtScroll Haggadah Treasury, 102–103.
39. Riskin, *The Passover Haggadah*, 90–91.
40. *ArtScroll Haggadah Treasury*, 97.
41. Etz Hayim, 358–377.
42. Riskin, *The Passover Haggadah*, 90.
43. Sperling, 193.
44. Frankel and Teutsch, 103.
45. Gross, 73–74.
46. Frankel and Teutsch, 104; *ArtScroll Haggadah Treasury*, 29.
47. Sperling, 182.
48. *ArtScroll Haggadah Treasury*, 104.
49. Rabbinical Assembly, 30.
50. Riskin, *The Passover Haggadah*, 104.
51. Kitov, 2:280.
52. Twerski, 140.
53. Rabbi Shimon bar Yochai (circa 250 C.E. is the reputed author of the Zohar; Simcha Bunam (1765–1827) was a Polish Hasidic master; Frankel and Teutsch, 102–103.
54. Philo (30 B.C.E.–40 C.E.), was a Jewish Hellenistic philosopher and Bible interpreter.
55. Rabbinical Assembly, 75.
56. Sperling, 187.
57. Rabbinical Assembly, 74.
58. Kitov, 2:281.
59. Frankel and Teutsch, 72.
60. See www.lisaekus.com/food_media_r esources/hadassahjewishholiday-cookbookrecipes.html; accessed October, 2003.
61. Ibid.
62. *ArtScroll Haggadah Treasury*, 124.
63. Rabbinical Assembly, 76.
64. Riskin, *The Passover Haggadah*, 114.
65. Frankel and Teutsch, 3.
66. Gelbard, 370.
67. *ArtScroll Haggadah Treasury*, 138.
68. Donin, *To Be a Jew*, 231.
69. *ArtScroll Haggadah Treasury*, 140.
70. For the attributes of God, see p. 128.
71. The 12 tribes of Israel are Reuben, Shimon, Levi, Judah, Dan, Naphtali, Gad, Asher, Issachar, Zebulun, Joseph, and Benjamin (Gen. 29–30, 35:16–18). However, for purposes of settling the Promised Land, Joseph received a double share that was passed on to his sons, Ephraim and Manasseh (Gen. 48:5–6). Therefore, the post-settlement listing of the 12 tribes includes Ephraim and Manasseh and excludes Joseph and Levi, the tribe that inherited the priesthood rather than any of the tribal lands and was scattered among the people.
72. The orders of the Mishnah are *Zera'im* (seeds), *Mo'ed* (festivals), *Nashim* (women), *Nezikin* (damages), *Kodashim* (holy things), and *Tohorot* (purities).
73. The books of the Torah are B'reishit (Genesis), Shemot (Exodus), Va-yikra (Leviticus), Ba-midbar (Numbers), and Devarim (Deuteronomy).
74. The Matriarchs are Sarah, Rebecca, Rachel, and Leah.
75. The Patriarchs are Abraham, Isaac, and Jacob.

76. Rabbinical Assembly, 128.
77. See www.sephardiconnect.com/pesah/mimouna.htm; accessed October 2003.

Fast of the Firstborn

1. Strassfeld, 16.

Prayer for Dew

1. *ArtScroll Siddur*, 702.

Omer Period

1. Frankel and Teutsch, 123.
2. Kitov, 2:363–366.
3. Frankel and Teutsch, 123.
4. Strassfeld, 53.
5. Ckatam Sofer is a major halakhic work of Moses Sofer (1762–1839), the leading figure of Hungarian ultra-Orthodoxy; see www.torah.org/advanced/haaros/lag.htm; accessed November 2003.
6. Strassfeld, 56.
7. Ibid., 62.
8. Ibid.
9. Waskow, *Seasons of Our Joy*, 177.
10. Kolatch, *The Jewish Book of Why*, 283.

Shavuot

1. Kolatch, *The Jewish Book of Why*, 216.
2. Strassfeld, 74.
3. Ibid.
4. Frankel and Teutsch, 153.
5. Strassfeld, 74.
6. Frankel and Teutsch, 153–154.
7. Lau, 334.
8. Strassfeld, 74.
9. Witty and Witty, 329; Strassfeld, 72.
10. Dosick, 179.
11. Kitov, 3:73.
12. Sperling, 204–205.
13. Ibid., 205.

Akdamut

1. Alternate translation.
2. *ArtScroll Siddur*, 714.
3. Waskow, 193.

Fast Days and Summer Observances

17th of Tammuz

1. Strassfeld, 87.

The Three Weeks

1. Strassfeld, 87.
2. Ibid.
3. Trepp, 206.

Tisha b'Av

1. Steinsaltz, 229–231; Frankel and Teutsch, 177; Strassfeld, 88.
2. Strassfeld, 89.
3. Waskow, *Seasons of Our Joy*, 212.
4. Ibid., 213.

Tu b'Av

1. Frankel and Teutsch, 182.
2. Strassfeld, 89.
3. Ibid., 89–90.
4. Ibid., 90.
5. Waskow, *Seasons of Our Joy*, 213.

Tzom Gedalyah

1. Strassfeld, 103.

10th of Tevet

1. Strassfeld, 85, 170.

Synagogue and Prayer

Synagogue

Overview

1. Trepp, 15.
2. Hammer, *Entering Jewish Prayer*, 62.
3. Millgram, *Jewish Worship*, 64.
4. Hammer, *Entering Jewish Prayer*, 63–65.
5. Millgram, *Jewish Worship*, 63.
6. Hammer, *Entering Jewish Prayer*, 65–70.
7. Millgram, *Jewish Worship*, 64–67.
8. Spiegel, 865.
9. Ibid., 66.
10. Donin, *To Pray As a Jew*, 12–14.
11. Hammer, *Entering Jewish Prayer*, 72–74.
12. Millgram, *Jewish Worship*, 552–553.

Synagogue Architecture

1. Frankel and Teutsch, 167.
2. Millgram, *Jewish Worship*, 551.
3. Steinsaltz, *A Guide to Jewish Prayer*, 197.
4. Millgram, *Jewish Worship*, 336.
5. Steinsaltz, *A Guide to Jewish Prayer*, 197.
6. Trepp, 16.
7. Sperling, 83.
8. Frankel and Teutsch, 45.
9. Steinsaltz, *A Guide to Jewish Prayer*, 299–300.
10. Frankel and Teutsch, 167–168.
11. Steinsaltz, *A Guide to Jewish Prayer*, 300.
12. Frankel and Teutsch, 167.
13. Millgram, *Jewish Worship*, 340.

Torah Scrolls and Ornaments

1. Cohen, 170.
2. *Etz Hayim*, 1484.
3. See www.jewishworldreview.com/cols/goldberg020598.html; accessed November 2003.
4. Kolatch, *This Is the Torah*, 91.
5. Ibid., 87.
6. *Etz Hayim*, 1485.
7. Kolatch, *This Is the Torah*, 97.
8. MT Sefer Torah 7:9.
9. Kolatch, *This Is the Torah*, 98–99.
10. Ibid., 98.
11. Ibid., 106–109.
12. Sperling, 82.
13. Cohen, 172.
14. Author's translation: "A time to be born." The form of the Hebrew verb is technically an infinitive ("to be"), not the basis of a gerund ("for being").
15. Kolatch, *This Is the Torah*, 111–114.
16. Author's translation: "Therefore, write down this song." The Hebrew word "shir" is generally translated as "song" rather than "poem," as in the biblical book, "Shir ha-Shirim" (Song of Songs).
17. Alternate translation.
18. Cohen, 173–176.
19. Kolatch, *This Is the Torah*, 57–58.
20. Alternate translation.
21. Millgram, *Jewish Worship*, 339.
22. Cohen, 176.
23. Frankel and Teutsch, 179–180.
24. Steinsaltz, *A Guide to Jewish Prayer*, 276.
25. Frankel and Teutsch, 178.

Ark

1. Frankel and Teutsch, 12.
2. Ibid., 12–13.
3. Millgram, *Jewish Worship*, 338.
4. Frankel and Teutsch, 13.
5. Ibid.
6. Kolatch, *This Is the Torah*, 68–70.
7. Frankel and Teutsch, 13.
8. Ibid., 13.

Bimah

1. Steinsaltz, *A Guide to Jewish Prayer*, 293.
2. Frankel and Teutsch, 20.
3. MT Tefillah 11:3.
4. EJ at "Ark."
5. Alternate translation.
6. Frankel and Teutsch, 20.
7. Ibid.
8. Kolatch, *This Is the Torah*, 82–83.

Mechitzah

1. Millgram, *Jewish Worship*, 339–340.
2. Steinsaltz, *A Guide to Jewish Prayer*, 290.
3. Dosick, 215.
4. Millgram, *Jewish Worship*, 340.
5. Ibid., 339,

Rabbi

1. Cohen, 212–214
2. This section was adapted with permission from Millgram, *Jewish Worship*, 116–119, 530–541.

Hazzan

1. Millgram, *Jewish Worship*, 518.
2. Cohen, 240–241.
3. Millgram, *Jewish Worship*, 519.
4. Steinsaltz, *A Guide to Jewish Prayer,* 322–323.
5. Millgram, *Jewish Worship*, 520.
6. Ibid., 521.
7. Ibid., 526.
8. Cohen, 248–249.
9. Ibid., 251–253.

Prayer

Overview

1. Hammer, *Entering Jewish Prayer*, 8.
2. Alternate translation.
3. Cohen, 139–141.
4. Heschel, *Man's Quest for God*, 13.
5. Originally, the Hebrew word "*mincha*" referred to the cereal part of the sacrifice offered twice daily in the Temple. Later it became associated only with the afternoon offering, either because of usage of the term in the story of the conflict between Elijah and the priests of Baal (2 Kings 18) or from an alternative meaning of the Hebrew root (to rest), which refers to the fact that the day is fading and figuratively coming to rest at that time. (Garfiel, 117–118)
6. Alternate translation.
7. Garfiel, 25.
8. Millgram, *Jewish Worship*, 26–27.
9. Ibid., 28.
10. MT Tefillah 4:16.
11. Martin, 20–21.
12. Millgram, *Jewish Worship*, 17–18.

Major Themes of Prayer

1. Hammer, *Entering Jewish Prayer*, 20–26.
2. Author's translation: "Holy, holy, holy! The Lord of Hosts! The whole earth is filled with His glory." In the Hebrew, the subject of the last sentence is traditionally "the earth." The Hebrew "k'vodo" is translated as "His glory" in traditional prayer books.
3. Author's translation: "Praised is the glory of God from His place." The Hebrew "mim'komo" literally means "from His place" in the translation used in traditional prayer books.

Language of Prayer

1. This section was adapted with permission from Millgram, *Jewish Worship*, 32–34.

Proper Form of Prayer

1. Millgram, *Jewish Worship*, 31.
2. Cited in Braude, *The Midrash on Psalms 2:19.*
3. Millgram, *Jewish Worship*, 24–25.
4. Ibid., 28–29; Hammer, *Entering Jewish Prayer*, 27–28.
5. MT Tefillah 5:5.
6. Ibid., 5:15.
7. E. Klein, 104–105.
8. Lutske, 261.
9. E. Klein, 95–98.
10. Millgram, *Jewish Worship*, 359.
11. Lutske, 259–260.
12. Author's translation: "Call out to the Lord with thanks, with the kinor sing [praises] to our God." The Hebrew word "todah" literally means "thanks"; the word "zamru" is usually translated as "sing," as in the zemirot (songs for the Sabbath table). It is difficult to ascertain the proper translation for the Hebrew word "kinor."
13. Generally translated as "shofar, harp, lyre, tambourine, stringed instruments, pipe, sounding cymbals, loud clashing cymbals."
14. Trepp, 23.

15. Donin, *To Pray As a Jew*, 20–21.
16. Hammer, *Entering Jewish Prayer*, 18–19.
17. Donin, *To Pray As a Jew*, 22.
18. Hammer, *Entering Jewish Prayer*, 19.
19. Ibid., 17.

Answer to Prayer

1. Millgram, *Jewish Worship*, 19.
2. Martin, 17.
3. Millgram, *Jewish Worship*, 20.
4. E. Klein, 7–8.
5. Ibid.
6. Millgram, *Jewish Worship*, 23.
7. Author's translation: "Behold, God is my salvation; I will trust and not be afraid; for God the Lord is my strength and song, and He has been my salvation."

Congregational Prayer

1. The Hebrew word "*tzibbur*" is an acronym for "*tzadikim, beinonim,* and *risha'im*" (righteous, average, and wicked), indicating that all three components have a place in the congregation of Israel.
2. Donin, *To Pray As a Jew*, 14–16.

Prayer as Polemic

1. Cohen, 46–48.
2. Ibid.
3. Ibid.

Siddur

1. This article was adapted with permission from Millgram, *Jewish Worship*.
2. Cohen, 239.
3. Ibid., 44–45.
4. Hammer, *Entering Jewish Prayer*, 97–98; Millgram, *Jewish Worship*, 383–384.
5. Ginzberg, *Saadia's Siddur*, 327.
6. Millgram, *Jewish Worship*, 385–388.
7. Ibid., 388–389.
8. Millgram, *Jewish Worship*, 389–390.
9. Ibid.

Minyan

1. *ArtScroll Siddur*, 990.
2. Millgram, *Jewish Worship*, 342–343.
3. Kolatch,*This Is the Torah*, 66–67.
4. Millgram, *Jewish Worship*, 342–343.
5. Steinsaltz, *A Guide to Jewish Prayer*, 312.
6. Millgram, *Jewish Worship*, 343.
7. Bloch, 77.
8. Note that when David had earlier counted his soldiers, which was necessary for making war and not a "frivolous" exercise, he was not punished (2 Sam. 18:1).

Kippah

1. Frankel and Teutsch, 91.
2. Donin, *To Be a Jew*, 180.
3. E. Klein, 107.
4. Sperling, 20.
5. Kolatch, *The Second Jewish Book of Why*, 52.
6. Witty and Witty, 82–83.
7. Frankel and Teutsch, 91.

Tallit

1. Sperling, 22.
2. Frankel and Teutsch, 169.
3. E. Klein, 110.
4. Ibid.
5. Ibid.
6. Ibid., 110–111.
7. Maimonides, *The Commandments*, 21.
8. Sperling, 20–21.
9. Maimonides, *The Commandments*, 22.
10. Author's translation: "May the angel who redeemed me from all harm, bless the youngsters."
11. MT Tzitzit 3:9.
12. Frankel and Teutsch, 170; Kolatch, *The Jewish Book of Why*, 105.

13. Kolatch, *The Jewish Book of Why*, 105.
14. *Etz Hayim*, 1469.
15. Sperling, 21.

Tefillin

1. Umberto Cassuto (1883–1951), Italian Bible scholar.
2. This area, known as the "third eye," is important in traditional medicine and spiritual philosophy.
3. Yehezkel Kaufmann (1889–1963), Ukrainian-born scholar and professor of Bible at Hebrew University, Jerusalem.
4. Garfiel, 70–71.
5. Sperling, 130.
6. E. Klein, 112.
7. Lutske, 119.
8. Michael, Gabriel, Raphael, Uriel, Tzadkiel, Yufiel, Raziel.
9. Sperling, 27–28.
10. Lutske, 121.
11. Frankel and Teutsch, 171.
12. *ArtScroll Siddur*, 6.
13. MT Tefillin 4:25.
14. Maimonides, *The Commandments*, 19.
15. Lau, 46.
16. Trachtenberg, 145–146. The root of the word means "defend" or "guard," as in "prophylactic," which connotes protection from disease.

Blessings and Benedictions

1. MT B'rakhot 1:4.
2. For example, giving charity; honoring or fearing one's father and mother; loaning money to the poor; judging a case in a court of law; returning a lost article; and rejoicing with the widow, orphan, or stranger.
3. Sperling, 110.
4. Millgram, *Jewish Worship*, 91.
5. Cohen, 45.
6. Rabbi Eliezer of Worms (1160–1237), a medieval German scholar.
7. Sperling, 31.
8. Riskin, *International Jewish Post*, March 30, 2001.
9. Cohen, 44–45.
10. Hammer, *Entering Jewish Prayer*, 92.
11. Millgram, *Jewish Worship*, 91.
12. *ArtScroll Siddur*, 224–231; Lau, 97–104.
13. Insert the appropriate word: "*li*" (me), "*le-avi*" (my father), "*le-imi*" (my mother), "*la-avotai*" (my ancestors), "*le-rabi*" (my teacher), or "*la-avoteinu*" (our ancestors).
14. Millgram, *Jewish Worship*, 91–92.
15. Donin, *To Pray As a Jew*, 65–66.
16. Ibid., 66.
17. Ibid., 67.

Amen

1. Donin, *To Pray As a Jew*, 227.
2. MT B'rakhot 1:13.
3. Donin, *To Pray As a Jew*, 227.
4. Ibid., 228.
5. E. Klein, 128.
6. Donin, *To Pray As a Jew*, 230.

Kaddish

1. Millgram, *Jewish Worship*, 153–154.
2. Ibid., 155.
3. Ibid., 155–156.
4. Ibid., 156.
5. Donin, *To Pray As a Jew*, 217-218.
6. Millgram, *Jewish Worship*, 483.
7. Alternate translation.
8. *ArtScroll Kaddish*, 32.
9. Ibid., 40.
10. Donin, *To Pray As a Jew*, 226.

Daily and Sabbath Prayers

Daily Order of Prayers

1. Steinsaltz, *A Guide to Jewish Prayer*, 84–89; Hammer, *Entering Jewish Prayer*, 102–103.
2. Ibid.

Morning Blessings

1. Millgram, *Jewish Worship*, 144.
2. Author's translation: "How goodly are your tents, O Jacob, your dwelling places, O Israel." The Hebrew "tovu" comes from "tov," which generally means "good. The word "places" is generally added in English translations to enhance the meter of the verse.
3. Donin, To Pray As a Jew, 185.
4. Witty and Witty, 87.
5. Donin, *To Pray As a Jew*, 186; *ArtScroll Siddur*, 14.
6. Millgram, *Jewish Worship*, 147.
7. Ibid., 148.
8. Donin, *To Pray As a Jew*, 187.
9. *ArtScroll Siddur*, 22.
10. Millgram, *Jewish Worship*, 149.
11. Ibid., 190; Sperling, 36–37.
12. *ArtScroll Siddur*, 49.
13. E. Klein, 44.
14. Ibid., 191–193.
15. Ibid., 194.
16. Hammer, *Entering Jewish Prayer*, 109.
17. Donin, *To Pray As a Jew*, 194–195.
18. *ArtScroll Siddur*, 19.
19. Donin, *To Pray As a Jew*, 196.

Mah Tovu

1. Riskin, "From Curse to Blessing," *International Jerusalem Post*, July 6, 2001, 39.

Pesukei de-Zimra

1. Hammer, *Entering Jewish Prayer*, 111–112.
2. Psalms 19, 34, 90, 91, 135, 136, 33, 92, 93.
3. Hammer, *Entering Jewish Prayer*, 113.
4. *ArtScroll Siddur*, 67.
5. Sperling, 39.
6. *ArtScroll Siddur*, 67.
7. Ibid., 78–79.
8. Donin, *To Pray As a Jew*, 173–174.
9. Ibid., 174.
10. Millgram, *Jewish Worship*, 166.
11. Ibid., 611.
12. *ArtScroll Siddur*, 82.

Barchu

1. Donin, *To Pray As a Jew*, 165.
2. *ArtScroll Siddur*, 84.
3. Ibid.
4. Gelbard, 74-75.

Ahavah Rabbah and Ahavat Olam

1. Hammer, *Entering Jewish Prayer*, 144.

Shema

1. Alternate translation.
2. Millgram, *Jewish Worship*, 73.
3. *ArtScroll Siddur*, 91.
4. *Etz Hayim*, 1024.
5. *ArtScroll Siddur*, 91; Sperling, 42.
6. Donin, *To Pray As a Jew*, 150.
7. *ArtScroll Siddur*, 92.
8. *Etz Hayim*, 1025.
9. E. Klein, 64.
10. Donin, *To Pray As a Jew*, 149.
11. Ibid., 148.
12. Hammer, *Entering Jewish Prayer*, 122, 131–132.
13. *ArtScroll Siddur*, 90.
14. Millgram, *Jewish Worship*, 444–446.
15. *ArtScroll Siddur*, 28.
16. Some cover their eyes with the edges of their fingers when reading the first verse of the *Shema* and then kiss the fingers when finished. The index, middle, and ring fingers are flexed to form the letter "*shin*"; the thumb is bent to form the letter "*dalet*"; and the fifth finger is bent to form the letter "*yud*," thus producing the word "*Shaddai*," a name of God (Gelbard, 45).
17. MT Keri'at Shema 2:2.
18. Donin, *To Pray As a Jew*, 147–148.
19. Gelbard, 46.
20. Ibid., 341.

21. Hammer, *Entering Jewish Prayer*, 135.
22. Alternate translation.
23. Hammer, *Enering Jewish Prayer*, 135–138.
24. Donin, *To Pray As a Jew*, 159.
25. Millgram, *Jewish Worship*, 100–101.
26. Donin, *To Pray As a Jew*, 163–164.
27. Ibid., 164–165; *ArtScroll Siddur*, 264–265.

Amidah

1. Donin, *To Pray As a Jew*, 71.
2. Cohen, 11.
3. Gelbard, 18.
4. Millgram, *Jewish Worship*, 104.
5. Cohen, 30.
6. Millgram, *Jewish Worship*, 107.
7. Ibid., 105–106.
8. Cohen, 40.
9. *ArtScroll Siddur*, 107.
10. Author's translation: "For the name of the Lord will I proclaim: ascribe greatness to our God." The Hebrew word "godel" derives from a root meaning "big" or "great."
11. According to tradition (*Shibalei ha-Leket*), the 18 blessings were the declarations of the angels on the following occasions (Sperling, 44–47):
    1. Shield of Abraham, when the patriarch was saved from the furnace of Kasdim.
    2. Resuscitates the dead, when God sent dew to revive Isaac, who was terrified that he was about to be sacrificed.
    3. The Holy God, when Jacob arrived at the gates of heaven and declared the divine holiness.
    4. Gracious giver of wisdom, for Gabriel teaching Joseph the 70 languages that he needed as the viceroy of Egypt.
    5. Desires repentance, when God accepted the penitence of Reuben for his sin against Jacob, his father, and rescinded the death sentence imposed by Heaven.
    6. Pardons abundantly, when God forgave Judah after he admitted the sin he had committed against Tamar.
    7. Redeemer of Israel, when God freed the Israelites from bondage in Egypt.
    8. Heals the sick, when God came to soothe the pain of Abraham after his circumcision.
    9. Blesses the years, when Isaac reaped an abundant harvest in the land of the Philistines.
    10. Gathers the dispersed of Israel, when Jacob was reunited with his sons Joseph and Shimon [who had been held hostage] in Egypt.
    11. Loves righteousness and judgment, when God gave the laws of the Torah to Moses.
    12. Breaks enemies and humbles the presumptuous, when the Egyptians drowned in the Sea of Reeds.
    13. Supports and stays the righteous, when Joseph closed the eyes of Jacob when his father died.
    14. Builder of Jerusalem, when Solomon erected the First Temple.
    15. Causes salvation to flourish, when the Israelites passed through the Sea of Reeds joyously singing hymns of praise to God.
    16. Hears prayer, when God answered the prayers of the Israelites suffering in abject slavery in Egypt.

17. Restores His Presence to Zion, when God came down from Heaven to the Tabernacle.
18. To whom it is fitting to give thanks, when Solomon dedicated the First Temple.
19. Blesses Israel with peace, when the Israelites entered the Holy Land.

12. Donin, *To Pray As a Jew*, 76–81.
13. E. Klein, 75.
14. *ArtScroll Shemoneh Esrei*, 251.
15. Donin, *To Pray As a Jew*, 104–105.
16. From Maimonides; see E. Klein, 87–88.
17. *ArtScroll Kaddish*, 46.
18. *ArtScroll Siddur*, 99.
19. Lau, 63.
20. Gelbard, 10.
21. Millgram, *Jewish Worship*, 358–359.
22. Lau, 63–64.
23. Hammer, *Entering Jewish Prayer*, 87.
24. Ibid., 192–194.
25. Ibid., 194–196.
26. Ibid., 196.
27. Millgram, *Jewish Worship*, 134.
28. 28. Author's translation: "Holy, holy, holy! The Lord of Hosts! The whole earth is filled with His glory." In the Hebrew, the subject of the last sentence is literally "the earth" and the verb for "filled" is passive. The Hebrew "k'vodo" is translated as "His glory" in traditional prayer books.
29. Ibid., 135.
30. *ArtScroll Siddur*, 100.
31. According to tradition, the evil king who promulgated the decree was miraculously killed by a snake that reached the royal bedchamber (Sperling, 145).
32. Donin, *To Pray As a Jew*, 124.
33. Millgram, *Jewish Worship*, 136.
34. Ibid., 445.
35. Donin, *To Pray As a Jew*, 159–160.
36. Millgram, *Jewish Worship*, 209–210; Donin, *To Pray As a Jew*, 131–132.
37. *ArtScroll Siddur*, 112.
38. Donin, *To Pray As a Jew*, 102.
39. Millgram, *Jewish Worship*, 138.
40. Hertz, 594.
41. Ibid.
42. Donin, *To Pray As a Jew*, 136.
43. Ibid., 135.
44. Millgram, *Jewish Worship*, 608.
45. Ibid., 139.
46. *ArtScroll Siddur*, 117.
47. Hammer, *Entering Jewish Prayer*, 186.
48. E. Klein, 86.

Tachanum

1. Donin, *To Pray As a Jew*, 202–203.
2. Millgram, *Jewish Worship*, 462.
3. *ArtScroll Siddur*, 132.
4. Author's translation: "fell on his face on the ground in front of the ark of the Lord." The Hebrew word "vayipal" comes from the root "nafal," which literally means "fall," a dramatic act rather than "lying on the ground."
5. Ibid., 132–133.
6. Ibid., 136.
7. Millgram, *Jewish Worship*, 462.
8. *ArtScroll Siddur*, 124.
9. These are days of rejoicing, for during this period Solomon dedicated the Temple in Jerusalem. Some do not recite *Tachanun* from Yom Kippur until the Second of Heshvan, because the month of Tishrei contains a substantial proportion of the joyous Jewish holidays (Sperling, 245–246).
10. During the years of wandering in the wilderness, Nisan was considered a month of festivity and holiness. For 12 days, the chiefs of the 12 tribes offered special sacrifices (one each day). This was followed

by the Passover festival (Sperling, 177).

11. I. Klein, 26–27; Donin, *To Pray As a Jew*, 207–210.

Torah Service

1. Donin, *To Pray As a Jew,* 231.
2. *Stone Chumash*, 1095.
3. Cohen, 190.
4. Kolatch, *This Is the Torah*, 352.
5. Donin, *To Pray As a Jew*, 233.
6. Cohen, 179–180.
7. The combined *parshiyot*, in which both portions share one or more mutual themes, are Vayakhel–Pekudei (Exod. 35–40), Tazria–Metsora (Lev. 12–15), Aharei Mot–Kedoshim (Lev. 16–20), Be-har–Behukkotai (Lev. 25–27), Hukkat–Balak (Num. 19–25), Mattot–Mase'ei (Num. 30–36), Nitsavim–Va-yelekh (Deut. 29:9–31:30) (Cohen, 180).
8. Alternate translation.
9. Gelbard, 120.
10. The right side is even given precedence in dressing. The right shoe is put on before the left; though if there are laces to be tied, the knot is first made on the left (since the knot of the tefillin is fastened on the left hand). When removing shoes, however, the left is always taken off first, lest the right foot be slighted if the left foot was still covered (Levush 2:4). In the ritual of *halitzah* (see p. 53), the right shoe is used (Yev. 104a) (Sperling, 16–17).
11. Kolatch, *This Is the Torah*, 74.
12. Ibid., 54, 71, 73.
13. Ibid., 239.
14. Steinsaltz, *A Guide to Jewish Prayer,* 153.
15. Readings from three Torah scrolls also occur when Rosh Hodesh Adar falls on a Sabbath that is also Shabbat Shekalim, and when Rosh Hodesh Nisan falls on a Sabbath, that is also Shabbat ha-Hodesh.
16. MT Tefillah 12:23; Cohen, 192.
17. Donin, *To Pray As a Jew*, 49.
18. Sperling, 81.
19. *Etz Hayim*, 1481.
20. Cohen, 186–187.
21. Donin, *To Pray As a Jew*, 50.
22. Ibid., 53–54.
23. Kolatch, *This Is the Torah*, 155–157.
24. Ibid., 167–168.
25. Israel Meir ha-Kohen, *Hafetz Hayim.*
26. *Biur Halakha* on S.A. OH 136, cited in Donin, *To Pray As a Jew*, 349, 350.
27. Ibid.
28. Kolatch, *This Is the Torah*, 186.
29. Millgram, *Jewish Worship*, 110.
30. Kolatch, *This Is the Torah*, 187.
31. Millgram, *Jewish Worship*, 109.
32. Donin, *To Pray As a Jew,* 240.
33. Millgram, *Jewish Worship*, 110.
34. Kolatch, *This Is the Torah*, 188–189.
35. Millgram, *Jewish Worship*, 183–184.
36. Kolatch, *This Is the Torah*, 136.
37. Ibid., 118, 134, 142.
38. *Etz Hayim*, 1484.
39. Kolatch, *This Is the Torah*, 137.
40. Biale, 26.
41. Kolatch, *This Is the Torah*, 46, 135.
42. Ibid., 131–132.
43. Millgram, *Jewish Worship*, 113–114.
44. Cohen, 190.
45. Sperling, 136.
46. Author's translation: *Mi She Berakh.*
47. Donin, *To Pray As a Jew*, 248.
48. Cohen, 199.
49. Donin, *To Pray As a Jew*, 240–241.
50. Cohen, 196–197.
51. Kolatch, *This Is the Torah*, 192.
52. Author's translation.
53. Donin, *To Pray As a Jew*, 254–255.
54. Kolatch, *This Is the Torah*, 148.

Chapter and Verses

1. Cohen, 181–182.

Haftarah

1. Donin, *To Pray As a Jew*, 242.
2. Kolatch, *This Is the Torah*, 199.
3. Ibid., 200, 368.
4. Millgram, *Jewish Worship*, 115.
5. *Etz Hayim*, 1486–1490.
6. Ibid., 208.
7. Donin, *To Pray As a Jew*, 242–243; Sperling, 139.
8. Donin, *To Pray As a Jew*, 243–245.
9. Ibid., 246–247.
10. Millgram, *Jewish Worship*, 186.

Av ha-Rachamim

1. *ArtScroll Siddur*, 456.

Yekum Purkan; Mi She Berakh

1. Millgram, *Jewish Worship*, 187.
2. Ibid., 188.
3. *ArtScroll Siddur*, 451.
4. Ibid.
5. Millgram, *Jewish Worship*, 188.
6. Author's translation: " … and save the son of Your maidservant." The Hebrew "hoshiyah," which is also used in the hoshanot on Sukkot, is often translated as "save." Kolatch, *This Is the Torah*, 160.

Prayer for the Government

1. Millgram, *Jewish Worship*, 189–190.
2. Donin, *To Pray As a Jew*, 253.
3. Millgram, *Jewish Worship*, 190.
4. Donin, *To Pray As a Jew*, 253–254.

U-va le-Tziyyon Go'el

1. *ArtScroll Siddur*, 154.
2. Millgram, *Jewish Worship*, 152–153.
3. Donin, *To Pray As a Jew*, 211–212.
4. Millgram, *Jewish Worship*, 609.

Ein Keloheinu

1. Witty and Witty, 181.
2. Donin, *To Pray As a Jew*, 214.
3. Ibid., 214–215.

Aleinu

1. Millgram, *Jewish Worship*, 455–456.
2. EJ at "Aleinu."
3. Millgram, *Jewish Worship*, 455.

Prayers Recited before Leaving the Synagogue

1. Author's translation: "Do not fear sudden terror, or the destruction of the wicked when it comes." The first part of the verse is a command in the Hebrew. The second half, which is in the indicative, reflects the presence of the word "ki," which in context means "when."
2. Author's translation: "Even in your old age." The Hebrew "ziknah" literally means old. For example, in the prayer Shema Koleinu (Hear our voices), we pray that God not cast us away "be-eit ziknah" (in our old age).
3. Sperling, 74–75; *ArtScroll Siddur*, 161–162.

Psalm of the Day

1. Sperling, 162.
2. Author's translation: "The earth and its fullness is the Lord's." The Hebrew "u-me-lo'o" comes from "malei," which means "full."
3. Author's translation: "Great is the Lord and highly to be praised." The Hebrew "u-me-hullal" is related to the Hallel (see page 162), which literally means "praise."
4. Author's translation: "God of vengeance." This is the more familiar translation of the Hebrew.
5. Author's translation: "The Lord reigns and is clothed in majesty [at the completion of Creation]." The Hebrew "malach" is usually regarded as a verb form.
6. *ArtScroll Siddur* 162-169.
7. Ibid., 162–169.
8. Donin, *To Pray As a Jew*, 260.

9. *ArtScroll Siddur*, 320.
10. Donin, *To Pray As a Jew*, 214.

Yigdal

1. Cohen, 46–47.
2. Idelsohn, 74.

Adon Olam

1. *ArtScroll Siddur*, 12.
2. Ibid., 295
3. Ibid., 12.

An'im Zemirot

1. Millgram, *Jewish Worship*, 484.

Bedtime Prayers

1. Ibid., 291.
2. *ArtScroll Siddur*, 289.
3. Millgram, *Jewish Worship*, 292.

Blessings before Eating

1. This section was adapted with permission from Donin, *To Pray As a Jew*, 305–309; I. Klein, 42–43; Lau, 86–91.
2. Author's translation: "... and the fat of the land." In context, Isaac is referring to the Land of Israel rather than to the entire earth. Lau, 86.

Grace after Meals

1. Sperling, 96.
2. *ArtScroll Siddur*, 182.
3. This practice is inferred from the verse, "Magnify the Lord with me and let us exalt in His Name together" (Ps. 34:4), which is recited after taking the Torah scroll out of the ark. Because the word "magnify" (*gadlu*) is an imperative in the second person plural, it cannot be used when there is only one other person beside the individual leading the *Birkat ha-Mazon*. Therefore, the *zimmun* cannot be recited unless there are at least three who have eaten at the table (Sperling, 91).

4. Millgram, *Jewish Worship*, 295.
5. Ibid., 295.

Shir ha-Ma'alot

1. Milgram, *Jewish Worship*, 196.
2. Ibid., 197.

Shehecheyanu

1. Cohen, 134.

Tefillat ha-Derech

1. Millgram, *Jewish Worship*, 471.
2. Witty and Witty, 489.

Thanksgiving Blessing

1. Donin, *To Pray As a Jew*, 249.
2. *ArtScroll Siddur*, 143.

Jewish Literature

Bible

1. Aughor's translation: Ketuvim. Ther e is no "th" sound in the Heberw language.

Ten Commandments

1. Alternate translation.
2. Frankel and Teutsch, 174.
3. Kolatch, *The Jewish Book of Why*, 125.
4. Frankel and Teutsch, 174–175.
5. Allusions to the Ten Commandments in the *Shema* (E. Klein, 65–66).

Masoretic Text

1. Kolatch, *This Is the Torah*, 213.
2. A Torah scroll is written without vowels or punctuation so that scholars can discover the endless array of profound ideas and teachings that are hidden in each verse (Sperling, 81). According to Natronai Gaon, the vowel signs limit the interpretations; each word of the Torah has "70 faces" (various ways of being interpreted) and also can be understood in ways different from the traditional vowel signs (Kitov, 3:176).

3. Kolatch, *This Is the Torah*, 214–221.
4. Genesis: 19:8,25,33; Exodus: 8:20, 11:6, 14:13, 25:39, 26:31; Leviticus: 27:9; Numbers: 4:49, 9:6, 13:22, 32:25, 33:8, 35:5; Deuteronomy: 3:20, 4:23,42, 17:19, 19:11.
5. Larger letters appear at Genesis: 1:1, 34:31, 50:23; Exodus: 11:18, 34:7, 34:14; Leviticus: 11:42, 13:33; Numbers: 13:30, 14:17, 27:5; Deuteronomy: 6:4, 18:13, 29:27, 32:6. Smaller letters appear at Genesis: 2:4, 23:2, 27:46; Exodus: 32:25; Leviticus: 1:1, 6:2; Numbers: 25:11; Deuteronomy: 9:24, 32:18. Dots appear at Genesis: 16:5, 18:9, 19:33, 33:4, 37:12; Numbers: 3:39, 9:10, 21:30, 29:15; Deuteronomy: 29:28; 2 Samuel: 19:20; Isaiah: 44:9; Ezekiel: 41:20, 46:22; Psalms: 27:13.
6. Genesis: 1,534 verses, 50 chapters, 12 portions; Exodus: 1,209 verses, 40 chapters, 11 portions; Leviticus: 859 verses, 27 chapters, 10 portions; Numbers: 1,288 verses, 36 chapters, 10 portions; Deuteronomy: 955 verses, 34 chapters, 11 portions. See Kolatch, *This Is the Torah*, 247–267.

Biblical Commentary

1. Holtz, 222.
2. Ibid., 228.
3. Ibid., 257.
4. Robinson, 305.
5. Ibid., 306.

Rabbinic Literature

1. Holtz., 129–131.
2. Ibid., 138–139.

Mishnah

1. Gross, 174–178.
2. *Zera'im* (Seeds), *Mo'ed* (Festivals), *Nashim* (Women), *Nezikin* (Damages), *Kodashim* (Holy Things), *Tohorot* (Purities).
3. Alternate translation.
4. Holtz, 132.

Baraita and Tosefta

1. Jewish Theological Seminary, "Introduction to the Talmud." www.JTS.com; accessed November 2003.

Talmud

1. Ibid.
2. A Moroccan scholar (1013–1103) who compiled the most important code prior to the *Mishneh Torah* of Maimonides.
3. Holtz, 139–143.
4. Ibid., 160.
5. *Etz Hayim*, 1475.
6. Holtz, 162.

Midrash

1. Holtz, 178–181.
2. Ibid., 181–184.
3. *Etz Hayim*, 1493.
4. Holtz, 186–189, 198.
5. Ibid., 201–204.

Thirteen Principles of Faith

1. Millgram, *Jewish Worship*, 421.
2. Ibid.
3. *ArtScroll Siddur*, 178–181.
4. Millgram, *Jewish Worship*, 422.

Mitzvot

Rabbinic Commandments

1. Maimonides, *The Commandments* (Positive), 266.

Reasons for Observance of the Mitzvot

1. Much of this section was adapted with permission from lectures by Byron Sherwin, Spertus Institute of Jewish Studies (Chicago).
2. An American rabbi, scholar, and theologian (1907–1972).
3. Alternate translation.

Performance of the Mitzvot

1. This article was adapted with permission from Chavel, 281–288.
2. Maimonides, *The Commandments* (Positive), 282–283.
3. Ibid., 285–286.
4. Alternate translation.
5. Maimonides, *The Commandments* (Positive), 285.
6. Ibid., 283–285.
7. Ibid., 287.
8. Ibid., 288.

Obligation of Women to Perform the Commandments

1. This article was adapted with permission from Biale, 10–43.
2. Kaufman, 211.
3. MT Talmud Torah 1:13.
4. A leading 12th-century French talmudic scholar.

Proper Behavior and Ethical Living

Gemilut Hasadim

1. The chancellor of The Jewish Theological Seminary, New York.
2. See www.tiwestport.org/torah/5763/simchattorah.html; accessed December 2003.

Tzedakah

1. Lecture by Byron Sherwin, Spertus Institute (Chicago).
2. Alternate translation.
3. *Matanot Aniyim* 10:18.
4. Ibid.
5. Ibid., 10:7–12.
6. Ibid., 9:1–3.
7. Ibid.

Hospitality

1. Telushkin, 534.
2. *ArtScroll Siddur*, 193.
3. Telushkin, 536.

Visiting the Sick

1. See www.ou.org/torah/tt/5762/vayera62; accessed on January 2003.
2. Rosen, 213.
3. Abrahams, 40.
4. Ben Samuel He-Hasid, 367.
5. Alternate translation.
6. This section is adapted with permission from lectures by Byron Sherwin, Spertus Institute (Chicago).
7. Author's translation.
8. This section is adapted with permission from lectures by Byron Sherwin, Spertus Institute (Chicago).
9. Author's translation. "Heal me, O Lord, and I shall be healed." This emphasizes the firm conviction of the speaker that he will be healed, rather than merely repeating the request for healing.
10. Preuss, 22–26.
11. Alternate translation.
12. Alternate translation.
13. Alternate translation.
14. A 12th-century Spanish physician and Hebrew writer.
15. *ArtScroll Shemoneh Esrei*, 133.
16. A 12th-century physician and translator from Arabic to Hebrew.

Lashon ha-Ra

1. Project Genesis.
2. Ibid.
3. A contemporary rabbi and physician who has authored many books and articles on Torah topics, psychology, and psychiatry.
4. Twerski, 70–71.

Washing the Hands

1. Alternate translation.
2. Lau, 24.
3. Lutske, 279–280.

Mikveh

1. Dosick, 269.
2. Ibid., 270.
3. Ibid.
4. I. Klein, 518–521.
5. Robinson, 246.
6. Dosick, 270.
7. Biale, 164–165.
8. Telushkin, 619.

Niddah

1. Biale, 147.
2. Ibid., 152.
3. Ibid., 153.
4. Ibid., 160.
5. Ibid., 162.
6. Ibid., 161–162.
7. Ibid., 169.
8. Ibid., 157–158.
9. Telushkin, 617.
10. Dosick, 272.
11. A second-century *tanna* and leader of the post-Bar Kokhba generation in the Land of Israel.

Impurity after Childbirth

1. *Etz Hayim*, 650.

Sha'atnez

1. Kolatch, *The Second Jewish Book of Why*, 286.
2. See www.faqs.org/faqs/judaism/FAQ/05-Worship/section-41.html; accessed on June 2003.
3. Maimonides, *The Commandments* (Negative), 40.
4. A late 13th-century or early 14th-century Italian kabbalist and halakhic authority.
5. Chill, 236–237.
6. Hertz, 844.

Jewish Courts and Judges

1. MT Sanh. 2:1–7.
2. Ibid.
3. Ibid.
4. Chill, 97.
5. Maimonides, *The Commandments* (Negative), 260.
6. Chill, 96.
7. *Etz Hayim*, 1101.
8. *Stone Chumash*, 1036.
9. Ibid.
10. Maimonides, *The Commandments* (Negative), 262.
11. *Stone Chumash*, 433.
12. Maimonides, *The Commandments* (Negative), 265.
13. Chill, 103.

Business Ethics

1. Chill, 252.
2. Maimonides, *The Commandments* (Negative), 257.
3. Jacobs, 63–64.
4. A 20th-century British rabbi and theologian.
5. Ibid., 64–65.

Prohibition against Lending at Interest

1. Alternate translation.
2. Maimonides, *The Commandments* (Negative), 213.
3. Hertz, 849.
4. Chill, 87.

Miscellany

Symbols of Jews and of Israel

Magen David

1. See www.aish.com/literacy/concepts/Star_of_David.asp; accessed November 2003.
2. Plaut, 51–52.
3. Ibid. 62–63.
4. Frankel and Teutsch, 162.

Israeli Flag

1. Mishory.

Hatikvah

1. The original version had different closing lines, which were changed after the establishment of the State of Israel: "Our hope is not lost—the

ancient hope to return to the land of our ancestors, to the city where David encamped" (Dosick, 335–336).

Menorah

1. Ginzberg, *Legends of the Jews*, 4:321.
2. Alternate translation.
3. Chill, 121.
4. Frankel and Teutsch, 106.
5. This menorah is designed after the one on the Arch of Titus, which symbolized the alleged invincibility of the Roman Empire. Ironically, that glorious state fell into ruins, whereas the Jewish people have survived (Robert Layman, personal communication, 2004). Before the menorah was chosen, other objects were put forth as possible emblems of the new State of Israel. These included a Torah scroll and the two tablets of the Ten Commandments (to symbolize the People of the Book), and the Burning Bush (to indicate that though persecuted for thousands of years, the Jews survived).

Mezuzah

1. Frankel and Teutsch, 109.
2. Alternate translation.
3. Gelbard, 109.

Magic and Superstition

Amulet

1. Trachtenberg, 144.
2. *Guide of the Perplexed*, 1:6.
3. Witty and Witty, 491.
4. Frankel and Teutsch, 70.

Evil Eye

1. Stone, 508.
2. See www.sefarad.org; accessed February 2004.
3. Schauss, 88–89.

Popular Superstitions

1. This article was adapted with permission from Lutske, 148–165.

Other Customs and Concepts

Beards

1. Dosick, 251.

A Chosen People

1. Alternate translation.
2. Alternate translation.

Conversion

1. Kadden and Kadden, 43–44.
2. Ibid.
3. Witty and Witty, 393.
4. Kadden and Kadden, 45; I. Klein, 440–441.
5. Kadden and Kadden, 46.
6. I. Klein, 440.
7. Ibid.
8. Trepp, 248.
9. Kadden and Kadden, 46–47.
10. Ibid., 47.
11. See www.us-israel.org/jsource/Judaism/Conversion.html; accessed March 2004.
12. Maimonides, *The Commandments* (Negative), 240.
13. *Stone Chumash*, 431.
14. Maimonides, *The Commandments* (Negative), 241.
15. This is permitted by a ruling of the Rabbinical Assembly Law Committee of the Conservative movement.
16. Gordon, 13.
17. The Conservative movement requires commitment and observance, but these requirements are not as stringently enforced as in Orthodox conversions (Robert Layman, personal communication, 2004).

Conversion of a Child

1. Kadden and Kadden, 48.
2. I. Klein, 445.
3. Ibid., 446.

Dreams

1. Frankel and Teutsch, 42.
2. Witty and Witty, 491–492.

Excommunication

1. Alternate translation.
2. Kolatch, *The Second Jewish Book of Why*, 58.
3. Ibid., 56–57.
4. Robinson, 463–466.

Golem

1. Frankel and Teutsch, 63.
2. See golem.plush.org.faq/; accessed November 2003.

Heavenly Bodies

1. Frankel and Teutsch, 165.
2. *Etz Hayim*, 7–8.
3. Frankel and Teutsch, 114.
4. Ibid., 113.
5. Frankel and Teutsch, 162–163.
6. Maimonides, *Eight Chapters*, 8.
7. Frankel and Teutsch, 197–199.

Kissing Holy Objects

1. Donin, *To Pray As a Jew*, 43–44.

Kitel

1. Frankel and Teutsch, 91–92.

The Messiah

1. Frankel and Teutsch, 107–108.
2. Telushkin, 546.
3. Ginzberg, *Legends of the Jews*, 4:233–235, 6:438.
4. Frankel and Teutsch, 108.
5. Ibid.
6. Frankel and Teutsch, 108–109.
7. *ArtScroll Siddur*, 465.
8. Frankel and Teutsch, 108–109.

When Will the Messiah Come?

1. Dosick, 49.

Mizrach

1. Gross, 589.
2. Frankel and Teutsch, 44.
3. Gross, 589.
4. Ibid.
5. Frankel and Teutsch, 45.

Names of God

1. *Stone Chumash*, 13–14.
2. Waskow, "The God Who Nurtures," 33.
3. Lutske, 181.
4. See www.jewfaq.org/name/htm; accessed November 2003.
5. Ibid.
6. Frankel and Teutsch, 118–119.
7. Lutske, 181–182.
8. See www.jewfaq.org/name/htm; accessed November 2003.
9. Robinson, 10; see www.jewfaq.org/name/htm; accessed November 2003.
10. Frankel and Teutsch, 119.

Numbers

1. Alternate translation. *"Echad"* is often the alterantive spelling in Jewish prayer books.
2. Frankel and Teutsch, 124.
3. Trachtenberg, 119.
4. Frankel and Teutsch, 176.
5. Ibid., 58–59.
6. Ibid.
7. Ibid., 55–56.
8. Isaacs, *The Jewish Book of Numbers*, 59, 62.
9. Frankel and Teutsch, 149.
10. Ibid., 150.
11. Alternate translation.
12. Alternate translation.
13. Isaacs, *The Jewish Book of Numbers*, 75.
14. The first group of 10 is Adam, Seth,

Enosh, Kenan, Mechalalel, Jared, Enoch, Methusaleh, Lamech, and Noah. The next group of 10 is Shem, Arpachshad, Shelach, Eber, Peleg, Reu, Serug, Nachor, Terach, and Abraham.
15. Frankel and Teutsch, 173.
16. Ibid.
17. Hosea, Joel, Amos, Obadiah, Jonah, Micah, Nachum, Habakkuk, Zephaniah, Haggai, Zechariah, and Malachi.
18. Frankel and Teutsch, 175.
19. Ibid., 47.
20. Ginzberg, *Legends of the Jews*, 3:165–166.
21. *Stone Chumash*, 895.
22. Frankel and Teutsch, 151.
23. Alternate translation.
24. Alternate translation.
25. Isaacs, *The Jewish Book of Numbers*, 184–185.
26. Ibid., 182–183.

Shalom

1. Alternate translation.
2. The president of the Sanhedrin (*nasi*) during the first half of the second century C.E.
3. Lutske, 335–336.
4. Appel, Don, and Jerry Herman, *Milk and Honey*, 1961.

Food

Overview

1. Roden, 22–24.

Characteristics of Jewish Cooking

1. Roden, 15–17.

Dietary Laws

1. *Stone Chumash*, 599.
2. Maimonides, *The Commandments* (Negative), 169.
3. *Stone Chumash*, 601.
4. Ibid., 599.
5. Chill, 176–177.
6. *Stone Chumash*, 599.
7. Ibid., 605.
8. Dosick, 264.
9. Obadiah ben Jacob Sforno (c.1470–c.1550), Italian biblical commentator and physician.
10. *Stone Chumash*, 1013.
11. Isaac ben Judah Abravanel (1473–1508), statesman, philosopher, and Bible scholar.
12. Chill, 411.
13. One of the second-century C.E. leaders of the post-Bar Kokhba generation who played a decisive role in the development of the Mishnah.
14. *Stone Chumash*, 1013.
15. Lau, 117–119.
16. Ibid.
17. Kolatch, *The Jewish Book of Why*, 94.
18. Chill, 8.
19. Ibid., 168.
20. Dosick, 264.
21. *Guide of the Perplexed*, 3:48.
22. Hertz, 318.
23. Chill, 114.
24. Hertz, 453.
25. *Guide of the Perplexed*, 3:48.
26. Maimonides, *The Commandments* (Negative), 169.
27. Sha'ar Shemini, 60–end.
28. *Guide of the Perplexed*, 3:48.
29. Maimonides, *The Commandments* (Negative), 170.
30. *Guide of the Perplexed*, 3:48.
31. Ibid.
32. *Etz Hayim*, 1464.
33. Cooper, 30.
34. Kolatch, *The Jewish Book of Why*, 85.
35. *The Jewish Dietary Laws*, 54.

Kashrut Certification

1. See www.jewfaq.org/kashrut.htm; accessed January 2004.
2. Witty and Witty, 429.

Seven Species

1. Chill, 111.
2. *Stone Chumash*, 1069.
3. Frankel and Teutsch, 16–17; see www.us-israel.org/jsource/Judaism/species.html; accessed February 2004.
4. Frankel and Teutsch, 16–17.
5. Frankel and Teutsch, 194.
6. See www.allhlwines.com/kosher.html; accessed December 2003; Roden, 634.
7. See www.jewfaq.org/kashrut.htm; accessed February 2004.
8. Cutler, 227.
9. Frankel and Teutsch, 128–129.
10. Ginzberg, *Legends of the Jews* 1:164.
11. *ArtScroll Tanach*, 1466.

Specific Foods

1. Frankel and Teutsch, 6.
2. Marks, 284–285; Shostek, 17–18.
3. Marks, 224.
4. Alternate translation.
5. Cutler, 362.
6. Alternate translation.
7. A major third-century Babylonian scholar.
8. Frankel and Teutsch, 25.
9. Marks, 185.
10. Frankel and Teutsch, 33.
11. Sperling, 224.
12. Marks, 122–123; Shosteck, 199–202.
13. Shosteck, 122.
14. Frankel and Teutsch, 62.
15. Cutler, 120.
16. Author's translation: "May they [*v'yidgu*] upon the earth." The Hebrew word is gramatically a verb rather than a noun plus an adjective.
17. Frankel and Teutsch, 55.
18. R. Schwartz, 103–104.
19. Frankel and Teutsch, 110.
20. MT Me'ilah 8:8.
21. *Guide of the Perplexed*, 3:46.
22. Ibid., 143.
23. Marks, 114.
24. Ibid., 114, 158.

Challah

1. Alternate translation.
2. Reider, 13–16.
3. Frankel and Teutsch, 68; Roden, 98.

Gefilte Fish

1. Shosteck, 73–74.
2. Marks, 72.

Plants and Animals

Plants

Trees

1. Frankel and Teutsch, 181.
2. *Etz Hayim*, 1104.
3. Frankel and Teutsch, 182.
4. Ginzberg, *Legends of the Jews*, 5:97–98.
5. *Stone Chumash*, 13.
6. Alternate translation: "it is a tree of life to all who hold fast to it, and its supports are *me-ushar*." Proverbs (11:30) also observes that "the fruit of the righteous is a tree of life; a wise man captivates people."

Specific Plants

1. *Stone Chumash*, 455.
2. Author's translation. "A righteous [man] shall flourish as a date palm, and grow mighty like a cedar in Lebanon."
3. Ginzberg, *Legends of the Jews*, 5:197–198.
4. Ibid., 3:169–170.
5. Patai, 340.
6. Frankel and Teutsch, 128.
7. Alternate translation.
8. Ibid., 139.
9. Moldenke and Moldenke, 5.
10. See www.eletra.com/gems/e_article000012014.cfm; accessed December 2003.
11. Alternate translation.

Animals

Cruelty to Animals

1. Alternate translation.
2. Alternate translation.
3. *Guide of the Perplexed*, 3:17.
4. Author's translation. "satisfies the desire of every living thing." The Hebrew word "*masbi'ah*' comes from a root meaning "satisfy." The Hebrew word "*ratzon*" simply means "wish" or "desire," rather than "heart's content."
5. Alternate translation.
6. R. Schwartz, 19, 28.
7. Ibid., 27.
8. Ibid., 29.
9. Ibid., 30.
10. Hertz, 844.
11. Maimonides, *The Commandments* (Negative), 213.
12. Alternate translation.
13. *Guide of the Perplexed*, 3:48.
14. Maimonides, *The Commandments* (Negative), 155.
15. Isaacs, *Animals in Jewish Thought and Tradition*, 82.
16. Author's translation. "... that the Lord is giving you." The Hebrew word "*natan*" means "give."
17. *Stone Chumash*, 1051.
18. Cited in Isaacs, *Animals in Jewish Thought and Tradition*, 129.
19. Maimonides, *The Commandments* (Positive), 217.
20. MT Shab. 21:9–10.
21. R. Schwartz, 27.

Specific Animals

1. Alternate translation.
2. Frankel and Teutsch, 17–18; Ben-Shaul, 32.
3. Toperoff, 18.
4. Frankel and Teutsch, 18.
5. *Stone Chumash*, 947.
6. Alternate translation.
7. Pinney, 182.
8. Toperoff, 21.
9. Ibid., 34.
10. Ibid., 36–37.
11. Alternate translation.
12. Toperoff, 186.
13. Ben-Shaul, 32.
14. Toperoff, 47.
15. Alternate translation.
16. *Stone Chumash*, 281.
17. Frankel and Teutsch, 40.
18. Ibid.
19. Toperoff, 50–51; *Stone Chumash*, 433.
20. Alternate translation.
21. *Stone Chumash*, 1057.
22. Ibid.
23. Alternate translation.
24. *Stone Chumash*, 279; Toperoff, 12.
25. *Stone Chumash*, 861.
26. Alternate translation.
27. Frankel and Teutsch, 15.
28. Ibid., 41.
29. Pinney, 162.
30. Toperoff, 55.
31. *ArtScroll Tehillim*, 835.
32. Ginzberg, *Legends of the Jews* 4:157, cited in Frankel and Teutsch, 41.
33. *Stone Chumash*, 599.
34. Toperoff, 103.
35. Chill, 429.
36. *Stone Chumash*, 1029.
37. Author's translation. "Some trust in chariots and some in horses, ..."
38. Toperoff, 124–125.
39. Alternate translation.
40. Frankel and Teutsch, 98–99.
41. *ArtScroll Haggadah Treasury*, 95-96.
42. Pinney, 220.
43. Author's translation. "blow a shofar in Zion ... ." Shofar is the Hebrew word used in the text.
44. Alternate translation.
45. *Etz Hayim*, 844.
46. Toperoff, 170–171.

47. Ibid., 139.
48. Frankel and Teutsch, 96.
49. Ibid.
50. Alternate translation.
51. Frankel and Teutsch, 43.
52. *Stone Chumash*, 402.
53. Frankel and Teutsch, 43.
54. Toperoff, 61.
55. Ibid.
56. Toperoff., 195.
57. Ibid., 145.
58. Pinney, 96.
59. Alternate translation.
60. *Stone Chumash*, 794.
61. Alternate translation.
62. Toperoff, 207–209.
63. Alternate translation.
64. Frankel and Teutsch, 136.
65. Ibid., 154.
66. Ibid., 149.
67. *Stone Chumash*, 17.
68. Ibid., 280.
69. Ibid., 851.
70. *Etz Hayim*, 889.
71. Frankel and Teutsch, 149.
72. Alternate translation.
73. *Stone Chumash*, 283.

Abbreviations

Ar.	Arachin (T)*
ARN	Avot d'Rabbi Natan (commentary on Mishnah tractate Avot)
Avot	*Pirkei Avot*
Av. Zar.	Avodah Zarah (T)
BB	Bava Batra (T)
Bek.	Bekhorot (T)
Ber.	Berachot (T)
Ber. R.	*Berachot Rabbah* (M)
Betz.	Beitzah (T)
BK	Bava Kamma (T)
BM	Bava Metzia (T)
Eccles. R.	*Ecclesiastes Rabbah* (M)
Eduy.	Eduyot (T)
EH	Even ha-Ezer (SA)
EJ	*Encyclopedia Judaica*
Er.	Eruvin (T)
Gen. R.	*Genesis Rabbah* (M)
Git.	Gittin (T)
Hag.	Hagigah (T)
Hal.	Hallah (T)
HM	Hoshen Mishpat (SA)
Hor.	Horayot (T)
Hul.	Hullin (T)
JT	Jerusalem Talmud

*(T) = book of Talmud (M) = Midrash (SA) = Shulchan Arukh

Ket.	Ketubot (T)
Kid.	Kiddushin (T)
Kil.	Kilayim (T)
Lev. R.	*Leviticus Rabbah* (M)
Ma'as. Sh.	Ma'aser Sheni (T)
Mak.	Makkot (T)
Mek.	*Mekhilta* (M)
Meg.	Megillah (T)
Men.	Menachot (T)
MK	Mo'ed Katan (T)
MT	*Mishneh Torah*
Ned.	Nedarim (T)
Nid.	Niddah (T)
OH	Orach Hayim (SA)
Ohol.	Oholot (T)
PdRE	*Pirkei de-Rabbi Eliezer* (M)
Pes.	Pesachim (T)
PR	*Pesikta Rabbati* (M)
RH	Rosh Hashanah (T)
SA	Shulchan Arukh
Sanh.	Sanhedrin (T)
Sem.	Semachot (T)
Shab.	Shabbat (T)
Shek.	Shekalim (T)
Shev.	Shevuot (T)
Sof.	Soferim (T)
Sot.	Sotah (T)
Suk.	Sukkah (T)
Taan.	Ta'anit (T)
Tanh.	*Tanhuma* (M)
Tehillim R.	*Tehillim Rabbah* (M)
Tob.	Tobit (part of Apocrypha)
YD	Yoreh De'ah (SA)
Yev.	Yevamot (T)

Bibliography

Agnon, Shmuel Yosef. *Days of Awe*. New York: Schocken, 1965.
Ben-Shaul, D'vora. "Lions and Tigers and Bears, Oh My!" *International Jerusalem Post*, August 10, 1001, p. 32.
Biale, Rachel. *Women and Jewish Law*. New York: Schocken, 1984.
Blech, Benjamin. *More Secrets of Hebrew Words*. Northvale, N.J.: Aronson, 1993.
Bloch, Abraham P. *The Biblical and Historical Background of Jewish Customs and Ceremonies*. New York: Ktav, 1980.
Braude, William G. *The Midrash on Psalms 2:19*. New Haven, Conn.: Yale University Press, 1959.
Buber, Martin. *Tales of the Hasidim*. New York: Schocken, 1947.
Chill, Abraham. *The Mitzvot*. New York: Bloch, 1974.
Cohen, Jeffrey. *Blessed Are You: A Comprehensive Guide to Jewish Prayer*. Northvale, N.J.: Aronson, 1993.
Cooper, John. *Eat and Be Satisfied*. Northvale, N.J.: Aronson, 1993.
Cutler, Daniel S. *The Bible Cookbook: Love of Food in Biblical Times Plus Modern Adaptations of Ancient Recipes*. New York: William Morrow, 1985.
Diamant, Anita. *The New Jewish Wedding*. New York, Fireside, 1985.
Diament, Carol, Claudia R. Chernov, Tamara Cohen, Rochelle Furstenberg, Daniel Gordis, Leora Tanenbaum, Jules Harlow, and the Women's Zionist Organization of America Hadassah, eds. *Pray Tell: A Hadassah Guide to Jewish Prayer*. Woodstock, Vt.: Jewish Lights, 2003.
Dobrinsky, Herbert. *A Treasury of Sephardic Laws and Customs*. Hoboken: Ktav, 1986.
Donin, Hayim. *To Be a Jew: A Guide to Jewish Observance in Contemporary Life*. New York: Basic Books, 1972.
———. *To Pray as a Jew: A Guide to the Prayer Book and the Synagogue Service*. New York: Basic Books, 1980.
Dorff, Elliott N. *Matters of Life and Death: A Jewish Approach to Modern Medical Ethics*. Philadelphia: Jewish Publication Society, 1998.

Dosick, Wayne. *Living Judaism: The Complete Guide to Jewish Belief, Tradition, and Practice*. San Francisco: Harper San Francisco, 1995.

Dresner, Samuel. *The Jewish Dietary Laws*. New York: Rabbinical Assembly of America, 1982.

Elbogen, Ismar. *Jewish Liturgy: A Comprehensive History*. Philadelphia: Jewish Publication Society, 1993.

Encyclopaedia Judaica. Jerusalem: Keter, 1972.

Etz Hayim. Senior editor David Lieber. Philadelphia: Jewish Publication Society, 2001.

Feinstein, David. *The Kol Dodi Haggadah*. Brooklyn: Mesorah Publications, 1990.

Feuer, Avrohom Chaim. *ArtScroll Shemoneh Esrei*. Brooklyn: Mesorah Publications, 2001.

Frankel, Ellen, and Betsy Platkin Teutsch. *The Encyclopedia of Jewish Symbols*. Northvale, N.J.: Aronson, 1992.

Frankl, Ludwig August. www.us-israel.org/jsource/History/isflag.html (accessed April 11, 2004).

Gale, Barak, and Ami Goodman. "The Trees Are Davening: A Tu B'Shvat Haggadah Celebrating Our Kinship with the Trees and the Earth." Available at www.coejl.org/celebrate/tub_haggadah.html (accessed February 2004).

Garfiel, Evelyn. *The Service of the Heart*. New York: Yoseloff, 1958.

Gelbard, Shemul Pinhas. *Rite and Reason: 1050 Jewish Customs and Their Sources*. Nanuet, N.Y.: Feldheim, 1998.

Ginzberg, Louis. *Legends of the Jews*. 7 vols. Philadelphia: Jewish Publication Society, 1909–1938.

———."Saadia's Siddur." *Jewish Quarterly Review* n.s. 33 (1942).

Goodenough, Erwin R. *Jewish Symbols in the Greco-Roman Period*. Ed. and Abr. Jacob Neusner. Princeton, N.J.: Princeton University Press, 1988.

Goodman, Philip. *Anthology for Hanukkah*. Philadelphia: Jewish Publication Society, 1976.

———. *Anthology for Passover*. Philadelphia: Jewish Publication Society, 1966.

———. *Anthology for Purim*. Philadelphia: Jewish Publication Society, 1964.

———. *Anthology for Rosh Hashanah*. Philadelphia: Jewish Publication Society, 1973.

———. *Anthology for Shavuot*. Philadelphia: Jewish Publication Society, 1974.

———. *Anthology for Sukkot and Simchat Torah*. Philadelphia: Jewish Publication Society, 1973.

———. *Anthology for Yom Kippur*. Philadelphia: Jewish Publication Society, 1971.

Gordon, Evelyn. "Who's a Jew?" *International Jerusalem Post*, March 15, 2002, p. 13.

Greenberg, Blu. *How to Run a Traditional Jewish Household*. New York: Simon & Schuster, 1983.

Groner, Jonathan. "Maoz Tsur Is a Tune That's Much More Than Meets the Ear." *Northern California Jewish Bulletin*, December 2000.

Gross, David C. *The Jewish People's Almanac*. New York: Hippocrene Books, 1988.

Grossman, Naomi. "The Gay Orthodox Underground." *Moment Magazine* (April 2001), 56–59.

Ha-Am, Ahad. *Al Parashat Derakhim*. Berlin: Judisher Verlag, 1921.
Hammer, Reuven. *Entering the High Holy Days*. Philadelphia: Jewish Publication Society, 1998.
———. *Jewish Prayer: A Guide to Personal Devotion and the Worship Service*. New York: Schocken, 1994.
Harvard Hillel Songbook. Boston: Godine, 1992.
Haut, Irwin H. *Divorce in Jewish Law and Life*. New York: Sepher-Hermon, 1983.
Heine, Heinrich. www.myjewishlearning.com/culture/food/Overview_Ashkenazi_Cuisine/German_Beginnings/Food_Cholent_Roden.html (accessed April 11, 2004).
Hertz, J. J. *The Pentateuch and Haftorahs*. London: Soncino, 1978.
Herzl, Theodore. *The Jewish State*. Mineola, NY: Dover Press, 1988.
Heschel, Abraham Joshua. *Man's Quest for God*. New York: Charles Scribner, 1954.
———. *The Sabbath: Its Meaning for Modern Man*. New York: Harper Torchbooks, 1966.
Hirsch, Samson Raphael. *Horeb: A Philosophy of Jewish Laws and Observances*. London: Soncino, 1962.
Holtz, Barry. *Back to the Sources*. New York: Summit Books, 1984.
Ibn Ezra, Abraham: *Commentary on the Torah*. Trans. H. Norman Strickman and Arthur M. Silver. New York: Mesorah, 1996.
Idel, Moshe. *Kabbalah: New Perspectives*. New Haven, Conn.: Yale University Press, 1988.
Idelsohn, A. Z. *Jewish Liturgy and Its Development*. New York: Dover, 1995.
Isaacs, Ronald. *Animals in Jewish Thought and Tradition*. Northvale, N.J.: Aronson, 2000.
———. *The Jewish Book of Numbers*. Northvale, N.J.: Aronson, 1996.
Jacobs, Louis. *Principles of the Jewish Faith*. Northvale, N.J.: Aronson, 1988.
Jakobovitz, Immanuel. *Jewish Medical Ethics*. New York: Bloch, 1959.
Jewish Theological Seminary. *Introduction to Talmud* [Internet Course]. www.jtsa.edu.Talmud.introduction (accessed November 2003).
Kadden, Barbara Binder, and Bruce Kadden. *Teaching Jewish Life Cycle*. Denver: A. R. E. Publishing, 1997.
Kaplan, Aryeh. *Made in Heaven: A Jewish Wedding Guide*. Brooklyn: Moznaim, 1983.
Kaplan, Mordecai. *Sabbath Prayer Book*. New York: Jewish Reconstructionist Foundation, 1945.
Kaufman, Michael. *The Woman in Jewish Law and Tradition*. Northvale, N.J.: Aronson, 1993.
Kitov, Eliyahu. *The Jew and His Home*. Trans. Nathan Bulman. New York: Shengold, 1963.
Klagsburn, Francine. *Jewish Days: A Book of Jewish Life and Culture around the Year*. New York: Farrar, Straus, Giroux, 1996.
Klein, Earl. *Jewish Prayer: Concepts and Customs*. Columbus, Ohio: Alpha, 1986.
Klein, Isaac. *A Guide to Jewish Religious Practice*. New York: Jewish Theological Seminary of America, 1979.
Kolatch, Alfred J. *The Jewish Book of Why*. Middle Village, N.Y.: Jonathan David, 1981.

———. *The Second Jewish Book of Why*. Middle Village, N.Y.: Jonathan David, 1985.
———. *This Is the Torah*. Middle Village, N.Y.: Jonathan David, 1988.
Lamm, Maurice. *The Jewish Way in Death and Mourning*. New York: Jonathan David, 1972.
———. *The Jewish Way in Love and Marriage*. New York: Harper & Row, 1980.
Lamm, Norman. *Judaism and the Modern Attitude to Homosexuality*. Jerusalem: Encyclopedia Judaica Yearbook, 1974.
Lau, Israel Meir. *Practical Judaism*. Jerusalem: Feldheim, 1997.
Lewittes, Mendell. *Jewish Marriage: Rabbinic Law, Legend, and Custom*. Northvale, N.J.: Aronson, 1994.
Lutske, Harvey. *The Book of Jewish Customs*. Northvale, N.J.: Aronson, 1986.
Maimonides, Moses. *The Commandments*. Trans. Charles Chavel. London: Soncino, 1967.
———. *The Eight Chapters*. Trans. Joseph Isaac Gorfinkle. New York: AMS Press, 1966.
———. *Guide of the Perplexed*. Trans. Shlomo Pines. Chicago: University of Chicago Press, 1963.
———. *Mishneh Torah*. Trans. Philip Birnbaum. New York: Hebrew Publishing, 1974.
Marks, Gil. *The World of Jewish Cooking*. New York: Simon & Schuster, 1996.
Martin, Bernard: *Prayer in Judaism*. New York: Basic Books, 1968.
Millgram, Abraham. *Jewish Worship*. Philadelphia: Jewish Publication Society, 1971.
———. *Sabbath, the Day of Delight*. Philadelphia: Jewish Publication Society, 1959.
Mishory, Alec. "The Flag and the Emblem." Available at www.israel-mfa.gov.il/mfa/go.asp?MFAH0cph0 (accessed January 2004).
Moldenke, Harold, and Alma Moldenke. *Plants of the Bible*. New York: Dover, 1986.
Nachmanides. *Commentary on the Torah*. Trans. Charles Chavel. New York: Shilo, 1975.
Orenstein, Debra. *Lifecycles Vol. 1.: Jewish Women on Life Passages and Personal Milestones*. Woodstock, Vt.: Jewish Lights Publishing, 1994.
Oshry, Ephraim. *Responsa from the Holocaust*. Trans. Y. Leiman. Brooklyn, N.Y.: Judaica Press, 1989.
Patai, Raphael. *On Jewish Folklore*. Detroit: Wayne State University Press, 1983.
Pedagogic Center of the Department for Jewish Zionist Education. 2002. www.jajz-ed.org.il (accessed October 2003).
Plaut, W. Gunther. *The Magen David*. Washington, D.C.: B'nai B'rith Books, 1991.
Podwal, Mark. *A Jewish Bestiary*. Philadelphia: Jewish Publication Society, 1984.
Pollack, Gloria. *The Jewish Festivals in Ancient, Medieval, and Modern Sources*. Brooklyn: Sepher-Hermon Press, 1997.
Press, Chaim. *What Is the Reason: Succot*. New York: Bloch, 1966.
Preuss, Julius. *Biblical and Talmudic Medicine*. Trans. Fred Rosner. New York: Sanhedrin Press, 1978.
Project Genesis. Available at www.torah.org/learning/lifecycles/milah/shalomz.html (accessed December 2003).

Rabinowicz, Rachel Anne, ed. *Passover Haggadah: The Feast of Freedom*. New York: The Rabbinical Assembly, 1982.

Rabinowicz, Tzvi. *A Guide to Life: Jewish Laws and Customs of Mourning*. Northvale, N.J.: Aronson, 1989.

Reider, Freda. *The Hallah Book: Recipes, History, and Traditions*. Hoboken, N.J.: Ktav, 1987.

Resnicoff, Steven H. "Jewish Law Perspectives on Suicide and Physician-Assisted Dying." *Journal of Law and Religion* 13, no. 289 (1988–1989): 230–267.

Riskin, Shlomo. "Breaking the Chains." *International Jerusalem Post*, August 31, 2001, p. 39.

———. "Count Your Blessings." *International Jerusalem Post*, March 30, 2001.

———. "From Curse to Blessing." *International Jerusalem Post*, July 6, 2001, p. 39.

———. *The Passover Haggadah*. New York: Ktav, 1983.

———. *Women and Jewish Divorce*. Hoboken, N.J.: Ktav, 1989.

Robinson, George. *Essential Judaism: A Complete Guide to Beliefs, Customs, and Rituals*. New York: Pocket Books, 2000.

Roden, Claudia. *The Book of Jewish Food*. New York: Knopf, 1997.

Rosen, Dov. *Shema Yisrael*. Trans. Leonard Oschry. Jerusalem: Shema Yisrael, 1972.

Rosenzweig, Franz. *The Star of Redemption*. Boston: Beacon Press, 1972.

Salkin, Jeffrey K. *Being God's Partner*. Woodstock, Vt: Jewish Lights Publishing, 1994.

_____. *Putting God on the Guest List*. Woodstock, Vt: Jewish Lights Publishing, 1996.

Schauss, Hayyim. *The Lifetime of a Jew*. Cincinnati, Ohio: Union of American Hebrew Congregations, 1950.

Scherman, Nosson. *ArtScroll Haggadah Treasury*. Brooklyn: Mesorah Publications, 1985.

———. *ArtScroll Kaddish*. Brooklyn: Mesorah Publications, 1991.

———, ed. *Stone Chumash*. Brooklyn: Mesorah Publications, 1994.

Scherman, Nosson, and Meir Zlotowitz, eds. *ArtScroll Machzor*. Brooklyn: Mesorah Publications, 1994.

———. *ArtScroll Siddur*. Brooklyn: Mesorah Publications, 1986.

———. *ArtScroll Tanach*. Brooklyn: Mesorah Publications, 2001.

———. *ArtScroll Tehillim*. Brooklyn: Mesorah Publications, 2001.

———. *ArtScroll Yom Kippur Reader*. Brooklyn: Mesorah Publications, 1992.

Scholem, Gershom. *Kabbalah*. New York: Quadrangle, 1974.

———. *Major Trends in Jewish Mysticism*. New York: Schocken, 1961.

———. *On the Kabbalah and Its Symbolism*. New York: Schocken, 1965.

Schwartz, Howard. *The Savage in Judaism*. Chicago: University of Chicago Press, 1990.

Schwartz, Richard. *Judaism and Vegetarianism*. New York: Lantern, 2001.

Sforno. *Commentary on the Torah*. Trans. Raphael Pelcovitz. Brooklyn: Mesorah, 1987.

Shosteck, Patti. *A Lexicon of Jewish Cooking*. Chicago: Contemporary Books, 1979.

Shoys, Hayim. *The Jewish Festivals: A Guide to Their History and Observance*. Trans. Samuel Jaffe. New York: Schocken, 1996.

Siegel, Richard, Michael Strassfeld, and Sharon Strassfield. *The Jewish Catalogue.* Philadelphia: Jewish Publication Society, 1973.

Soncino Talmud [CD-ROM]. Davka Corp. and Judaica Press, 1991–1995.

Sperling, Abraham Isaac. *Reasons for Jewish Customs and Traditions.* Trans. Abraham Matts. New York: Bloch, 1968.

Spiegel, Shalom. "On Medieval Hebrew Poetry." In *The Jews: Their History, Culture, and Religion.* Ed. Louis Finkelstein. Philadelphia: The Jewish Publication Society, 1960.

Steinsaltz, Adin. *The Essential Talmud.* New York: Bantam Books, 1976.

———. *A Guide to Jewish Prayer.* New York: Schocken, 2000.

Strassfeld, Michael. *The Jewish Holidays: A Guide and Commentary.* New York: Harper & Row, 1985.

Strassfeld, Michael, and Sharon Strassfeld. *The Second Jewish Catalog.* Philadelphia: Jewish Publication Society, 1976.

Telushkin, Joseph. *Jewish Literacy.* New York: William Morrow, 1991.

Tendler, Moses. *Medical Ethics.* New York: Federation of Jewish Philanthropies, 1975.

Toperoff, Shlomo Pesach. *The Animal Kingdom in Jewish Thought.* Northvale, N.J.: Aronson, 1995.

Trachtenberg, Joseph. *Jewish Magic and Superstition: A Study in Folk Religion.* New York: Behrman, 1939.

Trepp, Leo. *The Complete Book of Jewish Observance.* New York: Summit Books, 1980.

Twerski, Abraham J. *From Freedom to Bondage.* Brooklyn: Shaar Press, 1995.

Waskow, Arthur. "The God Who Nurtures at the Breast." *Jerusalem Report*, January 15, 2001, p. 33.

———. *Seasons of Our Joy.* New York: Bantam Books, 1982.

Wein, Berl. *Jerusalem Post*, March 23, 2001.

Weiss, Avraham. *The Prenuptial Agreement.* Cedarhurst, N.Y.: The Orthodox Caucus, 2002.

Weiss, Susan. "Sue the . . . !" *Jerusalem Report*, March 12, 2001, p. 55.

Wiesel, Elie. *The Jews of Silence.* Philadelphia: Jewish Publication Society, 1967.

Witty, Abraham B., and Rachel Witty. *Exploring Jewish Tradition.* New York: Doubleday, 2001.

Zohar. Trans. Harry Sperling. London: Soncino Press, 1949.

Weekly Torah and Haftarah Readings

TORAH	HAFTARAH
Genesis	
B'reishit (1:1–6:8)	Isaiah 42:5–43:11 (Ash) Isaiah 42:5–21 (Seph)
No·ach (6:9–11:32)	Isaiah 54:1–55:5 (Ash) Isaiah 54:1–10 (Seph)
Lekh L'kha (12:1–17:27)	Isaiah 40:27–41:16
Va-yera (18:1–22:24)	2 Kings 4:1–37 (Ash) 2 Kings 4:1–23 (Seph)
Chayyei Sarah (23:1–25:18)	1 Kings 1:1–31
Tol'dot (25:19–28:9)	Malachi 1:1–2:7
Va-yetzei (28:10–32:3)	Hosea 12:13–14:10 (Ash) Hosea 11:7–12:12 (Seph)
Va-yishlach (32:4–36:43)	Hosea 11:7–12:12 (Ash) Obadiah 1:1–21 (Seph)
Va-yeishev (37:1–40:23)	Amos 2:6–3:8
Mi-ketz (41:1–44:17)	1 Kings 3:15–4:1
Va-yiggash (44:18–47:7)	Ezekiel 37:15–28
Va-y'chi (47:28–50:26)	1 Kings 2:1–12
Exodus	
Sh'mot (1:1–6:1)	Isaiah 27:6–28:13; 29:22–23 (Ash) Jeremiah 1:1–2:3 (Seph)
Va-era (6:2–9:35)	Ezekiel 28:25–29:21
Bo (10:1–13:16)	Jeremiah 46:13–28
B'shallach (13:17–17:16)	Judges 4:4–5:31 (Ash) Judges 5:1–31 (Seph)
Yitro (18:1–20:23)	Isaiah 6:1–7:6; 9:5 (Ash) Isaiah 6:1–13 (Seph)
Mishpatim (21:1–24:18)	Jeremiah 34:8–22; 33:25–26
T'rumah (25:1–27:29)	1 Kings 5:26– 6:13
T'tzavveh (27:20–30:10)	Ezekiel 43:10–27

TORAH	HAFTARAH
Ki Tissa (30:11–34:35)	1 Kings 18:1–39 (Ash)
	1 Kings 18:20–39 (Seph)
Va-yak·hel (35:1–38:20)	1 Kings 7:40–50 (Ash)
	1 Kings 7:13–26 (Seph)
P'kudei (38:21–40:38)	1 Kings 7:51–8:21 (Ash)
	1 Kings 7:40–50 (Seph)
Leviticus	
Va-yikra (1:1–5:26)	Isaiah 43:21–44:23
Tzav (6:1–8:36)	Jeremiah 7:21–8:3; 9:22–23
Sh'mini (9:1–11:47)	2 Samuel 6:1–7:17 (Ash)
	2 Samuel 6:1–19 (Seph)
Tazri·a (12:1–13:59)	2 Kings 4:42–5:19
M'tzora (14:1–15:33)	2 Kings 7:3–20
Acharei Mot (16:1–18:30)	Ezekiel 22:1–19 (Ash)
	Ezekiel 22:1–16 (Seph)
K'doshim (19:1–20:27)	Amos 9:7–15 (Ash)
	Ezekiel 20:2–20 (Seph)
Emor (21:1–4:23)	Ezekiel 44:15–31
B'har (25:1–26:2)	Jeremiah 32:6–27
B'chukkotai (26:3–27:34)	Jeremiah 16:19–17:14
Numbers	
B'midbar (1:1–4:20)	Hosea 2:1–22
Naso (4:21–7:89)	Judges 13:2–25
B'ha·alot'kha (8:1–12:16)	Zechariah 2:14– 4:7
Sh'lach L'kha (13:1–15:41)	Joshua 2:1–24
Korach (16:1–18:32)	1 Samuel 11:14–12:22
Chukkat (19:1–22:1)	Judges 11:1–33
Balak (22:2–25:9)	Micah 5:6–6:8
Pinchas (25:10–30:1)	1 Kings 18:46–19:21
Mattot (30:2–32:42)	Jeremiah 1:1–2:3
Mas'ei (33:1–36:13)	Jeremiah 2:4–28; 3:4 (Ash)
	Jeremiah 2:4–28; 4:1–2 (Seph)
Deuteronomy	
D'varim (1:1–3:22)	Isaiah 1:1–27
Va-etchannan (3:23–7:11)	Isaiah 40:1–26
Eikev (7:12–11:25)	Isaiah 49:14–51:3
R'eih (11:26–16:17)	Isaiah 54:11–55:5
Shof'tim (16:18–21:9)	Isaiah 51:12–52:12
Ki Tetzei (21:10–25:19)	Isaiah 54:1–10
Ki Tavo (26:1–29:8)	Isaiah 60:1–22
Nitzavim (29:9–30:20)	Isaiah 61:10–63:9
Va-yeilekh (31:1–31:30)	Isaiah 55:6–56:8
Ha·azinu (32:1–52)	2 Samuel 22:1–51
V'zot ha-B'rakhah (33:1–34:12)	Joshua 1:1–18 (Ash)
	Joshua 1:1–9 (Seph)

Torah Readings for Holidays and Special Sabbaths

HOLIDAY	TORAH READING	ADDITIONAL READING	HAFTARAH
Sabbath and Rosh Hodesh	Variable	Num. 28:9–15	Isa. 66:1–24
Eve of Rosh Hodesh	Variable	—	I Sam. 20:18–42
Rosh Hashanah			
(1st day)	Gen. 21:1–34	Num. 29:1–6	I Sam. 1:1–2:10
(2nd day)	Gen. 22:1–24	Num. 29:1–6	Jer. 31:2–20
Yom Kippur			
(morning)	Lev. 16:1–34	Num. 29:7–11	Isa. 57:14–58:14
(afternoon)	Lev. 18:1–30	—	Jon.1:1–4:11; Mic. 7:18–20
Sukkot (1st day)	Lev. 22:26–23:44	Num. 29:12–16	Zech. 14:1–21
(2nd day)	Lev. 22:26–23:44	Num. 29:12–16	1 Kings 8:2–21
(intermediate Sabbath)	Exod. 33:12–34:26	Variable	Ezek. 38:18–39:16
Shemini Atzeret	Deut. 14:22–16:17	Num. 29:35-39	1 Kings 8:54–66
Simchat Torah	Deut 33:1–34:12 Gen 1:1–2:3	Num. 29:35–39	Josh. 1:1–18
Hanukkah			
(1st Sabbath)	Variable	—	Zech. 2:14–4:7
(if 2nd Sabbath)	Gen. 41:1–44:17	—	1 Kings 7:40–50
Shabbat Shekalim	Variable	Exod. 30:11–16	2 Kings 11:17–12:17
Shabbat Zachor	Variable	Deut. 25:17–19	1 Sam. 15:1–34
Shabbat Parah	Variable	Num. 19:1–22	Ezek. 36:16–38
Shabbat ha-Hodesh	Variable	Exod. 12:1–20	Ezek. 45:16–46:18
Shabbat ha-Gadol	Variable	—	Mal. 3:4–24
Passover (1st day)	Exod. 12:21–51	Num. 28:16–25	Josh. 5:2–6:1; 6:27
(2nd day)	Lev. 22:26–23:44	Num. 28:16–25	2 Kings 23:1-9, 21–25

(intermediate Sabbath)	Exod. 33:12–34:26	Num. 28:19–25	Ezek. 37:1–14
(7th day)	Exod. 13:17–15:26	Num. 28:19–25	2 Sam. 22:1—51
(8th day)	Deut. 15:19–16:17 (if Sabbath: 14:22–16:17)	Num. 28:19–25	Isa. 10:32–12:6
Shavuot (1st day)	Exod. 19:1–20:23	Num. 28:26–31	Ezek. 1:1–28; 3:12
(2nd day)	Deut. 15:19–16:17 (if Sabbath: 14:22–16:17)	Num. 28:26–31	Hab. 2:20–3:19
Yom ha-Atzmaut	Deut. 7:12–8:18	—	Isa. 10:32–12:6
Tisha b'Av			
(morning)	Deut. 4:25-40	—	Jer. 8:13–9:23
(afternoon)	Exod. 32:11–14; 34:1–10	—	Isa. 55:6–56:8
Afternoon of all fast days (not Yom Kippur)	Exod. 32:11–14; 34:1–10	—	Isa. 55:6–56:8

Orders of the Mishnah and Tractates of the Talmud

Zera'im (seeds)	
Berachot (Ber.)	Blessings and prayers
Pe'ah	Gleanings (laws of charity)
Demai (Dem.)	Produce not definitely tithed
Kilayim (Kil.)	Diverse kinds (prohibitions against crossbreeding and mingling of varied species of plants, animals, and clothing)
Shevi'it	Sabbatical year
Terumot (Ter.)	Gifts to the *Kohanim*
Ma'aserot (Ma'as.)	Tithes for the Levites and the poor
Ma'aser Sheni (Ma'as Sh.)	Second tithes (to be eaten in Jerusalem)
Hallah (Hal.)	Dough offering to the *Kohanim*
Orlah	Forbidden fruits of young trees (first four years)
Bikkurim (Bik.)	First fruits (offered at the Temple)
Mo'ed (festivals)	
Shabbat (Shab.)	Sabbath laws
Eruvin (Er.)	Permissible limits on the Sabbath
Pesachim (Pes.)	Passover (*hametz*, matzah, paschal sacrifice)
Shekalim (Shek.)	Shekel dues for the Temple and Temple ceremonies
Yoma	Yom Kippur (sacrifices and fast)
Sukkah (Suk.)	Sukkot (sukkah, four species)
Beitzah (Betz.)	General festival laws
Rosh Hashanah (RH)	New Year (prayers, shofar, fixing months and years)
Ta'anit (Taan.)	Fast days (other than Yom Kippur)

Megillah (Meg.)	Purim
Mo'ed Katan (MK)	Intermediate days of Passover and Sukkot (lit., "little festival")
Hagigah (Hag.)	Special sacrifices for the three pilgrimage festivals

Nashim (women)

Yevamot (Yev.)	Levirate marriage and *halitzah*; prohibited marriages
Ketubot (Ket.)	Marriage contract (mutual rights and duties of husband and wife)
Nedarim (Ned.)	Vows (making and annulling of vows)
Nazir (Naz.)	Nazirite vows
Sotah (Sot.)	Wife suspected of adultery
Gittin (Git.)	Divorce and the *get*
Kiddushin (Kid.)	Betrothal and marriage

Nezikin (damages)

Bava Kamma (BK)	Torts (damage to persons and property)
Bava Metzia (BM)	Civil law (lost and found property, fraud, usury, relations with workers)
Bava Batra (BB)	Property law (real estate, inheritance, sales, partnerships)
Sanhedrin (Sanh.)	Courts of justice, judicial procedure, criminal law
Makkot (Mak.)	Flagellation (punishment of criminals, cities of refuge)
Shevu'ot (Shev.)	Oaths
Eduyot (Eduy.)	Testimonies (various rabbinic teachings)
Avodah Zarah (Av. Zar.)	Prohibition of idolatry
Avot	Ethical teachings
Horayot (Hor.)	Erroneous rulings by the court on matters of religious law (and how to correct them)

Kodashim (holy things)

Zevachim (Zev.)	Sacrificial system in the Temple
Menahot (Men.)	Cereal offerings, tzitzit, tefillin
Hullin (Hul.)	Ritual slaughter of animals and the dietary laws
Bekhorot (Bek.)	Firstborn children and animals
Arachin (Ar.)	Laws of valuations or contributions to the Temple
Temurah (Tem.)	Substituting one animal offering for another

Keritot (Ker.)	Sins punishable by death or separation from the community
Me'ilah	Sacrilege against Temple property
Tamid (Tam.)	Daily offerings in the Temple
Middot (Mid.)	Architecture and measurements of the Temple
Kinnim (Kin.)	Bird offerings
Tohorot (cleanness/purity)	
Kelim (Kel.)	Ritual impurity of utensils
Oholot (Ohol.)	Ritual impurity related to a corpse
Nega'im (Neg.)	Leprosy
Parah	Red heifer
Tohorot (Toh.)	Ritual purification
Mikva'ot (Mik.)	*Mikveh* (bath for ritual purification)
Niddah (Nid.)	Family purity (menstruation and the monthly period of separation between husband and wife)
Machshirin	Liquids and foods subject to ritual uncleanness
Zavim (Zav.)	Discharges rendering a person ritually unclean
Tevul Yom (TY)	Various forms of ritual uncleanness
Yadayim (Yad.)	Ritual uncleanness of the hands
Ukzin	Fruits and plants subject to ritual uncleanness

Index

B